82
.10
1.00
.62
.60
.50
.82
.50
1.00
.45
40
.40
———
7.50

*studying*
### *TEACHING*

PRENTICE-HALL INTERNATIONAL, INC., *London*
PRENTICE-HALL OF AUSTRALIA, PTY. LTD., *Sydney*
PRENTICE-HALL OF CANADA, LTD., *Toronto*
PRENTICE-HALL OF INDIA PRIVATE LTD., *New Delhi*
PRENTICE-HALL OF JAPAN, INC., *Tokyo*

# *studying*

# *TEACHING*

**JAMES RATHS**
*Bureau of Educational Research
and Field Services*
*University of Maryland*

**JOHN R. PANCELLA**
*Science Department*
*Richard Montgomery High School*
*Montgomery County, Maryland*

**JAMES S. VAN NESS**
*Departments of History
and Secondary Education*
*University of Maryland*

**PRENTICE-HALL, INC., Englewood Cliffs, N. J.**

*To the life and work of Louis E. Raths*

*Any teacher who chooses to make a difference will make one.*—HAROLD CARTER

# Introduction

Methods courses in education have, for many years, been under serious attack both from within institutions of higher learning and from the outside—the lay public, the profession, and various councils, associations, or groups organized for the betterment of American education.

The arguments against methods courses do have some strong points on their side. First, it is indeed true that there are very few generalizations about teaching that have solid empirical support. The relationships between variables in the teaching-learning act are neither highly regular nor completely predictable. While this is true of most areas of study dealing with the human element, it seems especially true of education. Certain techniques may prove effective one day, ineffective the next. At times efforts on a teacher's part can help one-half the class attain the lesson's objectives, but actually hinder the progress of the other half. This complexity is perhaps the most frustrating aspect of teaching. Secondly, many students find methods courses impractical. Sometimes they summarize this feeling by stating that the courses are too theoretical. The sorry fact, which in a sense reflects the first objection, is that there is far too little theory in education. Theory, in part, describes relationships between variables. As noted above, all too few relationships have been identified and tested. Thus, methods courses become impractical when, instead of dealing with relationships between variables supported by data, they proceed with a problems approach leading to solutions on an *ad hoc* basis, rather than in terms of principles of teaching or learning.

If all of the above is in fact true, what is a proper role for methods courses today? Granting the above arguments, the editors of this book of readings make two assumptions about the teaching process. First, we are assuming that the better teachers in our schools are the ones who are rational about the decisions they make in the teaching act. They consider alternatives, weigh possible outcomes, and evaluate their decisions by collecting relevant evidence. From this assumption it follows that methods courses could be most effective in helping prospective teachers identify relevant variables within the teaching-learning process to which they may pay particular attention. In this way, teachers can learn ways to "monitor" their own teaching. Methods courses with this thrust will give students the ability to assess for themselves the kind of job they are doing in the teaching role. Lawrence Kubie suggests to psychiatric students that they must not limit their concern to merely observing themselves in relationship to their subjects. They must use their observations as a basis for introspection. "I always know that a young man has started the long road to becoming a psychiatrist," Kubie states, "when in the presence of a group of his peers he begins to say publicly and without defensiveness and without shame, 'What I said was not so bad, but why did I have to say it that way' or even, 'The way I said it was not so bad, but why did I have to look like that.' Something like this must happen in the process of learning how to become an educator." [1]

Taking its cue from Kubie, this book proposes some ways of helping teachers raise their level of awareness in the teaching act so as to improve their ability to review rationally the decisions they have made and the alternatives they have considered. In short, it is the editors' view that a proper role of methods courses is that of training education students in the various ways by which they may assess their own teaching.

A second assumption is that although there are few generalizations about teaching that are firmly supported by evidence, there are practices and techniques current in teaching that have been deemed successful, if not on factual grounds, at least by the impressions of experience. Are these impressions to be ignored? We think not. A second role of methods courses may be to present techniques and procedures as working hypotheses. The alternatives suggested by experienced teachers and education teachers may enlarge the number of choices that beginning teachers may consider and test. Thus, it is appropriate for a methods course to suggest various approaches to planning, testing, carrying out a discussion, etc., that student teachers may ultimately wish to try and to test in their own teaching.

In short, then, this book will attempt to present readings that suggest various methods by which teaching can be examined and described and to offer descriptions of procedures that may serve as a starting point for beginning teachers.

Henry Adams once said, "Teachers affect eternity; they never know where their influence will end." It is our belief that this is true and that

[1] Lawrence S. Kubie, "Research on Protecting Preconscious Functions in Education." Address to the A.S.C.D. Research Institute, Washington, D. C., April, 1960.

the role of the teacher is increasingly important in the world today. It is our fond hope that students using this text will derive greater satisfactions from their teaching as a result of considering the skills and concepts with which it is concerned.

.   .   .

The editors are greatly indebted to the authors and publishers of the articles which have been included in this book of readings. We are grateful for their generosity in so kindly permitting us to use their contributions.

J.R.

J.R.P.

J.S.V.N.

# Contents

Chapter Eight

# DISCIPLINE     375

*studying*
## *TEACHING*

**Chapter One**

# WHAT IS TEACHING ?

What is teaching? This difficult question has plagued man for years and still is, at best, difficult to answer. Obviously no definition fits all men, at all times, and for all purposes. An observer may tell a teacher who is giving a test that he will return "when some teaching is going on." This comment certainly reveals one notion about the teaching act. If you were told that someone was teaching in the room next door, what image would you have of his likely behavior? Is he standing or sitting? Talking or listening? Asking questions or answering them? Of course, the answer is not known. As a matter of fact, he may not even be in the room—and yet he considers himself teaching.

The problems associated with the difficulty of defining "teaching" carry over to the image a person has of himself as a teacher. If he cannot even define what he is supposed to be doing, can he really feel effective on the job?

Many times, teachers feel quite ineffective. The bright children in a class learn because they are bright; the slow children fail to learn because they are slow. Any exceptions to these generalizations are explained away in the patois of the profession—underachiever, striver, overly motivated, culturally deprived, etc. The teacher may begin to see himself as an extraneous, intervening variable without much direct effect on the outcomes of the teaching-learning act.

Surely the teacher makes a difference, and surely it is in a large part his teaching that makes the difference—not eye color, cut of clothes, nor ethnic background.

What, then, is teaching? The question may be directed to the goals of the teacher and to the actual behavior called "teaching." Is it the role of the teacher to change people? What is the difference between indoctrination and teaching? Can one be said to be teaching in the absence of learning? What are some of the tasks of the teacher? The readings in this chapter are meant to stimulate discussion concerning these and other questions and to suggest ways in which teachers and teaching might be viewed by observers.

# 1

# Teaching Machines

## HARRY S. BROUDY

When the teaching machine was introduced by S. L. Pressey and B. F. Skinner some time ago, it was a cloud no bigger than a man's hand on the educational horizon. Today it is a sizable cloud indeed. Experience with tape recorders, computers of all sorts, and general sophistication about the ways of a man and a machine promise a revolution in formal schooling.

Calm and judicious pedagogical voices dismiss the development as merely another adjunct to human teaching. They reassure the teacher that he or she will never be replaced (much as horse dealers were once assured that horses would never be replaced by motor cars). This reassurance is justified but it would be surprising indeed if the role of the teacher, like that of the horse, will ever be the same again.

For those who are not familiar with teaching machines, it need only be said that they are devices that by means of a tape or other contrivance present a task to the pupil. The task can be a problem in arithmetic, a word to be spelled, a choice among three or four forms of a sentence, the completion of a map.

Indeed, the variety of learning tasks is almost unlimited—provided only that there is a right answer. Usually in these machines the right answer is followed by a new task; the wrong answer keeps the pupil at the old task or directs him to finding out where he went wrong. The subtlety of the machine is not to be under-estimated. Suppose the task is spelling. A machine might ask for the spelling of "deceive," "receive," and "conceive," and then pop in "believe." Or if the task is arithmetic, problems can be varied almost endlessly by a careful program designer so that every variety of fraction, percentage, and number combination is represented by a task.

Furthermore, the reinforcement or reward need not be confined to the prosaic: "That is correct, proceed to the next problem." For the young

Harry S. Broudy, *Paradox and Promise: Essays on American Life and Education* (Englewood Cliffs, N.J.: Prentice-Hall, Inc., 1961), pp. 149–54. Reprinted by permission.

3

a comic book, a lollipop, or a brace of tickets to the movies could be served up at strategic moments, and no less ingenious rewards and punishments could easily be contrived for the more mature learners as well.

In other words, those who are muttering about the mechanical nature of the teaching machine are wasting their breath. It is mechanical, but not so stupid nor so rigid as the mutterers would like to believe. On the contrary, being a machine, it is thorough and uniform in its demands, rewards, punishments, and other ministrations. In short, when it works, it is extraordinarily efficient, something most human beings, including teachers, are not.

Oddly enough, the great vulnerability of teaching by machine, as one educator recently pointed out, is that, being machines, they will not work a good deal of the time. The out-of-order sign will always be on a fair proportion of them at any given moment, and teachers will have to become adept at the repair and maintenance of machines, just as they have been forced to become wise in the ways of tape recorders and movie projectors. Skilled technicians being scarce and highly paid, one wonders whether this trend may not solve the economic problem of teachers. By allowing them to retain their title as teachers and changing their function to that of mechanics, our society can have its cake and eat it too. By making teachers do the work of mechanics our citizens can, in all good conscience, pay them the wages of mechanics—something they feel they cannot do so long as teachers are merely instructors.

Properly used, the machines represent a liberation of the teachers, much as the mechanical marvels in agriculture have liberated farmers from drudgery and unproductive toil. If teachers do not readily apprehend this, it is, I believe, because they have conceived of teaching exclusively in terms of one phase of instruction. Seeing this phase of their work threatened by the encroachment of the machine, they are understandably perturbed, just as linotype operators are justifiably perturbed by machines that will make them dispensable.

If this phase of teaching is all there is to it, then one must say to teachers what one says to linotypists and other machine operators about to be displaced by labor-saving devices: "Friends, you are the victims of progress. Some of you will be absorbed in the new order of things. Others are doomed to suffer, but in the long run more people will be employed, more good will be produced, and more happiness will be distributed to more people. In the meantime, let us pass laws to alleviate your distress." Or to put it bluntly, if teaching is what a machine can do better than teachers are now doing, then the machine ought to be doing it.

There are, however, many facets to teaching. Practicing the right response or practicing the finding of the right response is only one facet—the one that is most adaptable to machines. But there is also the facet we call insight or understanding, and there is the facet we might call appreciation. For centuries good teachers have complained that all their time was used up in drill and practice. Suppose now they are freed by the machine to devote themselves to the understanding and appreciation phases of teaching. Will they rejoice at this opportunity or will they perhaps be frightened at having to do something other than perfecting their pupils in the right responses?

I suspect that this is too superficial a solution. Machines for drill, human teachers for insights and appreciation, sounds like a plausible division of labor, but are we so certain that machines cannot manage the other facets also?

What of the movement now well under way with generous impetus from Foundations to stage "educational spectaculars," so to speak? For example, what about the courses in physics in the grand manner that television has been exhibiting to a nationwide class at early hours of the morning? Cannot the student get his insights from this type of machine teaching? And would this not solve the problems of schools that cannot afford to build laboratories with high-grade equipment nor to hire topflight professors? The television presentation, on the other hand, spares no expense in the way of equipment, professors, assistants, planning, and whatever else it takes to explain and demonstrate the principles of physics.

Surely insight can be promoted in this way simultaneously for millions of viewers. And once the moment of insight has been achieved, supplementary practice on the problems and exercises could be programmed for machine teaching. All we would then need is the machine-tender teacher, the television-operator teacher, and the IBM test grader.

I repeat that those who shrink from these possibilities had better steel themselves to the realities they portend. Large-scale high school and college instruction may be impossible without machine duplication of a relatively small number of teaching performances. And does it matter really whether the pupil gets his principles of physics and chemistry, his mathematics and history, from a television lecturer or from a lecturer standing in the front of the room or hall?

To be sure, the possible ego damage to the local teacher or professor is fearful to contemplate. For the local instructor has to admit that he cannot give a first-rate lesson. High school teachers are more likely to be persuaded of this than college professors, so that unless the professors are themselves to be permitted to perform on television, the venture is in for rough sailing. Something similar to the disinclination of college professors to use textbooks they did not write may well set in. The planners of educational television had better look to their human relations experts before they prescribe it as a panacea for the college enrollment explosion.

Then is nothing educational safe from the machine, from the IBM punch card, and from the electronic brains? In principle, nothing. Anything that can be shown, played, or sung—literature, art, science—all can be adapted for machine duplication and perhaps presented better and certainly more elaborately than the average local schoolroom and teacher can do it.

In practice, however, it is hard to imagine a conversation between a machine and a pupil; it is difficult to imagine the machine and the learner growing together, interacting with each other so that the experience of each changes irreversibly with each moment of instruction. It is even more difficult to conceive of a machine toward which the pupil feels respect and from which he expects understanding and respect. It is difficult to imagine how a machine could, without a word, pass a judgment on a pupil that the pupil will feel more keenly than the most detailed of reports from the battery of tests that the electronic counselors can emit on a second's notice.

Whatever accrues from such conversation cannot be achieved by machines. When teacher and pupil are both part of a unified quest toward something higher than either of them, to use a notion of Froebel's, we are out of the realm of the machine. Particularly when the learning is an insight into values, does the machine have a hard time of it.

Consider, for example, the problem of instilling in a pupil a love of truth or of justice or of freedom. It is not difficult to make a film or to turn out literary materials containing the appropriate sentiments. And perhaps photogenic professors with a gift for the theatrical can, with the help of a Foundation grant, turn out a spectacular that will cause students to surge into streets hungering after justice and freedom. This type of teaching can arouse emotion and incite action. It does not, however, institute a relation between the teacher and pupil such that the meanings of truth and justice and freedom are sharpened by dialectic and honed by conversation. One must be able to talk back to Socrates.

The machine cannot serve the pupil as a life model which interacts with him as his friends do, as do a hero and his worshipers, as do the master and the disciple.

It is of some significance that we do not remember our great teachers as efficient teaching machines, but rather as personalities who literally "personified" for us something that we either valued at the time or came to value in later years. I am sure, to take a personal example, that there were many professors of philosophy who could have lectured as ably and

clearly as did the late Edgar Sheffield Brightman at Boston University. Even his own special insights into philosophical doctrines could be gleaned from his writings. Possibly television could convey the eager preoccupation with truth by a religiously and morally committed man. But what device could substitute for his dialogue with students in the class, in interviews, in conferences—some of them conducted in a taxicab on the way to lunch in a Chinese restaurant? How can we mechanize the heady sweetness of his praise for a sharp question or a good term paper? How could he, from a television screen, correct your impulsive comment, hasty generalization? How could he via television make you feel mature simply by taking what you said seriously enough to be mercilessly frank about it?

All of this comes to what? Being a highly individualized teacher, Professor Brightman contributed something unique to the learning situation he created. If this contribution was good, the loss of it is not reparable by substituting another teacher through television, tape, or anything or anyone else. It is one thing to put a Brightman *on* television; it is another to remove him from the classroom *by* television. Those who are enthusiastic about the potentialities of putting first-rate teachers on television or into some other form of teaching machine should not forget the possible irreparable loss they may occasion by removing first-rate teachers from the educational scene. Genuine individuals are not comparable and therefore not substitutable.

If a teacher is a source of nonstandardized insights; if the teacher is creative enough to produce a highly personal reaction to the world and to the subjects he teaches, then he is a valuable asset and not a machine at all. If he is an inciter to thought; if he can engage in enlightening dialogue; if he enacts a life style that persuades as it reveals, then it is not a teaching machine we are talking about. In this sense there is no more point in talking about any one type of "good" teacher than there is to talk about any one type of "good" artist or "good" personality. The goodness lies in their willingness, indeed, their inability to refrain from interacting with the young in an educative way, and this they do in as many ways as there are individual patterns in their respective lives.

Great and wonderful is the institution that attracts to its faculty a variety of personalities who exemplify the diverse patterns of the good life and who, by teaching, conduct their pupils on their own individual guided tour in the wisdom of the race. In such an institution each classroom is a new perspective from which the world looks new and fresh and revelatory. Great and wonderful are the years one is privileged to spend exploring the world in the company of such teachers. The pressure of life's business makes these years tragically few.

The advent of a teaching machine that can drill the learner with marvelous efficiency and has mechanical means of duplicating a lesson a millionfold through the miracles of electronics only serves to make us ask anew: Just what is teaching and what are teachers for? The answer is at once disturbingly old and suggestively new. Why, teachers teach *themselves.* They themselves are the only subject matter that they alone can teach.

# 2

# What *Is* a Good Teacher?

## LOUIS E. RATHS

When speaking about a *good teacher* we are probably thinking of many things —the teacher as a person, what he does in the classroom, how he interacts with other members of the faculty. We may also be thinking of him as a representative of the school in the community. We may be thinking of his background of experience and training. This article will concentrate on the most essential things which are expected of all good teachers as they work with children in the classroom.

What do we postulate as the functions of good teaching? This conception of good teaching will be greatly influenced by the culture to which we have been exposed and which we prize; good teaching depends upon one's philosophy of education and upon changing conceptions of what constitutes good teaching. No one pattern of good teaching exists. There are many different patterns—all of which are good.

Writings, conferences, and researches of the past fifty years constitute a base for making some generalized proposals about the functions of teaching, proposals unbiased in that they do not imply goodness or badness of teaching. Judgment of the quality of teaching will follow the collection of data which bear upon these functions. Assuming the following twelve functions to be of great importance in almost every teaching day, we would then want to observe teaching with these twelve points in mind. Our discussions with teachers and those responsible for teacher education programs would revolve around these twelve points. Teachers themselves would be looking at their own work in terms of these same points.

It would be unfortunate if teachers were to be rated by some only in these terms. If these are the deepest areas of concern the data we collect should be used as a basis for improvement. Teachers themselves will probably want help in one or more of the func-

Louis E. Raths, "What *Is* a Good Teacher?" *Childhood Education*, XL, No. 9 (May 1964), 451–56. Reprinted by permission of the Association for Childhood Education International, 3615 Wisconsin Avenue, N. W., Washington, D. C., and of the author.

tions. The points are proposed, not as a rating scale, but as a broad framework for teachers to discover more about themselves in relation to the functions of teaching.

1. Explaining, informing, showing how
2. Initiating, directing, administering
3. Unifying the group
4. Giving security
5. Clarifying attitudes, beliefs, problems
6. Diagnosing learning problems
7. Making curriculum materials
8. Evaluating, recording, reporting
9. Enriching community activities
10. Organizing and arranging classroom
11. Participating in school activities
12. Participating in professional and civic life

## EXPLAINING, INFORMING, SHOWING HOW

1. The good teacher is expected to be well informed in the areas in which he teaches. He is expected to be able to communicate information needed for background, enrichment, and motivation, and on many occasions to *explain* relationships to children. The very word "explain" indicates that it isn't a fact to be explained; it is helping children to understand causal relationships; correlations; dependency relations; relationships of opposites, of larger and smaller, of heavier and lighter. In *showing how*, requirements vary for different age and grade levels. For instance, the teacher may be showing children how to put on their boots and jackets or how to mix certain colors. He may be showing them how to handle the number system, how to analyze propaganda, how to draw maps, how to use a book, and how to interview. In addition to clearness and comprehensiveness of the presentation, we expect some effort in getting the children ready for

the demonstration. Most important of all, if the object is to show how, we expect the teacher to allow time in the curriculum for the children to practice until they have a certain grasp of the processes—enough so that they can do it at a level of quality which suits the purpose for the grade level at which it is being done. We expect all good teachers to do well at the task of informing, explaining, and showing how.

## INITIATING, DIRECTING, ADMINISTERING

2. One function of teaching is largely concerned with initiating, organizing, directing, and making many decisions. From the time he begins the day until he goes home at night the teacher faces decisions which might range from a thoughtful deliberation in making changes in a teaching schedule to a quick decision on sending an ailing child to the nurse's office, or what to do in the absence of a special teacher. His handling of the many unusual situations which turn up in the course of a week is indicative of his ability to reorganize and to direct.

It is becoming a much more common practice to include children in much of the planning of the school day. The teacher needs to initiate some of this work, to help get it organized and to direct it. In all these things he helps the children to see alternatives, to see additional resources and to anticipate consequences. Children look to the teacher for decision-making in many situations. There are decisions to give more time on dramatics or science. There are decisions involving the use of consultants, meeting with parents, referring of some children for outside help. Observing teachers give some clue to their resourcefulness in organizing, managing, and directing.

## UNIFYING THE GROUP

3. At the beginning of each school year the teacher is confronted with a number of children. It is his hope and that of the children that as they live together they will become a unified group. When the children identify with each other and when the teacher's concerns overlap the children's, there is good reason to hope that a group spirit will emerge. When the teacher is fair and just to all he is making a contribution to classroom morale.

Discipline problems begin to be solved as children see that permissiveness is controlled by purposes. Children see that they may do those things which contribute to the agreed-upon purposes and that activities which conflict with those purposes are frowned upon or restricted. When there are some subgroups, most children know what is going on in all of them. A rather wide variety of activities is going on, and children have a sense of participation. Having choices to make, they can frequently choose those in which they have some special skills or abilities to assert. Concentrated attention is relieved occasionally with games or with a dramatic presentation. There is a variety of teaching and learning procedures. Seating is not thought of as a permanent and fixed condition. The teacher is alert to the possibility of cliques and is doing many things to develop the idea of a group. An important task of the teacher is that of developing a group with a group spirit, an identification with common purposes and some common concerns.

## GIVING SECURITY

4. Many children are in need of a warm, friendly atmosphere. The teacher with love and affection in abundance is creating a climate which makes it easier for these children to learn. Some children are greatly in need of praise and recognition, and one task of the teacher is to differentiate instruction so that all children may have a sense of achievement and accomplishment. Those children who feel a sense of loneliness, isolation, and sometimes rejection need to be helped by teachers to feel that they belong, that they are wanted and needed. Some children are afraid of school, timid on playgrounds, fearful of many things in their lives. With them the teacher diminishes threats, warnings, or unusually heavy penalties and provides support and assurance instead. The teacher tries to help those children plagued by feelings of guilt and shame by showing that all of us make mistakes and that we can profit by them; by indicating that we are all human and that at different times most of us have had these feelings. There are some children who have little respect for themselves and who feel that they are not worth very much. Here, the teacher asks them for their opinions and sees to it that they assume some responsibilities. Many children have dozens of questions about their relationships to the world and to their inner selves. To the teacher with insight these questions are not irrelevant. And there are some children who have a deep sense of economic insecurity, who wonder if they can count on next week or next month to be as secure as the present week. The classroom teacher brings to children a sense of security in

the meeting of these needs. Whenever there are in children, cases of aggressiveness, withdrawing, submission, or psychosomatic disturbance, the teacher sees to it that the children's needs for special attention are met promptly.

There is pride in what the pupils are doing, and when they need protection the teacher protects them. In a classroom atmosphere which generates group cooperation rather than competition, children help each other. Because it is not altogether a teacher-dominated room—with all or nearly all questions coming from the teacher and every response going to him—children hold discussions with each other. It matters when a child is absent; it matters that birthdays are observed; it matters that returning to school after holidays is a time for reunion and rejoicing.

## CLARIFYING ATTITUDES, BELIEFS, PROBLEMS

5. It is not unreasonable to assume that most of our children are utterly confused by the many social influences surrounding them. Looking at so many different ways of living on TV; listening to many things on radio; reading comics which again introduce new and unusual ideas; moving from one place to another every few years and meeting new people and new teachers; experiencing directly or vicariously the difficulties of a broken family; having few places to play and little opportunity to talk things over with parents who might both be working; living in the aftermath of cruel war and hearing much about possible new wars; being close to and sometimes a participant in racial problems; living under the ominous threat of unemployment; often seeing the glittering array of tempting goods in stores and realizing how little of it

his own family has, the child of today must surely be very much confused. He hears nice things from the adults but sees and hears many things which contradict what they tell him.

To help clarify these matters, the teacher creates opportunities for children to state their attitudes, interests, and problems; to talk about their purposes and aspirations; to speak their beliefs and convictions; to indicate what they think might and should be done; to reveal and to share some of the deeper feelings they have; and to tell about the activities in which they are engaging and those in which they would like to share. As deeper expressions of personality come out, the teacher limits questioning and tries to find out how much self-expression means to the children, whether they want help, whether they have thought of alternative action in solving their problems and consequences of actions. He raises questions with the children which only they can answer, for the questions concern the values which children hold. He gives the children opportunities to compare, observe, classify, interpret and puts them in a position to analyze, criticize, and summarize. The teacher helps them to look for assumptions—those things which are taken for granted—and gives them opportunities to imagine and to create. There are problems to be solved and decisions of value to be made. In each specific instance a question or two is asked for the personal reaction of an individual or a small group and the responses are accepted by the teacher. As this is carried on day by day and week by week, the assumption is made that some of the confusion surrounding children is being cleared up. Even more important is the idea that it is possible to clear it up and children are experiencing a teacher who believes that this is indeed possible. At the same time children are becoming accustomed to saying what they believe, stating what they think; they are becoming adapted to living in a world where people are not all alike, and they are beginning to prize the differences.

## DIAGNOSING LEARNING PROBLEMS

6. In every classroom there are children who are not making the expected progress in their learning, growth, and development. As the teacher lives with these children, it is part of his task to have "hunches" and to suggest to himself possible courses of action. The teacher has to be alert to signs of ill health and sensitive to emotional problems of children. He has to be aware of limits of children's ability as well as of possible negative influences within the room, on the playground and at home. He has to feel his way around for evidence, lack of experience, and hence of maturity. The teacher faces behavior problems knowing that the behavior represents symptoms, that with the acting out of these symptoms children are asking for help. The naughty boy or girl is asking for help as much as the overshy and exclusively withdrawn. Apathy and flightiness, overconforming and overdissenting—all are taken as signs that the children want help in establishing direction. The impulsive child and the one who is always stuck, the one who seems to get little meaning out of the work, and the one who wool-gathers, the one who is loudly assertive, and the one who has little faith in his own ideas are asking for understanding. The prima donna, the rebel without a cause, the unpredictable student, the one who is unrevealing, the one who seeks the exclusive companionship of one other child, the cynic, and the futilitarian all seem to be asking for a more important part in the power structure of the group. The teacher is alert to children who need special help in skills prized by the group. The teacher is grateful to the school with facilities for extra help for children who need more help than the teacher in the crowded school day can give. Surely one of the most important functions of a teacher is to make diagnoses which relate to learning and growth and suggestions which enable children to feel a sense of accomplishment and of identity with their peers.

## MAKING CURRICULUM MATERIALS

7. All teachers recognize the inadequacy of the available books in meeting the needs of every child in the room. Every teacher is faced with the necessity of developing curriculum materials to supplement those provided by the local community. The teacher often hectographs or mimeographs materials which seem more appropriate for a particular group. He makes classroom tests; orders movies, slides, and weekly newspapers; makes arrangements for visiting speakers; tries to get display materials of articles which are produced locally or at a great distance. The teacher asks a great many questions which do not appear in the books and makes suggestions for individual study. In a hundred ways he is modifying the curriculum for the needs of his particular group. Curriculum making is an important function of teaching. If a teacher has some practice in this area and some confidence in his ability to work with children in the development of new materials, he is more able to meet the learning needs of all children in the group.

### EVALUATING, RECORDING, REPORTING

8. All teachers have the task of keeping records and making reports, of recording absences and tardiness. There is the oral report to individual children, sometimes to the whole class about their progress. There are reports to parents, written and oral. Directed toward the plans to make life more productive and zestful for the child, there are reports to go to the administrator and on occasions to other teachers. Reports are necessary which indicate the planning of the schedule and the curriculum, such as a daily log or a projection into the future. In some instances there are anecdotal records to keep track of the behavior of a child, to see if he has decided to change certain of his behaviors. In spring some kind of reporting is usually asked which involves decisions about promotions, retardation, and possible summer work. With respect to most of these things teachers come to their work well prepared, and what they do about this important task is largely dictated by local circumstances.

### ENRICHING COMMUNITY ACTIVITIES

9. Most parents believe that a community is better when it has better schools, but the belief has little worth if the school itself is not concerned with the quality of community life. A classroom teacher who identifies himself with the community is sensitive to its problems and how they are solved, its growth and aspirations. The teacher is concerned about playgrounds, libraries, parks, museums, community health, and transportation. As these things are discussed in school, the teacher is able to bring in appropriate illustrations from the community. Parents are frequent visitors and are thought of as colleagues with deep concerns about the education of their children. Community products are exhibited in the school.

There are field trips and visits to local institutions. The hobbies of mothers and fathers are sometimes shared with the children. Newcomers are oriented. Children who are leaving for another school get special attention and ways are sought to help them to a better start in a new location. In meetings with parents as much attention is paid to influential surroundings as to learning problems in the classroom. Harmonious relationships between school and community are a continuing, essential part of school life. When teachers have this concern, daily efforts are made to enrich the community—an important function of teaching.

### ARRANGING AND ORGANIZING CLASSROOM

10. It is the task of every teacher with the help of pupils to make the classroom a beautiful, pleasant place in which to live. Appearance and arrangement can make a great impression on a visitor. Ideally, the room seems a wonderfully pleasant place in which to learn: lighting is appropriate; colors are pleasing; equipment and supplies are at hand. The room can be quickly reorganized for a variety of activities. In such a room children feel at home. A room organization which is flexible and adaptable to different purposes brings an additional sense of security to children, who like the classroom better when they have shared in developing plans for its use. Many teachers initiate frequent change in the class-

room during the year; for them a room is not fixed for all time in the first month of school. Children's exhibits are changed from time to time. Committees of children have different responsibilities for different tasks in arranging their classroom.

## PARTICIPATING IN SCHOOL ACTIVITIES

11. In addition to all these classroom matters, there is the obligation of every teacher to participate in school activities, such as committee work, holiday programs to share in, lunchroom duty, bus duties, evening meetings. The teacher who believes that his tasks are fulfilled when he pays attention exclusively to his own classroom soon learns that there is the need to be concerned with the welfare of all children in all grades of the school. His participation in total school life is

regarded as one of the important tasks of teaching.

## PARTICIPATING IN PROFESSIONAL AND CIVIC LIFE

12. Every teacher is expected to enter wholly into professional life and to make his contribution to the improvement of the profession. He is expected to belong to professional societies, attend conferences, act in accord with professional ethics, keep up to date in the reading of literature, and make some attempt with his colleagues in the community to share new and pertinent research results. In addition, there is the usual expectation of his being a participating citizen in his community.

Those who discharge these responsibilities in an effective manner are making great contributions for good to a troubled world.

# 3

# Teaching, Acting, and Behaving

## THOMAS F. GREEN

Whatever men do may be viewed as conforming to certain generalizations of human behavior; generalizations, which describing and explaining what men have done, afford also some basis for predicting what they shall do. It may be questionable whether a social science is possible which treats of human behavior except in the aggregate and which therefore can explain or predict human behavior except in relation to large numbers and general tendencies. But this question does not concern me. I assume that whatever men may do, in every specific detail, can be *viewed* as conforming to certain generalizations or laws of human behavior even though we may not know what those generalizations or laws may be. When we observe any item of human behavior in this light, we observe it to "fall under" some general law or to be a "special case" of some generalization. The law or generalization may then be cited as an ex-

Thomas F. Green, "Teaching, Acting, and Behaving," *Harvard Educational Review*, XXXIV, No. 4 (1964), 507, 509. Reprinted by permission.

planation or part of an explanation to account for the occurrence of such behavior and to predict like behavior in the future.

But many times the same behavior, viewed as conforming to such a descriptive generalization, may also be viewed as done in *obedience* to certain rules or principles of action. When one views his own behavior in this light, then the principle or rule of action being "followed" or "applied" may be cited as his reason for acting as he did. There is a difference between someone giving an explanation as to why he acted as he did, and giving a good reason for acting as he did. The one involves the citation of a generalization or law of human behavior, and the other involves the citation of a rule of action. That there is a difference here is also clear when one considers that my explanation why A acted as he did may differ from A's reason for acting as he did, and indeed, my explanation may not even include *any* good reason for his action. And this can be true even when my explanation is correct or adequate and when A is in no way deceived concerning his "real" reason. That there is no contradiction in such a supposition shows that there is a difference between an explanation of human behavior and a reason for acting in a certain way; and this difference between explanation and reason is one way of displaying the difference between conformity to rule and obedience to rule. Either an explanation or a reason may be offered in answer to the question "Why did you do such and such?" because that question can be differently interpreted as a request for a cause or a request for a principle of conduct.

The concepts "explanation" and "reason," "behavior" and "action," "conformity to rule" and "obedience to rule" are ambiguous. It is clear, however, that in some sense each of these is a pair of contrasting concepts, and, moreover, that the contrast drawn in each pair is related to that in each of the other pairs. Thus, the contrast between conformity to a law of behavior and obedience to a rule of action is related to a possible contrast between giving an explanation of one's behavior and giving a reason for acting in a certain way. Similarly, the contrast between conforming to a rule and obeying a rule is the central distinction in a possible contrast between behaving and acting.

This contrast between conformity to rule and obedience to rule lies also at the heart of what we mean by teaching. For teaching is a rule-guided activity, or as I shall say, it is norm-regarding. That is to say, it is important for a teacher not only to understand some explanation of his behavior, but also to have some reasons for acting as he does; and these are different requirements. In a Freudian explanation as to why a gardener behaves as he does, the principles of good gardening may never enter. But presumably his *reasons* for doing as he does *must* include some reference to the principles involved in gardening. Gardening is a rule-directed activity. Similarly, an explanation of a teacher's behavior may have nothing to do with the principles of good teaching or the canons of inquiry. But one's reasons for teaching in a certain way must include some reference to such principles. We cannot understand teaching if we study it simply as a species of human behavior. It must be viewed also as a species of human action; that is, not simply as behavior conforming to some laws or generalizations of human behavior, but as conduct obedient to certain principles of action. Teaching, in short, is not simply norm-conforming; it is norm-obeying.

# 4

# Personal Thoughts on Teaching and Learning

## CARL ROGERS

This is the shortest chapter in the book but if my experience with it is any criterion, it is also the most explosive. It has an (to me) amusing history.

I had agreed, months in advance, to meet with a conference organized by Harvard University on "Classroom Approaches to Influencing Human Behavior." I was requested to put on a demonstration of "student-centered teaching"—teaching based upon therapeutic principles as I had been endeavoring to apply them in education. I felt that to use two hours with a sophisticated group to try to help them formulate their own purposes, and to respond to their feelings as they did so, would be highly artificial and unsatisfactory. I did not know what I would do or present.

At this juncture I took off for Mexico on one of our winter-quarter trips, did some painting, writing, and photography, and immersed myself in the writings of Søren Kierkegaard.

Carl Rogers, "Personal Thoughts on Teaching and Learning," *On Becoming a Person* (Boston: Houghton Mifflin Company, 1961), pp. 273–75. Reprinted by permission.

I am sure that his honest willingness to call a spade a spade influenced me more than I realized.

As the time came near to return I had to face up to my obligation. I recalled that I had sometimes been able to initiate very meaningful class discussions by expressing some highly personal opinion of my own, and then endeavoring to understand and accept the often very divergent reactions and feelings of the students. This seemed a sensible way of handling my Harvard assignment.

So I sat down to write, as honestly as I could, what my experiences had been with *teaching*, as this term is defined in the dictionaries, and likewise my experience with *learning*. I was far away from psychologists, educators, cautious colleagues. I simply put down what I felt, with assurance that if I had not got it correctly, the discussion would help to set me on the right track.

I may have been naive, but I did not consider the material inflammatory. After all the conference members were knowledgeable, self-critical teachers, whose main common bond was an interest in the discussion method in the classroom.

I met with the conference, I presented my views as written out below, taking only a very few moments, and threw the meeting open for discussion. I was hoping for a response, but I did not expect the tumult which followed. Feelings ran high. It seemed I was threatening their jobs, I was obviously saying things I didn't mean, etc., etc. And occasionally a quiet voice of appreciation arose from a teacher who had felt these things but never dared to say them.

I daresay that not one member of the group remembered that this meeting was billed as a demonstration of student-centered teaching. But I hope that in looking back each realized that he had lived an experience of student-centered teaching. I refused to defend myself by replying to the questions and attacks which came from every quarter. I endeavored to accept and empathize with the indignation, the frustration, the criticisms which they felt. I pointed out that I had merely expressed some very personal views of my own. I had not asked nor expected others to agree. After much storm, members of the group began expressing, more and more frankly, their own significant feelings about teaching— often feelings divergent from mine, often feelings divergent from each other. It was a very thought-provoking session. I question whether any participant in that session has ever forgotten it.

The most meaningful comment came from one of the conference members the next morning as I was preparing to leave the city. All he said was, "You kept more people awake last night!"

I took no steps to have this small fragment published. My views on psychotherapy had already made me a "controversial figure" among psychologists and psychiatrists. I had no desire to add educators to the list. The statement was widely duplicated however by members of the conference and several years later two journals requested permission to publish it.

After this lengthy historical buildup, you may find the statement itself a letdown. Personally I have never felt it to be incendiary. It still expresses some of my deepest views in the field of education.

I wish to present some very brief remarks, in the hope that if they bring forth any reaction from you, I may get some new light on my own ideas.

I find it a very troubling thing to *think*, particularly when I think about my own experiences and try to extract from those experiences the meaning that seems genuinely inherent in them. At first such thinking is very satisfying, because it seems to discover sense and pattern in a whole host of discrete events. But then it very often becomes dismaying, because I realize how ridiculous these thoughts, which have much value to me, would seem to most people. My impression is that if I try to find the meaning of my own experience it leads me, nearly always, in directions regarded as absurd.

So in the next three or four minutes, I will try to digest some of the meanings which have come to me from my classroom experience and the experience I have had in individual and group therapy. They are in no way intended as conclusions for someone else, or a guide to what others should do or be. They are the very tentative meanings, as of April 1952, which my experience has had for me, and some of the bothersome questions which their absurdity raises. I will put each idea or meaning in a separate lettered paragraph, not because they are in any particular logical order, but because each meaning is separately important to me.

a. I may as well start with this one in view of the purposes of this conference. *My experience has been that I cannot teach another person how to teach.* To attempt it is for me, in the long run, futile.

b. *It seems to me that anything that can be taught to another is relatively inconsequential, and has little or no significant influence on behavior.* That sounds so ridiculous I can't help but question it at the same time that I present it.

c. *I realize increasingly that I am only interested in learnings which significantly influence behavior.* Quite possibly this is simply a personal idiosyncrasy.

d. *I have come to feel that the only learning which significantly influences behavior is self-discovered, self-appropriated learning.*

e. *Such self-discovered learning, truth that has been personally appropriated and assimilated in experience, cannot be directly communicated to another.* As soon as an individual tries to communicate such experience directly, often with a quite natural enthusiasm, it becomes teaching, and its results are inconsequential. It was some relief recently to discover that Søren Kierkegaard, the Danish philosopher, had found this too, in his own experience, and stated it very clearly a century ago. It made it seem less absurd.

f. As a consequence of the above, *I realize that I have lost interest in being a teacher.*

g. When I try to teach, as I do sometimes, I am appalled by the results, which seem a little more than inconsequential, because sometimes the teaching appears to succeed. When this happens I find that the results are damaging. It seems to cause the individual to distrust his own experience, and to stifle significant learning. *Hence I have come to feel that the outcomes of teaching are either unimportant or hurtful.*

h. When I look back at the results of my past teaching, the real results seem the same—either damage was done, or nothing significant occurred. This is frankly troubling.

i. As a consequence, *I realize that I am only interested in being a learner, preferably learning things that matter, that have some significant influence on my own behavior.*

j. *I find it very rewarding to learn,* in groups, in relationships with one person as in therapy, or by myself.

k. *I find that one of the best, but most difficult ways for me to learn is to drop my own defensiveness, at least temporarily, and to try to understand the way in which his experience seems and feels to the other person.*

l. *I find that another way of learning for me is to state my own uncertainties, to try to clarify my puzzlements, and thus get closer to the meaning that my experience actually seems to have.*

m. This whole train of experiencing, and the meanings that I have thus far discovered in it, seem to have launched me on a process which is both fascinating and at times a little frightening. *It seems to mean letting my experience carry me on, in a direction which appears to be forward, toward goals that I can but dimly define, as I try to understand at least the current meaning of that experience.* The sensation is that of floating with a complex stream of experience, with the fascinating possibility of trying to comprehend its ever changing complexity.

I am almost afraid I may seem to have gotten away from any discussion of learning, as well as teaching. Let me again introduce a practical note by saying that by themselves these interpretations of my own experience may sound queer and aberrant, but not particularly shocking. It is when I realize the *implications* that I shudder a bit at the distance I have come from the common-sense world that everyone knows is right. I can best illustrate that by saying that if the experiences of others had been the same as mine, and if they had discovered similar meanings in it, many consequences would be implied.

a. Such experience would imply that we would do away with teaching. People would get together if they wished to learn.

b. We would do away with examinations. They measure only the inconsequential type of learning.

c. The implication would be that we would do away with grades and credits for the same reason.

d. We would do away with degrees as a measure of competence partly for the same reason. Another reason is that a degree marks an end or a conclusion of something, and a learner is only interested in the continuing process of learning.

e. It would imply doing away with the exposition of conclusions, for we would realize that no one learns significantly from conclusions.

I think I had better stop there. I do not want to become too fantastic. I want to know primarily whether anything in my inward thinking as I have tried to describe it, speaks to anything in your experience of the classroom as you have lived it, and if so, what the meanings are that exist for you in *your* experience.

# 5

# The Model of Good Teaching

MARIE M. HUGHES & ASSOCIATES

What is good teaching? The teacher-learner situation in its complexity, its flow, and its multiple relationships requires creativity on the part of the teacher. If teaching may be described as decision-making in interaction, then the product of the teacher's decision is the response he makes to the child or group with whom he is interacting. When the response is not routine or stereotyped, it is creative. The occasion is never quite the same and won't be again. The effort made to understand and to respond within the meaning of a specific and unique child must be a creative act to be successful. The measure, then, of good teaching is the quality of the response the teacher makes to the child or group with whom he is interacting. It is the child who is reaching out, seeking, raising the questions, trying out his ideas.

Marie M. Hughes and Associates, "The Model of Good Teaching," *Development of the Means for the Assessment of the Quality of Teaching in Elementary Schools*. U.S. Office of Education Cooperative Research Project No. 353 (Salt Lake City: The University of Utah, 1959), pp. 215–22. Reprinted by permission.

How does the teacher respond so that he can be used as a resource by the child? To become a man of autonomy and initiative, to become a man with confidence in himself, the child needs to have opportunities to try himself out by initiating ideas and actions which are successful most of the time. This he can do only if the teacher makes the appropriate response. The responses of the teacher may include:

Giving the child support by telling him things are going along well, by assuring him that his is a good idea

Giving him a direct answer to a question that he asks, or helping him locate the answer if it is not known by the teacher

Giving him a chance to elaborate his idea by asking him more about it in a nonthreatening and nonevaluative manner

Giving him an evaluation, either positive or negative, that points up specifically what is correct or incorrect; or by

Giving him a chance to relate to his own experience

If the child is to become a man who is "open to his experience," a man who can encompass much of reality, then as a child he must relate positively to more people, things, and situations. The teacher's response to him must be such that he wants to reenter the situation. When failure is more or less continuous, one reduces his level of aspiration and oftentimes withdraws from the situation. Therefore, the teacher's response must include:

Requiring from the child only that which he is capable of doing

Opening new possibilities to him without coercion

Withholding all sarcasm and ridicule

Interpreting to him the data in the situation of which he is aware

If the child is to become a man who has positive feelings toward himself and cherishes uniqueness in others, then the teacher's response to him must respect his own individuality. Such responses may include:

Giving the child some choice in what he is doing; for example, what he writes about, what he reads, the picture he paints

Expressing a belief in the child as a person

Listening to him

Accepting most of his ideas

Helping him gain competence in the things he cherishes

If the child is to grow into a man who possesses highly developed communicative skills, he must have opportunity to talk and to listen to others. The teacher's responses must include:

Seeking for his opinion and experience

Giving him an opportunity to use a variety of media of communication

Giving him a model of standard language usage

Providing him with a variety of books and other reading materials

Seeking to further his purposes in reading

Giving him opportunity to compare his reading with his new experience, to draw inferences and generalizations from his reading

Seeking the child's own idiomatic response in writing and other media of expression

If the child is to grow into a man who acts with an attitude of social responsibility the teacher's responses must include:

Setting of limits with him and for him

Clarifying standards with public criteria

Structuring the situation with clarity

Reprimanding with public criteria

Giving the child responsibility for others

Evaluating with discrimination

Good teaching, then, requires appropriate responsiveness to the data the child and group are placing in the situation. It is in this way that the exploring and searching activities of the child or group can be rewarded properly. When their own seeking activities are rewarded, they become involved and commit themselves further to the activity. We believe: "The child's capacity to create new and challenging problems for himself is his most potent source of continuous growth and development."[1] It is his own desire for growth that makes possible the constructively creative man.

Good teaching requires a reduction in the controlling functions exercised continuously by the teacher. We have shown how these controls extend to the exact wording of answers, to the minutiae of a problem for attention. We have shown that the child's explorations in the way of looking ahead, of relating to his own experiences are usually crushed as the teacher restructures the child back into the narrow path laid out for him. The stereotyped and repetitive question and answer blocks children's use of higher mental processes. They recall and repeat; they do not synthesize or generalize.

The extensive and pervasive control

[1]Manual Barkan, *Foundations of Art Education* (New York: The Ronald Press Company, 1955).

under which children live in the class-room keeps them dependent and prevents them from full participation in the subject matter (content) of the school.

Good teaching requires that the classroom be well managed so that the business of learning may receive full attention. This means that the teacher perform the functions of controlling with clarity and with consistency. It does mean that in the position of teacher with its superior-subordinate relationship, the power component be ameliorated through relating the direction or the command to situational factors or to the larger society.

It is quite probable that most teaching would be improved by the reduction of the present large number of controlling acts to one-third or one-half of what they now are.

Good teaching requires that the human environment be accepting of each individual, that in some way it tell him that he is important. This suggests that teachers not "pit" one group of children against another, but find ways to integrate the wide range of differences that are always present. It suggests a personal rapport between teacher and child. This personal rapport is built upon many little things. For example, the granting of a request other than routine says to the child, "I care for you. You count with me." Psychologists have noted that gratification in one area tends to instigate a feeling of well-being that extends into other areas of an individual's life.[2]

Individual rapport is built through

[2] Louis Barclay Murphy, *Personality in Young Children* (New York: Basic Books, Inc., Publishers, 1957), Vol. II, Chap. IV; and Bruno Bettleheim, *Love Is Not Enough* (New York: Free Press of Glencoe, Inc., 1950).

empathy and support from one who is a significant person in one's life. It is developed with interpretation of reality that enriches or makes the situation more for one.

Good teaching keeps the interpersonal relationships supportive within the classroom. There are common problems, concerns, and agreements because people have had a chance to talk and to listen to one another. There has been time to explore the opinions and wants of the group. Out of this, a shared-problem-solving attitude develops. To maintain a supportive climate the negative acts of sarcasm and threat must be abolished. A reduction in the number of admonishments and reprimands will make those used more effective, especially when they are linked to clearly stated situational factors.

The concept of functions performed in the classroom by the teacher in interaction makes it possible to relate action to the objectives toward which one is working.

The effects on children of the pattern of teaching functions to which they are subjected day after day and year after year are accumulative. Whether or not the "life space" permitted them in the classroom is sufficient to allow them to explore their own ideas, to solve problems of many kinds, to have some choice as to their own activities makes a real difference in their own involvement in the subject matter (content) of the school, in their attitude toward learning, and in their development of autonomy. Whether or not they are respected as individuals makes a difference in their development of confidence and positive self-concept.

What teachers do in the classroom makes a difference.

Good teaching requires that the

teacher be a well educated, mature person who has the insight and energy for this demanding job. Every decision made in the classroom should be a considered one. This undoubtedly means a smaller number of students in each classroom. Growth is wavering and uneven as well as forward; it goes by leaps as well as crawls. The specifics for a growing child are not entirely predictable. To provide for the differences that are the hopes of each generation requires more than a textbook and a dictionary. It requires the responsive human environment that fosters exploration and initiative.

# 6

# The N.E.A. Code of Ethics

Believing that true democracy can best be achieved by a process of free public education made available to all the children of all the people; that the teachers in the United States have a large and inescapable responsibility in fashioning the ideals of children and youth; that such responsibility requires the services of men and women of high ideals, broad education, and profound human understanding; and, in order that the aims of democratic education may be ·realized more fully, that the welfare of the teaching profession may be promoted; and, that teachers may observe proper standards of conduct in their professional relations, the National Education Association of the United States proposes this code of ethics for its members. The term "teacher" as used in this code shall include all persons directly engaged in educational work, whether in a teach-

"Ethics for Teachers: The N.E.A. Code," Personal Growth Leaflet No. 135 (Washington, D.C.: Senior Citizens of America, n.d.). Reprinted by permission.

ing, an administrative, or a supervisory capacity.

## ARTICLE I—
## RELATIONS TO PUPILS AND THE HOME

SECTION 1

It is the duty of the teacher to be just, courteous, and professional in all his relations with pupils. He should consider their individual differences, needs, interests, temperaments, aptitudes, and environments.

SECTION 2

He should refrain from tutoring pupils of his classes for pay, and from referring such pupils to any member of his immediate family for tutoring.

SECTION 3

The professional relations of a teacher with his pupils demand the same scrupulous care that is required in the confidential relations of one teacher with another. A teacher, therefore, should not disclose any information obtained confidentially from his pupils, unless it is for the best interest of the child and the public.

SECTION 4

A teacher should seek to establish friendly and intelligent cooperation between home and school, ever keeping in mind the dignity of his profession and the welfare of the pupils. He should do or say nothing that would undermine the confidence and respect of his pupils for their parents. He should inform the pupils and parents regarding the importance, purposes, accomplishments, and needs of the schools.

**ARTICLE II—**
**RELATIONS TO CIVIC AFFAIRS**

SECTION 1

It is the obligation of every teacher to inculcate in his pupils an appreciation of the principles of democracy. He should direct full and free discussion of appropriate controversial issues with the expectation that comparisons, contrasts, and interpretations will lead to an understanding, appreciation, acceptance, and practice of the principles of democracy. A teacher should refrain from using his classroom privileges and prestige to promote partisan politics, sectarian religious views, or selfish propaganda of any kind.

SECTION 2

A teacher should recognize and perform all the duties of citizenship. He should subordinate his personal desires to the best interests of public good. He should be loyal to the school system, the state, and the nation, but should exercise his right to give constructive criticisms.

SECTION 3

A teacher's life should show that education makes people better citizens and better neighbors. His personal conduct should not needlessly offend the accepted pattern of behavior of the community in which he serves.

**ARTICLE III—**
**RELATIONS TO THE PROFESSION**

SECTION 1

Each member of the teaching profession should dignify his calling on all occasions and should uphold the importance of his services to society. On the other hand he should not indulge in personal exploitation.

SECTION 2

A teacher should encourage able and sincere individuals to enter the teaching profession and discourage those who plan to use this profession merely as a stepping-stone to some other vocation.

SECTION 3

It is the duty of the teacher to maintain his own efficiency by study, by travel, and by other means which keep him abreast of the trends in education and the world in which he lives.

SECTION 4

Every teacher should have membership in his local, state, and national professional organizations, and should participate actively and unselfishly in them. Professional growth and personality development are the natural product of such professional activity. Teachers should avoid the promotion of organization rivalry and divisive competition which weaken the cause of education.

### Section 5

While not limiting their services by reason of small salary, teachers should insist upon a salary scale commensurate with the social demands laid upon them by society. They should not knowingly underbid a rival or agree to accept a salary lower than that provided by a recognized schedule. They should not apply for positions for the sole purpose of forcing an increase in salary in their present positions; correspondingly, school officials should not refuse to give deserved salary increases to efficient employees until offers from other school authorities have forced them so to do.

### Section 6

A teacher should not apply for a specific position currently held by another teacher. Unless the rules of a school system otherwise prescribe, he should file his application with the chief executive officer.

### Section 7

Since qualification should be the sole determining factor in appointment and promotion, the use of pressure on school officials to secure a position or to obtain other favors is unethical.

### Section 8

Testimonials regarding teachers should be truthful and confidential, and should be treated as confidential information by school authorities receiving them.

### Section 9

A contract, once signed, should be faithfully adhered to until it is dissolved by mutual consent. Ample notification should be given both by school officials and teachers in case a change in position is to be made.

### Section 10

Democratic procedures should be practiced by members of the teaching profession. Cooperation should be predicated upon the recognition of the worth and the dignity of individual personality. All teachers should observe the professional courtesy of transacting official business with the properly designated authority.

### Section 11

School officials should encourage and nuture the professional growth of all teachers by promotion or by other appropriate methods of recognition. School officials who fail to recommend a worthy teacher for a better position outside their school system because they do not desire to lose his services are acting unethically.

### Section 12

A teacher should avoid unfavorable criticism of other teachers except that formally presented to a school official for the welfare of the school. It is unethical to fail to report to the duly constituted authority any matters which are detrimental to the welfare of the school.

### Section 13

Except when called upon for counsel or other assistance, a teacher should not interfere in any matter between another teacher and a pupil.

SECTION 14

A teacher should not act as an agent, or accept a commission, royalty, or other compensation, for endorsing books or other school materials in the selection or purchase of which he can exert influence, or concerning which he can exercise the right of decision; nor should he accept a commission or other compensation for helping another teacher to secure a position.

ARTICLE IV—
STANDING COMMITTEE ON
PROFESSIONAL ETHICS

There is hereby established a Standing Committee on Professional Ethics consisting of five members appointed by the president.

It shall be the duty of the Committee to study and to take appropriate action on such cases of violation of this Code as may be referred to it. The Committee shall be responsible also for publicizing the Code, promoting its use in institutions for the preparation of teachers, and recommending needed modifications.

If, when a case is reported, it is found to come from a state which has an Ethics Committee, such case shall immediately be referred to said state committee for investigation and action. In the case of a violation reported from a state which has neither a code nor an ethics committee, or from a state which has a code but no ethics committee, the NEA Ethics Committee shall take such action as seems wise and reasonable and will impress members with the importance of respect for proper professional conduct. Such action shall be reported to the chief school officers of the community and the state from which the violation is reported.

The Committee is further vested with authority to expel a member from the National Education Association for flagrant violation of this code.

# ACTIVITIES

1. If you were to observe a teacher practicing his profession, what are some aspects of the classroom, the climate, the planning, the interaction between teacher and students, etc. to which you would pay particular attention?

2. What bases did you use to identify the areas named in answer to Question 1? Did research evidence give much direction? Did learnings from previous education courses suggest crucial areas to be observed?

3. Nathaniel Cantor[1] has suggested that the following statements are assumptions that serve as the basis for orthodox teaching:

### THE ASSUMPTIONS OF ORTHODOX TEACHING

a. It is assumed that the teacher's responsibility is to set out what is learned and that the student's job is to learn it.

b. It is assumed that knowledge taken on authority is educative in itself.

c. It is assumed that education can be obtained through disconnected subjects.

d. It is assumed that subject matter is the same to the learner as to the teacher.

e. It is assumed that education prepares the student for later life rather than that it is a living experience.

f. It is assumed that the teacher is responsible for the pupil's acquiring of knowledge.

g. It is assumed that pupils must be coerced into working on some tasks.

h. It is assumed that knowledge is more important than learning.

i. It is assumed that education is primarily an intellectual process.

Would teachers who taught in the way of Carl Rogers accept these assumptions? Would they add or eliminate some? How would you answer these questions in terms of the teaching described by Broudy, Hughes, L. Raths?

[1] Nathaniel Cantor, *The Teaching Learning-Process* (New York: The Dryden Press, 1953), pp. 59–72.

29

4. What are your assumptions about teaching?

5. Play the role of a teacher and instruct some fellow students. Listen to a tape recording of your lesson. What comments, questions, or other verbal behavior could be classified as an "act" according to Green? Which of the comments could be classified as a "response"?

6. Consider the validity of the following statement: "All the views of teaching presented in the chapter are subjective." Is there an alternative way of viewing teaching?

7. Common to most professions is a code of ethics; for the teaching profession such a code is advanced by the N.E.A. How specific are the principles of the N.E.A. Code of Ethics to the teaching profession? Could the tenets apply to any other profession as well?

## Chapter Two

# INTERACTION IN THE CLASSROOM

If you are interested in evaluating a teacher's effectiveness, you must be conscious of his behavior in the classroom. But classroom observation is not easy. How does one systematically observe the teacher and some thirty individual students? One possibility is to limit the observation to specific instances: giving praise, asking questions, criticizing. Such a procedure may be useful at times, but much which transpires in the classroom remains unrecorded. Who is to say that these unrecorded segments are less important in evaluating teacher effectiveness in the classroom than those which were recorded?

Still, the question remains, how can one systematically observe a teacher and some thirty individual students? Educational researchers have been working on this problem for over three decades. As they have gained experience and sophistication, they have moved closer to procedures which will promote systematic observation of the teacher-student interaction in the classroom. Although some still tend to emphasize particular aspects of this interaction, others have striven for a general descriptive observation system.

In the reports which follow you may find several techniques which will facilitate your observation of classrooms. As you read about them, you might ask yourself how a teacher could employ them in his own classroom while he is teaching. You might also look for agreement or discrepancies among the various research findings reported. Can you predict your reaction if you find two research reports in substantial agreement about how effective teachers behave? How will you react if two reports disagree? How do you suppose the researchers defined "effective teaching?" How would you define it?

# 7

# What Is Teaching ?  One Viewpoint

## MARIE M. HUGHES

Psychologists, other researchers, and curriculum workers are in agreement that a most important variable in the classroom is that of the teacher.

The teacher behavior in the classroom that is most pervasive and continuous is, of course, the verbal action. The verbal and the nonverbal behavior of teachers is, according to Mary Aschner, "the language of responsible actions designed to influence the behavior of those under instruction" (1).

Indispensable data then for a description and analysis of teaching are verbatim records of what the teacher said and did and the response made by a child or group, including children's initiatory actions directed toward the teacher.

### DATA OF THIS STUDY

The data of this study (2) were secured from 41 elementary teachers—7

Marie M. Hughes, "What Is Teaching? One Viewpoint," *Educational Leadership*, XIX, No. 4 (January 1962), 251–59. Copyright ©1962 by the Association for Supervision and Curriculum Development. Reprinted by permission.

men and 34 women. These teachers had classrooms in 19 buildings in 8 school districts.

The representativeness of the group may be judged from the fact they received their training degrees in 22 different states. Their age range was 25 to 50 years; their teaching experience, 5 years to 30 years; with a bimodal distribution at the ninth and fifteenth years. They were career teachers and judged good by supervisory and consultant staff members.

Three 30-minute records were secured from each of the teachers by two observers working at one time in the classroom with the teacher's cooperation and knowledge of the exact time the observers would arrive to take the record. In general, the records were taken several days apart.

A brief episode from one 30-minute record may provide a more adequate picture of the data with which we worked:

RECORD #2620, PAGE 2:

T.: Carl, do you remember the day you came to school and said you could play a tune on the piano? It was a tune we all knew and so we sang it with you. You found out you could play the same tune on the tone bells. I wonder if you'd play the same tune for us today.

T.: My! We liked to sing with you. Can we start our music time by your playing again and our singing with you? Why don't you play it on the tone bells?

Carl: I'd like to play it on the piano.

T.: Well, all right, you may play it on the piano if you'd rather. Do you want to play it all through once or shall we start right off together?

Carl: I'll play it through. (Played on piano "Mary Had a Little Lamb" with one hand.)

T.: That was very nice!

Carl: I think you could sing with me.

T.: All right, we'd be glad to. (Carl played and children sang.) Thank you, Carl.

Carl: You could even do all of it.

T.: You mean we could sing all of the verses?

Carl: I can even do "followed her to school one day . . . etc."

T.: I'm sure you can, Carl. Thank you very much.

What does the teacher do? It is obvious that there is a wide repertoire of behavior open to the teacher.

The teacher *tells* people what to do.

The teacher *sets* goals, the specifics of attention. "Today, we shall do the 25 problems on page 90."

The teacher *gives* directions. "Take your books out and open them to page 90." "Do not write your name."

The teacher *reprimands*. "Take your seat, Johnny."

The teacher *accuses*. "You didn't work very hard."

The teacher *admonishes*. This is, of course, before anything happens. "Don't forget to close the door." "Make sure you look up your words."

The teacher *supports* and *encourages*. "That's nice." "Good." "Fine." "OK." "I knew you could do it."

The teacher *grants* or *denies* requests.

The teacher *clarifies* and *elaborates* on the problem or content under discussion.

The teacher *asks* questions.

The teacher *gives* cues.

There are many ways to categorize or organize the verbal behavior and non-verbal behavior of a teacher. It is the point of view of this investigator that the superior-subordinate relationship in the teacher-learner situation, with its culturally bestowed power position

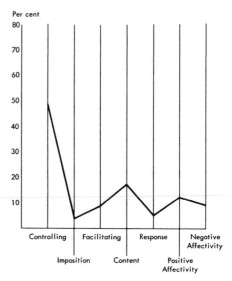

**Fig. 1.  Mean Distribution of Teaching Acts for 90 Minutes Observation for 35 Teachers**

over the child, makes it impossible for the teacher to act in the classroom without performing a *function* for some child, group, or the entire class as recipients. It is the teacher who holds the power to give aid or withhold aid; to judge and to punish; to gratify or to deny; to accept or to ignore the response of a child.

Actually, children who are not participants in a given episode of interaction with the teacher do respond to his behavior (3, 4).

The presumptuousness of looking at teacher behavior from the standpoint of functions performed for the child is recognized. The 30-minute consecutive record often made it possible to follow actions and reactions through an epi-

sode, and many times several episodes. In addition, for a four year period
there has been consistent effort through
interviews and paper and pencil tests
to discover children's views of typical
classroom situations. To date, responses

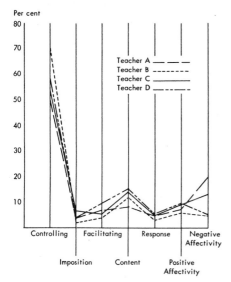

Fig. 2. **Distribution Patterns of Teaching Acts for Four Teachers High in Controlling**

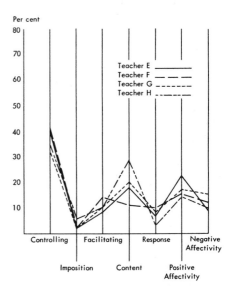

Fig. 3. **Distribution Patterns of Teaching Acts for Four Teachers Low in Controlling**

have been secured from some 1400
fifth and sixth graders in three states
(5, 6). Interviews have been held with
younger children, and with junior
high youths.

As expected, children react in an
individual manner; however, there is a
great range of intensity of reaction. In
general, there is a high degree of emotionality, with children responding to
elements in the situations that were not
intended or foreseen by adults. Another
tentative finding was that for any given
teacher behavior, from 7 to 20 per cent
of those to whom it was directed appeared to make no response. They were
not involved or they failed to identify
with the situation when given the opportunity in interviews or paper and pencil
test. The mode for this noninvolvement

was 14 per cent. Most of the teachers
are, of course, aware of the phenomenon of one or more children seeming
not to be "with it."

## DESCRIPTION OF TEACHING

Figure 1 presents the mean distribution of teaching acts performed by
the teachers during three 30-minute
periods of teaching. It is immediately
clear that the largest number of teaching acts falls within the category of
controlling functions. Figures 2 and 3
present the mean distributions of teaching acts for teachers who are among
the highest and those who are among
the lowest in the exercise of control
in the classroom. Since the present
report is devoted largely to an exposition of Controlling Functions, and the
Development of Content, a brief
definition of the other categories may
be useful.

TEACHER IMPOSITION

These are acts where the teacher projects himself into the situation. For example: In a few classrooms without routine procedures for supplies, the teacher might say over and over again, "Keep your seat, I'll bring it to you." Another is the expression of evaluation e.g., on reading a story in a foreign locale, "Their names are certainly queer." Moralizing is another act that falls in this category. As may be noted in the figures, very few teaching acts fall in this category.

FACILITATING

These acts may be thought of as management functions that are relatively neutral. All statements that designate time, change of schedule, and so forth. Those information seeking acts that are nonevaluative; that is, the child is free to have or not have it, e.g.: "Who brought lunch money?" Rhetorical questions of "Wasn't that fun?" "Did you enjoy it?" "We're finished, aren't we?" Such questions, if they evoke a response, secure a chorus of "yes" or "no" as expected. More often than not the teacher does not wait for an answer.

These management functions differentiate least among teachers and are the most stable with a teacher's series of records.

PERSONAL RESPONSE

This includes meeting the individual requests of children, listening to their personal interests and experiences unrelated to the content under consideration.

These are all positive responses and most often are interactions between a teacher and a single child.

POSITIVE AND NEGATIVE FUNCTIONS

These need little comment since they are the praise and reproof categories. It is realized that the use of positive and negative reinforcement controls behavior; however, by their very nature these teaching acts are, as a group, more affectivity-laden. Therefore, it was deemed desirable to trace them out separately.

Although space does not permit an elaboration of these last three categories, it is hypothesized that they have much to do with the personal liking or not liking of the teacher. There is something in a personal response that conveys the idea, "You count—you are important enough for me to listen to you, and to do something just for you."

Approval and acceptance were expressed most often in a stereotyped manner: "Fine," "Yes," "O.K." "Good," "All right." Such expressions without a definite referent served the purpose of allaying tension. It was one way of saying. "All is well."

It is hypothesized that the acceptance of reprimands of any degree of intensity depends to a large extent on the teacher's use of *public criteria*. If he makes clear the elements in the situation that call for certain required behavior, children may protest, but they can accept the reprimand as just. Consistency of teacher behavior is another element in fairness.

In general, more acts of positive affectivity were recorded for teachers than of negative affectivity; however, Fig. 2, depicting teachers high in control, shows two teachers who were more negative than positive in their teaching. The gross differences in distribution of teaching acts shown in Figs. 2 and 3 suggest that the classroom is quite different for the children in attendance.

## CONTROLLING FUNCTIONS

Our study showed that the teaching acts most frequently performed were those of control. By control, reference is not limited to discipline. Since these teachers were considered good teachers, their classes were well organized and generally attentive. By control is meant goal setting, directing the children to the precise thing to which they give attention. Not only is the content named for children, but they are held to a specific answer and processes of working. Such control is firm and pervasive. In many classrooms the control might be considered implacable. Sixty-eight per cent of the teachers had one or more of their records with 50 per cent or more of their teaching acts categorized as controlling.

The teacher most often wanted only *one* answer and refused all others. For example, a third grade was reporting on books read, then classifying them according to theme. One little girl made a few remarks about her book and then said, "It's a fantasy." The teacher immediately replied, "You mean imaginative, don't you?" No reward for the use of a divergent word or a suggestion of any relationship or differentiation between the two.

The control of content is exercised by the teacher in the structure of the *what* to give attention to. In a third grade arithmetic class each child had a foot rule. The teacher structured the group by saying. "Today, we are going to study the middle line. What is it called?" Several children answered. "One-third," "a fourth," "a half." One boy was busy measuring some paper on his desk and said, "This is $6\frac{1}{4}$ inches." (Correct) The teacher replied, "Just the middle line today. We just talk about the half."

As long as the question or statement that structures the class or the individual requires but *one* answer, the teacher is in absolute control. Nothing more may properly occur until the next question is asked. Such structure of content appears to evoke memory but little more in mental activity.

When structure is open, more than one answer is possible. Indeed, there may not be an absolutely right answer. For example, "What might happen if the new highway went across the state by one route instead of another?" Closed structure of content resulted in question and answer between teacher and class—it was strictly recitation. Open structure, with more than one answer possible, resulted in participation of several pupils before re-entry of the teacher in the situation. In other words, more ideas were generated and more pupils became involved in the work.

## CONTROL AS REGULATION OF WHO

Another phase of controlling behavior is that of regulating who will do what, answer questions, give the report, take lunch money to the office, etc. Such regulation can serve indirectly as punishment or as reward.

"Your work is finished, so you take the books to Mrs. Jones." At least a criterion of choice, "your work is done," is made public. In one episode the children were sharing their stories with one another and the teacher regulated after each story with, "Whom shall I choose, whom shall I ask to go next?" A child would then be named. As teacher choices followed one another, the excitement mounted over the who was to be next and not over the content of the stories.

Other teachers set up some *neutral* manner of regulating. "Write your names on the board when you are ready and we shall take them in order." Another teacher had children put a slip on a spindle. Their stories were then read in order of completion. Some teachers made charts of committees who worked at the various housekeeping and management chores a week at a time.

We found in one sixth grade that the students considered the teacher unfair. He was perplexed, so we tried to find out why this perception. It turned out that Lou and Hazel always got to answer the telephone. They sat next to the office and could answer without moving about unduly. This fact had not been shared with the children; consequently, all they saw was unfairness.

The use of *Public Criteria* for the controlling actions of the teacher is suggestive. It ameliorates the power of the teacher. It gives the authority an impersonal embodiment.

### CONTROL OVER MANY ACTIVITIES

The controls exercised are expressed in all kinds of activities. It was difficult to get hold of the criteria used by teachers in their expression of control.

A child was making cut-out paper pears to be placed in a cornucopia poster filled with fruits and vegetables. The teacher said, "Why don't you make them bigger?"

Child: I made them like they are on my grandfather's farm.
T.: Get the picture from my desk and make them big like that.

The teacher judged in cases of altercation or conflict of interest. Incidentally, the conflict of interest was frequently between teacher and child or group. To illustrate, a teacher said:

T.: Who do you wish to have help you with your reading?

Child: Madeline.
T.: How about Susan?
Child: Jane.
T.: Let's see. Mary would be a good one. Yes, go sit with Mary.

A junior high school teacher working with the English class putting out a paper said:

T.: Here are some interesting things about the Navy that we could put in the paper. Who wants to write it?
Agnes: I will. I read it and thought the boys might like it.
T.: No, you already have three things in. I'll write it myself.

We hypothesize that consistent use of *Public Criteria* might aid in reducing the conflicts with authority. *Public Criteria* are situationally placed:

T.: There is time for *one* story before noon.
T.: We had trouble with a certain kind of problem yesterday; therefore, we will work on similar problems today.
T.: The children using the saws are on the barn committee and must have them until they finish; therefore, you have to wait.

*Public Criteria* can also express the conventions and accepted ways of doing. "You have too many erasures on your paper to read it easily," instead of "*I* won't take a paper that looks like that."

### PLACE OF CONTROLLING FUNCTIONS

This investigator believes that it is the business of the teacher to manage (control, if you prefer) the classroom so that learning for all the children present may proceed. Controlling functions will undoubtedly constitute between 30 and 40 per cent of a teacher's behavior; however, the power component may be ameliorated through the use of:

Open-structure that permits some choice or requires more than one answer

Increased Regulation (*who* is to respond) that is neutral or done with public criteria that expresses the reason for the choice

Directions that are clear with limits set to reduce repetition of directions and lessen the number of reprimands

Rules that are group developed, situationally oriented, and enforceable. They should make sense to children

## DEVELOPMENT OF CONTENT

There is a relationship between the development of content and the nature of the control exercised by structure. When the structure permits no exploration on the part of children it serves to delimit and restrict.

A primary class was reading about a baby elephant. They discussed its age and other things pertaining to the picture of the baby elephant. Finally Ben spoke up an said:

Ben: Look, here is an elephant with a tusk.

T.: Yes, that elephant is on the other page. Read this page and find out what Baby Elephant did when she got to the monkey cage.

It might have been profitable to raise the question why one elephant had tusks and the other did not. It can be hypothesized that the mental processes evoked by the different situations are likewise different.

In another class the teacher and class were looking at a large map of the two hemispheres, when one child asked where the local town was. The teacher replied, "It is about here, but can't be seen on this map. I'll get you one and you can find it and other towns you know."

The teaching acts that develop content elaborate and add to the content or problem under consideration. Response is made to the data placed in the situation by the children. It is believed that children involved in content have something to say. They are encouraged in this by the teacher who respects their efforts. The teacher *stimulates* by offering several suggestions of ideas or of activities that might be done. The choice of doing, however, remains with the child. (It is, of course, proper to give a direction or an assignment, which then would be an act of control.)

Evaluation that keeps content as a referent is in this category. To illustrate, "You have used several kinds of sentence structure in your composition. Very good." The phrase, "That's good," spoken after a child has read the composition does not tell him whether he was good to have written it at all, or good to have read it, or just good to have gotten through the episode. In terms of compositions, he has received nothing definite that helps him move ahead with his writing. He has received teacher approval. With most of the evaluation made in the form of generalized approval or disapproval, such expressions foster dependence on teacher instead of judgment and interest in the content.

If children and youth are to become interested in subject matter for its own sake, do they not need to link their own experience and make their own personal inquiry in relationship to it? If children are not listened to, how can one know what concepts are developed or what interpretations are made?

An upper grade discussion had been going on concerning early California Indians.

T.: Incidentally, did the California Indians have a pretty easy life?

Arthur: No.

T.: Yes they did, Arthur. Don't you remember? Who can tell me about it?

What logic was Arthur using in his

reply? Was it strictly subjective, "I wouldn't have liked it," or had he assessed the situation with some judgment?

When do children use a variety of mental processes such as making comparisons, explaining with some logic, noting relationships, generalizing from a series of data? What kind of questions and teacher responses evoke what mental activity (7)?

Perhaps teachers need to develop what might be called *creative use of interruptions.*

Not long ago a mother reported the disgust of her kindergarten son whose teacher allegedly told him that he couldn't talk about dinosaurs until third grade. The child had been to the Dinosaur Monument and Museum with his family. While there, the father had bought each boy a book which had been read at home.

One can conjecture all kinds of reasons why the teacher did not wish to get off on dinosaurs. However, the question remains, "In what situations do teachers act in ways that children can see them as people who *aid* in their personal quest for knowing? Since this child's dinosaurs were tied to Vernal, Utah, it might have been very stimulating to listen to his story and also mention the Berea Tar Pits within the city of Los Angeles, as another locale where bones had been found.

It is, of course, possible that the child wanted attention only. Even so, the school can meet such personal needs of children through the use of their explorations and inquiries in the development of content. It is suggested that children's questions and remarks be integrated with the lesson plan of the teacher.

The present study of teaching found that the most prevalent series of teaching acts were in question-answer test or recitation situations. Far too many such situations were spent in working for the specific answer wanted by the teacher.

Of the total group of 41, only 3 teachers had all of their records with 20 or more of their teaching acts in this category of development of content. Seventy-four per cent of all records had 20 per cent or less of teaching acts falling in this category of exploration, amplification, utilization of children's questions and remarks, evaluation and stimulation. This category has been described as working with the content or problem and called *development of content.*

Some relationships of one category to another may be of interest. Development of Content and Negative Affectivity correlate—.42 significant at the .001 level in social studies. This relationship is not unexpected, since teachers who use many acts of Negative Affectivity are not responsive to children's ideas and explorations even in subject matter.

Personal Response is correlated —.35 with Controlling and a —.38 with Negative Affectivity. Again, this is not unexpected and it holds for all records regardless of kind of work the classes were doing.

The point of view expressed in this report is that teaching may be described in terms of functions the teacher behavior, verbal and nonverbal, performs for the child, group, or class to whom it is directed. It was found possible to categorize such teaching acts in seven categories: Controlling, Imposition, Facilitating, Development of Content, Personal Response, Positive Affectivity, and Negative Affectivity.

Control of the class was exercised in varied activities, but particularly in terms of *what* to give attention to and *who* was to do what; also, the *how* of doing was prescribed and enforced. Management of the classroom for learning is the teacher's job; therefore, control functions are necessary. It was suggested, however, that the power component the teacher holds may be reduced with changes in verbal behavior.

In dealing with subject matter, little attention was given to children's exploratory remarks or their questions. The questions teachers used for structure were usually closed; that is, asked for one *right* answer. It was suggested that one right answer evoked the use of recall as a mental process instead of stimulating a larger range of mental activity.

It was suggested that *responsiveness* on the part of the teacher to children's remarks, questions, personal experience (data they place in the situation) would lead them to greater involvement in content (subject matter) and stimulate use of higher mental processes.

Teachers demonstrated different patterns in teaching. Different patterns do affect the learning of children (8, 9).

**REFERENCES**

1. Aschner, Mary Jane, "The Language of Teaching," in *Language and Concepts in Education*, ed. by O. Smith and R. Ennis. Skokie, Ill.: Rand McNally & Co., 1961.

2. Hughes, Marie M. and Associates, *The Assessment of the Quality of Teaching: A Research Report*. U. S. Office of Education Cooperative Research Project No. 353. Salt Lake City: The University of Utah, 1959.

3. Kounin, J. and P. Gump, "The Ripple Effect in Discipline," *The Elementary School Journal* (Fall 1958), pp. 158–62.

4. Kounin, J., *et al.*, "Explorations in Classroom Management," *Journal of Teacher Education* (June 1961), pp. 235–46.

5. Carin, Arthur, "Children's Perceptions of Selected Classroom Situations." Doctoral Dissertation, University of Utah, June 1959.

6. De Vaney, Elena, "Perceptions Among Teachers and Students of Varying Cultural Backgrounds." Doctoral Dissertation, University of Utah, October 1960.

7. Aschner, M. J. McCue, "Asking Questions to Trigger Thinking," *N.E.A. Journal* (September 1961), pp. 44–46.

8. Flanders, Ned, *Teacher Influence: An Interaction Analysis*. U. S. Office of Education Cooperative Research Project No. 397. Minneapolis: University of Minnesota, 1960.

9. Sears, Pauline, "What Happens to Pupils Within the Classroom of Elementary Schools." Paper read at American Educational Research Association meeting, Los Angeles, June 30, 1960.

# 8

# Teacher Influence, Pupil Attitudes, and Achievement

## NED A. FLANDERS

### TEACHER INFLUENCE AND TALKING

#### COMMUNICATION AND TEACHER INFLUENCE

Step inside a classroom and what do you hear? The chances are better than 60 per cent you will hear someone talking if you are in an elementary or secondary school classroom.

If someone is talking, the chances are that it will be the teacher more than 70 per cent of the time. Yes, the teacher talks more than all the students combined. He manages class activities by giving directions. He expresses his ideas by lecturing. He stimulates student participation by asking questions. He clarifies student ideas by applying them to the solution of a problem. He praises and encourages students from time to time. On rare occasions he may clarify or diagnose the feelings and attitudes expressed by students or inferred from their behavior. He may also criticize the behavior of a student or class. All are types of teacher statements that can be heard in a classroom.

Most of the functions associated with teaching are implemented by verbal communication. Of course, nonverbal communication does exist and is not unimportant. The nod of the head to encourage student participation, the finger to the lips to warn against talking, the smile, and the frown, these all communicate to students. But nonverbal communication occurs less frequently than verbal communication and the two are usually highly correlated. The frown is most often associated with statements that express disapproval, the smile with statements of approval.

The first step toward systematic classroom management is made when a teacher understands how to control his verbal communication so that he can use his influence as a social force. Unfortunately, this kind of knowledge and the corresponding skill don't

Ned A. Flanders, *Teacher Influence, Pupil Attitudes, and Achievement*, Cooperative Research Monograph No. 12, Office of Education, U.S. Department of Health, Education and Welfare. (Washington, D.C.: Government Printing Office, 1965), pp. 1–23, 111–21.

always go together. As one teacher put it, "I know what I'm doing and I am usually aware of most mistakes that I make, but I don't know what to do about it."

The research reported in this monograph concerns the verbal statements of teachers as they occur in the spontaneous interaction of the classroom. We will explain what has been called a system of classroom interaction analysis, our method of recording and analyzing teacher statements. A theory of teacher influence or, more modestly, some hypotheses of teacher influence will be developed and tested. The data were obtained from research carried out in the Minneapolis and St. Paul public schools before March 1957 and after March 1958. Additional data came from research in Wellington, New Zealand, carried out under a Fulbright Research Scholarship during 1957.

Our basic purpose is greater understanding of the teacher's role, the control he provides while teaching, and the patterns of influence he uses in classroom management.

There are at least two theoretical models that are currently being used to understand interaction analysis data collected in a classroom. One model makes use of the logical steps of problem-solving and draws heavily from what we know about inductive and deductive reasoning, scientific method, procedures for defining terms, level of abstraction, and principles from the field of semantics. This approach is being used in the research of B. Othaniel Smith (14) at the University of Illinois.

The second model, the one we use, is based less on the intellectual skills mentioned above and more on a set of social skills used by teachers to control and manage class activities. This model is based on a psychology of superior-subordinate relationships, adapted to fit classroom conditions. An earlier development can be found in the 59th Yearbook, National Society for the Study of Educational Research (9).

The differences between these two models can be illustrated by the teacher's orientation to classroom behavior. Suppose a teacher becomes aware of intellectual confusion in the remarks of a student because the student uses the same word as if it had two quite different meanings. The teacher's knowledge and skill in defining words and his understanding of level of abstraction will help in diagnosing the intellectual aspects of the problem in terms of the first model. Just how he chooses to provide this information—by lecturing, by asking a series of questions so that the student can "discover" the difficulty, or by directing the student in some semantic exercise—is the kind of choice on which the second model is based. Here the teacher is concerned with his own behavior and how he can best use his authority to enhance student learning.

Neither model is "right" or "wrong," and an understanding of both models is likely to improve teaching. Each model is a frame of reference for organizing ideas about behavior; such an organization guides research. Research within either frame of reference is difficult and tedious; to work in both simultaneously would require more resources than were available at Minnesota when the research reported in this monograph was planned and conducted.

To summarize, this monograph is concerned with analyzing the spontaneous verbal communication of the teacher. A system of interaction analysis is used for this purpose. The procedure involves the classification of statements every 3 seconds and the tabulation of data in special matrices for later analysis. Measures of academic achievement and student attitudes are correlated with the verbal patterns observed in the classroom. Most of the conclusions refer to the role of the teacher in classroom management.

### EARLY RESEARCH ON CLASSROOM CLIMATE

Most research programs have antecedents in the work of other researchers. The research reported in this monograph is no exception. We are indebted to a number of individuals whose work has contributed to our thinking.

The term "classroom climate" refers to generalized attitudes toward the teacher and the class that the pupils share in common despite individual differences. The development of these attitudes is an outgrowth of classroom social interaction. As a result of participating in classroom activities, pupils soon develop common attitudes about how they like their class, the kind of person the teacher is, and how he will act in certain typical situations. These common attitudes color all aspects of classroom behavior, creating a social atmosphere, or climate, that appears to be fairly stable, once established. Thus, the word "climate"[1] is merely a shorthand reference to those qualities that consistently predominate in most teacher-pupil contacts and in contacts among the pupils in the presence or absence of the teacher.

---

[1] Climate is assessed either by analyzing teacher-pupil interaction and inferring underlying attitudes from the interaction, or by the use of a pupil-attitude inventory and predicting the quality of classroom interaction from the results. Its precise meaning, as commonly used, is seldom clear—just as its synonyms, "morale," "rapport," and "emotional tone," are also ambiguous. To have any meaning at all, the word is always qualified by an adjective, and it is in the choice of adjectives that researchers become reformers and too often lose their objectivity.

The earliest systematic studies of spontaneous pupil and teacher behavior that relate directly to classroom climate are those of H. H. Anderson and his colleagues, Helen and Joseph Brewer and Mary Frances Reed (2, 3, 4, and 5 in the bibliography at the end of this monograph); these studies are based on the observation of "dominative" and "integrative" contacts. It is essential to understand the qualitative differences between an integrative and a dominative social contact, because most of the research on classroom climate makes similar behavioral distinctions.

A preliminary study showed that it was possible to devise reliable measures of behavior of young children. Behavior was recorded as "contacts" divided into two groups of categories. If a child snatched a toy, struck a playmate, or commanded him, or if he attempted to force him in some way, such contacts were included under the term "domination." By such behavior he ignored the rights of the companion; he tended to reduce the free interplay of differences and to lead toward resistance or conformity in responding or adapting to another.

Other contacts were recorded which tended to increase the interplay of differences. Offering a companion a choice or soliciting an expression of his desires were gestures of flexibility and adaptation. These tended in the direction of discovering common purposes among differences. Such contacts were grouped under the term "socially integrative behavior." (5, p. 12)

The findings of Anderson are based on the study of preschool, primary school, and elementary school classrooms involving five different teachers and extending over several years. The imaginative research of Anderson and his colleagues has produced a series of internally consistent and significant findings: First, the dominative and integrative contacts of the teacher set a pattern of behavior that spreads throughout the classroom; the behavior of the teacher, more than of any other individual, sets the climate of the class. The rule is that a climate of domination incites further domination, and one of integration stimulates further integration. It is the teacher's tendency that spreads among pupils and is continued even when the teacher is no longer in the room. Furthermore, the pattern a teacher develops in one year is likely to persist in his classroom the following year with different pupils. Second, when a teacher has a higher proportion of integrative contacts, pupils show more spontaneity and initiative, more voluntary social contributions, and more acts of problem-solving. Third, when a teacher has a higher proportion of dominative contacts, the pupils are more easily distracted from schoolwork, and show greater compliance to, as well as rejection of, teacher domination.

A year or so after Anderson started his work, Lippitt and White (12), working with Kurt Lewin, carried out laboratory experiments to analyze the effects of adult leaders' influence on boys' groups. The laboratory approach used had certain advantages in studying the effects of the adult leader's behavior. First, the contrasting patterns of leader behavior were purified and made more consistent as a result of training and role-playing. Second, differences in the underlying personality and appearance of the adult leaders were minimized through role rotation. Third, the effect of the pattern of leader behavior was intensified, compared with the effect in an ordinary classroom, since there were only 5 boys to a group. Roughly speaking, the pattern Lippitt and White named "authoritarian leadership" consisted of dominative contacts; "democratic leadership" consisted of an integrative pattern; and "laissez-faire" consisted of irregular and infrequent integrative contacts with an element of indiffer-

ence to the total group that is seldom found in a classroom and was not present in the Anderson et al. studies.

Most of the conclusions of the Lippitt and White study and others confirm or extend the general conclusions of Anderson et al., with some semantic modification but very little change, if any, in behavioral meaning. From the point of view of classroom teaching, one interesting extension was the conceptualization of "dependence on the leader" by Lippitt and White. This is a state of affairs in which group members are unable to proceed without directions from the leader. Anderson et al. used the category "conforming to teacher domination" and thus noted similar events, but in the more concentrated social climates of the laboratory experiments, it was clearly seen that extensive compliance occurs when there is a generalizd condition of dependence.

These two mutually supportive and independent studies aroused considerable interest in the notion of social climate. Additional research revealed minor variations of the central theme already established. Withall (15) showed that a simple classification of the teacher's verbal statements into 7 categories produced an index of teacher behavior almost identical to the integrative-dominative (I/D) ratio of Anderson et al. Flanders (8) created laboratory situations in which contrasting patterns of teacher behavior were exposed to one pupil at a time. A sustained dominative pattern was consistently disliked by pupils: it reduced their ability to recall the material studied, and it produced disruptive anxiety, as indicated by galvanic skin response and changes in the heartbeat rates. The reverse trends were noted as pupil reactions to integrative contacts. Perkins (13), using Withall's technique, studied groups of teachers organized to discuss the topic of child growth and development. He found that greater learning about child growth and development occurred when group discussion was free to focus on that topic; groups with an integrative type of leader were able to do this more frequently than were groups led by a dominative type of leader.

In a large cross-sectional study that did not use observations of spontaneous teacher behavior, Cogan (6) administered to 987 eighth-grade students in 33 classrooms a single paper-and-pencil instrument that contained three scales: (*a*) a scale assessing student perceptions of the teacher; (*b*) a scale on which students reported how often they did required schoolwork; and (*c*) a scale on which students reported how often they did extra, nonrequired schoolwork. Cogan's first scale assessed traits which he developed in terms of Murray's list of major personality needs. There were two patterns in this scale. The items of one pattern were grouped as "dominative," "aggressive," and "rejectant." The second pattern was "integrative," "affiliative," and "nurturant"; these correspond to Anderson's dominative and integrative patterns. Cogan found that students reported doing more assigned and extra schoolwork when they perceived the teacher's behavior as falling into the integrative pattern rather than the dominative pattern.

All together, these research projects support the definition given earlier of classroom climate. The two teacher behavior patterns that create the contrasting classroom climates are shown below:

*The Integrative Pattern*
a. Accepts, clarifies, and supports the ideas and feelings of pupils.
b. Praises and encourages.
c. Asks questions to stimulate pupil participation in decision-making.

d. Asks questions to orient pupils to schoolwork.

*The Dominative Pattern*
a. Expresses or lectures about own ideas or knowledge.
b. Gives directions or orders.
c. Criticizes or deprecates pupil behavior with intent to change it.
d. Justifies own position or authority.

CONCEPTS FOR UNDERSTANDING CLASSROOM INTERACTION

One contribution of research on classroom climate has been the identification of different kinds of verbal statements that the teacher uses. This information has been used in the development of our system of interaction analysis.

A less consistent contribution of this early research concerns the words used to designate patterns of teacher behavior. In fact, there is quite a choice: Anderson (2)—"dominative" and "integrative"; Lippitt and White—"authoritarian," "democratic," and "laissez-faire" (12); Withall (15), Flanders (8), Perkins (13)—"teacher-centered" and "student-centered"; and Cogan (6)—"preclusive" and "inclusive." All these come from a short stroll in the conceptual garden of psychology; an overnight hike could extend the list indefinitely. Faced with such a choice, we might first pause to discuss the concepts used in this type of research.

Concepts used to describe teacher influence refer to a series of acts occurring during some time period. When a particular series occurs again and again, it becomes familiar to an observer and he can identify it. We call such a series a "pattern" of influence.

It is interesting to distinguish between an influence pattern and the concept of "role," as it is commonly used in the literature of social psychology. The difference is in the degree of behavioral specificity that is implied. For example, it may be said that a teacher plays in the classroom a "democratic" or "authoritarian" role. These concepts not only connote value judgments, but they are so abstract that they fail to denote very much about the behavior of the teacher. If someone tries to create either role, his choice of influence patterns depends primarily on his personal and often unique understanding of the concept. Such a choice involves too many alternatives; specificity is lacking.

The only path through these difficulties is to increase understanding by insisting that the concepts used have explicit behavioral meaning. In the rest of this section, certain concepts that refer to the teacher's behavior, the student's reactions, and the nature of the learning goals will be presented. In each instance, a description of behavior in a social setting will be given first. Next, concepts will be used to abstract the behavior events, and in the process, a theoretical definition of the concept will become clear. Finally, the procedures used in this study to measure or quantify the concept will be briefly stated.

The reader may wish to evaluate the development of these concepts by ' applying the following criteria. First, what are the concepts that are given theoretical meaning by analysis of the behavior that commonly occurs in a classroom? Second, are the procedures used for quantifying behavior that is associated with a concept (a) practical: that is, can they be used in a classroom; (b) representative: that is, do they adequately sample all behavior that could logically be associated with the concept; and (c) reliable: that is, can the error factor be determined and is it low, compared

with the differences studied? Third, can the concepts be organized into hypotheses or principles (cause and effect statements) to predict behavior or the consequences of behavior?

*Concepts for Describing Teacher Influence.* Teacher influence exists as a series of acts along a time line. It is most often expressed as verbal communication. In this study we assume that verbal communication constitutes an adequate sample of the teacher's total influence pattern. A single act of a teacher occupies a segment of time. Before this act a particular state of affairs exists; after the act is completed, a different state of affairs exists. Some acts are more potent than others and have greater consequences. Furthermore, a long series of similar acts may have more extensive effects than just an isolated few.

A researcher is free to choose concepts that will be used to describe the state of affairs before and after an act, and concepts that will be used to describe the act itself.

Suppose a teacher says, "Please close the door," to a student. The chances are that the student will close the door. Before this act of influence, the student was engaged in some activity, such as thinking or reading. But since he was expected to comply with the teacher's command, he interrupted his train of thought to get up and close the door.

Actually, this sequence of behavior is as complex as we wish to make it. We could theorize about the social expectations that exist when a teacher makes what adults call a reasonable demand of a student. Much could be said, if we had the facts, about how past contacts with other authority figures have helped to form this particular student's reactions to a command. It might be that the student resented this intrusion and chose to push the door so that it slammed, rather than gently closing it. A lesser degree of resentment could be expressed by an audible sigh followed by slow movements.

Because of all the concepts that could be used to describe behavior, there is a choice here along a continuum. The genotypic concepts that describe inner motives or feelings are at one end, and the phenotypic concepts that describe more superficial aspects of behavior are at the other end. The choice should fit the purpose. A psychiatrist would prefer certain concepts for his purposes that would probably be too genotypic for the majority of interpretations that a teacher needs to make.

Our choice in this instance leads to the following explanation. The teacher exerted *direct influence*, which restricted the *freedom of action* of the student, making him momentarily more *dependent* on the teacher. From this illustration we hope the reader will understand that an act of direct influence restricts freedom of action, usually by focusing on a problem and, in this case, it made the student more dependent on teacher influence for a short period of time.

By the way, you the reader may have felt uneasy when you thought of a teacher's restricting the freedom of action of a student. These are terms that often elicit value judgments. However, it seems sensible to assert that a student's freedom of action is restricted when he is told to shut the door. Nevertheless, it is difficult to make an objective description of such events.

Now, suppose the same door is closed, but with a completely different script. The teacher asks, "Does anyone feel a draft in here?" Johnny says, "Yes, it's cold. I think it's coming from

this open door." The teacher says, "Well, since it seems cold, please close the door." So Johnny gets up and closes the door.

The second example includes the same command and ultimately leads to the same compliance, yet most of us would agree that the state of affairs would be different at the termination of the episode. Consider, too, differences after a series of such episodes extending over hours, days, weeks, or the school year.

Again we face a choice in conceptualizing the behavior. Our choice is as follows: The command, "Close the door," was modified first by a question, "Does anyone feel a draft in here?" second, by a student response, "Yes, it's cold. I think it's coming from this open door," the latter phrase being a student-initiated idea; and third, by the teacher's acknowledging the student's idea, "Well, since it seems cold. ..." Taken all together, the teacher's acts of influence are more indirect than direct. While the student's freedom of action was restricted, his perception of this restriction was probably modified in the second example because he was solving a problem that he had helped to identify, rather than merely complying with the command of an authority figure. In fact, the teacher's behavior encouraged the student's initiative and, in this sense, his freedom of action was expanded. Later on, after more examples are given, we hope it will become clear that an act of indirect influence expands freedom of action and usually makes a student less dependent on the teacher. He often has greater orientation to a problem, because he helped to identify it.

Most teachers who hear these ideas expressed immediately conclude that indirect influence is superior to direct influence. We believe that the basis of this value judgment lies less in the ideas just expressed than in the social pressures that affect teachers' self-concepts. Most teachers apparently want to believe that they are "indirect teachers," even before they hear how these concepts are defined or are told about any research findings. If being an indirect teacher means consistently using indirect influence, we can state categorically that no such teacher exists, because no teacher employs a pure pattern of influence. All teachers establish some kind of balance based on a combination of direct and indirect influence.

At this point, further objection often arises. It seems obvious that any "intelligent teacher" would prefer to have his students "problem-oriented," as illustrated in the second episode, rather than "authority-oriented," as illustrated in the first episode. (The quotation marks are used here to emphasize how quickly abstract value judgments enter the discussion.) Our experience would suggest that, in the long run, most teachers want the students in their classes to react to the demands of problem-solving rather than to their own authority. Yet does it necessarily follow that indirect influence is superior to direct influence? Is the student in the first illustration any less "problem-oriented" than the student in the second?

Our system of interaction analysis provides an explicit procedure for quantifying direct and indirect influence that is closely related to the teacher behaviors identified by research on classroom climate. Direct influence consists of those verbal statements of the teacher that restrict freedom of action, by focusing attention on a problem, interjecting teacher authority, or both. These statements include lecturing, giving directions, criticizing, and justifying his own use of authority.

Indirect influence consists of those verbal statements of the teacher that expand a student's freedom of action by encouraging his verbal participation and initiative. These include asking questions, accepting and clarifying the ideas or feelings of students, and praising or encouraging students' responses.

*Concepts for Describing Student Dependence.* One way to start describing student reactions to teacher influence is to postulate that dependence is always present in some degree in any teacher-pupil relationship. The maturity and power advantages of a teacher, reinforced by social expectations, are such that the student anticipates teacher direction and supervision. The student is more often ready to comply with teacher influence than not, and when he does not comply, his anxiety increases because the teacher can control an effective system of rewards and punishments.

One way to describe the process of instruction is to say that the teacher strives to change the response pattern of a student from mere compliance to independent action, determined by the student's own analysis of the problems confronting him. A student who recognizes no learning problem is much more dependent on the teacher in deciding what is or is not acceptable behavior, and will solicit direction. On the other hand, a student hard at work on a problem responds to the requirements for its solution; these requirements form a set of criteria with which to evaluate his own behavior as well as that of the teacher.

The first complication of this over-simplification is that students differ in their ability to give up dependence on the teacher by shifting orientation to the problem-solving requirements. Some students can hardly separate the problem-solving requirements from teacher approval, and continually seek teacher support at nearly all stages of their activities. We call such students *dependent-prone*. Even the most skillful teachers find it difficult to stimulate self-directed problem-solving among highly dependent-prone students. Dependence-proneness is a personality trait that is established early in childhood, and the extent to which it can be modified by school experiences is unknown.

We must distinguish here between *compliance* and *dependence*. When a teacher directs, demands, or forces, compliance is not voluntary. But when a student imagines or expects that the teacher wants a job done in a particular fashion and voluntarily does what he imagines the teacher wants, his reaction is an act of dependence.

By way of illustration, let us apply the concepts of dependence-proneness, compliance, and dependent behavior to the episode of the boy closing the door. Most students, whether they are dependent-prone or not, will comply when told or asked to do something by the teacher. Most students, for example, will get up and close the door. This is an act of compliance. Suppose, however, that we could turn this episode into a little experiment in which closing the door gradually becomes more and more of an imposition. Suppose that we could move the door farther and farther away, put flights of stairs in the way as physical barriers, and, in general, make the task increasingly cumbersome and difficult. Even when the task became most difficult, a highly dependent-prone student would probably get up and close the door, but a student with low dependency-proneness might be stimulated to think of an alternative, such as "Let's close the window. That will stop the circulation of cold air." The dependent-prone student

has a lower threshold or resistance to compliance than the independent-prone.

Illustrating acts of dependence within the context of this episode becomes a bit absurd, since the episode involves only a simple act of common courtesy. But suppose that the student, with no sign from the teacher, simply volunteers to close the door, and that we can prove he wasn't doing it for his own comfort. Such an action is not compliance, but an act of dependence. A more typical dependent act in the classroom consists of soliciting approval and permission. For example, a student does an arithmetic problem and then asks the teacher; "Is this the way you wanted it done?"

Over a long period of time, continuous compliance will increase the incidence of dependent behavior. Students begin to anticipate teacher demands and respond dependently. Being ordered to act in a certain way and being subjected to standards of behavior imposed by an authority figure will, in the long run, set these expectactions. The more dependent-prone respond with compliance and acts of dependence. The more independent-prone will comply when forced, and, depending on other factors, may engage in subtle and not so subtle acts of aggressive counter-dependence, or rebelliousness.

*Compliance*, then, consists of doing what one is told to do by an authority figure. This type of behavior is best quantified by the analysis of spontaneous behavior, for example, by analyzing a tape recording or developing a system of observation.

*Dependent behavior* consists of voluntarily bowing to expected teacher influence or to imagined restraints associated with the teacher's authority. The problems of measurement are difficult, since acts of dependence must be separated from acts of compliance on the basis of difference in intent.

We might note here that conformity to group standards, real or imagined, often has a self-initiated and thus voluntary aspect to it. In this sense, acts of conformity and acts of dependence both differ from compliance because of the absence of a teacher directive and the presence of the pupil's intent to please. The imagined directive or group force-field that creates conformity and dependence can be just as potent and seem just as real for the pupil as those creating compliance.

*Dependence-proneness* is a personality trait representing the tendency of a student to engage in dependent acts. Dependence-proneness is a concept necessary to explain why some children respond dependently, and others do not, when exposed to identical social stimuli. Dependent behavior may be caused by a number of psychological forces, one of which is dependence-proneness.

In past laboratory experiments dependent behavior has been successfully measured by observing teacher-pupil contacts and noting, in particular, requests for help and solicitations of approval. Filson (7) used a paper-and-pencil questionnaire on which students indicated their need for approval and help, or their lack of it, during a teacher-directed learning task. We have been particularly unsuccessful in developing procedures for measuring dependent behavior in the classroom under field conditions.

In this study, dependence-proneness is measured by an attitude inventory consisting of 45 items. The reliability and validity of this scale have been cited by Flanders, Amidon, and Anderson (10) for seventh-grade and eighth-grade boys and girls.

*Concepts for Describing Learning Goals.* Learning goals are usually described in terms of curriculum organization and content. In all classroom activities the learning of certain skills, understandings, or facts is central to a plan for which the teacher has ultimate responsibility.

However, certain dimensions of learning goals, particularly the goal perceptions of the students and the teacher, can be conceptualized and measured without specifying the curriculum content involved. For example, the following dimensions of students' goal perceptions seem independent of content. First, there is a dimension of motivation; how attractive and interesting are these goals? Second, there is a dimension of realism; are the resources of time, ability, and energy adequate to reach a goal? Third, there is a dimension of clarity; how well do students understand the steps necessary to reach a goal and how clearly is the end product visualized?

The last-named dimension, goal clarity, received special emphasis in this monograph because variation of this variable is crucial to our hypotheses about teacher influence. In the analysis of results, we will distinguish between situations in which goals are presumed to be clear and those in which goals are presumed to be less clear.

The first two dimensions, motivation and realism, are ignored in our studies, even though they are important, because the consequences of their variation are more self-evident. Lewin (11) and many others have discussed goals with high positive valence which create strong motivation and result in greater progress in learning. The consequences of sufficient or insufficient time, ability, and energy are self-evident. The assumption that motivation and realism are approximately equal among the groups being compared later in this monograph seems to us quite reasonable. Certainly the students all had an equal opportunity for work, they often had more than enough energy, and individual differences were distributed within each class in a manner that did not seriously affect our results.

We assume that the dimension of goal clarity can be described by conceiving of a continuum that extends from *clear goals* at one end to *ambiguous goals* at the opposite end. We define having *clear goals* as a condition in which a student knows what steps are necessary to reach the goal and has a clear picture of the end product. Having *ambiguous goals* is defined as a condition in which a student is not sure of the steps necessary to reach the goal and has an uncertain picture of the end product. The perceptions of the students, not the teacher, are essential to any measure of the clarity or ambiguity of goals.

As goals become clear, a student at work on a problem can use his understanding of the problem-solving requirements to guide his own behavior or to evaluate teacher influence. In either case, he is less dependent on teacher influence. It seems reasonable to suppose that a student will benefit most from problem-solving experiences when he works at the lowest level of dependence on the teacher that both he and the teacher can tolerate that permits necessary coordination and maintenance of classroom learning activities. A certain amount of dependence is desirable and will always be present in the classroom, but the teacher can and should control the general level of dependence by appropriate use of teacher influence.

The level of dependence at some moment in the classroom is a function of the student's dependence-proneness, the restraints set by the teacher's pattern of influence, and the student's perception of the learning goal. In a specific situation, we assume the dependence-proneness of the student is "given," that is, fixed by the personality trait. The restraints set by the teacher are a function of his use of direct and indirect influence and the perception of this influence held by the student from past experience. When goals are ambiguous, the student is more likely to respond to teacher influence in a dependent fashion. When goals are clear he can evaluate teacher influence by analyzing the intent of the teacher in terms of the problem-solving requirements.

It takes time to establish a learning goal, to identify the steps of problem-solving, and to begin work activities. During this period of time, clear goals gradually emerge from ambiguous goals. Because the student expects to comply with the teacher's authority, an expectation founded on past experience with authority figures, he responds initially in a dependent manner or at least with compliance. The natural tendency of a teacher, when faced with a situation in which goals are ambiguous, is to establish clarity by using a pattern of influence that is primarily direct. Direct influence, under these circumstances, leads to higher levels of dependence that can interfere with self-directed problem-solving. In effect the student must take into consideration both the demands of the teacher and the demands of the problem. A dependent-prone student remains oriented to the demands of the teacher, even when goals become clear. Dependence, once established under these conditions, is difficult to reduce.

The case of closing the door can

again serve as an illustration. When the teacher said, "Please close the door," the student's orientation to action was in terms of compliance. In one sense, problem-solving was not possible for him unless he chose to make an issue out of complying. Repeated over and over again, such compliance increases dependence. In the second example of closing the door, the action taken was a solution to the problem of eliminating a cold draft. The teacher's indirect approach permitted the student to participate in the identification of the problem; when such an approach is used, students are more likely to suggest an alternative solution, such as closing a window. Dependence-proneness is thus held constant rather than being intensified. The point here is that the teacher's choice of direct or indirect influence while goals are still ambiguous is crucial to the control of dependence.

When the activity under consideration is an important part of the curriculum and not a routine closing of a door, the consequences of alternative teacher influence patterns are much more significant. Our observation of teachers in many classrooms gives us the conviction that teachers are more likely to exert direct influence while goals are ambiguous or when progress is halted and diagnosis needed. Add to this the tendency of students to comply and to become dependent, and a good deal of the dependent behavior that occurs in the classroom is explained.

Amidon (1) has successfully measured the goal perceptions of students during laboratory experiments involving eighth-grade students learning geometry. He manipulated the initial conditions by presenting information on tape recordings: one to create goal ambiguity and the other, goal clarity.

At different points during the learning activities, a paper-and-pencil scale was used to assess the students' perceptions of next steps and end products.

In the field studies to be reported in this monograph, conditions of greater goal ambiguity are presumed to exist during the initial two days of the 2-week units of study and during those periods in which the teacher introduces new material. During the middle and terminal phases of the 2-week unit of study, excluding the introduction of new material, greater goal clarity is presumed to exist.

*Concepts for Describing Teacher Flexibility and Homogeneous Classroom Activities.* Anyone who has observed many hours in a classroom soon notices that classroom interaction occurs in a sequence of activity periods. First, there may be a routine 3 to 5 minutes for settling down to work. Next, perhaps, homework is corrected and handed in. Next, a student or group may give a report. This may be followed by a 15-minute discussion, and so on. We have found it advantageous to tabulate interaction analysis data separately for these periods.

The main reason for separating data from different activities is that we can then discover whether a teacher shifts his balance of direct and indirect influence in various activity periods. Is a teacher more indirect when new material is being introduced? Is he more indirect when helping diagnose difficulties? Is he more direct when supervising seatwork? What about evaluating homework or test results?

Identifying activity periods is almost a second system of categorization that is superimposed on the system for classifying verbal statements. In junior-high academic classrooms, we use 5 activity categories: introducing new material; evaluating homework, tests, or learning products; other class discussion; supervising seatwork or group activities; and routine clean-up, passing of materials, or settling down to work. In general, a change from one activity to another is indicated by the statements made, a change of class formation, or a change in the communication pattern.

Tabulating data separately for homogeneous activities permits us to define teacher flexibility and measure it. Teacher flexibility is a measure of the change a teacher makes in his verbal influence from one activity period to another. We measure this by noting the ratio of indirect influence (I) to direct influence (D) in one activity period and comparing it with the corresponding ratio in other activity periods. If we wish to avoid a measure which is a ratio of a ratio, that is, an I/D ratio as a per cent divided by a per cent, we can compare changes in the per cent of indirect influence across different activities, and then make the same comparison for direct influence. Unfortunately, this does not eliminate the statistical problems. Distributions of I/D ratios, comparative per cents of indirect statements, and raw tallies all form a "J"-shaped curve.

HYPOTHESES OF TEACHER INFLUENCE
FOR THIS STUDY

In the preceding section, a series of concepts necessary to understand teacher influence were described and defined. Included among these concepts were direct and indirect teacher influence, freedom of action of the student, dependent and independent behavior, the personality trait of dependence-proneness, clear and ambiguous goals, and teacher flexibility.

These concepts are tools for thinking about teacher behavior.

In the long run, the purpose of testing hypotheses about teacher influence is to establish principles of teacher behavior that can guide a teacher who wishes to control his own behavior as part of his plan for classroom management. Each principle, if it is to be useful, must be a cause-and-effect statement. Accordingly, this report will express principles in statements that adhere to the following general pattern: if such and such is true, then action "X" will produce result "Y."

This study is concerned with the following hypotheses, which will be stated in terms of the concepts described in the preceding section:

*Hypothesis One:* Indirect teacher influence increases learning when a student's perception of the goal is confused and ambiguous.

*Hypothesis Two:* Direct teacher influence increases learning when a student's perception of the goal is clear and acceptable.

*Hypothesis Three:* Direct teacher influence decreases learning when a student's perception of the goal is ambiguous.

In these three hypotheses, the concept *learning* refers to the development of skills and understandings that can be measured by pre- and post-tests of achievement. In this project, tests were administered before and after a 2-week unit of study, so that an operational definition of learning consists of final achievement, adjusted for initial ability.

By way of brief review, the dynamic explanation of these hypotheses rests on the following reasoning: First, indirect influence increases learning when goals are ambiguous because less disabling dependence develops. During the initial stages of learning, goals are ambiguous. Indirect influence increases student freedom of action, allowing the student the opportunity to question goals and the procedures for reaching them. The net effect of this participation in clarifying goals is less compliance to authority per se and more attention to problem-solving requirements, or at least a more balanced orientation for those students who have high dependence-proneness.

Second, direct influence increases learning when goals are clear because the criteria for accepting or rejecting teacher influence as well as various alternative actions can be recognized in terms of the problem-solving requirements. The student is presumably oriented toward the problem; direct teacher influence is likely to be oriented toward the problem and be helpful; and the net effect is more efficient action toward problem solution. Dependence on the teacher remains steady or is decreased as a result of successful progress toward the goal.

Third, direct influence decreases learning when goals are ambiguous because it increases dependence sharply. The primary response of the student is compliance with teacher authority when goals are unclear. This, in turn, develops dependence. Unless the student understands the goal that the teacher has in mind, he has no other acceptable alternative, given our present cultural expectations. The high dependence that quickly develops means that the student is oriented more toward pleasing the teacher than toward meeting the problem-solving requirements.

These hypotheses are generalized predictions across a range of individual differences. The interaction between a teacher and a particular student in a specific situation is modified by unique personality characteristics and situational factors.

## RESEARCH TOOLS FOR ANALYZING CLASSROOM INTERACTION

The studies of classroom interaction reported in this monograph made use of the following research tools: first, an observation procedure called classroom interaction analysis; second, several student-attitude inventories assessing student perceptions of the teacher and the schoolwork; third, a dependence-proneness test used for scaling this attribute among students; and fourth, achievement tests used to measure learning achievement. Each of these will be described in turn.

### CLASSROOM INTERACTION ANALYSIS

The spontaneous behavior of a teacher is so complex and variable that an accurate description of it is most difficult to obtain. Even trained observers struggle with the same biases that distort the testimony of witnesses at the scene of an accident. Too often an observer's preconceptions of what he thinks should happen allow him to perceive certain behaviors but prevent him from perceiving others. Interaction analysis is an observation procedure designed to minimize these difficulties, to permit a systematic record of spontaneous acts, and to scrutinize the process of instruction by taking into account each small bit of interaction.

Classroom interaction analysis is particularly concerned with the influence pattern of the teacher. This might be considered a bias, but it is a bias of purpose and interest. Our purpose is to record a series of acts in terms of predetermined concepts.

The concepts in this case refer to the teacher's control of the students' freedom of action. Our interest is to distinguish those acts of the teacher that increase students' freedom of action from those acts that decrease students' freedom of action, and to keep a record of both. The system of categories is used by the observer to separate those acts which result in compliance from those acts which invite more creative and voluntary participation; at the same time, it prevents him from being diverted by the subject matter which is irrelevant to this study.

Interaction analysis is concerned primarily with verbal behavior because it can be observed with higher reliability than most nonverbal behavior. The assumption is made that the verbal behavior of the teacher is an adequate sample of his total behavior; that is, his verbal statements are consistent with his nonverbal gestures, in fact, his total behavior. This assumption seems reasonable in terms of our experience.

*The Procedure.* The observer sits in the classroom in the best position to hear and see the participants. At the end of each 3-second period, he decides which of a prescribed set of numbered categories best represents the communication events just completed. He writes this category number down while simultaneously assessing communication in the next period. He continues at a rate of about 20 to 25 observations per minute, keeping his tempo as steady as possible. His notes are merely a sequence of numbers written in a column, top to bottom, so that the original sequence of events is preserved. Occasionally, marginal notes are used to explain the class formation or any unusual circumstances. When there is a major change

in class formation, the communication pattern, or the subject under discussion, the observer draws a double line and indicates the time. As soon as he has completed the total observation, he retires to a nearby room and writes up a general description of each separate activity period. This includes the nature of the activities, the class formation, and the position of the teacher. The observer also notes any additional facts that seem pertinent to an adequate interpretation and recall of the total observation period.

*The Categories.* There are 10 categories in the system. Seven are assigned to teacher talk and two to student talk. The 10th category covers pauses, short periods of silence, and talk that is confusing or noisy. The category system is outlined in Table 1.

Of the seven categories assigned to teacher talk, categories 1 through 4 represent indirect influence, and categories 5, 6, and 7, direct influence.

Indirect influence encourages participation by the student and increases his freedom of action. To ask a question (category 4) is an invitation to participate and express ideas, opinions, or facts. It is true that a question can be so phrased as to leave very little freedom of action, but at least the student can refuse to answer, a reaction which reflects more freedom than does passive listening. The more general a teacher's question, the greater the opportunity for the student to assert his own ideas.

When the teacher accepts, clarifies, or uses constructively the ideas and opinions of students (category 3), they are encouraged to participate further. Often teachers act as if they do not hear what a student says; to acknowledge and make use of an idea is a powerful form of recognition. To praise or encourage student participa-

TABLE 1

**Categories for Interaction Analysis, 1959**

| | | |
|---|---|---|
| *Teacher Talk* | *Indirect Influence* | 1.* ACCEPTS FEELING: accepts and clarifies the tone of feeling of the students in an unthreatening manner. Feelings may be positive or negative. Predicting or recalling feelings are included.<br>2.* PRAISES OR ENCOURAGES: praises or encourages student action or behavior. Jokes that release tension, but not at the expense of another individual, nodding head or saying "um hm?" or "go on" are included.<br>3.* ACCEPTS OR USES IDEAS OF STUDENT: clarifying, building, or developing ideas suggested by a student. As teacher brings more of his own ideas into play, shift to category 5.<br>4.* ASKS QUESTIONS: asking a question about content or procedure with the intent that a student answer. |
| | *Direct Influence* | 5.* LECTURING: giving facts or opinions about content or procedure; expressing his own ideas, asking rhetorical questions.<br>6.* GIVING DIRECTIONS: directions, commands, or orders which students are expected to comply with.<br>7.* CRITICIZING OR JUSTIFYING AUTHORITY: statements intended to change student behavior from unacceptable to acceptable pattern; bawling someone out; stating why the teacher is doing what he is doing; extreme self-reference. |
| *Student Talk* | | 8.* STUDENT TALK—RESPONSE: talk by students in response to teacher. Teacher initiates the contact or solicits student statement.<br>9.* STUDENT TALK—INITIATION: talk initiated by students. If "calling on" student is only to indicate who may talk next, observer must decide whether student wanted to talk. |
| *Silence* | | 10.* SILENCE OR CONFUSION: pauses, short periods of silence and periods of confusion in which communication cannot be understood by the observer. |

\* There is NO scale implied by these numbers. Each number is classificatory, designating a particular kind of communication event. To write these numbers down during observation is merely to identify and enumerate communication events, not to judge them.

tion directly (category 2) is to solicit even more participation by giving a reward. The ability to use the feeling tone of a student constructively, to react to feeling and clarify it (category 1), is a rare skill. Teachers with this ability can often mobilize positive feelings in motivation and successfully control negative feelings that might otherwise get out of hand.

All the actions falling into categories 1 through 4 tend to increase and reward student participation, and to give students the opportunity to become more influential. The net effect is

greater freedom of action for the students.

Direct influence increases the active control of the teacher and often stimulates compliance. The lecture (category 5) focuses the attention of the students on ideas chosen by the teacher. To give directions or commands (category 6) is to direct the activities of the class with the intent of obtaining compliance. Category 7 refers to criticizing student behavior or justifying the teacher's use of authority. These actions concentrate authority in the hands of the teacher. Direct influence tends to increase teacher participation and to establish restraints on student behavior. The ensuing restriction of freedom may occur in the form of compliance to the teacher or of adjustment to the requirements of problem-solving activities. The net effect is less freedom of action for the students.

The division of student talk into categories 8 and 9 provides an automatic check on freedom of student action within the system of categories. Ordinarily, but not always, a pattern of direct teacher influence is associated with less student talk, which generally consists of responses to the teacher (category 8). A pattern of indirect influence is ordinarily associated with more student talk, which is often initiated by the students (category 9). The use of only two categories to record all kinds of student talk neglects a great deal of information, but the major purpose of these categories is the analysis of teacher influence. The greatest information will accrue from observation if category 9 is used sparingly and only on those occasions when the communication is truly student-initiated.

For example, the act of a student in answering a specific question asked by a teacher obviously falls into category 8. Even the act of giving an oral report may be placed in this category when the student is restricted to a specific outline and is probably responding to the teacher's directions.

Category 9 should be used by the observer only to indicate the student's spontaneous expression of his own ideas. General questions are often a clue that a student may be initiating his own ideas. When a teacher calls on a student who voluntarily raised his hand to speak and asks, "Have you anything to add, Robert?" the chances are that the use of category 9 is correct.

The purpose of category 10 is to record short pauses, silences, and periods of confusion as they occur during classroom interaction. It is not intended to record periods of silence or confusion lasting for more than 2 minutes. The continuous use of this category to designate long periods of silence serves no useful purpose.

The system of categories is designed for situations in which the teachers and the students are actively discussing schoolwork. It is an inappropriate tool when the verbal communication is discontinuous, separated by fairly long periods of silence, or when one person is engaged in prolonged lecturing or in reading aloud to the class. In situations in which two-way communication does not exist and is not likely to exist, the observer should stop and make a note of the exact time at which spontaneous interaction lapsed and the reasons for the interruption. The observer must remain alert to the resumption of spontaneous interaction.

*Marking Activity Periods.* Teacher influence is a pattern that is constantly changing over time. The most effective teachers, in fact, have a large repertoire of behaviors, and systematic observation shows that they can present many different influence patterns.

The identification of activity periods is one way that flexibility can be studied. In effect, a second system of categories is superimposed on the 10 interaction categories; this second system is likely to be different in each research study. For example, it may be sufficient in a study of high school mathematics classes to indicate periods of (*a*) settling down to work, (*b*) introducing new material, (*c*) teacher-directed discussion or work on material that is not new, (*d*) supervision and direction of individual seatwork, and (*e*) periods of evaluation, in which homework and test results are discussed.

In an elementary classroom, it would be reasonable to keep interaction data collected during show-and-tell separate from reading instruction, and these in turn from arithmetic, music, games, penmanship, etc.

If interaction analysis is to be used to discover whether a teacher's pattern of influence in planning work with students is different, for example, from his influence pattern while supervising work already planned, then even finer discriminations would be necessary to identify the boundaries of the required time periods.

One way to develop sensitivity to these different activity periods is to train the observer to draw a double line whenever there is a change in the class formation, the communication pattern, the subject matter to be learned, or in the presumed purpose of instruction. After the classroom visit is completed, the observer can use his double lines and marginal notes to recreate a brief chronology of the classroom activities. Interaction data gathered by this procedure can be grouped in a variety of ways for special comparisons.

No matter whether one is discussing a set of categories for interaction analysis or a set of categories for classifying activity periods, there are two requirements that must be satisfied in order to make generalizations about total class interaction. First, the system should be designed to include all possible events, that is, the categories should be totally inclusive. Second, a single event must be recorded in one, and only one, category so that the categories will be mutually exclusive.

Any system of observation that fails to meet the first requirement is selective, and under it the data are not representative of all the events that occurred. Failure to meet the second requirement produces an inconsistent enumeration of events; the comparison of category frequencies then becomes meaningless or at least biased in some unknown way.

## CONCLUSIONS AND IMPLICATIONS OF THE PROJECT

### METATHEORY

Theorizing about theory is not a common pastime, especially in the field of education, but some questions should be raised about the theoretical hypotheses around which this project is organized. What kind of theorizing will be of most help in creating a theory of instruction? Can the present hypotheses contribute to a theory of instruction? These two questions will occupy our attention for a page or two before we go on to discuss the conclusions and implications of the project.

To theorize about the behavior of a classroom teacher, one must draw from the fields of learning theory, motivation, personality, group dynamics, sociometry, and practically everything else, and direction signs are not well-posted.

Educators are not yet ready to start the ambitious task of developing a theory of instruction that takes into account all behavior that occurs in a classroom. In one bold step of oversimplification, we postulated that a theory of instruction must at least concern itself with the teacher's acts of influence and the reactions of the students, using the goals of learning as a reference for interpretation. There must be concepts that describe teacher influence, concepts that describe student reactions, and concepts that describe learning goals. In the analysis of behavior, the order is reversed. Given particular learning goals, students' perceptions of these goals are developed through classroom interaction. The work that follows also involves interaction. The analysis of student and teacher interaction is carried out in terms of the learning goals. We found that classroom behavior makes the most sense when viewed within this frame of reference.

In order to contribute to a theory of instruction, a hypothesis must propose dynamic cause-and-effect relationships among learning goals, teacher behavior, and student behavior. If the hypothesis is verified empirically, it can become a principle of instruction that a teacher can then use to predict the consequences of his own behavior under certain conditions. To illustrate, one of our hypotheses is that direct influence when goals are ambiguous produces high dependence on the teacher and less learning. Direct influence is a concept describing teacher behavior; it is operationally defined as the enumeration of a series of verbal statements occurring in sequence and theoretically defined as those acts which restrict alternative actions of the student. Goals are conceptualized along a continuum from ambiguous to clear, and are operationally defined in terms of the student's perceptions. Acts of dependence and learning are aspects of the student's behavior. Each can be assessed and given operational meaning by either paper-and-pencil tests or observation.

The ultimate value of this kind of engineering research will be tested by pragmatic criteria. As this chapter is being written, arrangements have been completed for an inservice training program in a nearby school district. The project will attempt to answer the question, if teachers learn our theories about the consequences of indirect and direct influence, will this help them control their behavior and become more effective teachers? The results of the present project will become part of the content of this inservice training.

SOME ASSUMPTIONS INHERENT IN OUR APPROACH

Certain assumptions are necessary in our analysis of teacher influence. First, acts of influence are expressed primarily through verbal statements. Nonverbal acts of influence do occur, but are not recorded by interaction analysis. The reasonableness of this assumption rests on the assertion that the quality of the nonverbal acts is similar to the verbal acts; to assess verbal influence therefore is to adequately sample all influence.

Second, how much teachers talk and what they say determine to a large extent the reactions of the students. This is another way of saying that the teacher is an influential authority figure. Given the teacher's position of authority, his greater maturity, and the common expectations of students, we find this assumption reasonable.

Third, an assumption necessary to the application of these research results in any program designed to increase teacher effectiveness is that teachers can control their verbal participation in the classroom. We believe that the average teacher can control his behavior and use it as a psychological force in classroom management. He can be indirect if he chooses, or direct, according to his assessment of the situation. What we hope to provide are principles which he can use in making the choice.

These assumptions focus our attention on the verbal participation of teachers and students. We are in the business of evaluating classroom communication in terms of the teacher's control. Our procedures tend to emphasize control processes and to ignore subject matter, or content. The latter is important, but so is the former, and we prefer to work on one thing at a time at our present stage of development.

MAJOR CONCLUSIONS OF THE 1955–57 STUDIES

The purpose of the early studies was to develop research tools and to use these tools to study relationships between teacher statements and average classroom scores on a pupil attitude inventory. These early studies were conducted in eighth-grade combined English/social studies in Minnesota and Standard Four elementary classrooms in New Zealand. A sample of Minnesota elementary classrooms provided additional interaction analysis data.

These early studies establish clear and significant relationships among teacher statements, pupil attitudes toward the teacher, and the classroom learning activities. Furthermore, the same relationships were shown to exist in more formal and less formal classroom situations in two countries some 8,000 miles apart.

It was shown that when a class scored higher on scales of teacher attractiveness, motivation for schoolwork, fair rewards and punishments, independence, and lack of disabling anxiety, its teacher showed more acceptance of, interest in, and constructive use of the student ideas expressed in classroom discussion. In New Zealand, the teachers of higher-scoring classes also gave fewer directions and made fewer criticisms. The incidence of corporal punishment was also much lower in high-scoring New Zealand classrooms. In the lower-scoring classrooms, the opposite trends occurred. The findings of these early studies were consistent with the research carried out almost 20 years before the present studies by H. H. Anderson and his colleagues.

If one accepts the assumptions and theoretical formulations presented in the first part of this monograph, one sees that these studies demonstrate a cause-and-effect relationship between teacher influence, as expressed by the verbal statements of teachers, and pupil attitudes, as measured by our paper-and-pencil instruments. At the different age levels that exist at primary, elementary, junior high, and senior high grade levels, across different combinations of pupil personality and individual differences, with different types of teaching styles, and even in two countries which differ in the formality of teacher-pupil relationships, students react similarly to the same differences in teacher influence.

These early studies did not include any measure of subject matter achievement. Such measures were purposely delayed until the larger field study could be conducted with the necessary experimental controls.

THE MAJOR CONCLUSIONS REGARDING ACHIEVEMENT

In this project we have isolated situations in which students learned more, and have compared these with situations in which students learned less. Our method of isolation was not to administer a test of achievement first and then study the differences in teacher behavior. Instead, we made theoretical predictions of the following sort.

First, we assessed acts of teacher influence as they occurred spontaneously in the classroom. By using the technique of interaction analysis, we were able to isolate teachers who had an above-average pattern of indirect influence. We found that they were far more flexible than those teachers who exerted below-average indirect influence. That is, they could be just as direct as the latter teachers in certain situations, but they could be far more indirect in other situations. The net effect was a higher average of indirect influence.

Second, we predicted certain patterns would occur among the more flexible teachers: (1) they would be most indirect while goals were being clarified and new content material was being introduced; (2) they would be most direct after goals had been clarified, while work was in progress.

Finally, we predicted that the students of those teachers who were less flexible would learn less, as measured by our achievement tests. It was on this basis that we isolated classes of higher achievement and classes of lower achievement.

When we initially contacted teachers to solicit their participation in the project, we expected certain types of students to learn more while working with direct teachers and other types of students to learn more while working with indirect teachers. We were wrong. All types of students learned more while working with the more flexible teachers. We also thought that classes in the field of mathematics might learn more while working with a direct teacher and that classes in the field of social studies would learn more while working with an indirect teacher. Again we were wrong. It is true that teachers of mathematics use time and methods differently than do teachers of social studies, but students of the more flexible teachers scored higher on the achievement tests in both content areas.

We are not yet prepared to discard the notion that particular types of students work more effectively toward learning goals with particular types of teachers even though our field studies failed to support it. In a series of experiments with geometry classes, we found significant differences indicating that dependent-prone students learned more than independent-prone students while working with a more indirect teacher. Perhaps subsequent experiments will reveal what types of students learn the most while working with direct teachers. Furthermore, there are a number of improvements that can be made in our methods of classifying students into types, and these should be tried out before discarding expectations which at first glance seemed quite reasonable.

With our present data, a factor-analysis can be made of student attitudes toward direct and indirect teachers. An item analysis of the factors in the M.S.A.I. test, made separately for our five types of students, may reveal that different attitudes do develop from contacts with different types of teachers, even though these attitudes did not affect achievement in this study.

## SOME IMPLICATIONS OF THE RESEARCH

*Implications for Classroom Teachers.* To those of us on the staff, the most interesting implication of the project concerns the timing of direct and indirect influence. We find this most interesting because our theoretical predictions are contrary to accepted teaching practice. Nearly all teachers agree that immediate action should be taken in any situation in which the learning goals are ambiguous and students do not know what to do. "Students who are unable to go on with their work are wasting time," the reasoning goes, "Something should be done!" So far we are all in agreement.

Should the initial contacts made by a teacher in such a situation be direct or indirect? Our theory suggests an indirect approach; most teachers use a direct approach. Teachers can find many justifications for their direct approach. Often they think that to tell the students what to do is only to remind them of something they already know. Sometimes teachers are quite sure that the students are lazy or are pretending confusion. A direct approach seems more efficient at the moment, and a teacher is a busy person. These and many other reasons are often mentioned by teachers as a justification for the following pattern: (a) the teacher decides students are confused; (b) the teacher makes his best guess on the cause of this confusion; and (c) the teacher, acting on his own diagnosis, proceeds to give information, direction, and, in some cases, criticism in order to reestablish patterns of work.

The two most common situations in which a teacher faces this choice are those in which new material is being introduced, such as a new topic, a new procedure, or a new method of problem-solving, and those in which a group already at work runs into difficulty—when Johnny won't cooperate, information cannot be found, the anwer doesn't check with an independent proof, materials are missing, and so forth.

It is obvious to any person with teaching experience that no valid generalizations can be made on how the teacher should handle these and similar situations. That is, it is obvious that there are some situations in which a teacher should be primarily direct and others in which he should be primarily indirect. However, we can make a statistical generalization which will hold for 100 such situations. In this study, the teachers of students who learned less employed a pattern of direct influence more often in such a situation. Our theory predicts higher achievement and less dependence when goals are clarified by an indirect approach.

An indirect approach stimulates verbal participation by students and discloses to the teacher students' perceptions of the situation. Such an approach not only provides the teacher with more information about students' understanding of a particular problem, but also often encourages students to develop more responsibility for diagnosing their difficulties and for suggesting a plan of action.

A direct approach increases student compliance to teacher opinion and direction. It conditions students to seek the teacher's help and to check with the teacher more often to be sure they are on the right track.

A second implication for classroom teachers is that the major differences in the use of influence between the teachers whose students learned the most and those whose students learned the least are illustrated by the use of actions classified under categories 1, 2, and 3. The direct teachers lack those social skills of communication that are involved in accepting, clarifying, and making use of the ideas and feelings of students. The indirect teachers have these skills, even though they are not in use most of the time. Although these skills are used sparingly, they are employed when needed.

Associated with this increased social

skill is less need for directions and criticism. The most direct teachers give twice as many directions as the most indirect, and express eight times as much criticism. These figures are consistent with what has been said about dependence. Lack of clarifying and using student ideas places the teacher in a position of giving more directions; in short, he must work harder to keep his students working successfully. When dependence is higher, progress by students depends much more on continuous teacher supervision.

There are interesting comparisons to be made between what we have found in this project and some of the more common criticisms of the public schools that have attained national prominence during the last several years. Some critics of the public schools have advocated that teachers "get tough," tell students what to do, and demand high standards. Our data show that higher standards can be achieved not by telling students what to do in some sort of misguided "get tough" policy, but by asking questions and then using student ideas, perceptions, and reactions to build toward greater student self-direction, responsibility, and understanding. If "getting tough" means helping students face the consequences of their own ideas and opinions, as contrasted against living with the consequences of the teacher's ideas and opinions, then indirect teachers are much tougher.

The third implication for classroom teachers that we would like to mention is that variability in teacher influence, or flexibility, is associated with teachers whose students learned the most. One consequence of this finding is that our better teachers were less alike and our poorer teachers were more alike. It suggests that creative

teaching is an expression of a particular teacher's personality, working with a particular group of students, in a particular subject.

We should emphasize again that our six most indirect social studies teachers fell clearly into two types. Three lectured much more and placed greater emphasis on content material, but all six shared the common characteristic of a higher I/D ratio. The more content-oriented teachers worked with student ideas less, but when they did, their pattern was essentially indirect. The other three teachers worked in a very different style that included 31.6 per cent student talk, the highest average in the entire study. The average student achievement of this latter group was a nonsignificant one-half point higher, indicating that achievement was high for two rather different styles of teaching. It also indicates that a variation from 20 per cent student talk in the content-oriented style to 31.6 per cent student talk in the other three classrooms is not associated with a significant difference in achievement.

The differences between the direct and indirect teachers may be interpreted in terms of the different roles the teacher is able to play in the classroom. The direct teachers could not shift their style of interaction as much as the indirect teachers. Because the direct teachers had fewer ways of working with students, they could provide only a limited number of roles. On the other hand, the indirect teachers were able to adopt many different roles, and they shifted from one to another in a manner consistent with the theories that have already been stated.

*Implications for Preservice and Inservice Education.* There is no substitute for knowledge of what is being taught. Two of the mathematics teachers were not adequately trained. One of these two classes showed an average mean gain in achievement that was last in rank order and *one-sixteenth* of the mean gain of the highest-ranking class. The other class was ninth in rank order. The teacher of this latter class used more social skill in guiding classroom communication. His attitude was, "I'm no math teacher, but we'll have to make the best of it and learn this material together." While his class exceeded the achievement of one or two other classes whose teachers had more extensive training in mathematics, the achievement could not match that of those classes whose teachers were both socially skillful and well-qualified.

The two cases just described illustrate a general implication of this project for the training of teachers. Teachers who are qualified in a content area should be exposed to some type of human relations training that will help them attain the following objectives: first, the ability to use the social skills of accepting, clarifying, and using the ideas of students in planning work and diagnosing difficulties; second, knowledge of those acts of influence that restrict student reactions and those that expand student reactions; and third, understanding of a theory of instruction that he can use, to control his own behavior as he guides classroom communication.

It is reasonable to suppose that these objectives cannot be reached without supervised practice. The person supervising this practice should be able to provide the practice-teacher with information about his own behavior. One way to do this is to use the technique of interaction analysis. The procedure is likely to involve threat for the practice-teacher and will require a skillful, indirect approach on the part of the supervisor.

One possible procedure would permit practice-teachers to try out different patterns of influence. Suppose that on one occasion the practice-teacher tried introducing material with a highly direct pattern and that on another occasion he tried with an indirect pattern. A qualified observer could collect interation analysis data, tabulate the two matrices, and discuss the resulting communication patterns with the practice-teacher. This could be done if all practice-teachers were trained to become reliable observers so that they could alternate between the roles of observer and teacher in teams of two.

*Implications for Merit Pay.* In the present decade, the issue of merit pay for gifted teachers will probably receive more and more attention. Already many school districts are experimenting with different systems. Since this study deals with teacher effectiveness, inferences about the merit pay issue are inescapable.

Two warnings should be issued to anyone who reads this project report and then makes inferences about merit pay. The first warning is that it is easier to identify poor teaching than good teaching. This study found that teachers were quite similar whose students learned the least and had the poorest attitudes toward the teacher and class activities. The teachers who presented the opposite picture were more flexible. By refining the research techniques of this project, reliable distinctions between high- and low-scoring classrooms could be made concerning the amount of students' talk, teachers' use of their time, and the distinction between the 8 and 9 categories of student talk (i.e., student response versus student initiation). The possibility of making such distinctions looks promising, but much more preliminary work will be necessary.

The second warning is that the correlations between various measures derived from interaction analysis, student attitude inventories, and tests of achievement are still so low that evaluation of an individual teacher is subject to considerable error, even though the general trends of the research are statistically significant. So much for the warnings.

The major aim of all systems of merit pay is to reward competence in such a way that all teachers who can improve their teaching skills will do so. A secondary objective, which is to give higher pay for more difficult jobs, must await a more dramatic modification of school organization leading to specialized teaching functions.

Our staff, after making such a close analysis of teacher-pupil contacts, has developed a number of basic beliefs about some of the issues of merit pay. First, programs for the improvement of instruction should be designed and controlled by teachers as part of their professional responsibility. Teacher control, rather than administrative control, is necessary because changing one's methods of teaching is very personal, often involves emotional adjustments, cannot be coerced by administrative fiat, and therefore must be a voluntary, self-directed process.

Second, no system of teacher evaluation will be accepted by teachers until it has been tested and found satisfactory by the teachers whose professional welfare will be affected. Teachers must have confidence in the valuative methods, criteria, and control before they will cooperate.

Third, a system of inservice training that teachers think is successful in helping improve their own ability to teach can become, with care, a steppingstone to a satisfactory system of rewarding the exceptionally competent. In our opinion, this means that merit pay would normally follow a 4- to 6-year active, voluntary inservice training program that, in the opinion of the majority of teachers, has been successful. As teachers experience success in improving their teaching and develop confidence in the criteria used to identify improvement, they will be closer to accepting a system that provides monetary reward for those who make the best progress.

It is our opinion that whenever systems of merit pay are forced from "the top down," the program will fail to meet its major objectives. Administrators and school boards following this path will meet with failure. In the same breath, it can be predicted that teachers who resist schedule policies that have served well in the past will be confronted with increasing criticism from the public and from school board members. Sooner or later the minimum teachers' salary will stop improving in relation to the general economy, and it will then be in the best interests of the profession to raise the ceiling of teacher income for those who are most qualified and most effective.

It follows from the foregoing assertions that the development of objective criteria and procedures to evaluate teacher effectiveness is a professional responsibility. The most rugged test of any procedure is an objective research program that not only provides evidence of the highest quality attainable, but also employs procedures that nearly all teachers can understand and use in a self-improvement program.

*The Implications of Interaction Analysis.* The system of interaction analysis used in this study is content-free. It is concerned primarily with the social skills of classroom management, as expressed through verbal communication. It is costly and cumbersome, and it requires some form of automation in collecting, tabulating, and analyzing the raw data. It is not yet a finished research tool.

Nevertheless, our staff has experienced minor triumphs that we will never forget. We have, for instance, played the following game with considerable success: A single observer collects interaction analysis data, tabulates a matrix, and presents the matrix at a staff meeting. The only information supplied to the staff is the presumed objective of the lesson, the grade level of the class, and the sex of the teacher. The observer who collected the data remains silent as the rest of the staff reconstruct the social interaction. Conclusions about the tempo or speed of interaction, the relative domination of the teacher, whether he asks long or short questions, how much he lectures, and many other aspects of interaction are listed. After the group has finished crawling out on the end of a limb, the observer corrects any misconceptions that may have developed. The number of correct speculations is usually very high, well over 80 per cent. Occasionally a single misconception colors other guesses until a picture develops that is quite incorrect, but these latter outcomes are remarkably infrequent.

Much of the inferential power of this system of interaction analysis comes from tabulating the data as sequence pairs in a $10 \times 10$ matrix. This is a time-consuming process. It can be and should be done mechanically by electronic computers. Once the high cost of tedious tabulation is under control, the problem of training reliable observers and maintaining their reliability will still remain.

We have reason to be optimistic about the value of interaction analysis.

Its potential as a research tool, however, for a wide application to problems in education remains to be explored.

## REFERENCES

1. Amidon, E. and N. A. Flanders, "The Effects of Direct and Indirect Teacher Influence on Dependent-Prone Students Learning Geometry," *Journal of Educational Psychology*, LII, No. 6 (December 1961), 286–91.
2. Anderson, H. H., "The Measurement of Domination and of Socially Integrative Behavior in Teacher's Contact with Children," *Child Development*, X, No. 2 (June 1939), 73–89.
3. —— and H. M. Brewer, "Studies of Teachers' Classroom Personalities, I: Dominative and Socially Integrative Behavior of Kindergarten Teachers," *Applied Psychology Monographs*, No. 6, 1945.
4. —— and J. E. Brewer, "Studies of Teachers' Classroom Personalities, II: Effects of Teacher's Dominative and Integrative Contacts on Children's Classroom Behavior," *Applied Psychology Monographs*, No. 8, 1946.
5. —— and M. F. Reed, "Studies of Teachers' Classroom Personalities, III: Follow-Up Studies of the Effects of Dominative and Integrative Contacts on Children's Behavior," *Applied Psychology Monographs of the American Psychological Association*, Stanford, Calif.: Stanford University Press, No. 11, December 1946.
6. Cogan, M. L., "Theory and Design of a Study of Teacher-Pupil Interaction," *The Harvard Educational Review*, XXVI, No. 4 (Fall 1956), 315–42.
7. Filson, T. N., "Factors Influencing the Level of Dependence in the Classroom." Unpublished Ph. D. Thesis, University of Minnesota, 1957.
8. Flanders, N. A., "Personal-Social Anxiety as a Factor in Experimental Learning Situations," *Journal of Educational Research*, XLV (October 1951), 100–110.

9. ——, "Diagnosing and Utilizing Social Structures in Classroom Learning," 59th Yearbook of the National Society for the Study of Educational Research, *Part II, The Dynamics of Instructional Groups*. Chicago: University of Chicago Press, 1960. Chap. IX, pp. 187–217.

10. —— and J. P. Anderson and E. J. Amidon, "Measuring Dependence Proneness in the Classroom," *Educational and Psychological Measurement*, XXI, No. 3 (Autumn 1961), 575–87.

11. Lewin, K., *A Dynamic Theory of Personality*. New York: McGraw-Hill Book Company, 1935. Chap. IV, pp. 114–70.

12. Lippitt, R. and R. K. White, "The 'Social Climate' of Children's Groups," in R. G. Barker, J. S. Kounin, and H. F. Wright, eds., *Child Behavior and Development*. New York: McGraw-Hill Book Company, 1943, pp. 458–508.

13. Perkins, H. V., "Climate Influences Group Learning," *Journal of Educational Research*, XLV (October 1951), 115–19.

14. Smith, B. O., "A Concept of Teaching," *Teachers College Record*, LXI, No. 5 (February 1960), 229–41.

15. Withall, J., "The Development of a Technique for the Measurement of Social-Emotional Climate in Classroom," *Journal of Experimental Education*, XVII (March 1949), 347–61.

# 9

# A Procedure for Assessing the Classroom Behavior of Students and Teachers [1]

HUGH V. PERKINS

## INTRODUCTION

The behavior of students and teachers in the classroom has been a focus of research for over two decades. A persistent methodological problem has been how to obtain reliable objective data on behavioral variables. The need for more refined instruments to measure these variables, the growing interest in pupil and teacher behavior in natural settings, and the specific requirements of a planned research project on underachievement led to the development of the procedure reported here.

A method frequently used to study what goes on in classrooms and groups has been the verbatim recording of verbal behavior by machine or stenographer: e.g., Lewin, Lippitt, and White (11), Anderson, Brewer, and Reed (1), and Withall (17) in their studies of social-emotional climate and, more

recently, Gallagher (6) and Spaulding (16) in their respective analyses of the quality of thinking and of the effective dimensions of the creative process.

Hughes (7) and Leacock (10) used anecdotal or narrative descriptions to obtain behavioral data that were less quantifiable but greater in scope. Frequently each pair of observers collate their independent records into a single report containing only those data common to the two records. Medley (13) described a technique called OScAR (Observation Schedule and Record) for measuring a teacher's behavior in the classroom. OScAR is a list of behaviors to be looked for plus a scoring system by which several correlated items form a composite scale that is more reliable and interpretable than any individual item.

[1] This reseach was supported by Public Health Grant MH 07344–01 and by the General Research Board and the Computer Science Center of the University of Maryland. The author gratefully acknowledges the contributions made to this study by Richard M. Brandt, Arianna Claypool, Angus McDonald, Jr., and Johanna C. Van Looy.

Hugh V. Perkins, "A Procedure for Assessing the Classroom Behavior of Students and Teachers," *American Educational Research Journal*, I, No. 4 (November 1964), 249–60. Reprinted by permission.

Other investigators have devised more convenient methods for quantifying and processing behavioral data by training observers to judge and categorize classroom behavior on the spot. In an instrument developed by Flanders (4a), the observer every three seconds assigns what is then taking place to one of ten categories, seven of which deal with behavior by the teacher. In the point-time sampling technique employed by Kowatrakul (8) and Sears (15), the observer watched one subject long enough to record an example of one type of behavior in a six-category instrument and then immediately passed on to the next subject. A recent advance is the use of kinescope recorder and television cameras mounted in classroom walls and operated by remote control (14). This technique provides sound films of classroom interaction without an outsider being present.

The purpose of the present study was to develop a procedure based on reliable and valid instruments for measuring student-behavior, learning-activity, teacher-behavior, and teacher-role variables presumed to be related to differential achievement.

## DEVELOPMENT OF INSTRUMENTS

Two instruments were developed: one entitled *Student Categories* and the other, *Teacher Categories*. The categories making up these instruments are listed and defined in Table 1.

The first nine student categories cover behavior and evolved as a refinement and an expansion of a set of six such categories reported by Kowatrakul (8) and Sears (15). The remaining six student categories cover learning activity.

The first ten teacher categories were based on the seven teacher-behavior

categories used by Flanders (4a) in analyzing classroom interaction. In research studies using the Bales-Gerbrands (2) interaction recorder, Lamb (9) and McKinstry (12) identified nine teacher-role categories. These nine categories were combined and refined into the five teacher roles listed in Table 1.

## COLLECTION OF DATA

Two-minute samples of the classroom behavior and learning activities of individual underachieving and achieving fifth-grade pupils were categorized during weekly observations in one or more of four academic subjects: language arts, arithmetic, social studies, and science. Efficient and objective categorization of 5 to 15 behaviors per minute was possible by using a Bales-Gerbrands (2) recorder, an electrically powered machine that moves tape (paper on which categorizations are recorded) at a constant speed, thereby enabling the duration of each behavioral response to be accurately measured.

At the same time that pupil behavior was being observed and categorized, a second trained observer, using another Bales-Gerbrands recorder, was categorizing the teacher's behavior and role in successive two-minute samples. The 72 pupils in the sample and their teachers were observed by two-member observer teams in 2,410 two-minute samples totaling 80 hours extending over five months—January to June 1963.

## RELIABILITY AND VALIDITY

The interobserver reliability of the four observers in the study was estimated by the following procedure. Each observer was paired successively

TABLE 1

| Student Categories | | Teacher Categories | |
| --- | --- | --- | --- |
| LISWAT | Interested in ongoing work: listening and watching—passive. | 1. | Does not accept student's idea, corrects it: rejection or correction of student's response. |
| REWR | Reading or Writing; working in assigned area—active. | 2. | Praises or encourages student or behavior: enthusiastic acceptance of student's response. |
| HIAC | High activity or involvement: reciting or using large muscles—positive feeling. | 2A. | Listens to, helps, supports, nurtures student: accepting, helping response; also listening to recitation. |
| WOA | Intent on work in another curricular area: school activity not assigned to be done right then. | 3. | Accepts or uses student's answer or idea. |
| | | 4. | Asks questions about content (what? where? when?): wants to find out whether student knows and understands material. |
| WNA | Intent on work of nonacademic type: preparing for work assignment, cleaning out desk, etc. | 4A. | Asks questions that stimulate thinking (why? how?): encourages student to seek explanations, to reason, to solve problems. |
| SWP | Social, work-oriented—PEER: discussing some aspect of schoolwork with classmate. | 5. | Lectures, gives facts or opinions about content: gives information in discussion, recitation, or committee meeting. |
| SWT | Social, work-oriented—TEACHER: discussing some phase of work with teacher. | 6. | Gives directions, commands, or orders with which student is expected to comply. |
| SF | Social, friendly: talking to peer on subject unrelated to schoolwork. | 7. | Criticizes or justifies authority: disapproves of conduct or work of student or group of students. |
| WDL | Withdrawal: detached, out of contact with people, ideas, classroom situation; daydreaming. | 10. | Is not participating in class activities: is giving test or is out of room—class silent or in confusion. |
| DISC | Large-group discussion: entire class discusses an issue or evaluates an oral report. | LDR | Leader-director—teacher initiative—active: conducts recitation or discussion, lectures, works with small groups. |
| REC | Class recitation: teacher questions, student answers—entire class or portion of it participating. | RES | Resource person—student-centered, lesser role than leader: helps group or committee, brings material, suggests. |
| IND | Individual work or project: student is working alone on task that is not a common assignment. | SUPV | Supervisor—teacher initiative, passive, role during seatwork: circulates to observe and help. |
| SEAT | Seatwork, reading or writing, common assignment. | SOC | Socialization agent: points to and reinforces social expectancies and rules; criticizes behavior. |
| GRP | Small-group or committee work: student is part of group or committee working on assignment. | EVL | Evaluator: listens and gives mark for oral report, individual or group; asks, "How many did you get right?" |
| REP | Oral reports—individual or group: student is orally reporting on book, current events, or research. | | |

with every other observer; each pair then participated in training sessions in which both members of the pair observed and categorized first a pupil's behavior and later the teacher's be-havior and role. The number of seconds that one member of a pair recorded behavior (or activity or role) in a specific category was correlated with the number of seconds that the other member recorded in the same category while simultaneously observing the same pupil or teacher.

For the *Student Categories*, product-moment coefficients for the various pairings of observers ranged from .88 to .99 for five 2-minute samples, with a mean of .97 (obtained by means of Fisher's $z$ transformation). For the *Teacher Categories*, the coefficients, again for five 2-minute samples, ranged from .83 to .98, with a mean of .94. Recordings occurred in 12 of the 15 categories in the student instrument and in 13 of the 15 categories in the teacher instrument. Since the scores used to compute these coefficients totaled the same amounts of time (120 seconds × 5) for every observer, the coefficients are higher than they would be had there been no time restriction.

A further estimate of reliability was obtained by computing coefficients between the scores (number of seconds) of the members of each pairing for each of the 12 most frequently used categories of the two instruments (77 per cent of all categorizations). These coefficients are given in Table 2.

The high interobserver coefficients for all pairings of the four observers for all categories combined and for 9 of the 12 most frequently used categories, considered individually, were accepted as establishing the reliability of both instruments and the objectivity of the four observers who used them.

Validity of the two instruments was established in several ways. First, since the definitions of each category describe the kinds of things students and teachers do in the classroom, the instruments have face validity. Second, the tally sheets of the categorizations made by the observers accounted for 120 seconds of student and teacher behavior for each time sample. This fact satisfied the criterion of inclusiveness of categories and provides fur-

TABLE 2

**Interobserver Reliability Coefficients for Most Frequently Used Categories**

| | OBSERVER PAIRINGS | | | | | | |
| CATEGORY | A-B | A-C | A-D | B-C | B-D | C-D | Mean |
|---|---|---|---|---|---|---|---|
| | | | *Student Categories* | | | | |
| Listening, watching | .98 | .98 | .67 | 9.8 | .98 | .98 | .97 |
| Reading or writing | .88 | .99 | .48 | * | .94 | 1.00 | .95 |
| High activity | .96 | .70 | 1.00 | .95 | 1.00 | 1.00 | .98 |
| Withdrawal | .99 | .76 | .99 | .75 | .92 | .75 | .93 |
| Recitation | 1.00 | 1.00 | * | 1.00 | 1.00 | 1.00 | 1.00 |
| Seatwork | * | * | * | * | .99 | 1.00 | .99 |
| | | | *Teacher Categories* | | | | |
| 2A. Listens, helps | .90 | .74 | .96 | .99 | .64 | .81 | .90 |
| 4. Asks questions | .45 | .65 | .52 | .83 | .96 | .88 | .78 |
| 5. Lectures | .40 | .40 | .41 | .92 | .77 | .76 | .67 |
| 10. Is not participating | * | 1.00 | .55 | * | .94 | 1.00 | .97 |
| Leader | .04 | .99 | .51 | 1.00 | * | 1.00 | .95 |
| Supervisor | * | .55 | .43 | .77 | .60 | * | .60 |

* This category was not used by either observer during the five 2-minute samples on which the coefficients of this pairing are based.

ther evidence of the validity of the instruments.

Finally, the learning-activity categories of the *Student Categories* and the teacher-behavior and -role categories of the *Teacher Categories* were validated against an external criterion. Three of the observers had each had more than 20 years' experience in public-school teaching or supervision. Without access to categorized data obtained by observation, each one wrote short descriptions of the 14 teachers and classrooms of the study, omitting all identifying data. The writer, serving as judge, matched the quantified data on learning activity, teacher behavior, and teacher role obtained from observations in each classroom with the 14 written descriptions of these teachers and classrooms prepared by the three observers. Eleven (79 per cent) of the 14 sets of data were matched correctly.

Later, the three observers, serving as independent judges, identified disguised written descriptions of the teachers that had been prepared from the quantified data for learning-activity, teacher-behavior, and teacher-role categories obtained in observations. Correct identifications were made for 12 (86 per cent) of the 14 teachers. Such a procedure was not feasible for the student-behavior categories because the kinds of quantified data obtained from observations could not be translated into descriptions that were sufficiently differentiated to permit adequate identification.

Possible experimental bias prevents accepting these agreements between the results obtained by instruments and classroom descriptions written by observers who participated in the study as conclusively showing that the instruments are valid. Further evidence of their validity will be presented in the next two sections of this report.

## FINDINGS

Since the total amount of observation time varied somewhat for different pupils and different teachers, the total amount of time for each category, pupil, teacher, and school subject was viewed as part of the whole and changed to percentages to achieve comparability. The behavior of underachievers and achievers in each of the 14 classrooms is reported in percentages by category and classroom in Table 3.

These data show that for approximately 75 per cent of the time the behavior of both underachievers and achievers was academic-work-oriented: listening and watching, reading or writing, high activity, or work with peers. A general pattern of pupil behavior in learning situations is discernible, but within this general pattern marked differences can be noted between and within classrooms. Mean differences between underachievers and achievers were significant for only two of the nine behavior categories: achievers engaged in significantly more social work with peers; and underachievers more frequently withdrew from the learning activity.

Testing the mean scores for underachievers and achievers of the proportionate amounts of time various learning-situation, teacher-behavior, and teacher-role variables were categorized was not a meaningful analysis since teacher behavior and role were regarded as responses to the total learning situation rather than as responses to specific underachieving or achieving pupils. Computation and analyses of $t$ values for 21 learning-activity, teacher-behavior, and teacher-role categories and 6 groupings for achievement and sex differences revealed that only 11 of the 126 $t$ values were significant. Seven of these 11 values related to categories that were used less than 5 per cent of the time. Since 2-minute observations were made alternately of underachievers and achievers, this general lack of significant differences suggests a fairly high degree of split-half reliability in the categorization of teacher behavior, role, and use of learning activity.

The great variability of percentages for each category of learning activity in Table 3 and each category of teacher behavior and role in Table 4 shows clearly the uniqueness of each classroom as a learning environment. The extensive use of recitation and seatwork (75 per cent of the time) and the infrequent use of discussion, individual work, group work, and oral reports are particularly evident in Table 3. In Table 4, the large percentages of listening-helping behavior shown for nearly all teachers would appear to be important in the facilitation of learning. In contrast, the low incidence of praise (1 per cent), asking "thinking" questions (1 per cent), and using pupil's answer or idea (4 per cent) reveals that other important ways of assisting children to learn were rarely used. The almost exclusive use of the leader and the supervisor roles (88 per cent) by these teachers parallels the high incidence of recitation and seatwork noted above. These findings raise the question whether greater variation and flexibility in types of learning activity and teacher role would stimulate learner curiosity and hence lead to increased learning.

The data in Tables 3 and 4 show that the instruments developed in this study do discriminate between underachieving and achieving pupils and between different kinds of teachers in terms of behavior, role, and learning situation

and thus provide further evidence of the validity of the instruments.

## DISCUSSION

How valid or representative is this picture of teacher behavior and classroom interaction as a picture of teachers, or teaching, in general? A partial answer may be found by comparing the results obtained by this set of *Teacher Categories* with those obtained by Hughes (7a) and Flanders (5b). Although many of the categories of the three instruments are similar, differences in their definition or use by each research worker and dissimilarity among the teacher groups in the three studies clearly indicate that comparisons among the studies will not be wholly valid. The comparisons drawn are of necessity crude and speculative. They are limited to teacher-behavior and teacher-function categories and were made between mean percentages in each category for the total sample of teachers in each study.

Hughes's *Provo Code* (7b) was developed from an analysis of trained observers' written records of 41 elementary teachers' classroom behavior; it consists of seven teacher-function categories: (1) Controlling, (2) Imposition, (3) Facilitation, (4) Content Development, (5) Personal Response, (6) Positive Affectivity, and (7) Negative Affectivity. As stated earlier, Flanders (4a) has seven teacher-behavior categories: (1) accepts feeling, (2) praises or encourages, (3) accepts or uses ideas of student, (4) asks question, (5) lectures, (6) gives directions, (7) criticizes or justifies authority; two categories of student behavior: (8) student talk—response, (9) student talk—initiation; and (10) silence or confusion. After data for categories 8 and 9 were

TABLE 3

**Percentage of Time Recorded in Each Behavior Category for Underachievers (U) and Achievers (A),\* by Classrooms; and Percentage of Time Spent in Each Learning Activity for Each Classroom**

| Class-room | Student Behavior† | | | | | | | | | | Learning Activity† | | | | |
|---|---|---|---|---|---|---|---|---|---|---|---|---|---|---|---|
| | LSWAT | REWR | HIAC | WOA | WNA | SWP | SWT | SF | WDL | DSCN | REC | IND | SEAT | GRP | REP |
| A U | 20.0 | 32.4 | 14.0 | 2.3 | 9.5 | 6.7 | 5.1 | 1.1 | 8.9 | 0 | 33.6 | 22.4 | 32.2 | 5.7 | 6.4 |
| A A | 26.6 | 37.5 | 11.2 | .8 | 9.3 | 7.1 | 2.0 | 1.8 | 3.7 | 0 | | | | | |
| B U | 22.6 | 47.3 | 11.1 | 3.5 | 5.9 | 2.1 | .5 | 1.0 | 6.0 | | 35.8 | 6.9 | 53.5 | .8 | 3.0 |
| B A | 19.2 | 46.4 | 12.4 | 6.8 | 4.9 | .3 | .6 | .5 | 8.7 | | | | | | |
| C U | 27.6 | 34.2 | 9.2 | 5.9 | 5.1 | 2.6 | 1.1 | 4.5 | 9.8 | 4.2 | 23.8 | 9.9 | 58.2 | 4.0 | 0 |
| C A | 37.8 | 30.5 | 5.7 | 3.7 | 7.8 | 1.7 | 2.0 | 5.1 | 5.6 | | | | | | |
| D U | 32.5 | 18.3 | 6.3 | 19.0 | 7.2 | .9 | .7 | 3.6 | 11.7 | 13.5 | 36.2 | 1.4 | 28.6 | 1.9 | 18.3 |
| D A | 43.1 | 22.4 | 4.1 | 5.1 | 4.6 | 2.8 | .7 | 3.9 | 13.3 | | | | | | |
| E U | 33.3 | 25.7 | 2.1 | 4.1 | 12.1 | 1.8 | 0 | 5.8 | 15.0 | 3.1 | 27.7 | 3.9 | 55.0 | 10.3 | 0 |
| E A | 33.4 | 33.2 | 3.1 | 3.9 | 6.4 | 2.3 | 1.4 | 5.0 | 11.6 | | | | | | |
| F U | 27.0 | 26.4 | 2.5 | 5.2 | 5.0 | 9.9 | .9 | 9.0 | 14.2 | 4.1 | 25.8 | 12.1 | 39.1 | 18.0 | 1.0 |
| F A | 27.1 | 24.9 | 4.2 | 12.3 | 4.0 | 8.8 | 2.0 | 6.9 | 9.7 | | | | | | |
| G U | 45.4 | 39.7 | 2.5 | .2 | 3.3 | 1.5 | .6 | .4 | 6.4 | 0 | 46.0 | 0 | 49.4 | 4.6 | 0 |
| G A | 59.2 | 30.1 | 2.8 | 0 | 2.4 | .6 | .5 | .4 | 4.0 | | | | | | |
| H U | 38.6 | 25.5 | 5.1 | 7.5 | 2.8 | .7 | 5.3 | 5.3 | 9.1 | 17.5 | 43.1 | 14.0 | 17.2 | 8.1 | 0 |
| H A | 45.1 | 21.5 | 8.2 | 2.9 | 5.6 | 5.1 | 3.2 | 4.0 | 4.4 | | | | | | |
| I U | 17.3 | 33.4 | 5.2 | 10.8 | 7.2 | 1.3 | 1.3 | 5.1 | 18.4 | 0 | 62.1 | 0 | 28.8 | .9 | 8.7 |
| I A | 26.9 | 34.5 | 6.8 | 4.0 | 5.1 | 4.5 | .6 | 3.3 | 14.4 | | | | | | |
| J U | 29.6 | 25.7 | 12.0 | 5.6 | 5.8 | 4.8 | 1.6 | 4.4 | 10.3 | 8.6 | 13.8 | .9 | 49.9 | 10.5 | 16.2 |
| J A | 26.6 | 22.8 | 13.0 | 2.7 | 4.3 | 9.7 | 3.7 | 6.3 | 10.9 | | | | | | |
| K U | 46.7 | 12.7 | 6.7 | .6 | 3.9 | 5.7 | 3.0 | 10.4 | 10.5 | 24.7 | 41.4 | 4.1 | 22.5 | 5.5 | 1.7 |
| K A | 39.7 | 16.1 | 7.5 | 5.0 | 4.5 | 3.8 | 1.3 | 10.2 | 11.8 | | | | | | |
| L U | 35.1 | 32.0 | 8.0 | .1 | 10.2 | 3.7 | 2.3 | 2.6 | 5.9 | 1.0 | 24.6 | 16.7 | 48.2 | 5.7 | 3.8 |
| L A | 28.6 | 41.0 | 6.6 | .2 | 9.4 | 5.3 | 2.1 | 1.5 | 5.4 | | | | | | |
| M U | 31.8 | 31.9 | 8.8 | .2 | 7.8 | 3.1 | 2.8 | 3.3 | 10.2 | 1.5 | 35.6 | 10.2 | 33.1 | 10.5 | 9.1 |
| M A | 32.0 | 35.2 | 6.7 | 3.1 | 6.4 | 6.2 | 1.4 | 2.6 | 6.3 | | | | | | |

\* All pupils in the fifth grade.
† See Table 1, left-hand column, for description of categories.

75

TABLE 3 (cont.)

| | 1 | 2 | 2A | 3 | 4 | 4A | 5 | 6 | 7 | 10 | LDR | RES | SUPV | SOC | EVL |
|---|---|---|---|---|---|---|---|---|---|---|---|---|---|---|---|
| O  U | 19.4 | 28.8 | 13.0 | 1.6 | 9.1 | 9.6 | 1.9 | 6.2 | 10.5 | .3 | 10.0 | 22.1 | 57.6 | 8.8 | 1.2 |
| O  A | 15.6 | 34.7 | 2.2 | 2.1 | 6.9 | 14.6 | 3.6 | 13.7 | 6.5 | 5.5 | 8.0 | 33.7 | 40.9 | 6.8 | 5.0 |
| $\bar{X}$  U | 30.5 | 29.6 | 7.6 | 4.8 | 6.8 | 3.9 | 1.9 | 4.5 | 10.5 | 5.5 | 6.8 | 12.2 | 13.9 | 4.7 | 6.1 |
| $\bar{X}$  A | 32.9 | 30.8 | 6.8 | 3.8 | 5.8 | 5.2 | 1.8 | 4.7 | 8.3 | 7.8 | | | | | |
| $s$  U | 9.1 | 8.5 | 4.0 | 5.2 | 2.8 | 3.1 | 1.6 | 2.9 | 3.5 | | | | | | |
| $s$  A | 11.3 | 8.4 | 3.5 | 3.2 | 2.0 | 3.9 | 1.1 | 3.7 | 3.6 | | | | | | |

TABLE 4

**Percentage of Time Recorded in Each Behavior and Role Category for 14 Fifth-Grade Teachers**

| Teacher | Behavior Category* | | | | | | | | | | Role Category* | | | | |
|---|---|---|---|---|---|---|---|---|---|---|---|---|---|---|---|
| | 1 | 2 | 2A | 3 | 4 | 4A | 5 | 6 | 7 | 10 | LDR | RES | SUPV | SOC | EVL |
| A | .7 | .1 | 35.2 | 2.3 | 12.8 | .7 | 14.1 | 12.4 | 1.5 | 20.2 | 45.1 | 0 | 43.3 | .8 | 10.9 |
| B | .3 | .3 | 35.8 | .9 | 15.3 | 0 | 6.8 | 10.4 | .7 | 29.4 | 41.9 | .6 | 54.2 | .9 | 2.5 |
| C | .6 | .4 | 13.3 | 1.8 | 6.7 | 1.5 | 23.8 | 6.8 | 4.1 | 41.1 | 31.3 | .4 | 57.7 | 3.3 | 7.2 |
| D | .1 | .5 | 46.5 | 5.4 | 7.4 | .5 | 13.5 | 7.3 | 1.6 | 17.1 | 50.2 | 12.6 | 33.2 | 1.3 | 2.7 |
| E | .1 | 6.5 | 29.0 | 5.0 | 6.4 | 1.0 | 14.9 | 3.7 | 2.4 | 30.9 | 57.5 | 0 | 38.4 | 1.6 | 2.4 |
| F | .2 | 0 | 15.0 | 3.4 | 5.0 | 2.2 | 7.2 | 8.0 | 3.9 | 55.0 | 35.9 | 7.4 | 49.0 | 2.8 | 4.9 |
| G | .6 | .4 | 29.0 | 6.7 | 21.1 | 3.1 | 17.8 | 13.4 | .8 | 7.3 | 64.5 | 0 | 33.9 | .6 | 1.0 |
| H | 1.9 | 1.2 | 51.2 | 7.7 | 9.4 | 1.4 | 15.4 | 4.5 | 1.6 | 5.7 | 61.8 | 25.2 | 11.6 | 1.4 | 0 |
| I | .4 | 0 | 19.5 | 1.9 | 16.4 | .4 | 29.8 | 10.7 | 14.5 | 6.4 | 71.4 | .2 | 16.0 | 12.3 | .1 |
| J | .2 | .5 | 33.9 | 3.1 | 4.8 | .4 | 17.9 | 4.2 | 1.3 | 33.9 | 42.2 | 6.4 | 48.4 | 1.0 | 1.9 |
| K | .8 | .5 | 28.4 | 6.6 | 14.0 | 3.2 | 20.1 | 8.6 | 3.1 | 14.6 | 66.2 | .9 | 23.9 | 2.6 | 6.4 |
| L | .4 | 1.3 | 52.4 | 3.1 | 16.5 | .3 | 7.6 | 6.0 | 3.9 | 8.6 | 31.6 | 18.1 | 42.1 | 4.1 | 4.0 |
| M | .3 | 1.0 | 57.2 | 4.8 | 9.9 | .2 | 17.0 | 4.5 | .8 | 4.3 | 63.0 | 9.6 | 21.5 | .8 | 5.1 |
| O | 0 | 0 | 45.7 | .7 | 7.5 | .8 | 19.3 | 10.3 | 2.1 | 13.6 | 42.4 | 4.4 | 48.3 | 2.6 | 2.3 |
| $\bar{X}$ | .5 | .9 | 35.2 | 3.8 | 10.9 | 1.1 | 16.1 | 7.9 | 3.0 | 20.6 | 50.4 | 6.1 | 37.3 | 2.6 | 3.7 |
| $s$ | .5 | 1.7 | 14.0 | 2.2 | 5.1 | 1.0 | 6.4 | 3.2 | 3.5 | 15.4 | 13.6 | 7.9 | 14.5 | 3.0 | 3.0 |

* See Table 1, right-hand column, for description of categories.

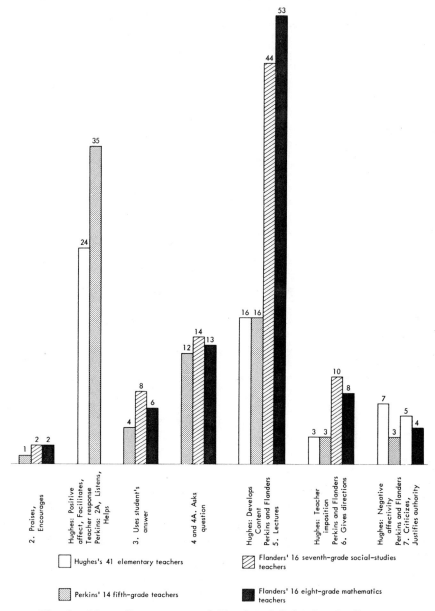

**Fig. 1. Mean Percentages of Teachers' Behavior in Four Studies of Classroom Interaction Grouped into Comparable Categories**

eliminated, the percentages of total time that behavior was assigned to each of the seven teacher categories were computed for two groups of teachers studied by Flanders ([5b] App., pp. 34-35): 16 seventh-grade social-studies teachers and 16 eighth-grade mathematics teachers. Data from the present study used in these comparisons were the mean percentages (reported in Table 4) for seven of the teacher-behavior categories of 14 fifth-grade teachers.

The bar graph in Fig. 1 shows mean percentages of various types of teacher behavior that may reasonably be compared. Although these comparisons may distort some of the categories or findings, it is interesting to note the high degree of similarity of classroom behavior among the teachers in the three studies. The proportion of time spent by Perkins' fifth-grade teachers was fairly close to, or the same as, that spent by Hughes's elementary teachers in each of the following grouped functions: listening-helping (facilitating learning, etc.); lecturing (developing content); and giving directions (teacher imposition). On the other hand, Hughes's teachers spent twice as large a proportion of time criticizing or reprimanding their pupils.

With regard to those categories common to Flanders' study and the present study, the results were similar for praising or encouraging, asking questions, and criticizing or justifying authority. Flanders' junior-high teachers greatly exceeded Perkins' fifth-grade teachers in using student's idea, lecturing, and giving directions. The similarities between the results obtained by the *Teacher Categories* instrument of this study and those obtained by Flanders and Hughes are further evidence of the validity of this instrument.

Figure 1 reveals rather striking differences between junior-high and elementary teachers in the ways that each group structures and influences the learning experiences in their respective classrooms. Flanders' teachers appear to play a more active role, as evidenced by their more frequent use of the stu-dent's ideas, of lecturing, and of giving directions. Hughes's and Perkins' elementary teachers made greater use of listening, helping, supporting, and clarifying. This difference may not be real since Flanders did not have a helping-supporting category as such and may have assigned helping and supporting the student to such categories as using student's idea, lecturing, or giving directions.

Although these comparisons are only suggestive, the similarities and differences that exist among teachers in behavior, function, role, and teaching process, as measured by these instruments, seem to promise further breakthroughs in studying teacher influence and effectiveness and in developing a theory of instruction.

An important advantage of the procedure developed in this study is that it yields data on behavior, role, and learning activity in quantified form. Although certain qualitative and unique aspects may be sacrificed by the categorization process, the objective data that are obtained permit rigorous testing of hypotheses. Another advantage is that simultaneous categorizations of student and teacher behavior on the paper tape of recorders provide a permanent record of teacher-pupil interaction that may be subjected to pattern and sequence analysis.

A disadvantage of the procedure is the large amount of clerical time required to measure the length of each line (in seconds) on the tape and to record the duration of each behavioral response on a tally sheet. This disadvantage could be reduced by more elaborate instrumentation using calibrated tape or punched cards.

### REFERENCES

1. Anderson, Harold H., Joseph E., Brewer, and Mary F. Reed, "Studies

of Teachers' Classroom Personalities, III," *Applied Psychology Monograph*, No. 11. Stanford, Calif.: Stanford University Press, 1946.

2. Bales, Robert F. and Henry Gerbrands, "The Interaction Recorder, an Apparatus and Check List for Sequential Content Analysis of Social Interaction," *Human Relations*, I (November 1948), 456–63.

3. Cogan, Morris L., "Research on the Behavior of Teachers: A New Phase," *Journal of Teacher Education*, XIV (September 1963), 238–43.

4. Flanders, Ned A., *Interaction Analysis in the Classroom: A Manual for Observers*. Minneapolis: College of Education, University of Minnesota, 1960(a).

5. Flanders, Ned A., *Teacher Influence, Pupil Attitudes, and Achievement*. Report of Cooperative Research Project No. 397. Washington, D. C.: U. S. Department of Health, Education, and Welfare, Office of Education, 1963. Minneapolis: University of Minnesota, 1960(b).

6. Gallagher, James J., *A System for Classifying Thought Process in the Content of Classroom Verbal Interaction*. Urbana, Ill.: Institute for Research on Exceptional Children, University of Illinois, 1962.

7. Hughes, Marie M., *Development of the Means for the Assessment of the Quality of Teaching in the Elementary Schools*. Report of Cooperative Research Project No. 353. Washington, D. C.: U. S. Department of Health, Education, and Welfare, Office of Education, 1960 (a). Salt Lake City: University of Utah, 1959 (b).

8. Kowatrakul, Surang, "Some Behaviors of Elementary School Children Related to Classroom Activities and Subject Areas," *Journal of Educational Psychology*, L (June 1959), 121–28.

9. Lamb, Howard E., "Self and Role Concepts Related to Behavior, Intelligence, and Academic Achievement."

Doctoral Thesis, University of Maryland, 1962.

10. Leacock, Eleanor, "Classroom Processes Study," *Theory and Research in Teaching*, ed. Arno A. Bellack. New York: Bureau of Publications, Teachers College, Columbia University (1963), pp. 112–17.

11. Lewin, Kurt, Ronald Lippitt, and Ralph K. White, "Patterns of Aggressive Behavior in Experimentally Created 'Social Climates,'" *Journal of Social Psychology*, X (May 1939), 271–99.

12. McKinstry, Clarence R., "The Behavior of Selected Fifth-Grade Students as Related to Subject Areas and Teacher Roles." Doctoral Thesis, College Park, Md., University of Maryland, 1962.

13. Medley, Donald M., "Experiences with the OScAR Technique," *Journal of Teacher Education*, XIV (September 1963), 267–73.

14. Schueler, Herbert, Milton J. Gold, and Harold E. Mitzel, *The Use of Television for Improving Teacher Training and for Improving Measures of Student Teaching Performance*. Improvement of Student Teaching, Phase 1. New York: Hunter College, City University of New York, 1962.

15. Sears, Pauline S., *The Effect of Classroom Conditions on the Strength of Achievement Motive and Work Output of Elementary School Children*. Report of Cooperative Research Project No. 873. Washington, D. C.: U. S. Department of Health, Education, and Welfare, Office of Education, 1963.

16. Spaulding, Robert, "Affective Dimensions of the Creative Processes." Paper presented to the Association for Supervision and Curriculum Development, March 1963.

17. Withall, John G., "The Development of a Technique for the Measurement of Social-Emotional Climate in Classrooms," *Journal of Experimental Education*, XVII (March 1949), 347–61.

# 10

# Feedback in Classrooms: A Study of Corrective Teacher Responses

## MORTON D. WAIMON

The efforts described in this paper grew out of an attempt to help prospective teachers study and understand interaction in classrooms, and to help them become more aware of pupil behavior in classrooms, and more sensitive to its meaning for teachers. It was felt that this could best be done by studying the teaching-learning process in actual classrooms. A method was developed, therefore, for describing, analyzing and interpreting observed classroom behavior.[1]

Basic to this observation of the teaching-learning process is the conceptualization of the classroom as an action system; that is, a phenomenon whose separate elements exist in dynamic relationship to one another and to the environment in which they are found.

Morton D. Waimon, "Feedback in Classrooms: A Study of Corrective Teacher Responses," *Journal of Experimental Education*, XXX, No. 4 (June 1962), 355–59. Reprinted by permission.

[1] Morton D. Waimon, "Observing the Classroom Action System," *Journal of Teacher Education*, XII (December 1961), 466–70.

The model developed for this work depicts three elements in the classroom action system: the teacher, the learners, and the behavior or classroom setting. It was used to demonstrate that a teacher's behavior influences the behavior setting and the behavior of learners; that a learner's behavior has an effect on the behavior setting and on how the teacher will act; and that the behavior setting itself limits the behavior of both teacher and learners. In other words, the three elements are mutually dependent each upon the others.

Although the education students involved in this investigation of the classroom studied the total action system, this paper is chiefly concerned with the way in which teachers are influenced by pupil behavior.

The learner obviously affects teacher behavior when he solicits help or asks a question. Less obviously, but perhaps of greater importance, all the learner's behavior provides the teacher with information about himself relative to that learning situation. He provides the teacher with clues about his present readiness to learn. This information, which is in the nature of a feedback to the teacher, is what prompts a teacher to change or modify something in the situation so that learning can occur.

When a teacher perceives that learning is not taking place, he makes corrective responses by changing something in the learning environment or by attempting to change some aspect of the learner's readiness. If we think of learning as occurring when learner's readiness and environment are brought into harmony, then we may view a teacher's corrective responses as maximizing the balance in the teaching-learning system.

This, then, is the conceptual framework which led us to ask the following questions:

1. What proportion of teacher behavior is corrective; that is, is made in response to pupil behavior which indicates that learning is not taking place?
2. What proportion of teachers' corrective responses is directed toward changing the environment?
3. What proportion of teachers' corrective responses is directed toward changing some aspect of the learner's readiness?
4. Which aspect of the environment is most frequently manipulated?
5. Which aspect of the learner's readiness is most frequently manipulated?

**PROCEDURES**

After an initial orientation and training period, teams of four members each were established to make classroom observations, and observation guides were distributed to each team. One member was to concentrate and record data on the teacher, two were to concentrate on the learners, the fourth on the behavior setting. Time sheets blocked off in five-minute intervals were used for recording, and an entire observation period lasted thirty

minutes. Immediately following the observation period, team members coalesced their data.

Teams were responsible for recording everything which took place during an observation period. Working as teams and having each member concentrate on one element of the action system helped in making the recorded accounts more complete and more accurate. The member responsible for the behavior setting had to identify the kind of lesson, unit or activity engaged in; the apparent goals and subgoals of the activity; the selection and organization of content; and the procedures followed, including the materials and equipment available for use. The member responsible for the teacher was to record everything the teacher said to an individual learner or to the class; all the teacher's non-verbal behavior relative to an individual learner or to the class; all the teacher's apparent feelings relative to an individual learner or to the class. The other two members divided the class between them to make observation easier, and were to record everything any learner said to the teacher or to the class; all significant nonverbal behavior of learners (that is, all behavior which was noticeable to the teacher and to the observers), and all apparent feelings expressed by any learner. At the end of the observation period, team members combined their records into a running account of everything that happened during the observation period. Observations were made in nineteen classes of the Laboratory School of Illinois State Normal University.

TREATMENT OF THE DESCRIPTIVE DATA

The descriptive records gathered by teams were divided into smaller units of behavior which were called behavior episodes. Behavior episodes may best be explained as samples of behavior, within the larger stream of behavior, which have a discernible beginning and end. For example, during an arithmetic lesson a pupil discovers he has no pencil; he tries to borrow one from his neighbor without success; he informs the teacher of his difficulty; is told to take one from the teacher's desk; he does so and returns to his seat to continue work. All the action aimed at securing a pencil is a behavior episode.

CLASSIFYING THE DATA

Team members then analyzed and classified their data several ways. First the records were read over to find pupil behavior, both verbal and nonverbal, which indicated that the pupil was not ready to learn in that situation. Each such response was starred. Expressions of boredom, disinterest or confusion, inattention, irrelevant behavior, questions regarding procedures or content were regarded as indications that a learner was not ready to learn; that is, not ready to make the correct response called for. Next the records were checked for teacher behavior which was made in response to starred pupil behavior. An "X" was placed beside each such teacher response.

Behavior episodes were then classified into three categories: Type A episodes are those episodes in which there was no evidence that any learner lacked readiness to learn in that situation. Learning proceeded smoothly without any apparent blocking. Type B episodes are those episodes in which a learner indicated a lack of readiness to learn, but in which the teacher did *not* respond to that specific pupil behavior. Type C episodes are those episodes in which a learner indicated a lack of readiness to learn and in which

the teacher *responded* to the specific pupil behavior.

Type C episodes were further evaluated to determine how often teachers responded to pupils' lack of readiness by attempting to change something in the environment, and how often the teacher's response tended to be directed toward the pupil himself.

When a teacher response was directed toward the environment, it was further classified into responses that change the goal, responses that change the content, or responses that change the procedures.

When a teacher response was directed toward the learner, it was further classified into responses that act on the pupil's equipment (that is, affect his physique, sense organs, or mental abilities), responses that act on pupil's needs and goals (that is, his need for affection, approval, independence, self-respect, or his immediate personal goals), or responses that act on the pupil's learned ideas and skills (that is, his previous learnings).

The following are examples of each type episode:

Type A—(All pupils ready. No corrective teacher responses made.)

T:       "What is the first number? Lynn?"
Lynn:   "Three."
T:       "Three what?"
Lynn:   "Three tens."
T:       "What does the 2 mean?"
Lynn:   "Two ones."
T:       "And what is the whole number? Three?"
Lynn:   "Tens."
T:       "And two . . . ?"
Lynn:   "Ones."
T:       "Make?"
Lynn:   "Thirty-two."
T:       "Good for you, Lynn."

Type B—(Lack of readiness shown, but no corrective responses made by teacher.)

T: (Reviewing spelling words.) *"Every*. Look at your own paper. If you look at someone else's paper that tells me you don't know how to spell it. *Begin, yesterday, . . .."*

Ricky: (Repeats all words without being asked.)

Scott, Jim, Brad: (Talked to each other.)*

Kerry: (Dropped his pencil; picked it up.)

Paul: (Opened his book before he was supposed to.)

Toni: "I got scared last night."*

Sandy: "My mommy made some popcorn balls for Halloween."*

T: "The last word is *invite*. All right, there are your words. Open your book to page 80 and check your words, and I will come around to see if you are a good checker-upper."

Type C—(Lack of readiness shown, and teacher makes corrective responses.)

T: (Writes 14 on the board.) "What is the name of this number? Anybody? Anyone can answer because the group is small."

Steve: "Twenty-four."*

T: "No, Steve, let's begin at one and count until we reach the number." X L(l.i.s.)

Steve: "1. . .2. . .3. . .4. . .5. . .6. . .7. . .8 . . .9. . .10. . .11. . .12. . .13. . .14"

T: "Fine, now we know how to proceed."

---

Polly: (Not paying attention)*

T: "Polly, look at this number right here. You're too busy watching over there. How many tens?" X L(n.g.)

Polly: "One."

T: "How many ones?"

Polly: "One."

T: "Now, ten and one are 11 in all."

---

T: (Reading to class from *Who's Who in Supermarket*. The Produce Department is mentioned.) "Do you all know what a Produce Department is? It's the name given to the department where fresh fruits and vegetables are sold. "Name something that is sold in the Produce Department. Steve?"

Steve: "Lettuce."

T: "Good. Janie?"

Janie: "Grapefruit."

T: "Yes. Willy?"

Willy: "Greeners."

T: "Greeners? What do you mean, Willy?"

Willy: "Greeners."

T: "Could you draw a picture of your vegetable? I'm afraid we don't quite understand your word." X E(p)

Willy: (Draws on board. His vegetable turns out to be a green onion.) "At our house, we call them greeners."

## FINDINGS

We found that out of a total of 865 behavior episodes, 402 were Type A episodes. That is, 46.5 per cent of the episodes observed were instances in which there was *no* evidence of lack of readiness on the part of learners. Learners indicated a lack of readiness in 463 episodes or 53.5 per cent of the total. In 96 episodes, or 11.1 per cent of the total, teachers made no response to the evidence of lack of readiness to learn in that situation (see Table 1).

The average number of episodes recorded in nineteen classes was 46 episodes. The average percentage of Type C episodes was 41 per cent with a standard deviation of 15 per cent.

Type C episodes totaled 367. Of these, 82 episodes or 22.3 per cent were episodes in which the teacher responded to pupils' lack of readiness by attempting to change something in the environment (E). In 285 episodes, or 77.7 per cent, the teacher responded to pupils' lack of readiness by attempting to change something about the learner himself. The average percentage of learner-directed teacher responses was 76 per cent with a standard deviation of 13.4 per cent.

Of a total of 82 teacher responses which attempted to change something in the environment (E), 53 responses, or 65 per cent, were a change of procedures; 25 responses, or 30 per cent, were a change of content; and only 4 responses, or 5 per cent, were a change of goals (see Table 2).

Of a total of 285 teacher responses which attempted to change some aspect of the learner's readiness (L), 140 responses, or 49 per cent, sought to change the learner's needs and goals; 138 responses, or 48 per cent, to change the pupil's learned ideas and skills;

and only 7 responses, or 3 per cent, were related to pupil's equipment (see Table 3).

The ratio of one subcategory of teacher response to the others varied widely among the observed nineteen classes, and no significant central tendency was found to exist.

## CONCLUSIONS

A conceptualization of the classroom as an action system wherein pupil behavior is viewed as feedback information used by teachers to make corrective responses is a promising one for the study of the teaching-learning process.

The stream of interaction between

TABLE 1

**Classification of Behavior Episodes**

| Type of Behavior Episode | | Number | | Per cent | |
|---|---|---|---|---|---|
| Type A | | 402 | | 46.5 | |
| Type B | | 96) | | 11.1) | |
| | | | 463 | | 53.5 |
| Type C | | 367) | | 42.4) | |
| | Total | 865 | | 100. | |

TABLE 2

**Classification of Environment-Directed Teacher Responses (E)**

| Aspect of Environment | | Number | Per cent |
|---|---|---|---|
| Goals (g) | | 4 | 5. |
| Content (c) | | 25 | 30. |
| Procedures (p) | | 53 | 65. |
| | Total | 82 | 100. |

TABLE 3

**Classification of Learner-Directed Teacher Responses (L)**

| Aspect of Learner's Readiness | | Number | Per cent |
|---|---|---|---|
| Pupil's equipment (e) | | 7 | 3. |
| Pupil's needs and goals | | 140 | 49. |
| Pupil's learned ideas and skills(l.i.s.) | | 138 | 48. |
| | Total | 285 | 100. |

teacher and learners can be divided into episodes and these episodes can be classified into three types: (1) Episodes in which there is no evidence of lack of readiness on the part of the pupils; (2) Episodes in which pupils indicate a lack of readiness, but in which teachers do not respond; (3) Episodes in which pupils indicate lack of readiness and in which teachers directly respond to that specific behavior.

In approximately 40 per cent of the instances observed, teachers' behavior was a direct response to learner behavior. This teacher behavior can be classified into (1) behavior which attempts to change the environment to suit the readiness of the learner (E), or (2) behavior which attempts to make the learner more ready for the environment. There is a tendency for teachers to try to change the learner's readiness when learning does not occur.

Teacher responses which manipulate the environment can be classified into the subcategories we used; that is, responses which (1) changed the goal, (2) changed the content, (3) changed the procedures.

Teacher responses which manipulate the learner can be classified into two of the subcategories which we used; that is, responses which act on (1) pupils' needs and goals, and (2) pupils' learned ideas and skills. The third category, pupils' equipment, is of questionable value since so few responses went into this category.

The ratio of one subcategory of teacher response to the others varied widely among the nineteen classes, as we have said. This wide variation suggests that type of teacher response may be related to some aspect not studied at this time, such as, subject matter being taught, grade level being taught, or years of teaching experience.

As a final conclusion, it is felt that direct study of the teaching-learning process in actual classrooms by prospective teachers is a valid and advantageous method of teacher training. And, it is feasible through the use of system analysis and the development of models to help in the conceptualization.

# ACTIVITIES

1. What different techniques are available to you in interacting with students in the classroom?

2. What are some ways you can monitor your conduct as a teacher?

3. Consider the following teaching episode. Do you think it demonstrates good teaching? What are some ways you might describe the teaching, withholding judgment for awhile? Use the Flanders framework and compare your ratings with those of your classmates. Devise your own scheme for cataloging interaction patterns. (Perhaps Chapter 6 of the *Handbook for Research on Teaching*, N. L. Gage, ed., will suggest alternatives for your analysis.)

*Class:*  30 ninth-grade social-studies students.

*Topic:*  Civil War

Teacher:  Do you think the Southern States were morally right in leaving the Union? Bob —

Bob:  No. They joined the Union—and they should have known they were going to have to stay in the Union in thick and thin. It's just like a marriage.

Teacher:  You feel the relationship of South Carolina to the United States was similar to that of husband and wife?

Bob:  I didn't say that—I meant the Constitution was like a wedding promise—it is binding.

Teacher:  Does it say in the Constitution that joining the Union is binding?

Bob:  It must. At least it's implied.

Teacher:  (talking to whole class) Shhh! Bob has brought up an interesting point—and very few of you are listening to it. Some of you don't even seem to care. You'll care next Friday when we have a quiz on this. Bob, would you repeat your position for the benefit of those who weren't listening.

| | |
|---|---|
| Bob: | I think the South was wrong in quitting the Union. |
| Sue: | Why do you think so? |
| Teacher: | He just told us why—if you had been listening. Any other person like to state his position? |
| Andy: | I disagree with Bob. |
| Teacher: | Tell us about your point of view. |
| Andy: | I think South Carolina did the right thing—if you don't stand up for what you believe in—other people may push you around. |
| Sally: | What time does this period end? |
| Teacher: | Will you people please keep your mind on the topic at hand. Andy—is it always "right" to take a stand? |
| Andy: | Yes—that's what I was taught. |
| Teacher: | Do you *always* take a stand on whatever you believe? |
| Andy: | I sure do. |
| Teacher: | Oh. I appreciate how you feel, Andy. Many others feel as you do. We have heard two views about the Civil War. Any others? (pause) Perhaps we should review some of the facts during the rest of the period. Who was the Republican candidate for President in 1860? |
| Carolyn: | Abraham Lincoln. |
| Teacher: | OK! Who was the Democratic candidate? |
| Tom: | U. S. Grant? |
| Teacher: | No—but was Grant ever a candidate for President? |
| Richard: | Yes—twice and he won. |
| Teacher: | Good for you Richard. Do you know who the Democratic candidate for President in 1860 was? |
| Richard: | Stephan Douglas. |
| Teacher: | Good. |

*. . . and on*

4. Collect, by tape recorder or other means, or make up similar classroom episodes. Avoid trying to label the episodes good or bad—but try to devise ways of describing the actual teaching.

5. Can you think of some ways a teacher could monitor his behavior in class other than those reported here?

6. If after obtaining a description of a classroom activity you wished to evaluate the quality of the teaching or the learning, what criteria would you employ?

7. Some of the observation scales may be too complex for convenient application. Can you suggest alternative scales which will emphasize those aspects of classroom interaction which seem most important to you?

## Chapter Three

# DECISIONS IN PLANNING

For many years, poor teaching was described in terms of the apparent effects it had on the psyches of students. Accounts of cruelty, sadism, insensitivity, and the like usually are characteristic of stories concerning inferior teachers. As of late, more and more investigators of teaching are beginning to realize that poor teachers have been inflicting "intellectual" injury upon students too. Many teachers are confusing the teaching of facts with the teaching of thinking.

Clearly, such confusion often is a reflection of a teacher's own miseducation. In the past, teaching of science, history, Enslish, and mathematics has reflected a concern for isolated topics and areas of study that lack relationships to larger ideas and understandings. Curriculum movements current in disciplines illustrate a refreshing trend away from such teaching. Scholars in specific disciplines are working closely with teachers to carefully correlate content with intellectual objectives. These new curricula define appropriate content for the purpose of illustrating or testing the objectives.

What are some ways teachers may monitor their planning to reflect upon the quality of curriculum decisions they are making concerning the goals of their teaching and the content used to attain their goals? What implications for planning do you see in the research data reported in the previous chapter on "Interaction in the Classroom"?

# 11

# The Aims of Education

## ALFRED NORTH WHITEHEAD

Culture is activity of thought, and receptiveness to beauty and humane feeling. Scraps of information have nothing to do with it. A merely well-informed man is the most useless bore on God's earth. What we should aim at producing is men who possess both culture and expert knowledge in some special direction. Their expert knowledge will give them the ground to start from, and their culture will lead them as deep as philosophy and as high as art. We have to remember that the valuable intellectual development is self-development, and that it mostly takes place between the ages of sixteen and thirty. As to training, the most important part is given by mothers before the age of twelve. A saying due to Archbishop Temple illustrates my meaning. Surprise was expressed at the success in after-life of a man, who as a boy at Rugby had been somewhat undistinguished. He answered, "It is not what they are at eighteen, it is what they become afterwards that matters."

In training a child to activity of thought, above all things we must beware of what I will call "inert ideas" —that is to say, ideas that are merely received into the mind without being utilised, or tested, or thrown into fresh combinations.

In the history of education, the most striking phenomenon is that schools of learning, which at one epoch are alive with a ferment of genius, in a succeeding generation exhibit merely pedantry and routine. The reason is, that they are overladen with inert ideas. Education with inert ideas is not only useless: it is, above all things, harmful—*Corruptio optimi, pessima*. Except at rare intervals of intellectual ferment, education in the past has been radically infected with inert ideas. That is the reason why uneducated clever women, who have seen much of the world, are in middle life so much the most cultured part of the community. They have been saved from this horrible burden of inert ideas. Every intellectual revolution

Alfred North Whitehead, *The Aims of Education* (New York: The Macmillan Company, 1929), pp. 1–3, 8–15. Copyright 1929 by The Macmillan Company, renewed 1957 by Evelyn Whitehead. Reprinted by permission.

which has ever stirred humanity into greatness has been a passionate protest against inert ideas. Then, alas, with pathetic ignorance of human psychology, it has proceeded by some educational scheme to bind humanity afresh with inert ideas of its own fashioning.

Let us now ask how in our system of education we are to guard against this mental dryrot. We enunciate two educational commandments, "Do not teach too many subjects," and again, "What you teach, teach thoroughly."

The result of teaching small parts of a large number of subjects is the passive reception of disconnected ideas, not illumined with any spark of vitality. Let the main ideas which are introduced into a child's education be few and important, and let them be thrown into every combination possible. The child should make them his own, and should understand their application here and now in the circumstances of his actual life. From the very beginning of his education, the child should experience the joy of discovery. The discovery which he has to make is that general ideas give an understanding of that stream of events which pours through his life, which is his life. By understanding I mean more than a mere logical analysis, though that is included. I mean "understanding" in the sense in which it is used in the French proverb. "To understand all, is to forgive all." Pedants sneer at an education which is useful. But if education is not useful, what is it? Is it a talent, to be hidden away in a napkin? Of course, education should be useful, whatever your aim in life. It was useful to Saint Augustine and it was useful to Napoleon. It is useful, because understanding is useful.

\* \* \*

I appeal to you, as practical teachers. With good discipline, it is always pos-sible to pump into the minds of a class a certain quantity of inert knowledge. You take a text-book and make them learn it. So far, so good. The child then knows how to solve a quadratic equation. But what is the point of teaching a child to solve a quadratic equation? There is a traditional answer to this question. It runs thus: The mind is an instrument, you first sharpen it, and then use it; the acquisition of the power of solving a quadratic equation is part of the process of sharpening the mind. Now there is just enough truth in this answer to have made it live through the ages. But for all its half-truth, it embodies a radical error which bids fair to stifle the genius of the modern world. I do not know who was first responsible for this analogy of the mind to a dead instrument. For aught I know, it may have been one of the seven wise men of Greece, or a committee of the whole lot of them. Whoever was the originator, there can be no doubt of the authority which it has acquired by the continuous approval bestowed upon it by eminent persons. But whatever its weight of authority, whatever the high approval which it can quote, I have no hesitation in denouncing it as one of the most fatal, erroneous, and dangerous conceptions ever introduced into the theory of education. The mind is never passive; it is perpetual activity, delicate, receptive, responsive to stimulus. You cannot postpone its life until you have sharpened it. Whatever interest attaches to your subject-matter must be evoked here and now; whatever powers you are strengthening in the pupil, must be exercised here and now; whatever possibilities of mental life your teaching should impart, must be exhibited here and now. That is the golden rule of education, and a very difficult rule to follow.

The difficulty is just this: the apprehension of general ideas, intellectual habits of mind, and pleasurable interest in mental achievement can be evoked by no form of words, however accurately adjusted. All practical teachers know that education is a patient process of the mastery of details, minute by minute, hour by hour, day by day. There is no royal road to learning through an airy path of brilliant generalizations. There is a proverb about the difficulty of seeing the wood because of the trees. That difficulty is exactly the point which I am enforcing. The problem of education is to make the pupil see the wood by means of the trees.

The solution which I am urging is to eradicate the fatal disconnection of subjects which kills the vitality of our modern curriculum. There is only one subject-matter for education, and that is Life in all its manifestations. Instead of this single unity, we offer children—Algebra, from which nothing follows; Geometry, from which nothing follows; Science, from which nothing follows; History, from which nothing follows; a Couple of Languages, never mastered; and lastly, most dreary of all, Literature, represented by plays of Shakespeare, with philological notes and short analyses of plot and character to be in substance committed to memory. Can such a list be said to represent Life, as it is known in the midst of the living of it? The best that can be said of it is, that it is a rapid table of contents which a deity might run over in his mind while he was thinking of creating a world, and had not yet determined how to put it together.

Let us now return to quadratic equations. We still have on hand the unanswered question. Why should children be taught their solution? Unless quadratic equations fit into a connected curriculum, of course there is no reason to teach anything

about them. Furthermore, extensive as should be the place of mathematics in a complete culture, I am a little doubtful whether for many types of boys algebraic solutions of quadratic equations do not lie on the specialist side of mathematics. I may here remind you that as yet I have not said anything of the psychology or the content of the specialism, which is so necessary a part of an ideal education. But all that is an evasion of our real question, and I merely state it in order to avoid being misunderstood in my answer.

Quadratic equations are part of algebra, and algebra is the intellectual instrument which has been created for rendering clear the quantitative aspects of the world. There is no getting out of it. Through and through the world is infected with quantity. To talk sense, is to talk in quantities. It is no use saying that the nation is large— How large? It is no use saying that radium is scarce,—How scarce? You cannot evade quantity. You may fly to poetry and to music, and quantity and number will face you in your rhythms and your octaves. Elegant intellects which despise the theory of quantity, are but half developed. They are more to be pitied than blamed. The scraps of gibberish, which in their school-days were taught to them in the name of algebra, deserve some contempt.

This question of the degeneration of algebra into gibberish, both in word and in fact, affords a pathetic instance of the uselessness of reforming educational schedules without a clear conception of the attributes which you wish to evoke in the living minds of the children. A few years ago there was an outcry that school algebra was in need of reform, but there was a general agreement that graphs would put everything right. So all sorts of things were extruded, and graphs were intro-duced. So far as I can see, with no sort of idea behind them, but just graphs. Now every examination paper has one or two questions on graphs. Personally, I am an enthusiastic adherent of graphs. But I wonder whether as yet we have gained very much. You can-not put life into any schedule of general education unless you succeed in exhibit-ing its relation to some essential charac-teristic of all intelligent or emotional perception. It is a hard saying, but it is true; and I do not see how to make it any easier. In making these little formal alterations you are beaten by the very nature of things. You are pitted against too skilful an adversary, who will see to it that the pea is always under the other thimble.

Reformation must begin at the other end. First, you must make up your mind as to those quantitative aspects of the world which are simple enough to be introduced into general educa-tion; then a schedule of algebra should be framed which will about find its exemplification in the these applica-tions. We need not fear for our pet graphs, they will be there in plenty when we once begin to treat algebra as a serious means of studying the world. Some of the simplest applications will be found in the quantities which occur in the simplest study of society. The curves of history are more vivid and more informing than the dry catalogues of names and dates which comprise the greater part of that arid school study. What purpose is effected by a catalogue of undistinguished kings and queens? Tom, Dick, or Harry, they are all dead. General resurrections are failures, and are better postponed. The quanti-tative flux of the forces of modern society is capable of very simple exhibi-tion. Meanwhile, the idea of the variable, of the function, of rate of change, of equations and their solution,

of elimination are being studied as an abstract science for their own sake. Not, of course, in the pompous phrases with which I am alluding to them here, but with that iteration of simple special cases proper to teaching.

If this course be followed, the route from Chaucer to the Black Death, from the Black Death to modern Labour troubles, will connect the tales of the medieval pilgrims with the abstract science of algebra, both yielding diverse aspects of that single theme, Life. I know what most of you are thinking at this point. It is that the exact course which I have sketched out is not the particular one which you would have chosen, or even see how to work. I quite agree. I am not claiming that I could do it myself. But your objection is the precise reason why a common external examination system is fatal to education. The process of exhibiting the applications of knowledge must, for its success, essentially depend on the character of the pupils and the genius of the teacher. Of course I have left out the easiest applications with which most of us are more at home. I mean the quantitative sides of sciences, such as mechanics and physics.

Again, in the same connection we plot the statistics of social phenomena against the time. We then eliminate the time between suitable pairs. We can speculate how far we have exhib-ited a real causal connection, or how far a mere temporal coincidence. We notice that we might have plotted against the time one set of statistics for one country and another set for another country, and thus, with suit-able choice of subjects, have obtained graphs which certainly exhibited mere coincidence. Also other graphs exhibit obvious causal connections. We wonder how to discriminate. And so are drawn on as far as we will.

But in considering this description,

I must beg you to remember what I have been insisting on above. In the first place, one train of thought will not suit all groups of children. For example, I should expect that artisan children will want something more concrete and, in a sense, swifter than I have set down here. Perhaps I am wrong, but that is what I should guess. In the second place, I am not contemplating one beautiful lecture stimulating, once and for all, an admiring class.

That is not the way in which education proceeds. No; all the time the pupils are hard at work solving examples, drawing graphs, and making experiments, until they have a thorough hold on the whole subject. I am describing the interspersed explanations, the directions which should be given to their thoughts. The pupils have got to be made to feel that they are studying something, and are not merely executing intellectual minuets.

# 12

# Thinking in Education

## JOHN DEWEY

### 1. THE ESSENTIALS OF METHOD

No one doubts, theoretically, the importance of fostering in school good habits of thinking. But apart from the fact that the acknowledgement is not so great in practice as in theory, there is not adequate theoretical recognition that all which the school can or need do for pupils, so far as their *minds* are concerned (that is, leaving out certain specialized muscular abilities), is to develop their ability to think. The parceling out of instruction among various ends such as acquisition of skill (in reading, spelling, writing, drawing, reciting); acquiring information (in history and geography), *and* training of thinking is a measure of the ineffective way in which we accomplish all three. Thinking which is not connected with increase of efficiency in action, and with learning more about ourselves and the world in which we live, has something the matter with it just as thought.... And skill obtained apart from thinking is not connected with any sense of the purposes for which it is to be used. It consequently leaves a man at the mercy of his routine habits and of the authoritative control of others, who know what they are about and who are not especially scrupulous as to their means of achievement. And information severed from thoughtful action is dead, a mind-crushing load. Since it simulates knowledge and thereby develops the poison of conceit, it is a most powerful obstacle to further growth in the grace of intelligence. The sole direct path to enduring improvement in the methods of instruction and learning consists in centering upon the conditions which exact, promote, and test thinking. Thinking *is* the method of intelligent learning, of learning that employs and rewards mind. We speak, legitimately enough, about the method of thinking, but the important thing to bear in mind about method is that thinking is method, the method of intelligent experience in the course which it takes.

John Dewey, *Democracy and Education* (New York: The Macmillan Company, 1916). Copyright 1916 by The Macmillan Company, renewed 1944 by John Dewey. Reprinted by permission.

I.

The initial stage of that developing experience which is called thinking is *experience*. This remark may sound like a silly truism. It ought to be one; but unfortunately it is not. On the contrary, thinking is often regarded both in philosophic theory and in educational practice as something cut off from experience, and capable of being cultivated in isolation. In fact, the inherent limitations of experience are often urged as the sufficient ground for attention to thinking. Experience is then thought to be confined to the senses and appetites; to a mere material world, while thinking proceeds from a higher faculty (of reason), and is occupied with spiritual or at least literary things. So, oftentimes, a sharp distinction is made between pure mathematics as a peculiarly fit subject matter of thought (since it has nothing to do with physical existences) and applied mathematics, which has utilitarian but not mental value.

Speaking generally, the fundamental fallacy in methods of instruction lies in supposing that experience on the part of pupils may be assumed. What is here insisted upon is the necessity of an actual empirical situation as the initiating phase of thought. Experience is here taken as previously defined: trying to do something and having the thing perceptibly do something to one in return. The fallacy consists in supposing that we can begin with ready-made subject matter of arithmetic, or geography, or whatever, irrespective of some direct personal experience of a situation. Even the kindergarten and Montessori techniques are so anxious to get at intellectual distinctions, without "waste of time," that they tend to ignore—or reduce—the immediate crude handling of the familiar material of experience, and to introduce pupils at once to material which expresses the intellectual distinctions which adults have made. But the first stage of contact with any new material, at whatever age of maturity, must inevitably be of the trial and error sort. An individual must actually try, in play or work, to do something with material in carrying out his own impulsive activity, and then note the interaction of his energy and that of the material employed. This is what happens when a child at first begins to build with blocks, and it is equally what happens when a scientific man in his laboratory begins to experiment with unfamiliar objects.

Hence the first approach to any subject in school, if thought is to be aroused and not words acquired, should be as unscholastic as possible. To realize what an experience, or empirical situation, means, we have to call to mind the sort of situation that presents itself outside of school; the sort of occupations that interest and engage activity in ordinary life. And careful inspection of methods which are permanently successful in formal education, whether in arithmetic or learning to read, or studying geography, or learning physics or a foreign language, will reveal that they depend for their efficiency upon the fact that they go back to the type of the situation which causes reflection out of school in ordinary life. They give the pupils something to do, not something to learn; and the doing is of such a nature as to demand thinking, or the intentional noting of connections; learning naturally results.

That the situation should be of such a nature as to arouse thinking means of course that it should suggest something to do which is not either routine or capricious—something, in other words, presenting what is new (and hence uncertain or problematic) and yet sufficiently connected with existing habits to call out an effective response. An effective response means one which accomplishes a perceptible result, in distinction from a purely haphazard activity, where the consequences cannot be mentally connected with what is done. The most significant question which can be asked, accordingly, about any situation or experience proposed to induce learning is what quality of problem it involves.

At first thought, it might seem as if usual school methods measured well up to the standard here set. The giving of problems, the putting of questions, the assigning of tasks, the magnifying of difficulties is a large part of school work. But it is indispensable to discriminate between genuine and simulated or mock problems. The following questions may aid in making such discrimination. (a) Is there anything but a problem? Does the question naturally suggest itself within some situation or personal experience? Or is it an aloof thing, a problem only for the purposes of conveying instruction in some school topic? Is it the sort of trying that would arouse observation and engage experimentation outside of school? (b) Is it the pupil's own problem, or is it the teacher's or textbook's problem, made a problem for the pupil only because he cannot get the required mark or be promoted or win the teacher's approval, unless he deals with it? Obviously, these two questions overlap. They are two ways of getting at the same point: Is the experience a personal thing of such a nature as inherently to stimulate and direct observation of the connections involved, and to lead to inference and its testing? Or is it imposed from without, and is the pupil's problem simply to meet the external requirement?

Such questions may give us pause in deciding upon the extent to which current practices are adapted to develop reflective habits. The physical equipment and arrangements of the average schoolroom are hostile to the existence of real situations of experience. What is there similar to the conditions of everyday life which will generate difficulties? Almost everything testifies to the great premium put upon listening, reading, and the reproduction of what is told and read. It is hardly possible to overstate the contrast between such conditions and the situations of active contact with things and persons in the home, on the playground, in fulfilling of ordinary responsibilities of life. Much of it is not even comparable with the questions which may arise in the mind of a boy or girl in conversing with others or in reading books outside of the school. No one has ever explained why children are so full of questions outside of the school (so that they pester grown-up persons if they get any encouragement), and the conspicuous absence of display of curiosity about the subject matter of school lessons. Reflection on this striking contrast will throw light upon the question of how far customary school conditions supply a context of experience in which problems naturally suggest themselves. No amount of improvement in the personal technique of the instructor will wholly remedy this state of things. There must be more actual material, more *stuff*, more appliances, and more opportunities for doing things, before the gap can be overcome. And where children are engaged in doing things and in discussing what arises in the course of their doing, it is found, even with comparatively indifferent modes of instruction, that childrens' inquiries are spontaneous and numerous, and the proposals of solution advanced, varied, and ingenious.

As a consequence of the absence of the materials and occupations which generate real problems, the pupil's problems are not his; or, rather, they are his *only as* a pupil, not as a human being. Hence the lamentable waste in carrying over such expertness as is achieved in dealing with them to the affairs of life beyond the schoolroom. A pupil has a problem, but it is the problem of meeting the peculiar requirements set by the teacher. His problem becomes that of finding out what the teacher wants, what will satisfy the teacher in recitation and examination and outward deportment. Relationship to subject matter is no longer direct. The occasions and material of thought are not found in the arithmetic or the history or geography itself, but in skillfully adapting that material to the teacher's requirements. The pupil studies, but unconsciously to himself the objects of his study are the conventions and standards of the school system and school authority, not the nominal "studies." The thinking thus evoked is artificially one-sided at the best. At its worst, the problem of the pupil is not how to meet the requirements of school life, but how to *seem* to meet them—or, how to come near enough to meeting them to slide along without an undue amount of friction. The type of judgment formed by these devices is not a desirable addition to character. If these statements give too highly colored a picture of usual school methods, the exaggeration may at least serve to illustrate the point: the need of active pursuits, involving the use of material to accomplish purposes, if there are to be situations which normally generate problems occasioning thoughtful inquiry.

II.

There must be *data* at command to supply the considerations required in dealing with the specific difficulty which has presented itself. Teachers following a "developing" method sometimes tell children to think things out for themselves as if they could spin them out of their own heads. The material of thinking is not thoughts, but actions, facts, events, and the relations of things. In other words, to think effectively one must have had, or now have, experiences which will furnish him resources for coping with the difficulty at hand. A difficulty is an indispensable stimulus to thinking, but not all difficulties call out thinking. Sometimes they overwhelm and submerge and discourage. The perplexing situation must be sufficiently like situations which have already been dealt with so that pupils will have some control of the meanings of handling it. A large part of the art of instruction lies in making the difficulty of new problems large enough to challenge thought, and small enough so that, in addition to the confusion naturally attending the novel elements, there shall be luminous familiar spots from which helpful suggestions may spring.

In one sense, it is a matter of indifference by what psychological means the subject matter for reflection is provided. Memory, observation, reading, communication are all avenues for supplying data. The relative proportion to be obtained from each is a matter of the specific features of the particular problem in hand. It is foolish to insist upon observation of objects presented to the senses if the student is so familiar with the objects that he could just as well recall the facts independently. It is possible to induce undue and crippling dependence upon sense-presentations. No one can carry around with him a museum of all the things whose properties will assist the conduct of thought. A well-trained mind is one that has a maximum of resources behind it, so to speak, and that is accustomed to go over its past experiences to see what they yield. On the other hand, a quality or relation of even a familiar object may previously have been passed over, and be just the fact that is helpful in dealing with the question. In this case direct observation is called for. The same principle applies to the use to be made of observation on one hand and of reading and "telling" on the other. Direct observation is naturally more vivid and vital. But it has its limitations; and in any case it is a necessary part of education that one should acquire the ability to supplement the narrowness of his immediately personal experiences by utilizing the experiences of others. Excessive reliance upon others for data (whether got from reading or listening) is to be depreciated. Most objectionable of all is the probability that others, the book or the teacher, will supply solutions ready-made, instead of giving material that the student has to adapt and apply to the question in hand for himself.

There is no inconsistency in saying that in schools there is usually both too much and too little information supplied by others. The accumulation and acquisition of information for purposes of reproduction in recitation and examination are made too much of. "Knowledge," in the sense of information, means the working capital, the indispensable resources, of further inquiry; of finding out, or learning, more things. Frequently it is treated as an end itself, and then the goal becomes to heap it up and display it when called for. This static, cold-storage ideal of knowledge is inimical to educative development. It not only lets occasions for thinking go unused, but it swamps thinking. No one could construct a house on ground cluttered with miscellaneous junk. Pupils who have stored their "minds" with all kinds of material which they have never

put to intellectual uses are sure to be hampered when they try to think. They have no practice in selecting what is appropriate, and no criterion to go by; everything is on the same dead static level. On the other hand, it is quite open to question whether, if information actually functioned in experience through use in application to the student's own purposes, there would not be need of more varied resources in books, pictures, and talks than are usually at command.

III.

The correlate in thinking of facts, data, knowledge already acquired is suggestions, inferences, conjectured meanings, suppositions, tentative explanations—*ideas*, in short. Careful observation and recollection determine what is given, what is already there, and hence assured. They cannot furnish what is lacking. They define, clarify, and locate the question; they cannot supply its answer. Projection, invention, ingenuity, devising come in for that purpose. The data *arouse* suggestions, and only by reference to the specific data can we pass upon the appropriateness of the suggestions. But the suggestions run beyond what is, as yet, actually *given* in experience. They forecast possible results, things *to do*, not facts (things already done). Inference is always an invasion of the unknown, a leap from the known.

In this sense, a thought (what a thing suggests but is not as it is presented) is creative—an incursion into the novel. It involves some inventiveness. What is suggested must, indeed, be familiar in *some* context; the novelty, the inventive devising, clings to the new light in which it is seen, the different use to which it is put. When Newton thought of his theory of gravitation, the creative aspect of his thought was not found in its materials. They were familiar; many of them commonplaces —sun, moon, planets, weight, distance, mass, square numbers. These were not original ideas; they were established facts. His originality lay in the *use* to which these familiar acquaintances were put by introduction into an unfamiliar context. The same is true of every striking scientific discovery, every great invention, every admirable artistic production. Only silly folk identify creative originality with the extraordinary and fanciful; others recognize that its measure lies in putting everyday things to uses which had not occurred to others. The operation is novel, not the materials out of which it is constructed.

The educational conclusion which follows is that *all* thinking is original in a projection of considerations which have not been previously apprehended. The child of three who discovers what can be done with blocks, or of six who finds out what he can make by putting five cents and five cents together, is really a discoverer, even though everybody else in the world knows it. There is a genuine increment of experience; not another item mechanically added on, but enrichment by a new quality. The charm which the spontaneity of little children has for sympathetic observers is due to perception of this intellectual originality. The joy which children themselves experience is the joy of intellectual constructiveness—of creativeness, if the word may be used without misunderstanding.

The educational moral I am chiefly concerned to draw is not, however, that teachers would find their own work less of a grind and strain if school conditions favored learning in the sense of discovery and not in that of storing away what others pour into them; nor that it would be possible to give even children and youth the delights of personal intellectual productiveness— true and important as are these things. It is that no thought, no idea, can possibly be conveyed as an idea from one person to another. When it is told, it is, to the one to whom it is told, another given fact, not an idea. The communication may stimulate the other person to realize the question for himself and to think out a like idea, or it may smother his intellectual interest and suppress his dawning effort at thought. But what he *directly* gets cannot be an idea. Only by wrestling with the conditions of the problem at first hand, seeking and finding his own way out, does he think. When the parent or teacher has provided the conditions which stimulate thinking and has taken a sympathetic attitude toward the activities of the learner by entering into a common or conjoint experience, all has been done which a second party can do to instigate learning. The rest lies with the one directly concerned. If he cannot devise his own solution (not of course in isolation, but in correspondence with the teacher and other pupils) and find his own way out he will not learn, not even if he can recite some correct answer with one hundred per cent accuracy. We can and do supply ready-made "ideas" by the thousand; we do not usually take much pains to see that the one learning engages in significant situations where his own activities generate, support, and clinch ideas—that is, perceived meanings or connections. This does not mean that the teacher is to stand off and look on; the alternative to furnishing ready-made subject matter and listening to the accuracy with which it is reproduced is not quiescence, but participation, sharing, in an activity. In such shared activity, the teacher is a learner, and the learner is, without knowing it, a teacher—and upon the whole, the less consciousness there is, on either side, of either giving or receiving instruction, the better.

IV.

Ideas, as we have seen, whether they be humble guesses or dignified theories, are anticipations of possible solutions. They are anticipations of some continuity or connection of an activity and a consequence which has not as yet shown itself. They are therefore tested by the operation of acting upon them. They are to guide and organize further observations, recollections, and experiments. They are intermediate in learning, not final. All educational reformers, as we have had occasion to remark, are given to attacking the passivity of traditional education. They have opposed pouring in from without, and absorbing like a sponge; they have attacked drilling in material as into hard and resisting rock. But it is not easy to secure conditions which will make the getting of an idea identical with having an experience which widens and makes more precise our contact with the environment. Activity, even self-activity, is too easily thought of as something merely mental, cooped up within the head, or finding expression only through the vocal organs.

While the need of application of ideas gained in study is acknowledged by all the more successful methods of instruction, the exercises in application are sometimes treated as devices for *fixing* what has already been learned and for getting greater practical skill in its manipulation. These results are genuine and not to be despised. But practice in applying what has been gained in study ought primarily to have an intellectual quality. As we have already seen, thoughts just as thoughts are incomplete. At best they are tentative; they are suggestions, indications.

They are standpoints and methods for dealing with situations of experience. Till they are applied in these situations they lack full point and reality. Only application tests them, and only testing confers full meaning and a sense of their reality. Short of use made of them, they tend to segregate into a peculiar world of their own. It may be seriously questioned whether the philosophies ... which isolate mind and set it over against the world did not have their origin in the fact that the reflective or theoretical class of men elaborated a large stock of ideas which social conditions did not allow them to act upon and test. Consequently men were thrown back into their own thoughts as ends in themselves.

However this may be, there can be no doubt that a peculiar artificiality attaches to much of what is learned in schools. It can hardly be said that many students consciously think of the subject matter as unreal; but it assuredly does not possess for them the kind of reality which the subject matter of their vital experiences possesses. They learn not to expect that sort of reality of it; they become habituated to treating it as having reality for the purposes of recitations, lessons, and examinations. That it should remain inert for the experiences of daily life is more or less a matter of course. The bad effects are twofold. Ordinary experience does not receive the enrichment which it should; it is not fertilized by school learning. And the attitudes which spring from getting used to and accepting half-understood and ill-digested material weaken vigor and efficiency of thought.

If we have dwelt especially on the negative side, it is for the sake of suggesting positive measures adapted to the effectual development of thought. Where schools are equipped with laboratories, shops, and gardens, where dramatizations, plays, and games are freely used, opportunities exist for reproducing situations of life, and for acquiring and applying information and ideas in the carrying forward of progressive experiences. Ideas are not segregated, they do not form an isolated island. They animate and enrich the ordinary course of life. Information is vitalized by its function; by the place it occupies in direction of action.

The phrase "opportunities exist" is used purposely. They may not be taken advantage of; it is possible to employ manual and constructive activities in a physical way, as means of getting just bodily skill; or they may be used almost exclusively for "utilitarian," i.e., pecuniary, ends. But the disposition on the part of upholders of "cultural" education to assume that such activities are merely physical or professional in quality is itself a product of the philosophies which isolate mind from direction of the course of experience and hence from action upon and with things. When the "mental" is regarded as a self-contained separate realm, a counterpart fate befalls bodily activity and movements. They are regarded as at the best mere external annexes to mind. They may be necessary for the satisfaction of bodily needs and the attainment of external decency and comfort, but they do not occupy a necessary place in mind nor enact an indispensable role in the completion of thought. Hence they have no place in a liberal education—i.e., one which is concerned with the interests of intelligence. If they come in at all, it is as a concession to the material needs of the masses. That they should be allowed to invade the education of the elite is unspeakable. This conclusion follows irresistibly from the isolated conception of mind, but by the same logic it disappears when we perceive what mind really is—namely, the purposive and directive factor in the development of experience.

While it is desirable that all educational institutions should be equipped so as to give students an opportunity for acquiring and testing ideas and information in active pursuits typifying important social situations, it will, doubtless, be a long time before all of them are thus furnished. But this state of affairs does not afford instructors an excuse for folding their hands and persisting in methods which segregate school knowledge. Every recitation in every subject gives an opportunity for establishing cross connections between the subject matter of the lesson and the wider and more direct experiences of everyday life. Classroom instruction falls into three kinds. The least desirable treats each lesson as an independent whole. It does not put upon the student the responsibility of finding points of contact between it and other lessons in the same subject, or other subjects of study. Wiser teachers see to it that the student is systematically led to utilize his earlier lessons to help understand the present one, and also to use the present to throw additional light upon what has already been acquired. Results are better, but school subject matter is still isolated. Save by accident, out-of-school experience is left in its crude and comparatively irreflective state. It is not subject to the refining and expanding influences of the more accurate and comprehensive material of direct instruction. The latter is not motivated and impregnated with a sense of reality by being intermingled with the realities of everyday life. The best type of teaching bears in mind the desirability of affecting this interconnection. It puts the student in the habitual attitude of finding points of contact and mutual bearings.

## SUMMARY

Processes of instruction are unified in the degree in which they center in the production of good habits of thinking. While we may speak, without error, of the method of thought, the important thing is that thinkings is the method of an educative experience. The essentials of method are therefore identical with the essentials of reflection. They are first that the pupil have a genuine situation of experience—that there be a continuous activity in which he is interested for its own sake; secondly, that a genuine problem develop within this situation as a stimulus to thought; third, that he possess the information and make the observations needed to deal with it; fourth, that suggested solutions occur to him which he shall be responsible for developing in an orderly way; fifth, that he have opportunity and occasion to test his ideas by application, to make their meaning clear and to discover for himself their validity.

# 13

# The Process of Education

## JEROME S. BRUNER

\* \* \*

To recapitulate, the main theme of this chapter has been that the curriculum of a subject should be determined by the most fundamental understanding that can be achieved of the underlying principles that give structure to that subject. Teaching specific topics or skills without making clear their context in the broader fundamental structure of a field of knowledge is uneconomical in several deep senses. In the first place, such teaching makes it exceedingly difficult for the student to generalize from what he has learned to what he will encounter later. In the second place, learning that has fallen short of a grasp of general principles has little reward in terms of intellectual excitement. The best way to create interest in a subject is to render it worth knowing, which means to make the knowledge gained usable in one's thinking beyond the situation in which the learning has

occurred. Third, knowledge one has acquired without sufficient structure to tie it together is knowledge that is likely to be forgotten. An unconnected set of facts has a pitiably short half-life in memory. Organizing facts in terms of principles and ideas from which they may be inferred is the only known way of reducing the quick rate of loss of human memory.

Designing curricula in a way that reflects the basic structure of a field of knowledge requires the most fundamental understanding of that field. It is a task that cannot be carried out without the active participation of the ablest scholars and scientists. The experience of the past several years has shown that such scholars and scientists, working in conjunction with experienced teachers and students of child development, can prepare curricula of the sort we have been considering. Much more effort in the actual preparation of curriculum materials, in teacher training, and in supporting research will be necessary if improvements in our educational practices are to be of an order that will meet the challenges of

Jerome S. Bruner, *The Process of Education* (Cambridge, Mass.: Harvard University Press, 1961), pp. 31–32. Reprinted by permission.

the scientific and social revolution through which we are now living.

There are many problems of how to teach general principles in a way that will be both effective and interesting, and several of the key issues have been passed in review. What is abundantly clear is that much work remains to be done be way of examining currently effective practices, fashioning curricula that may be tried out on an experimental basis, and carrying out the kinds of research that can give support and guidance to the general effort at improving teaching.

How may the kind of curriculum we have been discussing be brought within the intellectual reach of children of different ages? To this problem we turn next.

# 14

# Curriculum Decisions and Provision for Individual Differences

VIRGIL E. HERRICK

A teacher makes a number of educational decisions when dealing with the problem of individual differences in his classroom. These decisions are in different classes.

One class of decisions has to do with the selection of objectives, the topic being studied, the organizing center being used, the instructional plan considered appropriate, and the nature of the evaluation desired.

A second class of decisions has to do with how individual children are recognized and respected, how teacher and pupil roles are determined, and how the interpersonal dynamics of the classroom are directed to more adequate personal, social, and educational ends.

A third class of decisions has to do with the way children and teachers are grouped, the way time and space are used, and the way instructional materials and resources are obtained and related.

Every teacher has to deal with all three of these classes of decisions in the teaching that he does. Most, if not all, of the provisions for dealing with individual differences in the classroom fall in these categories.

It is the thesis of this article that all these classes of decision-making are important and related. No one class can be omitted from adequate educational planning for individual differences. Further, decisions in Class 1, which deal with goals and instructional strategies to accomplish them, and decisions in Class 2, which deal with individuals and with human dignity and respect, have first priority and should precede and control rather than follow decisions in Class 3, where administrative arrangements for children, teachers, time space, and materials are dominant considerations.

Too often we start with an administrative commitment to a teaching machine, to a teaching team and a group of ninety children (or for that matter,

Virgil E. Herrick, "Curriculum Decisions and Provision for Individual Differences," *The Elementary School Journal*, LXII, No. 6 (1962), 313–20. Copyright 1962 by the University of Chicago Press. Reprinted by permission.

to a group of twenty-five children); and then we consider what directives these decisions have for instruction rather than vice versa.

This thesis can be documented by examining briefly two decisions in Class 1 that confront every teacher every day that he teaches. These two decisions have to do with determining the nature and the level of the teacher's instructional objectives and the nature and the characteristics of the organizing centers he selects for teaching and learning.

Several other decisions in curriculum could have been used for this discussion. The nature and the priorities of the screens for selecting learning activities and the nature and roles of the teacher and the learner in the evaluation process in instruction would have served equally well. The conclusions growing out of the two areas selected will illustrate the point being made.

One of our most ancient and most persistent notions about the teaching-learning act is that it ought to be purposeful—goal-centered—and directed by significant educational objectives. Few disagree with this general proposition.

If this conception of the teaching-learning act is sound, a careful study of these objectives, their nature, and their use in making educational decisions should furnish many suggestions for providing for individual differences.

Nerbovig's(2) study of how teachers use objectives, Lund's (1) preliminary analysis of teacher-learning episodes, and our own studies of classroom behavior suggest several conclusions about how many teachers see and use objectives in their instructional practices.

1. Many teachers do not understand the difference between topics, areas, and objects as definitions of scope or of organizing centers for learning activi-

ties and important understandings and intellectual processes as definitions of instructional objectives. (*Addition is* a topic. *Chicago* is an area. The *earthworm* is an object.)

Teachers state their objective as "to teach Chicago" rather than seeing understandings like "Man works with other men to meet their common needs" as the objective and Chicago as a representative city that can be used to achieve some appreciation of this generalization.

Thus the phrases "to educate children," "to teach Chicago," or "to develop an understanding of the simple sentence" are not objectives. The first is a generality that states the total task of the school. The second is a possible organizing center to be used to develop certain understandings or objectives. The third avoids the issue: the objective is the understanding or idea of the simple sentence itself.

A teacher's statement of instructional objectives is more useful in making curriculum decisions if this statement does not include principles of learning, important organizing centers, a list of instructional materials, propositions about the good life, and the kitchen sink.

If a teacher can distinguish between important understandings and intellectual processes as objectives and the other necessary components of curriculum, he is freer to think imaginatively about many different topics, areas, objects, and centers of interest that can be used to include the individual differences of children and yet deal with the important understandings and thought processes of the educational program.

In providing for individual differences in the classroom, teachers must realize that in any comprehensive teaching act, several important curriculum decisions have to be made. Determining instructional objectives is only one of these decisions. Equally important is the realization that objectives can perform certain curriculum functions and that they cannot perform others. Failure to make these distinctions creates obstacles to providing adequately for the individual differences of children.

2. Many teachers fail to distinguish between objectives seen as facts and specific skills, and objectives seen as major concepts of the subject area and as key intellectual and social processes.

How a teacher sees and defines his instructional objectives plays an important part in determining how he will provide for the individual differences of children.

Stenographic records of classroom episodes were used to examine how teachers perform their many instructional tasks. The records used were taken from schools in "Prairie City," a typical midwestern community studied by the Committee on Human Development of the University of Chicago, and from schools in communities in Texas, Michigan, Illinois, and Wisconsin. Our analysis of these records shows three important findings.

First, many teachers see their content objectives at the level of the specific fact and thus deal with such objectives as "Robins have red breasts," "5 fours are 20," "the letter *h* is formed with a straight line and a half loop," and "Chicago is on Lake Michigan."

When a teacher sees his instructional objectives in this way, adaptations for individual differences are forced in certain directions. The teacher may vary the speed with which children move through these particulars. The teacher may make adaptations in instructional materials, workbooks, drill exercises, flash cards—so that the child can work on those things

which he does not know. The teacher may devise grouping procedures that will bring together children who are at about the same place in this hierarchy of things to know and to verbalize.

Some teachers see their objectives, however, at the level of such concepts as "a number may express either the idea of how many or the idea of relationship" or "the area of any rectangular surface is dependent upon the length of its base and height" or "man influences and is influenced by his environment."

When a teacher sees his instructional objectives on this more general level, his classroom provisions for individual differences tend to use a wider variety of related activities and experiences to help children deal with these understandings on many levels of conceptualization and in respect to many different sets of particulars. The teacher tends to see no single learning experience as having a one-to-one relationship to the mastery of these concepts. The way is opened for many possible adaptations in the learning experiences of children. If the teacher does not see how he can achieve his objectives through many possible instructional menas, the only alternatives open to him for variation in his teaching are children, time, and materials.

With this latter perception of objectives, teachers are more likely to see these broader objectives as having meaning for both the kindergarten child and the high-school senior. No time is spent in curriculum committees trying to define the level of understanding to be reached by first-, fourth-, or sixth-grade children. This important fact is always being defined by the children themselves. Thus, the child himself becomes an important agent in determining many of the necessary provisions for his own learning. Actually he is the only one who has much of the necessary information.

Second, many teachers who see their instructional objectives at the level of the fact tend to organize their instruction around these specifics directly and use instructional procedures that stress recognition, verbalism, and memory. Thus, this kind of teacher sees no problem in teaching "3 fours are 12" as "3 fours are 12" or "air has weight" as the verbalism "air has weight." His objective, therefore, becomes the unit of instruction to be taught directly.

Our analysis indicates that when a teacher sees his instructional objectives as learning specifics, this perception limits the possible ways in which he can provide for pupils' individual differences.

Third, many teachers who see their instructional objectives at the level of the fact tend to ignore the importance of the whole array of skills—language skills, thinking skills, social skills, and skills in the use of instructional materials that are regarded as important instructional objectives in every curriculum program.

Again, our data seem to indicate that when a teacher sees process objectives as a necessary part of any classroom activity, he tends to organize his classroom instruction around organizing centers that properly include these skills. His organizing centers thus tend to be more comprehensive and provide more opportunity for various levels of skill use, for many different vehicles for skill development, and for many more appropriate areas of skill application—all important conditions that would make possible desirable instructional provisions for individual differences.

In our examination of learning episodes, the importance of the role of the organizing center in the instructional process soon became apparent. The more we thought about objectives and

their nature and directives for instruction, the more we realized that if instructional objectives are important understandings and learning processes, then you did not teach them directly, but you had to select some vehicle or vehicles to provide the means for their accomplishment.

These vehicles—the questions the teacher asked, the example or problem posed, the objects to be examined, and the zoo to be visited and observed—all formed organizing centers to which the children and teacher related their activities and to which they applied their thinking, generalizing, and personal action.

An organizing center for instructional purposes is any object, idea, person, question, or instructional material used to relate and focus the thinking and the action of an individual or a group. Organizing centers can be defined better by their organizing functions than by their nature.

A picture is not an organizing center for instruction because it is a picture. Rather, it is an organizing center because the eyes and thoughts of a class of children focus on it and their learning behavior is related to it in some kind of active fashion.

If a picture is not the object of attention and educational action by some individual or group, it is not an organizing center. An object becomes an organizing center only when it becomes the focus for such action by these individuals. The nature of a center does not of itself make it a center; its nature merely permits and enhances such focusing and organizing behavior.

Nerbovig in her study found that teachers talked about teaching addition, the farm, electricity, and the seven basic foods as their objectives rather than identifying the understanding and the processes commonly assumed to be objectives (2, p. 122).

To us this finding indicated that many teachers start their educational planning with their organizing centers rather than with their objectives. Actually, this is a much more realistic and useful curriculum decision in their eyes than the decision that "a simple sentence is a single complete unit of thought."

These analyses forced the author to hypothesize that perhaps the most critical single decision a teacher makes about his teaching is the one dealing with the identification and the selection of a desirable set of organizing centers for giving meaning and scope to the learning activities of a group of children.

If an organizing center is to make it possible to meet the individual needs of the children who participate in its development, it should have the following characteristics:

1. *More than one dimension of accessibility.*

If an organizing center can be attacked in more than one way by the learner, its power to provide for individual differences is increased.

If a teacher poses a question as a center for thought and action and presents the question orally, he limits its accessibility. If he asks the question orally and also writes it on the chalkboard, he increases the accessibility of the question for learning. None of the child's energy has to go into remembering the question so that if the question has any significance for him, he is freer to concentrate his full attention on studying and resolving it.

Even though the teacher speaks and writes the question on the board, if the necessary information to deal with the question is provided only by the teacher, he limits its accessibility to children. If however, the necessary information to deal adequately with the question can be acquired by children through observation, manipulation, reading, and other sources of knowing, the accessibility of the organizing center to children for learning is correspondingly increased.

If the question is such that responses to it are limited to one word, *yes* or *no*, the capacity of the question to deal with individual differences is more limited than if this were not true.

If the map on the board is large enough for all to see and is placed properly, its accessibility to more than one child is increased. If the map it too small or is poorly placed, its accessibility for learning is decreased. Or, if work is to be done on the map, the map is more accessible to children if each child can have a copy than when this is not true.

An organizing center is more accessible to more than one child if it properly involves the participation of two or more individuals. Sending a note to the principal does not require the five children we sometimes send with it. One child can run this errand. We sometimes justify this action by claiming that the other four are getting better acquainted with their school environment. Organizing centers that consist of spelling words, vocabulary words in reading, combinations in arithmetic seldom involve more than one child and thus permit only certain limited adjustments to individual differences.

All that has been said may sound simple-minded, but it has become obvious to me that irrespective of how we manipulate the variables of ability and accomplishment, the number of individuals involved, the pacing of the learning process, and the materials and physical space, unless the organizing center for the learning is accessible to the children, no real provision for individual differences can be made.

2. *More than one level of accomplishment.*

If an organizing center is to have the capacity to provide for individual differences, it must have low catch-hold points and high ceilings. An earthworm can provide a challenge to a kindergarten child and to a college senior; to a child with limited experience and limited capacity to learn, as well as to a child with rich experience and gifted capacities. This principle applies to organizing centers like the common and persistent problems of living in social studies, creative writing in language arts, and learning more about our weather in science.

Many teachers, however, use organizing centers that have narrow limits for knowing and learning, such centers as spelling the word *cat*, locating the capital of Illinois, naming the parts of speech, or working examples in arithmetic. Each of these centers limits the child to one level of accomplishment. Each provides little opportunity for individual differences. The teacher's alternatives are to try these specific centers until he finds one the child can do or to spend enough time on one until the child finally grasps the proper response.

3. *More than one dimension of mobility.*
One of the most important problems in curriculum planning is to know how to insure proper continuity in a child's learning. Every teacher wants one lesson in reading to contribute to the next one. Every teacher wants to help every child transfer his knowledge of his own community to his attempts to understand the lives of people more remote in space and time.

If a teacher can select organizing centers that have the capacity to move in time, in space, in cultures, and in logic, these centers have greater capacity to provide for individual differences than when this is not true.

In social studies, for example, such centers as great people, great documents, cities, states, or countries are commonly used as organizing centers, but they have limited mobility. It is hard to move Madison, Wisconsin, anywhere else. But social functions, common geographic characteristics, or the common and persistent problems of living, all have the capacity to move in time, in space, in cultures, and in logic. They have greater capacity, therefore, for providing room and opportunity for encompassing meaningfully differences in children's background, ability, and development than centers that lack this capacity.

If we checked proposed organizing centers in social studies programs against this criterion, we would go a long way toward providing a more effective instructional base for dealing with individual differences in this field. Unless instruction is organized around centers that provide room for individuals to vary and to zoom in understanding as far as they can go, few effective instructional provisions can be made for individual differences.

4. *More than one degree of organizing capacity.*
Some teachers favor a main organizing center that has several important subcenters that have to be studied if the children are to get a proper understanding of the whole. The *home* is one good example. As children study the home, such subcenters as the responsibilities of children and parents in the home; how such problems as food, clothing, earning money, and recreation are handled; how the different rooms of the house are used; and how the house is placed in a community of houses—all provide a means for individual and/or small group study and exploration. Yet all these enterprises are seen as important and relevant parts of the main area of concern. It was felt that this kind of organizing center provided many more opportuni-

ties for providing for individual differences than an organizing center like *pets*. Yet a center like *pets* provides greater organizing scope than naming locations, describing objects, and drawing up lists—centers commonly used by many teachers.

This examination of how decisions in two common areas of curriculum planning can contribute to more adequate provisions for individual differences suggests the following conclusions:

1. The decisions the teacher makes about the important components of curriculum direct and limit the nature of the provisions that can be made for dealing with individual differences.

2. Teachers who see their instructional objectives at the level of factual specifics tend to provide for individual differences through variations in time, in amount to be learned, in numbers of children, and in instructional materials. The things to be learned tend to remain constant at the specific level for all children.

3. Teachers who see their instructional objectives at the level of important generalizations and key intellectual and social processes are more willing to explore a wider variety of means for accomplishing those objectives and are more willing to accept a wider range of levels of understanding and accomplishment.

4. The capacity of a learning center to provide for individual differences depends on the extent to which such centers meet the following criteria: they need to have more than one dimension of accessibility, more than one level of accomplishment, more than one aspect of mobility, and more than a single degree of organizing capacity.

When these conditions are met, the teacher has an organizing base for instructional activities that will include more than one child, provide room for many levels of contribution, permit children to move in many important directions, and help them explore an adequate number of important relationships. To me, the provision of this kind of instructional base lies close to the heart of our problem of providing adequately for the individual differences of children.

## REFERENCES

1. Herrick, Virgil E., and Grace Lund, "The Curricular Analysis of Teaching-Learning Episodes." Madison: University of Wisconsin, 1960, p. 25.

2. Nerbovig, Marcella H., "Teacher's Perception of the Functions of Objectives." Unpublished Ph.D. Dissertation, Department of Education, University of Wisconsin, 1956, p. 228.

# 15

# Teaching as Curriculum Decision-Making

## VIRGIL E. HERRICK

Joseph Schwab in his excellent paper on "Education and the Structure of the Disciplines"[1] shows the wide differences in experimentation and explanation of the organism by biologists when there are differences in conception of the organism. When the biologist conceived the organism as "many pairs of fixed and determinate cause-effect connections" then this conception led to an attempt to identify the causal factors. When the biologist conceived the organism "as a collection of equilibrium points around each of which a limited degree of variation occurs"; or "as a vastly complicated 'feedback' mechanism in which damage or change in one part would be followed by 'cor-

rection' changes in many others," then these conceptions lead to quite different approaches and explanations.

What is true of biologists and the ways in which they have conceived and studied the organism is even more true of educationists and the ways in which we have conceived and studied teaching. Barr,[2] in his final and most comprehensive review of teaching effectiveness and its correlates, identifies and places in context the many different motives and conceptions which have actuated the numerous studies of teaching and teachers over the past half century of research effort. It is very clear from this review and that of others[3,4] that teaching is conceived in

Virgil E. Herrick, "Teaching as Curriculum Decision-Making," in *The Nature of Teaching*, ed. Louise M. Berman (Milwaukee: School of Education, University of Wisconsin, 1963), pp. 66–81.

[1] Joseph J. Schwab, "Education and the Structure of the Disciplines," Parts I and II. A paper prepared for Project on the Instructional Program of the Public Schools, National Education Association, 1201 Sixteenth Street, N.W., Washington, D. C. (1961), p. 20.

[2] A. S. Barr *et al.*, *Wisconsin Studies of the Measurement and Prediction of Teacher Effectiveness: A Summary of Investigations* (Madison, Wis.: Dembar Publications, Inc., 1961), pp. 134–52.

[3] Arno A. Bellack and Dwayne Huebner, "Teaching," *Review of Educational Research*, XXX, No. 3 (June 1960), 246–57.

[4] Nathan L. Gage, ed., *Handbook of Research in Teaching*. A Project of the American Educational Research Association, N.E.A. (Skokie Ill.: Rand McNally & Co., 1963).

many different ways with resulting differences in what is emphasized and cherished as being significant in understanding and directing the teaching-learning process. It is clear, also, that we have moved from seeing effective teaching in terms of the qualities and behaviors of the person per se to considering effectiveness in teaching as the result of the dynamic interactions which exist between a number of vital aspects of the teaching-learning situation and a teacher.

Conceptions of teaching which emphasize this later point of view, while borrowing heavily from psychology, sociology, and philosophy for theoretical frameworks, have been concerned with actual classroom situations and with devising categories of behavior which explain and relate the complicated processes of classrooms.

Thus on our own campus we have a study of teaching which combines Rogers' concept of a teacher as providing a permissive and accepting environment and climate within which the learner can make discoveries for himself and learn to deal with his own personal-cognitive-social world more effectively with the concept of a communication model for dealing with the verbal interchange which takes place between teachers and children in the teaching act. Previous papers by Bills and Gerbner in the conference have provided many more examples of the importance of both of these points of view for teaching.

An examination of interaction studies of teaching have shown a concern for the logical operations involved in clarifying understanding,[5] the sending and receiving acts of the teacher,[6]

the integrative-dominative function of a teacher,[7,8] and the management of teachable groups.[9]

As laudable as it is to study teaching with some appreciation of the complex interactions of a personal, logical, social, and psychological nature which take place in the classroom situation with appropriate observational techniques, it is somewhat amazing that the conceptual structures used to analyze these records of classroom behavior have practically ignored many of the curricular operations so important in teaching. Many of the interactions contained in a running record of classroom behavior are influenced or determined by prior or on-the-spot decisions about the important curriculum operations.

The important findings of Anderson,[10] Lippitt,[11] Withall,[12] Flanders,[13]

---

Withall, *Mental Health Teacher Education Research Project* (Madison, Wis.: University of Wisconsin Press, 1960).

[7] Ned Flanders, *Teacher Influence, Pupil Attitudes and Achievement: Studies in Interaction Analysis* (Minneapolis: University of Minnesota Press, 1960).

[8] Marie W. Hughes *et al.*, *A Research Report: Assessment of the Quality of Teaching in Elementary Schools* (Salt Lake City: University of Utah Press, 1959).

[9] Herbert Thelen, *Teachability Groupings*. A Research Study Conducted under a Grant from the Cooperative Research Branch, U. S. Office of Education (Chicago: University of Chicago Press, 1961).

[10] H. H. Anderson and Helen M. Brewer, "Studies of Teachers' Classroom Personalities I, Dominative and Socially Integrative Behavior of Kindergarten Teachers," Applied Psychology Monographs 1945, No. 6. Also Studies Nos. II and III, 1946, No. 8, and 1946, No. 11.

[11] K. Lewin, R. Lippitt, and Sibylle K. Escalona, "Studies in Topological and Vector Psychology," Studies in Child Welfare, XVI, No. 3 (Iowa City: University of Iowa Press, 1940).

[12] John Withall, "Assessment of the Social-Emotional Climate Experienced by a Group of Seventh Graders as They Moved from Class to Class," *Educational Psychology Measurement*, XII (1952), 440–51.

[13] Flanders, *op. cit.*

---

[5] B. Othanel Smith *et al.*, *A Study of the Logic of Teaching: A Report on the First Phase of a Five-Year Research Project* (Urbana: Bureau of Educational Research, University of Illinois, 1960).

[6] John M. Newell, W. W. Lewis, and John

and Hughes *et al.*[14] in regard to autocratic-democratic,      dominative-inte-
grative, direct-indirect teaching are
dependent ultimately on a teacher's
choice of a curricular pattern and what
this means for her role in respect to the
learner as supportive and encouraging
rather than dominative and directive.
Her curriculum decisions will supply
organizing centers which permit or
obstruct exploration and progressive
goal definition; communication systems
which permit or obstruct meaning
clarification; role clarifications which
encourage or deny responsibility and
constructive    participation   in    the
learning act by all concerned. The
psychological and social parallelism
of autocratic-democratic, dominative-
integrative,    direct-indirect   can   be
matched and associated with similar
curricular    parallelisms    as    subject-
centered, child-centered, fact-centered,
problem-centered,      and      deductive-
inductive instructional planning and
teaching. The psychological, social,
and curricular referents are not unrelated dimensions in teaching but
should be a clear and necessary part of
any overall framework which places
each in its proper context. It is merely
proposed here that the curricular
decisions necessary to permit and give
significant direction to any psychological and social choice of democratic,
integrative, and indirect patterns of
classroom instruction should be a part
of any adequate concept of teaching.


## THE REQUIREMENTS OF AN
## ADEQUATE FRAMEWORK

In thinking about what constitutes
an adequate framework for teaching,
it is useful to ask the prior curriculum
question—What are the necessary com-

[14] Hughes *et al.*, *op. cit.*

ponents of teaching? One needs to
know what is involved or what kind of
categories of things one must deal
with in any adequate concept of teaching. Answers to this question provide
one with one class of referents for
curriculum theory building.

Since much of our thinking about
teaching has focused on the teacher in
her classroom, it is useful to keep this
vantage point and consider the question of the components of teaching
from this orientation. With this focus
it is possible to identify the following
aspects of teaching:


DIFFERENT CLASSES OF OBJECTS

Three classes of objects are found
in the teaching situation. The first
class is obviously of primary consideration.

*Class One.* Dynamic, purposive
human beings. Humans having a personality, goal perceptions, and a self-
concept. In relation to the teaching
act, humans can be further divided
into four levels of relationship to it:
(a) teacher and learners directly involved, (b) principal, supervisors,
janitor, etc., who usually operate in
a secondary relationship, (c) parents
and other adults having primary
relationship to a child, and (d) other
adults concerned with education.

*Class Two.* Objects devised to
contain and develop educational
programs—frequently highly self-contained. Textbooks, workbooks, films
and film strips, teaching machine
programs, etc.

*Class Three.* Objects not specifically
designed to convey educational programs—chairs, desks, tables, pictures,
blocks. Objects have unitary characteristics, occupy space, and can be selected
for various purposes and arranged in
various physical patterns. Usually, too,

these objects have implicit functions of their own which may or may not be consistent with their selected educational function in the classroom.

### A Geographic Space and Structure

Teaching always takes place somewhere and demands space and some arrangement of objects in this space. The nature and amount of geography available or used for teaching obviously is a factor in it. Grouping and classification of pupils are frequently geography problems and every teaching plan has a geographic dimension of time, space, and physical structure.

*or grouping*

### A Social Space and Structure

Many studies of group dynamics and the sociology of the classroom have concerned themselves with the social structure and climate of classroom behavior. Perhaps the most important part of the social structure of a classroom is its power structure and the related authority or prestige roles played by teachers and students. A third factor to consider in the social space and structure of a classroom is that it exists in relation to other social systems which make up a school and its related social communities.

### A Communication System with Appropriate Signs and Symbols

It is clear that one of the most important aspects of teaching is its communication system. A child as well as teachers have to learn its nature and uses in the educational process.

### An Educational Structure

The overriding structure of a classroom is the educational plan or program with its objectives, curricular areas, teaching plans and instructional strategies. It is this all-inclusive structure which should encompass the other components of the classroom and give them meaning and function.

### Important Dimensions

In each of the necessary components above, a number of important dimensions are found—the dimension of feeling, the dimension of ideas and related cognitive processes, and a dimension of value.

These dimensions need a location and necessary referents to make them meaningful and available for study and modification. It is rather futile to deal with these dimensions as unique units of teaching.

This list, I am sure, can be improved and structured better, but it is valuable for our purpose in that it identifies some of the things which are always present in every act of teaching, good or bad, and irrespective of any concept of instruction and irrespective of where the act takes place. This list helps explain, too, why many of the researches on teaching have attempted to seize on one or a limited combination of these components—the teacher, the child, the social system, the cognitive domain, the teaching plan—for their research targets and thereby assumed that this target was sufficient in itself to explain and predict teaching.

## CRITERIA FOR AN ADEQUATE FRAMEWORK

This concept of the components of the classroom teaching-learning situation is based on the assumptions that (1) teaching is a complex multidimensioned act, (2) it is concerned primarily with the efficient achievement of educational objectives, (3) it involves the responsible decision-making and action of a teacher, and (4) it can take place in different kinds of social-physical settings and can be directed by different educational rationales.

## CRITERIA FOR A FRAMEWORK OF TEACHING

In view of these assumptions of the teaching-learning situation, what are the criteria any adequate framework for teaching must meet? It is proposed that an adequate framework for teaching:

1. Must be comprehensive in the sense that it includes and finds a place for all other subsystems important in teaching.

2. Must be more than a research rational—must be *developmental* in the sense that it permits going behind the specific teaching act to the phases of conceptualizing, structuring, acting, evaluating, and programming by both teacher and pupil.

3. Must be open-ended, nonvaluing, and reasonably nonstructured—but permit supplying many different valuing structures and rationales to its framework leading to many specific answers and plans for teaching consistent with such value orientations.

4. Must be meaningful in relation to general education and the foundational areas for teaching. It should serve as a means for relating and forming a unified structure of knowledge and values about life and education, as well as about teaching and curriculum planning.

5. Must have high face validity for dealing with both the act of teaching and for the study and development of our metaknowledge about how to plan

and deal with the teaching act more effectively.

## A PROPOSED FRAMEWORK

It should be clear to everyone that we are not at a place where we can say with confidence that we have a framework for teaching which would meet all of these criteria. We do feel, however, that such a framework should be organized around the common operations of curriculum instruction. These operations provide the important hook-on points for the various valuing structures and form the referents for the important curricular and instructional decisions made by anyone dealing with the teaching-learning act. These operations have high face validity, are open-ended, and relatively nonstructured and can be used to relate the contributions of general education as well as the foundational areas of education to the teaching act.

The following operations are proposed as forming the broad reference points for curriculum planning and for teaching. This listing does not imply any significant ordering or structuring. It should be clear to any teacher that you do not always begin with purposes and end with evaluation in every teaching act.

1. *The Perception of the General and Specific Operations Involved in the Planning and Design of Curriculum and the Teaching-Learning Act.* Relation to past + future

Most lists of curricular operations suggest by their arrangement that they were developed in some isolated and independent fashion. Seldom, if ever, is this true. Most teaching operations are developed in light of some perceived overall curricular or teaching model or a design which sets the conditions for determining objectives, nature of learning development, and the roles of the teacher and learner in the instructional process.

This design perception by the teacher exists on many levels of competence and insight. One level would be the limited recognition by the teacher that she was teaching arithmetic, rather than social studies or science. Another level would be a teacher who saw herself teaching arithmetic, paying particular attention to addition, and using the method of discovery in developing the necessary concepts. Another preliminary teaching plan is represented by a teacher who wanted to move from a consideration of north Europe to south Europe, contrasting the physical and social conditions which account for the likenesses and differences in the way people live.

Still another level of conception could be represented by a teacher who starts with a framework of questions and planning processes she and a group of children will consider in identifying problems to be examined, ways in which selections will be made, and in developing plans for dealing with these problems in effective ways.

The main point here is that prior commitments to curricular patterns exist in varying degrees of completeness to form the general context within which the specific planning and action of the classroom take place.

The second point of importance is the suggestion that planning and designing functions are a part of the specific curricular operations of the teaching act. There is no such thing as an unplanned curriculum or incidental teaching. There are only two planning alternatives open to a teacher—either she knows in general the curriculum pattern she will use or she knows the way in which such plans are developed with children.

2. *The Operations Involved in Goal*

*Setting, Objective Determining, or Outcome Determination.*

It should be clear to curriculum people who have studied a wide array of classroom records that few teachers start their planning with a set of instructional objectives. They are much more likely to start with topics, objects, or a section of a textbook as an initial step. Then, this topic or story is examined to see what important outcomes may grow out of its study. Frequently in this latter case, the learner assumes a responsible role for identification and statement of outcomes. Of course, it is clear that, classically, it is possible to start with objectives and then proceed to a consideration of the learning experiences which will enable children to perceive and understand them.

Again it should be clear that the way in which a teacher deals with the goal-setting phase of teaching sets up important conditions which will support either the direct or indirect teaching acts reported by Flanders,[15] the clarifying of understanding operations of Raths,[16] or the logical questions of Smith.[17] The findings of such studies as those done by Withall,[18] Anderson,[19] and Lewin and Lippitt[20] can be examined and partially explained on this same basis.

An important part of the goal setting operations of curriculum is the realization by the teacher that a necessary aspect of any set of objectives are those dealing with the intellectual, social, and communication processes important in learning and education. This realization and use of such objectives to plan and structure teaching

---

[15] Flanders, *op. cit.*
[16] Louis Raths, "What Is Teaching," mimeographed paper, New York University.
[17] Smith, *et al.*, *op. cit.*
[18] Withall, *op. cit.*
[19] Anderson and Brewer, *op. cit.*
[20] Lewin, Lippitt, and Escalona, *op. cit.*

operations will make a great difference in the nature of the teacher-
student interaction observed and
recorded in such studies. Again it is
argued that this kind of curricular
perception is a prior and necessary
consideration by a teacher or research
worker in any attempt to understand
and to deal with the teaching act
effectively.

When a teacher assumes a responsibility for developing effective methods
of inquiry in addition to important
concepts, then her curriculum planning
must be the kind which selects organizing centers which will permit observation, experimentation, and testing of
hypotheses. This commitment will lead
to teaching structures which will encourage certain kinds of questions,
patterns of teacher-student interaction,
and learning roles assumed by students.
When teachers do not see these process
objectives as being important, then
different teaching patterns and behaviors tend to follow.

3. *Operations Involved in the Selection
and Evaluation Phases of Curriculum Planning and Teaching.*

Every important curriculum operation involves the making of choices
and evaluations by those who are
involved. When a teacher is considering the nature of the question she is
going to ask to start a given lesson, her
choice is based on a consideration of
the kind of objectives to be achieved,
the kind of object, topic, problem,
etc. to be developed, the direction in
which the learning action might move,
as well as her assessment of her children,
their interests and backgrounds.

If her teaching conception includes
the importance of maximizing the role
and responsibility of the learner in
the making of choices and in the evaluation of consequences, then it is very
likely that the nature of classroom
interactions will be very different than

if the teacher's conception were that
these selection and evaluation procedures were primarily her function as
the key figure in such decision-making,
or worse, being made by the nature of
the instructional materials she is using.

The examination of classroom episodes shows that many of the teacher's
acts are concerned with reinforcing
and giving cues to the direction she
wishes the class to go or to the shutting
off of avenues of discussion and exploration which seem to be leading away
from the central topic or purpose.
These boundary- and direction-deter-
mining functions are based on selection and evaluation procedures and
may be the exclusive responsibility of
the teacher or they may involve the
student in varying degrees of responsibility and control. If this latter is
done, then increasingly the teacher
moves to a consideration with the students of how such decisions should be
made and how the students can use
this kind of understanding to deal with
similar problems in the future. Again
this kind of curriculum conception and
decision-making will result in interaction patterns which will differ in significant ways from those of a teacher who
holds a different concept of teacher-
student roles in decision-making.

Many of the studies of teaching have
made much of the authority figure and
normative behavior of the teacher in
the teaching act. The curricular parallelism has to do with the operations
related to evaluation and the nature
of the part the teacher plays in it. Playing one role, she becomes the authority
figure and assumes much of the dominative behavior associated with this role.
Playing another role in this same process, she assumes much of the integrative and supporting behavior associated
with a different teaching pattern.

Again it is the thesis of this paper
that an understanding of the important

components of the curricular evaluation operations would place both these roles in the same context and would explain the resulting differences.

For example, the essential aspects of evaluation include (1) identified objectives, (2) the definition of these objectives into behaviors which would characterize them, (3) a set of observations of the behavior of individuals being evaluated in appropriate situations, (4) the development of criteria for determining the degree of adequacy of observed behavior, (5) the valuing of these behaviors in light of the identified objectives and in relation to the criteria or norms, and (6) the use of these evaluations in determining and directing future behavior.

In relation to these aspects of evaluations a number of roles can be played— the role of the individual being observed and judged, the role of the determiner of the objectives and their definition, the role of the observer, the role of the determiner of the norms or criteria of adequacy, the role of the judger of the acts being observed, and finally the role of the individual who uses these evaluations to direct his future actions. It is clear that a single individual must play all these roles in self-evaluation. It is clear also that in most teaching, the teacher is the goal and norms determiner and definer, the observer of the action, and the appraiser of the action. All the learner does is to behave according to goals unknown to him, to be judged on bases unavailable for his present and future use, and to direct his future behavior toward equally unknown educational objectives.

It is possible, therefore, to develop a particular curricular-evaluation model for the normative and authority roles played by teachers in the array of teacher interaction studies by identifying the roles the teacher or student plays in dealing with the necessary dimensions of the evaluation process. The use of any of these curricular-evaluation models by a teacher would direct and differentiate her teaching behavior and communication systems in this area of the teaching process. From this point of view also, an acceptant and supportive teacher is one who helps a student distinguish his own sense of worthwhileness from his behavior related to his achievement of educational goals and permits their evaluation on constructive educational norms rather than on punitive and personal bases. This is merely another kind of curricular-evaluation model for dealing with the evaluation dimensions of the teaching-learning act. It is proposed, therefore, that our conception of teaching should include a consideration of these operations and the nature of the understandings and decisions which will result in more educationally valid evaluation models and consequently more educationally valid teaching behavior.

4. *Operations Involved in Organizing Curriculum Components into Educational Structures and Teaching Patterns.*

The decisions related to organizing and developing learning experiences with children form the central focus for all curriculum and teaching operations. Decisions as to objectives, evaluations, and overall orientations have their ultimate consequence in what one does about organizing and developing the teaching act with children.

Four decision areas may be identified in the organizing operations. These decision areas have to do with (1) determining what is involved, (2) selecting organizing centers, and (3) determining the continuity or sequence dimension. Obviously these decision points are not unrelated and certain decisions made in area one provide the basic working materials

organizing centers = focal point

for dealing with decisions in areas two and three.

*The Decision of What Is Involved.* This question is seldom discussed in books on curriculum, but examination of curriculum plans and teaching episodes reveals that the way in which this question is perceived and answered limits and directs the way in which the teaching-learning act is organized.

On one level of curriculum decision-making, this question is illustrated by a teacher considering how she is going to deal with the topic of weather. One way of considering weather is to see it as being composed of (1) air mass and its movement, (2) temperature and its source, and (3) moisture and its sources. One test of the adequacy of this conception of the necessary components of weather is to consider the question that if one could control the movement of air, temperature, and moisture, would it be possible to create the kind of weather one would want? However one would answer this question it should be clear that this conception of essential components would furnish the kinds of phenomena to observe, the conditions to be related, and possible organizational patterns to be considered in any teaching about weather.

On a more general level, if one sees social studies as dealing fundamentally with human relationships including such dimensions as common and persistent problems of living, social processes for dealing with such problems, geographic, political, and social areas within which these problems occur, subject matter about these aspects, and the tools and skills of social inquiry and analysis, then this array of components provides the building blocks for organizing and structuring social studies programs and teaching. If one starts with political or geographic areas as the important organizational reference, then this leads to a different

way of organizing social studies than if one sees the common and reoccurring problems of living as the fundamental organizing elements. This follows also if the subject matter and its major organizing generalizations were used as the major organizing base. The point here is that the selection of a particular aspect of social studies as the major organizing referent leads to different organizing structures but that each structure would include all of the necessary components at some point. This same proposition can be illustrated using conceptions of necessary components for the language arts, mathematics, and science.

*The Decision About the Organizing Centers.* Our study of teaching episodes indicates that one of the key decisions a teacher makes has to do with the organizing centers used to start and develop the lesson. The decision as to the kind of organizing center selected has a lot to do with the way individual differences are handled and how more than one child is included in the teaching-learning act.[21]

An organizing center is the point where all the important aspects of the teaching act can be related and given focus. Some centers are of such a nature and character that they permit this; others, while serving as organizing centers in the teaching act, are incapable by their very nature to permit this organizing to occur. One example of this lack of capacity is found in a social studies episode mentioned previously where the teacher wanted to go from north Europe to south Europe and to contrast the ways in which people deal with their problems of living. This teacher used the question: "What is the name of a country which was a

[21] Virgil E. Herrick, "Curriculum Decisions and Provisions for Individual Differences," *The Elementary School Journal*, LXII, No. 6 (March 1962), 313–20.

world power at the time of Christopher Columbus?" as the initial organizing center for the lesson. Attempts to follow this question with its clues lead the class to Genoa, Italy in one direction and to South America, speaking Spanish, in the other. While both of these directions were logical by following certain of the teacher's clues, they were not the country (Spain) desired by the teacher. Later parts of the episode reveal further that what she really wanted as an organizing center was "peninsula" in order to contrast peninsulas in south Europe and north Europe. Spain was valuable in her teaching plan only because it is on a peninsula.

The point of this illustration for our discussion is that "a country" is an organizing center which by its nature makes it impossible to move from north Europe to south Europe. "A country" does not have the capacity to move anywhere. This decision to use "a country" leads to a guessing contest on the part of students, the identification of Spain as a country which leads nowhere, and finally the giving up of this line of development in some frustration and starting over with another organizing center. Any teacher knows that most groups can tolerate only so many false starts before going to pieces.

A second illustration as to the importance of the organizing center in curriculum decision-making for teaching comes from teaching episodes dealing with reading, spelling, and arithmetic taken from many different schools. Some episodes covering lessons in science and hygiene at the secondary school level and a few in history and geography in the middle grades make the same point. The common characteristic of these episodes is the many independent highly restrictive organizing centers used to organize and develop the learning activities for a single lesson. An example is the reading lesson dealing with vocabulary. Each new word served as an independent center introduced one at a time by the teacher with little relationship between words. The spelling lesson used words in the same way, the arithmetic lesson used a list of examples (basic addition facts), and the hygiene lesson was concerned with words like intelligence, heredity, environment, as points to organize the discussion and thinking of the students.

This second illustration shows the importance of selecting an organizing center which is sufficiently comprehensive to include more than one child and which would lead to the involvement of a number of subcenters. A teaching plan which is organized around a large number of specific and relatively unique organizing foci can lead only to one kind of teaching and interaction pattern almost irrespective of the teacher's personality and feelings about children. There are, further, only a limited number of communications possible and it is rather impossible to find methods of inquiry relevant to dealing with these objects of educational concern.

*Decisions Regarding Patterns of Relationships and Sequence in Organization.* A number of structures and continuities are possible in every lesson or class taught by a teacher. The selection of a given one will permit the understanding and participation of students in its development or it will restrict and obstruct such participation and seeing of relationships and consequences.

A common sequence is merely the arrangement of limited learning episodes in time and in physical proximity to each other. Other more promising continuity structures use organizing themes like common and persistent problems of living as a basis for moving from one geographic area to another, from one culture to another, and from one time to a past or future. Other centers for developing teacher-learning structures are common geographic characteristics, continuing operations, and key organizing concepts. Illustrations of organization centers which are limited in continuity and organizing possibilities are people, great documents, specific geographic areas, specific cities, political areas, objects of specific character and the like. Similar analyses of permissive or restrictive organizing centers can be made in each content field.

5. *Operations Involved in Placing Curriculum Plans into Action.*

It should be recognized that curriculum planning and teaching are a part of the same action pattern. Planning prior to the teaching act provides the rationale and framework within which teaching takes place. In the interaction between the teacher, students, and the centers of attention and related feedbacks, changes in the direction, pacing, depth, relationship patterns, continuity, and degree of involvement factors always take place. It is merely argued that the thoughtful consideration of the key operations and related decisions in planning of the teaching act by the teacher and increasingly by the students is the context in which teaching must be considered and improved.

## CONCLUSIONS

This paper has argued for teaching seen as a set of curriculum decisions dealing with important operations of the teaching-learning act. An attempt has been made to describe the criteria which should be met by an adequate framework for understanding and improving teaching. A number of curricular operations are described and examined to show the extent to which decisions made in dealing with these operations would limit and direct the teaching act. It is claimed that on the basis of the analysis of a wide number of learning episodes that the curriculum decisions made in these episodes account for the interaction patterns, teacher-learner roles, and continuity structure found there.

The proposed framework has had some empirical testing in our undergraduate program of educating elementary school teachers for the past ten years. In the junior year sections where it was used, the instructors in the senior block semester reported that the students from these sections were different from others in that they had a "way of analyzing and validating their teaching," seemed able "to go behind their teaching and plans to the bases for developing them" and were "creative and imaginative" in devising and trying out different ways of teaching.

This on-the-spot subjective type of evaluation is further substantiated by a comparison of the performance of a section using this framework to analyze teaching behavior as observed in a closed circuit television program with other sections of similar background and ability. The comparison was based on their performance in tests on educational psychology and child development. The group with the framework to tie together their observations and analysis and their related course work in curriculum and learning was significantly better than all other sections. No one should draw cause and effect conclusions here, but it seemed that the operational framework was one of the important variables. A program of teacher education is obligated to develop a framework which would help students to relate the foundation areas of knowledge to the teaching act, to understand and appreciate their own general education, and to deal with the important planning and action phases of their growing maturity and competence as professional persons.

The knowledge developed as ways to deal with the decision areas of curriculum and teaching is the professional knowledge of teacher education and is more than the subject matter of the content fields or of the psychological or social foundations. A framework such as the one proposed here is sufficiently comprehensive to include in some meaningful fashion all the complex elements of teaching in a way that provides the teacher on all levels of professional competence with a powerful tool for skillful action and for professional growth. This framework assumes that there are always better answers to be made to these persistent and common operations to all education, teaching, and living. This concept demands all the best contributions of our knowledge, all the directives of our important values, and best of all, frees the intelligence and creativity of the teacher and student to achieve more significant and vital learning for themselves and for others. Any concept of teaching, irrespective of the importance of its specialized concern, which does less than this is inadequate to give form and direction to the program of teacher education of this and other universities and colleges of this land.

# 16

# Ausubel's Subsumer Theory of Learning: A Basis for the Teaching of Meaningful Verbal Material

JAMES RATHS

While there are clearly many educational philosophies and theories of learning from which a teacher may choose to use a guide for selecting and planning educational experiences, it is clear that a profusion of reality factors found in today's schools strictly limit the choices a teacher may make operational in a classroom. Whether dedicated to the humanist view, the progressive philosophy, or the phenomenological position, a teacher is faced with

The original ideas presented in this paper stem from the work of two leaders in the field of learning, D. P. Ausubel and Walter B. Waetjen. Professor Ausubel has written a very stimulating book summarizing his theory for the teaching and learning of meaningful material. Most of this paper is drawn from this source. Professor Waetjen has contributed a paradigm postulating the relationship of the cognitive structure to new stimuli and the role that epistemic behavior plays in incorporating new material into the cognitive structure. A slightly modified version of Professor Waetjen's paradigm is included in this paper.

While the author gives credit to both these men for their contributions, it is clear that neither of them can be held responsible for the manner in which their original ideas are expressed in this paper.

classes of 30 to 40 students and with community pressures to teach content that is fairly well set and standardized. These obstacles, and many similar reality factors associated with schools and teaching, serve to inhibit the introduction of many modern notions into the classroom.

Many educationists deplore the existing state of affairs. These people have made a major effort through preservice programs to affect changes in the teaching practices found in public schools. It is the author's point of view that many of the ideas advocated in preservice courses in education are inconsistent with the realities found in the schools. To implement change in the current basic organizational patterns of the schools by training preservice teachers in the ideas of progressive education for instance is clearly ineffective in its impact on the schools and on the teachers.

This paper will attempt to elucidate a theory of learning that seems more relevant to teachers faced with the following givens—a rather well defined curriculum that must be "covered" and hopefully taught to a large group of youngsters. At best, the implications of this theory for teaching are vague and obscure, but the fact that this is a theory of learning that seems quite relevant to the existing situation that our students face in classrooms makes it a worthwhile one to examine and pursue.

The purpose of this paper is to clarify and expand some of the statements found in Ausubel's theory of learning (1). C. D. Hardie once suggested that the structure of theory in the natural sciences consists of statements or postulates about unobservable entities that direct researchers in their observation of observable phenomena (5). Ausubel's theory presupposes such a nonobservable entity—the cognitive structure. A cognitive structure is the totality of an individual's existing knowledge organized in terms of highly generalized concepts under which are subsumed concepts of a less generalized nature as well as specific facts. The major organizational principle of the cognitive structure, in other words, is that of progressive differentiation of a body of knowledge from regions of greater generality to lesser generality—each linked to the next higher step in the hierarchy through a process of subsumption. It is important to point out that Ausubel does not mean that the levels are deductively related—one being derivable from another. The relationship is rather analogous to a filing system or an outline in that one concept is included within another more general one.

As a learner internalizes new material he places a value on it along a continuum going from highly general and inclusive to not very general and specific. Another dimension of material found in the cognitive structure is that of abstractness. This continuum, ranging from the concrete to the abstract, is different than the continuum going from the general to the specific.

If this theory adequately describes the way a student internalizes new material, then teachers must organize their teaching in such a way that they are confident their students possess in their cognitive structures highly general concepts under which they may subsume new material. Ausubel refers to these general elements as "advanced organizers."

For example, Ausubel used as an advanced organizer for a lesson dealing with the metallurgical properties of carbon steel, a passage placing emphasis on the major similarities and differences between metals and alloys. He found this material effective in anchoring the content of the lesson (2). As another example more relevant to the secondary school, teachers of geometry may teach the basic elements of proof—axioms, definitions, and theorems in mathematical and nonmathematical contexts before geometric proofs are introduced. This prior learning may serve to anchor the geometric concepts presented later in the year.

Advance organizers, Ausubel suggests, may be expository or comparative in nature. An expository organizer provides a hierarchical series of organizers in descending order of inclusiveness—each organizer preceding its corresponding unit of detailed material in the lesson. The comparative organizer suggests ways the previously learned concepts are basically similar or different from the new material. Historically relevant material or summaries or overviews which are presented at the same level of inclusiveness as the material to be learned are not considered to be advance organizers.

If a person has no cognitive structure relevant to the new material that is being presented to him, he will use strategies to master the material that can be found in the psychologies of rote learning. However, such knowledge of rote learning, it is held, does not give teachers insights into the dynamics of learning potentially meaningful material. Ausubel's theory is an attempt to fill that gap.

The following diagram endeavors to explain ways in which new material is incorporated into cognitive structure. Example A suggests that the material is not really new and that it is so readily subsumed into existing cognitive structure that a student may incorporate it almost immediately without much effort on his part. Example B portrays the internalization of material that is incorporated by a student only after some active process designed to fit the material into the existing cognitive structure. This active process may be one of asking questions or testing ideas

or merely thinking about how this new idea relates to the familiar material. The new learnings in this case do not fit the structure immediately, and a student plays an active role in trying to organize it into his structure.

Example C shows new material that does not fit the cognitive structure at first and even after an active process on the student's part to make it fit. The material is not internalized. Two outcomes may result in this case. First, generally anxiety is aroused. Feelings of anxiety may cause a student to withdraw from the learning situation. Sometimes we say he becomes blocked. Secondly, as shown in the line marked C', a student may review the new material with a wider focus than at first, taking into account more and more details in an effort to incorporate the new material into his structure (7).

LEARNING OUTCOMES

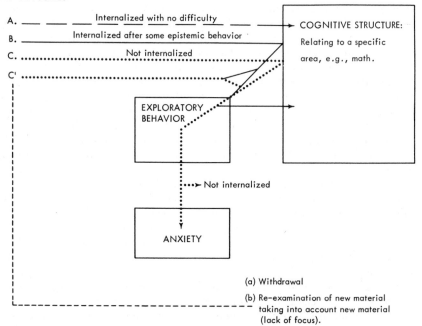

*Adapted from Waetjen (7).

**Fig. 1.   The Incorporation of Material into Cognitive Structure**

The lowering of discrimination that is reflected in this behavior may serve to alter the material through additions of perceptions and biases in a way that facilitates its incorporation into his cognitive structure. In these cases, C and C', the student is manifesting symptoms of learning disabilities. According to Ausubel's theory, they can be remedied by a teacher's strategy in organizing his presentation of content.

## IMPLICATIONS

The theory of learning stated above seems to have implications for many areas of a teacher's concern. These implications are briefly spelled out as follows:

### READINESS

It follows from this theory that readiness for learning is a function of previous learning experiences as well as maturity. Do youngsters have in their cognitive structure elements of a degree of inclusiveness that will enable them to subsume or incorporate the new material? Do youngsters have in their cognitive structure elements of a degree of abstractness that will enable them to handle the new material that is to be presented? If either of these questions is answered in the negative, it may be said that the youngsters are not ready for the learning experience. Both requisites, that of maturity (a factor in determining the ability of a student to handle abstract concepts, Inhelder [6]), and previous learnings (a factor in establishing advanced organizers), must be met before a youngster is "ready" to learn.

### ATTENTION SPAN

Attention span may be considered to be the amount of time a person spends fitting novel material into his cognitive structure. His attention span may appear short if he has no difficulty incorporating the new material into his cognitive structure. An example of this is the bright student in a review class. He shows signs of inattention. Another example is the case in which an individual has little or no existing cognitive structure under which to subsume the new material. An illustration of this would be a student naïve to mathematics sitting in on an advanced mathematics seminar. He, too, would show signs of inattentiveness. If after much effort a student is still unable to incorporate new material into his cognitive structure, he may develop anxieties leading to signs of withdrawal.

### PSYCHOLOGY OF SELF

*place a value on knowledge*

The extent to which a person can tolerate the anxieties of being unable to fit the new material into the existing cognitive structure may be related to current notions of the psychology of self that have become prevalent in the literature. Psychologists have for some time been puzzled by the discrepancies in learning abilities of people with equal intelligence. Nonintellectual factors have been surveyed to explain the observed differences. The psychology of self suggests that individuals have a unique attitude or stance that reflects attitudes toward thinking, learning and problem solving. Cartwright (3) has called this stance an "address of life." There may be a relationship between the ability to tolerate new material that does not fit into the cognitive structure and this quality.

### CURIOSITY

Curiosity can be defined as a drive to fit new material into the current cognitive structure of the individual. The extent to which a student puzzles, manipulates, studies, and reflects on new material in order to fit it into his cognitive structure may be an indicator of his curiosity. If this indicator is valid, then it would follow that curiosity is not an all-pervasive trait. A person must be curious about *something*. He is curious about those things for which he has a tentative cognitive structure that includes highly general elements under which new phenomena can be incorporated.

## RESEARCH SUGGESTED BY AUSUBEL'S THEORY OF LEARNING

A major problem in the examination of Ausubel's theory is to find hypotheses that stem from the theory that are testable. The problem is intensified in this case because of the obscure nature of the concept "organizer." Does an organizer function equally effectively for everyone? If Ausubel is saying that everyone has his own personal organizer, then his theory certainly would give little direction for teachers in the classroom. If, on the other hand, he is saying that a teacher can find organizers for students naïve to the new material to be taught, and that these organizers will facilitate learning, then teachers may find his ideas very productive and useful in a classroom. A first step may be one of trying to identify students who seem to learn using a style that reflects use of cognitive organization. The following procedure may produce two samples of youngsters with different learning styles. First, match secondary school youngsters on self-concept and general anxiety variables. Next, select those pairs of youngsters matched on these variables who show markedly different test anxiety scores. It may be reasonable to assume that the two populations of youngsters—one with high test anxiety and the other with low test anxiety—but with equivalent self-concept and general anxiety scores will use different learning styles in mastering new material. Interviews or schedules may be used with each of the pairs of students to find indicators of the use of advance organizers in a particular learning exercise. Such populations may also be generated by identifying those students with nearly equal test scores on a given achievement test but whose retention scores are vastly different. We may assume that the ways in which these students mastered the new material were quite different and the group that was able to retain the information made use of advance organizers. Perhaps these organizers could be discovered through an interviewing process.

## CONCLUSION

John Dewey railed against such ideas as this one of Ausubel's in that it placed great emphasis on the teacher's role in the learning situation and almost none on the student's privilege of learning. "It takes, in brief, everything educational into account save for its essence . . ." (4). If what Dewey says is true, it validly describes the ongoing emphases of our public schools. Are we able to help our teachers do an excellent job in the schools of today at the same time we are working to revise the goals of the public schools? It would seem a shame if we had to choose between these alternatives.

## REFERENCES

1. Ausubel, D. P., *The Psychology of Meaningful Verbal Learning.* New York: Grune & Stratton, Inc., 1963.

2. Ausubel, D. P., "The Use of Advance Organizers in the Learning and Retention of Meaningful Verbal Material," *Journal of Educational Psychology* (October 1960).
3. Cartwright, Roger, "Promoting Student Thinking," *Journal of Educational Sociology* (September 1963).
4. Dewey, John, *Democracy and Education.* New York: The Macmillan Company, 1916.
5. Hardie, C. D., "Reply to George L. Newsome, Jr.," *Studies in Philosophy and Education* (September 1963).
6. Inhelder, Barbel, and J. Piaget, *The Growth of Logical Thinking from Childhood to Adolescence.* New York: Basic Books, Inc., Publishers, 1958.
7. Waetjen, Walter B., "Curiosity and Exploration: Roles in Intellectual Development and Learning." Paper presented to A.S.C.D. Research Institute, Washington, D. C., April 1963.

# 17

# Planning for Individualizing Instruction

JAMES RATHS

It has long been argued that teachers should individualize their instructional practices. This generalization is the cliché of all clichés, often heard at professional meetings and P.-T.A. Programs. The question is of course, "How?" Education professors urge that teachers must "understand" children. It is very difficult to find out what is meant by understanding in this context, but it generally means that teachers will be familiar with general rules of development that may predict certain behavior patterns of youngsters. Some argue that individualization begins with finding out where children are, assigning them material that is to be learned next, and finally assessing how well the material has been learned. Of course, all of this is to be done individually, because no two people learn alike. Such prescriptions are of course nonsense. Not only do teachers have too little time to work with individuals in such a fashion but the profession has not provided teachers with instruments or techniques that will enable them to measure just "where" a student "is" in a given subject area. Anything a

teacher does is sheer guesswork on that score.

It is our suggestion that individualization of instruction takes place, in terms of the teaching act, more after the assignment than before it. We observed a gym teacher who had a sixth-grade class jumping over a rope. After everyone jumped over the rope, he would raise it several inches. In a short time, most of the group were sitting on the side; the rope had been placed too high for them to even attempt the jump. However, there were some boys who were still able to jump over the rope with fancy barrel rolls. The instructor stopped the class at this point and asked the group how they could place the rope so that everyone could participate. They decided to place the rope on a slant. In this manner, the most able athletes would be challenged at the high end and everyone else in the class could find a place over which he could successfully jump. It is our contention that the teacher in heterogeneous classes must make assignments analogous to the slanting rope. Under such assignments, students themselves will determine their own level according to ability and interest. Such assignments include comparing, summarizing, planning, classifying, defending a position, imagining, and others mentioned in Louis Raths' article appearing on pages 294 to 295. In brief, these assignments have many acceptable levels of achievement. Everyone can "get over them" at the level they choose to work. The key to the assignments is that there is not one answer or one way of completing the assignments. A question asking students to compare Virginia and Maryland may be answered in a rather trivial way by a mediocre student, but the attempt may be accepted as a comparison. If the assignment is to list the seven major products of Virginia, and if a student is only able to list six, then the student has not completed the assignment and presumably he has not done acceptable work.

The teaching skills that this approach demands are those associated with the clarifying process (see p. 319). By becoming fluent in ways to accept students' efforts without always judging them as good or bad, a teacher will be able to truly "individualize" his instruction.

# 18

# The Unit Process

ELIZABETH BERRY

## I

It was about a year ago that I addressed a group of English teachers in a Southern state. I spoke on trends in teaching English in the United States. More specifically, I discussed unit teaching, integrated programs, creativity, and the role of psychology and guidance in a modern English program. My audience were attentive enough, but I sensed an indifference to what I had to say. When I asked for comments, several said that they had been doing unit teaching. In fact, this seemed to be the consensus of the group. They apparently wanted to know what else could be done.

I was somewhat baffled; for I knew that once they understood unit teaching they would know what else could be done. Finally one of the teachers came to my rescue. She suggested that I have each person take a piece of paper and

Elizabeth Berry, "The Unit Process," *Educational Forum*, XXVII, No. 3, Part I (1963), 357–66. Reprinted by permission of the publisher, Kappa Delta Pi, an Honor Society in Education.

write a question pertaining to unit teaching that he would like to have discussed. This was done. As I examined the questions, I noticed that a number of them were the perennial ones: How can the English teacher create interest in Julius Caesar? How should book reports be made? How much grammar should be covered each year? Should all seniors be required to read "The Eve of Saint Agnes"? Should literature be taught chronologically or according to types? All of these questions revealed a complete lack of knowledge of unit teaching. Finally, I came to some more forward looking questions, posed by one who said, "Exactly what is a unit?" "How do you go about teaching a unit?" "What is the process?"

It was these latter questions that gave me a clue to the difficulty. I read them to the group and asked for discussion. What is a unit? What is unit teaching? What is the process? Many and varied were the answers I got. Some thought that unit teaching meant taking a topic and sticking to it for a month or so. Thus they conceived of teaching a unit on *Ivanhoe* or *Verbs*. Some thought that the prime purpose of unit teaching was to provide for individual differences, little realizing that this was only a secondary matter and that any teacher regardless of method could provide for individual differences if he so wanted to. Of course, some of the teachers had occasionally read an article on a unit some English teacher had taught. Perhaps they had tried such a method, but out of the context of the philosophy involved. Many of these teachers were simply taking suggested methods and trying to incorporate them into the traditional philosophy that had guided their former teaching. Such procedures had led to further confusion of the ends and means desired, since methods emerge from philosophy and give it meaning. The value of our discussion lay in the frankness with which these teachers were willing to face their problem. It was not easy for one of them to pave the way and say: Exactly what is a unit? What is unit teaching? What is the process?

I would like to say this at this time. I know of no way to straddle the fence in the teaching of English. It is imperative that philosophy and methods are consistent if worthwhile results are to come. There is no such thing as an effective teacher of English using an eclectic approach. To be eclectic is but to admit that one possesses neither a good working knowledge of existing philosophies nor has yet created a sound one of his own. As one distinguished educator recently said, "To be eclectic is to operate with no philosophy at all." Since very few educators in any generation are able to deal with the difficulties involved in the establishment of a new philosophy, it would be safe to say that the majority of English teachers in America today are modern English teachers, traditional English teachers, or confused English teachers. To those who are modern English teachers, to those who are confused English teachers, and to those who may wish to examine a viewpoint contrary to their own, I address the forthcoming remarks.

## II

Grasp of the real significance of unit teaching lies in an understanding of the philosophic point of view with which it is associated. In recent years there has been an intensification of the argument concerning traditional versus modern education. This argument has special significance to English teachers because the unit method of teaching English advocated in the N.C.T.E. curriculum guides stems from the modern philosophy of education set forth by John Dewey many years ago. Let me be clear at this point. John Dewey did not introduce unit methods of teaching; but he did set forth the philosophy from which the unit process could naturally emerge. Unfortunately, John Dewey was far in advance of the educators of his time. Only a few understood what he had to say. Too often, he was misquoted, misunderstood. Too often, in the years of his day he was blamed for ideas and practices that he mightily condemned. Even John Dewey's most severe critics seldom doubted the validity of the educational philosophy he expressed. They blame him not for setting forth a false philosophy, but rather for recommending educational theory and practice that the average teacher is not intelligent enough to comprehend and use. It is not the purpose of this paper to debate the intelligence of classroom teachers. I will leave this debate to some of the critics of John Dewey who have brought it up. There are probably many factors involved. Cultural lag in social change, overcrowded classrooms, psychological fear of change, these and other factors doubtless played a part. For some reason or other, it has taken most educators at least forty years to free themselves sufficiently to look at Dewey in perspective and discover what he actually said. Those who have done so are amazed at the soundness of his thought.

According to John Dewey, the argument is not progressive versus traditional education; and let me be quick to add that John Dewey belonged to neither progressive nor traditional school of thought. The argument is not whether or not children should master fundamental skills and facts. Both Dewey and his opponents recognized that students had to possess facts and skills to think effectively. The argument is not whether or not children should be taught to think. Both Dewey and his opponents thought children should be taught to think. The basic argument in educational method and practice concerns the nature of education. The basic argument between Dewey and the traditionalists he condemned is *a difference in theory of how people think.*

The guidance of learning to think in the classroom has for long been under the dominance of formal logic, especially on the upper levels. Formal traditional logic is the science of valid inference as distinguished from a systematic psychological study of how the mind works. Descartes, as long ago as 1637, distinguished between that logic which is useful in explaining to others what is already known and the logic which appears in learning something new. The distinction did not affect teaching until comparatively modern times. John Dewey paved the way. Dewey wanted a functional curriculum not, as many of his critics allege, because he was concerned to make pleasurable pupil activity a substitute for thought, but rather, because he wanted a school pro-

gram which would provide the young with conditions essential to reflective thinking. According to Dewey, thinking is not listening, it is not memorizing, it is not reciting. Thinking is not formal logic. Although all of these skills are phases of the thinking process, they are not reflective thinking. Thinking is a process through which meanings are developed, clarified, and tested by firsthand experience in problem-solving. For all practical purposes, Dewey considered reflective thinking and problem-solving one and the same.

The foregoing discussion provides background material, but still the reader is likely to ask: "But what does this have to do with the English class?" "What does it have to do with unit teaching?" "How does the mind actually work?" "What is the thinking process?" I believe that it was Kilpatrick who once said, "We learn what we live, we learn each item we live as we accept it, and we learn it to the degree that we accept it." I will answer these questions then by relating to you how I myself came to clarify my own knowledge of the philosophy of education which underlies the unit process.

It was eight years ago that I took a graduate course in philosophy of education with John Childs. As I have previously emphasized, unit teaching stems from the philosophy of education set forth by John Dewey; and John Childs was one of his disciples. John Childs believed that Dewey's philosophy had often been misinterpreted and misapplied. He said so, and he set about to straighten out the thinking of this graduate class. Inadvertently, he did this to me. Our class was a large one, about two hundred students. It was the last class that Childs would teach before age made it mandatory for him to retire. In order to be heard in this small auditorium classroom, it was necessary for class members to stand to recite. Each session began with some puzzling problem or question that the professor brought to light. It was about the fourth week of class that John Childs tried to evoke a discussion on "How people think," for he knew that this was the root of misinterpretation in educational thought. No student volunteered to recite, so he called upon me. I was not prepared, so I told him so. Still he insisted. Again I protested that I was not prepared to recite. Still he insisted. All eyes were upon me. I was desperate. There seemed no way out. Slowly, I got up. I had not the least idea what I would say. I had not read the weekly assignment. As I rose to my feet, I thought to myself, "How do I think?" I was no longer concerned with how other people think. If ever I needed to think, it was then. It was only a few seconds that I desperately dwelled on this topic. How do I think? How does my own mind work? In a flash, the answer came. I think when I am confronted with a problem. Slowly, I looked at the professor, "Thinking originates when a person has a problem. His problem arises out of his everyday experiences in living. This is where he gets his problem." John Childs looked at me and said, "Excellent." In reality he was a very kind man who knew how to give a student support at the proper time. Then, he said, "What do you do when you are confronted with a problem?" Again, I thought of my own situation in the classroom. I recalled that I had hesitated when asked to recite, and in my hesitation I had noted the choices of behavior open to me. I could get up and try to recite, even though I had not read the text. I could refuse to recite and hold my ground. Or I could leave the class. I could think of no other ways to handle the situation. I tried to refuse to recite, but John Childs failed to accept my refusal. I decided that leaving the class would

create an emotional tension for the professor, students, and me. Furthermore, it would be a cowardly way out. I saw only one other choice, to try even if I exposed my ignorance. I therefore made that choice. As I reconstructed these recent experiences, all of a sudden, I could give my answer, "When a person has a problem, he makes an analysis of the situation. From this analysis, he is able to determine the best course of action. A person then acts upon his decision." John Childs looked at me and said, "But suppose he fails?" Quickly, I recounted my own experiences, and I said, "Then he goes back and reexamines the situation and decides upon an alternate course of action." And John Childs asked, "When does he know he has made the right choice?" Automatically, I answered, "If it solves his problem. If he gets the results he is after. If it works." And then I added. "To the extent that his thinking processes are adequate and to the extent that his psychological state of mind is sound, to that extent will his actions and results reflect the best interest of himself and society." I thought a moment more and said, "If his problem is satisfactorily solved, he will doubtless make a generalization or try to apply the knowledge gained to new situations of similar nature. He might tell his friends about it when they are confronted with similar problems. In any event, he stores up the knowledge he has gained through first hand experience in problem-solving for future use."

John Childs went over the thinking process, using more technical terms than I might apply. After class, I hurried to the library, rushed to the card catalogue, then to the shelf. I was eager to get John Dewey's book *How We Think*. I relaxed as I read a summary of the thinking process. He had said what I had said, only years before. I had discovered what he had discovered;

furthermore, I had discovered the key to the unit process. Unit teaching is problem-solving, and problem-solving is reflective thinking. This is the greatest skill of them all—the ability to solve problems. The steps in problem-solving may be stated thus: (1) Thinking originates when a person is faced with a problem, puzzling situation, or dilemma that requires solution. (2) The next step is its location and definition. (3) A further analysis of the problem leads to suggestions of a possible solution or a plan of action. (4) There is then development by experimentation, fact-finding, and reasoning of the bearings of the suggestion or plan of action, and (5) finally, further analysis, experimentation, and observation lead to acceptance or rejection of the proposed solution, hypothesis, or plan.

### III

These are the major steps of the scientific method of inquiry, of reflective thinking, of problem-solving. It is easy to see how they apply in the acquisition of scientific knowledge, and it is easy to see how the science teacher can apply these principles in a scientific classroom. The English teacher is therefore likely to say, "But isn't that a method of science?" To those, I reply, "Don't let the word *scientific* mislead you. On first thought, you may think that the scientific method of inquiry is good only for scientists. You may say that only science is objective, language is not. But if you think again, you will realize that whatever objectivity may mean, it does not mean the absence of a point of view. The methods of science are also the methods of exposition. All truly great articulate men from Shakespeare to Einstein have known the importance of intuition as well as cognition. They know that their dreams as well as their logic come to repair them and help them out. They are not afraid to dream in symbols of great power, for they know that their contributions and achievements are dependent upon both feeling and form. The method of scientific inquiry, problem-solving, reflective thinking—call it whatever you like—is also the method of unit teaching in English."

The foregoing illustration and explanation are included with purpose. While it may sound easy enough to verbalize the thinking process; it is far from easy to understand it. Otherwise so many people would not be living in confusion today. Those English teachers who do not fully understand the problem-solving or reflective thinking process should take careful note of their own actions until they develop an awareness of it. In the final analysis, living a life is continuous problem-solving. Sometimes several problems are in the process of solution all at once. For the person who is a good problem-solver, life proceeds in an orderly fashion. He uses his communication skills to solve his problems by reflective thinking. On the other hand, a fuzzy thinker lives in chaos. To develop a sensitivity to the thinking process, the English teacher must examine his own daily activities. Examples similar to these will serve the purpose. (1) It is a Friday evening, you are expecting a weekend guest. There are a number of things that you must do before your guest arrives Saturday morning on the eleven o'clock train. How do you proceed? (2) One of your students has become a discipline problem in your fourth-period English class. What steps do you take in the solution of this problem? (3) You will soon finish your master's degree. You would like to locate in another area where salaries are better. You are uncertain, however, where you should go. How will you solve this problem? (4) You have been asked to speak at the next P.-T.A. meeting on the topic "Current Issues and Problems in the Teaching of English." How do you prepare for this meeting? (5) In your city an election is being held on the issue of fluoridation of the city water supply. You know nothing about fluoridation but you realize that you should go to the polls and vote. How do you proceed? (6) You would like to buy a new car. You are not certain which make or model is best. You have considered changing from the standard model to a compact. How will you proceed to a solution of this problem? (7) You are overweight. You ought to lose about twenty-five pounds. You have decided to give this matter consideration. What do you do? These are but typical problems that any number of English teachers might face. An educated person approaches these problems in an orderly way. He mentally or otherwise defines his problem, analyzes it from many angles, decides upon a solution, follows through, and evaluates results, as a clue to future action. On the other hand, the uneducated person employs other methods. He may go to a fortune teller, ask a friend to make the decision for him, avoid the problem and refuse to admit he has it, let his problems pile up until he is forced to act from outside pressures, trust to luck to guide him, or employ the method of trial and error. Unless he is lucky, he eventually becomes one of the neurotic personalities of our time. Then he rationalizes his mistakes and frequently says, "That's the way the cookie crumbles."

## IV

Unit teaching first came into educational discussion about 1926, and Morrison was the first to write about it. Early attempts at unit teaching, however, were quite different from the better methods that are known today. Early units were formal in nature and often followed the traditional school in actual method. The five steps of Herbart—preparation, presentation, comparison, generalization, and application—were sometimes used. These formal units were generally teacher conceived and dominated. Students assumed a passive role. Unit teaching as it was first known was primarily a different organization of subject matter. The teaching method showed little change.

In the 1930's and 1940's, English teachers who were studying guidance began to see that nondirective guidance techniques could be an effective English approach. They saw that many of the problems dealt with in guidance offices and homerooms were primarily the problems of all students, and that these problems are also the very content of language and literature in the English classroom. They began to see that the close relationship between guidance and the teaching of English lies in the fact that the English teacher by virtue of the very tools with which he deals—reading, writing, speaking, listening, observing, demonstrating, thinking—plays a vital role in the personal and social development that lies at the very heart of the guidance philosophy. They saw that the tools of guidance are the tools of language. In other words, the tools of language are the key to self-realization. Further analysis revealed that the guidance process itself was a process of problem-solving, and that for all practical purposes, nondirective guidance is a reflective thinking process. To these English teachers it became obvious that the focus in English should be upon the power of language in the life of the student, for it is through the language arts that the student is able to get life into manageable form and become that which he has in him to be. Such a philosophy did not mean that there was no need for specialized guidance services in the school, but it did emphasize that the English teacher had a definite guidance function. Thus came into existence guidance units in English.

In 1950, Smith, Stanley, and Shore first wrote about process units, and with their writing came increasing interest in the actual process by which the unit is taught. At about the same time, Alberty was writing about problem-solving units in the core curriculum and again emphasizing the importance of both content and process. Although there has been a great deal of argument regarding types of units, such argument is not pertinent to the issues presented here. Regardless of the nature of the material dealt with in the unit, whether it be a concrete problem, abstract problem, theme, or experiment, it is the unit process that is of the essence. The real contribution of these various men and movements was to increasingly emphasize problem-solving or reflective thinking as the heart and core of all unit teaching. As time passes on, increasingly English teachers are using a reflective thinking or problem-solving approach as they are able to comprehend it.

While the actual problem-solving processes may vary a little with each different subject area, the English teacher is most concerned with how they apply to the teaching of English. It is for this reason that I give an illustration of the earlier and the revised unit approach—the first is the formal teacher-dominated approach; the second is the more recent problem-solving approach.

A few years ago I visited and observed in the classroom of an English teacher who was conducting a unit on "The Role of the Newspaper in the World Today." This teacher began the unit by announcing that the students were going to undertake a unit on the aforementioned title. The teacher spent considerable time telling the students why it was important for them to make a study of the newspaper, then she told them that the next day the class would set up objectives for the unit study.

In the meantime, class members were to give some attention to the objectives. The next day in class, the students agreed upon a list of objectives for the unit, questions they wished to answer. It was interesting to note that their questions were primarily material that the teacher had given them in the lecture the day before. The teacher then announced a series of activities that the class would undertake in the study of the unit. These activities proceeded in a systematic way. As each activity was undertaken, the teacher brought to the class any materials needed, gave specific instructions on how each piece of work was to be done, and saw that these activities were carried out. Some of the activities undertaken included the daily reading of the local newspaper and a discussion of local news items. No attention was given to the accuracy of reporting. There seemed to be a feeling that if an article appears in the press it is valid. A local newsman spoke to the class and built up a strong argument for his paper and the press in general. He was a delightful speaker and won the support of the group. The students then wrote letters to the editor on a rather noncontroversial subject. The letters were graded, returned to the students, and presumably mailed. Students were encouraged to write articles of school interest for the school newspaper. Several did. Some vocabulary words relating to the press were studied. During the month that the unit was in progress, the daily work laboriously dragged on. By the end of the unit, the students were restless and ready for a change. The teacher, realizing that the students had lost interest, decided to bring the unit to an end with a class evaluation. In the evaluation, the students agreed that they had learned how to read the newspaper, recognized the importance of reading, and expected to confirm their interest by making a daily reading of the newspaper a part of their lives. The teacher then announced that it was time to move on to another unit, which would be a study of *Macbeth*.

After I had observed the teaching of the newspaper unit, I determined to try this unit using a different approach, method, and plan. I decided to use the unit process. My own personal goals were not only to help students improve their use of specific language skills, but also to make them critical readers of newspapers. From past experiences, I knew that many of the students believed that anything in print was truth. They had probably developed such a belief because most of their educational experience had been rooted in a firm belief in the word of the press. Many had gone through school proving their points with such remarks as this, "I can prove it because I read it in . . . . . ." Also I had observed that many of my students equated being arrested with being guilty, considered all advertising as an honest presentation of fact, thought almost any sale a good buy, and generally felt that the highest honor that a girl could achieve would be a photograph in the society section.

Now I could have told the students the strengths and weaknesses of a newspaper, of its worth and limitations. But I knew that learning comes from within, not from without, and that students are more apt to use fruitfully knowledge gained through self-discovery. For this reason, I presented the unit in a problem-solving context. I did this by making reprints of articles on the same subject but from different newspapers.

I used three different newspapers for this and selected an article from each on the same topic but with varying interpretations. I passed out reprints of the first article for the class to read. Class discussion followed, but there were few comments. In general, the class members agreed with the reporter. I then gave them a second article to read. There were some comments that this article was not in complete agreement with the first, but not much excitement about it. Then I gave them the third article. But this time students were puzzled at discrepancies and differences of opinion in reporting the news. I let them wrangle over these differences in class discussion before I took action. In other words, I allowed them to come face to face with a felt difficulty and problem. Finally I halted the discussion and said, "What is the issue in this discussion? What is it that you want to know? Let's define the problem."

Now the students entered the second phase of the unit process, when they defined the problem as they saw it in view of their recent experiences. I did not define the problem for the students. Through the use of the chalkboard to examine carefully selected answers, I patiently took time for the students to agree upon a statement of the problem and a series of questions that they should answer if they were to become intelligent readers of the news. Now I asked how the class could proceed to make a study of this problem so as to gain the needed insight. The students suggested numerous ways: (1) Daily reading of different papers to see differences or similarities in reporting. (2) Reading news magazines for a similar purpose. (3) Searching for books in the library that discuss the magazine and newspaper field. (4) Calling in local reporters for class interviews. (5) Getting personal accounts of news reporting from biographies of famous newsmen. (6) Interviewing people in the community who had complained about being misrepresented in the news. (7) Practicing news reporting themselves to see what difficulties arise. I shared in the suggestions for this cooperative research, but I did not dictate them. For I did not wish to kill initiative and creativity.

Next the class cooperatively agreed upon a plan of action. They then proceeded to carry out their plans, and I acted as a catalyst and guide. As the students began the study and exploration, they found a need to go to the library for resource materials pertaining to the problem at hand. The librarian helped the students find books and materials relating to their study. Perhaps it was necessary for both librarian and students to consult the card catalogue, the *Reader's Guide*, encyclopedias, and bibliographies. In addition, students used the library to investigate current magazines and newspapers. It was through the resources of the library, for example, that they were able to compare original articles with *Reader's Digest* condensations of them. It was from the *Reader's Guide* that students discovered articles on "How to Read the Chicago Tribune" and "All the News That Fits the Pattern" (April and May issues of *Harpers*, 1949). The students found especially helpful William H. Burton's *Education for Effective Thinking* and S. I. Hayakawa's *Language in Thought and Action*. Copies of Liebling's *The Press* and Edgar Dale's *How to Read a Newspaper* were also found on the library shelves.

In addition there were the autobiographies of newsmen and journalists telling their own personal experiences in the newspaper field. The unit took the students to the school library, to the public library, and into the community. It made them active researchers and problem-solvers. This is quite a contrast to the self-contained English classroom where students are spoon-fed from a single text or several volumes that the teacher himself has brought to them for use. The unit process makes students active seekers of knowledge, makes them creators of their own textbooks as they synthesize the source material.

As the unit proceeded, the students set up class discussion periods, small group discussion periods, panel discussions, class interviews, as well as written assignments to share their knowledge. As the unit ended they evaluated what they had learned about the original problem. Also they established guidelines for the evaluation of newspapers that would guide their future reading.

One final thought in conclusion. You have heard arguments in recent years concerning whether or not high school students should write research papers—some teachers say yes, some say no. I think such statements in themselves indicate a lack of clarification of the unit process. Students taught by the unit process write research papers from early school years on through the senior high school days. Properly done, a research paper is a write-up of a unit of study conducted by the unit process.

# 19

# Writing Objectives

## JAMES RATHS

*Clarity is all-important*

In writing lesson plans, objectives should be a teacher's initial consideration. Objectives, when clearly stated, not only give teachers directions for planning and students directions for studying, they also suggest ways in which teachers may evaluate their teaching. How can objectives be expressed clearly? Two criteria for writing goals follow:

1. Objectives should include the behaviors students are expected to display after they have mastered the material to be learned.

Goals are frequently stated in terms that are difficult to translate into anticipated responses of students at the close of the unit. For example, a goal such as "to teach the understanding of the causes of the Great Depression of 1929" does not suggest what a student will be expected to do once he has gained the desired "understanding." Words such as "understanding," "appreciating," "knowing" are difficult to translate into meaningful and testable objectives.

Some teachers assert that their goals cannot be stated in terms that describe the hoped-for behaviors of students. Although this may be true, it nonetheless places these teachers in the awkward position of not knowing whether their methods have been effective or not.

To further illustrate this idea, the ensuing examples demonstrate some poorly stated goals and some goals stated in terms of expected behaviors of students.

### Poorly Stated Goals

a. To understand the principles of the simple lever.
b. To know the meaning of Keat's "Ode on a Grecian Urn."
c. To comprehend the digestive system of the human body.
d. To appreciate the meaning of democracy.

### Clearly Stated Goals

a. To be able to diagram the 3 classes of simple levers.
b. To be able to translate Keat's poem into prose.
c. To be able to diagram the major parts of the digestive system.
d. To be able to compare the communistic and democratic forms of government.

2. The statement of desired behav-

iors ideally should include the situation in which the behaviors are to occur.

This second criterion increases the likelihood that students will grasp the practical application of a teacher's goals in the classroom. In brief, its application suggests what conditions will be part of the evaluation of the goals. For instance, some teachers allow open books in examinations, others permit students to prepare crib-sheets, while still others do not condone any student access to material in a test situation. To meet this criterion, objectives that include a description of student behaviors might also include the following phrases:

a. Given equations of the form
   $AX^2 + BX + C = 0,$
b. Given a poem, . . .
c. Without the aid of notes, . . .
d. Given evaluative criteria, . . .

Goals which meet these two criteria will greatly assist teachers in deciding on the methods they wish to use in their teaching and in devising test items to evaluate student achievement.

## REFERENCE

Mager, R. F., *Preparing Objectives for Programmed Instruction*. San Francisco: Fearon Publishers, Inc., 1962.

# 20

# Systematic Planning and Classifying Objectives

JOHN R. PANCELLA

In order for lesson and unit objectives to be meaningful to the teacher the objectives should support and be supported by the method and technique of the teaching act. This is not always obvious from looking at lesson plans. Objectives may contain comments such as "teaching for understanding of world problems," "providing experiences for better citizenship," or "to help the students understand the physical world." Comments such as these may be difficult to rationalize in terms of the content being taught if only facts and knowledge are emphasized. Usually the finale is a test which measures achievement of the facts, and does not reveal whether or not the goals and objectives were attained. How can teachers identify objectives and relate them to content? How can the objectives be planned so that they can be taught successfully? How can teachers determine their success or failure in reaching their goals? The latter might be indicated by testing what was taught. Such a notion will be explored in Chapter Four. There are techniques, however, which might help the teacher prepare for the total sequence of planning-teaching-testing.

One means of systematically planning a unit of work is to use a grid form for the outlay of content versus abilities. Such a matrix is illustrated on p. 146.

By indicating the number of lessons or activities in the appropriate boxes a teacher can see at a glance whether or not all the abilities desired as objectives are being implemented. The matrix also will visually portray the degree to which emphasis is being placed on certain areas. The decisions to teach for the selected abilities and the items to be stressed are made by the teacher.

If it becomes important later that the test questions closely parallel the pattern on the grid form, a plot of test items can be compared with the unit plan. For example, suppose most of the information is presented for students to memorize and evaluate, i.e., columns headed "Identify Central Issues" and "Evaluate Evidence of Authority." Would it be useful to construct an examination which contains mostly questions on the other columns?

| CONTENT AREA \ CRITICAL ABILITY | Identify Central Issues | Recognize Underlying Assumptions | Evaluate Evidence or Authority | Recognize Limitation of Data | Establish Relationships | Draw Warranted Conclusions |
|---|---|---|---|---|---|---|
| CULTURE CONCEPT (10 per cent) | | | | | | |
| ECONOMIC AFFAIRS (40 per cent) Systems Business Organizations Labor Problems Agriculture Consumer | | | | | | |
| POLITICAL AFFAIRS (40 per cent) Systems Government and Business Civil Liberties International Relations | | | | | | |
| SOCIAL AFFAIRS (10 per cent) Family Education | | | | | | |

**Fig. 1. Grid Form for the Construction of the Test of Critical Thinking in Social Science. The aim of the Social Science Committee was that the number of items for each ability would be approximately equal. P. L. Dressel and L. B. Mayhew,** *General Education: Explorations in Evaluation* **(Washington, D.C.: American Council on Education, 1954), p. 48, Fig. 1.**

Would it be useful to have most of the questions on the content area of "Culture Concept"? It would seem unlikely that such a plan would reflect back to the teacher how effective the teaching was for reaching goals and objectives such as "To have the students learn critical abilities for analyzing situations."

Thus, two reasons for classifying objectives might emerge:

1. For monitoring the teaching of skills, abilities, and thinking tasks which students are to gain with the content.

2. To use the planning at a later time for testing and determining whether or not successful teaching for goals has occurred.

A major difficulty in identifying the objectives is communicating the differences between types of thinking tasks. One system of classifying objectives according to a cognitive hierarchy is the "Taxonomy of Educational Objectives" (see condensed version in this chapter). The Taxonomy was developed on the presupposition that there is a structure to the cognitive process which is analyzable. Thus each thinking level builds on the previous ones. Six levels are defined: Knowledge (1.00), Comprehension (2.00), Application (3.00), Analysis (4.00), Synthesis (5.00), and Evaluation (6.00). This system is unlike the Dewey decimal classification for categorizing library materials, which is based on arbitrary divisions. The Taxonomy is a ladder of thought. Analysis (4.00) includes the first three levels; knowledge (1.00) is the base for all the levels.

These levels could be substituted for the column headings for critical abilities in the grid form. The plan could then be developed emphasizing selected content for those levels chosen by the teacher as goals. It may be that only the first three levels are applicable to a subject topic. The decision to use various levels should be left to the teacher. This necessarily depends upon whatever rationale the teacher selects.

The following are examples of objectives from a literature unit, classified by the six major levels of the Taxonomy.

1.00 To know the contemporary poets and their writing styles.

2.00 To gain the ability to interpret the writings of contemporary poets.

3.00 To use the rules of writing verse to describe selected poems.

4.00 To study poems and determine how they were constructed from their component parts.

5.00 To write creatively in a style unique to each student.

6.00 To evaluate writings for internal consistency of writing style and word usage.

There are other systems of classifying objectives such as the "Levels of Performance" by Bradfield and Moredock (see "Levels of Performance in Teaching," by Fred W. Fox, in this chapter). A system could be simplified to (1) Knowledge and Understanding, (2) Application, and (3) Inquiry. How would these systems be used to classify the objectives given above?

As will be discussed in Chapter Four, test items can be similarly classified according to the levels in order to plan tests for monitoring what was taught. The grid form and systems of classifying objectives, although flexible enough to be adapted by the individual teacher for each analyzable situation, do not constitute the only methods for planning. Instead, they are techniques for helping the teacher answer his own question, "What are some other ways I can use to look at my teaching?"

# 21

# Taxonomy of Educational Objectives

## BENJAMIN S. BLOOM, EDITOR

## COGNITIVE DOMAIN

### KNOWLEDGE

*1.00 Knowledge.* Knowledge, as defined here, involves the recall of specifics and universals, the recall of methods and processes, or the recall of a pattern, structure, or setting. For measurement purposes, the recall situation involves little more than bringing to mind the appropriate material. Although some alteration of the material may be required, this is a relatively minor part of the task. The knowledge objectives emphasize most the psychological processes of remembering. The process of relating is also involved in that a knowledge test situation requires the organization and reorganization of a problem such that it will furnish the appropriate signals and cues for the information and knowledge the indi-

vidual possesses. To use an analogy, if one thinks of the mind as a file, the problem in a knowledge test situation is that of finding in the problem or task the appropriate signals, cues, and clues which will most effectively bring out whatever knowledge is filed or stored.

*1.10 Knowledge of Specifics.* The recall of specific and isolable bits of information. The emphasis is on symbols with concrete referents. This material, which is at a very low level of abstraction, may be thought of as the elements from which more complex and abstract forms of knowledge are built.

*1.11 Knowledge of Terminology.* Knowledge of the referents for specific symbols (verbal and nonverbal). This may include knowledge of the most generally accepted symbol referent, knowledge of the variety of symbols which may be used for a single referent, or knowledge of the referent most appropriate to a given use of a symbol.

*To define technical terms by giving

Benjamin S. Bloom, ed., "Condensed Version of the Taxonomy of Educational Objectives," in *Taxonomy of Educational Objectives: Handbook I, Cognitive Domain* (New York: David McKay Co., Inc., 1956), pp. 201–7. Reprinted by permission.

*Illustrative educational objectives selected from the literature.

their attributes, properties, or relations.

*Familiarity with a large number of words in their common range of meanings.

*1.12 Knowledge of Specific Facts.* Knowledge of dates, events, persons, places, etc. This may include very precise and specific information such as the specific date or exact magnitude of a phenomenon. It may also include approximate or relative information such as an approximate time period or the general order of magnitude of a phenomenon.

*The recall of major facts about particular cultures.

*The possession of a minimum knowledge about the organisms studied in the laboratory.

*1.20 Knowledge of Ways and Means of Dealing with Specifics.* Knowledge of the ways of organizing, studying, judging, and criticizing. This includes the methods of inquiry, the chronological sequences, and the standards of judgment within a field as well as the patterns of organization through which the areas of the fields themselves are determined and internally organized. This knowledge is at an intermediate level of abstraction between specific knowledge on the one hand and knowledge of universals on the other. It does not so much demand the activity of the student in using the materials as it does a more passive awareness of their nature.

*1.21 Knowledge of Conventions.* Knowledge of characteristic ways of treating and presenting ideas and phenomena. For purposes of communication and consistency, workers in a field employ usages, styles, practices, and forms which best suit their purposes and/or which appear to suit best the phenomena with which they deal. It should be recognized that although these forms and conventions are likely to be set up on arbitrary, accidental,

or authoritative bases, they are retained because of the general agreement or concurrence of individuals concerned with the subject, phenomena, or problem.

*Familiarity with the forms and conventions of the major types of works, e.g., verse, plays, scientific papers, etc.

*To make pupils conscious of correct form and usage in speech and writing.

*1.22 Knowledge of Trends and Sequences.* Knowledge of the processes, directions, and movements of phenomena with respect to time.

*Understanding of the continuity and development of American culture as exemplified in American life.

*Knowledge of the basic trends underlying the development of public assistance programs.

*1.23 Knowledge of Classifications and Categories.* Knowledge of the classes, sets, divisions, and arrangements which are regarded as fundamental for a given subject field, purpose, argument, or problem.

*To recognize the area encompassed by various kinds of problems or materials.

*Becoming familiar with a range of types of literature.

*1.24 Knowledge of Criteria.* Knowledge of the criteria by which facts, principles, opinions, and conduct are tested or judged.

*Familiarity with criteria for judgment appropriate to the type of work and the purpose for which it is read.

*Knowledge of criteria for the evaluation of recreational activities.

*1.25 Knowledge of Methodology.* Knowledge of the methods of inquiry, techniques, and procedures employed in a particular subject field as well as those employed in investigating particular problems and phenomena. The emphasis here is on the individual's knowledge of the method rather than his ability to use the method.

*Knowledge of scientific methods for evaluating health concepts.

*The student shall know the methods of attack relevant to the kinds of problems of concern to the social sciences.

*1.30 Knowledge of the Universals and Abstractions in a Field.* Knowledge of the major schemes and patterns by which phenomena and ideas are organized. These are the large structures, theories, and generalizations which dominate a subject field or which are quite generally used in studying phenomena or solving problems. These are at the highest levels of abstraction and complexity.

*1.31 Knowledge of Principles and Generalizations.* Knowledge of particular abstractions which summarize observations of phenomena. These are the abstractions which are of value in explaining, describing, predicting, or in determining the most appropriate and relevant action or direction to be taken.

*Knowledge of the important principles by which our experience with biological phenomena is summarized.

*The recall of major generalizations about particular cultures.

*1.32 Knowledge of Theories and Structures.* Knowledge of the *body* of principles and generalizations together with their interrelations which present a clear, rounded, and systematic view of a complex phenomenon, problem, or field. These are the most abstract formulations, and they can be used to show the interrelation and organization of a great range of specifics.

*The recall of major theories about particular cultures.

*Knowledge of a relatively complete formulation of the theory of evolution.

INTELLECTUAL ABILITIES AND SKILLS

Abilities and skills refer to organized modes of operation and generalized techniques for dealing with materials and problems. The materials and problems may be of such a nature that little or no specialized and technical information is required. Such information as is required can be assumed to be part of the individual's general fund of knowledge. Other problems may require specialized and technical information at a rather high level such that specific knowledge and skill in dealing with the problem and the materials are required. The abilities and skills objectives emphasize the mental processes of organizing and reorganizing material to achieve a particular purpose. The materials may be given or remembered.

*2.00 Comprehension.* This represents the lowest level of understanding. It refers to a type of understanding or apprehension such that the individual knows what is being communicated and can make use of the material or idea being communicated without necessarily relating it to other material or seeing its fullest implications.

*2.10 Translation.* Comprehension as evidenced by the care and accuracy with which the communication is paraphrased or rendered from one language or form of communication to another. Translation is judged on the basis of faithfulness and accuracy, that is, on the extent to which the material in the original communication is preserved although the form of the communication has been altered.

*The ability to understand non-literal statements (metaphor, symbolism, irony, exaggeration).

*Skill in translating mathematical verbal material into symbolic statements and vice versa.

*2.20 Interpretation.* The explanation or summarization of a communication. Whereas translation involves an objective part-for-part rendering of a communication, interpretation involves a reordering, rearrangement, or a new view of the material.

*The ability to grasp the thought of the work as a whole at any desired level of generality.

*The ability to interpret various types of social data.

*2.30 Extrapolation.* The extension of trends or tendencies beyond the given data to determine implications, consequences, corollaries, effects, etc., which are in accordance with the conditions described in the original communication.

*The ability to deal with the conclusions of a work in terms of the immediate inference made from the explicit statements.

*Skill in predicting continuation of trends.

*3.00 Application.* The use of abstractions in particular and concrete situations. The abstractions may be in the form of general ideas, rules of procedures, or generalized methods. The abstractions may also be technical principles, ideas, and theories which must be remembered and applied.

*Application to the phenomena discussed in one paper of the scientific terms or concepts used in other papers.

*The ability to predict the probable effect of a change in a factor on a biological situation previously at equilibrium.

*4.00 Analysis.* The breakdown of a communication into its constituent elements or parts such that the relative hierarchy of ideas is made clear and/or the relations between the ideas expressed are made explicit. Such analyses are intended to clarify the communication, to indicate how the communication is organized, and the way in which it manages to convey its effects, as well as its basis and arrangement.

*4.10 Analysis of Elements.* Identification of the elements included in a communication.

*The ability to recognize unstated assumptions.

*Skill in distinguishing facts from hypotheses.

*4.20 Analyses of Relationships.* The connections and interactions between elements and parts of a communication.

*Ability to check the consistency of hypotheses with given information and assumptions.

*Skill comprehending the interrelationships among the ideas in a passage.

*4.30 Analysis of Organizational Principles.* The organization, systematic arrangement, and structure which hold the communication together. This includes the "explicit" as well as "implicit" structure. It includes the bases, necessary arrangement, and the mechanics which make the communication a unit.

*The ability to recognize form and pattern in literary or artistic works as a means of understanding their meaning.

*Ability to recognize the general techniques used in persuasive materials, such as advertising, propaganda, etc.

*5.00 Synthesis.* The putting together of elements and parts so as to form a whole. This involves the process of working with pieces, parts, elements, etc., and arranging and combining them in such a way as to constitute a pattern or structure not clearly there before.

*5.10 Production of a Unique Communication.* The development of a communication in which the writer or speaker attempts to convey ideas, feelings, and/or experiences to others.

*Skill in writing, using an excellent organization of ideas and statements.

*Ability to tell a personal experience effectively.

*5.20 Production of a Plan, or Proposed Set of Operations.* The development of a plan of work or the proposal of a plan of operations. The plan should satisfy requirements of the task which may be given to the student or which he may develop for himself.

*Ability to propose ways of testing hypotheses.

*Ability to plan a unit of instruction for a particular teaching situation.

*5.30 Derivation of a Set of Abstract Relations.* The development of a set of abstract relations either to classify or explain particular data or phenomena, or the deduction of propositions and relations from a set of basic propositions or symbolic representations.

*Ability to formulate appropriate hypotheses based upon an analysis of factors involved, and to modify such hypotheses in the light of new factors and considerations.

*Ability to make mathematical discoveries and generalizations.

*6.00 Evaluation.* Judgments about the value of material and methods for given purposes. Quantitative and qualitative judgments about the extent to which material and methods satisfy criteria. Use of a standard of appraisal.

The criteria may be those determined by the student or those which are given to him.

*6.10 Judgments in Terms of Internal Evidence.* Evaluation of the accuracy of a communication from such evidence as logical accuracy, consistency, and other internal criteria.

*Judging by internal standards, the ability to assess general probability of accuracy in reporting facts from the care given to exactness of statement, documentation, proof, etc.

*The ability to indicate logical fallacies in arguments.

*6.20 Judgments in Terms of External Criteria.* Evaluation of material with reference to selected or remembered criteria.

*The comparison of major theories, generalizations, and facts about particular cultures.

*Judging by external standards, the ability to compare a work with the highest known standards in its field— especially with other works of recognized excellence.

# 22

# Levels of Performance in Teaching

FRED W. FOX

New developments in science programs are being received generally with enthusiasm. Teachers feel that good science is being taught, and in addition there is the satisfaction to students and teachers alike that the courses are intellectually stimulating. One is taught to think as well as to learn about the world of nature. Even apart from "the new programs" any teacher gains satisfaction from moving his teaching from the end of the spectrum which demands rote learning, imitation, or repetition of facts presented, to the other end which promotes critical thought and analysis, discovery, or creativity.

At which end of the spectrum do we as teachers perform or expect our students to perform? Are we satisfied to teach as we were taught, or do we use our teaching abilities uniquely and imaginatively according to our personal and community resources and the special needs of our students? Do students sit at their desks day in and day out simply giving back to us what is in their texts, or are they investigating with materials and equipment, testing, gathering data, making judgments, predicting, and discovering? What is the level of performance in our classes?

One of the most imaginative and striking analyses by which we may quickly judge our teaching has been devised by James M. Bradfield and H. Stewart Moredock.[1] It is titled "Levels of Performance" for this discussion. Look at Table 1, p. 155, and ask yourself: At which level do I expect my students to perform?

It has been the writer's experience that both practicing teachers and teachers in training have been caught up by Bradfield and Moredock's imaginative ordering of potential classroom experiences. Science teachers who have studied the analysis have suggested a variety of implications for their teaching. Some of these follow:

[1] James M. Bradfield and H. Stewart Moredock, *Measurement and Evaluation in Education* (New York: The Macmillan Company, 1957), p. 204.

Fred W. Fox, "Levels of Performance in Teaching," *The Science Teacher*, XXXII, No. 4 (April 1965), 31–32. Reprinted by permission.

## "LEVELS OF PERFORMANCE"
## USES FOR THE ANALYSIS

### 1. EVALUATION

The original authors entitled the outline as "Performances Indicating Different Levels of Understanding of a Given Subject." Thus the "levels" were to be considered as standards or criteria against which to judge the work of our students. It is probably safe to say that our tests and examinations usually measure our students' abilities at Levels I and II. Bradfield and Moredock, of course, suggest that we evaluate student performance on more data than are accumulated through tests, quizzes, and examinations.[2] Our students work in the laboratory, enter discussions, prepare reports, read, and engage in a variety of activities beyond mere recitation (usually a Level I performance) and test-taking. In using the "Levels of Performance" analysis in evaluation, key questions become: What sources of evidence of student performance are there for rendering teacher judgments, and how do I make a record of such evidence of student behavior?

### 2. GOALS FOR SCIENCE TEACHING

It is quite apparent that we cannot evaluate student effort at the upper levels of performance if we never arrange for our students to operate there. Converting these levels of performance to teaching goals is a distortion of the original authors' intent. Science teaching objectives should be in a context of the field of science knowledge, the means of deriving

[2] For an additional discussion of sources of evidence for judging student work, see John S. Richardson, *Science Teaching in Secondary Schools* (Englewood Cliffs, N.J.: Prentice-Hall, Inc., 1957), Chap. VII.

it, its social implications, and its application to the solution of our daily problems. But many of us could improve our teaching simply by stating and living up to such a statement as: "I am going to teach science in such a manner that students have to explain, justify, predict, estimate, interpret, and make critical judgments."

### 3. METHOD OF TEACHING

The tremendous implication of raising the level of performance in our classroom is that we must change our method of teaching. Obviously it would be unfair to evaluate student behavior at the upper levels if students had not been permitted to develop skills at those levels. Evaluation apart, the significance of the "levels" is that laboratory work must become more vital, challenging, stimulating. Demonstrations can no longer be routine. Students will have to be given opportunity to solve problems for which there are no simple solutions. They will have to read, discuss, investigate, try out, argue, take trips, look at, listen to, improvise, succeed, fail. Only by changed methods in most of our classes will students have opportunity to compare, discriminate, reformulate, interpret, predict, discover, create— that is, to perform at a "higher level."

### 4. FINDING SATISFACTION IN TEACHING

No teacher likes to be accused of teaching as he was taught, nor does he like to believe that he teaches in a dull and perfunctory manner. The teacher who is gaining personal satisfaction from his teaching, who talks enthusiastically to his colleagues about his work, or who has a reputation among his students as a top teacher in the school, is exactly the same teacher who is himself teaching at a high level of perform-

TABLE 1

**Levels of Performance***

| Level | Performance |
|---|---|
| I | Imitating, duplicating, repeating. |
| | This is the level of initial contact. Student can repeat or duplicate what has just been said, done, or read. Indicates that student is at least conscious or aware of contact with a particular concept or process. |
| II | Level I, plus recognizing, identifying, remembering, recalling, classifying. |
| | To perform on this level, the student must be able to recognize or identify the concept or process when encountered later, or to remember or recall the essential features of the concept or process. |
| III | Levels I and II, plus comparing, relating, discriminating, reformulating, illustrating. |
| | Here the student can compare and relate this concept or process with other concepts or processes and make discriminations. He can formulate in his own words a definition, and he can illustrate or give examples. |
| IV | Levels I, II, and III, plus explaining, justifying, predicting, estimating, interpreting, making critical judgments, drawing inferences. |
| | On the basis of his understanding of a concept or process, he can make explanations, give reasons, make predictions, interpret, estimate, or make critical judgments. This performance represents a high level of understanding. |
| V | Levels I, II, III, and IV, plus creating, discovering, reorganizing, formulating new hypotheses, new questions and problems. |
| | This is the level of original and productive thinking. The student's understanding has developed to such a point that he can make discoveries that are new to him and can restructure and reorganize his knowledge on the basis of his new discoveries and new insights. |

ance. He compares the variety of teaching techniques he knows are available for his use and with discrimination selects those most suitable for his students and his experience and resources. He critically judges the content of the many science courses he may choose for his students. At his best, the teacher resourcefully departs from the traditional and the routine and creates new and imaginative approaches to both content and method in teaching.

He critically questions the commonplace teaching doctrines of his time (and even the not-so-commonplace) and searches for unique ways to solve teaching problems. And in this spirit of his own creativity he finds at the same time poise and confidence that his profession is worthy of his energy and devotion and that education under his direction is serving its proper ends.

What is your "level of performance"?

# ACTIVITIES

1. What are some planning techniques you may use in your teaching?
2. What are some ways you may monitor your planning?
3. Plan lessons for teaching identical concepts according to the notions of Dewey and Bruner.
4. What makes an idea "inert" according to Whitehead?
5. Suggest ways a teacher may implement the ideas of Ausubel cited by James Raths. What are some requisites for using his ideas? How can a teacher check to see if his use of advanced organizers has been effective?
6. Many teachers concern themselves with planning units. What is a "unit"? Are the ideas presented in this chapter antithetical to "unit" planning? Define your answer.
7. How does the concept of unit in Berry's article compare with others in this chapter? How does it compare with your concepts of unit?
8. Using the grid-form technique, develop a unit in your teaching field.
9. Classify the "Critical Abilities" of the Dressel and Mayhew grid form according to Bloom's Taxonomy.
10. Review the lesson plans at the end of this chapter in the light of Herrick's discussion.

    a. What decisions has the teacher made in each lesson plan according to each of the three classes mentioned in Herrick's article on organizing centers?
    b. Has the teacher differentiated between topics and important understandings?
    c. Has the teacher differentiated between concepts and skills?
    d. What has the teacher used as an organizing center?

11. Classify the goals of the lesson plans at the end of this chapter according to the Taxonomy.

    a. Discuss differences in the classification that are found in your group.

b. Most of the goals in traditional teaching can be classified under Knowledge (1.00). Why do you suppose this is true? How could you find out if your hunch is valid?

12. Analyze other lesson plans according to the paragraphs above.
13. What are some generalizations worth teaching? What content would best illustrate these generalizations?

## Sample Lesson Plan 1

### TENTH-GRADE BIOLOGY—INTRODUCTION TO CLASSIFICATION SYSTEMS

OBJECTIVE

Students are to discover the structure of a classification system.

MATERIALS

Student data book.
Each table has a small pan which contains approximately fifty mixed buttons.

PROCEDURES

Each pair of students is to group the buttons in any way they wish according to specific characteristics. (Some may begin with color, or size, or number of holes, etc.)

Toward the last 15 minutes of the class period several students will present their classification scheme. (Ask for their rationale for selecting their grouping.)

Look for the following ideas to emerge from student discussions.

1. Before a classification system can be developed, materials must be present to be classified.
2. A system will proceed from general to specific, or from simple to complex.
3. The basic elements of the different systems developed by different students will probably include *shape, size, color,* and *form and/or structure.* (These four categories are common to other systems of other items, such as school buildings, automobiles, plants and animals, etc.)

ASSIGNMENT

Read Chapter 6—"Classifying Living Things."
Answer the following question: In what way is the system for classifying living things related to the system for classifying buttons?

# Sample Lesson Plan 2

**TWELFTH-GRADE AMERICAN LITERATURE**

ASSIGNMENT FOR TODAY

Learn spelling words, p. 73.

METHODS

1. Give spelling quiz
2. Show filmstrip on ship "Constitution"
3. Play record of poem "Old Ironsides"
4. Role-play how the crew of the "Constitution" would have reacted to the poem.
5. Questions to ask in class:
    a. What words are unclear?
    b. Where did the author live?
    c. Why did the author write the poem?
    d. Would a poetry editor print this poem if it were written today?
    e. Did you like the poem?

ASSIGNMENT FOR TOMORROW

Look up the words you do not know in the poem " Old Ironsides " and learn the correct meanings.
Memorize the first stanza of " Old Ironsides."
Read " Casey at the Bat."

# Sample Lesson Plan 3

**ELEVENTH-GRADE U. S. HISTORY**

STUDENT ASSIGNMENT FOR TODAY

Bring in two news stories and one editorial dealing with the same subject or event.

CLASSROOM ACTIVITIES

1. Show aerial and ground photographs of New York City. Then show artists' sketches of the same areas. Discuss similarities and differences.

2. Select a panel of students to read their articles and editorials. Have the students consider whether the news stories presented the same picture. Was the difference of purpose evident in the editorial as compared to the news story?

3. Give out three groups of in-class assignments:

Group 1: Write a news story on the basis of the information given on a handout sheet (to be given to students).

Group 2: Write a favorable editorial dealing with some aspect of the news story outlined on the handout sheet.

Group 3: Write an unfavorable editorial dealing with some aspect of the news story outlined on the handout sheet.

4. Have various students in Group 1 read their news stories and call on students in Groups 2 and 3 to state whether they would accept them for publication in their paper.

5. Reconsider some of the news stories and editorials read by the panel.

ASSIGNMENT FOR TOMORROW

Read the selection in the book: "Propaganda and the American Revolution."

## Chapter Four

# TESTING AND GRADING

Evaluating student work is one of the most pressing realities of teaching. For the purpose of effecting such evaluations the test has been devised. A common premise that seems an almost universal tacit agreement between students and teachers at all levels is that a test should reflect the teaching which precedes it. Because teachers almost always test for what they have taught, a review of their tests should enable them to monitor the objective on which they are apparently placing the greatest emphasis. If a teacher has stressed thinking, concern for generalizations, and high-level skills, it is considered manifestly unfair to test only for the memorization of facts. If a teacher has stressed memory skills on his test, he would not be testing adequately for those high-level skills he may have set as a goal. Thus, here is yet another way a teacher may assess his own behavior in terms of his goals.

Must tests reflect teaching? Is it ever fair to teach for a test? Can grades be assigned on an objective basis? At times, the grade a student receives may affect his life deeply. Grades may determine his job opportunities, his chances for admission to the college of his choice, and perhaps even more important, his views of his own adequacy. Because of this, and because of the great emphasis currently placed on tests as a source of grades, it is incumbent upon each teacher to check the precision of his tests. Tests can be analyzed easily and inspected for reliability and content validity. Some ways for doing this will be reviewed in this chapter.

# 23

# Uses of Tests

DOLPH CAMP

Each year millions of standardized and other tests are administered to pupils at all grade levels in the United States and to adults seeking employment or advancement. Unfortunately, in some schools the test results are not being used. Some school officials apparently believe that the test results are "top secret" information since they lock them away in their files. Others apparently consider the results merely as a necessary part of a pupil's official cumulative record—to be entered in his folder in the office, but not always made easily accessible to his homeroom and other teachers. In an increasing number of schools, however, administrators, teachers, and—in schools fortunate enough to have them—trained counselors are using the test results to good advantage.

Tests can be used in many ways.

Dolph Camp, "Uses of Tests" in *Understanding Testing*, ed. Kenneth F. McLaughlin, Office of Education, U.S. Department of Health, Education, and Welfare (Washington, D.C.: Government Printing Office, 1963), pp. 12–13.

This article discusses briefly only six of the major uses: identification, classification, selection, evaluation, planning, and adjustment. Even though classification and selection may be considered as subsections of identification, and adjustment as a subsection of planning, each of these uses is of sufficient importance to merit independent treatment here.

## IDENTIFICATION

Standardized tests may be used, along with other data, to identify pupils with superior talents and those with low ability. For each of these groups, as well as the groups with average abilities, multiple aptitude tests may be used to identify the particular types of abilities each pupil possesses. A pupil with superior talents may be good in English, much better in mathematics, and still better in science, and one with low ability may be weak in history, weaker in English, and still weaker in mathematics. What-

ever the pupil's abilities are, a good
multifactor or multiple aptitude
battery will depict their pattern.

## CLASSIFICATION

Some schools practice homogeneous
grouping of pupils; that is, they assign pupils to classes on the bases of
mental ability, achievement, test
scores, or earlier class grades, because
they believe that better instruction is
possible if there is a narrow range of
abilities among the pupils in a class.
Such arrangements prevent any one
level of students from setting the pace
for the class. If the slow learner sets
the pace, the superior student wastes
time and loses interest. If the superior student sets the pace, the slow
learner becomes discouraged because
he finds it impossible for him to keep
up. Finally, if the average student
sets the pace of instruction, the fast
learner is bored and the slow learner
discouraged. For the instructional
program based on a narrow range of
abilities among the members of each
class, standardized tests may be used
along with other data in classifying
students into categories based on different levels of ability.

## SELECTION

Tests may be used along with other
data in selecting pupils for a college
or university, filling a position in industry, or assigning persons to specialized positions in the Armed
Services. Basic to the operation of selection is the fact that there must be more
people than there are places to fill.
The educational institution, the industry, or the Armed Services set the
requirements and select the test in
order to determine those who meet,

or most nearly meet, the requirements.

The high school or college counselor
uses test results in helping a pupil
make plans or adjustments. He begins
with the pupil's abilities and personality
traits and helps select situations in
which such abilities and personality
traits can best function. For example,
if a pupil prefers small classes and likes
to know all of his group, perhaps he
would be more successful and happier
at a small college rather than at a
large university.

The personnel director of a steel
mill, for example, must find men with
certain aptitudes or the skills required
for a specific job. In other words,
since the requirements of the job are
of utmost importance, he looks for
persons who possess the qualities it
requires.

The problem of fitting employees to
positions is different for the Armed
Services. Here, the number of persons
available is known, the number of
positions to be filled is known, and
all persons in the Service must have
an assignment. From a large group
of men and women with varied backgrounds, either volunteers or draftees,
the Service must match each person
to the job for which he is best suited
or to the job where he is most needed
at the moment, depending on his particular combination of skills.

With large numbers of men and
women to be considered, test results
are helpful in matching talents with
job needs or as a basis for transfers.

## EVALUATION

Standardized tests may be used in
evaluating instruction. Through the
use of test results pupils, classes, and
even schools may be compared with
fixed standards. Through tests, the
level of mastery of essential content

by a pupil may be compared with the level which has already been established for his grade or age group. Such a comparison shows whether the pupil is underachieving, achieving beyond his expectancy, or achieving according to his potential.

Through the use of test results a class average may be compared with the averages of preceding classes in order to determine whether changes in methods of instruction are having the desired effect.

Occasionally a principal will find it helpful to compare the average achievement of his school in various subjects with the averages of other schools in his geographical area, whether city, county, or state. However, in tables of norms, all schools lose their identity so that no school may say that it is better or poorer than the schools of any other particular school system. This is as it should be, since there are too many variables which could account for the differences in average achievement between any two particular schools.

## PLANNING

Perhaps the most important use of tests is that of supplying basic data to pupils, counselors, and parents to aid them in educational and vocational planning. Almost every college or university maintains a profile of abilities a student should have to succeed in its various departments or schools. College officials can compare an applicant's profile with its standard profile to determine in which department or school he is likely to succeed or whether he is likely to succeed in any of them.

A similar use of tests may be made by the industrial counselor who attempts to assist a youth or an adult in

obtaining suitable employment, or by a recruiting officer in the Armed Services assisting a new volunteer in choosing a military specialty in line with his abilities and interests and the current needs of the Services.

## ADJUSTMENT

An important use of tests is in assisting people—children, youth, or adults—in making necessary adjustments. For this purpose test results are used by such people as counselors in educational institutions, personnel managers in industry, and psychologists in clinical counseling. For example, a pupil may be attempting courses of study too difficult for him, a man who is at present a plumber may be in a position not requiring his abilities and interests, and needs to change jobs, or a housewife may become frustrated with everyday problems confronting her. In dealing with these people and helping them make adjustments, counselors and clinicians find standardized tests useful.

## CAUTIONS IN USING TESTS

Used properly, standardized tests are valuable tools in educational programs, in industry, in the Armed Services, and in psychological and psychiatric clinics. But, some caution should be observed in their use.

Those administering standardized tests must follow the directions in the test manual exactly. If they do not, the test loses its effectiveness for it will be impossible to make valid comparisons of the test scores obtained with the published standards.

No one should depend on tests alone in making any important career decision. Test results should be used

along with such background and educational information as that included
in a cumulative record. School marks,
data from questionnaires, rating scales,
autobiographies, and anectodal records
yield valuable information for counseling.

Caution should be observed in the
interpretation of test results. It is
difficult to set an exact cutting score
(that is, a minimum score which
must be obtained in order to be considered) as a requirement for entrance
into an educational institution, a
course of study, or a job. Instead
of an IQ or a percentile score, it is
usually considered better to use a
range of IQ scores or a percentile band
in making decisions on requirements.

Caution should be observed in the
reporting of test results in schools.
Counselors and other test users should
have a well-formulated policy on
reporting scores. In particular, the
policy statement should answer these
and other questions: Should parents
be given the test scores? Should a
pupil be given his own scores? Should
all teachers be given all the scores?
Although these questions are not
discussed here, they should be considered in reporting test results, for all

users should exercise maximum caution
to see that the persons concerned are
helped instead of hurt as a result of
testing.

Tests should be safeguarded. The
reputable test publisher does not sell
his tests to unqualified or unauthorized
persons. The use of good tests can be
impaired by negligence in the local
handling of them. When students
or others have studied a particular
test in advance, its measuring value
has been lessened and the results
are often worthless. There are not
many closed tests, and tests available
on the open market must be safeguarded by persons administering
them.

Today, schools are overcrowded,
there is a shortage of well-trained
teachers and counselors, and schools
are assuming greater responsibilities
for pupil welfare. Many schools are
administering tests on a gradewide or
schoolwide basis and using the test
scores in conjunction with other information for a number of such useful
purposes as have been discussed.
However, test users must be cautioned
that tests are a means to an end and
not an end in themselves.

# 24

# Planning Tests

JOHN R. PANCELLA

Once a teacher has his teaching objectives well in mind, his next efforts are usually directed to the question, "How may I evaluate the teaching and learning in my class to determine if the objectives have been obtained?" Most teachers answer this question to their own satisfaction by using tests. This section deals with ways a teacher may evaluate his tests to see if they are at all adequate for the purposes for which they are used.

## FACE VALIDITY

A most important question asks, "Is the test measuring what I want it to measure?" To determine this is exceedingly difficult in most measuring situations involving the assessment of personality traits, motivation, curiosity, etc. In achievement testing, however, the answer is not quite so difficult. It is a fairly easy matter to establish "face" validity of an achievement test. Face validity, in a few words, is merely proof that the test "covers" the material. Perhaps we will be able to illustrate a

way of establishing face validity by considering a specific example. Let us assume that of ten lessons in a science unit, four had lesson objectives concerned with the teaching of applications (level 3.00) and that the lessons were planned to accomplish these objectives through laboratory techniques. It would hardly seem consistent for a teacher, wishing to design a test to measure the attainment of these objectives, to make all questions on his test recall questions (level 1.00). The same logic would suggest that a test composed of synthesis questions (level 5.00) would be equally inappropriate. A teacher may establish the content validity of a test by categorizing the questions according to taxonomic scheme such as Bloom's—and thereby demonstrate that indeed his test is measuring at a cognitive level that is congruent with his purposes.

Along another dimension—that of content. Again, consider a teacher devising a test for a unit dealing with a Shakespearean play. Class objectives may have dealt with many aspects of the play—the author, the historical setting, the imagery, the plot, the characters, etc. Clearly a test would not have face validity if it concentrated most of its questions in any one of these important areas. Just as a test should reflect the cognitive level goals that a teacher sets, so it must reflect the content covered in class. A test that meets these objectives is said to have face validity.

Teachers examine the face validity of the tests they write, by making use of a grid described below. On one dimension, the teacher may enter various process dimensions. (Our example has made use of those of the Taxonomy.)

perusal of lesson plans may be of some help in making the determination. Now, if the teacher is planning a 100 item test, the grid suggests that 5 items concern recall of information concerning the causes of the war; 5 items dealing with the facts and figures, etc., of the military campaigns, and so on. A grid such as this one guards against an imbalance in the writing of a test —that would be the case if all the items were dealing with the military campaigns or if all the questions were recall questions. A test such as that may be appropriate in terms of its face validity for a course dealing centrally with the

TABLE 1

|  | Knowledge (per cent) | Comprehension (per cent) | Evaluation (per cent) |
|---|---|---|---|
| Causes of the War | 5 | 10 | 10 |
| Military Campaigns | 5 |  | 10 |
| Life on the Home Front |  |  | 10 |
| International Diplomacy | 5 | 5 | 5 |
| National Politics | 5 |  | 5 |
| Reconstruction | 5 | 10 | 10 |
| Total | 25 | 25 | 50 |

Along a second dimension, content topics and areas of study are listed. Before writing an examination, the teacher may indicate how many questions he wants in every cell of the grid. This decision gives direction for the writing of items. For example, suppose a history unit on the Civil War is the focus of a teacher's concern for writing a test. He may identify the cognitive levels that reflect his teaching purposes and the content areas that he feels received the most emphasis in his teaching. His grid might look as shown in Table 1.

Of course there is nothing magical about the percentages assigned to each cell. Each teacher must decide which content objectives and cognitive objectives most suitably reflect the emphases given in the teaching of the unit. A

remembering of facts and figures of the military campaign, but not for the course reflected in the assignment of percentages in the grid.

Testing is ordinarily considered a chore in teaching. Perhaps the suggestions outlined here might foster renewed interest in classroom testing and help teachers monitor their own teaching decisions through a review of the questions they ask on tests.

**REFERENCES**

1. *Making the Classroom Test: A Guide for Teachers*, 2nd ed., Evaluation and Advisory Service Series No. 4, Princeton, N.J.: Educational Testing Service, 1961.
2. Diederich, Paul B., *Short-cut Statistics for Teacher-made Tests*, 2nd ed., Evaluation and Advisory Service Series No. 5,

Princeton, N.J.: Educational Testing Service, 1960.

3. Wood, Dorothy Adkins, *Test Construction: Development and Interpretation of Achievement Tests.* Columbus, Ohio: Charles E. Merrill Books, Inc., 1961.

# 25

# Interpretation of Test Results

KENNETH F. MCLAUGHLIN

## ERROR ANALYSIS MADE INSIDE THE CLASSROOM

Paul B. Diederich suggests that an error analysis of a test can be done during classroom time by having each pupil *watch* a paper other than his own.[1] If the teacher is only interested in an overall "error analysis," i.e., in how many pupils chose any one of the *wrong* responses to a test question, then the teacher only needs to call out, "Item 1, 'b' is the correct answer. Each of you holding a paper in which item 1 was *missed*, raise your hand." Then he, or a class monitor, can quickly count the raised hands, record the number beside the test question, and proceed to the other questions. Thus, in a few minutes, the items missed by

the greatest number have been identified. After the papers are returned to the students, the teacher can quickly go over those questions which were missed most often and explain why they are incorrect.

## ITEM ANALYSIS METHODS

There are several methods for analyzing objective test results which make it possible to determine one or more of the following points:

1. *Difficulty* of an item—The per cent of the students of the class answering the question correctly.
2. *Discriminating power* of the correct answer —The capacity of an item to distinguish between good and poor students; the per cent of the highest scoring students answering the question correctly as compared with the per cent of the lowest ranking students answering the question correctly.
3. *Effectiveness* of each response for each test item—The *number* of students selecting each response (each response should be chosen at least once).
4. *Identification* of each student making a

Kenneth F. McLaughlin, *Interpretation of Test Results*, Bulletin 1964, No. 7, U.S. Department of Health, Education, and Welfare (Washington, D.C.: Government Printing Office, 1964), pp. 34–46.

[1] Paul B. Diederich, *Short-Cut Statistics for Teacher-Made Tests*, Evaluation and Advisory Service Series, No. 5 (Princeton, N. J.: Educational Testing Service, 1960), p. 3.

correct or incorrect choice for each item—Permits an individually designed corrective procedure for each student.

In a few school systems it is now possible to carry out an item analysis entirely by means of an attachment to a test scoring machine or by the use of automatic data processing equipment. In other schools where such services are not available it may be necessary to use other methods. In fact, much student interest may be aroused by carrying out such procedures during the classroom period when the scored papers are returned. It has been found that pupils at all grade levels, from the primary grades through graduate school, cooperate willingly. The students are interested in learning how many of their peers missed each item, why they made an incorrect choice, and the best answer for each question. If such an analysis has been completed for the teacher's own objective test, he immediately has information which can assist him to improve his test items for future use. He can then build up a test file of items of a known quality and difficulty which will discriminate between his good and poor students.

## "High-Low" Analysis

For some tests the teacher will find it helpful to use the classroom procedure which Diederich calls a "high-low" type of item analysis.[2] This method will reveal both the difficulty and the discriminating power of each item.

To determine the discriminating power of an item, it is necessary to split the class into two sections—those with high scores and those with low scores. The separation point is the middle or median score for the class. To find the median score the following steps are

necessary. Determine the range of scores of the class, that is, the highest and lowest scores, and record them at the top and bottom of the blackboard. Write all possible scores occurring in this interval in a column, beginning with the highest score at the top of the board and continuing to the lowest. Divide the number of class members by two to determine how many papers must be tallied in order to find the middle one. Beginning with the highest score, ask how many students made each score and record the results. As soon as the cumulative total number of papers equals half the class, the middle score can be determined without completing the distribution of scores.

If there are several students' papers at this middle score, collect these papers first. Then collect all papers in two groups—those above the middle score and those below. Distribute all papers above the median score on one side of the room, and those below the median score on the other side. Then assign the several papers with the median score to the high and low sides at random so that the total number of papers on each side is the same. If there should be an odd number of papers in the class so that they cannot be evenly divided, the discarding of the one paper remaining will leave one student to act as a recording monitor at the board.

It is possible to get a certain amount of teamwork in this operation if a captain is appointed for each of the two groups. The teacher, or the class member with no paper, can write the question numbers in a column on the board and make four column headings:

$$H \qquad L \qquad H + L \qquad H - L$$

These headings stand for:

H—the number of the "high" group

[2] *Ibid.*, pp. 3–10.

who mark the item correctly

L—the number of the "low" group who mark the item correctly

H + L—"difficulty index," the total number who marked the item correctly

H − L—"discrimination index," how many more of the "high" group than of the "low" group marked the item correctly

When the teacher asks, "How many have item No. 1 correct?" each student with the correct answer on the paper he is watching raises his hand. The captain of the high group calls his number—the "H" score. The captain of the low group calls his number—the "L" score. These two numbers are written on the board and then the recorder computes and calls out the two scores for "H + L" and "H−L."

These four numbers are always obtained in the same order. Each student writes these four numbers on the answer sheet below each question as it is computed by the board monitor. Each member of the class checks on the sum and difference. With a little practice, Diederich[3] says, this item analysis can be carried out for a one-period test in about 10 to 20 minutes depending on the number of items. This is much faster than the operation could be completed by the teacher. At the same time, an excellent learning situation develops since each student becomes involved in the test results for the class as a whole and wishes to know why he has missed some of the items.

If an item is acceptable for inclusion in later tests, "high-low" differences should be equal to at least 10 per cent of the size of the class.[4] For example, with a class of 36 the differences should be equal to at least 4. However, because of the large value of the "standard error," an item, the "true" difference of which would turn out to be 6, might in some cases give a value of less than 4. In other words, if the difference is small, one should examine the item closely. If it seems to be a well-constructed item, it should be retained. Diederich suggests that "not more than a fifth of the items in the final test should fall below the suggested standard and the *average* high-low difference should be above 10 per cent of the class, preferably 15 per cent or more."[5]

The H + L number, which indicates the total number of students choosing the correct answer, indicates the *difficulty* of the item for the class. The larger the number, the easier the item. In most cases, an item which 90 per cent of the class marks correctly is too easy. On the other hand, if less than 30 per cent of the class marks it correctly, it is probably too difficult.[6]

Occasionally, especially with a teacher-made objective test, a greater number in the low group will obtain the correct answer than in the high group. Then the H − L becomes negative, as in question 4 in Table 1, which is called "negative discrimination." When this occurs, the item needs further investigation. Careful examination of such an item may reveal that a few changes will improve it so that it need not be discarded. To determine what changes are necessary, the teacher might ask each member of the class why he chose one of the incorrect responses, and determine whether or not the key response was poorly written. For example, the correct response of the answer key might not attract the better students if some of the supposed incorrect choices, or distractors, were actually correct. A rewritten item may be placed in the teacher's item file and tried again in a later examination.

---

[3] *Ibid.*, p. 7.
[4] *Ibid.*, p. 8.

[5] *Ibid.*, p. 9.
[6] *Ibid.*, p. 8.

In Table 1 the results of the analysis of several test questions are given for a class with 36 students. Item 1 is an easy

which must be taught again, or if it is referring to an insignificant detail which should not have been included.

TABLE 1
**Examples of High-Low Item Analysis [N = 36]**

| Question | H | L | H + L | H − L |
|----------|-----|-----|-------|-------|
| 1 | 18 | 18 | 36 | 0 |
| 2 | 16 | 4 | 20 | 12 |
| 3 | 13 | 9 | 22 | 4 |
| 4 | 7 | 13 | 20 | −6 |
| 5 | 9 | 7 | 16 | 2 |
| 6 | 5 | 7 | 12 | −2 |
| 7 | 9 | 9 | 18 | 0 |
| 8 | 6 | 2 | 8 | 4 |

item (H + L = 36), since all members of the high and low group marked it correctly. It has the highest possible difficulty index—36—which indicates an easy item. (The lower the H + L score, the more difficult the item.) Since all students in each half marked the correct answer, it certainly will have no influence in discriminating between the high and low groups. Unless one desires to begin the test with an easy item, this item would not be used in another test.

Item 7 is harder than item 1, with a difficulty index of 18. Since H = 9 and L = 9, H − L is 0. Therefore, this item will not discriminate between the two groups and would not be used in its present form.

Item 2 is of average difficulty and is the most discriminating item illustrated, with H − L = 12.

Items 3 and 8 just barely meet the criteria for the level of discrimination (H − L) with the suggested value of 4 (i.e., 10 per cent of 36 is 3.6, which is rounded to 4). Item 8 is more difficult than item 3, as shown by the indices of 8 and 22, respectively. In fact, a test should not include many items as difficult as item 8. The teacher might examine this item to determine whether it is measuring a fundamental concept

Items 4 and 6 are examples of "negative discrimination." More students in the *lower* group selected the right answer than in the upper group. Although the difficulty indices suggest that the items are not easy, these items should be rejected until they are examined and rewritten.

Item 5 is more difficult than questions 1 through 4; however, since the discrimination index is only 2, it would not be used in future tests without some revision.

"ALTERNATE RESPONSE" ANALYSIS

The alternate responses, or choices, prepared for multiple-choice items often include those responses which students have been known to make most often in short-answer or free-response questions. For example, in mathematics or science the most frequent incorrect answer choices are those which would result if common errors were made in arriving at a solution. (In order to prevent a student from spending too much time on a problem, the last choice is often "none of the above.") The teacher may be more interested in the *kinds* of student errors than he is in knowing merely that a certain number of students missed a question. In this situation, the analysis would be carried out in this manner by the teacher: "Question No. 1—How many students selected choice 1?" (pause and record), "How many students selected choice 2?" (pause and record), and so on, for each of the choices for each question. Since in most cases the majority of the class will choose the correct response, the response count takes only a few minutes.

ITEM ANALYSIS BY TEST SCORING MACHINE

If a school system or a school has the IBM 805 Test Scoring Machine, it may have available the attachment called the Graphic Item Counter. This attachment provides one of the quickest and most accurate ways for making an item analysis. After separating the scored test papers into upper and lower groups on the basis of the total test scores, the machine operator can obtain the number of students in each group marking each response to each question. This information can be obtained for 18 5-choice questions at one time, since there are 90 counters available. If 4-choice, 3-choice, or 2-choice questions are asked, one run of the answer sheets through the machine will handle 22, 30, or 45 questions, respectively. If one wishes to learn only how many students answered each question correctly, as many as 90 questions may be analyzed at one time.

The procedures suggested before are for use with a single class or a department in one school. In developing and standardizing a new test, more cases would be needed than those of a single classroom and the procedures should be followed which are described briefly in *Understanding Testing*[7] or

given in detail in *Educational Measurement*.[8] In making an item analysis for a single classroom, it seems appropriate to divide the class into halves—upper half and lower half. If an item analysis is based upon a test administration to 400 or more students, then the upper and lower 27 per cent of the total group will give the best results.

An Item Analysis Sheet can be mimeographed with the headings and form given in Fig. 1. By using legal size paper, it is possible to analyze 10 questions in each column.

The figures for the "No." columns under "Upper Group" and "Lower Group" are obtained directly from the Graphic Item Count Record. The "No." under "Total Group" is the sum of the quantities under "No." in the Upper Group and Lower Group. The per cents are obtained by dividing the recorded numbers by the number in the upper or lower groups and in the total group. An example will make these calculations clear.

Suppose that there are 40 students in a class and the division into halves places 20 students in the Upper Group and 20 students in the Lower Group. In item 1, choice 1 was marked by 15 students in the Upper Group and 5 students in the Lower Group. In the Total Group, 20 (15 plus 5) marked choice 1. Choice 2 was marked by 1 student in the Upper Group and 1 student in the Lower Group which gives a sum of 2 for the Total Group. This procedure continues for each choice for each item in the test.

For rapid computation one can easily construct a table of per cents corresponding to the number of students

[7] Kenneth F. McLaughlin, "How Is a Test Built?" in *Understanding Testing* (Washington,

D.C.: U.S. Government Printing Office, 1962), pp. 4–7. U.S. Office of Education, OE–25003.

[8] Frederick B. Davis, "Item Selection Techniques," in *Educational Measurement* (Washington, D.C.: American Council on Education, 1951), pp. 266–328.

ITEM ANALYSIS SHEET

| Item No. | Choice | Upper group No. | % | Lower group No. | % | TOTAL GROUP No. | % | Item No. | Choice | Upper group No. | % | Lower group No. | % | TOTAL GROUP No. | % |
|---|---|---|---|---|---|---|---|---|---|---|---|---|---|---|---|
| 1 | ①︎ | 15 | 75 | 5 | 25 | 20 | 50 | | 1 | 3 | 15 | 1 | 5 | 4 | 10 |
| | 2 | 1 | 5 | 1 | 5 | 2 | 5 | | 2 | 1 | 5 | 2 | 10 | 3 | 8 |
| | 3 | 3 | 15 | 7 | 35 | 10 | 25 | 11 | 3 | 6 | 30 | 4 | 20 | 10 | 25 |
| | 4 | 1 | 5 | 5 | 25 | 6 | 15 | | 4 | 2 | 10 | 1 | 5 | 3 | 8 |
| | 5 | | | 2 | 10 | 2 | 5 | ✓✓ | ⑤ | 8 | 40 | 12 | 60 | 20 | 50 |
| | 1 | | | | | | | | 1 | | | | | | |
| | ②︎ | 20 | 100 | 18 | 90 | 38 | 95 | | 2 | | | 1 | 5 | 1 | 3 |
| 2 | 3 | | | 1 | 5 | 1 | 3 | 12 ✓ | ③ | 8 | 40 | 6 | 30 | 14 | 35 |
| | 4 | | | | | | | X | 4 | 10 | 50 | 12 | 60 | 22 | 55 |
| | 5 | | | 1 | 5 | 1 | 3 | | 5 | 1 | 5 | | | 1 | 3 |

○ Correct item choice

✓ Item discrimination less than desired

✓✓ "Negative" discrimination

X A "large number" choose the same incorrect choice

Example: Choice 1 is the correct answer for item No.1. 75% of the upper group and 25% of the lower group choose choice 1. These values lie in the 20–80 range, requiring a difference of 15% or more to be acceptable (75–25=50). Therefore, the item underlines{discriminates} satisfactorily. The total group % for the correct answer, choice 1, is 50. Hence the difficulty index is 50%.

Requirements for
Satisfactory Item Discrimination
(for correct choice)

| Range of values (Upper group and lower group) | Difference (Upper group minus lower group) |
|---|---|
| 90–100 | 5 or more |
| 80–90 | 10 or more |
| 20–80 | 15 or more |
| 10–20 | 10 or more |
| 0–10 | 5 or more |

**Fig. 1. Sample Item Analysis Sheet**

in half of the total group, going from 1 (which is 5 per cent) to 20 (which is 100 per cent). Then one fills in the % columns in the item analysis sheet for the Upper Group and Lower Group. (If this is done with a colored pencil, later analysis will be easier. In Fig. 1 the % columns have been shaded.) In item 1 this becomes for choice 1, 75 and 25; for choice 2, 5 and 5; for choice 3, 15 and 35; etc. The sum of the per cents in either of these columns should not exceed 100 by more than 3 per cent, which is the maximum which might occur in some classes because of rounding errors. The total may be less than 100 if one or more students omit a question.

Another table of per cents should be constructed corresponding to the number of students for the total group, in this case going from 1 (which is 2.5 per cent, rounded to 3 per cent) to 40 (which is 100 per cent). Then one fills in the % column under Total Group. (One can save these tables and develop new ones as they are needed when class size changes—because of absences at test time or changes of class size in a new school year.)

It has been shown in the literature that the test best able to put a class of students in rank order is one which has item difficulties spread over most of the range, but which has an average item difficulty of 50 per cent, with the greatest number clustering about 50 per cent.

As the next step, examine each test item in figure 1 and code it as suggested: A circle (O) around the correct answer choice; no further mark if the item appears satisfactory; a single check ($\checkmark$) if the item discrimination is less than desired; a double check ($\checkmark\checkmark$) if there is negative discrimination; and an "X" if a "large number" select the same incorrect choice.

In item 1 the correct answer is choice 1; 75 per cent of the Upper Group and 25 per cent of the Lower Group marked it correctly. Since there is a difference of 50 per cent (75 minus 25), which is much greater than the suggested minimum difference of 15 per cent, this item discriminates satisfactorily and would be a good one to include in future tests —if its other responses are satisfactory. Each of the other choices was operating since each was chosen at least once by some member of the class.

Item 2, with choice 2 as the correct one is an easy item—95 per cent of the total group of students marked it correctly. The *larger* the per cent the *easier* the item. The item does discriminate satisfactorily at this level, since there is a difference of 10 per cent (100 minus 90). Choices 1 and 4 should

be reexamined, since no one chose them. Some test constructors believe that a few easy items of this difficulty level at the beginning of a test helps to put the examinees at ease. Almost every student's score is raised one point by such an item and his relative rank may not be changed at all when one considers the complete test.

Item 11, the number of the item at the top of the second column in the Item Analysis Sheet, shows that each choice was selected by some of the students. The double check ($\checkmark\checkmark$) indicates that there is a "negative discrimination" with this item, which means that more students in the Lower Group chose the keyed answer than in the Upper Group. As a result, one obtains a discrimination index of minus 20 per cent (40 minus 60). This item does not assist in ranking the students in the proper order, but rather makes the rankings less dependable. The difficulty index, as shown in the Total Group % column is 50 per cent, the same as item 1—but this item 11 should *not* be used. One should examine items of this type to be sure that one has not made an error in developing the answer key. Because of rounding the Total Group % for all choices is 101.

Item 12 is an example of a question which does not discriminate at the desired level of 15 per cent but only 10 per cent (40 minus 30). However, if reconsideration of the item shows that it is a good item and important to the course, retain it. Choice 1 should be changed—it was so poor that no one selected it. Choices 2 and 5 are chosen by only one student each and are much weaker than choice 4. Choice 4 must be considered, since it has been marked with an "X." Why did so many students in both the Upper and Lower Groups select it? Is it the statement of a commonly accepted fallacy? Is it so ambiguous that in one sense it may really be correct? Does this question cover a basic part of the course which needs reteaching? Has this question been keyed properly? If choice 4 should be determined to be correct rather than choice 3, then one would have "negative discrimination" as in question 11. Since one student in each group omitted the question the Total Group % is 96.

Comments should be made concerning test items omitted by the student. As one becomes experienced in examining an Item Analysis Sheet, he quickly becomes aware of the few items which many students failed to answer because of the low numbers in the Total Group % column. If the test is timed, these items would come, in most cases, near the end of the test. If they occur randomly throughout the test, the teacher should examine the lesson plans to be certain that they have been previously covered—and then reteach them if necessary.

When the item analysis has been completed, a summary table of marks may be made of the number of single or double checks or X's. As one becomes more skillful in constructing one's own tests and using again items which have been tried out and found successful he will discover the number of marks diminishing. However, it will be a rare occasion when, for any given class, there will be no marks. This would also be true of standardized tests which can be analyzed in a similar manner in order to discover the weak points and errors in thinking of the students.

If each item used on a test is typed or pasted on a separate card, cataloged as to topic, and the aforementioned kinds of information concerning discrimination and difficulty recorded, it is possible to build a pool of *good* items which can be used in later classes. By recording when the item is used, the repetition of the same items in succeeding terms or years can be avoided. If the foregoing analysis shows that an item is poor, it should not be used unless it is rewritten.

### ITEM ANALYSIS BY TYPEWRITER

If a teacher wishes to make an item analysis himself, he can speed up the procedure by using what is called the "typewriter method." This method will be described in detail.

After sorting the papers in order, according to their scores, highest to the lowest, divide the papers into two halves at the median, as described previously for the "High-Low" Analysis. Select the pile of answer sheets for the "high" group first, still arranged with the highest score on top. Sit at a typewriter and select any set of five keys—if five-choice multiple-choice items have been used. For example, one might choose to use the keys on the typewriter with the letters or symbols at the "home position" for the right hand corresponding as follows:

| Answer choice | 1 | 2 | 3 | 4 | 5 |
|---|---|---|---|---|---|
| Typewriter key | j | k | l | ; | ¢ |

If a student omits an item, then strike the space bar.

Beginning with the paper of the first student with the highest score under the left hand use a finger to guide down the answer column question by question. In typing with the right hand one will feel uncertain for the first two or three papers but will soon establish a typing pattern. For example, the teacher looks at the response to question 1, observes that choice 2 was selected, and types "k"; for question 2 he observes that the student selected the last, or fifth, choice, so he types "¢"; for question 3, with choice 1 indicated type "j"; question 4 was omitted, so one uses the "space bar";

for question 5, with choice 3, type "l"; for question 6, with choice 4, type ";"; for question 7, with choice 1, type "j" as in question 3, etc. This procedure should be continued until a symbol or space has been made for one response for each item for a single student on the same line. One may also type the student's name, if desired. The responses for 30 items, including the seven above, might look like this with an extra space following

question 15 being included as a tallying aid:

k𝑒j l;jlklj;lkj ;k𝑒j;kljk𝑒;jklj

The next highest test paper of the "high" group should be recorded in the same manner on the second line (do not double-space). This routine should be continued until the responses to each question for each paper in the "high" group have been recorded. Thus, the responses of every student to

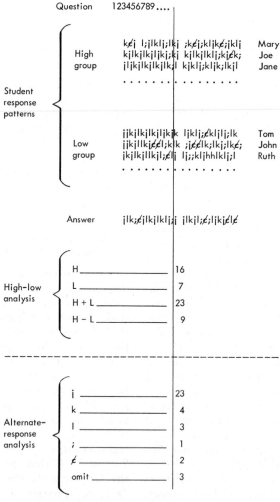

Fig. 2. Sample of an Item Analysis by Typewriter with a Detailed Analysis of Item 15 [N = 36]

each question are always in the *same* vertical column, one below the other. At the end of the "high" group, triple-space and proceed in the same manner for the "low" group.

Experience has shown that it is sometimes helpful to space systematically for each paper as one records letters for the answers. For example, if regular IBM answer sheets are used, space after items which are multiples of 15, i.e., after items 15, 30, 45, 60, etc. If answer sheets designed for a specific standardized test are used, the spacing will vary. If one uses an answer sheet of his own construction, an appropriate place to space might be at the end of each column of answers. This provides a visual check for the end of each group of questions. If the teacher's own answer sheet has been keyed with the correct responses, double-space and type it in the same relative position below the answer rows for the "high" and "low" groups.

Figure 2 shows part of an Item Analysis by Typewriter for 30 questions, with details for question 15. Note the separation of the "high" and "low" groups and that "H" and "L" are in the same order, from top to bottom, as the groups at the top of Fig. 2. A straightedge placed on the paper vertically and

to the left or right of each question's responses permits a rapid count of the number of responses for each group which are the same as that of the answer key. The interpretations made previously for the "High-Low" Analysis now apply.

At the bottom of Fig. 2 it is shown that with this typewritten method it is also possible to make the "alternate response" analysis by adding a row for each possible response choice below the "High-Low" Analysis. One counts and records the number of responses for each choice or omitted item. One can then discover the most common errors of the class.

This method can also be used to give error analysis information. With the vertical straightedge in position it is possible to circle or underline in red the incorrect responses. Since each row corresponds to a single student, individual help can be given as needed to each student on the specific topics or areas covered by each item.

In other words, with a little preplanning and with *one* handling of the test papers it is possible to use this typewriter method to derive a great amount of useful information. Other kinds of interpretations will suggest themselves as one uses this technique.

# 26

# Evaluation in Social Sciences

HARRY D. BERG

## THE USE OF TESTS IN INSTRUCTION

Tests are intended to evaluate the outcomes of instruction. The kinds of questions discussed in this chapter, then, will be most valid if the learnings and skills needed to deal with them are subjects of instruction. When emphasis on note taking in the classroom is followed by the thought type of examinations, the results will be destructive of student morale and disquieting to the teacher. Thought-provoking classroom discussions followed by memory tests will cause students to refrain from discussion in favor of listening for the instructor's remarks and explanations. Neither is good educational practice. Instruction and evaluation should reinforce each other.

This chapter does not intend to go into methods of instruction. How-ever, it should not be presumptuous to point out a few ways in which test items and exercises, themselves, may be used for nontesting purposes. Such procedure is particularly valid if the testing materials come close to defining the behavior we are interested in developing.

A common practice is to discuss a test in class as soon after giving it as possible. (It would be most desirable, of course, if students could learn of their errors at the time of making them. But without special devices this is not feasible.) Motivation is usually high, and if the test has been made up of thought items a good deal of learning can be expected to take place. A thought item, incidentally, might be defined as one which is worth discussing in class after testing.

Test items can also be used profitably for nongrading purposes at the time a topic is being discussed. The value of this procedure can be increased if the students are given study questions geared to the item exercises. In such cases the latter might be used as a study self-check.

Harry D. Berg, "Evaluation in Social Sciences," in *Evaluation in Higher Education*, ed. Paul L. Dressel and Associates (Boston: Houghton Mifflin Company, 1961), pp. 109–11. Reprinted by permission.

A more formalized method of diagnosing student difficulties for instructional purposes involves the use of a 5″ × 8″ index card on which the student is to record the reasons for selecting a particular answer to an objective test item. In effect, the item becomes the subject of an essay—a device occasionally appropriate for use in essay tests. The student's response may then be evaluated as indicated below. The technique is also useful in revising items for future use.

Name_____ Date_____
Question No._____Choice 1 2 3 4 5
               (Circle one)
Reasons for choice (Use back of card if necessary.)

The completed cards may be scored in terms of four categories:

1. R-R. These cards have the correct answers and the students' justifications are sound (right answer—right reasoning).
2. R-W. These cards have the correct answers, but the described reasoning is weak or wholly irrelevant and could not have led to the choice of the correct answer (right answer—wrong reasoning).
3. W-R. These cards have incorrect answers, but seemingly the reasoning is sound. In other words, looking at the reasoning alone would lead one to

believe that the student had reasoned well and should have chosen the correct answer (wrong answer—right reasoning).
4. W-W. These cards have incorrect answers and the reasoning is wholly inappropriate (wrong answer—wrong reasoning).

These results are useful for class discussion as well as for instructional planning.

**SUMMARY**

Instruction and testing are sometimes viewed as dichotomous, with instruction being devoted to providing answers and the student's mastery being later determined by questions directly pointing to the answers already provided. Instruction should be aimed at development of student abilities to relate knowledge to problem situations, and testing should both encourage this development and determine whether and to what extent it has taken place. The number and scope of social science problems in the world today to which such ability is both relevant and necessary are sufficient reason to orient instruction to the objectives and approaches to them suggested in this chapter.

# 27

# Levels of Questioning

## RICHARD L. CARNER

Miss Brown, the third grade teacher, finished her lecture on Columbus and pointed to the words printed in two neat rows on the chalkboard.

"When you write your compositions about Columbus these lists will help you spell any of the words you don't know."

A bright-eyed blonde girl, obviously bursting with some information or question about Columbus, eagerly waved her hand in the teacher's direction. She had already raised her hand twice during the lecture only to be ignored. Miss Brown looked at the girl and said, "I'm sorry, Nancy, we don't have any time for questions this morning."

At this point it occurred to me that none of the other children had asked any questions about Columbus nor had there been any discussion between the teacher and pupils.

"Before we write our compositions

Richard L. Carner, "Levels of Questioning," *Education* (May 1963), pp. 546–50. Copyright ©1963 by The Bobbs-Merrill Company, Inc., Indianapolis, Indiana. Reprinted by permission.

for today," continued the teacher, "I want each of you to tell me something he has learned about Columbus."

By the time the first row had finished it was apparent that each pupil had gone through this same procedure many times. The facts gushed forth in an incredibly monotonous fashion as twenty-four little tape recorders parroted the teacher's lecture.

"Columbus sailed to America in 1492."

"Columbus was born in Genoa."

"There were three ships, the 'Nina,' the 'Pinta,' and the, uh—" Robert furtively searched the chalkboard for his answer, "the 'Santa Maria.'"

In spite of the fact that there had been errors in the statements made by some of the pupils, there was no attempt to correct or question, or discuss any aspect of this historic voyage. After the last pupil had said something about Columbus, each child went to work immediately upon his composition.

Lunch time was at hand when they were completed and I was invited to examine them. With much pride, Miss Brown pointed out how neatly they were written. What she did not point out was that eighteen of the twenty-four compositions had the same title and that most of them were mere lists of unorganized facts which had been dutifully regurgitated by the pupils. There was little or no evidence of creativity in the pupils' writing and certainly limited evidence that they had done any critical thinking about the importance of Columbus' voyage to the new world.

In subsequent observations in this and other classrooms in the system, it became increasingly apparent that reading followed the same pattern where ability to indicate the "facts" was accepted as evidence that thinking had taken place.

## THE TEACHER'S ERRORS

The majority of teachers today could quickly enumerate the classical errors made by Miss Brown.

First, she had equated rote memory with understanding and the development of lasting and useful concepts.

Second, she has assumed that communication input is a passive act with no need for questioning, discussion, or clarification.

Third, and perhaps most important, Miss Brown was blithely unaware that she was contributing to the development of uncritical minds which were conditioned to readily and easily accept all information without question.

Fourth, there was no evidence of teacher-pupil planning or a mutual understanding of the purpose for the lecture beyond that of writing the daily composition.

Fifth, the compositions provided evidence that creativity and originality had been stifled and sacrificed in the

concern for reproducing the facts.

While this particular classroom is not fictional, it and others like it are rapidly becoming extinct simply because teachers are keenly aware of the importance of developing thinking skills from the very first day a pupil enters school.

One of the major avenues through which we can help guide and shape pupils' thinking is by recognizing the importance of proper questioning and that pupils must be taught how to question themselves to stimulate more productive thinking. However, questioning *is* an art and will be most effective when the teacher understands the thought processes through which the learner must progress in a given learning situation.

## TEACHER–PUPIL ROLES

The teacher's role in developing the thinking skills of her pupils must be an active one. First, she must understand better the thinking processes that are required in a given learning situation.

For example, if children read about an arithmetic principle, the verbs *speculate, guess,* or *imagine* would not be as germane as *recall, associate,* and *generalize.* In making functional use of a principle in an actual mathematical problem one would find the words *hypothesize, deduce, solve,* and *verify* to be of value, whereas *orient, observe, regard,* or *deliberate* would be less appropriate in the thinking process.

The same thing is true with all other areas of learning where certain specific modes of behavior or thinking best describe the processes through which an individual must progress in order to solve a problem successfully. Consequently, it is necessary for teachers to decide which *types* of thinking are required before questions can be asked which will channel the thinking process in the right direction.

Another aspect of the problem concerns the pupil himself and is, in the long run, perhaps the most important consideration of all. It is one thing to be able to respond to questions posed by the teacher but quite another to question one's self independently about the material being read.

Since there is little doubt that questioning activates the thinking processes, it is evident that mature, critical reading depends upon the ability to ask the proper question at the proper time. The ability to ask these vital questions does not occur automatically and, consequently, children must be taught how to ask questions at the various levels and how limited or extensive the answers may be.

In addition to asking questions directly related to the reading material, pupils should learn also to ask (and answer) such basic questions as:

"What is my purpose for reading this book, article, or story?"

"What type of reading material is it —narrative, expository, or technical, etc."

"What is the most effective way to deal with this material in terms of its type and my purpose in reading it?"

## LEVELS OF QUESTIONING

Although questions may be asked across ·an entire spectrum, from concrete to highly abstract, there is a notable tendency to overemphasize the kind of question which is readily supported by the facts or details to be found in the reading. While stressing these questions reduces controversy, it also has the unfortunate result of limiting the opportunity to develop higher-level thinking skills which are so important in critical reading. Consequently, teachers need to be more conscious of the level of question which is most suited to a particular reading or learning situation.

### LEVEL I—CONCRETE

The type of questions used at this level usually elicit responses which are characteristic of concrete thinking where there is a primary concern for observable, tangible, or obtainable details. In this kind of thinking one is dealing with relatively simple ideas, objects, processes, or concepts which most often do not require evaluation, judgment, or drawing conclusions. As a result, the learner's role in this type of thinking is that of absorbing the details or particular properties of a specific learning situation within a rather narrow context.

Teachers who limit their questions to *where, what, who, when* limit the possible answers to place, fact, person, or time. "Where was Mary?" "What was Mary doing?" "What color sweater was Mary wearing?" "Who was wearing the red sweater?" or "When did Mary return home?" are frequently the only kind of probing that the teacher does to evaluate comprehension. This "stick-to-the-facts" approach, if used exclusively, tends to reinforce the kind of reading which fails to penetrate beyond the literal meaning and which depends mainly upon the rote memory processes.

Teachers should not infer that Level I questions do not constitute a legitimate means to assess understanding of what is read. There are many occasions when specific, concrete anwers are desirable and necessary. For example, reading which is primarily concerned with following directions depends upon a concrete step-by-step understanding. Therefore, questions which focus upon specifics at each step are needed simply because the desired end result will not follow without comprehending the details and their sequence.

LEVEL II—ABSTRACT

The kind of questions asked at this level aid in the development of abstract thinking skills and require pupils to go beyond the specific or detail level of comprehension in order to generalize, classify, or relate these specifics into meaningful patterns. Since this is the case, teachers must be sure that their questions do not freeze pupils on one level while their expectancy for pupils' comprehension is one another.

Questions which are designed to elicit abstract thinking should lead the pupil to explore the "hows" and "whys" of a problem as well as the "whats."

If the question, "How are the economies and cultures of the Laplanders and Eskimos alike?" is asked, it is necessary for the pupil to do more than recite facts since he must select the likenesses as well as reject the differences. This is an obvious aid in the development of concepts because the pupil must classify or categorize the common elements of the two societies.

An answer to "Why are their cultures similar?" makes possible a generalization or principle which may have utility value whenever the pupil deals with a similar problem.

Thus it can be seen that *how* questions often relate to specific facts and that *why* questions force the attention to cause-and-effect relationships.

To ask a contractor, "How did you build this church?" might yield a complex of concrete details. But the question, "Why did you build this church?" would result in exposing the cause-and-effect relationships existing in the aesthetic values held by the contractor as well as other motivational forces which influenced his decision to build the kind of church he did.

Other Level II questions which the teacher may ask are specifically designed to promote certain kinds of abstract thinking. These questions would aid pupils in:

1. *Perceiving relationships* which exist among (1) discrete facts, (2) characters in a story, (3) past and current events, (4) spatially oriented objects such as homes, planets, and countries, and (5) situations.

2. *Sensing continuity and sequence* in events, plots, argumentation in support of opinion, and logical solutions to problems.

3. *Making inferences* about an author's purposes for writing, the things which motivate the characters in a story, or possible reasons why certain situations exist.

4. *Drawing sound conclusions* based upon both their own experience and a thorough understanding of the implications and facts which they have read.

5. *Evaluating* the validity of an author's argument or opinion through an examination of his reasoning or by making a comparison with other sources of information.

LEVEL III—CREATIVE

Questions which are asked at this level require answers which are more creative by nature and may demand both concrete and abstract thinking. It should be kept in mind that one of the major characteristics of creative thinking is the reorganization of concepts into novel patterns. In the hierarchy of questions it is possible to ask, teachers have been most reluctant to probe the creative realms where answers are not comfortingly right or wrong.

An open-end type question is most effectively used where a less rigidly structured answer is expected. Questions which begin, "What would happen if—" have been successful in stimulating creative thinking since it places no pressure on the individual to give "correct" answers. Instead, the pupil is free to explore all ramifications of a problem such as what possible results, limitations, or advantages there would be in altering an original situation.

To stimulate creative thinking, the teacher can follow up the reading of a story by asking such questions as "What do you think would have happened in the story if Billy were older? Younger? Stronger? Weaker?"

Such questions can also be used in content areas such as science to enable pupils to hypothesize new or different applications of principles learned. The question, "What other uses could be made of this (process, instrument, or machine)?" opens up many possible answers because it does not restrict the pupil to a specific context.

This type of thinking lies at the heart of scientific inquiry and must be encouraged from the beginning of formal education. What better result can there be from teaching science than to cause pupils to *think* like scientists?

## SUMMARY

Since children come to school with a seemingly inexhaustible supply of questions, every effort should be made to teach them to sharpen and focus these "whys" as an aid to thinking. Miss Brown's remark, "We don't have any time for questions," is both a contradiction and a denial of a desirable outcome of good teaching.

The evidence that good teaching has taken place is reflected more in the kinds of questions pupils ask than in the abundance of pat answers they can produce. Only when teachers and pupils understand and use better techniques of questioning as part of the reading process will each pupil's real potential be achieved.

## REFERENCES

1. Carner, Richard L., "Concepts—The Alpha and Omega of Reading," *The Allyn and Bacon Reading Bulletin*, No. 107. Boston: Allyn & Bacon, Inc., 1961.
2. Lorge, Irving, "The Teacher's Task in the Development of Thinking," *The Reading Teacher*, XIII (February 1960).
3. Russell, David, *Children's Thinking*. Boston: Ginn and Company, 1956.
4. Stauffer, Russell G., "Children Can Read and Think Critically," *Education*, LXXX (May 1960), 522-25.

# 28

# Grading Alternatives

JOHN R. PANCELLA

One of the paradoxes of the teaching profession is that almost every teacher can intuit which students are really good, which are really poor, and which are mediocre. Therefore a problem arises in grading tests, because the mores of the teacher-student relationship almost forbid a teacher to make grade assignments on an intuitive basis. Classroom ethics demand that teachers consider more than their intuition in handing out rewards and punishments. The guidelines for this procedure are based on more than mere whimsy or circumstance. There is a great deal of evidence in support of the idea that as teachers make public their criteria for distributing rewards and punishments, anxiety levels are lower and children seem to learn more effectively. The question, then, is not so much whether one method of distributing grades is better than another, but rather, whether students understand the methods that the teacher is planning to use. This section will include a brief résumé of several alternatives a teacher may consider for assigning grades to students.

1. One way to grade is to mark according to fixed percentages selected in advance. For instance, 90 per cent and above is A, 80–89 per cent is B, and so on. The scores of other pupils are not considered as a basis for comparison. Each student competes against a fixed standard. This method is used quite often by teachers in schools and colleges; however, it has several serious drawbacks. First, the difference between an 89 and a 90 may be small compared to the standard error (precision) of the test, and yet vastly different grades will be assigned unfairly and invalidly to pupils receiving those scores. Secondly, there is nothing magical about 90 per cent alone. The question "90 per cent of what" directs us to examine the test itself. How difficult were the items and how strictly was the key applied to the students' answers? Almost any teacher in any situation can write a test that everyone will pass or that everyone will fail. This means that the rigid standards of 90 per cent, etc. are not so rigid but merely reflect a flexibility in writing tests rather than in assigning grades.

**187**

2. A second means of grading which is just as arbitrary as that discussed above, but which gives the illusion of being quite sophisticated is the "normal" curve technique. This procedure assumes that the class reflects ability grouping similar to the distribution of intelligence in the general population. More specifically, the assumption asserts that there are few students in the class in the A and F categories; more students in each of the B and D categories; and most of the students fall in the C range. A teacher calculates the standard deviation[1] of the distribution of test scores and assigns grades on a basis similar to this:

A—Mean plus 1 1/2 standard deviation units

B—Mean plus 1/2 standard deviation units

C—Mean plus and minus 1/2 standard deviation units

D—Mean minus 1/2 standard deviation units

F—Mean minus 1 1/2 standard deviation units

This procedure almost always assumes someone is going to get A and someone is going to fail. The basis for assigning grades is one of comparing one student's achievement with the class record. This method would suggest that two students with identical achievement levels assigned to two different classes might end up with completely different grades. This would occur if one student was in a "bright" section while the other student was in a "slow" section. The latter student's score would look good in comparison to his student colleagues, whereas the first student's grade might

[1] See Paul B. Diederich, *Short-Cut Statistics for Teacher-Made Tests* (Princeton, N.J.: Educational Testing Service, 1960), pp. 19–20, for suggestions for calculating the standard deviation of a distribution.

suffer when compared to his fellow students.

3. Another method for assigning grades incorporates aspects of both of those previously mentioned. It consists of placing the raw scores of a test along a continuum. Teachers using this procedure make two decisons. First, where are there significant enough gaps between scores to draw lines distinguishing students who deserve one level of grade and those deserving another level? Second, once the lines have been drawn, which letter grade will be assigned each group recognized by the gap-scanning (see Table 1)? It is possible for a teacher to decide that while he recognizes three groups, they achieved so well he will label the groups A+, A and A—. On another test, he may feel that the performance was particularly weak, and he might assign only C, D, and F grades to the group.

Nothing in this paragraph is meant to imply that this procedure is strictly objective. It is our contention that all methods are subjective—with the subjective element taking effect in various dimensions of the testing-grading process. Some subjectivity enters into the writing of the test in the first alternative mentioned, specifically, at the level of judging the quality of work the various groups represent. Teachers using this method must plan their tests in such a way that the middle person in the group gets approximately 50 per cent of the test correct. Only if this condition is met will the gaps between groups be wide enough to allow teachers to draw meaningful distinctions between groups. We are assuming that the purposes of tests of this sort are essentially for the assigning of grades.

In sum, no method is foolproof or perfectly objective. We hope that someday teachers will be able to lay

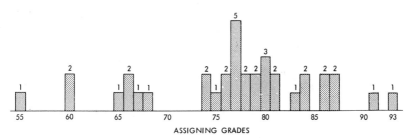

ASSIGNING GRADES

**Table 1.**

aside the impossible task of labeling students' work with A's or B's while they continue to describe the quality of a student's work in grosser and perhaps more valid ways, e.g., pass and fail. Until that time, teachers need to know the assumptions underlying the grading system they are using and to be aware of the importance of making their system public to their students.

# 29

# Marks on Term Papers in the Liberal Arts

## ARNOLD M. ROTHSTEIN

It has been said that ". . . the ideal training for the ideal citizen [is a] good sound liberal education."[1] To provide ideal training requires, in the first place, liberal teachers. Unfortunately, according to one view, the education of teachers "is corrupted by a curriculum, a program of pedagogy which is a methodology of teaching."[2]

The implication here is that exposure to a liberal arts curriculum will have a broadening and liberating effect. This investigation attempted to explore how this effect is achieved.

A professor's assignments often reflect his conception of course purpose(s). Accordingly, markings by professors on term papers which *they* had assigned were examined, with a view to ascertaining the relationship between the assignments and the purposes of the liberal arts course.

Thirty-six undergraduate term papers from the humanities, natural sciences, and social sciences were read and carefully analyzed.[3] The students received eight A's, twenty-two B's, five C's, and one P (passing). If one considers B a good grade, at least 80 per cent of the papers were rated as good, while *no* paper was rated as poor. The professors' markings and comments were catalogued and tabulated. Fifty-three per cent of a total of 329 markings related to mechanics of writing: spelling, punctuation, grammar, and usage; 28 per cent consisted of value statements

Arnold M. Rothstein, "Marks on Term Papers in the Liberal Arts," *Journal of Teacher Education*, XVI, No. 2 (June 1965), 249–50. Reprinted by permission of the publisher.

[1] Center for the Study of Democratic Institutions, "The University—An Interview with A. Whitney Griswold, President of Yale University" (New York: Fund for the Republic, 1961), p. 21.

[2] *Ibid.*, p. 14.

[3] The papers were written by thirty-six students and marked by thirty-six different professors. Twenty-five students were from a private liberal arts college in a metropolitan area and eleven were from a public liberal arts institution in the same area. Seventeen sophomores, eleven juniors, five freshmen, and three seniors produced seventeen papers for courses in the humanities, thirteen for courses in the social sciences, and six for courses in the natural sciences.

such as "Good," "Weak," "Tighten your organization," "Improve your style," "Be less superficial," "Reveal yourself more"; 13 per cent endorsed or questioned the assertions of the students; 5 per cent dealt with matters of form and style. Commentary tended to be profuse when the professor disagreed with the student or appeared to be justifying his assignment of a particular grade. Both markings and commentary appeared to be used merely as a record of achievement symbolized by the letter grade.

In assaying what further work could have been done on the papers, they were subjected to detailed analysis.[4] Altogether, 1,558 additional markings might have been made which would have called attention to thinking processes.

The papers were coded according to the following scheme.[5]

1. Attributive statements were identified—those which ascribed or imputed motivation or feeling to another.
2. Extreme statements were marked—superlatives, all, none, always, never.
3. Generalities were scored—people, we, they, Negroes, groups, nations.
4. Qualifying statements were checked—maybe, perhaps, might, probably.
5. If-then hypotheses were identified, e.g., "If I didn't see them, they weren't there."
6. *Or* statements were identified—"There are only two possibilities," the polarization of issues into two values.
7. Analogies were underscored—just as, like, the same as, you might as well say.

It is significant that the range of

ratios of possible markings to actual markings was from 2:1 to 100:1, with a mean potential of nearly 5:1. Under the coding analysis for expressions relating to thinking processes, *no* paper had less than a total of seven markings. In contrast, in the tabulation of the markings of the professors (excluding the letter grade), twenty-one of the thirty-six papers contained less than a total of seven markings, and five of the twenty-one contained no markings at all.

The writer has employed the system of coding papers indicated herein with much success in several undergraduate courses. Parts of the system are gradually introduced until, over the period of a semester, students are able to react to the entire system. The writer has found it provides students with an opportunity to analyze what they say, to uncover their assumptions, and to draw inferences therefrom. They get a chance to reflect on and react to what they have written. From student reactions in general, an impression has been received that little attention has been given in previous training to the forms of thinking. To be sure, teachers claim that they teach students to think,[6] but one can only wonder *how.* For example, it would be instructive to know how the hortatory injunctions, "Improve your style" and "Reveal yourself more," actually help the student to think.

Should the mechanics of writing, form and style, the writer's assertions—what the professors looked for in the papers—not have been looked for? Without doubt, these matters deserve attention. The question is rather what else might have been looked for. More than 50 per cent of the investigator's markings identified extreme statements, found in all but one of the papers

---

[4] Each paper was read three times: once for general comprehension and twice for distinctive analysis, the cataloguing of the professors' markings, and the coding scheme used by the investigator.

[5] Acknowledgment of indebtedness is made to Louis E. Raths, distinguished professor of education, Newark State College, who developed the scheme.

[6] Thinking involves several mental processes.

studied, and attributive statements, found in all but two. Here was potential for instruction.[7]

The implications of language for revealing the mental processes of students dare not be overlooked, and a means is here proposed whereby an assignment is not terminated, either for professor or student, merely because a grade has been recorded. Exhortations, such as "Improve your thinking," are relegated to the scrap heap; instead markings are used which lay the exercise open to further analysis and reflection to provide practice in using important mental processes.

Objections and criticisms may be anticipated. Admittedly, the investigation is limited in scope and method, but it can serve as a springboard for future exploration. Some may object that the thirty-six professors did not mark papers very well, that this may be *just* an indication of poor teaching. Another criticism might point to purpose: The investigator analyzed the papers in one way and the professors in another. It might also be argued that concern with mental processes as such provides the structure for an entire course, probably logic or composition. But should not *all* courses have logic? At least one professor of logic believes it is precisely because schools do not emphasize thinking that we need courses in logic.[8] Moreover, compartmentalization is not a little to blame for the student's seeing spelling and punctuation as belonging within the confines of the appropriate course—

"Spelling counts only in the spelling course." The perversity of student nature being what it is, could one hope for transfer of grandiose proportions if logic courses were made mandatory? Is it not likely that student reaction would be—"Thinking counts only in the thinking course?"

The criticism of the liberal arts champion contains an implied objection to the investigation. Referring to the need for gifted teachers, he states: ". . . the solution to the problem of an adequate number of properly trained teachers in the universities lies first in the change of the curriculum for the training of high school teachers."[9] The question is, How is the curriculum to be changed?

The common conception of curriculum views it as organization of content: the means by which the content is disseminated is considered subsidiary. And so, traditionally, curricular revision has been seen as augmenting, deleting, or shifting of the content. A curriculum is made liberal by widening the number and scope of course offerings; rarely is change in method conceived of as a means of liberalizing.

As one examines the way in which the term papers were marked by the professors, one can see that their teaching practices reflect more of a parochializing effect than an encouragement of thoughtfulness. On the other hand, the analysis undertaken by the investigator, requiring a shift not in content but in method, has a liberalizing effect, with autonomy as a distinct goal.

The investigation tends to reaffirm what has long been known. It is not the specific course nor the specific content within a course that is crucial.

[7] Perhaps we all need training in differentiating between what is observational and what is inferential; confusion of the ascriptive and the descriptive is often the hallmark of the undisciplined. Upon momentary reflection, the symbiotic nature of certain ways of speaking (thinking) and prejudice becomes evident.

[8] Cynthia Schuster, "Can We Teach the High School Student to Think?" *Educational Research Bulletin* No. 37 (April 1958).

[9] Center for the Study of Democratic Institutions, *op. cit.*, p. 15.

What is all-important is the quality of the work pursued.[10] Teaching practices determine to a significant degree whether effects shall be parochial or liberal. There may be faith that a liberal arts course broadens, releases, and emancipates, but some evidence should be forthcoming that the liberalizing *effect* is distinct from method, that it depends upon *arts* which are liberal and not upon a teacher who is liberal.

[10] Lamar Johnson, "Criteria for Defining New Type Courses," *School and Society*, XLII (September 14, 1935); Lawrence A. Lowell, "College Studies and Professional Training," *Educational Review*, XLII (October 1911). President Lowell pointed out that it made little difference what specific courses were taken in preparation for advanced study, since transfer of the knowledge was questionable, but that it did matter whether attention was paid to mental processes, the skills of which could be transferred widely.

# ACTIVITIES

1. What are some testing and grading techniques you may use in your teaching?

2. What are some ways you may monitor your testing and grading?

3. Categorize each of the following according to Bloom's Taxonomy. (Suggested answers follow.) Also, try out the category systems suggested by the Fox article and the Carner article included in this section.

a. List five reasons why the assembly-line method of manufacture is so widely used by American industry.

b. The "initiative," "referendum," and "recall" were incorporated into state constitutions primarily during the:
   - (a) New Deal
   - (b) Progressive era
   - (c) Civil War
   - (d) Jacksonian era

c. Briefly outline relations between America and Mexico over Texas to 1836.

d. What are the implications in the case of the Charles River Bridge vs. Warren Bridge (1837)?

e. You turned four pieces of work 8″ long between centers, and all pieces showed a taper on the end nearest the tailstock. In order to correct this inaccuracy (eliminate the taper) you should adjust the taper attachment:
   - (a) away from you
   - (b) toward you
   - (c) to your left
   - (d) to your right

f. What were the proslavery arguments? Were they realistic?
   - (a) historical justification
   - (b) scriptural justification
   - (c) benefits whites and Negroes alike
   - (d) economic advantages of the institution
   - (e) necessary to the Southern way of life

g. Evaluate the qualities of agar as a culture medium for growing bacteria.

h. What disadvantages could you see in using live animals as "cultivating media" for growing bacteria?

**194**

i. Would these disadvantages outweigh the advantages? Why?

j. Why can bacteria be used in industry?

k. In 1795 the Conspiracy of Equals led by one Grachus Babeuf failed badly and would earn little more than a mention in a history of the Revolution except that, in retrospect, Babeuf appears as the first modern exponent of what system? Can you see this system in operation today?

l. In your opinion what were the six most important political and social features brought about by the French Revolution?

m. The fight for American independence has been called a revolution, an international war, and a civil war. Which one of these three interpretations do you agree with, and why? I will accept any answer if you can give valid reasons for your choice.

n. Do you feel that the treatment received by the Loyalist from the Colonist was fair or unfair? State your reasons. I will accept any answer if it is well thought out and substantiated.

o. What suggestion would you make to help spur the feudal economy most?

p. Which of the following can be concluded from Jefferson's "principles of government?"

    (a) Honest friendship with all nations rules out the necessity of entangling alliances.

    (b) State governments should have the supreme power in dealing with foreign countries.

    (c) All men are equal in the eyes of the law of the land.

    (d) None of the above.

q. Match the following:

| | |
|---|---|
| Peaceable Coercion | Embargo Act |
| Continental System | Charles Pinckney |
| Election of 1800 | Louisiana Purchase |
| Election of 1804 | Thomas Pinckney |
| Treaty of San Ildefonso | Napoleon |

r. If President DeGaulle were suddenly to begin practicing impressment of American seamen, what would America's course of action be? Briefly explain, giving reasons for your conclusion.

s. In your own words, explain how you would construct a "soundproof" room. Evaluate the problem carefully and give the types of materials used and the reasons for their use.

t. What alternative courses of action would you seriously consider and which one would you choose concerning the Negro problem. This includes such issues as Negro troops, slaves in rebel states, slaves in loyal states, etc.

u. You are asked to formulate a bill in which the voting age is reduced to 18. Explain how you would go about getting advocates for your bill in both a state and a national situation.

v. Describe briefly women's rights and how they have increased since 1789. Do you think women should have equal rights with men? Explain.

w. You are in the South Atlantic and you are in a warm current. Are you near South America or Africa?

x. You read in a book that penguins have been found on some islands parallel to Central America. What conclusion could you draw concerning ocean currents?

y. Write two or three sentences to tell what you have found most interesting about your study of ocean currents.

## SUGGESTED ANSWERS FOR ACTIVITY 3.

| | | |
|---|---|---|
| a. 1.00 | j. 2.00 | s. 3.00 |
| b. 1.00 | k. 1.00 and 5.00 | t. 5.00 |
| c. 1.00 | l. 2.00 | u. 5.00 |
| d. 2.00 | m. 2.00 | v. 2.00 and 5.00 |
| e. 3.00 or 4.00 | n. 6.00 | w. 3.00 or 4.00 |
| f. 1.00 and 6.00 | o. 4.00 | x. 3.00 or 4.00 |
| g. 6.00 | p. 2.00 | y. ? May be 6.00 or in Affective |
| h. 4.00 | q. 1.00 | Domain |
| i. 6.00 | r. 4.00 | |

*Note:* These "solutions" are not professed to be irrevocably correct. In some cases the level of the question will depend on what is assumed to be the intended thinking task, and not what has actually occurred in answering the questions. Readers may justify other levels than those shown here.

4. A class of 32 students was given an objective mastery test of ten multiple choice questions with five alternatives each. The following is the analysis of correct answers for each test item. What conclusions do the data suggest for each item?

| | (Test Item) | | | | | | | | | |
|---|---|---|---|---|---|---|---|---|---|---|
| | 1 | 2 | 3 | 4 | 5 | 6 | 7 | 8 | 9 | 10 |
| Correct Answer in Upper 16 | 16 | 16 | 10 | 2 | 12 | 0 | 13 | 4 | 10 | 8 |
| Correct Answer in Lower 16 | 16 | 12 | 5 | 12 | 10 | 0 | 3 | 6 | 4 | 4 |

5. The following are analyses of three of the test items indicated above. Correct key answer is marked with asterisk (*). What conclusions do the data suggest for each item?

Item 8

| | 1* | 2 | 3 | 4 | 5 |
|---|---|---|---|---|---|
| Upper 16 | 4 | 1 | 1 | 8 | 2 |
| Lower 16 | 6 | 0 | 3 | 3 | 4 |

Item 9

| | 1 | 2 | 3 | 4 | 5* |
|---|---|---|---|---|---|
| Upper 16 | 0 | 3 | 2 | 1 | 10 |
| Lower 16 | 1 | 7 | 4 | 0 | 4 |

Item 10

| | 1 | 2* | 3 | 4 | 5 |
|---|---|---|---|---|---|
| Upper 16 | 0 | 8 | 1 | 6 | 1 |
| Lower 16 | 3 | 4 | 2 | 2 | 5 |

6. The following scores represent the number correct out of 100 items on midsemester tests in various courses. What decisions would you make concerning the assignment of letter grades?

| Course A | Course B | Course C | Course D |
|----------|----------|----------|----------|
| 98 | 93 | 75 | 55 |
| 97 | 89 | 75 | 54 |
| 97 | 88 | 75 | 53 |
| 96 | 88 | 75 | 53 |
| 95 | 88 | 75 | 50 |
| 95 | 87 | 74 | 50 |
| 94 | 81 | 74 | 50 |
| 93 | 81 | 74 | 50 |
| 92 | 81 | 74 | 50 |
| 88 | 80 | 74 | 49 |
| 84 | 80 | 74 | 49 |
| 81 | 80 | 73 | 49 |
| 77 | 79 | 73 | 48 |
| 75 | 79 | 73 | 47 |
| 74 | 79 | 73 | 47 |
| 68 | 79 | 70 | 46 |
| 68 | 75 | 70 | 46 |
| 68 | 75 | 70 | 46 |
| 67 | 75 | 70 | 46 |
| 67 | 75 | 69 | 46 |
| 65 | 74 | 65 | 45 |
| 64 | 73 | 65 | 45 |
| 59 | 73 | 65 | 45 |
| 59 | 73 | 64 | 45 |
| 58 | 73 | 63 | 45 |
| 57 | 68 | 62 | |
| 57 | 67 | 62 | |
| 50 | 67 | 49 | |
| 40 | 66 | | |
| | 64 | | |
| | 64 | | |

7. Check the face validity of several classroom tests. How well do the tests conform to the goals of the course?

8. Collect papers handed back by professors in various courses. Do the professors' comments on these papers support or refute Professor Rothstein's thesis articulated in his article in this chapter?

9. Write several test questions for each of the categories in Bloom's Taxonomy.

10. Collect tests administered by teachers and professors. Classify the questions according to the Taxonomy.

11. Examine several standardized tests in your subject area. For what purposes were the tests designed? Do the items seem to contribute to the purposes?

12. The scope of this text is necessarily limited in the measurement area. Find several sources dealing with measurement and testing and compare

their definitions of validity, reliability, objectivity, and practicality. Apply these definitions to the tests examined above.

13. Devise another scheme for classifying test items other than the ones mentioned in this chapter. Try it on the sheet of practice questions.

14. Do you find it easier to select the level and write the test question or to assign levels to questions already written? Explain your choice.

15. Look at the end-of-chapter questions in textbooks popular for the course you will teach. What levels are they? What might the results reflect about the text content?

16. Could a system of classification such as Bloom's be useful in evaluating textbooks? How could this aid in planning?

17. Can you cite examples of teaching in which the test questions may not reflect the goals of the course?

18. What are some reasons for testing besides those cited in Camp's article?

19. Consider the following dialogue between two teachers.

> *Smith:* "In my English classes an 'A' is 90 per cent and above. I teach a tough course."
>
> *Jones:* "My standards are a little higher. I have college prep kids and it takes 95 per cent or above to get an 'A.'"

What are your comments on these assertions? Do you agree or disagree that Jones is a "tougher" grader than Smith? Does Jones have higher standards than Smith? What suggestions could you offer to help these teachers clarify their statements or monitor their teaching?

## Chapter Five

# TEACHING METHOD

A teacher once began a lesson by asking, "What should we talk about today?" as he leaned on a huge, huge lump of coal he had placed on his desk. Needless to say, the students' questions were directed toward the lump of coal and coincidently to the teacher's lesson plan on carbon. This is an example of a gimmick that teachers discover for themselves, steal from colleagues, or share in professional meetings. "Schemes" such as these help motivate students, assist teachers in making their teaching more individual, and they clearly are a part of every successful teacher's repertoire. However, it is impossible to particularize successful stratagems for young teachers to use. They are so specific to a definite topic or so reflective of the individual's personality that they defy cataloging. This section is dealing instead with ideas related to teaching methods that are reflective of the ways in which knowledge is generated in the disciplines. The methods of inquiry and discovery are the assumptions basic to each field, the rules for collecting evidence, and the postulates for drawing references.

What are some ways that you may introduce methods into your courses?

# 30

# Method and Technique in Teaching

EARL S. JOHNSON

Between the "immanent future" and the "immanent past" stands the "insistent present." "The present contains all there is. It is holy ground; for it is the past, and it is the future."[1] The question to be faced is, what to do *now*? Teachers have to understand what it means to teach. To this co-experience, for it is always teaching-learning, there are four faces: what to teach? why teach it? whom do we teach? and how? The quick answers to these questions are: reliable and useful knowledge, a philosophy of life, all God's children, and method and technique.

But quick answers are not good

Earl S. Johnson, "A View of the Future of the Social Studies," in *New Viewpoints in the Social Sciences*, ed. Roy A. Price (Washington, D.C.: National Council for the Social Studies, 28th Yearbook, 1958), pp. 225-32. Reprinted by permission of the author and the publisher.

[1] These are Whitehead's words to which may be added: "The communion of saints is a great and inspiring assemblage, but it has only one possible hall of meeting, and that is the present." *The Aims of Education and Other Essays* (New York: New American Library of World Literature, Inc.), pp. 14-15.

enough. Teachers have suffered too long from quick answers. They need to know with the utmost clarity, insight, and precision what the teaching-learning act is and what happens in and because of it.

It is necessary to start with a definition. The teaching-learning act in the social studies is a *transaction* between reliable and useful knowledge and immature human beings who are in the process of becoming better and wiser selves; this transaction is mediated by the process of *psychologizing* through which the subject matter of the social sciences and the humanities is restated into experience. Whatever else it be, this is certainly not a quick answer. But it is the one about which teachers of the social studies must be clear, insightful, and precise. It may be found in John Dewey's *The Child and the Curriculum.*[2]

Here, Dewey's "the child" and "the curriculum" will be replaced by "the need for knowledge" and "reliable and

[2] This essay, along with *The School and Society*, may now be had in the Phoenix Books paperback series of the University of Chicago Press.

useful knowledge." Between these two polar terms the shuttle of the process of psychologizing weaves an education. It is this dialectic which will be dealt with. The polar terms and their sub-terms may be juxtaposed as follows.[3]

### The Need for Knowledge

1. "an immature, underdeveloped" human being
2. "a somewhat narrow world of personal contacts"—"a world of persons with their personal interests"
3. "affection and sympathy"
4. the "little span of personal memory and tradition"
5. a "familiar physical environment"
6. "things held together by the unity of the personal and social interests which carry life along"
7. "the child's own world . . . the unity and completeness of his own life"
8. "the vital ties of affection, the connecting bonds of activity"

### Reliable and Useful Knowledge

1. "certain aims, meanings, values incarnate in the matured experience of the adult"
2. "a realm of facts and laws"—"material stretching back indefinitely in time, and extending outwardly indefinitely in space"
3. "truth, in the sense of conformity to external fact"
4. "the long centuries of the history of all peoples"
5. "the wide world—yes, even to the bounds of the solar system"
6. "facts torn away from their original place in experience and arranged with reference to some general principle"
7. "various studies [which] divide and frac-tionize the world for him"
8. "logically ordered facts . . . to be inter-preted in relation to [a] principle"

What a distance apart these poles and their subterms are. The task of teaching is, as has been suggested, to effect a transaction between them. This is the process of psychologizing,

the process of restating subject matter into human experience. But it is a joint and mutual process, a two-way street on which teacher and taught meet. This is the "feed" and "feed-back" process as it relates to pedagogy rather than to technology. But this is a genuine "feed" and "feed-back," not rote teaching or rote learning, not teacher citing and student re-citing but a joint adventure in ideas and ideals. How, from such a conception, anyone could derive the cliché, "teach the child and not the subject matter," escapes the wildest and most irresponsible imagination.[4]

But this process goes on between unequals. They are a "superior" teacher and an "inferior" student. What these words mean is implicit in the subterms given. The teacher's obligation is to reduce these inequalities or disparities or, in so far as possible, abolish them. This obligation falls upon the teacher as the person in the transaction who is "able to see the end in the beginning." Dewey observes that "to see the outcome is to know in what direction the [student's] present experience is moving, provided it move normally and soundly." Here is where present and future are joined, for "the far-away point, which is of no significance to us simply as far away, becomes of huge importance the moment we take it as defining a pres-ent direction of movement. Taken in this way it is no remote and distant result to be achieved, but a guiding method in dealing with the present.[5]

The four faces of teaching-learning again claim attention. The order in which they were stated is meant as no fixed order—from most to least im-portant. Any attempt to arrive at a

---

[3] The subterms are taken, verbatim, from John Dewey, *The Child and the Curriculum* (Chicago: University of Chicago Press, 1902), pp. 5-6.

[4] This cliché states the view of "either-or." The facts demand the view of "both-and." For this see Dewey, *op. cit.*, pp. 9-11.

[5] *Ibid.* p. 13.

fixed and hierarchical order would be preliminary to impotence; hence, they are treated in the order which is *convenient* rather than "right," that is, according to some "first principles" which the writer does not know.

First, what to teach? However much it is conditioned by why, for whom, and how, and each of these in turn conditioned by every other, there is something called reliable and useful knowledge. This the teacher ought to know. If this can, in the first instance, be acquired in terms of its teachability as well as in terms of its reliability and usefulness, well and good. But there is much doubt that it can be, at least *ab initio*. It should be voted against whenever it appears to be serving the principle that the education of teachers of the social studies should be merely task-oriented. Such a principle is too *ad hoc*, too practical, and too restricted. This is not to say that teachers need less education in the practice of their art. It is, rather, to emphasize the prior need for profound substantive knowledge and skill in analysis, so that the teacher has a firm place to stand in the social sciences and the humanities. If these fields are taught by masters of their art, so much the better. But there is need for insistence upon the prerequisite that substantive knowledge and analytical skill be attained in a program whose focus and purpose are with the theory and practice of loving and thinking about the Great Oughts of democratic humanism, not in the "training" of teachers. If it contributes to their *education*, it will contribute to their preparation *for* teaching. This philosophy is based on the motto, *Primum vir esto*—First, let him be a man. This demands a general education, about which more will be forthcoming.

So much and all too briefly about what is taught. Next, why teach it? The answer, which will have to be too quick to suit the demands of the question, is this: because it is necessary for the student's growth in goodness and wisdom in a society which is dedicated to the philosophy of democratic humanism. But what and why are interdependent as means and ends. H. G. Wells tells of the conditions and means which will help understand better the why of teaching.

I want simply this world better taught. . . . I will not suppose that there is any greater knowledge of things than men actually possess today, but instead of its being confusedly stored in many minds and books and many languages, it has all been sorted and set out plainly so that it can be easily used. . . . When I ask you to suppose a world instructed and educated in the place of this old traditional world of unguided passion . . . a world taught by men instead of a world neglected by hirelings, I do not ask you to imagine any miraculous change in human nature. I ask you only to suppose that each mind has the utmost enlightenment of which it is capable instead of its being darkened and overcast. Everyone is to have the best chance of being his best self. Everyone is to be living in the light of the acutest self-examination and the clearest mutual self-criticism.[6]

Next, for whom? Again, the answer must, perforce, be too quick. The boys and girls from both sides of the tracks; those whose fathers support the family by the use of their hands and those who support it by the use of their heads; the sons and daughters of those who borrow and those who lend; those who come from life circumstances with little or no margins of moral or material security and those who, for whatever reason, have an abundance of both; those with only a blurred picture of their careers and

[6] H. G. Wells, *The Undying Fire* (New York: The Macmillan Company, 1919), pp. 182, 184.

those whose picture is clear; those who view the school as something only to be endured until they can "get a job" and those who genuinely enjoy and respect it; those who have a distaste for, or at best an attitude of sufferance toward the teacher and those who respect the person and the role of the teacher; those who are "dull" and those who are "bright"; and those who are "hand-minded" and those who are "head-minded." All and each are to get the education which their talents and capabilities warrant which is not the *same* education, except that it be one which permits both appreciation and understanding of the values of a humane life as each can love and know them.

And now, to the *how* of it. In this face, to a degree not found in any other single one, all the faces are reflected. It traces to and depends on the *what* from which it gets the substance that is to be psychologized—restated into experience. Thus it traces to and depends on the *for whom*, the many kinds of human beings whose experience the substance is to affect. It also traces to and depends on the spirit and philosophy of democratic humanism, that which must pervade the climate in which teaching-learning goes on and from which it gets it dedication and its goals.

It is desirable now to trace the *how* of teaching-learning along the axis of *what* and *for whom*. In order to do this, it is necessary to explore the meaning of the terms, *method* and *technique*. One does not need to accept them as terms; only to follow the argument through which this author undertakes to show that each has a unique meaning, and how they become integrated in the process of psychologizing. In effect, the terms are *accidents*, but the processes which they symbolize are *essences*.

By the term *method* is meant that phase of the education of the teacher, as *intellectual*, by which substantive knowledge, analytical skill, and insight are acquired. That it combines both science and art is not only admitted but affirmed. Proof of this is given by Professor Robert Redfield in his paper, "The Art of Social Science," in which he recognizes "the relationship of social science to humanistic endeavors and include[s] in the preparation of social scientists, as such, a humanistic education.[7]

The term *technique* here refers to that phase of the education of the teacher, as *teacher*, by which the science and art of instruction is acquired and continually improved in practice. It is the teacher's tool as "psychologizer." Note the term, "psychologizer" not *psychologist*. That the former requires knowledge of psychology is admitted, but that it also requires knowledge in the other social sciences and in the humanities is mandated. William James wrote that, "To know psychology . . . is absolutely no guarantee that we shall be good teachers."[8] "Psychology," he says, "is a science, and teaching is an art; and sciences never generate arts directly out of themselves. An intermediary inventive mind must make the application, by using its originality.[9] The application of what? The application of substantive

[7] Robert Redfield, "The Art of Social Science," *The American Journal of Sociology* LIV, No. 3 (November 1948), 181-90.

[8] William James, *Talks to Teachers on Psychology: And to Students on Some of Life's Ideals* (New York: Holt, Rinehart & Winston, Inc., 1914), p. 9.

[9] *Ibid.*, p. 7. He continues: "The science of logic never made a man reason rightly, and the science of ethics (if there be such a thing) never made a man behave rightly. . . . A science only lays down lines within which the rules of art fall, laws which the follower of the art must not transgress. . . ." *Ibid.*, p. 8.

knowledge, analytical skill and insight into human experience as the social sciences and the humanities deal with it. All the subterms under the poles of *Useful and Reliable Knowledge* and *The Need for Knowledge* are now brought into interaction. The transaction between them is now in process. In this process "for whom" becomes "with whom"— teacher and taught engaged in the mutual and reciprocal experience of teaching-learning.

What is processed in this process? A character? Yes, but in the very long run, for learning to be the architect of a character is the task of life, not only the assignment of school. Is the moral-intellectual independence of the student from the teacher also processed? It is, for it is one of the great ends of schooling and, in the measure in which it is achieved, the inequality between teacher and student is reduced and, we hope, ultimately abolished.

What else? In the words of John Dewey:

Events turn into objects, things with a meaning. They may be referred to when they do not exist, and thus be operative among things distant is space and time, through vicarious presence in a new medium.[10]

This is the process by which percepts are put into families and become concepts—the acid test of education wherever and under whatever auspices it goes on. This is the process in which the transfer of learning goes on, through which useful and reliable knowledge is transmuted into ideas, attitudes, ideals, and patterns of action. This is the process by which issues are settled, anxieties relieved, desires subjected to critical and disciplined examination, and curiosities satisfied. This is the process by which the Word becomes

[10] Dewey, *Experience and Nature*, *op. cit.*, p. 166.

flesh, all in the context of the rhythm of "romance, precision, and generalization."

Thus it is that "teaching has to depend on learning for its technique."[11] This is the learning of the *learned* as well as of the *learner*, of both the teacher and the taught. Thus, method and technique are joined until one can hardly tell which is which.[12]

But if they become almost indistinguishable why bother to separate them and treat them as if they were things apart? Because we ought to know what is joined if we would fashion and control the joining. Furthermore, technique (wrongly conceived) is, far too often, held to be enough. This is implied in the cliché "teach 'em what they know" which presumes that the teacher does not need to know other than or more than what "they" know. If this is all the teacher needs to know it isn't much, if anything, beyond common-sense knowledge. If so, Heaven help the students! There is, however, just enough truth in this cliché to make it dangerous. If it means that the teacher ought to *begin* with what "they" know it makes sense. But if it means that the teacher ought to *stop* there, it makes nonsense. What "they know" they often don't know as to its factuality but more importantly as to its meaning.

Technique must not be used as a lame and inadequate substitute for method, as these terms have been defined previously. Nor can it, now defined in its lowest terms, be permitted

[11] See Whitehead, *op. cit.*, Chap. III.
[12] Whitehead's observations on this process are: "You cannot put into life any schedule of general education unless you succeed in exhibiting its relation to some essential characteristic of all intellectual or emotional perception. . . . The process of exhibiting the application of knowledge must, for its success, essentially depend on the character of the pupils and the genius of the teacher." *Ibid.*, pp. 20, 21.

to be only devices and tricks of procedure with which the "trained" but still uneducated teacher tries to eke out inadequate knowledge.[13]

Criticism of those who hold that technique is enough, good or bad in quality, should be complemented by criticism, equally forthright, of those who hold that method is enough. There is nothing "just as good as"

[13] See Fred Clarke, *Foundations of History-Teaching* (London: Oxford University Press, 1929), p. 25. To commit this error is tantamount to one's redoubling his efforts when he has forgotten his aims or never had the knowledge which would give them to him. To commit the error of "only *method*" is equivalent to believing that students are intellectually superior to their teachers.

either technique *or* method. Teachers must have both.

The task of illustrating fully how method and technique merge in the process of psychologizing is too complex and formidable to undertake here. Instead, and more significant for present purposes, there is reason to inquire further into the need that the cloak of fact-and-value be repaired. Although this will require a discussion of method somewhat more than of technique, both will be treated. There is a sense in which method may be viewed as prior to technique because method, with the nature of the learners and the genius of the teacher, is that from which technique takes its instructions.

# 31

# The Act of Discovery

### JEROME S. BRUNER

Maimonides, in his *Guide for the Perplexed*,[1] speaks of four forms of perfection that men might seek. The first and lowest form is perfection in the acquisition of worldly goods. The great philosopher dismisses such perfection on the ground that the possessions one acquires bear no meaningful relation to the possessor: "A great king may one morning find that there is no difference between him and the lowest person." A second perfection is of the body, its conformation and skills. Its failing is that is does not reflect on what is uniquely human about man: "he could [in any case] not be as strong as a mule." Moral perfection is the third, "the highest degree of excellency in man's character." Of this perfection Maimonides says: "Imagine a person being alone, and having no connection whatever with any other person; all his good moral principles are at rest, they are not required and give man no perfection whatever. These principles are only necessary and useful when man comes in contact with others." "The fourth kind of perfection is the true perfection of man; the possession of the highest intellectual faculties. . . ." In justification of his assertion, this extraordinary Spanish-Judaic philosopher urges: "Examine the first three kinds of perfection; you will find that if you possess them, they are not your property, but the property of others. . . . But the last kind of perfection is exclusively yours; no one else owns any part of it."

It is a conjecture much like that of Maimonides that leads me to examine the act of discovery in man's intellectual life. For if man's intellectual excellence is the most his own among his perfections, it is also the case that the most uniquely personal of all that he knows is that which he has discovered for himself. What difference does it make, then, that we encourage discovery in the learning of the young? Does it, as

Jerome S. Bruner, "The Act of Discovery," *Harvard Educational Review*, XXXI, No. 1 (Winter 1961), 21-32. Reprinted by permission of the author and the publisher.

[1] Maimonides, *Guide for the Perplexed* (New York: Dover Publications, Inc., 1956).

Maimonides would say, create a special and unique relation between knowledge possessed and the possessor? And what may such a unique relation do for a man—or for a child, if you will, for our concern is with the education of the young?

The immediate occasion for my concern with discovery—and I do not restrict discovery to the act of finding out something that before was unknown to mankind, but rather include all forms of obtaining knowledge for oneself by the use of one's own mind—the immediate occasion is the work of the various new curriculum projects that have grown up in America during the last six or seven years. For whether one speaks to mathematicians or physicists or historians, one encounters repeatedly an expression of faith in the powerful effects that come from permitting the student to put things together for himself, to be his own discoverer.

First, let it be clear what the act of discovery entails. It is rarely, on the frontier of knowledge or elsewhere, that new facts are "discovered" in the sense of being encountered as Newton suggested in the form of islands of truth in an uncharted sea of ignorance. Or if they appear to be discovered in this way, it is almost always thanks to some happy hypotheses about where to navigate. Discovery, like surprise, favors the well prepared mind. In playing bridge, one is surprised by a hand with no honors in it at all and also by hands that are all in one suit. Yet all hands in bridge are equiprobable: one must know to be surprised. So too in discovery. The history of science is studded with examples of men "finding out" something and not knowing it. I shall operate on the assumption that discovery, whether by a schoolboy going it on his own or by a scientist cultivating the growing

edge of his field, is in its essence a matter of rearranging or transforming evidence in such a way that one is enabled to go beyond the evidence so reassembled to additional new insights. It may well be that an additional fact or shred of evidence makes this larger transformation of evidence possible. But it is often not even dependent on new information.

It goes without saying that, left to himself, the child will go about discovering things for himself within limits. It also goes without saying that there are certain forms of child rearing, certain home atmospheres that lead some children to be their own discoverers more than other children. These are both topics of great interest, but I shall not be discussing them. Rather, I should like to confine myself to the consideration of discovery and "finding-out-for-oneself" within an educational setting—specifically the school. Our aim as teachers is to give our student as firm a grasp of a subject as we can, and to make him as autonomous and self-propelled a thinker as we can—one who will go along on his own after formal schooling has ended. I shall return in the end to the question of the kind of classroom and the style of teaching that encourage an attitude of wanting to discover. For purposes of orienting the discussion, however, I would like to make an overly simplified distinction between teaching that takes place in the *expository mode* and teaching that utilizes the *hypothetical mode.* In the former, the decisions concerning the mode and pace and style of exposition are principally determined by the teacher as expositor; the student is the listener. If I can put the matter in terms of structural linguistics, the speaker has a quite different set of decisions to make than the listener: the former has a wide choice of alternatives for structuring, he is anticipating paragraph content while the listener is still intent on the words, he is manipulating the content of the material by various transformations, while the listener is quite unaware of these internal manipulations. In the hypothetical mode, the teacher and the student are in a more cooperative position with respect to what in linguistics would be called "speaker's decisions." The student is not a bench-bound listener, but is taking a part in the formulation and at times may play the principal role in it. He will be aware of alternatives and may even have an "as if" attitude toward these, and as he receives information he may evaluate it as it comes. One cannot describe the process in either mode with great precision as to detail, but I think the foregoing may serve to illustrate what is meant.

Consider now what benefit might be derived from the experience of learning through discoveries that one makes for oneself. I should like to discuss these under four headings: (1) The increase in intellectual potency, (2) the shift from extrinsic to intrinsic rewards, (3) learning the heuristics of discovering, and (4) the aid to memory processing.

## 1. INTELLECTUAL POTENCY

If you will permit me, I would like to consider the difference between subjects in a highly constrained psychological experiment involving a two-choice apparatus. In order to win chips, they must depress a key either on the right or the left side of the machine. A pattern of payoff is designed such that, say, they will be paid off on the right side 70 per cent of the time, on the left 30 per cent, although this detail is not important. What is important is that the payoff sequence

is arranged at random, and there is no pattern. I should like to contrast the behavior of subjects who think that there is some pattern to be found in the sequence—who think that regularities are discoverable—in contrast to subjects who think that things are happening quite by *chance*. The former group adopts what is called an "event-matching" strategy in which the number of responses given to each side is roughly equal to the proportion of times it pays off: in the present case R70:L30. The group that believes there is no pattern very soon reverts to a much more primitive strategy wherein *all* responses are allocated to the side that has the greater payoff. A little arithmetic will show you that the lazy all-and-none strategy pays off more if indeed the environment is random: namely, they win 70 per cent of the time. The event-matching subjects win about 70 per cent on the 70 per cent payoff side (or 49 per cent of the time there) and 30 per cent of the time on the side that pays off 30 per cent of the time (another 9 per cent for a total take-home wage of 58 per cent in return for their labors of decision). But the world is not always or not even frequently random, and if one analyzes carefully what the event-matchers are doing, it turns out that they are trying out hypotheses one after the other, all of them containing a term such that they distribute bets on the two sides with a frequency to match the actual occurrence of events. If it should turn out that there is a pattern to be discovered, their payoff would become 100 per cent. The other group would go on at the middling rate of 70 per cent.

What has this to do with the subject at hand? For the person to search out and find regularities and relationships in his environment, he must be armed with an expectancy that there will be something to find and, once aroused by expectancy, he must devise ways of searching and finding. One of the chief enemies of such expectancy is the assumption that there is nothing one can find in the environment by way of regularity or relationship. In the experiment just cited, subjects often fall into a habitual attitude that there is either nothing to be found or that they can find a pattern by looking. There is an important sequel in behavior to the two attitudes, and to this I should like to turn now.

We have been conducting a series of experimental studies on a group of some seventy school children over the last four years. The studies have led us to distinguish an interesting dimension of cognitive activity that can be described as ranging from *episodic empiricism* at one end to *cumulative constructionism* at the other. The two attitudes in the choice experiments just cited are illustrative of the extremes of the dimension. I might mention some other illustrations. One of the experiments employs the game of Twenty Questions. A child—in this case he is between 10 and 12—is told that a car has gone off the road and hit a tree. He is to ask questions that can be answered by "yes" or "no" to discover the cause of the accident. After completing the problem, the same task is given him again, though he is told that the accident had a different cause this time. In all, the procedure is repeated four times. Children enjoy playing the game. They also differ quite markedly in the approach or strategy they bring to the task. There are various elements in the strategies employed. In the first place, one may distinguish clearly between two types of questions asked: the one is designed for locating constraints in the problem, constraints that will eventually give shape to a hypothesis; the other is the

hypothesis as question. It is the difference between, "Was there anything wrong with the driver?" and "Was the driver rushing to the doctor's office for an appointment and the car got out of control?" There are children who precede hypotheses with efforts to locate constraint and there are those who, to use our local slang, are "potshotters," who string out hypotheses noncumulatively one after the other. A second element of strategy is its connectivity of information gathering: the extent to which questions asked utilize or ignore or violate information previously obtained. The questions asked by children tend to be organized in cycles, each cycle of questions usually being given over to the pursuit of some particular notion. Both within cycles and between cycles one can discern a marked difference on the connectivity of the child's performance. Needless to say, children who employ constraint location as a technique preliminary to the formulation of hypotheses tend to be far more connected in their harvesting of information. Persistence is another feature of strategy, a characteristic compounded of what appear to be two components: a sheer doggedness component, and a persistence that stems from the sequential organization that a child brings to the task. Doggedness is probably just animal spirits or the need for achievement— what has come to be called *n-ach*. Organized persistence is a maneuver for protecting our fragile cognitive apparatus from overload. The child who has flooded himself with disorganized information from unconnected hypotheses will become discouraged and confused sooner than the child who has shown a certain cunning in his strategy of getting information—a cunning whose principal component is the recognition that the value of information is not simply in getting it

*developing a pattern of behavior*

*intellectual persistence*

but in being able to carry it. The persistence of the organized child stems from his knowledge of how to organize questions in cycles, how to summarize things to himself, and the like.

Episodic empiricism is illustrated by information gathering that is unbound by prior constraints, that lacks connectivity, and that is deficient in organizational persistence. The opposite extreme is illustrated by an approach that is characterized by constraint sensitivity, by connective maneuvers, and by organized persistence. Brute persistence seems to be one of those gifts from the gods that make people more exaggeratedly what they are.[2]

Before returning to the issue of discovery and its role in the development of thinking, let me say a word more about the ways in which information may get transformed when the problem solver has actively processed it. There is first of all a pragmatic question: What does it take to get information processed into a form best designed to fit some future use? Take an experiment by Zajonc[3] as a case in point. He gives groups of subjects information of a controlled kind, some groups being told that their task is to transmit the information to others, others that it is merely to be kept in mind. In general, he finds more differentiation and organization of the information received with the intention of being transmitted than there is for information received passively. An active set leads to a transformation

related to a task to be performed. The risk, to be sure, is in possible overspecialization of information processing that may lead to such a high degree of specific organization that information is lost for general use.

I would urge now in the spirit of a hypothesis that emphasis upon discovery in learning has precisely the effect upon the learner of leading him to be a constructionist, to organize what he is encountering in a manner not only designed to discover regularity and relatedness, but also to avoid the kind of information drift that fails to keep account of the uses to which information might have to be put. It is, if you will, a necessary condition for learning the variety of techniques of problem solving, of transforming information for better use, indeed for learning how to go about the very task of learning. Practice in discovering for oneself teaches one to acquire information in a way that makes that information more readily viable in problem solving. So goes the hypothesis. It is still in need of testing. But it is an hypothesis of such important human implications that we cannot afford not to test it—and testing will have to be in the schools.

## 2. INTRINSIC AND EXTRINSIC MOTIVES

Much of the problem in leading a child to effective cognitive activity is to free him from the immediate control of environmental rewards and punishments. That is to say, learning that starts in response to the rewards of parental or teacher approval or the avoidance of failure can too readily develop a pattern in which the child is seeking cues as to how to conform to what is expected of him. We know from studies of children who tend to be

---

[2] I should also remark in passing that the two extremes also characterize concept attainment strategies as reported in *A Study of Thinking* by J. S. Bruner *et al.* (New York: John Wiley & Sons, Inc., 1956). Successive scanning illustrates well what is meant here by episodic empiricism: conservative focusing is an example of cumulative constructionism.

[3] R. B. Zajonc (Personal communication, 1957).

early over-achievers in school that they are likely to be seekers after the "right way to do it" and that their capacity for transforming their learning into viable thought structures tends to be lower than children merely achieving at levels predicted by intelligence tests. Our tests on such children show them to be lower in analytic ability than those who are not conspicuous in overachievement.[4] As we shall see later, they develop rote abilities and depend upon being able to "give back" what is expected rather than to make it into something that relates to the rest of their cognitive life. As Maimonides would say, their learning is not their own.

The hypothesis that I would propose here is that to the degree that one is able to approach learning as a task of discovering something rather than "learning about" it, to that degree will there be a tendency for the child to carry out his learning activities with the autonomy of self-reward or, more properly, by reward that is discovery itself.

To those of you familiar with the battles of the last half-century in the field of motivation, the above hypothesis will be recognized as controversial. For the classic view of motivation in learning has been, until very recently, couched in terms of a theory of drives and reinforcement: that learning occurred by virtue of the fact that a response produced by a stimulus was followed by the reduction in a primary drive state. The doctrine is greatly extended by the idea of secondary reinforcement: any state associated even remotely with the reduction of a primary drive could also have the effect of producing learning.

There has recently appeared a most searching and important criticism of this position, written by Professor Robert White,[5] reviewing the evidence of recently published animal studies, of work in the field of psychoanalysis, and of research on the development of cognitive processes in children. Professor White comes to the conclusion, quite rightly I think, that the drive-reduction model of learning runs counter to too many important phenomena of learning and development to be either regarded as general in its applicability or even correct in its general approach. Let me summarize some of his principal conclusions and explore their applicability to the hypothesis stated above.

I now propose that we gather the various kinds of behavior just mentioned, all of which have to do with effective interaction with the environment, under the general heading of competence. According to Webster, competence means fitness or ability, and the suggested synonyms include capability, capacity, efficiency, proficiency, and skill. It is therefore a suitable word to describe such things as grasping and exploring, crawling and walking, attention and perception, language and thinking, manipulating and changing the surroundings, all of which promote an effective—a competent—interaction with the environment. It is true of course, that maturation plays a part in all these developments, but this part is heavily overshadowed by learning in all the more complex accomplishments like speech or skilled manipulation. I shall argue that it is necessary to make competence a motivational concept; there is *competence motivation* as well as competence in its more familiar sense of achieved capacity. The behavior that leads to the building up of effective grasping, handling, and letting go of objects, to take one example, is not random behavior that is

---

[4] J. S. Bruner and A. J. Caron, "Cognition, Anxiety, and Achievement in the Preadolescent," *Journal of Educational Psychology*, unpublished.

[5] R. W. White, "Motivation Reconsidered: The Concept of Competence," *Psychological Review*, LXVI (1959), 297-333.

produced by an overflow of energy. It is directed, selective, and persistent, and it continues not because it serves primary drives, which indeed it cannot serve until it is almost perfected, but because it satisfies an intrinsic need to deal with the environment.[6]

I am suggesting that there are forms of activity that serve to enlist and develop the competence motive, that serve to make it the driving force behind behavior. I should like to add to White's general premise that the *exercise* of competence motives has the effect of strengthening the degree to which they gain control over behavior and thereby reduce the effects of extrinsic rewards or drive gratification.

The brilliant Russian psychologist Vigotsky[7] characterizes the growth of thought processes as starting with a dialogue of speech and gesture between child and parent; autonomous thinking begins at the stage when the child is first able to internalize these conversations and "run them off" himself. This is a typical sequence in the development of competence. So too in instruction. The narrative of teaching is of the order of the conversation. The next move in the development of competence is the internalization of the narrative and its "rules of generation" so that the child is now capable of running off the narrative on his own. The hypothetical mode in teaching by encouraging the child to participate in "speaker's decisions" speeds this process along. Once internalization has occurred the child is in a vastly improved position from several obvious points of view—notably that he is able to go beyond the information he has been given to generate additional ideas that can either be checked immediately from experience or can, at least, be used as a basis for formulating reasonable hypotheses. But over and beyond that, the child is now in a position to experience success and failure not as reward and punishment, but as information. For when the task is his own rather than a matter of matching environmental demands, he becomes his own paymaster in a certain measure. Seeking to gain control over his environment, he can now treat success as indicating that he is on the right track, failure as indicating he is on the wrong one.

In the end, this development has the effect of freeing learning from immediate stimulus control. When learning in the short run leads only to pellets of this or that rather than to mastery in the long run, then behavior can be readily "shaped" by extrinsic rewards. When behavior becomes more long-range and competence-oriented, it comes under the control of more complex cognitive structures, plans and the like, and operates more from the inside out. It is interesting that even Pavlov, whose early account of the learning process was based entirely on a notion of stimulus control of behavior through the conditioning mechanism in which, through contiguity, a new conditioned stimulus was substituted for an old unconditioned stimulus by the mechanism of stimulus substitution, that even Pavlov recognized his account as insufficient to deal with higher forms of learning. To supplement the account, he introduced the idea of the "second signaling system," with central importance placed on symbolic systems such as language in mediating and giving shape to mental life. Or as Luria[8] has put it, "the first signal system [is] concerned with directly

---

[6] *Ibid.*, pp. 317-18.

[7] L. S. Vigotsky, *Thinking and Speech* (Moscow, 1934).

[8] A. L. Luria, "The Directive Function of Speech in Development and Dissolution," *Word*, XV (1959), 341-464.

perceived stimuli, the second with systems of verbal elaboration." Luria, commenting on the importance of the transition from first to second signal system, says: "It would be mistaken to suppose that verbal intercourse with adults merely changes the contents of the child's conscious activity without changing its form. . . . The word has a basic function not only because it indicates a corresponding object in the external world, but also because it abstracts, isolates the necessary signal, generalizes perceived signals and relates them to certain categories; it is this systematization of direct experience that makes the role of the words in the formation of mental processes so exceptionally important."[9, 10]

It is interesting that the final rejection of the universality of the doctrine of reinforcement in direct conditioning came from some of Pavlov's own students. Ivanov-Smolensky[11] and Krasnogorsky[12] published papers showing the manner in which symbolized linguistic messages could take over the place of the unconditioned stimulus and of the unconditioned response (gratification of hunger) in children. In all instances, they speak of these as *replacements* of lower, first-system mental or neural processes by higher order or second-system controls. A strange irony, then that Russian psychology that gave us the notion of the conditioned response and the assumption that higher order activities are built up out of colligations or structurings of such primitive units, rejected this notion while much of American learning psychology has stayed until quite recently within the early Pavlovian fold (see, for example, a recent article by Spence[13] in the *Harvard Educational Review* or Skinner's treatment of language[14] and the attacks that have been made upon it by linguists such as Chomsky[15] who have become concerned with the relation of language and cognitive activity). What is the more interesting is that Russian pedagogical theory has become deeply influenced by this new trend and is now placing much stress upon the importance of building up a more active symbolical approach to problem-solving among children.

To sum up the matter of the control of learning, then, I am proposing that the degree to which competence or mastery motives come to control behavior, to that degree the role of reinforcement or "extrinsic pleasure" wanes in shaping behavior. The child comes to manipulate his environment more actively and achieves his gratification from coping with problems. Symbolic modes of representing and transforming the environment arise and the importance of stimulus-response-reward sequences declines. To use the metaphor that David Riesman developed in a quite different context, mental life moves from a state of outer-directedness in which the fortuity of stimuli and reinforce-

---

[9] *Ibid.*, p. 12.
[10] For an elaboration of the view expressed by Luria, the reader is referred to the forthcoming translation of L. S. Vigotsky's 1934 book being published by John Wiley & Sons, Inc., and the Technology Press.
[11] A. G. Ivanov-Smolensky, "Concerning the Study of the Joint Activity of the First and Second Signal Systems," *Journal of Higher Nervous Activity*, I (1951), 1.
[12] N. D. Krasnogorsky, *Studies of Higher Nervous Activity in Animals and in Man*, Vol. I (Moscow, 1954).

[13] K. W. Spence, "The Relation of Learning Theory to the Technique of Education," *Harvard Educational Review*, XXIX (1959), 84-95.
[14] B. F. Skinner, *Verbal Behavior* (New York: Appleton-Century-Crofts, 1957).
[15] N. Chomsky, *Syntactic Structure* (The Hague: Mouton & Co., 1957).

ment are crucial to a state of inner-directedness in which the growth and maintenance of mastery become central and dominant.

*a sense, developed thru experience - a feeling for*

### 3. LEARNING THE HEURISTICS OF DISCOVERY

*rightness (intuition)*

Lincoln Steffens,[16] reflecting in his *Autobiography* on his undergraduate education at Berkeley, comments that his schooling was overly specialized on learning about the known and that too little attention was given to the task of finding out about what was not known. But how does one train a student in the techniques of discovery? Again I would like to offer some hypotheses. There are many ways of coming to the arts of inquiry. One of them is by careful study of its formalization in logic, statistics, mathematics, and the like. If a person is going to pursue inquiry as a way of life, particularly in the sciences, certainly such study is essential. Yet, whoever has taught kindergarten and the early primary grades or has had graduate students working with him on their theses—I choose the two extremes for they are both periods of intense inquiry—knows that an understanding of the formal aspect of inquiry is not sufficient. There appear to be, rather, a series of activities and attitudes, some directly related to a particular subject and some of them fairly generalized, that go with inquiry and research. These have to do with the *process* of trying to find out something and while they provide no guarantee that the *product* will be any *great* discovery, their absence is likely to lead to awkwardness or aridity or confusion. How difficult it is to de-

[16] L. Steffens, *Autobiography of Lincoln Steffens* (New York: Harcourt, Brace & World, Inc., 1931).

scribe these matters—the heuristics of inquiry. There is one set of attitudes or ways of doing that has to do with sensing the relevance of variables—how to avoid getting stuck with edge effects and getting instead to the big sources of variance. Partly this gift comes from intuitive familiarity with a range of phenomena, sheer "knowing the stuff." But it also comes out of a sense of what things among an ensemble of things "smell right" in the sense of being of the right order of magnitude or scope or severity.

The English philosopher Weldon describes problems solving in an interesting and picturesque way. He distinguishes between difficulties, puzzles, and problems. We solve a problem or make a discovery when we impose a puzzle form on to a difficulty that converts it into a problem that can be solved in such a way that it gets us where we want to be. That is to say, we recast the difficulty into a form that we know how to work with, then work it. Much of what we speak of as discovery consists of knowing how to impose what kind of form on various kinds of difficulties. A small part but a crucial part of discovery of the highest order is to invent and develop models or "puzzle forms" that can be imposed on difficulties with good effect. It is in this area that the truly powerful mind shines. But it is interesting to what degree perfectly ordinary people can, given the benefit of instruction, construct quite interesting and what, a century ago, would have been considered greatly original models.

Now to the hypothesis. It is my hunch that it is only through the exercise of problem solving and the effort of discovery that one learns the working heuristic of discovery, and the more one has practice, the more likely is one to generalize what one has learned into a style of problem solving or inquiry that serves for any kind of task one may encounter—or almost any kind of task. I think the matter is self-evident, but what is unclear is what kinds of training and teaching produce the best effects. How do we teach a child to, say, cut his losses but at the same time be persistent in trying out an idea; to risk forming an early hunch without at the same time formulating one *so* early and with so little evidence as to be stuck with it waiting for appropriate evidence to materialize; to pose good testable guesses that are neither too brittle nor too sinuously incorrigible; etc., etc. Practice in inquiry, in trying to figure out things for oneself, is indeed what is needed, but in what form? Of only one thing I am convinced. I have never seen anybody improve in the art and technique of inquiry by any means other than engaging in inquiry.

## 4. CONSERVATION OF MEMORY

I should like to take what some psychologists might consider a rather drastic view of the memory process. It is a view that in large measure derives from the work of my colleague, Professor George Miller.[17] Its first premise is that the principal problem of human memory is not storage, but retrieval. In spite of the biological unlikeliness of it, we seem to be able to store a huge quantity of information—perhaps not a full tape recording, though at times it seems we even do that, but a great sufficiency of impressions. We may infer this from the fact that recognition (i.e., recall with the aid of maximum prompts) is so extraordinarily good in human beings—particularly in comparison with spon-

taneous recall where, so to speak, we must get out stored information without external aids or prompts. The key to retrieval is organization or, in even simpler terms, knowing where to find information and how to get there.

Let me illustrate the point with a simple experiment. We present pairs of words to twelve-year-old children. One group is simply told to remember the pairs, that they will be asked to repeat them later. Another is told to remember them by producing a word or idea that will tie the pair together in a way that will make sense to them. A third group is given the mediators used by the second group when presented with the pairs to aid them in tying the pairs into working units. The word pairs include such juxtapositions as "chair-forest," "sidewalk-square," and the like. One can distinguish three styles of mediators and children can be scaled in terms of their relative preference for each: *generic mediation* in which a pair is tied together by a superordinate idea: "chair and forest are both made of wood"; *thematic mediation* in which the two terms are embedded in a theme or little story: "the lost child sat on a chair in the middle of the forest"; and *part-whole mediation* where "chairs are made from trees in the forest" is typical. Now, the chief result, as you would all predict, is that children who provide their own mediators do best—indeed, one time through a set of thirty pairs, they recover up to 95 per cent of the second words when presented with the first ones of the pairs, whereas the uninstructed children reach a maximum of less than 50 per cent recovered. Interestingly enough, children do best in recovering materials tied together by the form of mediator they most often use.

One can cite a myriad of findings to indicate that any organization of in-

[17] G. A. Miller, "The Magical Number Seven, Plus or Minus Two," *Psychological Review*, LXIII (1956), 81-97.

formation that reduces the aggregate complexity of material by embedding it into a cognitive structure a person has constructed will make that material more accessible for retrieval. In short, we may say that the process of memory, looked at from the retrieval side, is also a process of problem solving: how can material be "placed" in memory so that it can be got on demand?

We can take as a point of departure the example of the children who developed their own technique for relating the members of each word pair. You will recall that they did better than the children who were given by exposition the mediators they had developed. Let me suggest that, in general, material that is organized in terms of a person's own interests and cognitive structures is material that has the best chance of being accessible in memory. That is to say, it is more likely to be placed along routes that are connected to one's own ways of intellectual travel.

In sum, the very attitudes and activities that characterize "figuring out" or "discovering" things for oneself also seems to have the effect of making material more readily accessible in memory.

# 32

# Teaching Social Studies Through Discovery

## BYRON G. MASSIALAS & JACK ZEVIN

The study reported here is grounded in some of the hypotheses advanced by Jerome Bruner in his recent work. According to him, the highest state of human autonomy and perfection is achieved when the child begins to discover for himself regularities or irregularities in his physical and sociopolitical environments. While no earthshaking scientific discoveries should be expected, the person who is engaged in this process is given the opportunity to make leaps into the unknown and uncontrolled world, and he learns the value of formulating plausible hypotheses about human interactions. It is maintained that when facts and details are put into a structured pattern, they are retained longer and can be retrieved easier when needed.[1]

The study was conducted in a Chicago public high school over a period of one academic year, and it attempted to explore further the dimensions and the implications of teaching a course in world history through discovery or, what Bruner calls, the process of "figuring out." While the general nature of the study was exploratory, some questions provided the focus of the investigation. Some of these questions were: (1) To what extent are high school sophomores with slightly above average ability capable of participating in discovery and in inquiry? (2) How can historical materials be presented in such a way that while some cues will be offered, the story will not be given away, and the student will be prompted to study independently and to acquire the heuristics of learning? (3) To what extent do the style and method of discovery operate as a potent

Byron G. Massialas and Jack Zevin, "Teaching Social Studies Through Discovery," *Social Education*, XXVIII, No. 7 (November 1964), 384-87, 400. Reprinted by permission of Dr. Massialas and the publisher.

[1] Jerome S. Bruner, "The Act of Discovery," *Harvard Educational Review*, XXXI (Winter 1961), 21-32. (See Reading 31, this vol.) For more details on the philosophical and psy-

chological assumptions underlying the method, see B. G. Massialas, "Teaching History as Inquiry," in Shirley H. Engle, editor, *New Perspectives in World History*. Thirty-Fourth Yearbook (Washington, D.C.: The National Council for the Social Studies, 1964).

motivational device in learning? Before dealing with these questions and presenting relevant classroom discussion, let us briefly identify some instructional procedures and classroom mechanics which will help the reader reconstruct the teaching experience.

The class was composed of 35 students, most of them about 15 years old, enrolled in a required modern world history course. The course began with the Reformation, and it generally followed the sequence of historical topics; selected social events were chosen to be investigated in some depth. All the aesthetic products of culture including art, music, literature, and architecture were drawn upon for classroom material; however, the study emphasized the use of historical documents in developing the student's ability to discover and explain his political and social environment. Secondary sources—e.g., textbooks, excerpts from monographs, magazine articles—were used only insofar as they related to the problem under attack, and they were introduced after the initial encounter with the "discovery episode." On the average, a new discovery episode was introduced every two weeks, and in the main, it consisted of a historical document, the origin, referent, and author of which were carefully deleted. The students were challenged to gather all the missing information. Although a discovery episode presupposed some general knowledge, it was not necessary for the student to have had special training or familiarity with the problem under consideration. In a situation such as this, the instructor performs a nondirective role in that he explicitly refuses to answer any of the students' questions. His task in the classroom is twofold: (1) to instigate and challenge the students, and (2) to moderate the discussion.

In order to illustrate the flow of classroom discussion during a discovery session, parts of the student dialogue are here reproduced. In this particular case, the students were given ten brief poems[2] and were asked to read them carefully. The participants were encouraged to discover a plausible choice for the cultural origin of the following poems.

1.

My Thoughts turn to the Ancient Capital
    Long life and peace during your reign
O, Emperor.

2.

The beginning of all art
    A song when planting a rice field
in the country's inmost part.

3.

Is there, I wonder
    A man without a pen in hand—
The moon tonight!

4.

On the temple bell
    Resting, sleeping,
a firefly.

5.

A Great Lord—And Who
    makes *Him* get off his horse?
—cherry blossoms do!

6.

Snow yet remaining
    The mountain slopes are hazy—
It is evening.

7.

A crossroad sermon! True,
    It's rigamarole—but then
It's tranquil too!

8.

So brilliant a moonshine

[2] These poems were taken from Harold G. Henderson, *Introduction to Japanese Haiku* (New York: Doubleday & Company, Inc. [Anchor Books], 1962). The selection of material was based primarily on two criteria: (a) availability of data pertaining to a central or common theme, e.g., the feudal system in Japan; and (b) careful avoidance of clues which would "give away" the puzzle.

When I am born again—
A hilltop pine!

9.

To the Great Lord's hall
Five or six horsemen hurry hard—
A storm wind of fall.

10.

As he snoozes, the mountain stream he
uses
To wash his rice,
No simple peasant, this!

The discussion that ensued was tape-recorded and transcribed. Selected parts of the transcription are given below.

FIRST DAY

*Teacher:* Please read this. (*five minutes of silence*) Well now, everyone finished? What do you think of this reading? What are these?

*Tim:* This must be a collection of poems.

*Teacher:* Why?

*Tim:* Because each of these little pieces is in verse. Some rhyme.

*George:* But they're so vague. What are we supposed to do with them?

*Teacher:* Whatever you like. Are they really vague?

*Gwen:* I don't think so. Some of the poems are very interesting, maybe difficult to interpret, but interesting.

*Sylvia:* Yes, I think we can find clues if we try.

*George:* Clues for what? All this is still vague.

*Bill S.:* Yes, what are we supposed to find out? What do these mean? Where are they from? Who wrote them? When were they written?

*Teacher:* All of you should be able to supply your own answers to these questions. Who would like to make the first attempt? (*a moment of silence*)

*Carolyn:* Well, they're all poems, so they must have been written by a poet.

*Bill S.:* That's some help! How do you know they're not written by one and the same poet? They all look the same to me, same three lines, same style, all short and vague.

*Carolyn:* But they're on different subjects

and they give different feelings. Each one gives me a different feeling.

*Bill S.:* Does that mean they can't be by one poet expressing himself on different subjects?

*Sylvia:* I have a different idea. Maybe these poems are all by different poets, but may seem to be the same because of the style. What I mean is that maybe these are the usual kind of poem for this country.

*Gwen:* Or, it could just be the style of a particular poet.

*John:* I think this is getting us nowhere. Let's forget about the poet and try to find out where it's from.

*Bob:* But these poems are too vague.

*Diane:* We're back to that again.

*Teacher:* Well, does everyone agree with this, or can someone offer advice or evidence to help us out? Where are these from?

*Sharon:* They are from Europe because an Emperor is mentioned, and lords are also mentioned a couple of times. This means there must have been an autocracy in this country. Many countries of Europe had monarchs and lords.

*Bernard:* At one time almost every European country had this kind of government. Maybe these poems are from Russia. Russia had an Emperor and nobles running it for a long, long time.

*Diane:* I think that this is from France or Germany, or Austria during the Middle Ages, because the lords seem to be very powerful; they are able to command cavalry men and to own large halls. Maybe the emperor referred to is Charlemagne.

*Gwen:* I think you're getting on the wrong track. This is no European set of poems, certainly not American!

*Teacher:* Why?

*Gwen:* Well, you're missing a lot of important parts of the poems that seem not to be European at all. What about the mention of a temple? Since when are Medieval churches called temples? And what about the reference to rice in one of the poems? Rice wasn't one of the European's main dishes, at least as far as I know.

*Eddie:* Rice is from the Orient, from China. The Chinese eat lots of rice. The poems must be translated from Chinese.

*Steve:* They could also be from Japan or India. I've read somewhere that these two countries produce and eat rice as their main dish.

*Mary:* I read recently that Southeast Asia produces a lot of rice. Vietnam exports rice, and eats some of it.

*Helen:* I have a suggestion, but not of another country. I think we should try to get the meaning and message of each poem and then find out where they're from. Let's start with poem 1 and work our way down.

It is apparent that the first day is spent on orientation and organization of the materials at hand. During the introductory phases of the discovery episode, the students are encouraged to come to grips with the responsibility of exercising independent judgment in pursuing a course of action. The teacher and the material, which includes only limited clues, create a sense of puzzlement. The students begin to suggest modes of attack and try to capitalize on the available springboards. For example, John proposes that the focal point of investigation should change from a quest to identify the poet to an inquiry into the national origin of the poems. This suggestion is taken up by several members of the class—e.g., Gwen, who in her first reaction to the poem, offers a hypothesis which harmonizes several problematic bits of data and refutes previous conjectures. At this point other students attempt to validate and to narrow down the proposition that the poems are of non-Western source. Helen, following up this line of investigation, concludes the deliberations of the first day by suggesting that each poem be thoroughly scrutinized and analyzed before returning to the main source of perplexity.

SECOND DAY

*Here the students are considering Helen's suggestion, and they are studying each poem in*

*depth. Only discussion relating to three of these poems (8, 9, and 10) is reproduced here.*

*Helen:* This poem (Number 8) is written by a Buddhist or a Hindu because it contains a belief in rebirth. As far as I know, only these two religions teach this belief.

*George:* I think it's called reincarnation. That means that you are born over and over again into new bodies or forms, although your soul remains the same.

*Helen:* Well, I think this poet is a Buddhist or Hindu because he believes this idea. He wants to be born again as a pine tree on a hilltop so he can enjoy beautiful moonlit nights. Does anyone disagree?

*Mary:* I don't. Now we have a better idea of where these poems are from. They have to be from the Orient, and they have to be from a country with Buddhists or Hindus living in it. They can't be from anywhere else.

*Gwen:* Yes, and according to the ninth poem, these would have to be from a country in which great lords are important people. The ninth poem repeats the fourth poem, and the great lord is said to own a hall. This must be like a castle.

*Steve:* The lord seems to have soldiers or cavalry working for him. Then the poem changes subject and tells of a storm wind of the fall.

*Gwen:* Maybe the poet is trying to tell us in a roundabout way that a war or fight is brewing. That's why the cavalry is reporting to the great lord. I don't think his poem is peaceful like the others at all. It's a poem that tells us of troubles in the country. People were fighting each other and each great lord probably had soldiers working for him.

*Sharon:* That's called a feudalistic system. These poems have to be from a feudalistic country. We have to find out which Oriental countries were feudalistic—or still are.

*George:* That might be a help. Find out which Oriental countries had feuding societies and feudal lords.

*Sharon:* I agree about the wars, but I don't think your suggestion will help because all those feudal societies used to have little wars.

*Steve:* Like England during the War of

the Roses and France during the tenth and eleventh centuries?

*Tim:* I think you are right. You have also missed something important. If there are great lords in this country, there are most likely other lords, lesser ones in the setup as well. This sounds very close to feudalism. Usually, however, feudalism is a system of many powerful nobles and a weak king.

*Sharon:* Well, that fits pretty well. We definitely know that the lords of this country are powerful, armed, and have castles of some kind, while the emperor is spoken of as being in his ancient capital. It seems to me that he's out of the picture.

*Bill:* But we really can't tell for sure.

*Sharon:* Well, at least we know that the nobility is powerful, and if that's true, then the emperor must have that much less power or say-so on everything.

*Teacher:* Good point. Now what about a volunteer for the last poems?

*Bernard:* The last one is about a lazy peasant. I guess it's a kind of joke because the peasant is taking a nap while the water washes his rice, which I guess is in some sort of sack hanging in the water. Say! That's pretty clever.

*Diane:* Some people, including the poet, must have thought peasants were simple-minded, and the poet is showing us that this isn't so, because here's a peasant who can get his work done and sleep at the same time.

*Bernard:* By the way, I think this poem and the second one about rice prove that rice is very important in the life of the people of this country, and it also shows that these two poems are by different people.

*Mary:* Why do you say that? We decided before that we couldn't be sure of that.

*Bernard:* Well, in the second poem those who plant the rice are praised and in the last poem peasants are made fun of.

*Karen:* That could still be that same poet in a different place or mood.

In the above discussion the students are subjecting the poems to a detailed examination. All shades of meaning and locational clues are explored. In

part, they seem to be working in sequential steps or plateaus; once they have determined that the poems are of Buddhist or of Hindu origin then they strike out to reach a new plateau which would incorporate more data and eliminate fruitless speculations. In their attempt to explain the existence of "great lords" they begin to draw certain logical inferences, e.g., if powerful lords are in control the monarch must be correspondingly weak. It should also be noted that in the process of "figuring out" the puzzle, the participants draw from personal accumulated knowledge which, on several occasions, provides the missing parts and clarifies certain ambiguities and vagueness in the material. For example, they are trying to interpret the poems in terms of a theory of feudalism. The discussion pertaining to the last poem is a clear illustration of an attempt to reconcile contradictory information and place it in the framework of a more inclusive and warranted hypothesis.

THIRD DAY

*Teacher:* Now that you've analyzed all of the poems, where do you think they're from?

*George:* We've ruled out the West, and this has to be from countries under the influence of Buddhism or Hinduism, the only religions preaching reincarnation.

*Eddie:* That limits our choices to India, China, or Japan.

*Eileen:* Or Southeast Asia. The question is which one?

*Steve:* It seems as though each of these places fills the bill. All are countries that are literate, religious, feudalistic at one time or another, and dependent on rice for a main part of their diet.

*Eddie:* Well, wait a minute. Now that I think of it, China may not be a good choice. It doesn't fit in with what we've been saying about these poems. China had a very powerful emperor who ruled through a civil service. As far as I know there was no nobility in China except for the emperor's household.

*Bill V.:* But wasn't there an earlier period in Chinese history in which feudalism was the form of government?

*Mary:* Well, at least we can eliminate most of Chinese history.

*Tim:* I think it's India. Great Lord could be a translation for Maharaja, but I'm not sure if India has had emperors. Did it?

*Teacher:* You can find out, can't you?

*Bill S.:* Oh, please tell us where it's from. I can't wait any longer.

*Teacher:* But why should I when you can find out for yourself? Doesn't someone have any helpful suggestions?

*Diane:* I think it's from India, too. The mention of rice, temples, peasants, and the religious tone to several of the poems make me think of India.

*Gwen:* But what you've said could apply to almost all of Asia, India, and the East.

*Tim:* I think we can rule out China altogether because I remember reading that Buddhism and the idea of rebirth were introduced into China after China already had a system of absolute emperors who ruled through a civil service, and I think there were no powerful nobles.

*Bob:* If all of that is correct, then China is ruled out, but that still leaves us with Japan, India, and Southeast Asia.

*Mary:* These poems must be from a mountainous country because of the mention of mountains in several of them.

*Gwen:* Northern India is very mountainous, so are parts of Southeast Asia, and all of Japan is that way.

*Randy:* Maybe it's Japan. Up until very recently Japan was a feudal country with lords, barons, and soldiers called Samurai, including a very shy, weak emperor. It is also a Buddhist country filled with ancient temples and preachers of religion. Japan sounds like a very good choice.

*Bill S.:* It could still be Northern India or Southeast Asia some time long ago.

*Bernard:* I believe there were emperors in India rather recently, called Moguls, or something like that.

*Karen:* What about the style of these poems? They seem pretty unusual. Maybe we can check into this by looking at sample poems from all over Asia until we hit on the same type. Maybe that will help us find a definite answer.

(Bell rings.)

During the third day of class deliberations, the students begin to limit the range of alternative choices or hypotheses; based on the previous analysis, they assert that the country in question will have to be Oriental, and that it will have to be under the cultural influence of Buddhism and/or Hinduism. Once this has been determined, a search for specific countries within the given cultural region takes place. Here they attempt to match alternative countries with the criteria that they have established. They further delimit the field of choice by rejecting those Oriental nations which deviate from the image they have constructed based on their interpretation of the poems. Throughout this process, they draw inferences which aid them in the defensible elimination of unwarranted hypotheses, e.g., the rejection of China as a possible choice by Tim and Bob, which takes the form of what Hunt and Metcalf call an "if-then generalization."[3] The primary goal of the group is the discovery of an answer that harmonizes all the evidence and integrates the ten poems. However, they soon realize that whatever data are at their command, they are not sufficient to support conclusively any of the proposed solutions. The realization of this difficulty motivates them to seek additional sources, especially those which include more detailed and authoritative information.

FOURTH DAY

*Bill W., Steve, Tim, and Karen:* We have final proof. We found it.

*Karen:* We checked these poems against

[3] Maurice P. Hunt and Lawrence E. Metcalf, *Teaching High School Social Studies* (New York: Harper & Row, Publishers, 1955).

Indian, Chinese, Japanese, and any other Oriental types of poems we could find, and we found out that this type of poem is Japanese only, and is called a *haiku*.

During the last phase of the discussion, the students offer concluding suggestions which are based on newly obtained evidence. For the most part, the additional proof was the result of the collation of the poems under investigation with all other relevant material which was accessible in the library. This line of inquiry was in part instigated by Karen's suggestion at the conclusion of the third day, which directed attention to the form and style in addition to the content of the poems.

## SUMMARY

The following four points provide the major results of this research:

1. Without exception the students were able to participate directly in the process of discovery and inquiry. This process entailed a number of related tasks—identifying and defining the problems at hand, devising alternative plans of attack, formulating working hypotheses from the given data and their previous learning experiences, testing the hypotheses by drawing logical inferences and by gathering relevant information, and arriving at a theory or "grand generalization" which draws together all bits of data and supporting hypotheses. It is interesting to note that the process of discovery moves from a stage of hunch and intuition to a stage of in-depth analysis and, finally, to the point where knowledge-claims are based on concrete, documentary evidence. While this is the general direction followed in the discovery episode, speculative or "intuitive" thinking may be found, to a great or lesser degree, in all of the phases; when there is a gap in knowl-

edge the student reaches out into unchartered and largely unknown realms of interpretation and thinking. From this observation the complementary nature of intuitive and analytic thinking may be seen.

2. Historical materials are used as raw data or as archeological remains from which students may reconstruct a society at a given place and period. The historical document furnishes the springboards for inquiry into human thought and action and the evolution of social institutions. In the process of reconstructing the event, historical hypotheses are often checked against contemporary phenomena; the students employ both historical and social science concepts, research techniques, and methods of analysis.

3. The way material is presented, coupled with the nondirective behavior of the teacher, leads to the creation of a new psychological climate. The students now become increasingly independent and they begin to question the authority of secondary material. They generally adopt an attitude of intelligent doubt, and they tend to propose new ideas and explanations that must be carefully defended. The class is given the opportunity to exchange ideas and analyze different views and interpretations.

4. The method of discovery has a highly motivating effect on students. Almost without exception, the students, directly or indirectly, demonstrate a great deal of personal involvement with the material under discussion. During the duration of the study there was wide classroom participation and intensive utilization of library resources. The motivating effect of the discovery episode is due, in large part, to the game-like situation which reinforces the element of perplexity and incentive to explore. The teacher indirectly encourages student exploration

by stubbornly refusing to provide ready-made answers.

The reader should keep in mind the exploratory nature of this study and the fact that the writers are offering observations based on rather limited samples. This research should, hopefully, provide a point of departure for further experimentation in this area. It would be advisable to undertake further study in which a variety of materials is given to students who represent all levels of education and who have a wide range of intelligence.

# 33

# Learning by Discovery: Rationale and Mystique

DAVID P. AUSUBEL

At the appropriate time and place, and for carefully designated purposes, learning by discovery has its defensible uses and undoubted advantages. This is what I will refer to as its rationale. But for a long time, and in many different guises learning by discovery has also been both a fad and a religion. Some of its proponents have elevated it into a panacea, making exaggerated claims for its uses and efficacy that go far beyond the evidence as well as far beyond all reason. It purportedly can do things for which it was never originally intended and is even ill-adapted—and for reasons that border either on mystical veneration of its alleged effects on the learning process, or on sheer sentimental fantasy about the nature of the child and of the educative process. This is what I mean when I talk about its mystique. The chief aim of this article is to distinguish between the rationale and the

David P. Ausubel, "Learning by Discovery: Rationale and Mystique," *Bulletin of the National Association of Secondary-School Principals* (December 1961), pp. 18-58. Copyright. Washington, D.C. Reprinted by permission.

mystique of the so-called discovery method of teaching.

## HISTORICAL ANTECEDENTS

Before attempting to set forth the rationale and mystique of the discovery method, I think it might be helpful briefly to consider the more important of the numerous educational movements and currents of thought from which it has evolved. Some of its historical antecedents are relatively recent, whereas others have flourished for centuries. Unfortunately, also, not all of these precursory trends are logically compatible with each other.

The Progressive Education movement obviously furnished several major strands in the design of the discovery method. One aspect of this movement was a growing dissatisfaction with the empty formalism of much educational content in the latter part of the nineteenth century and the early part of the twentieth century; with stultifying drill and catechism-like methods of teaching; with the curriculum's lack of relatedness to the everyday experience of the child, his physical world, and social environment; and with pupils' rote verbalization and memorization of ideas for which they had no adequate referents in experience. Overstatement of the realities underlying this dissatisfaction constituted the basis of the later mystique that *all* verbal learning is little more than glib verbalism and parrot-like recitation. This led, in turn, to the exaggerated emphasis that progressivists placed on relating the curriculum to the physical and social environment of the child; on direct, immediate, and concrete experience as a prerequisite for meaningful understanding; on active learning and inquiry; and on incidental learning and learning in natural, uncontrived situations. From this type of emphasis grew activity programs and project methods, and the credo of "learning for and by problem solving" as the principal objective and method, respectively, of the educational enterprise. Two final by-products of this point of view were deification of the act of discovery associated with the inductive and incidental learning methods of teaching, and extrapolation to the secondary-school and university student of the elementary-school child's dependence on recently prior concrete, empirical experience in the comprehension and manipulation of ideas. As we shall see later, both of these developments became extremely important components of the mystique of learning by discovery.

Such modern proponents of the discovery method as Gertrude Hendrix acknowledge their historical and ideological kinship to the Progressive Education movement, but are quick to disassociate themselves from some of the basic assumptions made by the inductive and incidental learning approaches to instruction. Hendrix

quite rightly points out that the main fallacy of the inductive approach lies in the teacher's use of the pupil's ability to verbalize a discovery as the "criterion by which [she] recognizes that discovery has taken place"(17, p. 296). And in referring to the incidental learning that purportedly occurs in the course of a pupil's involvement in a project or activity program, Hendrix correctly berates the advocates of this method because "all too often they took no responsibility for seeing that instances of the same generalization came along close enough together for the learner to become aware of either concepts or principles"(17, p. 293).

A second aspect of the Progressive Education movement relevant to the evolution of the discovery method was the child-centered approach to instruction that originated in the educational philosophies of Rousseau and Froebel. The adherents of this approach emphasized the importance of structuring the curriculum in terms of the nature of the child and his participation in the educative process, that is, in terms of his current interests, his endogenously derived needs, and his state of intellectual and emotional readiness. According to this point of view, the educational environment facilitates development best by providing a maximally permissive field that does not interfere with the predetermined process of spontaneous maturation. The child himself, it is asserted, is in the most strategic position to know and select those educational ingredients that correspond most closely with his prevailing developmental needs, and hence are most conducive to his optimal growth. Propositions such as these obviously make a fetish of autonomy and self-discovery, and regard as little short of sacrilege any form of guidance or direction in learning, and particularly the communication of insights or generalizations by teachers to pupils. Herein lies in part the origin of the mystique that expository teaching is inherently authoritarian, and that self-discovered insights are uniquely and transcendentally endowed with meaning and understanding that can be achieved through no other means. Hendrix, for example, castigates didactic exposition of generalizations as "authoritarian" and as only "satisfying to someone who *is already aware* of the ideas being presented"(17, p. 296). This same mystique also underlies the quite different educational doctrine that it is authoritarian and undemocratic for a knowledgeable person to communicate his knowledge to other persons lacking his particular background of thought and study, and that the latter individuals can learn more through "democratic discussion," that is, by talking off the tops of their heads and pooling their ignorance.

These two strands of the Progressive Education movement—emphasis on the child's direct experience and spontaneous interests, and insistence on autonomously achieved insight free of all directive manipulation of the learning environment—set the stage for the subsequent deification of problem solving, laboratory work, and naïve emulation of the scientific method. Many mathematics and science teachers were rendered self-conscious about systematically presenting and explaining to their students the basic concepts and principles of their fields, because it was held that this procedure would promote glib verbalism and rote memorization. It was felt that if students worked enough problems and were kept busy pouring reagents into a sufficient number of test tubes, they would somehow spontaneously discover in a meaningful way all of the important concepts and generalizations they

needed to know in the fields they were studying.

Of course, one had to take pains to discourage students from rotely memorizing formulas, and then mechanically substituting for the general terms in these formulas the particular values of specified variables in given problems. This would naturally be no less rote than formal didactic exposition. Hence, in accordance with the new emphasis on *meaningful* problem solving, students ceased memorizing formulas, memorizing instead type problems. They learned how to work exemplars of all of the kinds of problems they were responsible for, and then rotely memorized both the form of each type and its solution. Thus equipped, it was comparatively easy to sort the problems with which they were confronted into their respective categories, and "spontaneously proceed to discover meaningful solutions"—provided, of course, that the teacher played fair and presented recognizable exemplars of the various types.

Similarly, as the terms "laboratory" and "scientific method" became sacrosanct in American high schools and universities, students were coerced into mimicking the externally conspicuous but inherently trivial aspects of scientific method. They wasted many valuable hours collecting empirical data which, at the very worst, belabored the obvious, and at the very best, helped them rediscover or exemplify principles which the teacher could have presented verbally and demonstrated visually in a matter of minutes. Actually, they learned precious little subject matter and even less scientific method from this procedure. The unsophisticated scientific mind is only confused by the natural complexities of raw, unsystematized empirical data, and learns much more from schematic models

and diagrams; and following laboratory manuals in cookbook fashion,
without adequate knowledge of the
relevant methodological and substantive principles involved, confers about
as much genuine appreciation of scientific method as putting on a white
"lab" coat and doing a TV commercial
for "Roll-Aids."

As a result of the superstitious faith
of educators in the magical efficacy
of problem-solving and laboratory
methods, we have produced in the past
four decades millions of high-school
and college graduates who *never* had the
foggiest notion of the meaning of a
variable, of a function, of an exponent,
of calculus, of molecular structure,
or of electricity, but who have done all
of the prescribed laboratory work,
and have successfully solved an acceptable percentage of the required problems in differential and integral
calculus, in logarithms, in molar and
normal solutions, and in Ohm's Law.

One basic lesson that some modern
proponents of the discovery method
have drawn from this educational
disaster is that problem solving per se
is not conducive to meaningful discovery. Problem solving can be just
as deadening, just as formalistic, just
as mechanical, just as passive, and
just as rote as the worst form of verbal
exposition. The type of learning
outcomes that emerges is largely a
function of the structure, the substance, the organization, and the spirit
of the problem-solving experiences
one provides. However, an equally
important lesson which these same
proponents of the discovery method
refuse to draw is that, because of the
educational logistics involved, even the
best program of problem-solving
experience is no substitute for a mini-
mally necessary amount of appropriate
didactic exposition. But this minimum

will never be made available as long
as we adhere to the standard university
formula of devoting one hour of exposition to every four hours of laboratory
work and paper-and-pencil problem
solving.

Historically, the discovery method
may also be considered, in part, a
revolt against the prevailing educational
psychology of our time, which is largely
an eclectic hodgepodge of logically
incompatible theoretical propositions
superimposed upon a sterile empiricism. Perhaps the most outrageous
example of this unconscionable eclec-
ticism has been the six-decade campaign
sparked by Teachers College to integrate Thorndikian connectionism and a
wildly extrapolated neo-Behaviorism
with the major tenets of Progressive
Education. But the transparent soph-
istry that resulted from the attempt to
reconcile such antithetical sets of
principles as the Law of Effect, drive
reduction, stimulus-response and rote
learning theory, the transfer of identical
elements, and trial-and-error learning,
on the one hand, and progressivist viewpoints regarding meaningful understanding of ideas, active inquiry, and
autonomous discovery, on the other,
tended to alienate some of the more
independent-minded educational psychologists in the Progressive Education camp. Some defected to psychoanalysis, spawning a weird synthesis of
Deweyism and Freudianism, whereas
others were attracted by the greater
emphasis on cognition and insightful
problem solving which characterized
such field theorists and Gestalt theoreti-
cians as Tolman, Lewin, Köhler,
Wertheimer, and Katona. Also included
among the defectors were many vigor-
ous supporters of the discovery method,
who viewed the extrapolation of rote
learning theory to verbal classroom
learning as sufficient proof of the

essentially rote nature of verbal learning, and as ample justification for designing nonverbal discovery techniques of teaching.

A final current of educational thought influencing the evolution of the discovery method was the militant sentimentality underlying the currently popular educational objective of making *every* child a critical and creative thinker. This objective is, in part, a wish-fulfilling extension of our present-day preoccupation with actualizing the creative potentialities of gifted children. But it also harks back to certain conceptions within the mental measurement movement and to the official environmentalistic bias of Progressive Education. (At Teachers College, we must remember, Darwin and Mendel have always occupied prominent positions in the gallery of ideological villains.) If, for example, we accept the premise that the structure of intellect can be analyzed into a multiplicity of separately identifiable cognitive abilities or factors (as many as 120 according to Guilford [14]), the conclusion seems inescapable that simply on the basis of probability almost every child is destined to become a genius or a near-genius with respect to at least one factor; and even if a particular child were to receive an unlucky shake of the genic dice, a benevolent educational environment would certainly make up for the difference.

RATIONALE

As I suggested earlier, my unhappiness with the discovery method is not a generalized phenomenon. I do not disapprove of it under any and all circumstances. What I do object to are some of its unwarranted assumptions, overstated claims, inadequately tested propositions, and, above all, to some

of the reasons advanced for its efficacy. I will consider these latter matters shortly under the general headings of mystique and evidence.

But let us begin on a more positive note and examine first the legitimate claims, the defensible uses, and the palpable advantages of the discovery method. In the early, unsophisticated stages of learning any abstract subject matter, particularly prior to adolescence, the discovery method is invaluable. It is also indispensable for teaching scientific method and effective problem-solving skills. Furthermore, various cognitive and motivational factors undoubtedly enhance the learning, retention, and transferability of meaningful material learned by discovery.

Why are discovery methods so valuable in teaching difficult and abstract subject-matter content to children, especially in fields such as mathematics with their own distinctive terminology and symbolic systems?

In the absence of prior discovery and nonverbal experience, children approximately below the age of twelve[1] tend to find directly presented verbal constructs of any complexity unrelatable to existing cognitive structure, and hence devoid of potential meaning.[2] Until they consolidate

[1] "The designation of age level here is solely for purposes of convenience, and is not meant to imply that the change is abrupt or that overlapping of learning processes does not occur between children in adjacent age groups. Nor does it imply that the transition is reflective of "internal ripening" and hence takes place invariably at this age. The precise age *around* which the transition occurs depends on the nature of the child's prior experience and education and on such individual differences as IQ. The only necessary assumption, therefore, is that a gradual qualitative transition in mode of learning takes place as children reach a certain level of cognitive sophistication, and that the age at which this change is most salient varies with both individual capacity and experience" (2, p. 20).

[2] See, for example, Piaget (28, 29) and Serra (30).

a sufficiently large working body of key verbal concepts based on appropriate experience, and until they become capable of directly interrelating abstract propositions without reference to specific instances, children are closely restricted to basic empirical data in the kinds of logical operations they can relate to cognitive structure. Thus in performing "class-inclusive and relational operations," they generally require direct experience with the actual diverse instances underlying a concept or generalization, as well as proximate, nonverbal (rather than representational) contact with the objects or situations involved (20). During the elementary-school years, directly presented and verbal materials are too distantly removed from empirical experience to be relatable to cognitive structure (2, p. 20).

Furthermore, for children who are still functioning at Piaget's level of concrete operations, nonverbal, intuitive discovery and application of principles, prior to formal verbalization, *is* often desirable, *in addition to* the use of concrete-empirical props. In learning more complex and abstract ideas far removed from everyday experience, it is plausible to suppose that subverbal insights acquired through discovery experience may serve as a facilitating transitional phase in the achievement of full verbal understanding. Verbalization of principles before this nonverbal insight is sufficiently consolidated may both interfere with the process of consolidation and impede transfer because it is self-evident that relatively well-established intuitive awareness of a principle is more functional and transferable to analogous situations than is a marginal type of verbal understanding. Also, if the verbalized principle is prematurely available, many pupils, especially those who are anxiety ridden or anxious to please, will be tempted to memorize the words rotely and abandon the quest for meaningful understanding.

This does not necessarily mean, however, that actual discovery is [always] required before meaningfulness is possible. As long as direct, nonverbal contact with the data is an integral part of the learning situation, derivative verbal concepts and generalizations may often be meaningfully apprehended even though they are presented rather than discovered. But since discovery probably enhances both retention and transferability . . . [in more difficult and abstract learning tasks], and since the time-consuming empirical aspect of the learning must take place anyway, it is . . . [desirable] in these circumstances to encourage pupils independently to complete the final step of drawing inferences from data (2, p. 21).

In lesser degree, this same rationale also applies to adolescents and adults who are relatively unsophisticated in the basic concepts and terminology of a given discipline. The older individual, however, has the benefit of greater general cognitive sophistication and linguistic facility, as well as of past successful experience in meaningfully relating abstractions to each other without the aid of concrete, empirical experience. Hence, he will move through the intuitive, subverbal phase of insightful understanding much more rapidly than the comparably unsophisticated child, and, unlike the latter, will soon dispense with this phase entirely.

The discovery method also has obvious uses in teaching problem-solving techniques and appreciation of scientific method. There is no better way of developing effective skills in hypothesis making and testing; desirable attitudes "toward learning and inquiry, toward guessing and hunches, toward the possibility of solving problems on one's own . . .; [and] attitudes about the ultimate orderliness of nature and a conviction that order can be discovered"(7, p. 20). As a matter of fact, this is the major rationale for laboratory work. Except in the case of children and unsophisticated older persons, subject-matter content can be both transmitted and illustrated much more efficiently by means of exposition, demonstration, and schematic models.

Independent problem solving, furthermore, is perhaps the only feasible way of testing whether students *really* comprehend meaningfully the ideas they are able to verbalize. But here we have to be careful not to fall into a trap. To say that problem solving is the only practical method of measuring the meaningful understanding of ideas is *not* the same as saying that the learner who is unable to solve a representative set of problems *necessarily* does not understand, but has merely memorized the principles exemplified by these problems. Successful problem solving demands many *other* abilities and qualities, such as reasoning power, perseverance, flexibility, improvisation, sensitivity, and tactical astuteness, *in addition to* meaningful comprehension of the underlying principles. Hence, failure to solve the problems in question may reflect deficiencies in these latter factors rather than lack of genuine understanding.

Finally, in spite of the inconclusive empirical evidence, when all is said and done, and one has properly discounted the exaggerated claims made for the unique virtues of learning by discovery, as well as the fanciful reasons offered for same, it still seems

plausible to suppose that the greater effort and vividness associated with independent discovery lead to somewhat greater learning and retention. One might expect the advantages conferred by discovery techniques to be even greater with respect to transferability, since the experience gained from · formulating a generalization from diverse instances . . . obviously facilitates

the solution of problems involving this generalization (2, p. 22).

The crucial points at issue, however, are not whether learning by discovery enhances learning, retention, and transferability, but (a) whether it does so *sufficiently*, for learners who are capable of learning principles meaningfully *without* it, to warrant the vastly increased expenditure of time it requires; and (b) whether, in view of this time consideration, the discovery method is a feasible technique for transmitting the substantive content of an intellectual or scientific discipline to cognitively mature students who have already mastered its rudiments and basic vocabulary. It is largely to an exploration of these issues that the remainder of this article is devoted.

## MYSTIQUE

For purposes of analysis, the mystique of learning by discovery may be conveniently divided into nine propositions.

### ALL REAL KNOWLEDGE IS SELF-DISCOVERED

The most general and metaphysical of the nine propositions is the familiar assertion that to possess knowledge *really* or acquire an idea, the learner must discover it by himself or through his own insight. This proposition stems in part from the deification of the act of creative discovery in the problem-solving, activity-program approach to teaching, and from John Dewey's extreme preference for problem-solving ability, rather than ability to acquire knowledge, as the proper criterion of intelligence. It is also partly derived from the child-centered and client-centered doctrines that the individual himself is best equipped to regulate the process of learning about himself and his universe, and, therefore, that any tampering with this autonomy, is, by definition, detrimental to learning outcomes.

More recently, a sentimental type of Rousseauean mysticism and primitivisms has become fashionable, and has been superimposed upon the aforementioned ideological substrate. It is best exemplified by Jerome Bruner's statement that:

... if man's intellectual excellence is the most his own among his perfections, it is also the case that the most uniquely personal of all that he knows is that which he has discovered himself . . . [Discovery creates] a special and unique relation between knowledge possessed and the possessor (8, p. 22). . . . The transition to adulthood involves an introduction to new realms of experience, the discovery and exploration of new mysteries, the gaining of new powers. This is the heady stuff of education and it is its own reward (9, p. 76).

In accordance with this conception of the true nature of genuine knowledge, Bruner formulates the objectives of education as follows:

School should provide not simply a continuity with the broader community or with everyday experience. It is the special community where one experiences discovery by the use of intelligence, where one leaps into new and unimagined realms of experience, experience that is discontinuous with what went before (9). . . . Education must also seek to develop the processes of intelligence so that the individual is capable of going beyond the cultural ways of his social world, able to innovate, in however modest a way, so that he can create an interior culture of his own. For whatever the art, the science, the literature, the history, and the geography of a culture, each man must be his own artist, his own scientist, his own historian, his own navigator (9, p. 59).

Now these are lofty and poetically expressed sentiments, and anyone but a clod would regret having to assume the role of wet blanket by interposing such mundane considerations as validity and practicality. It is perfectly true that one cannot simply soak up one's culture like a piece of blotting paper and expect it to be meaningful. But who advocates doing anything of the kind? The very processes of perception and cognition necessarily require that the cultural stimulus world must first be filtered through each individual's personal sensory apparatus and cognitive structure before it can have any meaning. Meaning can never be anything more than a *personal* phenomenological product that emerges when potentially meaningful ideas are integrated within an individually unique cognitive structure. Invariably, therefore, the achievement of meaning requires translation into a personal frame of reference, and reconciliation with established concepts and propositions. All of this goes on in any program of meaningful expository teaching, and is obviously a far cry from the strawman picture of passive absorption which Bruner draws to disparage this method and thereby enhance the relative attractiveness of learning by discovery. Most of what anyone *really* knows consists of insights discovered by *others* which have been communicated to him in meaningful fashion.

Quite apart from its lack of face validity, the proposition that every man must discover for himself every bit of knowledge that he *really* wishes to possess is, in essence, a repudiation of the very concept of culture. For perhaps the most unique attribute of human culture, which distinguishes it from every other kind of social organization in the animal kingdom, is precisely the fact that the accumulated discoveries of millennia can be transmitted to each succeeding generation in the course of childhood and youth, and need not be discovered anew by each generation. This miracle of culture is made possible only because it is so much less time-consuming to communicate and explain an idea meaningfully to others than to have them rediscover it by themselves.

Within each generation, therefore, we can only expect a given individual to internalize meaningfully a reasonable fragment of the total fabric of the culture that is expounded to him by the various educational agencies. If we are at all concerned with the breadth of his knowledge, we cannot possibly expect him to discover everything he is expected to know. The obligation of going beyond one's cultural heritage and contributing something new is an obligation that applies to an entire generation, not to each of its individual members. Hence, as we shall see later, the school cannot realistically set for itself the goal of having *each* child "leap into new and unimagined realms of experience" and emerge with ideas that are "discontinuous with what went before." The school can only hope to help one child in a thousand do this, or, more likely, one child in a million.

MEANING AS AN EXCLUSIVE
PRODUCT OF CREATIVE,
NONVERBAL DISCOVERY

A related proposition that relies somewhat less on flat epistemological assertion, and is more naturalistically grounded, holds that abstract concepts and propositions are forms of empty verbalism unless the learner discovers them directly out of his own concrete, empirical, nonverbal experience (6, p. 112). Another slightly different

way of expressing the same idea is to say that "generalizations are products of problem solving . . . and are attainable in no other way" (6, p. 119). Careful analysis of this proposition reveals, in my opinion, that it rests on three serious logical fallacies: (a) a straw-man representation of the method of verbal learning; (b) the failure to distinguish properly between reception and discovery learning, on the one hand, and the prevailing tendency to confuse the reception-discovery dimension of the learning process with the rote-meaningful dimension, on the other; and (c) unwarranted generalization of the distinctive conditions of learning and thinking in childhood to adolescence and adult life.

The use of the old straw-man technique was, of course, the simplest and most effective way of discrediting the method of verbal exposition. Instead of describing this procedure in terms of its essential characteristics, it became fashionable to picture it in terms of its worst abuses. Examples of such abuses were naturally not very difficult to find, since an appreciable number of teachers still rely on rote verbal learning in teaching meaningful subject matter. Some of the more flagrantly inept practices include "premature use of verbal techniques with cognitively immature pupils; arbitrary . . . presentation of unrelated facts without any organizing or explanatory principles; failure to integrate new learning tasks with previously presented materials; and the use of evaluation procedures that merely measure ability to recognize discrete facts or to reproduce ideas in the same words or in the identical context as originally encountered"(2, pp. 23-24).

Nevertheless, even though it is entirely proper to caution teachers against these kinds of abuses, it is highly casuistic to represent them as inherent in the method itself. An approach to teaching which is rational and appropriate on logical and psychological grounds should not be branded as worthless and discarded simply because, like all pedagogical techniques in the hands of incompetent or unintelligent teachers, it is subject to misuse.

A second reason why meaning is commonly perceived as an exclusive product of problem-solving and discovery techniques of learning is because widespread confusion exists regarding basic distinctions between reception and discovery learning, and between rote and meaningful learning. This confusion, of course, is largely attributable to the lamentable tendency on the part of many educational psychologists to interpret meaningful school learning in terms of the same concepts used to explain instrumental conditioning, paired-associate learning, rote serial learning, maze learning, and simple discrimination learning.

"Because most of the understandings that learners acquire both in and out of school are presented rather than discovered"(2, p. 16), it is crucially important to differentiate between reception and discovery learning. In reception learning (rote or meaningful), the learner is not required to discover what he learns, but need only internalize what is presented to him so that it is available and reproducible at some future time. In discovery learning, on the other hand, the substance of what is to be learned must first be independently discovered by the learner before he can internalize it.

The first phase of discovery learning, therefore, involves a process quite different from that of reception learning. The learner must rearrange a given array of information, integrate it with existing cognitive structure, and reorganize or transform the integrated combination in such a way as to create a desired end product or discover a missing means-end relationship. After this phase is completed, the discovered content is internalized just as in reception learning (2, p. 16).

Now this distinction between reception and discovery learning has absolutely nothing to do with the rote-meaningful dimension of the learning process. Hence it is erroneous to assume that reception learning is invariably rote and that discovery learning is invariably meaningful. *Both* kinds of learning can either be rote *or* meaningful depending on the conditions under which the learning occurs. Reception or discovery learning is meaningful provided that the learner adopts a set to incorporate the substantive import of the learning task within his cognitive structure, and that the task itself is potentially meaningful, that is, logically or nonarbitrarily related thereto. It is rote, on the other hand, if the task consists of purely arbitrary associations, as in paired-associate, puzzle-box, or serial learning, and also (regardless of how much potential meaning the task has), if the learner adopts a set merely to internalize it in an arbitrary, verbatim fashion. It should be clear up to this point, therefore, that verbal reception learning is not necessarily rote in character, and can be meaningful even when not preceded by problem-solving or discovery experience.

But in discussing the legitimate rationale of the discovery method, it will be remembered that I placed certain developmental limits on meaningful verbal reception learning. I pointed out then that learners who have not yet developed beyond the concrete stage of logical operations are unable to incorporate within their cognitive structures a relationship between two or more abstractions, unless they have the benefit of recently prior concrete, empirical experience. Such learners, therefore, cannot meaningfully comprehend verbally or symbolically expressed propositions without the aid of these concrete-empirical props, although they by no means have to discover these propositions autonomously in order to understand them meaningfully. As every elementary-school teacher knows, meaningful verbal reception learning—without any problem-solving or discovery experience whatsoever—is perhaps the most common form of classroom learning, provided that the necessary props are available.

Beginning in the junior high school period, however, and becoming increasingly more true thereafter, prior empirical and nonverbal experience is no longer essential before concepts and generalizations become potentially meaningful. It is true, of course, that the pupil's established verbal concepts must have been preceded sometime in the past by direct, nonverbal experience with the data from which they were abstracted; but once these concepts are sufficiently well consolidated, and the pupil is able to manipulate and interrelate them adequately on a purely abstract basis, new learning material is logically relatable to cognitive structure without any direct or nonverbal *current* reference to empirical data. The adolescent, unlike the typical elementary-school child, *is* capable of performing logical operations on verbal propositions(20). His concepts and generalizations, therefore, tend more to be second-order constructs derived from relationships between previously established verbal abstractions already one step removed from the data itself(20). And since he is freed from dependence on direct, nonverbal contact with data in independently discovering meaningful new concepts and generalizations, he is obviously also liberated from this same dependence in the much less rigorous task' of merely apprehending these constructs meaningfully when they are verbally presented to him (2, p. 21).

This is the point at which some of the more zealous proponents of Progressive Education took a disastrously false turn. John Dewey had correctly recognized that meaningful understanding of abstract concepts and principles in childhood must be built on a foundation of direct, empirical experience and, for this reason, advocated the use of project and activity methods in the elementary school. But he also appreciated that once a firmly grounded first story of abstract understandings was established, it was possible to organize secondary and higher education along more abstract and verbal lines. Unfortunately, however, although Dewey himself never elaborated or implemented this latter conception, some of his disciples blindly generalized childhood limiting conditions, with respect to meaningful verbal reception learning, broadly enough to encompass learning over the entire life span. And this unwarranted extrapolation, frequently but erroneously attributed to Dewey himself, provided a pseudo-naturalistic rationale for, and thus helped perpetuate, the seemingly indestructable myth that, under any and all circumstances, abstractions cannot possibly be meaningful unless preceded by direct, empirical experience.

THE DISCOVERY METHOD
IN TRANSMITTING
SUBJECT-MATTER CONTENT

Educators who are convinced that abstractions are mere glib verbalisms unless independently discovered by the learner have no other logical alternative than to advocate the use of discovery techniques—in high school and university as well as in the elementary school—as a principal method of transmitting the substantive content of subject matter. Easley

(12, 13), for example, argues strenuously for reorganizing, in whole or in part, the curriculum of science, mathematics, and other secondary-school and college level subjects along the lines of inductive discovery. He also insists that nonverbal understanding and application of principles should be required of and demonstrated by students before they are permitted to use them in verbal form.

But whereas the frequent use of discovery techinques in the transmission of complex and abstract subject-matter content can be defended in the elementary school, on the grounds that the acquisition and transfer of subverbal insight may possibly facilitate the later acquisition of verbal understanding, it is difficult to rationalize the same practice in high school and beyond. It is true, as already pointed out, that the utilization of subverbal insight by older individuals might be temporarily helpful in the early, unsophisticated stages of learning a difficult new discipline. Nevertheless, since discovery methods are incomparably more time-consuming than didactic verbal exposition, and since the cognitively mature individual does not linger very long in the unsophisticated state that is benefited by prior acquisition of subverbal insight, the use of these methods as a *primary* means of transmitting subject-matter content is as unfeasible as it is unnecessary. If secondary-school and university students were obliged to discover for themselves every concept and principle in the syllabus, they would never get much beyond the rudiments of any discipline. However, as is similarly the case in the elementary school, teachers who do not regard completely *autonomous* discovery as sacrosanct could greatly mitigate the time-consuming disadvantage of discovery methods by the judicious use of prompts or hints.

Some discovery enthusiasts[3] grudgingly admit that there is not sufficient time for pupils to discover everything they need to know in the various disciplines, and hence concede that there is also room for good expository teaching in the schools. In practice, however, this concession counts for little, because in the very next breath they claim that the acquisition of actual knowledge is less important than the acquisition of ability to discover knowledge autonomously and propose that pedagogy and the curriculum be reorganized accordingly. Hence, in spite of the formal bow they make to didactic exposition, it is clear that they regard the acquisition of problem-solving ability (9, p. 77; 35, pp. 6, 7, 32) as more basic than the acquisition of subject matter. There is, after all, only so much time in a school day. If the school takes as its principal function the development of discovery and inquiry skills, how much time could possibly remain for the teaching of subject matter?

SUBVERBAL AWARENESS
AS THE KEY TO TRANSFER

We have seen, up to this point, that the reasoning underlying the mystique of discovery as a prerequisite for meaning has rested either upon bald metaphysical assertion, or upon unwarranted pseudonaturalistic assumptions regarding the nature of understanding and knowledge. Gertrude Hendrix tried to fill this theoretical void by constructing a more systematic and sophisticated pedagogic rationale for the discovery method than had been attempted heretofore. She did this by adapting to the problem of transfer the time-honored

[3] See, for example, Bruner (7, p. 21); Suchman (35, p. 32).

labeling theory of the function of language in thought. Hendrix denies that verbal generalizing is the primary generator of transfer power. . . . As far as transfer power [is] concerned the whole thing [is] there as soon as the nonverbal awareness [dawns]. . . . The separation of discovery phenomena from the process of composing sentences which express those discoveries is the big new breakthrough in pedagogical theory (17, pp. 292, 290).

The "key to transfer," Hendrix states, is a "subverbal internal process—something which must happen to the organism before it has any new knowledge to verbalize" (15, p. 200). Verbalization, she asserts further, is not only unnecessary for the generation and transfer of ideas and understanding, but is also positively harmful when used for *these* purposes. Language only enters the picture because of the need to attach a symbol or label to the emerging subverbal insight so that it can be recorded, verified, classified, and communicated to others; but the entire substance of the idea inheres in the subverbal insight itself. The resulting problem then, according to Hendrix, becomes one of how to plan and execute teaching so that language can be used for these necessary secondary functions "*without* damage to the dynamic quality of the learning itself" (17, p. 292).

How plausible is this proposition? Let us grant at the outset that a subverbal type of awareness or insight exists, and that this type of insight is displayed by rats, monkeys, and chimpanzees in experimental learning situations, and by household pets, saddle horses, barnyard animals, wild beasts, children, and adults in a wide variety of everyday problem-solving situations. But is it because of this type of insight that human beings have evolved a culture and have achieved

some progress in such fields as philosophy, chemistry, physics, biology, and mathematics, quite beyond anything yet approached by horses, chickens, or apes? Or is it because of the qualitatively superior transfer power of verbal or symbolic generalization?

The principal fallacy in Gertrude Hendrix' line of argument, in my opinion, lies in her failure to distinguish between the labeling and process functions of language in thought. She writes:

We have been a long time realizing that subverbal awareness of a class, or a property, or a relation *had* to be in *some*one's mind before anyone could have thought of inventing a word for it anyway. In the natural order of events, the abstraction forms first, and *then* a name for it is invented (16, p. 335).

Now what Hendrix is referring to here is simply the labeling or naming function of language in thought. The choice of a particular arbitrary symbol to represent a *new* abstraction obviously comes *after* the *process* of abstraction, and is not organically related to it. But this is not the *only* role of language in the abstraction process, nor is it the *first* time that it is used in this process. Verbalization, I submit, does more than verbally gild the lily of subverbal insight; it does more than just attach a symbolic handle to an idea so that one can record, verify, classify, and communicate it more readily. It constitutes, rather, an integral part of the very process of abstraction itself. When an individual uses language to express an idea, he is not merely encoding subverbal insight into words. On the contrary, he is engaged in a process of generating a higher level of insight that transcends by far—in clarity, precision, generality, and inclusiveness—the previously achieved stage of subverbal awareness.

The old philosophical notion that

words merely mirror thought or clothe it in outer garments is charmingly poetic but has little functional utility or explanatory value in the modern science of psycholinguistics. Even the seemingly simple act of making a choice of words in developing an idea involves complex processes of categorization, differentiation, abstraction, and generalization, the rejection of alternative possibilities; and the exclusion of less precise or overinclusive meanings. All of these processes contribute to and help account for the qualitatively superior transfer power of symbolic generalization.

Although the transfer power of symbolic generalization operates at many different levels of complexity and sophistication, even the simplest level transcends the kind of transfer that can be achieved with subverbal insight. Consider, for example, the transfer power of the word "house," which most preschool children can use correctly. Obviously, before the child ever uses this word, he has some unverbalized notion of what a house is. But I submit that, once he attains and can meaningfully use the verbal concept of "house," he possesses an emergent new idea that he never possessed before—an idea that is sharper, clearer, more precise, more inclusive, more transferable, and more manipulable for purposes of thinking and comprehension than its crude subverbal precursor. He can now talk about the idea of "house" in the abstract, devoid of all particularity, and can combine this idea with concepts of form, size, color, number, function, etc. to formulate relational propositions that could hitherto be formulated with only the greatest difficulty. That verbal concepts of this nature are more transferable and more manipulable than subverbal insights is demonstrated by numerous experiments on the effects

of verbalization on children's ability to solve transposition problems.[4] Knowledge of underlying verbal principles also enhances the learning of relevant motor performance; and the availability of distinctive verbal responses facilitates rather than inhibits concept formation and conceptual transfer.[5]

Not all ideas, however, are acquired quite as easily as the concept of house. As he enters school, the child encounters other concepts of much greater abstractness and complexity, e.g., concepts of addition, multiplication, government, society, force, velocity, digestion, that transcend his immediate experience and language ability. Before he can hope to acquire a meaningful grasp of such abstractions directly, that is, through direct verbal exposition, he must first acquire a minimal level of sophistication in the particular subject-matter area, as well as graduate into the higher level of intellectual development, i.e., the stage of formal logical operations. In the meantime he is limited to an intuitive, subverbal kind of understanding of these concepts; and, even though convincing empirical evidence is still lacking, it is reasonable to suppose that preliminary acquisition and utilization of this subverbal level of insight both facilitates learning and transferability, and promotes the eventual emergence of *full* verbal understanding. (Gertrude Hendrix, of course, would say that *full* understanding was already attained in the subverbal phase, and that verbalization merely attaches one to subverbal insight.)

Now, assuming for the moment that Hendrix' experimental findings are

---

[4] See, for example, Spiker and Terrill (31); Weir and Stevenson (38).
[5] See Ausubel and Fitzgerald (4) for a review of these findings.

valid, how can we explain the fact that immediate verbalization of newly acquired subverbal insight renders that insight less transferable than when verbalization is not attempted? (15). First, it seems likely that verbalization of nonverbal insight, before such insight is adequately consolidated by extensive use, may interfere with consolidation at this level, as well as encourage rote memorization of the ineptly stated verbal proposition. Even more important, however, is the likelihood that a verbally expressed idea—when ambiguous, unprecise, ineptly formulated, and only marginally competent—possesses less functional utility and transferability than the ordinarily more primitive and less transferable subverbal insight. This is particularly true in the case of children because of their limited linguistic facility and their relative incompetence in formal propositional logic.

Drawing these various strands of argument together, what can we legitimately conclude at this point? First, verbalization does more than just encode subverbal insight into words. It is part of the very process of thought which makes possible a qualitatively higher level of understanding with greatly enhanced transfer power. Second, direct acquisition of ideas from verbally presented propositions presupposes both that the learner has attained the stage of formal logical operations, and that he possesses minimal sophistication in the particular subject matter in question. The typical elementary-school child, therefore, tends to be limited to an intuitive, subverbal awareness of difficult abstractions. The older, cognitively mature individual, however, who is also unsophisticated in a particular subject-matter area is able to dispense with the subverbal phase of awareness rather quickly, i.e., as soon as he attains the

necessary degree of sophistication; and once he attains it, he probably short-circuits the subverbal phase completely. Lastly, immediate verbalization of a nonverbal insight, when this latter insight is newly acquired and inadequately consolidated, probably decreases its transferability. This phenomenon can be explained by means of the general developmental principle that an ordinarily higher and more efficient stage of development, while still embryonic and only marginally competent, is less functional than an ordinarily more primitive and less efficient phase of development. Running, for example, is eventually more efficient than creeping, but if a one-year-old infant had to run for his life, he would make better progress creeping.

Gertrude Hendrix, however, comes out with somewhat different and more sweeping conclusions from the same set of data. First, she regards nonverbal awareness as containing within itself the entire essence of an emerging idea, and insists that language merely adds a convenient symbolic handle to this idea. Second, she generalizes children's dependence on a preliminary subverbal stage of awareness, to all age levels, to all degrees of subject-matter sophistication, and to all levels of ideational difficulty. Actually, this subverbal stage is highly abbreviated, both for young children learning less difficult kinds of abstractions and for older, cognitively mature individuals working in a particular subject-matter area in which they happen to be unsophisticated; and it is bypassed completely when this latter sophistication is attained. Finally, she interprets her experimental findings regarding the inhibitory effects of immediate verbalization on the transferability of subverbal insight, as providing empirical *proof* of her thesis that both the substance of an idea and the essential basis of its transfer power are present in their entirety as soon as nonverbal awareness emerges. In my opinion, these findings do nothing of the kind. They merely show that a relatively clear subverbal insight, even when only partially consolidated, is more functional and transferable than an ambiguous, inept, and marginally competent verbally expressed idea.

Unlike Gertrude Hendrix, therefore, I would conclude that secondary-school and college students, who already possess a sound, meaningful grasp of the rudiments of a discipline like mathematics can be taught this subject meaningfully and with maximal efficiency through the method of verbal exposition, supplemented by appropriate problem-solving experience; and that the use of the discovery method in these circumstances is inordinately time-consuming, wasteful, and rarely warranted. Why do discovery techniques seem to work so well in programs such as the one devised by the University of Illinois Committee on School Mathematics? For one thing, the students entering the program, being victims of conventional arithmetic teaching in the elementary schools, do *not* have a sound, meaningful grasp of the rudiments of mathematics and have to be re-educated, so to speak, from scratch. For another, I have a very strong impression that as the program develops, the discovery element becomes progressively attenuated, until eventually it is accorded only token recognition. Lastly, stripped of its quite limited discovery aspects, the UICSM approach is a much more systematic, highly organized, self-consistent, carefully programmed, abstractly verbal system of verbal exposition than anything we have known to date in secondary-school mathematics. If it

proves anything, the success of this program is a testimonial to the feasibility and value of a good program of didactic verbal exposition in secondary-school mathematics, which program is taught by able and enthusiastic instructors and, in its early stages, makes judicious use of inductive and discovery techniques.

PROBLEM-SOLVING ABILITY
AS THE PRIMARY GOAL
OF EDUCATION

A fourth proposition underlying the mystique of learning by discovery is the belief that the development of problem-solving ability is the primary goal of education, and that somehow in the course of implementing this objective, the learner acquires all the of really important subject-matter content he needs to know. But although these two objectives are related and, in a sense, mutually supportive, they are far from being identical. Hence it cannot be assumed that methods promoting one objective necessarily promote the other. For this reason alone, "the process and goal of education" can hardly be considered "one and the same thing" (9, p. 77), as Bruner claims they are. The mere statement of any goal, furthermore, neither specifies the optimal methods whereby it can be achieved nor indicates the intervening process.

Quite apart from its usefulness in problem solving, the acquisition of knowledge as an end in itself must be considered a major goal of education. A large proportion of what any individual learns in the course of a lifetime has no immediate utility and is not applicable to any pressing problem of adjustment. Nevertheless, human beings are strongly motivated to learn so that they can better understand themselves, the universe, the human condition, and the meaning of life. Hence, if we are concerned with achieving this particular aim of education, we cannot leave its implementation to problem-solving and discovery techniques. The use of these techniques, as already pointed out, furthers the problem-solving objective of education, but, except in the elementary school and under other special circumstances, is not very efficient for transmitting subject-matter content. It is also important to appreciate at this point that typical problem-solving activity is most useful in dealing with everyday problems of living, and in illustrating, reinforcing, and testing for meaningful comprehension of concepts and principles. But only in the hands of particularly creative individuals does it constitute a practical method of acquiring ideas that are important enough to include in the learner's store of knowledge.[6]

In the realm of educational theory, if not in actual practice, the impact of Dewey's exaggerated emphasis on problem solving still continues to disturb the natural balance between the "transmission of the culture" and the problem-solving objectives of education. Enthusiastic proponents of the discovery method still assert that "more basic than the attainment of concepts is the ability to inquire and discover them autonomously" (35, p. 32). And to this Bruner adds:

Whatever [program] is introduced [in the schools] let it be pursued continuously enough to give the student a sense of the

power of mind that comes from a deepening of understanding. It is this, rather than any form of coverage over time that matters most (9, p. 77).

These somewhat extreme value judgments regarding the principal function of the school inspire, in turn, correspondingly one-sided proposals with respect to curriculum and pedagogy. Suchman, for example, contends that,

the schools must have a new pedagogy with a new set of goals which subordinates retention to thinking. . . . Instead of devoting their efforts to storing information and recalling it on demand, they would be developing the cognitive functions needed to seek out and organize information in a way that would be most productive of new concepts (35, pp. 6–7).

The development of problem-solving ability is, of course,

a legitimate and significant educational objective in its own right. Hence it is highly defensible to utilize a certain proportion of classroom time in developing appreciation of and facility in the use of scientific methods of inquiry and of other empirical, inductive and deductive problem-solving procedures. But this is a far cry from advocating that the enhancement of problem-solving ability is the major function of the school. To acquire facility in problem solving and scientific method, it is not necessary for learners to rediscover every principle in the syllabus. Since problem-solving ability is itself transferable, at least within a given subject-matter field, facility gained in independently formulating and applying one generalization is transferable to other problem areas in the same discipline. Furthermore, overemphasis on developing problem-solving ability would ultimately defeat its own ends. It would leave students with insufficient time in which to learn the content of a discipline; and, hence, despite their adeptness at problem solving, they would be unable to solve simple problems involving the application of such content (2, p. 23).

[6] "The inductive derivation of concepts and generalizations from diverse instances is an exception to this statement, but is only a conspicuous feature of concept attainment during childhood (before a really large quantity of subject matter is incorporated). For the most part in the formal education of the individual, the educating agency merely transmits ready-made concepts, categorical schemata, and relational propositions." (Ausubel, 1961, p. 21).

Some advocates of the discovery method favor a type of guided practice in the "heuristics of discovery" that is reminiscent of the faculty psychology approach to improving overall critical thinking ability through instruction in the general principles of logic. Once the heuristics of discovery are mastered, they constitute, according to Bruner, "a style of problem solving or inquiry that serves for any kind of task one may encounter" (8, p. 31). Similarly, Suchman's inquiry training program "is not proposed as a new way to teach science, but as a way of teaching basic cognitive skills . . . [that belong] in the science program and in every other curriculum area that requires . . . reasoning and the formulation and testing of hypotheses" (35, p. 32).

One principal difficulty with this approach, as the faculty psychologists discovered, is that critical thinking ability can only be enhanced within the context of a specific discipline. Grand strategies of discovery do not seem to be transferable across disciplinary lines—either when acquired within a given discipline, or when learned in a more general form apart from specific subject-matter content. This principle has been confirmed by countless studies and is illustrated by the laughable errors of logic and judgment committed by distinguished scientists and scholars who wander outside their own disciplines. From a purely theoretical standpoint alone, it hardly seems plausible that a strategy of inquiry, which must necessarily be broad enough to be applicable to a wide range of disciplines and problems, can ever have, at the same time, sufficient particular relevance to be helpful in the solution of the specific

problem at hand. And from the standpoint of elementary-school children, one wonders whether grand strategies of inquiry pitched at this level of abstraction can be meaningful enough to be used successfully in problem solving.

A second significant difficulty with this approach is that its proponents tend to confuse the goals of the scientist with the goals of the science student. They assert that these objectives are identical, and hence that students can learn science most effectively by enacting the role of junior scientist. The underlying rationale is that all intellectual activity regardless of level is of one piece, and that both creative scientists and elementary-school children rely heavily on intuitive thinking. Bruner is an eloquent spokesman for this point of view:

> Intellectual activity anywhere is the same, whether at the frontier of knowledge or in a third-grade classroom. What a scientist does at his desk or in the laboratory, what a literary critic does in reading a poem are of the same order as what anybody else does when he is engaged in like activities—if he is to achieve understanding. The difference is in degree, not in kind. The schoolboy learning physics *is* a physicist, and it is easier for him to learn physics behaving like a physicist than doing something else (7, p. 14).

Suchman also explains that the ultimate goal of his inquiry training program is for children to discover and formulate explanations which represent

> the causality of a single instance in terms of broad universal principles and generalizations. This is the unification of concepts for which the scientist strives. It can and, in our opinion, should be the ultimate goal of children's inquiry as well (35, p. 13).

In the first place, although it is true that all kinds of meaningful activity have certain attributes in common, differences in the level of abstraction, generality, and sophistication involved may very well give rise to qualitative as well as quantitative differences between them.

Second, I cannot agree that the goals of the research scientist and of the science student are identical. The scientist is engaged in a full-time search for new general or applied principles in his field. The student, on the other hand, is primarily engaged in an effort to learn the same basic subject matter in this field which the scientist had learned in his student days, and also to learn something of the method and spirit of scientific inquiry. Thus, while it makes perfectly good sense for the scientist to work full time formulating and testing new hypotheses, it is quite indefensible, in my opinion, for the student to be doing the same thing—either for real, or in the sense of rediscovery. Most of the latter's time should be taken up with appropriate expository learning, and the remainder devoted to sampling the flavor and techniques of scientific method. It is the scientist's business to formulate unifying explanatory principles in science. It is the student's business to learn these principles as meaningfully and critically as possible, and *then*, after his background is adequate, to try to improve on them if he can. If he is ever to discover, he must first learn; and he cannot learn adequately by pretending he is a junior scientist.

Lastly, there is in my opinion a world of difference between the intuitive thinking of elementary-school children and the intuitive thinking of scholars and scientists. The elementary-school child thinks intuitively or subverbally about many complex, abstract problems, not because he is

creative, but because this is the *best he can do* at his particular stage of intellectual development. The intuitive thinking of scientists, on the other hand, consists of tentative and roughly formulated "hunches" which are merely preparatory to more rigorous thought. Furthermore, although the hunches themselves are only makeshift approximations which are not very precisely stated, they presuppose both a high level of abstract verbal ability as well as sophisticated knowledge of a particular discipline.

### EVERY CHILD A CREATIVE AND CRITICAL THINKER

I have already alluded to the fact that one of the currently fashionable educational doctrines giving support to the discovery method movement is the notion that the school can make every child a creative thinker and help him discover discontinuously new ideas and ways of looking at things. Creativity, it is alleged, is not the exclusive property of the rare genius among us, but a tender bud that resides in some measure within every child, requiring only the gently, catalytic influence of sensitive, imaginative teaching to coax it into glorious bloom.

This idea rests on the following questionable assumptions: that one can be creative without necessarily being original; that all discovery activity, irrespective of originality, is qualitatively of one piece—from Einstein's formulation of the theory of relativity to every infant's spontaneous discovery that objects continue to exist even when they are out of sight; that considering the multiplicity of abilities, every person stands a good chance, genetically speaking, of being creative in at least one area;

and that even if uncooperative, good teachers can take the place of missing genes.

Hohn's use of the term "creativity" is typical of the prevailing tendency in "discovery" circles to "democratize" the meaning of this concept. A child behaves creatively in mathematics, according to Hohn, when he proposes alternative approaches, grasps concepts intuitively, or displays autonomy, flexibility, and freedom from perseverative rigidity in his discovery efforts (19, pp. 103-4). Now one can define words in any way one chooses, and hence can define creativity so that it means nothing more than "autonomous and flexible discovery." But if this is *all* one means, would it not save endless confusion if one used these particular words instead of a term which both connotatively and denotatively implies a rare form of originality?

As a matter of fact, the very same persons who use "creativity" in the more "democratic" sense of the term also imply in other contexts that the encouragement of true creativity (i.e., in the sense of original accomplishment) in *every* child is one of the major functions of the school. This view is implicit in Bruner's position that the school should help every child reach discontinuous realms of experience so that he can create his own interior culture. It is also implicit in the goal that Suchman proposes for his inquiry training program; namely, that children should be trained to formulate the same kinds of unifying concepts in science which are produced by our most creative scientists. And it is made unambiguously explicit in the following statement by Bruner:

A small part, but a crucial part of discovery of the highest order is to invent and

develop models or "puzzle forms" that can be imposed on difficulties with good effect. It is in this area that the truly powerful mind shines. But it is interesting to what degree perfectly ordinary people can, given the benefit of instruction, construct quite interesting and, what a century ago, would have been considered greatly original models (8, p. 30).

How reasonable then is the goal of "teaching for creativity," that is, in the sense of singularly original achievement? A decent respect for the realities of the human condition would seem to indicate that the training possibilities with respect to creativity are severely limited. The school can obviously help in the realization of existing creative potentialities by providing opportunities for spontaneity, initiative, and individualized expression; by making room in the curriculum for tasks that are sufficiently challenging for pupils with creative gifts; and by rewarding creative achievement. But it cannot actualize potentialities for creativity if these potentialities do not exist in the first place. Hence it is totally unrealistic, in my opinion, to suppose that even the most ingenious kinds of teaching techniques that we could devise could stimulate creative accomplishment in children of average endowment. Since creative potentialities are, by definition, sparsely distributed in the population, instances of true creativity can be anticipated no more frequently among the clientele of our schools than among any other population of human beings.

Even "teaching for *critical* thinking" and "teaching for problem solving" are somewhat grandiose slogans, although obviously much more realistic than "teaching for creative thinking." To be sure, the critical thinking and problem-solving abilities of most pupils can be improved. But this is a far cry from saying that most pupils can be trained to become good critical thinkers and problem solvers. Potentialities for developing high levels of these abilities are admittedly much less rare than corresponding potentialities for developing creativity. Nevertheless, there are no good reasons for believing that they are any commoner than potentialities for developing high general intelligence. Also, in my opinion, variability in genic endowment is probably responsible for more of the measured variance in critical thinking or problem-solving ability than is variability in educational experience.

Aptitude in problem solving involves a much different pattern of abilities than those required for understanding and retaining abstract ideas. The ability to solve problems calls for qualities (e.g., flexibility, resourcefulness, improvising skill, originality, problem sensitivity, venturesomeness) that are less generously distributed in the population of learners than the ability to comprehend verbally presented materials. Many of these qualities also cannot be taught effectively. Although appropriate pedagogic procedures can improve problem-solving ability, relatively few good problem solvers can be trained in comparison with the number of persons who can acquire a meaningful grasp of various subject-matter fields (2, p. 23).

From the standpoint of enlightened educational policy in a democracy, therefore, it seems to me that the school should concentrate its major efforts on teaching both what is most important in terms of cultural survival and cultural progress and what is most teachable to the majority of its clientele. As improved methods of teaching become available, most students will be able to master the basic intellectual skills as well as a reasonable portion of the more important subject-matter

content of the major disciplines. Is it not more defensible to shoot for this realistic goal, which lies within our reach, than to focus on educational objectives that presuppose exceptional endowment and are impossible of fulfillment when applied to the generality of mankind? Would it not be more realistic to strive first to have each pupil respond meaningfully, actively, and critically to good expository teaching before we endeavor to make him a good critical thinker and problem solver?

I am by no means proposing a uniform curriculum and pedagogy for all children irrespective of individual differences. By all means let us provide all feasible special opportunities and facilities for the exceptional child. But in so doing, let us not attempt to structure the learning environment of the *non*exceptional child in terms of educational objectives and teaching methods that are appropriate for either one child in a hundred or for one child in a million.

EXPOSITORY TEACHING
AS AUTHORITARIANISM

Advocates of the discovery method also take advantage of the opprobrium associated with authoritarianism in education to discredit didactic exposition and to further their own cause. In doing this, they not only rely on the straw-man technique of representing a highly exaggerated "tell'm and drill" approach as typical of expository teaching, but also assert that expository teaching is *inherently* authoritarian. When a teacher stands in front of a classroom and presents facts, concepts, and principles, he is, according to Gertrude Hendrix (17, pp. 290, 296, 298) and others, behaving in an authoritarian fashion. This is presumably so because he is allegedly coercing pupils, by the prestige of his position and by his power to dispense reward and punishment, into unquestioningly accepting on faith his own version of "the truth," instead of giving them an opportunity to discover it for themselves. Bruner puts it this way:

Insofar as possible, a method of instruction should have the objective of leading the child to discover for himself. Telling children and then testing them on what they have been told inevitably has the effect of producing bench-bound learners whose motivation for learning is likely to be extrinsic to the task at hand—pleasing the teacher, getting into college, artificially maintaining self-esteem (9, p. 77).

In the first place, I submit that this distressing picture of expository teaching is a bit overdrawn. I do not deny that schools and colleges abound in such teachers. But this characterization is certainly not true of all didactic exposition, nor is it inherent in the method itself. Second, there is nothing inherently authoritarian in presenting or explaining ideas to others as long as they are not obliged, either explicitly or implicitly, to accept them on faith. Didactic exposition has always constituted the core of any pedagogic system, and, I suspect, always will, because it is the only feasible and efficient method of transmitting large bodies of knowledge.

The deference to authority implied in accepting already discovered relationships has been condemned out of all reason. If students were required independently to validate every proposition presented by their instructors before accepting it, they would never progress beyond the rudiments of any discipline. We can only ask that established knowledge be presented to them as rationally and nonarbitrarily as

possible, and that they accept it tentatively and critically as only the best available approximation of the "truth" (2, p. 22).

## DISCOVERY ORGANIZES LEARNING EFFECTIVELY FOR LATER USE

I turn now to four propositions recently propounded by Jerome Bruner(8) which, taken together, may be said to constitute a proposed psychological rather than philosophical rationale for the discovery method. First, Bruner hypothesizes that,

emphasis upon discovery in learning has precisely the effect upon the learner of leading him to be a constructionist, to organize what he is encountering in a manner not only designed to cover regularity and relatedness, but also to avoid the kind of information drift that fails to keep account of the uses to which information might have to be put (8, p. 26).

However, learning by discovery, in my opinion, does not *necessarily* lead to more orderly, integrative, and viable organization, transformation, and use of knowledge. It does so only insofar as the learning situation is highly structured, simplified, and skillfully programmed to include a large number of diversified exemplars of the same principle, carefully graded in order of difficulty. But under these circumstances, one must, in all fairness, attribute these latter outcomes to the teacher's or textbook writer's organization of the data from which the discovery is to be made, rather than to the acts of discovery itself.

As a matter of fact, *pure* discovery techniques, as employed by scholars and scientists, could only lead to utter chaos in the classroom. Put a young physics student into a bathtub and he is just as likely to concentrate on the soap bubbles and on the refraction of light as on the displacement principle that he is supposed to discover. In the UICSM program, therefore, students are given a prearranged sequence of suitable exemplars, and from these they "spontaneously self-discover" the appropriate generalization. Elementary-school pupils in the Inquiry Training Program are similarly shown a carefully prepared demonstration film illustrative of a given principle in physics and are then permitted to ask questions answerable by "yes" or "no." Under both of these conditions pupils are engaging in "true," autonomous discovery in the same sense that a detective independently "solves" a crime after a benevolent Providence kindly gathers together all of the clues and arranges them for him in the correct sequence. This type of discovery is perfectly compatible with the automated teaching movement (despite the howls of anguish which teaching machines elicit from discovery enthusiasts) and is obviously a far cry from the kind of discovery that takes place in research laboratories.

Now, in making these observations, I certainly do not wish to create the impression that I quarrel with the UICSM method of inducing discovery, or that I favor the use of raw, unselected, and unorganized data in discovery programs. I quarrel only with Bruner's interpretation that the organizing and integrative effects of learning by discovery are attributable to the act of discovery per se, rather than to the structure and organization which are put there by the programmers of such curriculums as the UICSM and the Physical Science Study Committee courses in secondary-school mathematics and physics respectively.

## DISCOVERY AS A UNIQUE GENERATOR OF MOTIVATION AND SELF-CONFIDENCE

Bruner (7, 8, 9) and other discovery enthusiasts (35, p. 3; 17, pp. 292-93) perceive learning by discovery as a unique and unexcelled generator of self-confidence, of intellectual excitement, and of motivation for sustained problem solving and creative thinking. I have already acknowledged that discovery techniques are valuable for acquiring desirable attitudes toward inquiry, as well as firm convictions about the existence and discoverability of orderliness in the universe. It is also reasonable to suppose that successful discovery experience enhances both these attitudes and convictions and the individual's feeling of confidence in his own abilities. On the other hand, there is no reason to believe that discovery methods are unique or alone in their ability to effect these outcomes.

As every student who has been exposed to competent teaching knows, the skillful exposition of ideas can also generate considerable intellectual excitement and motivation for genuine inquiry, although admittedly not quite as much perhaps as discovery. Few physics students who learn the principle of displacement this way will run half-naked through the streets shrieking, "Eureka." But then again, how many students of Archimedes' ability are enrolled in the typical physics or mathematics class? How comparable to the excitement of Archimedes' purely autonomous and original discovery is the excitement generated by discovering a general formula for finding the number of diagonals in an $n$-sided polygon after working problems one through nine in the textbook? And what happens to Archimedes Junior's motivation and self-confidence if, after seventeen immersions in the tub, he has merely succeeded in getting himself soaking wet?

Careful study of the psychological experiment cited by Bruner (8, pp. 23-24), by way of illustrating the allegedly unique motivational and inspirational values of discovery methods, leaves me no more convinced than I was before. Bruner describes a psychological experiment in probability learning with a two-choice apparatus in which "the payoff sequence is arranged at random and there is no pattern. Some subjects quickly begin to catch on to the fact (and rightly so in this case), that "things are happening quite by chance . . . [and] very soon revert to a much more primitive [and empirically more successful] strategy wherein *all* responses are allocated to the side that has the greater payoff." Other more trusting and optimistic souls, however, persist in believing that "there *is* some pattern to be found in the sequence . . . i.e., that regularities are discoverable," and hence keep trying one unsuccessful hypothesis after another, in each of which "the number of responses given to each side is roughly equal to the proportion of times it pays off."

"What has [all] this to do with the subject at hand?" asks Bruner.

For the person to search out and find regularities and relationships in his environment, he must be armed with an expectancy that there will be something to find and, once aroused by expectancy, he must devise ways of searching and finding. One of the chief enemies of expectancy is the assumption there is nothing one can find in the environment by way of regularity or relationship (8, p. 24).

I can thoroughly appreciate the logic of this argument, but I still cannot see what relevance it has for the issue regarding the unique motivational virtues of the discovery method. All Bruner is saying here is that, in the absence of a firm conviction about the existence of discoverable regularities in a particular problem-solving situation, one will resort to simple trial-and-error behavior—just like Thorndike's cats in the puzzle-box. But why should discovery methods necessarily inspire any more confidence in the existence of discoverable regularities in the universe than the method of didactic exposition which, after all, is dedicated to the presentation and explication of these regularities? It is true that successful discovery experience strengthens such confidence; but unsuccessful experience has precisely the opposite effect—as demonstrated by the resurgence of magical and superstitious thinking that follows in the wake of failure to find patterns of orderliness in nature.

### DISCOVERY AS A PRIME SOURCE OF INTRINSIC MOTIVATION

A related motivational proposition put forth by Bruner states that "to the degree that one is able to approach learning as a task of discovering something rather than 'learning about it,' to that degree will there be a tendency for the child to carry out his learning activities with the autonomy of self-reward or, more properly, by reward that is discovery itself" (8, p. 26). Bruner feels that learning by discovery frees the child from the immediate control of such extrinsic motives as high marks, desire for parental and teacher approval, and a need to conform to the expectations of authority figures. In support of this hypothesis, he cites research data showing that early "overachievers" in school tend to be conformists, to overdevelop rote abilities, and to be deficient in analytic and critical thinking ability (8, p. 26).

In my opinion, however, there is no existing or necessary association between a discovery approach to learning and intrinsic motivation, on the one hand, and a reception approach to learning and extrinsic motivation, on the other. But because of certain cultural influences on personality development in our type of social system, I would tend to postulate precisely the opposite kind of relationship; namely, that discovery learning is more often associated with extrinsic motivation than is reception learning. Whether an individual primarily manifests intrinsic or extrinsic motivation in learning, it seems to me, is largely a function of two factors: (a) how much intrinsic self-esteem he possesses, and hence how great his relative need is for compensatory extrinsic status; and (b) the strength of his cognitive needs in their own right, that is, his need to acquire knowledge and to understand his environment as influenced by genic and temperamental determinants and by previous, satisfactory learning experience.

On these grounds, I would think that a more plausible interpretation of Bruner's data is that it is the learner who is lacking in intrinsic self-esteem who develops an overpowering need, both for such external symbols of achievement as high grades and teacher approval and for the glory and prestige associated with independent discovery in our culture. Hence the overachiever is typically a child who is deficient in intrinsic self-esteem. He relies unduly on rote memorization both because it is the surest route to the high marks

and the teacher approval he craves, and because (on account of his anxiety and impaired self-esteem) he lacks the courage and self-confidence to improvise in novel, problem-solving test situations (5). At the same time, however, to bolster his impaired self-esteem, he aspires to the prestige and status which, in our culture, can only be achieved through the exercise and hypertrophy of White's so-called "competence motive," which Bruner equates with the drive to discover (8, pp. 27-28).

What I am suggesting, therefore, is that rather than being uniquely powered by intrinsic motives, learning by discovery or overvigorous exercise of the drive for competence reflects a lack of intrinsic self-esteem and a compensatory need to overachieve with respect to the external symbols and trappings of successful accomplishment. To be sure, there are individuals who are driven to discover principally because of a compelling need to express their individuality or creative urges, to find the answers to haunting problems, or to discharge their feelings of moral obligations to the social community. But in our particular culture with its emphasis on status, prestige, ego aggrandizement, and material rewards—especially among individuals who lack intrinsic self-esteem—such motives for discovery tend to be the exception rather than the rule.

DISCOVERY AND THE
" CONSERVATION OF MEMORY "

In the last of his four propositions, Bruner claims unique retention advantages for material learned by the discovery method. And again he illustrates his point by citing an experiment of questionable relevance to the principle he proposes. Pairs of words are presented to twelve-year-old children:

One group is simply told to remember the pairs, that they will be asked to repeat them later. Another is told to remember them by producing a word or idea that will tie the pair together in a way that will make sense to them. A third group is given the mediators used by the second group when presented with the words, to aid them in tying the pairs into working units (8, p. 31).

The wholly predictable results were that the uninstructed children remembered least, and that the "children who developed their own [mediators] for relating the members of each word pair . . . did better than the children" who were given the mediators by exposition (8, p. 32).

Why don't these findings support Bruner's proposition regarding the beneficial influence of discovery on retention? First, the learning task in this experiment is hardly comparable to the situation where children must discover a generalization inductively and autonomously. In Bruner's experiment, the entire content of what is to be learned is *given* and the child need only supply a mediating link from his own cognitive structure which is sufficiently inclusive to subsume both members of the word pair. Now isn't this precisely the paradigm for meaningful reception learning in which materials are presented, and the learner then tries to incorporate them into his own cognitive structure by relating them to more inclusive established ideas? The superior retention of the children who used mediators, as compared to those who were uninstructed, is attributable to the facilitating effect on retention which occurs when one helps learners convert an ostensibly rote reception learning task into a more meaningful type of reception learning. The discovery

variable, in my opinion, is not implicated at all in this experiment.

Second, the superior retention of the word pairs related to the *self*-constructed mediators simply reflects the value of using more stable, relevant, and familiar subsumers within cognitive structure as anchoring posts for new learning materials. Mediators that children choose themselves are obviously more relevant and familiar to them than mediators suggested to them by others. The fact that they are *self*-constructed is quite beside the point.

Lastly, even within the framework of a reception learning interpretation, we should be careful about generalizing these findings to classroom pedagogy. In a short and easy learning task dealing with familiar materials, it is quite feasible for children to construct their own organizing concepts. But one could not legitimately conclude from this experiment that it would also be feasible for them to construct their own organizers for large bodies of complex and unfamiliar learning materials in subject-matter areas where their level of sophistication is necessarily low.

## RESEARCH EVIDENCE

I now propose to examine a representative sample of the more significant published research bearing on the discovery method. The professional literature on "learning by discovery" regrettably exemplifies, as clearly as any research in education, the all too frequent hollowness of the hallowed phrase, "research shows."[7] Careful examination of what research supposedly "shows" in this instance yields these

[7] See Martin Mayer (26, p. 67), for a critique of the phrase, "research shows."

three disheartening conclusions: (*a*) that most of the articles most commonly cited in the literature as reporting results supportive of discovery techniques actually report no research findings whatsoever, consisting mainly of theoretical discussion, assertion, and conjecture; descriptions of existing programs utilizing discovery methods; and enthusiastic but wholly subjective testimonials regarding the efficacy of discovery approaches; (*b*) that most of the reasonably well-controlled studies report negative findings; and (*c*) that most studies reporting positive findings either fail to control other significant variables or employ questionable techniques of statistical analysis.

In view of the apparently sound theoretical reasons listed earlier (under "rationale") for predicting modest advantages in learning, retention, and transferability attributable to the use of discovery techniques, these largely equivocal and negative findings are somewhat disappointing. In many cases, of course, findings are equivocal simply because of failure to control such other relevant variables as the rote-meaningful, the inductive-deductive, the verbal-nonverbal, and the intramaterial organization dimensions of learning, while varying the reception-discovery factor. In other instances, it is quite possible that negative findings are less indicative of inadequacies in the underlying theory than of inadequacies in research design, which unfairly load the dice against the possibility of confirming hypotheses. And as far as long-term curriculum studies are concerned, one might anticipate that any short-term advantages accruing from the use of discovery techniques per se would be more than offset by its time-consuming aspects, and the consequent low rate of acquiring subject-matter content.

## LONG-TERM STUDIES

Despite their frequent espousal of discovery principles, the various curriculum reform projects have failed thus far to yield any research evidence in support of the discovery method. This is not to say that the evidence is negative, but rather that there just isn't any evidence, one way or the other—notwithstanding the fact that these projects are often cited in the "discovery" literature under the heading, "research shows." For one thing, the sponsors of some of these projects have not been particularly concerned about *proving* the superior efficacy of their programs, since they have been thoroughly convinced of this from the outset. Hence, in many instances they have not even attempted to obtain comparable achievement test data from matched control groups. And only rarely has any effort been expended to prevent the operation of the crucial "Hawthorne Effect," that is, to make sure that evidence of superior achievement outcomes is attributable to the influence of the new pedagogic techniques or materials in question, rather than to the fact that the experimental group is the recipient of *some* form of conspicuous special attention; that *some*thing new and interesting is being tried; or that the teachers involved are especially competent, dedicated, and enthusiastic, and receive special training, attend expense-free conventions and summer institutes, and are assigned lighter teaching loads.

But even if the sponsors of the curriculum reform movements were all imbued with missionary research zeal, it would still be impossible to test the discovery hypothesis within the context of curriculum research. In the first place, a large number of other significant variables are necessarily operative in such programs. The UICSM program, for example, not only relies heavily on the principle of self-discovery of generalizations, but also on an inductive approach, on nonverbal awareness, on abundant empirical experience, on careful sequential programming, and, above all, on precise, self-consistent, unambiguous, and systematic verbal formulation of basic principles. To which variable, or to which combination of these variables and the "Hawthorne Effect" should the success of this program be attributed? Personally, for reasons enumerated earlier in this article, I would nominate the factor of precise and systematic verbal formulation rather than the discovery variable. (Students enrolled in the UICSM program learn more mathematics, in my opinion, *not* because they are required to discover generalizations *by themselves*, but because they have at their disposal a systematic body of organizing, explanatory, and integrative principles which are not part of the conventional course in secondary-school mathematics. These principles illuminate the subject for them and make it much more meaningful, coherent, and exciting.) Finally, "measurement is [always] a difficult problem [in such research] because standardized achievement tests both cover various traditional subject-matter units deliberately ignored by these new curricula, as well as fail to measure knowledge of the more modern concepts, which they emphasize" (4).

Preliminary findings of the Inquiry

Training Program also fail to support the discovery hypothesis(33). Inquiry training did not significantly improve the quality of the questions asked by the subjects or facilitate their grasp of concepts. It is true that those pupils who were trained in the particular inquiry techniques employed did ask a significantly greater number of the right kinds of questions in the criterion situation than did pupils in the control group. But isn't this precisely what they were trained to do? Pupils who are trained to ~ask certain kinds of questions in one situation will naturally tend to ask more of the same kinds of questions in an analogous criterion situation than will pupils who do not receive this particular inquiry training. The transfer value of such training can only be demonstrated by using criteria which are both more independent of the particular training procedures employed, and more reflective of its goals than of its techniques. Currently, therefore, more definitive evidence of transfer is being sought.

A number of long-term curriculum studies in the older literature are frequently cited as providing empirical support for the discovery method. Using basically identical research designs, McConnell (25), Thiele (37), and Swenson (36) compared the so-called "drill" and "generalization" methods of teaching number facts to second-grade pupils. The drill approach emphasized rote memorization and mechanical repetition of authoritatively presented facts and rules, whereas the generalization method stressed meaningful perception of relationships and derivation of generalizations. Pupils taught by the generalization method also had the added benefit of concrete props in the McConnell study, and of organized grouping of materials in the Swenson study. A well-known study by G. Lester Anderson(1) was also conducted along very similar lines, but used fourth-grade pupils.

Needless to say, the generalization method was found to be superior in all four studies, except in criterion situations calling for immediate and automatic recall of knowledge relatively unchanged in form from that learned in the training situation. Much more salient than the discovery variable in each of these studies, however, was the rote-meaningful factor; and in two of the studies, the differential availability to the "generalization" group of concrete visual aids or to organized grouping of learning materials, further complicated interpretation of the findings. It should also be remembered that it is precisely in relation to this age group of young learners first entering the stage of concrete logical operations, and still completely unsophisticated in a new, difficult, and abstract subject matter, that the efficacy and feasibility of the discovery method are least disputed. The time-cost factor is relatively unimportant at this age level, both because large bodies of subject matter cannot be learned through expository teaching anyway, and because a transitional phase of subverbal, intuitive understanding is developmentally necessary in the acquisition of complex abstractions. However, it would be quite unwarranted to generalize from these findings that meaningful expository teaching of twelfth-grade mathematics is less efficacious than learning by discovery.

SHORT-TERM STUDIES

The well-known Gestalt writings on insightful problem solving by Köhler (24), Wertheimer(39), Duncker(11), and Katona (21) are traditionally cited in the "discovery" literature as supportive of the discovery method of teaching. Actually, however, the Gestalt emphasis on insight deals only with the rote-meaningful dimension of problem solving and has no bearing whatsoever on the relative efficacy of the expository (reception) and discovery approaches. As pointed our earlier, both reception and discovery learning may each be rote or meaningful, depending on the conditions under which learning occurs. The Gestalt theorists merely insist that the concept of insight is more valid than the Thorndikian trial-and-error or the Hullian point of view in explaining problem-solving behavior that lies within an organism's verbal or subverbal reasoning ability.

Köhler's, Wertheimer's, and Duncker's monographs also do not really report research findings in the usual sense of the term. They are, rather, elaborate and sophisticated analyses of the nature and conditions of insightful problem solving from the Gestalt point of view, which use observations, informal experiments, anecdotes, and demonstrations to illustrate the principles under discussion. Katona's studies, on the other hand, are more genuinely experimental but, at the very most demonstrate that understanding of a principle, as opposed to rote memorization, leads to superior retention[8] and transfer. One experiment in particular shows that a rotely memorized verbal princi-

---

[8] A neo-behaviorist explanation of this "superior retention" finding is that understanding of a principle reduces the sheer volume of *what* has to be remembered by rendering the details of the learning task reconstructable from memory of the principle itself (Osgood, 27, p. 570). The writer's own interpretation stresses the nonarbitrary and substantive incorporability (anchorability) of meaningfully learned material within cognitive structure.

ple is less transferable to new problems than is mere empirical experience with problems exemplifying the principle in question(21). But this only indicates that meaningful understanding of a principle, even when unverbalized, is more transferable than rote memorization. It does not suggest that newly emerging nonverbal awareness is *always* more transferable than verbal understanding.

This latter study by Katona is reminiscent of Gertrude Hendrix' previously discussed experiment(15), but Hendrix carried the design and argument one step further. She also included another control group of subjects who *first* acquired *meaningful* nonverbal awareness of a principle, and *then* attempted immediate verbalization. She showed that her experimental subjects, who were sent out of the room while these control subjects were attempting to verbalize nonverbal awareness, were not only superior in transfer power to the control subjects who had merely learned the principle through verbal exposition, but were also superior to this other control group as well, which had acquired nonverbal awareness *prior* to verbalization. Hendrix interpreted her findings to mean that the full transfer power and substance of an idea are already present in the emerging subverbal insight, and that this dawning subverbal awareness, when left unverbalized, is *invariably* more transferable than when put into words. I have already explained in detail why I think that immediate verbalization of insight reduces transferability *only* when pupils are in the process of learning difficult abstract propositions, or when older individuals are in the early unsophisticated stages of learning a new discipline, and why I believe that verbalization enhances transferability under *all other* circumstances.

At this point I only wish to consider methodological and statistical aspects of Hendrix' experiment.

In reporting her study, Hendrix frankly acknowledged the difficulty of devising both "a good behavioral test for the achievement of unverbalized awareness," and a suitable test of transfer. There was also the formidable problem of deciding "whether subjects were obtaining the correct answers through counting or through applying the generalization" (15, p. 203). With respect to the maintenance of necessary controls, Hendrix freely admitted, furthermore, that it was difficult to prevent "communication and discussion among members of the different method groups in the time interval between learning and testing," and to administer the various tests and experimental procedures without revealing to the subjects that an experiment was in progress(15, pp. 203-4).

In addition to all of these acknowledged measurement, evaluation, and control problems, only forty subjects were available for all three groups, and even this relatively small number was achieved only by pooling results from three very different kinds of experimental populations, for whom a test of homogeneity of variance was not even reported. Both the small experimental population, and the undetermined comparability of its three separate components, rendered untenable Hendrix' assumption that random assignment of subjects to the three treatment groups equalized these groups with respect to the influence of the uncontrolled variables.

Lastly, the difference on the transfer test between the "verbal exposition" group and the "nonverbal awareness group" was only significant at the .12 level, and the corresponding difference between the "nonverbal awareness" group and the group which had verbalized their nonverbal awareness was only significant at the .33 level. Mathematicians, of course, may have their own norms of which I am unaware, but neither of these [*] levels of significance is regarded very seriously by either statisticians or educational research workers. Taking all of these factors into consideration, therefore, the experimental foundations for the far-reaching conclusions which Hendrix draws from these findings can hardly be considered impressively firm.

We come finally to a series of experimental studies in which varying amounts of guidance were furnished to different groups of subjects in problem-solving situations. Stacey (32) studied the effects of directed versus independent discovery on solving a group of meaningful problems, each of which required subjects to identify the one item in a set of five that did not "belong." He found that active participation and self-discovery were more efficacious for learning than was "passive participation involving only recognition or identification of information" presented to the learner. This finding, of course, was wholly predictable, since the fostering of such complete passivity in problem-solving experience as providing the correct answer for each problem as well as the reason for same is self-evidently inadvisable and is seldom if ever practiced today. But even so, surprisingly enough, significant differences were *not* found between these extreme treatment groups on a transfer test.

Using similar kinds of material, but with college students rather than sixth-grade pupils, Craig(10) obtained results even less favorable for the discovery method. His "directed" group, which received a brief verbal explanation of principles during the training period, learned and retained significantly more principles than did his "independent group" which had no help whatsoever in the training situation. As in the Stacey study, however, the two groups were not significantly different with respect to mean score on a transfer test. Kittell's findings in a similar type of experiment with sixth-grade pupils(23) were, if anything, even more damaging to the discovery cause than were Craig's. The group in his experiment which received an "intermediate" amount of guidance, but nevertheless an amount which was somewhat *greater* than that received by Craig's "directed" group (i.e., explanation of principles *plus* organization of materials) was superior in learning, retention, *and* transfer to groups receiving either less or more direction. Pooling the findings of these three studies, therefore, the evidence seems to support the conclusions that in this type of problem-solving exercise, guidance in the form of providing information about underlying principles facilitates learning, retention, and possibly transfer more than either the provision of less guidance or the furnishing of specific rules for each of the problems.

Haselrud and Meyers(18) recently conducted a coding study, with college students, which was explicitly designed to rebut the Craig and Kittell findings. However, their subjects exhibited significantly better learning on problems where the coding rule was given than where it had to be independently derived. Furthermore, on a delayed transfer test, there was *no* difference whatsoever in the number of correct code identifications made for the problems learned originally with the rule given and the problems learned originally by independent derivation of the code. Nevertheless, on the grounds that the *gain* from the first to the second test was greater for those problems where the rule had been independently derived, the investigators concluded that principles which are independently derived are more transferable than principles for which the rule is given. This, in my opinion, is equivalent to saying that, of two matched race horses trained by methods A and B respectively, who are tied at the end of the criterion race, the horse trained by method B is *really* superior because at the half-way mark he was one lap behind the horse trained by method A, but nevertheless caught up to him by the end of the race.

A final study in this area by Kersh(22) yielded results practically identical to those of Craig, Kittell, and Haselrud and Meyers on the test of original learning, but results opposite to those of Kittell on the delayed retest. By using an ingenious research design, however, Kersh was able to explain this latter finding on the basis of the greater interest and motivation, on the part of the "independent discovery" group, to continue practicing the task during the test-retest interval. Kersh concluded that discovery experience per se does not enhance understanding or meaningfulness.

## SUMMARY AND CONCLUSIONS

Learning by discovery has its proper place among the repertoire of accepted pedagogic techniques available to teachers. For certain designated purposes and for certain carefully specified learning situations, its rationale is clear and defensible. But learning by discovery also has its own elaborate mystique. Its legitimate uses and advantages have been unwarrantedly extrapolated to include both educational goals and levels of intellectual maturity, levels of subject-matter sophistication, and levels of cognitive functioning for which it is ill-adapted—and for reasons which derive from sheer dogmatic assertion; from pseudonaturalistic conceptions about the nature and conditions of intellectual development, from outmoded ideas about the relationship between language and thought; from sentimental fantasies about the nature of the child and the aims of education; and from uncritical interpretation of the research evidence.

The discovery method can be used most effectively when the learner is in the concrete stage of logical operations and is dependent both on concrete-empirical props and on a preliminary phase of intuitive, subverbal insight for the learning of complex abstractions. It can also be advantageously employed in the early stages of teaching older individuals a difficult new discipline in which they are as yet very unsophisticated. The latter stage, however, is as temporary as the subject-matter unsophistication itself, and cannot be considered a developmental type of limiting condition as in the case of younger learners.

Because of its serious time-cost disadvantage, learning by discovery cannot possibly be a feasible method of teaching subject-matter content—except, of course, in the two circumstances just mentioned. The time-cost factor outweighs by far any modest "vividness," motivational, and problem-solving advantages associated with its use.

The discovery method also has obvious uses and advantages in teaching problem-solving techniques and methods of scientific inquiry within a given discipline, and in testing for meaningful comprehension of material learned through didactic exposition. Although the promotion of problem-solving ability is a legitimate educational objective in its own right, it can hardly be considered a primary goal of education. Also, since problem-solving methods are not feasible for transmitting large bodies of subject-matter content, we cannot depend on students somehow acquiring all of the subject matter they need to know during the course of involvement in a discovery program. Even from the standpoint of enhancing problem-solving ability and even among a population of gifted pupils, excessive emphasis on discovery methods would ultimately defeat its own ends because students would not acquire enough of the knowledge they need to solve problems adequately.

Programs dedicated to teaching the "heuristics of discovery" fail to appreciate that critical thinking ability can only be enhanced within the context of a specific discipline. Furthermore, since the major goals of the science student, unlike those of the scientist, are not to formulate and verify new principles but to learn the rudiments of a scientific discipline as well as something of the spirit and methods of scientific inquiry, he cannot accomplish these objectives by playing the role of junior scientist.

The proposition that, *really* to possess an idea or to call it one's own, one must discover it oneself, is not only lacking in face credibility, but also repudiates the basic educational assumption on which the transmission of human culture rests; namely, that the accumulated discoveries of mankind can be effectively learned through verbal exposition and need not be rediscovered anew by each individual in every generation. Most of the knowledge anyone *really* possesses is discovered and transmitted to him by others; all we can reasonably expect most individuals to do, as far as making knowledge their own is concerned, is to integrate this knowledge meaningfully within their own cognitive structures.

Meaningful knowledge is not an exclusive product of creative nonverbal discovery. For potentially meaningful *presented* material to become meaningful knowledge, the learner need only adopt a set to incorporate its substantive import nonarbitrarily within his cognitive structure. The assertion that abstract concepts and generalizations are forms of glib verbalism unless the learner discovers them himself is predicated (a) on a misrepresentation of verbal learning as a passive, rote phenomenon; (b) on confusion between the reception-discovery and the rote-meaningful dimensions of learning; and (c) on unwarranted generalization to adolescents and adults of children's dependence on concrete-empirical props in comprehending and manipulating abstract ideas.

Gertrude Hendrix' proposition that both the substance of an idea and its transfer power reside entirely within "dawning subverbal awareness," rests, in my opinion, on an outmoded nominalistic conception of the role of language in thought. Verbalization does more than attach a convenient symbolic handle to an idea; it is, rather, part of the very process of thought itself and makes possible a qualitatively higher, more precise, more general, and more transferable type of understanding. However, premature verbalization of a subverbal insight by a child or unsophisticated adult could conceivably inhibit transfer because an ambiguous, ineptly stated, and marginally competent verbal representation of an idea probably has less functional utility in problem solving than the ordinarily more primitive and less efficient subverbal representation of the same idea.

The organizing and integrative effects of learning by discovery are not attributable to the act of discovery per se, but to the careful sequential organization and selective schematization which are deliberately introduced into the so-called "discovery" curriculums by their sponsors. The use of "pure" discovery techniques, as employed by scholars and scientists, could only lead to utter chaos in the classroom. Contrary, also, to the assertion of discovery enthusiasts, there is nothing *inherently* authoritarian in presenting ideas or knowledge to others, as long as they are not obligated to accept it on faith.

Discovery methods are, by no means, unique in their ability to generate self-confidence, intellectual excitement, and sustained motivation for learning. Good expository teaching can accomplish these very same objectives. It is also unrealistic to attribute to contrived discovery experiences in the classroom the same kind of inspirational stimulation that is generated by "real" discovery in the research laboratory. Neither are discovery methods unique in inducing intrinsic as against extrinsic motivation for learning. As a matter of fact, it is precisely the individual in our type of culture who lacks intrinsic self-esteem and has strong compensatory needs for prestige, status, and ego aggrandizement who is most likely to strive for the glory associated with original discovery.

Actual examination of the research literature allegedly supportive of learning by discovery reveals that valid evidence of this nature is virtually nonexistent. It appears that the various enthusiasts of the discovery method have been supporting each other research-wise, by taking in each other's laundry, so to speak; that is, by citing each other's opinions and assertions as evidence and by generalizing wildly from equivocal and even negative findings. The different curriculum reform projects using discovery techniques have not attempted the well-nigh impossible task of isolating the effects of the discovery variable from the effects of other significant variables and, in most instances, have not even attempted to collect adequate control data with which to evaluate the efficacy of a given project as a whole. Studies comparing "drill" and "generalization" methods of teaching the number facts have provided evidence about rote versus meaningful learning rather than evidence about the effectiveness of the discovery method; and, in any case, these studies deal with an age group and type of learning for which the value and feasibility of self-discovery are least disputed.

Findings from short-term research studies are similarly disappointing. Because of questionable methodological and statistical points in Hendrix' experiment regarding the relative transferability of verbalized and unverbalized subverbal insight, any psychological or pedagogic inferences from the reported data are, in my opinion, completely unwarranted. Lastly, research on meaningful verbal and symbolic problem solving indicates, on the whole, that providing guidance to the learner, in the form of verbal explanation of the underlying principles, almost invariably facilitates learning and retention, and sometimes transfer as well. *Self*-discovery methods, in contrast, are relatively much less effective.

Discovery methods are often rationalized in terms of the currently fashionable slogan that the school's chief responsibility is to make every child (or nearly every child) a critical and creative thinker. This incredible notion is based on the assertion that all discovery activity, irrespective of degree of originality, is qualitatively of one piece; on a watered-down, more "democratic" definition of creativity, broad enough to include *any* type of independent discovery; and on naïve *tabula rasa* conceptions of human plasticity which hold that, even if a given child has no creative potentialities, inspired teaching can create them anyway. Actually, creativity is a rare gift. The school can only help in actualizing its expression in those rare individuals who already possess the necessary potentialities.

There is a pressing need in these troubled times to dispense with sentimental fantasy and euphoric slogans and to get on with the realistic business of education. This means helping schools do well the kinds of jobs that schools can *really* do; namely, developing more efficient and appropriate ways of selecting, organizing, and presenting significant knowledge to students so that they can learn and retain it meaningfully—both as an end in itself and as a basis for future learning and problem solving.

## REFERENCES

1. Anderson, G. L., "Quantitative Thinking as Developed Under Connectionist and Field Theories of Learning," *Learning Theory in School Situations*, University of Minnesota Studies in Education. Minneapolis: University of Minnesota Press, 1949, pp. 40-73.

2. Ausubel, D. P., "In Defense of Verbal Learning," *Educational Theory*, XI (1961), 15-25.

3. —— and D. Fitzgerald, "Meaningful Verbal Learning and Retention," *Journal of General Psychology*, LXVI, 2nd half (April 1962), 213-24.

4. —— and D. Fitzgerald, "Meaningful Learning and Retention: Intrapersonal Cognitive Variables," *Review of Educational Research*, XXXI (December 1961).

5. ——, H. M. Schiff, and M. Goldman, "Qualitative Characteristics in the Learning Process Associated with Anxiety," *Journal of Abnormal and Social Psychology*, XLVIII (1953), 537-47.

6. Brownell, W. A. and G. Hendrickson, "How Children Learn Information, Concepts and Generalizations," *Learning and Instruction*, Forty-Ninth Yearbook, National Society for Study of Education, Part I (1950), pp. 92-128.

7. Bruner, J. S., *The Process of Education*. Cambridge, Mass.: Harvard University Press, 1960.

8. ——, "The Act of Discovery," *Harvard Educational Review*, XXXI (1961), 21-32.

9. ——, "After Dewey What?" *Saturday Review* (June 17, 1961), pp. 58-59; 76-78.

10. Craig, R. C., "Directed *versus* Independent Discovery of Established Relations," *Journal of Educational Psychology*, XLVII (1956), 223-34.

11. Duncker, K., "On Problem-Solving," *Psychological Monographs*, LVIII, No. 270, (1945).

12. Easley, J. A., Jr., "Is the Teaching of Scientific Method a Significant Educational Objective?" *Philosophy and Education* (I. Scheffler, ed.). Boston: Allyn and Bacon, Inc., 1958.

13. ——, "The Physical Science Study Committee and Educational Theory," *Harvard Educational Review*, XXIX (1959), 4-11.

14. Guilford, J. P., "Three Faces of Intellect," *American Psychologist*, XIV (1959), 469-79.

15. Hendrix, Gertrude, "A New Clue to Transfer of Training," *Elementary School Journal*, XLVIII (1947), 197-208.

16. ——, "Prerequisite to Meaning," *Mathematics Teacher*, XLIII (1950), 334-39.

17. ——, "Learning by Discovery," *Mathematics Teacher*, LIV (1961), 290-99.

18. Haselrud, G. M. and Shirley Meyers, "The Transfer Value of Given and Individually Derived Principles," *Journal of Educational Psychology*, XLIX (1958), 293-98.

19. Hohn, F. E., "Teaching Creativity in Mathematics," *Arithmetic Teacher*, VIII (1961), 102-6.

20. Inhelder, Bärbel and J. Piaget, *The Growth of Logical Thinking from Childhood to Adolescence*. New York: Basic Books, Inc., Publishers, 1958.

21. Katona, G., *Organizing and Memorizing*. New York: Columbia University Press, 1940.

22. Kersh, B. Y., "The Adequacy of 'Meaning' as an Explanation for the Superiority of Learning by Independent Discovery," *Journal of Educational Psychology*, XLIX (1958), 282-92.

23. Kittell, J. E., "An Experimental Study of the Effect of External Direction During Learning on Transfer and Retention of Principles," *Journal of Educational Psychology*, XLVIII (1957), 391-405.

24. Köhler, W., *The Mentality of Apes*. New York: Harcourt, Brace & World, Inc., 1925.

25. McConnell, T. R., "Discovery *vs.* Authoritative Identification in the Learning of Children." *University of Iowa Studies, Studies in Education*, IX, No. 5. Iowa City: University of Iowa, 1934.

26. Mayer, M., *The Schools*. New York: Harper & Row, Publishers, 1961.

27. Osgood, C. E., *Method and Theory in Experimental Psychology*. New York: Oxford University Press, Inc., 1953.

28. Piaget, Jean, *The Psychology of Intelligence*. New York: Harcourt, Brace & World, Inc., 1950.

29. ———, *The Construction of Reality in the Child*. New York: Basic Books, Inc., Publishers, 1954.

30. Serra, Mary C., "A Study of Fourth-Grade Children's Comprehension of Certain Verbal Abstractions," *Journal of Experimental Education*, XII (1953), 103-18.

31. Spiker, C. C. and G. Terrell, "Factors Associated with Transposition Behavior of Preschool Children," *Journal of Genetic Psychology*, LXXXVI (1955), 143-58.

32. Stacey, C. L., "The Law of Effect in the Retained Situation with Meaningful Material," *Learning Theory in School Situations*. University of Minnesota Studies in Education. Minneapolis: University of Minnesota Press, 1949, pp. 74-103.

33. Suchman, J. Richard, "Training Children in Scientific Inquiry." Paper presented to the Society for Research in Child Development, March 1959. Urbana: College of Education, University of Illinois.

34. ———, "Inquiry Training in the Elementary School," *Science Teacher*, XXVII (November 1960), 42-47.

35. ———, "Inquiry Training: Building Skills for Autonomous Discovery." Urbana: College of Education, University of Illinois, June 1961.

36. Swenson, Esther J., "Organization and Generalization as Factors in Learning, Transfer, and Retroactive Inhibition," *Learning Theory in School Situations*. University of Minnesota Studies in Education. Minneapolis: University of Minnesota Press, 1949, pp. 9-39.

37. Thiele, C. L., *The Contribution of Generalization to the Learning of the Addition Facts*. Contributions to Education, No. 763. New York: Bureau of Publications, Teachers College, Columbia University, 1938.

38. Weir, Morton W. and Harold W. Stevenson, "The Effect of Verbalization in Children's Learning as a Function of Chronological Age," *Child Development*, XXX (1959), 143-49.

39. Wertheimer, M., *Productive Thinking*, enl. ed. New York: Harper & Row, Publishers, 1959.

# 34

# The Child and the Inquiry Process

## J. RICHARD SUCHMAN

Man's ability to understand and control his environment depends on how well he has conceptualized it—how closely his conceptual systems correspond to reality. When one person tries to shape the concepts of another by talking to him or showing him something or giving him something to read, we call it teaching. When a person tries to promote these conceptual changes for himself by gathering and processing information, the activity becomes inquiry.

If man could not inquire, he could not gather and process data, raise and test hypotheses, build theories and test them empirically; all of his learning would have to be programed for him by others. Data would have to be fed to him, inferences would have to be drawn for him, and he would have to be told at every turn what conclusions

could be drawn. In short, he would be totally dependent as a learner and a thinker. It is obvious therefore that being able to inquire is a necessary condition for the independence and autonomy of learning.

Inquiry is a fundamental form of learning. Long before the child begins formal education he is gathering data from his environment. The infant grasps a pot, picks it up, feels it, turns it over, puts blocks in it, dumps them out, and so forth. These interactions with the environment help to form intuitive schemata by which the child begins to internalize the properties of his environment.

## ASSIMILATION
## AND ACCOMMODATION

As he grows older, the child learns to become more systematic in his searching and in his collection and processing of data. As his conceptual systems become broader and more complex, the methods by which he acquires and organizes data become

J. Richard Suchman, "The Child and the Inquiry Process," in *Intellectual Development: Another Look*, ed. A. Harry Passow. Washington, D.C.: Association for Supervision and Curriculum Development, 1964. Copyright © 1964 by the Association for Supervision and Curriculum Development. Reprinted by permission.

more sophisticated. As a result he is able to build more elaborate and accurate conceptual structures which reflect more closely the complexities of the real world.

In analyzing the act of inquiry it is helpful to think in terms of two basic processes. The first of these consists of taking in and incorporating what we perceive in terms of what we know and understand. We process data in terms of our conceptual systems. A child sees an object that has a wooden handle and a long metal blade attached to it. It looks to him very much like a knife. We can say that the child has assimilated his perception of the object in terms of a well-established conceptual system related to knives. The process of assimilation goes on continuously as we encounter familiar objects, events, and situations. As long as we have the appropriate conceptual categories and models, there is no conflict, and assimilation occurs without difficulty.

Supposing that when the object is held over a flame, the blade bends downward. If the child has had experience with objects that melt and slump downward as the result of melting, he can apply this model to the perceived event and still can *assimilate* this experience. Next we plunge the blade into a tank of water whereupon it straightens out to its original shape. Then we place the blade back over the flame in an inverted position, and this time it bends upward instead of downward. If the perceiver is a sixth-grade child, it is very likely that this experience will come as something of a shock. He is now confronted by a *discrepant event,* one which he could not have predicted and is not able to explain within the framework of his existing conceptual models. He faces a dilemma in the form of an experience which he cannot *assimilate.* Moreover,

before he is able to assimilate this experience he will have to learn more about the properties of the blade and the circumstances under which the bending took place. He may have to create a new conceptual model by combining parts of old models. If he has no teacher to engineer this conceptual reorganization for him through explanation and demonstration, he will have to do this for himself by experimenting and gathering data, by trying out various combinations of conceptual models, and testing each of these experimentally until he finally arrives at a point where he has a model that seems to match the event.

This process of reshaping and reorganizing conceptual structures until they fit and account for perceived events is known as *accommodation.* Inquiry involves both assimilation and accommodation in complementary roles. The inquirer, faced with a discrepant event, may first attempt to break it down into component parts, to analyze it in terms of variables which he has already conceptualized. In the case of the knife that is not a knife (it is actually a bimetallic strip), he may try to find out what the blade is made of or how it is put together. He may try to determine the changing temperature of the blade or the temperature of the water in the tank. He may wonder about the size and shape of the blade and try to find out more about changes in these conditions throughout the observed event. Through the process of analysis he may have obtained enough information about the event to assimilate it entirely. If he is aware of the fact that metals expand with increase in temperature, and the fact that two different metals may expand at different rates, and if, in addition, he discovers that the blade is made of two different metals welded together, he may arrive at the hypothesis that the bending was caused by stresses produced by the differential expansion within the blade. Analysis of this kind paves the way for conceptual reorganization. Yet before the child is able to assimilate the event, he must pull together the results of his analysis. To these analyzed data he tries to apply various combinations of explanatory conceptual models until he has constructed one that seems to account for what he has perceived. Accommodation provides for the necessary restructuring of concepts that enables the child to assimilate formerly discrepant events.

Through the dual processes of assimilation and accommodation a person is able to build theories, test them, incorporate them within a broader conceptual system and use them in finding greater meaning and unity in experience.

## INQUIRY IN CONTRAST
## TO ENGINEERED LEARNING

It is possible for a teacher to engineer conceptual reorganization in a child and to bring about the child's accommodation to discrepant events by programing a series of experiences, by drawing on past experiences, and by focusing attention through verbal instruction and exposition on selected aspects of his environment. In order to be effective in doing this, however, it is important for a teacher to be reasonably well acquainted with the existing conceptual structures of the learner and to keep a constant check on the conceptual modifications that are taking place at every step along the way. This is very difficult even when the teacher-pupil ratio is one-to-one. It of course becomes more difficult as the number of pupils increases.

When the mode of learning is inquiry, however, the process of data gathering, analysis, and experimentation is under the control of the learner himself. He is free to reach out in whatever direction he chooses for data and to gather this information in whatever sequence is most meaningful to him. Through inquiry, the learner influences and actually programs his own learning in terms of his own cognitive needs as dictated by his style of learning and his informational needs of the moment.

To summarize thus far, inquiry can be regarded as a fundamental learning process, which is under the autonomous control of the learner and promotes conceptual growth through the dual and complementary functions of assimilation and accommodation.

## DEVELOPMENTAL CHANGES
## IN INQUIRY

The course of development of thinking, as described by Inhelder and Piaget(11), moves from the highly egocentric, intuitive and concrete toward the more decentralized, analytical and abstract. There is no mode of mental activity in which these developmental trends are more evident than the process of inquiry. At a very early age this process is seen as taking the form of sensorimotor learning. This is the seemingly disorganized interaction with the environment through which the child builds a repertoire of intuitive schemata representing the properties of his environment. These schemata are by-products of his attempts to manipulate and control his environment. Later, during the preschool years, data gathering takes on a somewhat more organized form. This stage is called "preoperational" because the child is still concerned with producing an effect rather than seeing a relationship. As yet he is unable to see his manipulations as tentative and reversible. He does not regard them as operations that can be done and undone or as experiments that can be replicated.

Once the child crosses over into operational thinking, his inquiry takes on more of the character of research. He can subdivide his activity into separate operations and can examine the effects of each operation independently from that which precedes or follows it. He is therefore able to experiment in a somewhat controlled fashion. At first he performs only concrete operations; that is, he manipulates the environment directly and groups his findings in ways that are likely to yield new ideas and conceptual organizations. In looking for an explanation of the bimetal strip, he might try varying the temperature first in one direction and then in another and observing the consequences of these changes. From this information, he might hypothesize a systematic relationship between temperature and the bending of the blade.

As the child approaches adolescence he becomes capable of going beyond concrete operations to the point where he can manipulate ideas and propositions and test hypotheses through formal logical operations. Thus, while the child at the stage of concrete operations might discover through the manipulation of materials that a bimetal strip will bend only when two different metals are used, the adolescent who has arrived at the level of formal logical operations might be able to deduce this same conclusion logically.

The metals must bend because they are fixed to each other along a common surface. The area of one becomes greater than the area of the other because they expand at different rates. Some internal stress must be produced. The only configuration that would permit the common surface to remain unchanged while one metal becomes larger than the other would be that of concentric circles.

The formal logical process by which the adult arrives at the conclusion that the blade had to bend seems far removed from the almost random exploratory manipulations of the infant, but they are both forms of inquiry because the learner increases his understanding of his environment through *self-directed* actions. There are many important changes in the way the autonomy of the learner is translated into plans and actions, into strategies and schemata. The infant centers on objects and comes to sense their properties intuitively by playing with them. The older child seeks to control the objects of his environment and learns how his manipulations as causes correlate with outcomes as effects. In time he abstracts from observed relationships concepts of causality. Perhaps it is more accurate to say that he constructs or invents these conceptual models of causality. Yet they are shaped by the events that he creates through his operations. He produces the data he needs in shaping, trying out, testing and revising his conceptual models of the real world. The mature mind can go one step further and test the validity of a construct or test a hypothesis logically, and completely bypass certain empirical or concrete operations.

## MOTIVATION OF INQUIRY

Throughout these changes in the *form* of inquiry, its motivational basis is subject to very little change. The motivation to inquire is rooted partly in the need to assimilate perceived objects and events. At all levels of inquiry we pursue meaning; that is, we seek to relate new experience to old conceptual structures. Regardless of the level of sophistication that the pursuit takes, the activity of gathering and processing information is exciting and pleasurable. The ability to assimilate discrepant events is intrinsically rewarding, and the construction of new conceptual models that enable one to find new meaning in old events creates in the learner a sense of power. These are satisfactions that result from the act of inquiring or its immediate consequences and serve to motivate learning when it occurs in the inquiry mode.

One of the by-products of recent investigations dealing with new methods of instruction in science, mathematics, and social studies has been the almost universal recognition by the researchers of a kind of motivation that was not found in the traditional learning situation. Bruner(3) has been one of the most articulate in describing this phenomenon. These new teaching methods have all involved the more or less inductive approach in which new understandings come to light through a form of discovery by the individual learner. It was sensed by Bruner and others that the act of discovery had a number of highly desirable consequences not the least of which was a high level of motivation. He noted that discovery tended to produce much activity and interest, a sense of intellectual potency in the learner, an increasing faith in the regularity of the universe. This faith seemed to promote a feeling of confidence in the child that prompted him to pursue his learning activities in search of more and more of these regularities.

Just what is discovery? Is it a highly creative act that involves the sudden recognition of something very new and unique? Or is it simply the recognition of order in what formerly appeared to be chaos? The term is used in a great many ways so that now it seems to be unwise to use it to describe any particular cognitive act. Yet the sense of discovery, the "aha" feeling does seem to turn up only under certain circumstances. It seems to happen only when assimilation is finally achieved after it is first blocked. When the discrepant event is suddenly rendered assimilable through cognitive reorganization there is a release of tension and a feeling of satisfaction.

Here then is reward that is directly associated with the process of inquiry. So long as a child can believe that a new discovery can result from inquiry, he will inquire without any outside pressure to do so.

Yet is there a motivation entirely *intrinsic in the act* of inquiry itself? Is the expectation of closure a necessary condition for the motivation of search? Hunt(10) suggests yet another motivating force. He calls it the "motivation inherent in information processing and action." What he is saying in effect is that we have a need for cognitive activity, a need that can be met only by the intake of data, the processing of it, the drawing of inferences from it, and the making of decisions. Another way of saying this might be that we have the need to inquire, not because inquiry leads to the joyous experience of discovery but simply because inquiry itself is a highly satisfying and stimulating activity.

One may then raise the question that if Hunt is right, why do we not find our schools filled with inquirers gathering data and satisfying this need? One answer may be that inquiry would be the dominant mode of learning in the school except that we have done a highly effective job of preventing this from taking place by utilizing ego and social needs to motivate children to conform rather than to inquire, to store facts and generalizations rather than to search and discover for themselves. Perhaps it has been that by providing a climate hostile to inquiry we have succeeded in preventing this motivational force from promoting inquiry activity and permitting children to develop the skills of inquiry and the attitudes that lead to its use.

Alpert(1) has addressed himself to the problem of motivating curiosity in the schools. He suggests that we do this by utilizing the child's dependency on the teacher for social support. According to his plan the teacher acts toward the child *as though* the child is a curious person. The purpose is to shape the child's self-concept so that he comes to see himself as curious and then begins to take on curious behavior to correspond with this new self-image.

The theoretical implications of such an approach are most interesting. Can one expect a person to become curious because he has come to see himself as a curious person? Can we get a child to alter his self-image simply by giving social reinforcement to a new image? Will any resulting behavior change persist when the teacher is no longer around to reinforce the new self-image? We do not have answers to these questions, but it does seem that a more direct approach to promoting curiosity in anybody is to confront him with an event or object that is *discrepant enough to make him curious*—to build up irresistible pressures in the child to find a way of assimilating the event. As Bruner and others point out, the child who attains new understandings for himself gains a sense of intellectual power (Bruner [3]), mastery (White [20]), or accomplishment (Erikson [5]). The new self-image that results grows out of what the child knows he has actually done. He sees himself as a curious person and an autonomous inquirer because he

*has been* curious and autonomous. Once this image is established it is likely to promote more of the same kind of behavior.

## INQUIRY AND COGNITIVE STYLE

The element of autonomy that characterizes inquiry has special psychological significance for conceptual growth because it allows the learner to adapt the learning process to his immediate cognitive needs. These needs are in part a function of the way the learner thinks. Each learner has a style of conceptualization which strongly influences the mode by which he gathers, processes, and uses data. In other words, because inquiry is a self-directed mode of learning, it permits the learner to adapt the process of learning to match his own particular style of thinking.

Jerome Kagan at the Fels Research Institute and Irving Sigel at the Merrill-Palmer Institute have sampled these styles through a variety of instruments designed to reflect the basis upon which a subject prefers to associate elements of his perceived environment. They have been able to distinguish two and possibly three fundamental styles. These styles can best be illustrated by a sample test item. A child is presented with a card on which appear three pictures—a garden, a rake, and a fork. The child is asked to pick the two pictures that seem to go together and to give the reason for associating these two. If the child picks the rake and the garden because a rake is used in a garden, he is relying on past associations. He is linking together entities which have been contiguous in his experience. This style is called "relational" because linkages are made on the basis of directly observed relationships and do not require the use of conceptual systems or abstractions. The relational thinker does not stray too far from his perceptions and the associations that have grown out of them.

If the child says that the fork and the rake go together because they both have tines, he is making his association on the basis of a breakdown of perceived wholes into meaningful components. This style is called "descriptive-analytical" because the associations are formed through the analysis of experience. He has linked the fork and the rake on the basis of a component characteristic of each of them which he was able to respond to only because he had first dissociated the parts of both objects and then compared them in terms of one or more of these parts. The relational thinker is more likely to rely heavily on impressions while the analytical thinker tends to reflect on his percepts within a systematic framework of conceptual categories.

Kagan, Sigel, and Moss(12) found these styles to have consistency within individuals over time and over a wide range of cognitive tasks. Boys tend to be more analytical than girls, and both become less relational and more analytical with age.

These styles affect the inquiry process. Children show inquiry strategies that correspond to these cognitive styles. A study by Suchman and Kagan found that children with highly analytical styles of thinking tended to inquire more analytically, gathering data primarily for the purpose of analysis. The relational (low analytical) children were more inclined to form hypotheses based on impressions, bypassing the analytical process. The children selected inquiry strategies that best suited their styles of thinking. Further investigations of the relationship between cognitive styles and inquiry are now in progress.

## INQUIRY AND CONCEPTUAL GROWTH

It is well-known that you can get a child to become aware of a relationship or principle by exposing him to enough situations where the principle is operant. In time he will abstract the concept or generalize over the experiences. If the instances are carefully selected, one can guide or engineer the discovery of new relationships. Beberman's(2) and Hendrix's(9) approach to teaching algebra is based on this. They take the position that there is little point in talking about, let us say, the commutative principle unless the pupils have almost an intuitive understanding of just what the principle is. Too often when this is taught through a verbal didactic method, the pupils acquire merely a superficial, mechanistic understanding. They know what they have to do to get the answer but they do not know *why*. Beberman's method literally engineers the students into discovering the principle themselves. His pupils are given a series of mathematical operations to perform which can be done with simple arithmetic. The problems are arranged in order of increasing difficulty in that the numbers get larger and more difficult to handle arithmetically. However, it is possible to discover a short-cut that simplifies the calculation. By discovering this shortcut, the pupil has discovered the algebraic principle.

Without the benefit of a carefully programed set of experiences, one must go through a less-directed series of operations to arrive at a given concept. Before arriving at such a concept one might have to construct a number of intermediate and inadequate solutions in a succession of conceptual reorganizations. Is there any advantage in such trial-and-error thinking?

Smedslund(15) wondered about this and tried to determine whether the emerging concept is different in the one case in which it results from a simple generalization drawn from a set of positive instances and in the other case in which it is the end product of a series of conceptual reorganizations. He worked with preschool children and used the concept of the conservation of weight. He got one group of children to discover empirically that the weight of a plasticene ball does not change as its shape is modified. He contrasted this with another group whose members had come to internalize the concept of the conservation of weight through the natural processes by which such concepts become internalized (Piaget [14]). He found that concepts that are easily formed by simple generalizations are more readily discarded when data are discrepant to the concept. But when the concepts result from the resolution of conflicts in successive accommodations as in the normal course of conceptual growth, a conceptual structure is not easily given up even in the face of a heavy weight of discrepant data. Smedslund sneaked a little piece of clay away from the plasticene ball so that the children would not know he had done this. He then changed the shape of the ball and weighed it for the children so that they could see that its weight had changed as the shape was changed. Those children who had formed the concept of the conservation of weight simply through the generalization over several positive instances were quite ready to give up this concept in the face of *one discrepant event*. The other group, however, refused to accept the data as valid and raised rather strong doubts

as to the honesty of the experimenter presenting the demonstration.

This suggests certain weaknesses in any learning situation in which the conceptual increments toward each new structure are preprogramed for speed and ease of learning. It almost seems that when conceptual structures are formed by outside agents that obviate the learner's own accommodative struggles, the new concept is not hard-won or self-structured. It is less a part of the learner, less useful to him (Festinger [6]). He is therefore more willing to relinquish the concept if new data challenge its validity.

The step-by-step path toward conceptual growth is typical of most teacher-directed learning. The primary objective is the attainment of a new concept. This attainment is engineered by starting with the familiar and moving with or without discovery toward the unfamiliar with the purpose of assimilating this in the framework of existing structures. The assumption is that all learners begin with conceptual structures and cognitive styles that are enough alike to permit a standard sequence of operations (or lesson plan) to bring them to the same level of conceptualization.

Yet children's conceptual models differ enormously in structure. Take the relatively simple phenomenon of floating bodies. What makes an air bubble rise to the surface of a liquid? Some children have very diffuse notions that involve the "lightness of air" or the "tendency for gases to rise." Some believe that water pressure has something to do with it and that water pressure acts only in a downward direction. Some children understand the depth-pressure relationships in liquids, but fail to see this at all as related to gravity.

If a child is going to reorganize his concepts of floating or sinking, he will have to be able to proceed from where he is and not from some hypothetical point of ignorance. He must have the opportunity to try out his conceptual models by using them to design experiments and make predictions. He must be free to gather the data he needs to resolve his cognitive conflicts until he has evolved a conceptual system that lets him assimilate what he sees. In short, a realistic approach to conceptual growth must allow the learner to gather and process data in accordance with his cognitive needs of the moment, and this suggests he should be utilizing some form of inquiry.

## MEANS OF PROMOTING INQUIRY

There is a wide range of cognitive skills involved in the inquiry process. This includes the gathering, organizing, and processing of data, the trying out of conceptual models, the restructuring of these models to accommodate to new data, and the testing of models for validity. At times it is necessary to use exacting methods of sampling, control, and analysis. At other times a wild intuitive leap might be the operation most needed. There are broad strategies and special tactics that help to make inquiry more productive. The one most dependable characteristic of inquiry is that there is no one fixed method of operation. To build and strengthen inquiry skills, one would be hard-put in trying to identify a set of specific component skills that would have to be independently exercised and strengthened. Even if it were possible to make children more perceptive or flexible by giving them special exercises in this kind of activity, it is very doubtful whether such a piecemeal

approach would make a significant difference in the inquiry of children.

The element of creativity seems to play an important role in the inquiry process. Both in searching for new data and in restructuring conceptual systems to accommodate to new data the inquirer must act creatively. Torrance(19), Getzels and Jackson(7), and Guilford(8) have made notable advances in identifying the conditions that appear to affect the creative process. Torrance lists the following conditions as necessary "for the healthy functioning of the preconscious mental processes which produce creativity":

1. The absence of serious threat to the self, the willingness to risk
2. Self-awareness—in touch with one's feelings
3. Self-differentiation—sees self as being different from others
4. Both openness to the ideas of others and confidence in one's own perceptions of reality or in one's own ideas
5. Mutuality in interpersonal relations—balance between excessive quest for social relations and pathological rejection of them – *i.e. get along well with others*.

These conditions seem to center about the ego and suggest that creativity increases as the ego is freed from inhibition and external domination, yet stays open to the intake of ideas from the outside.

Getzels and Jackson lend further support to the notion that creativity is promoted more through environmental conditions than through specific training. I quote from their book:

Without passing premature judgment on the possibility of some positive effects from special instruction, we hold that boldness in thinking, free reign to the imagination, and creativity in performance will not be easily coming through piecemeal lessons and artificial stimulants. What is needed is a change in the entire intellectual climate in which we—the parents and the teachers—as well as the children function.

The findings of these researches point to the significance of attitudes and climates. They speak of the positive effects of "intellectual playfulness on creativity." Quoting again:

The relevant educational issue might well be: Are there certain areas of instruction in which opportunities are provided for "discovering" as well as for "remembering"? Is there provision in the curriculum for playing with facts and ideas as well as for repeating them? Can we teach students to be more sensitive to the nature of problems? Can we teach them that a problem may have several different interpretations and solutions? Even if there is only one right answer as in a mathematics problem, can a student solve the problem in a number of different ways?

The buildup of a given set of response patterns is a lot simpler to achieve than the promotion of creative thinking. In the case of the former, high pressure through strong and repeated reinforcements will generally have the desired effect. But high pressure has a way of interfering with creativity in forcing children to rely on stereotyped behavior. Creativity seems to occur most readily under conditions of low pressure.

One aspect of climate received extensive treatment in the research of Bruner et al.(4) as reported in *A Study of Thinking*. One of the more significant outcomes of these studies was the identification of several search and concept attainment strategies and the recognition of the fact that the kinds of strategies used by the subjects were determined in part by the "payoff matrix." That is, the way the subjects went about gathering data was largely a function of the kinds of performances that were being rewarded. When speed was rewarded, the subjects took greater

risks and adopted a gambling strategy to save time. They leaped in to test hypotheses that had a far less than 50-50 chance of being valid. They also started testing hypotheses after they had gathered only a small proportion of the available data. But when the time pressure was off and accuracy and economy of operations were made the important criteria for success, the strategy shifted. Stress on the economy of operations encouraged some to try to retain a maximum amount of data in their heads, although cognitive strain of this kind was generally avoided. When freedom from error was an important success criterion, the subjects took a slower but safer route.

These findings suggest that inquiry strategies are flexible and can be adjusted to the demands of the problem situation. The so-called "scientific method" is not a fixed sequence of operations such as (a) "define the problem," (b) "formulate hypotheses," and (c) "gather data," etc. Scientists have reported that *their* methods vary widely according to *their* problems, just as the strategies of Bruner's subjects do.

MacKinnon(13) also found no set patterns in the searching and thinking of highly creative architects and engineers. He concluded that:

If the widest possible relationships among facts are to be established, if what I would call the structure of knowledge is to be grasped, it is necessary that the student have a large body of facts which he has learned, as well as a large array of reasoning skills which he has mastered. . . . A knowledgeable person in science is not merely one who has an accumulation of facts, but rather one who has the capacity to have sport with what he knows, giving creative rein to his fancy in changing his world of phenomenal appearances into a world of scientific constructs.

Bearing in mind that the process of inquiry has a large creative component, yet cannot depart from the realm of logic and reason, we shall turn now to the problem of developing inquiry in the elementary school.

### THE INQUIRY TRAINING PROJECT

The Inquiry Training Project (Suchman [16, 17, 18]) came into being because it seemed that the process of inquiry is basic to all intellectual activity, and because our pilot studies showed that elementary school children at the level of the intermediate grades did not seem to be either willing or able to inquire productively even when they were faced with events that aroused their curiosity. When they did make attempts to obtain closure, these attempts were highly dependent in the sense that the children merely asked for explanations. Apparently they had been accustomed to having their conceptual growth engineered for them by teachers and did not know how to achieve this autonomously by asking questions to gather information.

Although it has been modified in many ways since the time of its inception in 1957, Inquiry Training still retains the same basic form with which it started. The children work as a group. A concrete problem is posed in the form of a motion picture film of a physics demonstration. This film is designed to puzzle the children. The event is not one which an elementary school child would easily explain simply by observing. Many of the critical variables, the nature of the materials used, the conditions of the materials and the changes in these conditions, are not observable in the film and must be verified in other ways.

The children are asked to find out why the events in the filmed episode occurred. The problem posed to them is one of constructing an explanatory system. In order to gather the information that they need they must ask questions. We restrict them to questions that can be answered by "yes" or "no" to prevent them from falling back into the open-ended type of inquiry in which the responsibility for structuring is in the teacher's hands. The yes-or-no question forces the children to think through and structure their own questions.

Inquiry sessions last between 30 and 60 minutes and each one is based on a different problem film. In structuring the inquiry sessions we try to provide the following three conditions:

1. *A problem that is real and meaningful to the children*, a discrepant event that they are unable to assimilate because: (*a*) they have not fully analyzed the event in terms of all the relevant variables, and (*b*) because they do not have the necessary conceptual models to assimilate the event in the way that they initially perceive it. The problem therefore is one of having to analyze and accommodate before assimilation can take place.
2. The second condition is the *freedom* given the children to gather whatever data they want in whatever sequence they desire. No attempt is made to guide or program the data given to the children beyond what is presented within the film itself. This condition allows the individual child to search in whatever direction he wants in gathering data to satisfy his own cognitive needs.
3. The third condition is *a responsive environment*. We attempt to provide the information asked for by the children as promptly and as accurately as possible so that the inquiry process is not blocked by delays or frustrations.

No external reinforcements or pressures are built into the program.

Inquiry is motivated primarily by the satisfactions intrinsic in the process itself. Part of this, we believe, is gained through the progress the children make toward greater understanding of the problem episode. The other part of the motivation comes from the excitement inherent in gathering and processing data. Of course, one cannot keep out ego and social motivation. Children ask questions to impress other children with what they know, and many are driven by the need to have the satisfaction of finding the "right answer." However, the teacher tries to protect the children from these and other extrinsic pressures to allow the satisfaction to grow out of the activities themselves and not to have it artificially generated by outside agents.

The inquiry sessions enable the children to learn some of the effects of various strategies of data gathering and processing. However, this awareness of the dimensions of the inquiry process and the logical structures that are used in the construction of explanatory systems can be developed more rapidly and effectively if the children's attention is brought back to the process of inquiry itself after they are no longer engaged in the science problem. A "critique" is given as a follow-up of the inquiry session. A tape recording of the inquiry session is played back to the children so that the group can observe the effects of various types and groupings of questions. In examining and evaluating their own question asking, the children are able to see many of the dimensions of strategy.

The inquiry sessions and the follow-up critique sessions fulfill the major requirements of Inquiry Training. The children have a series of experiences in attempting to construct explanatory models for observed events and have a way of reviewing, examining, and analyzing their previous inquiries so that they can be more effective and planful in future inquiry sessions.

In the academic year of 1960-61, we conducted an experiment to determine the effects of Inquiry Training over a 24-week period (Suchman [18]). Twelve teachers were especially trained over the summer, and each week during the experiment they spent an hour providing Inquiry Training for a full classroom of children. Each school that had an Inquiry Training group also had a control group. The control groups were given the same science content through the same films used to pose the Inquiry Training problems, but no practice or critiques relating to inquiry itself were given.

Evaluation of Inquiry Training posed a problem. None of the standardized aptitude or achievement tests could measure the kinds of changes Inquiry Training effects in the children. Of special concern were the changes in the inquiry process itself, in the willingness and ability of the children to gather data autonomously and to attempt to build explanatory models on their own. There was interest too in conceptual growth, not in how many facts and generalizations the children had stored and could report verbally, but in the actual change in the children's internalized structure of physical relationships.

We had to devise our own instruments and it was this problem that gave the study some of its biggest headaches. To measure these two kinds of outcomes, we constructed two very different kinds of tests.

The analysis of the inquiry process could only be based on a sample of the child's inquiry. The "Questest" was designed to obtain just such a sample. Special problem films were used. Each child was given the test individually. He was shown the test film and then given 25 minutes to ask questions to gather the data he needed and to construct his explanatory system. We tape-recorded these individual inquiry sessions and used the tape as the basis of our analysis of each child's inquiry behavior.

While we actually identified some 12 question types that could be clearly differentiated, it is more meaningful to point out the 3 major categories of questions. One of these was *verification.* This category included all questions that are attempts to identify and analyze the parameters of the problem episode; questions about the names of objects, the materials they were made out of, the conditions of objects such as temperature, pressure, shape, size; the events of the episode, and the properties of objects in the episode.

The second major question type was what we call the *implication* question. These questions are probes used to test out ideas of causal relationships. They go beyond the verification of what happened into the realm of why things happen. Implication questions have two important subdivisions. Some questions in this category are attempts to verify relationships between variables in a direct, abstract way. This question type is called "abstract-conceptual." An example of this would be: "Does the bending of the blade have anything to do with the heat?" The question is, in effect, a direct request for the verification of an idea. Abstract-conceptual questions are requests for judgments about causation and therefore short-circuit the process of inquiry. Because the questioner obtains a direct evaluation of his hypothesis he avoids the necessity of testing the hypothesis experimentally, of gathering data, and making his own inferences.

The second type of implication question is called "concrete-inferential." These questions are more like experiments. An example would be: "If we made the flame hotter, would the blade bend further?" In this case the child is manipulating a variable and simply asking if a particular outcome would be the result of his manipulation. But he makes his own inference as to causality from the data he obtains.

Our attempt in Inquiry Training was to increase the amount of verification and the amount of experimentation and to decrease the abstract-conceptual "brain-picking" kind of questioning.

In our analysis of the Questest protocols for the experimental and the control groups, we found first of all that in every case the inquiry-trained groups asked significantly more questions than the controls. It was necessary therefore to control for fluency in comparing the groups in terms of the frequencies of the major question types. We found that where fluency was high the inquiry-trained groups asked significantly more verification questions than the controls and significantly less abstract-conceptual implication questions than the controls. There was no noticeable difference between the two groups in the use of experimentation.

With respect to conceptual growth, our finding was that in most cases conceptual growth through the inquiry approach was about the same as the growth attained under the more traditional didactic methods. We did have two groups, however, in which the inquiry-trained children had significantly higher scores on the concept test than the control children.

Of course, the real test of Inquiry Training would be the degree to which a child is able to transfer his inquiry skills to problems in other content areas. If inquiry is a mode of behavior and can be developed and strengthened through practice and through the deliberate shaping of strategies and techniques, then this behavior should be applicable in a wide range of problem situations.

We are now engaged in an investigation to test the transfer effects of Inquiry Training. New problem films are now being developed in economics and biology. Sometime next year we will give a group of sixth-grade children Inquiry Training using our physics films and then determine how effective they are in solving economics and biology problems through the inquiry approach.

## IMPLICATIONS FOR CURRICULUM

We do not see the specific techniques and methodology of Inquiry Training as we have used it thus far as the significant outcome of our work. We have been far more concerned with the theoretical implications of our findings. What has impressed us most in our observation of the inquiry process is that the autonomy of the learner has enormous importance for both motivation and conceptual growth. Take away from the child the element of choice in the learning process and you destroy one of the most potent forces for keeping the child involved in learning and for giving him an opportunity to influence the course of his own learning. Self-direction in learning is not a case of the blind leading the blind because the learner is in a position to know the nature and the location of his conceptual gaps. He is sensitive to his own informational needs. If he is not given an opportunity to modify and at least to some extent to direct his own data intake, his learning experiences may well miss the mark by a wide margin. We have just begun to explore the

possibilities of introducing the inquiry approach and Inquiry Training into the curriculum. This approach should not be brought in as a thing apart from "regular subjects," as a "gimmick" or special shot in the arm. Possibly what is needed is an inquiry-centered curriculum in which the children would find themselves launched into areas of study by first being confronted by concrete problem-focused episodes for which they would attempt to build explanatory systems. Part of their data gathering might well be in the question-asking mode and certainly along the way time would have to be spent in building inquiry skills through critiques and other such procedures. Yet there would also be room for helping the children enlarge their conceptual systems through more teacher-directed means. At times the teacher might work with groups in developing new conceptual models or in identifying variables that might be useful for analysis of the problem episode. Of course, the children would still be using the library and other materials, but always in relation to a particular problem of inquiry. Learning would always be in connection with moving from concrete events toward the construction of an explanatory model. Yet neither the analysis of the concrete events nor the particular models constructed to explain them would be the most important outcome of these inquiries. There would be three and possibly more by-products that would have far greater significance.

First there would be the development and strengthening of the inquiry process itself. Since learning would always be couched within the inquiry framework, the children would become more autonomous learners and their motivation in the process of learning would be greater. The second by-product would be the self-image that would develop in the children as a result of a greater autonomy in learning. The children would emerge with a sense of intellectual potency and a faith in the regularity of the universe and a greater skepticism toward any explanatory system as a final and ultimate truth. They would learn to question and test and to see themselves as able to move from data to theory under their own power. This should boost their self-confidence for making further inquiries and for resisting efforts by others to program them into accepting a predetermined conclusion.

A third consequence of such a curriculum would be the development of a greater depth of understanding of principles and concepts within the disciplines of study relevant to the problems posed for inquiry. The child who inquires into the bimetallic strip can never emerge with a complete explanation of the events observed, but he can come to grips with such fundamental physical principles as conduction, the theory of molecular structure, the relationship between volume and temperature in matter, the principles governing stress and strain in metals. In Bruner's terms he will penetrate the structures of the disciplines concerned and become rather intimately involved with some segments of those structures.

Finally, the inquiry-centered curriculum would break away from the rhetoric of conclusions which now dominates so much of the curriculum and would put the process and products of scientific inquiry back into their proper relationship.

## REFERENCES

1. Alper, R., "The Shaping of Motives in Education." Speech prepared for the Fifth A.S.C.D. Curriculum Research Institute, 1960.

2. Beberman, M., *An Emerging Program of Secondary School Mathematics.* Cambridge, Mass.: Harvard University Press, 1958.

3. Bruner, J. S., "The Act of Discovery," *Harvard Educational Review,* XXXI (1961), 21-32.

4. —— *et al., A Study of Thinking.* New York: John Wiley & Sons, Inc., 1958.

5. Erikson, E., *Childhood and Society.* New York: W. W. Norton & Company, Inc., 1950.

6. Festinger, L., *A Theory of Cognitive Dissonance.* Evanston, Ill.: Row, Peterson & Company, 1957.

7. Getzels, J. W., and P. W. Jackson. *Creativity and Intelligence.* New York: John Wiley & Sons, Inc., 1962.

8. Guilford, J. P., *et al.,* "A Factor-Analytic Study of Creative Thinking," *Reports from the Psychology Laboratory.* Los Angeles: University of Southern California Press, 1952.

9. Hendrix, Gertrude, "Learning by Discovery," *Mathematics Teacher,* LIV (1961), 290-99.

10. Hunt, J. McV., "Piaget's Observations as a Source of Hypotheses Concerning Motivation." Paper read at the Annual Meeting, American Psychological Association, 1962.

11. Inhelder, Bärbel and J. Piaget, *The Growth of Logical Thinking from Childhood to Adolescence.* New York: Basic Books, Inc., Publishers, 1958.

12. Kagan, J., H. Moss, and I. Sigel, "The Psychological Significance of Styles of Conceptualization." A paper read at a Conference on Basic Cognitive Processes sponsored by the Social Science Research Council, 1961.

13. MacKinnon, D., "Fostering Creativity in Students of Engineering," *Journal of Engineering Education,* LII (1961), 129-42.

14. Piaget, J. and Bärbel Inhelder, *Le Développement des quantités chez l'enfant.* Dalachaux et Niestle, 1941.

15. J. Smedslund, "The Acquisition of Conservation of a Substance and Weight in Children," *Scandanavian Journal of Psychology,* II (1961), 156-60.

16. Suchman, J. R., "Inquiry Training in

the Elementary School," *Science Teacher*, XXVII, No. 7 (1960), 42-47.

17. ——, "Inquiry Training: Building Skills for Autonomous Discovery," *Merrill-Palmer Quarterly*, VII (1961), 147-69.

18. ——, "The Elementary School Training Program in Scientific inquiry." Illinois Studies in Inquiry Training.

Urbana: University of Illinois, 1962.

19. Torrance, E. P., *Guiding Creative Talent*. Englewood Cliffs, N. J.: Prentice-Hall, Inc., 1962.

20. White, R. W., "Motivation Reconsidered: The Concept of Competence," *Psychological Review*, LXVI (1959), 297-333.

# 35

# The Illinois Studies in Inquiry Training

## J. RICHARD SUCHMAN

We have been trying to develop inquiry skills in elementary school children. This began back in 1957 when we were disturbed by the findings of some studies. One of these found that 97 per cent of the questions asked in the classroom were asked by the teacher. Another found that as children moved from the first grade to the sixth grade, they become less empirical and based more hypotheses and tests of hypotheses on conclusions of authorities and less on their own empirical operations.

Over a period of years we have identified what seem to be necessary conditions for inquiry to occur in classroom settings, and we have tried to build a program that creates these conditions. The conditions are essentially these:

1. We find that the children need some kind of *focus* for their attention, some kind of problem or stimulus, and preferably, although not necessarily, one that is discrepant to the schemata or conceptual systems of the

child. In other words, one that cannot be readily assimilated.

2. They need the condition of *freedom*. We have broken freedom down into two parts, one of which is a kind of external freedom, that is, physical freedom to reach out for desired data and information and to acquire it at any rate in any sequence the child wishes. This is antiprograming in a sense. Internal freedom is something that follows as a consequence. We found that when you give children external freedom, they are inhibited for a time and do not avail themselves of it because they have been conditioned to follow the teacher's lead and to conform. But eventually, as they explore and find that external freedom does exist, they begin to build up what we call autonomy in their operations. They make decisions and try to satisfy their own cognitive needs by gathering the kinds of information they want. They also exercise freedom in trying out ideas.

Two kinds of scanning are used: scanning the field for data, and scanning the store of ideas for conceptual models. These comprise two parts of

J. Richard Suchman, "The Illinois Studies in Inquiry Training," *Journal of Research in Science Teaching*, II, No. 3 (September 1964), 230-32. Reprinted by permission.

the inquiry cycle. A child absorbs a percept and he tries to find a model he can use to assimilate it. Then, providing assimilation is incomplete, he performs some action to generate new data. At the same time that he acquires new data, he scans for new models on which to test the data. He endeavors to match the data coming in with the models being tried out. At some point the match between the data and a model is made.

3. The third condition is what O.K. Moore calls the "responsive environment." The child needs to have an environment where, when he reaches out for data, he procures something. He does not return with empty hands.

These, then, are three conditions for inquiry: the focus, the freedom to operate, and the responsive environment. If we provide these conditions we find that children inquire at elementary school age, and that inquiry will progress at a rate that far exceeds what would happen if one did not have these conditions. I am not going to say that they are necessary, but they are clearly conducive.

I would like to comment briefly on the motivation operating in this situation. One of the outcomes of creating these conditions is that you obtain a shift in motivation. When you have a teacher programing the learning experiences of the children (deciding what happens next), and when you have children following the teacher's lead, much of the motivation falls into what we call the social-ego category. The children look for rewards from the teacher and from the situation, extrinsic to the learning activity itself. When you go into the inquiry mode, you start with a problem and the children are free to attack it and build their constructs as they see fit. The motivation becomes more cognitive and takes two forms. One is the motivation of closure to close the gap and to make

the match between what is perceived and what is known. But we found that beyond this, after the children had found a reasonable degree of closure, they continued to inquire, to pull in data, and to process them. They were motivated, it seemed, by the act of inquiry itself. We were particularly curious about this.

The motivation seems to have different flavors. One is a pleasant sense of confidence a child gets in processing data even if no great problems bother him. The child picks away at an old alarm clock, takes it apart, and puts it back together, not because he is trying to build a grand theory of alarm clocks but because it is fun and because processing the kinds of data he is getting from these manipulations is very satisfying to him. He continues to do it without any real problems to prod him. There is also a sense of power and excitement in being able to do this. To borrow a phrase that J. McV. Hunt at Illinois uses, "we see in children a motivation inherent in information processing and action" and it seems to be a growing kind of motivational force that after a while tends to supplant the motivation of closure. In the beginning it seems highly important to give children problems that are discrepant in order to provide strong early interest. But after a while it becomes less necessary and children start structuring problems for themselves without having to be given one to start.

The procedure used for making children aware of the inquiry process is something we once termed Inquiry Training. (We have been sorry about the word "training" ever since.) We have produced a series of films starting with physics (we now have economics and biology, also) which are designed as discrepant events. They pose episodes which the children cannot assimilate without accommodating, or at least analyzing the event itself until assimilation is possible. The film is then the focus and offers the initial motivation. Next, we provided the freedom by allowing the children to ask yes-and-no questions to gather their data. These are questions phrased to be answered by "yes" or "no," but the teacher may qualify the answers where necessary. The questions are not attempts to elicit explanations or theory from the teacher but are strictly for data gathering, e.g., "Was the blade made of steel?"

One of our films is about a bimetal blade. When it is heated it bends downward, and when it is inserted into a tank of water, it straightens out. The demonstrator turns it over and puts it back on the flame. This time it bends upward, and when placed in water it once more straightens out. To the children who do not know anything about a bimetal blade, this is a discrepant event.

They continue from there, using "yes" or "no" questions. They cannot ask "was it because." If they start such questioning we tell them that it is their job to find explanations. "See if you can construct a theory. If you have one, you ought to be able to test it experimentally." Their experiments, too, are conducted through "yes" and "no" questions. "If we put the blade into a refrigerator would the same thing happen?" Such a question is the equivalent of an empirical test of a hypothesized relationship. The responsive environment is created by the teacher who answers the questions. As the children ask questions they build little theories which they test themselves.

We are now doing a study of the transfer of the effects of Inquiry Training with physics films, to see what influence this has on the ability to inquire into economics and biology problems. This is being done as a controlled study, in which we are comparing children who had experiences with physics to those who had not and checking the effects. So far, although the data are not all in, one thing is very clear: inquiry skills do transfer, not method per se, but a kind of attitude, a sense of self-confidence that the child has in his own ability to handle data and to build and test theories. The trained child is more willing to try out ideas after he has had this kind of experience. As far as transfer of method or approach is concerned, we do not know how much carries over. Such strategies are very hard to identify and to measure, so I am not so sure if we are going to see evidence of the transfer of methods.

We conducted a pilot study last summer with approximately 14 children to investigate the effects of cognitive style on inquiry. We had about 49 variables dealing with cognitive style, such as schematesizing, leveling, sharpening, field dependency, etc., in addition to data from the Primary Mental Abilities test. An intercorrelation matrix, including inquiry and other cognitive variables, yielded three correlation clusters suggesting three factors relevant to success in inquiry. One is the cognitive control dimension: the ability to handle and manipulate data. A second correlation cluster suggested the existence of an impulsivity factor, the capacity to leap beyond data to generate abstractions. Impulsivity leads to moving away from the data rather than "zeroing in" on it. In the inquiry process the child must shift back and forth from high cognitive control to impulsivity. If you never leave the data you will never construct theory. This ability is related to a third factor which we have identified as autonomy. If the child is high on cognitive control, impulsivity, and autonomy, we find him to be a more effective inquirer than a child who is low on any one of the three.

# ACTIVITIES

1. Describe some of the methods and techniques you may use in your classroom.

2. What are some of the procedures you may follow to monitor your teaching technique?

3. By what means are you able to evaluate the method you are using in your teaching?

4. In both the inquiry and discovery processes the students collect and evaluate data. What is the main difference by which data are collected in the two methods? Are there other differences as well as similarities?

5. Design teaching situations for your subject area which utilize organizing centers for (a) the process of discovery, (b) the process of inquiry.

6. Do the above for other thinking processes such as comparing and analyzing.

7. Review the articles by J. Raths and Herrick in the chapter "Decisions in Planning." Use an advanced organizer in your subject area for various methods.

8. What is the relationship between advanced organizer and subsumer theory?

9. The following are classroom activities which may routinely be used in various subject areas. Perhaps you have observed others. Categorize each as method or technique.

   a. Debate
   b. Use of audiovisual material such as movies, tapes, phonograph recordings, etc.
   c. Analyzing poetry
   d. Writing an essay on a topic new to the student
   e. "Pass-the-ball" questioning for review
   f. Individual laboratory research on an unknown variable

g. Written test
h. Oral test
i. Learning a new dialect in language class
j. Designing offense plays in basketball
k. Math problems for homework
l. Small-group discussion
m. Recitation of memorized information
n. Teacher-designed demonstration
o. Student-designed demonstration
p. Using programed materials for lessons
q. Student report
r. Role-playing
s. Visiting lecturer
t. Field trip

10. Examine some lesson plans and categorize instructional approaches as methods or techniques.

11. Observe some classroom teaching and categorize teaching acts as method or technique.

12. Suppose you are observing the following: A sixth-grade teacher has provided students with sealed cigar boxes which contain objects unidentified to the students. The students are busily shaking, tilting, and revolving the boxes in an endeavor to determine as much as possible about the contents. Is this method or technique? What thinking is going on? Speculate as to the lesson objective. Explain your answers in terms of what you have read.

13. You are observing a tenth-grade math class. The teacher previously has related to you that students have been having some difficulty understanding fractions. In this class the teacher has posted two full-page newspaper advertisements of different automobiles. The students were asked, "What do you see here that is similar? What do you see here that is different?" What do you think the teacher is trying to accomplish? Is this method or technique? Why? Could it be an advanced organizer?

# Chapter Six

# TEACHING FOR VALUING AND THINKING

The teaching profession has dedicated itself to develop in students a sense of values and a habit of critical thinking. In fact, these attributes are considered of such importance that the Educational Policies Commission of the National Education Association has made each of them the subject of its recent yearbooks. Although such statements are intended to stimulate, teachers occasionally may have a feeling of frustration because they do not always see how their teaching contributes to the achievement of the goals they have set themselves. This section suggests some alternatives open to teachers in the areas of valuing and thinking.

Many educators believe that to promote thinking and to accelerate valuing, teachers must allow students to do a great deal of verbalizing about their experiences: what they have seen, what they have heard, what they have read, and what they have imagined. You may have noticed from earlier articles included in this collection that, nevertheless, a student's chance to verbalize is at a minimum in many classrooms. It has also been found that in the areas of thinking and valuing, teachers can optimize their effectiveness by withholding critical judgments. Both of these aspects of the teaching-learning encounter, the amount of student talk and the amount of teacher criticism, may be used to monitor a classroom. What are some other processes observable in a classroom that may mirror a teacher's efforts to advance goals of thinking and valuing?

# 36

# Sociological Knowledge and Needed Curriculum Research

## LOUIS E. RATHS

### THE SOCIAL CONTEXT OF VALUES AND THINKING

Throughout the free world most people believe that social arrangements, laws, and institutions are made for man. Not the other way round. We believe that these social arrangements are means for the creating of individuals. Not the only means, perhaps, but a powerful resource for the creation of changed personalities. In his *Reconstruction in Philosophy*, written more than forty years ago, Dewey viewed social institutions in their educative effect; with reference to the types of individuals they foster. "The question is one of specific causations. Just what response does *this* social arrangement, political or economic, evoke, and what effect does it have upon the disposition of those who engage in it? Does it re-

Louis E. Raths, "Sociological Knowledge and Needed Curriculum Research," in *Research Frontiers in the Study of Children's Learning*, ed. James B. Macdonald (Milwaukee: School of Education, The University of Wisconsin-Milwaukee, 1961), pp. 20-48. Reprinted by permission.

lease capacity? If so, how widely?"[1]

I shall assume that the curriculum research that is "needed" will be related to the "types of individuals whom we wish to foster," and that shortcomings are in some ways related to the social arrangements and institutions and laws of our society. In my discussion I shall focus upon the school, but any reference to personality development assumes the wider social matrix.

The sociological research relating to social class structure, based for the most part, on Warner's scheme of identifying class status, has been directly related to the functioning of the school. The evidence is clear that in its distribution of rewards and punishments, the former go out of all proportion to the middle and upper middle class students; the penalties, go, out of all proportion, to the lower social classes. There is evidence that our tests of intelligence are biased in the kinds of problems presented, and in the words chosen to present those problems. The bias is in the direction of favoring the middle

[1] John Dewey, *Reconstruction in Philosophy*.

and the upper class children. Participation in extracurricular activities is shown to distinguish between lower and middle class children. Prizes, honors, and awards go in much higher proportion than their numbers suggest to the middle and upper class children. The high grades on reports to parents, and reports to colleges, go to the children of the middle and upper classes in much larger numbers than their proportion of the school population. The curriculum materials represented by the beginning primers and readers are shown to be a product of middle class living; hence probably of more interest to middle class children than to others.

Other items might be added to this list. Taken together, what bearing do they have upon Dewey's question about specific causation? Granting that the schools are functioning in this way, are they, then, releasing capacity? What are the effects upon children who participate in this social institution?

The evidence indicates that the school is selective in *releasing capacity*. In its functioning, the school shows a sensitivity to the welfare of the children of the middle class. An examination of "dropouts" shows that many more of the lower class children leave school before finishing. We know also that for every high school graduate who goes to college, there are two with equal intelligence scores and scholastic background who do not go, and primarily because of inadequate finances.

The elementary schools, the junior high schools, the senior high schools, a teacher's college, all show a relatively consistent pattern in this regard. Those who write materials for the schools, those who make the tests, the teachers, the administrators, and even the guidance personnel, display a similar consistency in their higher regard for children of the middle and upper social classes. Given such a consistent

pattern of functioning, is it possible that children of the lower social classes are unaware of the discrimination? What effects must this be having upon their development of *democratic* attitudes? upon loyalty to the school? upon their social relationships with each other? What rather large generalization might they draw about the "social system" in which they live? upon the integrity and sincerity of the status figures in the school?

And must it not also leave them with some sense of unworthiness? Year after year, in class after class, in academic and nonacademic matters of the school, they are rated low. As the years pass, must they not come to believe that they must in some ways merit these low ratings? that they are indeed inferior and unworthy? Instead of releasing capacity, I would infer that this treatment of many children restricts and constrains the release of capacity. We need curriculum research which explores a great variety of teaching and testing materials that are appropriate for lower class children. We need to know when and how to use these materials to release capacity. We need to reexamine the extracurricular programs to find ways of making them representative of the entire student population. We need annual accountings of ways in which high and how grades, rewards and penalties, praise and blame, are distributed to the children in the schools.

In the past few years there has been much talk of the lack of values in our children. Jacobs[2] summarized a series of studies which were concerned with the measurement of certain changes in college, and he concluded that in general not much change takes place. Judith Schoelkopf[3] found that children

[2] Jacobs, *"Changing Values In College"* (New York: Harpers Magazine, 1957).
[3] Schoelkopf. Unpublished Ph. D. Dissertation, New York University.

who were rated as severely overinhibited in their behavior showed little evidence of change between the years of two and one-half and six and one-half. Another group, characterized as severely underinhibited, made very few changes during the same four-year period. Those of us who have been visiting and observing schools for a period of years have experienced reports in faculty meetings which indicate that for a great many children the characterizations, year after year, are pretty much the same.

In these specific cases, some of the characterizations suggest the absence of release of capacity. One cannot say, however, that this is the fault of the school alone. In the absence of valid and reliable research evidence, we cannot make a claim against any one or several of the social institutions and arrangements of our society. We do know that certain undesirable kinds of behavior persist in the children under our care and tutelage.

What are some of the social conditions in general, which seem to have a bearing upon this lack of desirable change? We do know that about 20 per cent of our children move to a new residence every year, and we have little knowledge of the impact of this moving upon the growth and development of the children who move. We do know that approximately one in seven mothers is working, and that many of them will not be at home when children return from school. How does this affect the development of values? In approximately one-seventh of our families the home is "broken": either the father or the mother (or both) are not a part of the child's home; separation, divorce, mental illness and confinement to an institution, and death take a heavy toll and threaten the integrity of family life.

In terms of *where* our families are settling, the situation is again one that raises questions. One-fourth of our families now live in our new suburbs—and most of these cannot be called communities in the old sense of that term. We cannot depend upon these new centers of living to develop in our children a sense of values which will give direction to their lives. Almost 60 per cent of our families live in metropolitan centers; the cities are trying to squeeze their budgets for more adequate education of youth, for better housing and recreation, but, in general, they are fighting a losing battle, and they are now turning more and more toward the idea of securing federal assistance. What does this resettling of our families mean for the growth and development of the children, and what does it mean for curriculum research?

It must mean a great deal to the friendship and acquaintance problems of children. As we meet this new social phenomenon, can we not take an increased interest in the human relationships of these children, both in and out of school? Can we avoid the temptation of overorganizing the lives of these children? Can we provide more opportunities for them to be associated with each other in ways which they, themselves, might organize? How does all this affect junior and senior high school students as contrasted with those of elementary school age? We need this information and I suggest that we need it now.

In this century children have been exposed to ways of life that were alien to small communities at the turn of the century. It seems to me that it is now much more difficult for children to internalize the mores of their community. The movies, silent and talkies, have brought a bewildering variety of ways of life to nearly all of our children. Which is right? What is best? The new highways and other means of transportation have reshuffled our population and the ensuing new and different interactions have brought to the attention of the people involved many new ways of behaving. The radio, and later— television, increased greatly the range of choices in human behavior for hearing and viewing by children.

The press in American life is no longer what it once was. At the turn of the century our small town press was parochial and provincial. Today it is the purveyor of happenings the globe over. Moreover, it has lost a great deal of its respect and prestige. It probably stimulates little thought, and there is little or no consideration by the press of matters of values. The hodgepodge which the press now represents contributes to the confusion in values.

The place of work in the development of personality has lost much of its significance. It used to be that the struggle for survival gave meaning to life. Our children are largely divorced from the realities of that struggle, if indeed it continues to exist. In the absence of any such continuing motivation for work, we are inclined not to ask about the meaning of life. Then too, much of the work that many educated people do today could be done with much less schooling. Moreover, there is abroad in the land the idea that schools have little to do with the development of character: those who go to school many more years may indeed develop little more virtue. Our children see, daily, apparently well-educated persons extolling the advantage of one cigarette filter over another, one skin cream over another. Payola, bribes, rigged contests, surely must have effects on the kinds of children developing in our culture.

Could the children too be saying: "It isn't what you know, it's who you know that counts"; "it's money that talks"; "everything's a racket"; "you can't win"; "it's all right if you don't get caught"; "what's the gimmick?"

At any rate, the failure of our social institutions to free the capacities of the young for change, and the kinds social conditions which are prevalent at home and abroad in our time, point toward two important foci for education: *the development and clarification of values, and the development of thinking processes.* We assume that both processes will be carried forward in a context of significant world problems, national and local problems, and problems that have great personal significance for the students.[4]

## VALUES

The many and conflicting patterns of life to which our children are exposed, the lack of a strongly integrated community, the reduced impact of the family and the church, the deterioration of the relation between education and virtue, the worldwide upheavals, all point to the realm of values as a needed research in curriculum.

How can we go about it? Attempts to identify the "values" of people have proved almost fruitless. In general pencil-and-paper procedures have been followed, and the results represent pencil-and-paper opinions of students. We may get a starting direction by examining the concept of health, physical health. It is almost impossible to define the term so that it has practical meaning for an individual. Our needs for rest vary greatly; in terms of food, there can be no universal standard in terms of particulars of diet; in terms of energy output, again, great differences.

Suppose, however, we ask about deviations from health? about sickness?

[4] See, for example, C. Wright Mills, *The Sociological Imagination,* and Allen Wheelis, *The Quest For Identity,* for meaningful statements of the need for value clarification in terms of a societal perspective.

Here, we secure a much greater amount of agreement. In the area of values, by analogy, we would not seek to identify the values of children. Instead, we would ask: *When children have not developed values, how might it show up in their behavior?* And, if there is a widespread lack of value development in our culture, might not the symptoms vary, and wouldn't many children be afflicted?

This would suggest that we must be guided by a concept of value. Even though doctors tend more to agree on symptoms of illness, in the background there is at least the assumption that a treatment of the causes will be associated with a diminution of the symptoms. We need a guide on which to base our educative work with students. I have borrowed heavily from Dewey and my additions seem to me to be necessary.

1. A value implies prizing and cherishing. We may indeed have an attitude toward the lower social class, and may be acting upon that attitude, but if we do not prize it, if it is an attitude which we wish were different, then it cannot be called a value. Prizing and cherishing are, therefore, a requirement of a value. In addition:

2. A value implies choice after deliberation. It involves answering the question: Should I choose this? It frequently involves the anticipation of consequences and a reflection upon the desirability of the choice. It is weighing, and judging, before the choosing. If a person is responding impulsively, instinctively, reflexively, we should not associate the response with valuing. There is involved an intellectual emphasis upon sizing-up, upon judging alternatives in relation to ends sought. In addition:

3. A value—as such—implies recurrence of the valuing act. To choose something *once*, is hardly indicative that the something has the status of a value. We associate the concept of value with trend, with repetition, with a certain style of life. We infer that Jones or Smith values something because there is some emphasis on kinds of choices by Jones and Smith. Thus far we have said that a value must be: prized and cherished, reflected-upon, and repeated. There is more to the concept. In addition:

4. A value penetrates our living. If it is indeed a value of ours, we may allot some of our finances to support what is valued; we plan our time so that the value may be experienced in our living; we may develop new acquaintance and friendship patterns which are consistent with our values. We do reading, writing, speaking, collecting, and many other things, in support of values. We don't necessarily do all of these in support of any one value, but where we value, our lives are influenced. Values penetrate our living. In addition, and, finally:

5. When asked about our values, we affirm them. Having reflected upon them, prized them, repeatedly chosen them, having lived them—quite naturally—we affirm them when asked or challenged. We know what we are for. We have not only the moral courage, but in our lives we have demonstrated the moral energy.

*This is a large order.* If it takes *all five* criteria to determine a value, how many values do you have? It's my guess that you don't have many, and you are far from being alone in this regard. As was said earlier, it has become very difficult to develop values, and you and I are no exceptions.

The definition may be all the more welcomed if some time is given to some assumed synonyms of the word. Attitude is often associated with value. A father may have certain attitudes toward interracial marriage. As he examines them, he may feel that this is an awful risk. When asked for advice by his son, he might say, "This is a tremendously serious thing and you should think about it deeply." The son might then say, "What do you really think?" And the father might respond: "Frankly, I'm against it." But, if the son were to add, "Father, are you glad that you are of this opinion?" it is possible that the father would say that he wished he were different. In other words, he possesses an attitude that he does (not) prize, and in this case, as in many others, an attitude is not the equivalent of a value.

Beliefs are sometimes thought of as values. The point is here made that they are indeed values, if, and only if, they meet the five criteria which have been proposed. And I suggest that all of us have many so-called "beliefs" which are not values at all. They are securely compartmentalized and have little traffic with our lives.

So it is with many of our activities. There are many people who are in bridge clubs and play quite regularly, but who almost hate the thought of going—when the time comes for the game. They *do* things that look like interests, but which surely are not valued.

Here, the activity is carried out, but the prizing does not take place, and the reflection leads to another and quite different course of action.

Attitudes may become values, *when* they meet all five criteria. Interests may become values when they meet the criteria. Purposes, and aspirations too, may become values as they encompass the criteria. Feelings, activities, and beliefs may also become values. These are seven common ways in which personality expresses itself. Some of these expressions may be of the valuing kind. When they are not, it is suggested that we confine ourselves to the terms attitudes, interests, purposes, aspirations, feelings, activities, or beliefs. These are

good terms, but there is no need to confuse any or all of them with the concept of value.

$30°/o$

## YOUNGSTERS WITH VALUE PROBLEMS

If we use these criteria as a basis for exploring the lives of children, what will we find in the behavior of children who have "missed out" in the creation of values? Shall we find, as we did in the case of children with emotional needs, that certain patterns of behavior are common to them? The preliminary evidence suggests that we may be on the right road if we think of the following kinds of persistent behavior as in some way a concomitant of the absence of values:

1. CHILDREN WHO ARE APATHETIC, LISTLESS, DULL

They don't care much about activities going on around them. They look out the window; they fool with things in their pockets; they stare at books instead of reading them attentively. Nothing seems to be giving any direction to their lives. It is suggested that these children are in need of value development.

Before listing other behaviors symptomatic of a lack of value development, let me add that in every case I would apply two precautions: first, there should be a careful physical examination, to be sure that the symptoms of apathy are not related to physical defect or malfunctioning; and second, there should be clear evidence that a child is not severely disturbed emotionally. It might be inferred that these two exceptions may very well include all or nearly all of the cases of apathy and indifference. There is some evidence to the contrary.

## 2. EXTREMELY FLIGHTY CHILDREN

They seem to be interested in almost everything but, just for a moment or two; then they shift to something else. They seem to have no stable interests or concerns. They flit from one thing to another, and their teachers are apt to say: "I wish to high heaven that they would settle down for just a few minutes." Here, and in all other cases, we must make sure that there is no physical malfunctioning which might be causing the behavior, and no serious emotional difficulty.

## 3. CHILDREN WHO ARE EXTREME OVERCONFORMERS

Not having any values of their own, these children carry on their lives by trying to identify the values of their teachers, and then giving a kind of lipservice to these concepts. They will say or write what the teacher seems to want or to prize.

## 4. NAGGING DISSENTERS

These children are not rebels for a cause. They seem to pick on the teacher as a authority figure. They nag, carp, dissent. The teacher knows what they are against, but almost never does she know anything that they are *for*. One gets the clear feeling that these children are not dissenting after clear deliberation; that they are not dissenting because of conflict of principles. In other words, their dissent is not value-oriented. They are in need of guidance toward the development of values.

## 5. EXTREME HESITANCY, DOUBT, UNCERTAINTY

In the presence of a choice-situation, they cannot make up their minds. They want help. They don't know what they want, what they like, and they don't know what they want to try. In the absence of a value-base, it is indeed difficult to make choices, and in almost every classroom there are children of this kind. It is suggested that they need help in the development of values.

## 6. PERSISTENT, CONTINUING UNDERACHIEVEMENT

Where we have fairly clear evidence of ability, and almost chronic underachievement, it is a good hunch to suspect that guidance in value-development is needed. Having no values to guide their hour-by-hour, and day-by-day activities, these people are apt to aim at "getting by" and even to miss this goal on occasion. In our suburban schools especially, this category often includes 15 per cent, or more, of the children in the secondary levels. With the effort to help these children to develop values, will the pattern of underachievement change? As in all other cases, here too, we must take pains to investigate physical and emotional health before we decide that it is quite surely a value-related behavior.

## 7. THE ROLE-PLAYERS AND POSEURS

In our classrooms we not infrequently find children who seem to take the role of "the class fool." They mimic other children and sometimes the teacher; they pretend to be the characters in a story that is being read; or in a movie that is being seen. Having no real self to play, they play many selves. In their continuing trial of new and different roles they may be trying to find a role that suits them. They seem to need help in the creation of values, the ultimate basis for a *self*.

## 8. VERY, VERY INCONSISTENT CHILDREN

These children seem to change their beliefs, their attitudes, their feelings from day to day, and sometimes, from hour to hour. They are for integration, and a short time later, for segregation. Now they are loud for peace; yesterday it was for all-out war. There is little repetition of their views, and little penetration into life, and so far as we can infer, little or no deliberation before making their choices known. I suggest that here are children who need help in the development of values.

These *eight* behavior patterns (and there must be others) illustrate what may very well be the natural consequences of a culture that has been and is now in confusion. The family, the school, the church, the government, the communications media, the industries, seem less and less to stand for anything. In the absence of a unified outlook, there is little or nothing that can be internalized by our children as they grow through the culture. There is less "growing up" than we would want. It is becoming more and more difficult for children to acquire values which give direction and zest to life.

I think we must assume that the school, like every other institution, has some responsibility in this matter. We are, therefore, back to John Dewey's idea that the function of social institutions and arrangements is to help create personality; that in association with young learners we should be helping them to arrive at a sense of discrimination, a basis for making choices that are relevant to the worth of their lives.

What should the schools do? A good first step would be to make the best possible approximation concerning the frequency of these types of behavior in every classroom. We could indeed count the children who are like the ones described. Are teachers competent to identify them? With some help and some preparatory and exploratory activities, I believe they are in the best

position. You must remember, too, that we are looking for the extremes of behavior. We are not asking teachers to make ultrafine discriminations, and whenever they are in doubt, we should advise them to exclude the child in question.

After the audit is made, we shall have some of the extent of the problem. Our own preliminary estimates in the upper grades of the elementary school suggest that about 30 per cent of the children are so-called value-related behavioral types. This, I submit, makes it a very serious problem indeed. It is, of course, possible, that first approximations will vary considerably from community to community, and that in some areas the problems will be more or less acute.

## DEVELOPING VALUES

Let us assume that the problem is worthy of attention in terms of numbers of children involved. What next? Succeeding steps have to do with curriculum materials and teaching methods. If the social background has been reflected reasonably, there are some cues to follow. If we want these children to have a deeper understanding of themselves, and a better comprehension of their own epoch, it will be necessary to introduce curriculum materials which are consistent with these ends. And, in addition, the curriculum materials must provide the opportunity for children to express attitudes, feelings, beliefs, interests, purposes, aspirations, and to discuss their activities, in and out of school. When any of these are expressed by a child, the teacher listens, and her subsequent questioning represents an effort to find out if values are involved. She tries to find out if the child prizes or cherishes his belief or attitude or interest; she asks about one or two alternatives; she asks how long this has been a matter of concern: how often it comes up; she asks if he is doing anything about it in his life or if he needs any help to get it into his life's functioning; and she tries to sum up his views, thus giving him the chance to affirm or deny or reject what is attributed to him. This is the way in which the definition of value is useful in the clarifying processes.

There are many other ways to help children to clarify, and teachers have been using them for years; not in a systematic, focused way, perhaps—but with some effectiveness. We can repeat back to children, in exactly their own words, what they have said, and ask: "Is this what you mean?" When children *hear* what they have said, they often restate it with modifications which seem more clearly to express what they want to say.

We can say back to the children *in our words*, what we interpret as their meaning, and ask if this represents their point of view. Sometimes we quite consciously distort what they have said, and ask if this is what they mean.

On other occasions we ask children for definitions of a term they have used. We ask them to give examples or illustrations of the point they are trying to make. Our assumption is that as children try to make things more clear to us, they must first make them more clear to themselves, and this is the process of clarifying. We cannot do this, of course, unless children have an opportunity to say or to write about matters of concern to them; and we cannot carry the process forward unless we *listen* to what they are saying.

This listening is no easy task, and it is my opinion that we don't do nearly enough of it. There is an old saw to the effect that the best education would consist of Mark Hopkins at one end of a log, and a student at the other. No one takes the time to indicate what Mark did at his end of the log, and what the student *did* at the other end. To be effective, I think Mark would have to ask very intelligent questions, and then he would have to listen very carefully, and then he would have to react in ways which would help the student to clarify his meanings.

Sometimes we help the student to clarify by asking him to tell more about what he has said. We say, sometimes, that we don't see where it leads, what the consequences will be. We sometimes ask what is good about the particular interest, or attitude, or purpose, or activity. On occasion we ask if he believes that every one should accept his idea and why. At other times we raise questions about possible assumptions which he is making. We might ask about the importance or significance of the idea. We could ask him to tell us how he happened to get involved with the idea, or project, or belief.

There may be times when we sense some inconsistency in what the student is saying, and we bring this to his attention and ask him to try and straighten it out. If the occasion seems to warrant it, we might ask him to present the idea to the class, or to put it in writing. If he has talked for some length, we suggest that he boil it down into a summary. Sometimes we ask if he needs help in getting something started to test the idea.

There are two ideas to keep in mind about this questioning and clarifying procedure: (1) we never carry on an extended interview with a student in a classroom situation; one, two, or three questions at the most, consuming perhaps two or three minutes at the most; and (2) we don't argue with the student about what he says in reply and we don't reject it. Instead we say something to the effect that now we see it more clearly; now we understand him better. Where he has avoided replying we suggest that perhaps we might talk about it another time.

## THINKING AND VALUES

At this point, I must digress momentarily from the value theme, and address myself to some thinking processes. The two are always interlocked, if our concept of value is accepted. Hence, we believe that all value-type curriculum/ materials should have, and will have a problematic character. They present a situation which involves thinking. We can best insure this if we are guided by some criteria for making assignments which emphasize thinking.

What follows is only suggestive. There are many other kinds to consider, but these, I believe, are adaptable to all classes in the school, at every age level, and relevant to all subject areas without exception.

### 1. COMPARING

When students are put in the position where two or more things must be contrasted and compared; where they must seek out similarities and differences, we assume that thought processes are called for. Comparing one demonstration with another; one proof with another; one short story with another; one character with another; one translation with another; one diet with another; one form of life with another; one art form with another; one symphony with another; one poem with another . . . all of these . . . involve sensitivity, discrimination, judgment, and the support of that judgment by the materials under consideration. Moreover, if the student is asked what similarities and differences are significant, he is entering the world of value judgments. In his writing, he is almost cer-

tain to make a number of such value-type judgments, and one or two or three of these can be utilized by the teacher for clarification, using the types of questions suggested in preceding paragraphs.

### 2. SUMMARIZING

When students are asked to summarize an experience, when they are asked to summarize a story, a discussion, a chapter in a text, or a demonstration, they have to make discriminations. What will they retain? What will they leave out? What will receive greatest emphasis in the summary? least emphasis? A few will try to avoid summarizing; they will attempt to restate every detail, and these students must be asked to try again, and to do it in summary form. Here again, the teacher is almost sure to find a number of value judgments, and the processes of clarification can begin.

### 3. OBSERVING

If students are required to make observations of the world around them; if they must visit stores, and shops, and labs, and farms, and exhibitions, the problem of writing up one's observations requires organization, discrimination, emphasis. As they write, almost always, value judgments are made, and these become the basis for the clarifying procedures.

### 4. CLASSIFYING

To be required to make one's own categories is a rather high-level assignment, but it is within the abilities of most of us. In spelling, children might be asked to classify a list of words; in arithmetic, a list of problems. In a short story assignment, we might ask students to make a list of all the adjectives used in associations with a character, and to ask for some classification of the words. We could again classify diets; we could ask for discussion of a large area and, as different topics are mentioned, write them on the blackboard. If a large list results, we might ask the students to try to arrange the topics under headings which seem relevant to them. Here, as in the other cases, almost always value judgments are made, and can become the basis for the suggested clarification procedures.

### 5. CRITICIZING

Where students are asked to criticize, there are deep challenges to thought. The materials must be carefully examined and points selected for criticism; the criticism in turn must be defensible, and arguments against the criticism must be anticipated. Moreover, almost always some value judgments are made, and the teacher will find it relatively easy to try to clarify some of these statements.

### 6. PROBLEM SOLVING

Students are presented with a problem and are asked: what would you do in this situation and give your reasons for your action; or they may be asked to anticipate the consequences when different solutions are presented. As in the other cases, this requires reflecting, weighing, identifying facts and assumptions, and a judgment which represents a synthesis of all the factors entering into the situation. Where students indicate choices, preferences, what they are for or against, what they like or dislike, what they hope or fear, they are using value-type expressions and these can be clarified by the teacher.

### 7. ANALYZING

On some occasions we give to children a set of categories and ask them to analyze materials with those categories in mind. Often, this is done in the analysis of propaganda. Sets of pictures might be analyzed in terms of color, mood, media, space relations, and other criteria. Criteria for social class identification might be put forth, and the students required to apply them to characters in short stories and novels and plays. There are literally dozens of applications of this function, and in nearly all cases thought is required, and judgments are made. These can be clarified by the teacher.

### 8. IMAGINING

This category is limited only by the imagination of the teacher. Sometimes the so-called desert-island type of question is asked; or students are asked to tell what they would do if they had unlimited power and unlimited resources in certain situations; or, what they would do if they had twenty-four hours to live. They are asked to recall their most wonderful, or their most dire experiences, or the scariest, or the newest and most startling or surprising incident in their lives. In all of these, and hundreds more like them, students are making value-type expressions and these can be clarified.

### 9. PLANNING

This might involve the planning of a paper by making a preliminary outline; it might encompass the planning of a research. It might involve planning for the weekend, or for shorter and longer vacation periods. It might involve the planning of some money-raising project for the class or the school.

It might deal with one or several kinds of possible civic improvements: safety and traffic control; recreation facilities and management, and a host of other ideas. In all of them there is opportunity for students to think and to express value judgments, some of which the teacher can attempt to clarify.

## 10. INTERPRETING DATA

Here the idea is to present to students some systematic, organized data which have been collected and published. Only the data are given to students, and they are asked what inferences or conclusions can be drawn. After they have written their inferences, they are furnished with those inferences drawn by the writer of the article, and they are asked to compare their own, with those of the author. This is an exercise which requires precision in thinking, and when the comparisons are made, students often make value-type judgments which can then be clarified. They data may take the form of tables, graphs, charts, prose passages, cartoons, and maps. This form of assignment is excellent for teaching students some of the principles of interpreting data.

## 11. DOING RESEARCH

In some circumstances this can take the form of polling or interviewing; it might involve the construction of a questionnaire designed to find out how students spend their out-of-school hours, or how they spend their money. It might involve studies of soil productivity; it might encompass original problems which require the use of laboratory equipment and supplies. Whatever the problem proposed for inquiry, here again, there is great opportunity for thought, and as in all researches,

many value-type judgments have to be made, and these can be identified and efforts made to clarify them.

## 12. REACTING TO CODING

We have had great success with a method of coding the written papers of students. We put the symbol X in the margin where every student has used such extreme expressions as: all, every, never, none, always, each, etc., and we ask him to rewrite such sentences on a separate page and to answer two questions about them: (1) In what ways are these sentences alike? And (2) does he wish to change any of them, and if so—which ones—and what change does he wish to make. We use the code symbol Q in the margin where the student has used qualifying expressions: it seems, I feel, perhaps, maybe, could, might, some, etc., and we ask him to answer the same two questions about sentences so coded. We suggest that there is no necessity for him to change anything. If, after reexamining what he has written, he wants to make no changes, he is assured that this is his privilege, and that it is perfectly all right.

We use other code symbols for a great variety of thinking expressions: a V for value-type expressions; an A for attributions to other people. We use I-T for if-then sentences; E-O for either-ors. A mimeographed sheet containing fifty or more of these kinds of expressions is used as a guide for the reading of student papers. So far, we have made it a practice to take note of only a few types in each piece of writing completed by a student. Over a period of a semester, however, we try to bring to his attention just about all of the kinds which are on the mimeographed guide sheet.

We have found this as useful at the

*clarification process*

graduate level as at the elementary school level. It suggests that in our teaching, all along the line, not much attention has been given to forms of thinking represented in the writings of students. We do not read carefully what they have written; or if we do read it carefully we do not annotate it critically, and ask for reconsideration of coded sentences.

Thus far we have talked about values and the lack of value development, and what tends to show up in the behaviors of students as a consequence. Our hypothesis is a simple one: If students with behaviors of the kind put forth are exposed to thinking situations; if their written papers and oral comments are used as a basis for clarification with the questions suggested in the previous pages (and if the student's responses are accepted), then the frequency and intensity of these behaviors will diminish.

To test this hypothesis these students will have to be identified. Once or twice a day, for a period of an entire semester, some of the clarifying procedures will be utilized with these students. At the end of that time, the hypothesis states, these students will have changed their own behavior patterns. In other words, the teacher is not *trying* to change their specific acts. The teacher helps them to clarify their attitudes, their feelings, their purposes and aspirations, their interests and beliefs. As this is done, the student sees himself more clearly. He is now free to choose; to change or not to change.

Experimentation with this theory has been very, very limited. The available, and admittedly limited, data are encouraging. Students have changed significantly. It has been voluntarily commented upon by parents, by other teachers not aware that a hypothesis was being tested, and by the principal

and counseling office. Underachievers have shown a significant gain at the high school level. In the elementary school at Scarsdale, N. Y., a number of children in Grades 3, 4, and 5, seemed to change markedly, in their school behavior.

We have no information on the stability of these changes. Our designs were such that we cannot even say that we have clarified the values of the experimental students. We can say: that as students are worked with in the specified ways, the behavior of the students changed. To bring zest and purpose into the lives of students; to reduce apathy, flightiness, overconforming, nagging dissent, role-playing, great uncertainty, and even extreme inconsistency is perhaps enough, and much more than we have been able to accomplish heretofore.

It is possible, too, that our experimental teachers are extraordinary persons, teachers of the genius type. They say, however, that in former years they did not succeed with children of the kind worked with. Moreover, it is their belief that the great majority of teachers can learn to work with children in ways that emphasize the clarifying processes.

## YOUNGSTERS WITH THINKING PROBLEMS

And now, for a concluding section, which returns to the emphasis on thinking. Is there any analogy with the valuing process, in terms of behavioral types? We now hypothesize that there is. It is believed that through some combination of circumstances in the growing-up process, a number of children have not been required to master even some of the elementary thinking processes. Not having become proficient in them, not habituated to their use, how do these chronic "nonthinkers" behave in terms of characteristic patterns? We see some clearly recognizable cases, almost stereotypes of the poor thinking kind.

### 1. THE VERY IMPULSIVE CHILD

First, assuring ourselves that there is no physical cause, and that the child does not have severe emotional difficulties, we proceed on the assumption that he needs frequent opportunity to think. Teachers often say about him: he jumps the gun; he flies off at the first suggestion; if he would only take time to think for a minute. We suggest that teachers improvise some of the twelve thinking situations for this kind of child every day for a period of a semester. Developing a curriculum for him, which requires comparing, summarizing, observing, criticizing, analyzing, classifying, imagining, problem solving, interpreting data, doing research, and reacting to coding, are the first steps in the reconstruction of his impulsivity. These thinking operations require the taking of thought, the consideration of alternatives, the anticipation of difficulties—all of which slow down the impulsive person. As he is helped with these operations, the hypothesis states, the impulsiveness will decline in frequency.

### 2. THE OVERLY DEPENDENT CHILD

This child very, very often asks the teacher for help. Over and over again, he seems to be stuck. He seems to need help at every stage. The teacher often urges him to try to think things out for himself, and this does little good. He has been told this many times. We suggest that what he needs is a great emphasis upon the thinking-type situations which have been outlined at some length. As he works on his own ob-

servations, his own summaries, his own comparisons, he will be learning how to use his intelligence, and the hypothesis implies that as this process goes forward, day after day, he will become more independent, more self-directing.

### 3. THE RIGID, "IN-A-RUT" CHILD

When this child makes a mistake of some kind and is asked to start over again, he is quite apt to repeat his errors. He doesn't like to try something new; to try *another* way. There is a lack of flexibility about his approach to thinking, a narrowness which almost precludes thinking. He seems to be in a rut of his own making. The theory suggests that he too needs a variety of assignments encompassing many diverse thinking functions, and as he carries on the required operations, he will get out of his rut.

### 4. HE MISSES THE MEANING

Sometimes, when a joke is told in the classroom, and the children laugh, this child is apt to ask: "What are they laughing at?" He very frequently does not catch the meaning of a situation. In a summarizing situation, he is apt to repeat every tiny detail because he doesn't see the larger meanings. The causes may in some instances be physical or emotional, but if these can be ruled out, it may be inferred that he has not been required, nor has he learned to carry on the functions of interpretation, analysis, and criticism. Day after day, he needs a curriculum which is related to the twelve thinking assignments. His papers need to be scrutinized carefully and coded in terms of the thinking errors he is making. Under these circumstances, it is hypothesized that he will come to see the significant meanings in situations in which he is a participant.

### 5. THE LOUD, DOGMATIC, AND OVERASSERTIVE CHILD

In adult life he is a commonly appearing type. As arguments run low, or as the argument appears to be lost, his voice rises in volume, and perhaps, in stridency. He seems to be cocky; overly confident of his views, his conclusions, or recommendations. He wants to win or to dominate and cares little or nothing about logic and thinking if they happen to be in the way of winning. He often gets his way through his arrogance and he seems to conclude that his reasoning was the better kind. He is difficult to work with when reliance is placed upon exhortation, or cajolery. He reverts, again and again, to his characteristic behavior. To help him to reconstruct his habits, it seems necessary to get him on a regimen of thinking situations, and then to code his thinking so that he can see it, and appraise it for himself. Under these circumstances, he will probably reduce the bombast in his behavior, and introduce greater sensitivity to the analysis of the problematic situation.

### 6. THE UNDERCONFIDENT CHILD

Assuming again, that physical and emotional causes have been eliminated, this child is probably in need of rigorous training in thinking. At the moment, he has little confidence in his ability to think. He is apt to say, at the close of the meeting that he wanted to suggest something, but he didn't know how it would be received. Perhaps he might be laughed at, or ridiculed. He isn't sure that his thoughts are worth listening to. He isn't able to appraise his own analysis, or his own recommendations. Habitually, he is quiet and withdrawn in thinking situations. He too, it is presumed, needs assignments, day after day, of the kind previously described, and as he carries these out, he will develop the courage to say what he thinks, what he believes, what he is for and against.

### 7. HE CAN'T CONCENTRATE ON MEANS AND ENDS

At the time and the moment when it is most needed, he fails to concentrate on the matter at hand; a mistake is made which often imperils the whole enterprise or ruins the project at hand. Means are not connected with ends at every step of the way; a kind of thoughtlessness enters in; carelessness takes over. The connections between the immediate doing, and the long-range goal are not sensed. He himself often says that he tries hard but he always makes some mistake; that he is never satisfied with the quality of his final product; that something always goes wrong. As a matter of routine we are apt to tell him that he must pay closer attention, that he has to be more careful, that he should concentrate, and even as we are thus trying to persuade him into more adequate action, we realize, deep down, that it isn't going to do much good. This child needs a rigorous and long-range exposure to thinking situations of the kinds previously outlined. Teachers need to examine his thinking carefully; to code it for him; to reflect it to him. We must face him with his own thinking; we must let him see it and appraise it. Under these circumstances he might reconstruct his careless habits, and change his behavior.

### 8. THE "ANTI-THINK" CHILD

We have children who don't want to think. They're against it. They want things spelled out for them, on principle. "Isn't it the teacher's job to tell us what to do?" Confronted with the need for making some plan, alone, or in consort with others, he says, "Why all the talking? Why don't we just go ahead and *do* something?" They are action-oriented and in effect, lesson learners—in school. They dislike the need for suspending judgment, for considering alternatives, for examining the relationships of means to ends. In the parlance of our times, he is an anti-egghead. We suggest that this child has not had repeated opportunities to learn how to use reason. He needs the discipline of a curriculum which day after day focuses upon the thinking-type situations which have been presented in previous pages. Under that discipline, it is hypothesized that he will find satisfaction in pausing for reflection; he will find stimulation in a situation that is puzzling; he will want the challenges that are inevitably associated with thinking one's way toward more adequate solutions.

## SUMMARY

The curriculum should contain many more opportunities for the clarification of values, and the clarification of thinking. These opportunities should be related to the world conflicts, the culture conflicts, to regional, state, and local issues, and to problems of great personal concern to students. Questions of a kind facilitating clarification have been set forth. Ways of handling student responses have been outlined. The kinds of assignments which put an emphasis upon thinking have been described, and a number of ways of coding student papers have been presented.

It was suggested that certain types of behavior are associated with lack of value development:

1. Apathy, dullness
2. Flightiness
3. Overconforming
4. Nagging dissent
5. Extreme uncertainty
6. Underachievement
7. Role-playing
8. Great inconsistency

When these kinds of children have been indentified, it was hypothesized that if teachers will work persistently on the processes of value clarification, changes will take place in the behavior of children. These symptoms will decline and zest and purpose and direction will characterize the lives of the children. On the basis of very meager experimental evidence, there is hope that four out of five such children will change significantly.

It has also been suggested that certain types of behavior are associated with absence of, or neglect of thinking. These were listed as:

1. Impulsiveness
2. Overdependence
3. Rigidity, rut
4. Missing meaning
5. Loud, assertive
6. Fearful, underconfident
7. Lack concentration
8. The "anti-think"

Here it was hypothesized that if teachers were to see to it that these children were exposed over and over again to thinking-types of assignments, and that if the responses of the students were coded, and if the students were then confronted with instances of their own patterns of thinking, significant change would begin to take place in these designated behavior patterns.

If we assume the responsiblity for the development of personality through our social institutions, and if we recognize the behavioral symptoms as a resultant of current social conditions, then we are obligated to do our part in carrying forward two major emphases: the exploration of the significance and meaning of life to our students, and requiring of them the continuing utilization of higher mental processes. Nothing less is good enough. Nothing less will prepare us for an understanding of ourselves, in relation to the epoch in which we live. Nothing less will prepare us for our awesome responsibilities on the world stage.

Those with responsibility for curriculum development and research in the area of curriculum may profitably experiment with these ideas from the kindergarten through the graduate levels of instruction.

# 37

# The Reflective Teacher

LAWRENCE E. METCALF

It is easy for a modern educator to conclude that there are no horizons in the social studies today, except those that have been lost since the Eight Year Study. There are no large and exciting projects in social studies education such as are believed to be taking place in science and mathematics. With the assistance of Sputnik and the Cold War, science and mathematics have stolen all the headlines. Yet there are unrecognized horizons for the social studies in certain quiet developments now occurring at the level of basic research into the nature of teaching and subject matter. These developments are producing certain refinements in the theory and practice of reflective teaching.

The classical theory of reflective thinking as a method for teaching concepts and generalizations has been put by John Dewey.[1] Recent research

Lawrence E. Metcalf, "The Reflective Teacher," *Phi Delta Kappan*, XLIV, No. 1 (October 1962), 12-20. Reprinted by permission.

[1] John Dewey, *How We Think* (Boston: D.C. Health & Company, 1910, 1933).

on the logic and linguistics of teaching point toward certain refinements in Dewey's basic theory, although some of the investigators perceive themselves as anti-Dewey, or at least as having gone beyond Dewey. The import of these studies for teaching the social studies is not entirely clear, but at least two broad lines of development are beginning to suggest themselves. First, it is already clear that the traditional course in methods of teaching will have to give more attention than it has to the logical foundations of method. The methods course will become less technical and more theoretical in its content, a development that could silence those superficial critics of education who have claimed that all we need do to save the public schools is to eliminate courses in methods of teaching in favor of additional courses in "solid liberal arts content." The second development that is beginning to emerge is a preference for conceptual over factual content in both the elementary and secondary schools. No one has yet dared to suggest a similar reform at the college level.

The movement toward an emphasis upon the logical as well as the psychological aspects of teaching method, recent though it is, has already resulted in the publication of a methods textbook by Hullfish and Smith which assumes that reflective thinking is the only educational method.[2] This book is largely concerned with the problem of warranted belief, and how teachers may help students determine whether there is any warrant for holding certain beliefs. The authors of this book classify beliefs into three kinds, the analytic, synthetic, and evaluative. The procedures for verification of a belief vary with each type. In fact, verification has three different meanings. It is significant, particularly for the social studies, that the authors believe that all three kinds of belief can be verified, and they discuss the logical problems involved in each kind of verification.

Their discussion of the difference between the form and the function of a belief is also significant for the social studies teacher who favors reflection as a method of teaching. How is it possible for a statement that is synthetic in form to function as if its form were analytic? This possibility becomes a reality for the person who holds a synthetic belief not only without any evidential ground but also without any notion of the kind of factual knowledge that would make it necessary for him to give up his belief. A defining attribute of any belief that functions as analytic is that its possessor will not modify or reject it in the light of his experience with it. In Hullfish and Smith's terms, it is held in such a way that it is treated as true "come what may in experience." To illustrate the matter further, the principle of identity or noncontradiction as we find it stated in logic is analytic in both form and function. But a statement that is obviously synthetic in form, such as, "Negroes are intellectually inferior to whites," is held analytically by any person who lacks a concept of evidence. Many high-school students lack this concept, and a social studies teacher who would have students reflect upon their prejudices may first find it necessary to teach the nature of evidence.

In his essay on the uses of subject matter, Henderson has suggested a taxonomy of belief that is more complete than Hullfish and Smith's.[3] He has defined eight kinds of statements, and has labeled them as follows:

1. Statements
   1.1 Analytic
      1.11 Singular
      1.12 General
   1.2 Contingent
      1.21 Singular
      1.22 General
2. Prescriptions
   2.1 Singular
   2.2 General
3. Value Statements
   3.1 Singular
   3.2 General

Since he refers to these as statements of knowledge, he evidently shares with Hullfish and Smith the idea that value judgments and definitions, as well as propositions, may be verified in some way. He does not discuss the problems of verification where values and definitions are concerned, matters which receive considerable attention from Hullfish and Smith. It should be noted that Henderson uses the term *contingent* for those statements that Hullfish and Smith have called syn-

[2] H. Gordon Hullfish and Philip G. Smith, *Reflective Thinking: The Method of Education* (New York: Dodd, Mead & Co., 1961).

[3] Kenneth Henderson. "Uses of 'Subject Matter,'" in B. O. Smith and R. H. Ennis (eds.), *Language and Concepts in Education* (Skokie, Ill.: Rand McNally & Co., 1961).

thetic. Whether they are called contingent or synthetic, they amount to what logical positivists mean by testable propositions. Henderson also differs from Hullfish and Smith in making a distinction between prescriptions and evaluations, and between statements that are singular or general in their subject.

## THE VALUE OF CLASSIFYING STATEMENTS

The classification of statements, whether the statements represent knowledge, belief, or opinion, is useful in at least one regard to all teachers of social studies who seek reflection. It would be a mistake for a teacher to ask a student to present evidence in support of his analytic statement. An analytic statement usually takes the form of a definition, and for such a statement it would be more appropriate to ask for an example or an illustration. Bruner's work on concept attainment also suggests the appropriateness of asking for defining attributes, and to note whether the student can distinguish between the defining attributes of a concept and its nondefining or noisy attributes.[4] If a teacher wants a student to reflect upon a contingent statement, he will ask the student what else must be true if the statement is true. Hullfish and Smith make the same point when they say that every synthetic statement implies a prediction. The simple statement that "It is raining" implies that other things will be true if, indeed, it is raining. Ennis has defined critical thinking as the correct assessing of statements, and has identified 12 different kinds of judgment to be made by those who think critically

about the statements they encounter.[5] The point must be well taken that a teacher who seeks reflection in his students cannot succeed if he treats all statements as if they were of the same kind.

Henderson's concept of a contingent general statement is especially significant for those teachers of history who claim that a reflective study of the past increases student's understanding of the present. A contingent general statement, *if it is expressed in the present tense,* is the only kind of statement in history that arches through time, and breaks down the wall of separation between past and present. The statement that "Unless American soldiers fought like Indians, the red men usually defeated them," is contingent general in form, but its subject matter is in the past. But a statement that "Roman Catholic loyalty helps a presidential candidate of the Roman Catholic faith more than Protestant prejudice hurts him" (a statement that has received some confirmation from Louis Bean's study of the election returns of 1928 and 1960), in addition to having a contingent general form is cast in the present tense, and thus has a subject matter that is not limited to the past. Courses in history that fail to emphasize the study of such statements, what they mean and whether they are true, cannot back up the teacher's claim that an understanding of history clarifies present-day problems.

One can infer from the textbooks that are popular with teachers of social studies that the teachers of these courses prefer contingent singular to contingent general content. These are the "facts" that teachers believe students must learn in order to acquire enough background

---

[4] J. S. Bruner, Jacqueline J. Goodnow, and G. A. Austin, *A Study of Thinking.* (New York: John Wiley & Sons, Inc., 1956).

[5] R. H. Ennis, "A Concept. of Critical Thinking," *Harvard Educational Review,* XXXII, No. 1 (Winter, 1962).

to think about current problems. Typical content in high-school American history courses is illustrated by statements such as the following, each of which is taken from one of the leading textbooks in the field:

After the capture of Mexico City it was some months before a Mexican government could be found to sign a peace.

The most famous of the railroad consolidators was Cornelius Vanderbilt (1794-1877), who built up the New York Central system.

The Roosevelt Corollary was first put into effect in Santo Domingo.

The advance of labor unions was aided by the National Labor Relations Act (also called the Wagner Act) passed by Congress in 1935.

World War II did not inspire the enthusiasm and idealism of either the War Between the States or World War I.

The usefulness of this kind of content is reduced to a minimum when teachers require that it be learned apart from and prior to reflection. Hullfish and Smith put the issue clearly and succinctly:

... Some critics say, for instance, that, since thinking cannot go on in a vacuum, students must first be given the facts they may later use in thinking. Now, of course, the alternatives are not gaining facts apart from thought or thinking apart from facts. The question is how facts are to be best gained. This introduces a third alternative, using facts within a reflective process.

The use of facts within a process of reflection gives the facts some kind of order. There are two kinds of order suggested by Henderson, Hullfish, and Smith in their taxonomies. One kind results in concepts, the other in generalizations. Much of the literature on teaching the social studies has not distinguished between these two kinds of order. In fact, it is not unusual to find in a textbook on teaching the social studies that the teaching of con-

cepts and generalizations is treated as a single topic. Bruner has defined a concept as a category, which suggests that the teaching of concepts would require students to engage in acts of classfication. Students, for instance, would use their information about events as part of the basis for grouping them according to their common attributes. If imperialism is defined by attributes *a*, *b*, and *c*, then any event which possesses these attributes would be classified as an instance of imperialism. The author of this article has suggested that the sorting of events is one of the processes with which a teacher is concerned when he teaches a concept.[6] The kind of order which results from classification is basic to all thinking and cognition, and it focuses instruction upon the study of analytic statements. Such statements are never true in the sense that they have evidence to back them up, but rather they are what Hullfish and Smith have described as formal truths. Such statements are *necessarily* true because of the way in which terms are defined, and because of the way in which we have *chosen* to structure experience. Bruner puts the point well when he says that concepts are not discovered; instead, they are created.

## BACKING UP CONTINGENT GENERAL STATEMENTS

A second kind of order is obtained when contingent singular content is organized and presented according to the generalizations (contingent general statements) toward which they point. The statement that government deficits foster inflation under the conditions of full employment or imperfect competi-

[6] L. E. Metcalf, "Teaching Economic Concepts in the Social Studies," *The Illinois Councilor*, XXI, No. 1 (March 1960).

tion is an example of contingent general content. This kind of statement may be tested empirically and found to be probably true or false. Sometimes evidence is unavailable, and in this case we reserve judgment. The teaching of generalization includes two aspects. One aspect is concerned with what the statement says. This requires the learning of analytic statements (concepts). In the example above, students must define deficit financing, full employment, and imperfect competition. From the subject matter of economics students can learn the correct meanings of these terms. Bruner calls these correct meanings official definitions, to set them apart from the opinions students may have about the meaning of full employment, etc. But the teaching of generalizations, unlike the teaching of concepts, does not stop with definitions. The second and crucial aspect is empirical. It seeks to answer the question: Is it true that deficit-financing has certain consequences under certain conditions? At this stage of instruction the reflective teacher wants to know whether students have evidence to back up their contingent general statements.

## THE " WHAT," BUT NEVER THE " WHY "

If teachers of social studies insist upon teaching the facts out of all relationship to concepts or generalizations, they cannot expect students to grow in their understanding of social phenomena regardless of whether the phenomena are in the past or the present. If this kind of instruction occurs in a history course devoted to the pleasures of chronological narrative, the teachers may be entertaining, interesting, metaphorical, and even poetic, but their students will not develop any capacity to generalize their learning. They may

at best learn a great deal about *what* happened, although this can hardly happen if terms are never defined, but they can never learn *why* anything happened, because their content has no power to explain or predict events. The reason why this is so is suggested clearly by Swift's study of the teaching of explanations.[7,8,9]

High-school social studies are so much devoted to contingent singular content that they seldom try to explain why events have occurred except in a descriptive sense, and Swift has observed that many teachers and textbook writers cannot tell the difference between an explanation and a description. In order to tell the difference, and also in order to assess the correctness and adequacy of any explanation, one needs a model from which to work. Swift has borrowed his model from Hempel, and has studied the problem of teaching historical explanations as an aspect of instruction in critical thinking.

Hempel's model, which he borrowed from the physical sciences, and which he suggests as a research tool for professional historians, casts explanations into the form of a syllogism, the major premise of which is a contingent general statement. For reasons already offered, the author of this article believes that this contingent general statement should be expressed in the present tense. Other criteria are implicit in Hempel's model. The major premise should be testable and true (Hempel refers to explanations that rest upon an untestable premise as a pseudo-

[7] L. F. Swift, "Explanation as an Aspect of Critical Thinking in Secondary School Social Studies." Unpublished doctoral dissertation, University of Illinois, 1959.

[8] L. F. Swift, "Explanation," in B. O. Smith and R. H. Ennis, eds., *Language and Concepts in Education* (Skokie, Ill.: Rand McNally & Co., 1961).

[9] L. F. Swift, "The Teaching of Explanation in History," 1958. (Unpublished.)

explanation). The minor premise, which describes the existence of the antecedent conditions for the occurrence of the event to be explained, should also be historically true. Finally, a description of the event to be explained should follow logically from the truth of the major and minor premises. Swift has summarized the meaning of this kind of explanations as "a deductive argument possessed of empirical content."

The explanations offered by high-school social studies textbooks are usually incomplete by Hempel's standards, and require "filling in." These incomplete explanations usually imply, but do not state openly, a general law. Such explanations may abound even in the writings of historians who deny that there are any laws in history. A typical example of an incomplete explanation is the statement, "The Pilgrims came to the New World to escape religious persecution." This sentence standing as it is will make sense to most high-school students. They will believe it in the sense of not doubting it, and may even commit it to memory as an item of information. If this incomplete explanation is cast as a syllogism, doubt flows in from all directions.

Major Premise: If a group of people is persecuted for its religious beliefs, it will migrate to a new territory where it will be free to practice its religion.
Minor Premise: In 17th-century England a group of people called the Puritans were persecuted for their religion.
Conclusion: The Puritans migrated to the New World.

The teacher needs to raise only a few questions about this syllogism before the students sense its inadequacy. Many people who have been perse-cuted for their religious and other beliefs have not migrated. In fact, many of the Puritans did not, and hence we reserve the term *Pilgrim* for those who did.

The discovery of negative cases always calls for the rejection or modification of a proposition. It is not easy in the social studies to find propositions for which there are no negative cases. It is even difficult to frame propositions precisely enough to distinguish between negative and positive cases. We often settle for propositions that are grossly probable in their truth. Sometimes we are no more precise than to distinguish between the possible and the impossible, or the probable and the improbable, without specifying except in a very rough form the probability that a certain kind of event will occur under certain conditions. If the major premise in the above syllogism is modified so that it becomes a probabilistic rather than a certain truth, it might read as follows: If a group of people is persecuted for its religious beliefs, it *usually* migrates to a new territory.

The term *usually* gives us trouble, for it leaves unanswered the question, "How many negative cases would make it necessary for us to reject the probable truth of our premise?" Clearly, we would have to reject the premise if the number of negative cases exceeds the number of positive cases. But this observation raises the further question, "What constitutes a representative and adequate sample of cases?" What history, and how much history, would students have to study in order to test fairly the truth of a premise? Teachers of social studies are not yet well trained in logic or sampling and probability theory, and this is the kind of content that belongs in the methods course of the future.

The use of a qualifying term gives us another kind of trouble. It destroys the logical tightness of a syllogism. A description of the event to be explained cannot be deduced from premises that are merely probable in their truth. At best we can conclude that a certain kind of event is likely to occur under certain conditions. Unless we can identify conditions that account for negative cases we are forced to treat the major premise as a plausible hypothesis rather than a principle or general law. This may be the only kind of truth commonly available from the subject matter of the social studies. Nagel's analysis of explanation in the social sciences has explored thoroughly the limits of knowledge in history.[10] Given this state of affairs, the use of Hempel's model helps students to learn the extent to which their social studies content is a reliable guide for conduct, and better grounded than "common sense," if not as well established as physics or chemistry content.

[10] Ernest Nagel, *The Structure of Science* (New York: Harcourt, Brace & World, Inc., 1962).

There are many other considerations to be faced by a reflective teacher of the social studies, and basic research has begun to explore their dimensions. Unfortunately, limitations of space do not permit their treatment in this article. But it should be clear from what has been reported here that the new horizons for the social studies are in methods of teaching. The suggested reforms in method also call for revisions in social studies content, and the teacher of the future, in addition to knowing a lot of history, will also need to know more social science than has been required of him in the past. It goes without saying that he will have to be well trained in logic, linguistics, and the philosophy of science. As long as the social-studies curriculum devotes most of its instructional time to history he will need to be a student of theories of history, and what history is, and what kinds of history there are, and how history is different from such social sciences as sociology and economics.

# 38

# Promoting Student Thinking

## ROGER CARTWRIGHT

Thinking seems to be near or at the core of practically every important educational aim, yet much criticism from within and without education repeatedly asserts a failure to develop intelligence to anywhere near assumed potential. Such a gap between acknowledged goal and daily classroom practice may well result, in part, from confusion over various definitions of thinking. This account illustrates the use of one specific breakdown of thinking with a college education class, and suggests some implications for the role of thinking as a guiding *design* in the reconstruction of curriculum.

Underlying the notion of thinking as developed here are the ideas that it comprises a basic, pervasive style of address to life, that it nearly always manifests specific characteristics (akin to Dewey's "habits") which tend to perseverate and strongly influence behavior, and that when nurtured on a variety of tasks and experience it

offers almost unlimited possibilities for greatly expanded functioning in the service of clarified values, purposes, beliefs, and needs.[1]

This approach rests, in turn, on certain broad and fundamental assumptions with regard to the potency and extent of resources within individuals when these resources are given opportunities to function—the idea of *releasing capacities* already "there." The notion is held that the impulse to be active—to analyze, compare, predict, formulate, explore, synthesize, reflect, clarify, and choose—has its locus within the student; he is the "prime mover." Moreover there is everywhere within this viewpoint the idea of a highly significant relationship between the nature of the thinking

[1] Hilgard sees a significant relationship between Dewey's concern for the promotion of discriminating reason and " . . . new emphases within learning theory upon ego aspects of learning, upon searching behavior and intelligent problem-solving, upon learning in social contexts," p. 331, *Theories of Learning*, Ernest R. Hilgard. 1956. Cf. also *Explorations in Evaluation*, Paul L. Dressel and Lewis B. Mayhew, American Council on Education, 1954.

Roger Cartwright, "Promoting Student Thinking," *Journal of Educational Sociology*, XXXVI, No. 1 (September 1962), 33-41. Reprinted by permission.

being carried on (or the lack of thinking) and the characteristic and enduring behavior of the individual.[2]

The question may then be asked:
"If a group of college students preparing for teaching were confronted with
many and varied situations which
involved identifying of habitual ways
of thinking and behaving, and the
clarifying of one's values, beliefs, attitudes, needs and purposes—and were
this done in a framework which related
professional course content and personal concerns—how would these students react? If the curriculum was
planned so these students repeatedly
faced situations of doubt, uncertainty,
dilemma, disagreement, conflict, and
imbalance, and were asked to actively
resolve such conflicts in terms of reflective thinking and value clarifying—

[2] General support for this viewpoint may be
found in the more recent writings of Gordon W.
Allport, Gardner Murphy, Hadley Cantril,
Lawrence K. Frank, Margaret Mead, A. H.
Maslow, Lawrence J. Kubie, Marie Jahoda,
Carl R. Rogers, Earl C. Kelley, Alan Wheelis,
and others, writing from many perspectives:
educator, psychologist, social psychologist,
psychiatrist, anthropologist, etc. Shoben has
aptly put the case for intelligent thinking as a
basic style of address to life:
  "The contradiction lies in this: Our cognitive
  talents are part of our behavior and, consequently, in the service of our motives.
  Thought and speech, however simple or
  however complex, are instrumental to the
  fulfillment of our desires or to our defenses
  against anxiety or threatened self-esteem. . . .
  Yet these same cognitive abilities are the
  means by which we master our motives,
  transcend our defenses and attain an objective
  and dispassionate comprehension of our
  world. And in such mastery, transcendance
  and attainment lies our fundamental humanity." E. J. Shoben, Jr., "A Review," Basic
  Book News, XV, No. 10 (June 1959).
Much of the newest A.S.C.D. Yearbook reflects
strong concern that education attend closely
to the support and nurture of what Allport has
called "propriate striving." Cf. Perceiving,
Behaving, Becoming: A New Focus for Education,
Assoc. for Supervision and Curriculum Development, 1962.

how would such experiences cumulatively affect their thinking?

In pursuit of answers to these questions, a methodology for promoting
thinking was developed which attempted to marshal materials and techniques in a guiding design for an
education course.[3] Three key elements
made up its heart:

I. ELEVEN THINKING OPERATIONS

(1) Making observations of direct,
first-hand experience, (2) Summarizing, (3) Comparing, (4) Confronting
an analysis of one's own thinking-
related patterns of expression, (5)
Classifying, Sorting, Categorizing, (6)
Analyzing writings for ways of thinking,
(7) Identifying and analyzing problems; formulating hypotheses and ways
of testing these, (8) Interpreting raw
data, (9) Identifying and weighing
assumptions, (10) Collecting data, and
(11) Stating and defending a position.

II. FIVE BASIC AIMS[4]

(a) To create conditions under which
    students will be led to identify and
    clarify their own values, needs, at-
    titudes, purposes, beliefs, and ways of
    thinking, and to reflect upon and
    question these.

(b) To increase the student's awareness and
    understanding of the values, needs,
    purposes and ways of thinking of his
    peers.

(c) To aid the student in becoming con-
    versant with important issues, princi-
    ples, and people in the field of educa-
    tion.

[3] While designated as a "Resource Unit" it
is important to distinguish the obligatory
nature of the governing design for application
of the methodology from the many resource
units which commonly constitute optional
reservoirs of content.

[4] Developed to cover major areas which
contribute to student maturity and teaching
competency.

(d) To help the student to gain knowledge about the age level of children he will teach; about their stages of development, their needs, abilities, thinking, interests, ways of maturing.

(e) To help students to relate personal and professional concerns to broader social-cultural surroundings.

### III. Two associated Theories of Thinking and Valuing[5]

These relate significant changes in behavior to a persistent application of techniques designed to promote critical thinking and value clarification. The theories postulate seven "thinking-related" and seven "value-related" behaviors recognized as widespread and as detrimental to classroom learning and sound growth. A set of hypotheses link change in these habitual ways of behaving to the student's repeated and varied experience with the thinking operations and value-clarifying techniques. The suggestion is that a student who is characteristically impulsive, who "leaps before he looks," will tend over time to exhibit less impulsiveness and greater thoughtfulness as he confronts many exercises in which he is called upon to think in the ways indicated above, to examine and evaluate such thinking, and to do this in a context which calls on him to relate his perceived values, beliefs, needs, and purposes to course content.

Underlying the close, reciprocal relationship of these two theories is the idea that thinking cannot be meaningfully considered apart from those situations which call it forth and to which it is addressed.[6]

Central to this act of relating "thinking-in-process" to both a personal nexus of values and to course content was a "reflecting process" in which some seventeen "Value-Clarifying Questions"[7] were used again and again, by instructor and by students, in classes and in individual conferences. Over and over again, students were urged to respond verbally and in short writings to problems, dilemmas and conflicts of value, attitude, belief, to state "how they saw it," and at this point were supported in their efforts to clarify thinking and values as these questions were asked: "Is this something you cherish?" "How has this found expression in your life?" "Have you thought a lot about this?" "Where do you think that might lead?" "Do you want me to assume . . . ?"

The eleven ways of thinking and five Basic Aims were key "tools" used to work the "ground" or topical "terrain" prescribed for the course. By means of these, ten major categories for resource materials were set up. These included (a) Presentation of a Point of View, (b) Children's Writings, (c) College Students' Writings, (d) Observations (with assigned focus), (e) Writings by Professionals in the

---

[5] Developed by Professor Louis E. Raths, New York University. These provide a base in theory for systematic use of the design.

[6] Dressel and Mayhew state "Critical thinking cannot ignore values. Rather, attempts at critical thinking should cause each student to examine and define his own value position since it is irretrievably interwoven into the thinking he does and the solutions that he reaches." They add that critical thinking can occur in the context of many different value systems but that ". . . thinking is not truly critical unless it recognizes the existence of several value systems and the acceptance—too often unconscious—of one of them," p. 278, *Explorations in Evaluation*, Paul L. Dressel, Lewis B. Mayhew.

[7] These questions sought to get at whether the matter under discussion was prized and cherished by the individual, whether it was the product of reflection, if it had penetrated areas of his life, if he would affirm it upon challenge, and questions which sought elaboration of meaning through example, judgment on assumptions, prediction, evaluation of past experience, etc.

Field, (*f*) Research Data and Reports (with and without conclusions), (*g*) Textbooks, School Documents, and other Educational Materials, and so on. Assignments were developed and card-filed under each heading as material was sought and assessed in terms of its relevance to the Basic Aims, the Course Guide, and its potential in terms of thinking assignments. For example, two professional papers (Category *e*) might be compared by the student (Thinking Operation 3) with resultant inquiry (using selected clarifying Questions) into the student's chosen bases for comparisons and their significance to professional tasks on the one hand, and the student's own life experience and values on the other. These same papers might also serve fruitfully a need to examine for stated and unstated assumptions (Thinking Operation 9), to summarize as to key points (Thinking Operation 2), or be used as a basis for analysis of expressions which seem related to thinking patterns.[8]

These varied thinking assignments were used in every class session over one term and also constituted the central focus of short individual conferences held weekly with each student.[9] A strong effort was made to see that each student had a balanced experience in all the thinking operations. As students were confronted with children's writings, their own and their peers' writings, raw research data, sample textbooks, intraschool staff documents, and opportunities for observing children directly, they were repeatedly asked

such questions as "Would you compare . . . ?" "Could you state the problem here?" "What did you observe that you prized?" "How would you classify?" "Is he assuming . . . (and if so, what is the merit?)" "What can be inferred from this data?" "Where might those ideas have come from (in your experience)?" and "Where will these attitudes lead?" Through frequent short writings in class, students were asked to examine their own and their fellows' papers for patterns of expression which, it was hypothesized, relate significantly to thinking habits, and to summarize, weigh and interpret such use, to do this freely, "as they saw it." No censure or didactic analysis and use of "ideal models" of good thinking was used. They were given many opportunities to reflect again, to reaffirm, deny or change statements they had made as these were reflected back to them and in each case their judgment was accepted, and there was determined effort to avoid evidence of disapproval; there was no grading. In every case possible, support was given to the "thinking-in-process," as the student was encouraged to use candor in examining value-bases and explore relationships between self-discovered thinking habits and his purposes, goals, attitudes and beliefs.

Thus as students dealt with course content week by week they were (1) continually confronted with the need to think in a variety of ways and to identify and reflect upon their thinking, and (2) supported as they strove to more clearly identify thinking tendencies and to clarify values. Of critical importance in this systematic effort to encourage productive self-insight was the instructor's own spirit of support and reassurance. As they dealt with thinking exercises which called for the clarifying and weighing of values, students exhibited a wide range of behaviors: shyness, assumed diffidence,

[8] Reference is to "Some Tentative Patterns of Expression Which Often Relate to Thinking," a compilation of some eleven patterns of expression which appear to bear a relationship to characteristic thinking. Developed by Professor Louis E. Raths, New York University.

[9] Class met twice a week in two-hour sessions, less five field observations in schools.

belligerence, eagerness, strong doubt, uneasiness, anger, delight, humor. Repeated efforts were made to communicate the idea that the student's thinking was being honored, that no one could think for him, that his efforts at self-insight and self-direction were highly respected and encouraged, that his opinions and doubts were extremely important and worth time and careful consideration, and that no one could "give" him values but that he himself had plenty of power and could do the job.

## EVALUATION

In addition to protocols of student conferences and logs of class sessions, three other methods of evaluation were tried:

(1) In the Interpretation of Data Test (2.51, 2.52), a combining of probabilities for part scores (according to Lindquist) resulted in significance (5 per cent level) in all four score areas: General Accuracy, Beyond the Data, Caution, and Crude Error.

(2) Panel judgments on matched before-and-after thinking assignments from three selected thinking operations indicated substantial gains in Formulating the Problem (Operation 7), and some gains in Comparing (3), but no detectable trend in Observing (1).

(3) Thinking-Related Behavior Scales. These eleven-paragraph self-rating scales represented an expansion of the seven behaviors hypothesized in the Thinking Theory as relating to faulty thinking or lack of thinking. Major gains were made by the X class in two of the seven categories, *Confused* and *Impulsive*. Results in *Misses the Meaning* were inconclusive, and the remaining four categories were infrequently selected. Data on total gain supported the idea that the Resource

Unit was a factor in contributing to student growth in those behaviors students selected for rating.

In a special effort to test the Thinking Theory, six students from the X class were chosen on the basis of having rated themselves most severely (negatively) in terms of one or more behaviors. Throughout the semester, extra attention was given to them in terms of opportunities to practice thinking and valuing. It was hypothesized that five out of these six "specials" would demonstrate a gain of at least three points or more on the rating scale and that if this condition was not met, the methodology was to be regarded as having failed to effect change in terms of the Thinking Theory. Data supported the hypothesis: five out of the six students made gains ranging from four to eight points of positive change. In total cases of gain, the X class stood well above an average for equated groups of six from each of four comparison classes.

## IMPLICATIONS

Much controversy has arisen over assertions that college instruction too often fails to touch the lives of students at anywhere near a significant level; that there frequently appears a sort of conformity without significant purpose, a situation in which opinions are bland and beliefs casual. Inherent in some descriptions of student attitudes and behavior are strong suggestions of a lack of self-esteem coupled with a failure to utilize thinking in the service of increasingly clarified purposes and values.[10] Acknowledging that many

[10] See for instance Tead's reaction to Philip E. Jacob's study, *Changing Values in College:* "Emphasis on Values in College Teaching," pp. 14-20, *The Journal of Higher Education*, Ordway Tead (January 1960).

potent factors are at work in the culture which affect student thinking and commitment, it is necessary, in the writer's view, to accept a strong responsibility to reconstruct curricula for teacher training so that students will become involved at significant levels of motivation.

Unfortunately, concern about student thinking and commitment may find ready expression in encouraging study *about* thinking and an eager introduction of preferred *models* of thinking, but such efforts somehow fail to come to grips with the need to engage students in much on-the-spot thinking and encourage them as they attempt to appraise thinking habits and refine thinking in the service of clarified values and purposes. Too frequently, it is said, classes follow a monotonous round by which information is meted out to be collected again at examination time—and many students are able to play this game well without much recourse to thinking. Where students have thus adjusted to get by "successfully" it is not surprising that there is not only reluctance to try something new, but accompanying feelings of lack of worth—almost a dishonoring of capacities to think and value, to create and clarify important goals and purposes.

Can a *design* for curriculum development promote a dual emphasis on thinking and values to such degree that students are clearly manifesting a much higher caliber of thinking and of value-awareness and commitment? Such was the ambitious premise which, in part, underlay this study. The short-term data, while in no way statistically dramatic, suggest the worth of a large number of far more discriminating field trials over areas, ages, and time. What if such a systematic emphasis on thinking represented a common denominator throughout the student's range of courses? What if such respect-

ful questioning and clarifying were carried on through high school? begun in kindergarten? The suggestion is that the value of such experience might well cumulate and reinforce self-insight and self-direction and find highly effective expression as the student dealt with professional training. A stubborn problem intrudes here: the development of techniques for evaluation which will reflect with precision the student's gain in thinking as he puts such released capacity to work on professional tasks.[11]

Will the introduction of a systematic, guiding focus on thinking assignments in some way curtail the richness of course content?[12] In this study, far from restricting, it appeared to open up further avenues, to stimulate reflection and exploration, and to engender a quality of student responsibility rather rare in the writer's experience.

## THEORY—PUT TO WORK

Brownell,[13] Tyler,[14] Dressel and Mayhew,[15] and Carroll fairly repre-

[11] A majority of those working in the field of thinking seem agreed that in general thinking tests represent an analysis of product, and inferences about process need to be (though not always are) heavily qualified.

[12] The question may be construed (for fun) in the sense of inversion: too much thinking will drive all content out—which exposes the fallacy since thinking must be *about something*, albeit it does not follow that content *must* be thought about; other, routine operations can be performed upon it.

[13] William A. Brownell, "The Study and Guidance of Learning in Children," *Education 2000 A.D.*, ed. Clarence W. Hunnicutt (Syracuse, N.Y.: Syracuse University Press, 1956).

[14] Ralph Tyler: Comment summarized in a review of Conference Proceedings: "Research on College Influences on Personality: Report on the Andover Conference, March 26-28, 1959," Lloyd Morrisett, Jr., *Items*, Social Science Research Council, XIII, No. 3 (September 1959), 28-31.

[15] Dressel and Mayhew, *op cit.*, p. 284.

sent a common concern for the development of theory which is "born in the classroom," which is probing for greater insight into teaching, and which finds its way directly back to application in efforts to promote change in behavior.[16] The associated theories of thinking and valuing which formed the "theory-base" for this investigation are seen as promising examples along these lines: the characteristic behaviors described are drawn from teachers' experiences in many, many classrooms. The hypotheses relate systematic practice of certain methodology (teaching insights) to student change in behavior.

[16] Dressel and Mayhew call for ". . . research . . . undertaken to the end goal of providing insights for teachers." They emphasize "It should be applied research having very definite practical goals in view. Research findings need to be written in such a way that their implications for classroom teaching stand clear." Dressel and Mayhew, *op. cit.*

Now suppose that a group of college students were taught these theories and given many opportunities to try them out, not only with each other but in field situations with children: schools, settlement houses, playgrounds, etc. Would these students then be making a test of theory under meaningful circumstances? Would such experience with these theories find expression in the ways in which these young teachers subsequently dealt with the children in their classes? The suggestion is that such a chain-reaction or "enabling" process might have great repercussions in terms of helping many, many children in thinking and value-clarifying, and constitute one potent "empowering" factor toward "Education for Maturity."[17]

[17] Cf. "Are We Educating for Maturity?" Lawrence S. Kubie, *N.E.A. Journal* (January 1959).

# 39

# A Strategy for Developing Values

JAMES RATHS

This paper deals with a strategy for helping children to develop their own values. Recognition of the importance of children's values has been with us for years. "A great and continuing purpose of education has been the development of moral and spiritual values" (5). With this pronouncement, the Educational Policies Commission opened its 1957 report. As important as developing values seems to be to the DAR and the VFW, to the FBI and the HUAC, the area is even more important to us as educators, it seems to me, because of its implications for the learning process. Let me briefly spell out some of these implications.

First, Kubie (12) suggests that learning is swift, spontaneous and automatic. At times, learning is blocked—many times by what Kubie calls preconscious motives and drives. He recommends that teachers concern themselves with developing self-knowl-

edge on their students' part to remove blocks to learning—to free children so that they may learn in a spontaneous fashion. Second, Ginsburg (7) suggests that good mental health, assumed to be a necessary condition for learning, is merely a process of living up to a set of values. Finally, several researchers, following the ideas of Louis Raths, have identified pupil behaviors associated with a lack of values (9, 11, 13, 14). These classroom behaviors, including overconforming, indifference, flightiness and several others, it is argued, interfere with concentration, involvement, and openness in the learning process. Therefore, value development, it seems, should be one of the many central concerns of teachers.

While the area of value development has been a major concern of educators for many years, the public and many professional people, too, have had a feeling that our efforts in this area have not been too effective. The studies summarized by Jacob in his *Changing Values in College* tend to support this hunch (8). Teachers have been unable, it seems, to translate their genuine con-

James Raths, "A Strategy for Developing Values," *Educational Leadership*, XXI, No. 8 (May 1964), 509-14. Copyright ©1964 by the Association for Supervision and Curriculum Development. Reprinted by permission.

cerns about the value problem into effective patterns of action in their classrooms.

Essentially, there are four basic approaches to the development of values current in our schools. These methods include the teaching of values by the lecture method, by use of peer-group pressure, by finding or setting examples for children to respect and emulate, and by a reward and punishment rationale. These methods are neither mutually exclusive nor exhaustive of all the approaches we use in schools, but they seem to me to be among the most prevalent in our classrooms.

## METHODS IN USE

Perhaps the most common approach is the use of lecture methods. Teachers seem ever ready to tell students what they should believe or how they ought to act. It is easy to burlesque this method in harsh tones. Actually, it may be employed by the kindest, most sincere teachers as well as by the overly self-righteous, would-be reformers found on some school faculties. While it is possible to cite cases in which a lecture or even a "bawling out" did bring about changes in students' values, basically this method is not too successful. Attesting to this is the common cry of ·many teachers—"You can't *tell* those kids anything." In general, this remark has been found to be accurate.

Teachers' judgments and convictions seem, from a student's point of view, to be out of the framework of things. (Analogously, it may be akin to the feelings teachers in the field have of the "should's and should not's" of professors from schools and colleges of education.) Jones(10) has suggested a basis for explaining the ineffectiveness of the lecture method. He states that a teacher must be emotionally accepted by his students before he can contribute much to their development of self. By their moralizing and preaching, teachers may set themselves apart emotionally from their students. To the extent that teachers are not accepted by their students, it can be presumed that they will have little effect upon students' values. Students may leave the lecture all full of enthusiasm about what the teacher said, but they may not internalize what they admire and all too often they do not.

A second approach to the value development problem has been in the main popularized by exponents of the core curriculum. During a special period of the school day, students address themselves to self-evaluations and group evaluations. They are encouraged to speak freely, frankly and openly to the entire class judging their own behavior, criticizing group performances, and perhaps pledging themselves to future improvements. In general, such statements are accepted by the teacher with little or no comment while other pupils are free to make suggestions, recommendations, and comments.

The pressure of group approval or disapproval is a powerful force in bringing about changes in values. This method seems successful in some cases but it has some disturbing by-products. The most distressing of these is the tacit approval of the teacher of the notion that group consensus is correct or at least worthy of very serious consideration. This method, in effect, helps develop "other directed" persons. Another disadvantage inherent in this group technique is the passive role of the teacher. In a sense, the insight, experience, and skills of the teacher are muted. In their place, naïve students play the dominant role in value development, and they do it quite unconsciously.

A third approach for developing students' values is one of acquainting students with examples of exemplary behavior. Instances of model behavior may be drawn from history, literature, and legend or, more directly, from examples set by teachers.

Literature for all levels of schooling has been selected for the past several hundred years on the basis of the ethical and moral lessons with which it dealt. As in other methods discussed previously, some students are truly inspired by these vicarious experiences but we have little evidence that attributes found in a student's reading are readily transferred to daily life.

Teaching values by a living example is a related tactic. Here it is assumed that "values are caught, not taught." It is argued that as teachers demonstrate values, students will learn to prize these values. Surely people have been inspired by the goodness of a teacher with whom they have had the good fortune to be associated. However, teachers, especially in secondary schools, have little opportunity to demonstrate many key values. Problems that represent the real issues of life rarely present themselves in a 50-minute subject-matter period in such a way that students can observe their teacher's handling of them. It would truly be unfortunate if we had to rely on this approach as the only positive way teachers can help youngsters develop a set of values.

A fourth method deals with indoctrination and habit formation. Here it is assumed that when students are required to follow rules and regulations, when they are punished for infractions and praised for obedience, they will take on the values associated with the requirements. We are all familiar, however, with what students do when they are free *not* to obey the rules.

It is my contention that these four methods are rather ineffective. Perhaps their relative ineffectiveness arises partially because they are based on the assumption that the knowledge of ethical and moral choices necessarily leads to ethical and moral conduct. As pointed out many years ago by John Dewey(4), this assumption has little basis in fact.

Yet more important, these methods seem intent on utilizing external factors, such as lectures or peer-group pressures, to develop values. Friedenberg(6) analyzes the current problems in developing values as follows:

 . . . it is the inner discipline that is lacking; the school fails to provide a basis for it. The undisciplined behavior which sometimes results is often a sign of the anguish which results from having no core *of one's own.* [Emphasis added.]

The most promising approach would seem to be one that attempts to help each student build his own value system. This idea is supported by Allport(2) who asserts that no teaching is more important than that which contributes to a student's self. Clearly, this statement echoes the ideas of Kubie mentioned in the opening paragraphs. Are teachers able to help children in this way? B. O. Smith has said that teachers use little psychological knowledge beyond that found in common sense. What knowledge can we, as teachers, use in this area? Louis Raths has developed a teaching method designed to provide some direction for teachers who are interested in helping students develop their own value systems (15, 16, 17).

## USE OF CLARIFICATION PROCEDURES

The teacher's role in this method is neither that of preacher nor that of passive listener. Instead the teacher strives to (*a*) establish a climate of psychological safety, (*b*) apply a clarification procedure. An elaboration of these procedures follows.

## ESTABLISHMENT OF PSYCHOLOGICAL SAFETY

### NONJUDGMENTAL ATTITUDES

It has been said that teachers have difficulty responding to an idea without saying, "That's good," "That's bad," or "What good is it?" To provide an atmosphere in which children will feel free to express themselves without threat of ridicule and derision, teachers must refrain from making harsh unnecessary judgments. Of course at times some judgments become necessary in situations in which the health and/or safety of students are threatened in any real sense.

### MANIFESTATIONS OF CONCERN

While the teacher may be nonjudgmental, it is important for him to be concerned with the ideas expressed by his students. If the concern is apparently lacking, then often the number of student ideas shared with a teacher tends to diminish. Perhaps students are reluctant to share their ideas with someone who is not interested in them. One of the most effective ways to show concern for a student's ideas is to *listen* to them. Busy teachers sometimes overlook this basic and effective technique for communicating interest to their students. Another method for a teacher's communicating his concern for a student's ideas is to *remember* them. As a teacher is able to cite a student's idea in a later conversation, the student cannot help but feel genuinely flattered and impressed.

### OPPORTUNITIES FOR THE SHARING OF IDEAS

Teachers must organize their courses in such a way that children have the opportunity to express their opinions, purposes, feelings, beliefs, hunches, goals, and interests about moral issues. These attitudinal-type statements may then be examined by the child who expressed them with the teacher acting somewhat as a catalytic agent in the process. Some methods used by teachers in various researches by classroom teachers include: (*a*) question-answer discussion periods involving moot questions for the class to consider; (*b*) special written assignments; (*c*) role-playing techniques; (*d*) behavior manifestations of individuals or groups that may indicate attitudes, e.g., cheating or being tardy.

The task of finding issues that children may react to is no small problem. While our lives are filled with many, many moral and ethical questions to consider, even within our formal disciplines, it is difficult to find these issues in our textbooks, or *Weekly Readers*. Alexander(1), a textbook consultant for the New York City schools, has found that "few or no serious problems" are present in our current textbooks.

## CLARIFYING STRATEGIES

### ASKING QUESTIONS

The teacher may attempt to clarify the ideas elicited from his students by asking probing questions. The key criterion for selecting these questions is that they must be questions for which only the student knows the answer. Of course, to be effective they must be asked in a nonjudgmental manner. If a student seems seriously challenged by one of the questions, the teacher should make efforts to "save face" by accepting his bewilderment. For example, the teacher may pass on by saying, "That's a hard question for anyone to answer, isn't it?" "Let's think about it for a while and maybe an answer will come to us later." A list of questions that a teacher may ask is included below. Of course, this list is not exhaustive, and teachers may add to it as they become more fluent in the use of this procedure.

1. Reflect back what the student has said and add, "Is that what you mean?"
2. Reflect back what the student has said with distortions and add, "Is that what you mean?"
3. "How long have you felt (acted) that way?"
4. "Are you glad you think (act) that way?"
5. "In what way is that a good idea?"
6. "What is the source of your idea?"
7. "Should everyone believe that?"
8. "Have you thought of some alternatives?"
9. "What are some things you have done that reflect this idea of yours?"
10. "Why do you think so?"
11. "Is this what you really think?"
12. "Did you do this on purpose?"
13. Ask for definitions of key words.
14. Ask for examples.
15. Ask if this position is consistent with a previous one he has taken.

It is important that teachers ask these questions of students who express ideas with which they agree as well as with those students who express ideas with which they disagree.

## CODING WRITTEN WORK

Researchers have found the coding of written work very effective in value clarifying. Whenever students seem to express an attitude, belief, goal, purpose, interest, or aspiration, teachers may mark a V + or V − in the mar-

gin to reflect this idea back to the student. This code works much like other more familiar codes we already use in our schools, e.g., WW for wrong word, or SP for misspelled word. There is one crucial difference. When a teacher marks WW in the margin, there usually *is* a wrong word. When a teacher marks V + in the margin, it is understood that she is really asking, "Do you believe this?" or "Do you want to change it?"

## ACCEPTANCE WITHOUT JUDGMENT

It has been found that teachers feel awkward trying to draw the clarification exchange to a close. The verbal interaction between teacher and student is not to win an argument or to gain a debating point. The purpose of the exchange is to clarify students' ideas. It is important that teachers find a way to accept the students' ideas without communicating agreement or praise of them. In a sense, the exchange does not have an ending. Neither the teacher nor the student arrives at a conclusion. Neither is there a need for summarizing. Questions left unanswered are thought about and dwelt on by the student (and perhaps the teacher) at night before going to sleep, or during moments of quiet during the day. Some ways that have been found successful in closing an exchange are as follows:

1. Silence with a nod.
2. "Uh-huh."
3. "I see."
4. "I understand you better now."
5. "I can see how you would feel that way."
6. "I understand."
7. "I can see that it was difficult for you to decide that way."

In summary, the clarification procedure developed by Louis Raths attempts to elicit from students statements of an attitudinal nature and to clarify these statements for the student. By developing an emotional acceptance of himself on the part of his students, and by asking students questions which will serve to clarify their own purposes, goals, attitudes, beliefs, etc., teachers can play an effective role in developing values in their classrooms.

This procedure can be time-consuming or it may also take just a few seconds. For example, consider the following hypothetical exchange:

Student: I hate math.
Teacher: You have never liked math?
Student: Well, I did like it at one time.
Teacher: What changed your mind?
Student: I don't know.
Teacher: Oh.

Without trying to lecture the student about what he "ought" to like, without preaching about the dangers inherent in not liking math, the teacher is attempting to help the student understand his own preferences and values.

In passing, it may be appropriate to add that several researches (9, 11, 13, 14) have successfully attempted to test these ideas in classrooms in New York State and Wisconsin. Other studies are needed, of course, to test further the efficacy of this procedure. The experiences of a number of researches in this field suggest also that learning to use the process of clarifying is not easy. It is clearly a difficult matter to enter into a significant interaction with a student. The problem is much less that of identifying with a student, but one of identifying with the student's concerns, of listening, and of taking seriously what he has said and reacting thoughtfully to it.

It must be clear that teachers who apply the clarification procedure must have a tremendous respect for their students. As teachers agree or disagree with students' expressed ideas

they must be able to consider them as tenable ones to hold. If teachers believe it is their role to "convert" students to a "right way" of thinking, then it seems they must basically disrespect the view their students hold now. The distinction I am trying to make is one between accepting and respecting. It would seem possible for me to respect the views of a colleague, let us say, without accepting those views. This is the spirit that I believe must dominate a teacher's conversations with his students. Of course, this statement must be modified to the extent that a student's view may threaten the health or safety of himself or society. It is my contention that such cases are rare in classrooms. Yet there is still plenty of room for many safe differences of opinion and behavior between students and teachers.

Most of us have become accustomed to the association of teaching with changes in student behavior. Too frequently, quite without being aware of it, we look for "instant" changes. We hope for miracles on the "values front." We do not pay enough attention to the fact that it took many years for our students to learn their present almost valueless behavior, and that it may take a long sustained effort to help students to develop serious purposes and aspirations through the clarifying processes. For a free society, opportunities to clarify and to choose must be created again and again.

Norman Cousins (3) has written about his concern for the predatory quality of life in human form. He suggests that what makes our society so much like a jungle is the misfits who exert power over honest men.

There are those . . . who insist on projecting their warped ideas to the people around them. They are the agents of chaos. . . . Maybe this is what makes a jungle a jungle.

Cousins continues to say that the way out of the jungle is not just emptying it of these misfits. "There must be some notion about what is to take the place of the jungle. That is why ideals and goals are the most practical things in the world. They conquer the jungle, make men mobile, and convert humans from fawning and frightened animals into thinkers and builders." As teachers learn to develop the ideals, goals, and values of students by applying the clarification procedures outlined in this paper, they may perhaps become truly "influential Americans."

### REFERENCES

1. Alexander, Albert, "The Gray Flannel Cover of the American History Text," *Social Education*, XXIV, No. 11 (January 1960).
2. Allport, Gordon, *Becoming: Basic Considerations for Psychology of Personality.* New Haven, Conn.: Yale University Press, 1955.
3. Cousins, Norman, "Hoffa, Hegel and Hoffer," *Saturday Review* (April 20, 1963).
4. Dewey, John, *Moral Principles in Education.* Boston: Houghton Mifflin Company, 1909.
5. Educational Policies Commission, *Moral and Spiritual Values in the Public Schools.* Washington, D.C.: National Education Association, 1957.
6. Friedenberg, Edgar Z., *The Vanishing Adolescent.* New York: Dell Publishing Co., Inc., 1962.
7. Ginsburg, Sol. W., "Values and the

Psychiatrist," *American Journal of Orthopsychiatry*, XX (July 1950), 466.
8. Jacob, Philip E., *Changing Values in College.* New York: Harper & Row, Publishers, 1957.
9. Jonas, Arthur, "A Study of the Relationship of Certain Behaviors of Children to Emotional Needs, Values, and Thinking." Unpublished Ed. D. thesis, New York University, 1960.
10. Jones, Vernon, "Character Education," *Encyclopedia of Educational Research*, Chester Harris, ed. New York: The Macmillan Company, 1960.
11. Klevan, Albert, "An Investigation of a Methodology for Value Clarification: Its Relationship to Consistency of Thinking, Purposefulness, and Human Relations." Unpublished Ed.D. thesis, New York University, 1958.
12. Kubie, Lawrence, "Are We Educating for Maturity," *N.E.A. Journal* (January 1959).
13. Raths, James, "Underachievement and a Search for Values," *Journal of Education Sociology*, XXXIV, No. 2 (May 1961).
14. ——, "Clarifying Children's Values," *National Elementary Principal*, LXII, No. 2 (November 1962).
15. Raths, Louis E., "Values and Teachers," *Education Synopsis* (Spring, 1957).
16. ——, "Sociological Knowledge and Needed Curriculum Research," *Research Frontiers in the Study of Children's Learning*, J. B. Macdonald, ed. Milwaukee: School of Education, The University of Wisconsin-Milwaukee, 1960.
17. ——, "Clarifying Values," *Curriculum for Today's Boys and Girls*, R. S. Fleming, ed. Columbus, Ohio: Charles E. Merrill Books, Inc., 1963.

# ACTIVITIES

1. What are some activities you may plan for your classes that would promote valuing and thinking?

2. What are some of the methods that enable you to monitor your teaching for efforts to promote valuing and thinking?

3. Assume that a teacher's response to a student's statement of belief can be categorized as (1) accepting (without judgment); (2) judgmental, either plus or minus; (3) reflecting, or (4) argumentative—raising objections to the student's view. Observe a classroom and attempt to find if this category system is efficacious. Listen to a tape recording of your own teaching and attempt to categorize your responses.

4. Assume that the following comments are made by a student in your class. Assume also that the comment is relevant and germane to the class discussion. If a teacher wished to clarify the student's idea, what would be his best response? Circle your judgment. (Assume all teacher statements are made in a nonemotional way.)

   1. "I don't want to salute the flag."
     a. I'm sure some Americans feel that way.
     b. Do you think this is a patriotic attitude?
     c. Just this flag or any flag?
     d. I don't see how you can feel that way.
   2. "Writing a letter to a congressman is a waste of time."
     a. Someday you'll learn to appreciate our form of government.
     b. Do you feel this way about all congressmen or special ones?
     c. Imagine a Russian writing to his government.
     d. What do some of you other children think about this?
   3. "The government has no right to tell a private businessman what to do."
     a. What do you mean by the words "no right"?
     b. Is your father in business?

    c. Did the government ever tell your father what to do?

    d. A great many people feel as you do.

4. "Negroes have made great contributions to our society."

    a. The history of America is a story of the contributions of persons of all races and religions.

    b. Give me some examples and tell why you think they are great.

    c. More and more people are beginning to realize this fact.

    d. Did you hear that on television?

5. "The Supreme Court has banned prayer in the public schools.

    a. I don't think that is exactly what the Supreme Court decision says.

    b. Was the Supreme Court decision unanimous?

    c. I can see that the decision makes you feel badly.

    d. What does this mean for your school?

6. "Let's demonstrate our view by picketing the White House.

    a. Should we bother the President with this now that he is so busy with other problems?

    b. Are there other ways to demonstrate your views?

    c. You certainly seem to think your views are important.

    d. Picketing really never accomplished anything, did it?

5. Some educators feel that it is most important to teach process-thinking, valuing, inquiring, etc. Sometimes this position is considered to be antithetical to that which emphasizes subject matter. In your view, are these positions inconsistent?

6. It has been said that no textbook or course of study contains "thinking." Thinking takes place when students "interact" with the content of a textbook. What assignments seem most productive to promote deep and intellectual interactions? Suggest some in the content areas in which you are most interested.

7. If it is desirable for a teacher to be acceptive of students' responses, what types of questions lead to students' responses that are most difficult to accept? What kinds of questions facilitate attaining the desired acceptable replies?

8. Write down some of your beliefs concerning teaching and education. Which of these beliefs are synthetic according to Metcalf's view; which of these are analytic? What evidence can be gathered or cited to support the analytic beliefs you hold?

## Chapter Seven

# MEETING THE EMOTIONAL
# NEEDS OF CHILDREN

A perennial issue on the educational scene is the degree to which a teacher should play "psychologist." On the one hand, persons argue that elementary- and secondary-school teachers are not prepared to deal with the emotions of children, and any such problem should be referred to proper authorities. Although most teachers concede that they are not trained as psychologists, they do advance the point of view that they can act effectively and safely in giving students support and encouragement. Does such support constitute therapy? Perhaps that is the issue.

Activities designed to give support and encouragement to students have been subsumed under the broader heading of "meeting the emotional needs of students." Many curriculum plans over the past thirty years have been based on the premise that they were doing just that. But what are needs and how are they identified? Is there a distinction between a need for oxygen and a need for a feeling of belonging and group acceptance? To what degree should education meet the needs of students? Finally, does the teaching of skills, concepts, and understandings conflict with meeting a student's needs? These are questions that every teacher must consider.

# 40

# "Need" and the Needs-Curriculum

## B. PAUL KOMISAR

Individuals involved in all aspects of education reveal a considerable concern about needs. The administrator considers the needs of his faculty before submitting a budget. The school counselor decides the cases of academic tragedy and vocational aspiration with which he daily contends by recourse to his clients' needs. The curriculum supervisor exhorts teachers to meet the needs of their pupils, and it is announced to the public with dreary regularity that this is what teachers are doing. Programs at all levels of instruction from the nursery to the graduate school find their justification in the needs of the student or society or, more popularly, in both. Not to be outdone by the defenders of practice, the espouser of innovation employs similar warrant for *his* proposals. Nor is the critic (of theory or practice) a laggard in this regard; he is just as apt to castigate his victim for meeting

needs as for failing to do so. And, of course, there is no dearth of candidates eager to list for us the pupils' needs. Indeed, no committee report or textbook seems to be considered complete without at least one such list, though their authors seems divided on whether it is brevity or profusion that indicates success in this endeavor.

It is not my intention to add to these agitations or lists of what students need. Instead I will examine what we *mean* when we say pupils need something. This will be a study of the ways the word "need" is used in education. In the final section of this essay I will go a step further and apply the results of the analysis to the claim that public education should meet the needs of students.

The senses of "need" we will examine fall roughly into two categories. The first includes what I will call the prescriptive uses. Here we find, for example, the cases where "he needs discipline" is roughly equivalent to "he must have discipline" or "discipline is necessary for him." In the second category will fall the motivational uses of "need";

B. Paul Komisar, "'Need' and the Needs-Curriculum," in *Language and Concepts in Education*, eds. B. O. Smith and Richard Ennis (Skokie, Ill.: Rand McNally & Co., 1961), pp. 24-42. Reprinted by permission.

that is, its uses to refer in some way to motives. Here an assertion that pupils need affection is similar to saying that pupils want or seek out affection. This classification is crude but it will do for a beginning.

## 1. PRESCRIPTIVE USES OF "NEED"

A fruitful way of clarifying the use of an expression is by a study of the challenges which can be raised against statements made with the expression. I will be following this procedure in the subsequent examination. I will take up in turn some of the more important objections that might properly be raised against assertions of the form "he needs X." From these challenges and the accompanying answers, it will be possible to infer some of the criteria for the use of "need."

OBJECTIVE

When we refer to something as a need (or say that a subject needs something), we might be asked what it is needed for. In the case of "this pupil needs to study," we might be asked what objective studying is to serve for the pupil. As a test of the assertion itself, this makes "he needs to study," different from "he is six feet tall." A request for the consequences of being six feet tall is simply a request for additional information; it is not an attempt to evaluate the statement "he is six feet tall." For the fact that being tall makes a boy a likely basketball prospect is not part of the criteria for saying "he is six feet tall." The opposite is true of "he needs to study." If we are told that no objective is to be served by studying, that studying is not needed *for* anything, then this does constitute grounds for a denial of the assertion itself ("if nothing is to

come of it then he doesn't *need* to study").[1]

One of the criteria, then, for calling something a need is that it be related to some further state of affairs. I will refer to this state of affairs as the objective, although it may be a complex situation. The objective can be the achievement of a new state of affairs ("he needs drill to develop skills"). It may be the maintenance of an already existing state ("he needs to study in order to continue his fine record"). Or the objective may be the avoidance of some possible future state ("he needs recognition lest emotional frustration result").

Quite often we fulfill this criterion by making the objective part of the assertion itself ("he needs a course in history to graduate"). Even when we do not make the objective explicit, it is frequently implied by the context of our statement. But the absence of a challenge on this point only means that the condition has been fulfilled. Ultimately, if the objective is not made clear, or at least indicated, we can ask "what is that needed for?" We can press for an answer to our question, however elusive and difficult to articulate the objective may be. For by virtue of our language, that which is not needed for anything is not needed.

NECESSITY

When we say that a pupil needs something, we are relating that thing

[1] "But what are 'requirements'? They are the things that must be done in order to secure certain ends; they do not exist except in relation to those ends. If different ends are sought, the 'requirements' become different." Bertrand Russell, "Reply to Criticisms," in *The Philosophy of Bertrand Russell*, Paul A. Schilpp, ed. (Evanston, Ill.: The Library of Living Philosophers, Inc., 1946), p. 732.

to some objective. But *how* are they related—that which we call a need to the objective for which it is a need? Consider the claim "you need vitamin pills to improve your health." There are two ways of defeating it; that is, there are two ways of supporting the counterclaim that pills are not needed.

1. We might argue that vitamin pills have no effect on a person's physical or emotional state. If this argument could be made to stick, the prescription would stand refuted.

2. But even if we were to grant that the pills have a tendency to enhance health, we could defeat the claim by showing other feasible ways to achieve the same end. A demonstration of equally possible alternatives in some situation also refutes any claim that one alternative is *needed*.

Both of these cases involve a denial of necessity in some situation. The first claims that what is called a need will not assist in realizing the objective at all. The second claims that it is not the only way of helping to achieve the objective. It is clear now what the relation between need and objective must be. The object or activity or state of affairs we refer to as a need must be necessary to the objective, in the sense that its presence contributes to the achievement of the objective, while its absence renders the objective unattainable.

This second criterion is less stringent than it might appear. We are not called upon to guarantee the objective, except in very special cases in which we claim to be doing this ("*all* you need is practice").[2] Normally it is the necessary, not the sufficient conditions

[2] All uses of "need" in questions which request requirements fall into this special class. In asking for needs, we always seem to be requesting the necessary *and* sufficient conditions. The significance of this fact, if it is a fact, eludes me.

we prescribe (though a list of needs might satisfy both conditions). To announce that all candidates for graduation need twenty credits does not thereby guarantee graduation to all who fulfill the requirement. There may be additional requirements, other needs for the same objective. All we are committed to in our announcement is that with that many credits it remains possible to graduate, and that without them one cannot graduate.

But even this claim has an important reservation. When I say you need something, I mean that it is necessary in some more or less determinate situation. We are dealing with contextual necessity here. So what appear at first glance to be alternatives to needs, can often be eliminated by the practical exigencies of the specific situation. Take the case of a teacher who asserts that a pupil needs to join a special remedial class in order to accelerate his learning. It is no criticism of this assertion to say that the same result can be achieved with intensive personal tutoring. In most school situations this alternative is unrealistic, impossible to achieve. So in this situation it *is* the special class that is needed. There may be conceivable alternatives in some concrete situation, but if only one is feasible then that one is needed.

A word, finally, about two senses in which we might speak of something as necessary. There is the familiar notion of empirical necessity which exists between events in the natural world. When an event regularly precedes another event which would otherwise fail to occur, we speak of the relation as an empirically necessary one. The same is true of analytic necessity or necessity by rule. Here also only one path can be followed to a certain result, but this is the "can" of custom or culture. Thus it is empirically possible for a man to steal money to support his family, but cultural rules (laws, in this case) proscribe this practice. We will be returning to this point in a later section for, as it turns out, rules play an important role in prescription.

## DEFICIENCY

There is a third way of challenging assertions of the form "he needs $X$." They can be countered with the claim that the condition has already been realized and hence not needed any longer. For example, the assertion "John needs to complete the final assignment" is wrong if the assignment is already complete.

From this we can infer a third criterion supervising the use of "need." Before we can properly say of someone that he needs something, the subject must be deficient in, or lack, whatever we prescribe. More accurately, the use of "need" presupposes a deficiency, without which it is a mistake to say a need exists.[3]

This third criterion seems to be trivial and obvious, but there is one consideration that makes it worth our attention. Educators occasionally define a need as "a condition of deprivation or lack." On this view, when we use "need" to prescribe for a student, we are merely reporting that the student is lacking in some respect. On this definition, the two assertions "John needs this book" and "John doesn't have this book" say the same thing. However, they do not. It is true that one *criterion* for saying successfully "John needs this book" is that John does not have the book, but the original assertion does not say this. For I could *agree* that John lacks the

book yet *disagree* that he needs it. (One of the other conditions for making the prescription might be unfulfilled.)

This attempt to establish synonymity between statements of the form "$X$ needs $Y$" and "$X$ lacks $Y$" ignores the fact that whenever we are told that someone is bereft ("he is without a college education"), we can still properly ask if it is needed. This request is not meaningless, for there is an important difference between the two forms of expression. But the question "does John need attention?" *after being told he requires it, is* meaningless, heralding a failure in communication. For unless we are questioning the criteria ("does he *really* need it?"), the two assertions ("he needs ..." and "he requires ...") mean the same thing.

There are two temptations, I believe, which lead to this assimilation of "need" and "lack." First, there are some objectives so commonly accepted in a society that the mere realization that someone it deficient in them prompts us immediately to prescribe for alleviation of the condition. But this does not mean that *all* lacks are important. Nor does it mean that it is the deficiency alone which implies the need. It is only that the other conditions necessary for the use of "need" are obviously present and taken for granted. Secondly, we sometimes employ "lack" in assertions that are very similar to prescriptions. For example, we say "he lacks adequate medical care" not only to report a deficiency but to point out such a condition is unjustified. This is still not the same as "he needs more medical care," but the two assertions are very close. The one recognizes an unacceptable situation; the other takes action to remove it. However, even this does not justify equating "lack" with "need," for it is the presence of such adjectives as "adequate" and "suffi-

---

[3] This applies to the objective as well. If the objective is already attained, then clearly prescriptions made in its name are spurious.

cient" which turns mere lacks into serious shortages.

### RULES

There is, finally, a fourth condition which prevails when we use "need" in its prescriptive sense. Consider the case of a supervisor telling a teacher that members of her class need drill to improve their spelling. The teacher goes on to plan activities, demand student compliance, apply sanctions for failure, and generally evaluate students on their proficiency. The teacher is obviously not responding to the assertion "the class needs drill" as she would to a mere *report* that drill improves spelling.

In the above case the question of whether or not to increase the skill in spelling is simply not treated as a matter for debate. The decision has already been made. It is presupposed that the objective must be achieved. This introduces a new factor. Not only does the use of "need" presuppose an objective; it frequently presupposes an obligation or even a compulsion to achieve the objective as well.

Before discussing this point in greater detail, contrast the spelling situation with another which does not involve such a presupposition. An adviser tells a student, "You need more practice if you expect a career in music." There is no presupposition here concerning whether or not the student must go on in music. The adviser is simply giving information, reporting that some condition is necessarily dependent on another.

What is present in the spelling case and not present in the counseling situation is an underlying commitment to achieve the objective. As usual, the logical force of this point is revealed when we examine the challenge that might arise. Consider again the spelling

example and suppose, simply for the sake of argument, that we did not care whether students spelled correctly. This would be sufficient grounds for denying that the class needs drill. Note that this kind of challenge is irrelevant in the counseling situation. Since the counselor does not assume an obligation to attain a goal, jeopardizing the goal does not invalidate the assertion.

In some cases then the correctness of a prescription hinges on whether the presupposition—that the objective must be achieved—is justified. When the presupposition is challenged, what sort of defense can be made for it? If a teacher is challenged on this point ("why must students learn to read?"), there is a sense in which the reply "because I say so" would not be wholly inappropriate. For what the teacher is saying, in effect, is that he is responsible for seeing to it that certain objectives are achieved. These general social expectations constitute the teacher's authority and justification for imposing further requirements, giving directives, prescribing needs.

This point is made clearer, I think, when we look at a simpler case. A player in a card game may tell another that he needs to take one card. The person uttering the directive is presupposing that each player must have a certain number of cards. If someone were to challenge this assumption ("why must I have five cards?"), the objector would be referred to the rules of the game in which this was stipulated. In applying rules to persons clearly bound by them, we get directives. One needs to do $X$ because $X$ is itself dictated by the rules or because $X$ is in some way necessary to what the rule does stipulate.

Though schools are more complicated than card games, they are in this respect similar. The host of social expectations and subordinate regulations comprising school policy function as do the rules in games to justify prescriptions.

## TYPES OF PRESCRIPTIONS

Thus far I have been discussing prescription as if it were one job, a singular task which we do with language. Under the general rubric of prescription, however, different uses of "need" can be distinguished.

(1) "Need" occurs in assertions whose major function is to make rules or state them. An academic committee may decree, for example, that a certain average is needed for continued residence in a university. Here the committee is not reporting a requirement; they are literally making one. But "need" is also employed in the statement of a rule, in a report that such and such is a rule. I will call this the rule sense or rule use of "need."

(2) The application of general rules in specific situations to yield detailed requirements for particular subjects is what I called earlier the directive use of "need." There are variations in the way rules apply in different cases. I have been focusing attention on cases in which the objective is stipulated by rule or social expectation and "need" is used to prescribe the empirically necessary means. Other patterns are possible. In some cases rules may dictate both the objective and means. Finally, no objective may be involved, only a rule stipulated requirement.

In distinguishing the rule use of "need" from the directive use, I don't mean to be emphasizing the performatory character of rule making. The performatory element is important but there are directive cases also in which it is present. In some unusual circumstances "higher authority" must judge whether a rule applies to a subject, and even how it applies. But where the performatory element is common in the rule use, it is necessarily rare in the directive use. For we *make* rules of a general sort just to avoid the necessity for individual judgments in each specific case.

The differences I do want to emphasize between (1) and (2) are those that exist between a rule and the application of a rule. Typically, rules do not refer to particular subjects but to roles or positions. Also, but not invariably, rules differ from directives in that they stipulate only a *type* of required action or performance.

(3) In the counseling situation we encountered a third, the *informative* sense of "need." Here "need" is used to report, not impose, requirements. Thus we inform those not bound by rules what would be required of them if they were so bound ("if you join the club, you will need to attend meetings"). Or we can specify what is necessary to some goal even though the goal is not being sought ("to get good grades, one needs to study").

The difference between (2) and (3) is the difference between the hypothetical and categorical mood. Cases of (3) tell us what *would* be needed *if* certain conditions existed. Cases of (2) state what we *do* need *because* these conditions *do* exist. However, the actual form of the prescription may be misleading. In some contexts "need" may be used informatively to make a seemingly categorical assertion. "Students need affection," for example, may be elliptical, a condensed version of the hypothetical "if students are to achieve emotional security, affection is necessary." We depend on the context of the utterance to determine whether the actual form of the assertion is misleading.

Despite the differences between

these uses, they are all prescriptive in the ordinary sense of that term. A rule is said to prescribe or proscribe certain actions, and we are also said to prescribe when we apply the rules to specific individuals. Similarly a doctor is said to prescribe for a patient although the prescription is not binding on us. This reveals the ambiguity in the ordinary sense of prescription, but more importantly for present purposes, it helps explain why some challenges are not relevant to every case wherein "need" is used prescriptively.

In the preceding sections it was shown that there are at least four possible challenges one can legitimately make to the prescription "these students need $X$." We can ask what objective $X$ is to serve and question whether $X$ is necessary to the attainment of the objective. Also an inquiry can be made as to whether the students really lack $X$ or the objective. And finally we can ask for the rules or social expectations that make the achievement of $X$ obligatory. Thus, in response to the claim "this class needs instruction in science," the following questions might be raised:

(a) What objective is served by science instruction? (Suppose that the objective is development of scientific attitudes.)
(b) Is science instruction necessary to achieve the attitudes? (Will it contribute to their development at all? Is it the *only* feasible way to develop them?)
(c) Have students already had the instruction? Do they already possess the attitudes?
(d) What rules or expectations make the attainment of these attitudes mandatory?

Now it can be seen that not all challenges are relevant or relevant in the same way to each prescriptive use. Let me list some of the exceptions.

(1) When "need" is functioning informatively, challenge (d), the request for justification, does not apply as it does in directive cases. In directive cases the rules justify the *demand* or *insistence* that something be achieved. In informative cases the rules justify my *claim* or *prediction* as to what will be demanded; the rules do not justify my imposition for there is no imposition.

(2) The deficiency challenge, challenge (c), is irrelevant to statements of rules. For example, the rule that all club members need to pay dues is properly asserted even when it has been obeyed. Actually the rule is the general formula which tells us what to say and do when dues have not been paid.

But if a rule does not presuppose an existent deficiency, it does assume the expectation of one. It would be pointless to establish rules for cases that are unlikely to arise (e.g., "all high school students need to know how to talk").

(3) On some occasions of the rule use it is inappropriate to invoke challenge (a) and request the objective of the need. For some needs are "ultimate." Some rules do not specify what must be done to achieve a given end; they simply assert what must be done. However, these cases are apt to be rare, for "need" tends to be a relative term. We reserve it for cases when "$X$ is needed *for* $A$." To make simple demands or commands we tend to employ the more imperative expressions "must," "have to," and "is mandatory."

In addition to exceptions to the challenges, there are also additional challenges. The directive "you need to do $X$" is unjustified if you are not bound by the rules from which the prescription was generated. Similarly, any rules made by a group lacking legitimate authority are invalid.

These do not exhaust the exceptions

or additional challenges but they round out the picture of prescriptive sense of "need."

## 2. MOTIVATIONAL USES OF "NEED"

As far as his professional language is concerned, the educator stands at halfway house. Some of the concepts he uses have been borrowed from the social sciences. To this extent there tends to be disparity between the talk of the teacher and the layman. However, words common to everyone also find a place in educational discussions. No concept reveals this linguistic divergence better than the one we are presently scrutinizing. For there is nothing particularly technical about the use of "need" to prescribe. "He needs a job" is the kind of assertion anyone might properly make. But an educator who says that pupils need recognition may not mean pupils *require* it, in the prescriptive sense, but rather that pupils want or seek it out. This motivational sense of need we owe to the psychologist.

Here, as in the previous section, we find not one but three uses:

(a) Sometimes "need" reports or refers to a motive, so that the assertion "John needs (or has a need for) X" is a report of what John desires.

(b) Also, it is often *claimed* that "need" is used to refer to "deficit states" or "conditions of lack."

In both (a) and (b) need is an event or occurrence. That is, need assertions on either use are reports of states of affairs transpiring at the time the assertion is made. Or suitably tensed, the assertion may report past or future *events*.

(c) "Need" can and does operate in a dispositional sense also, as when it is used to report that a subject is prone to want a certain thing from time to time. In this sense "John needs

affection" does not mean that John now desires affection, only that he is inclined to desire it periodically. In the dispositional sense a need is a trait, a propensity, a predilection, not an event.

Despite the dual use of "need" as event and as trait, there has not been, to my knowledge, any attempt to alter the commonly accepted grammar of the term to give it a present continuous tense. Thus we do not say "he is needing" when reporting a contemporary episode, as we do with the terms "boxing," "running," "falling," etc. Consequently the same form— "he needs"—is utilized to report motives and dispositions.

We will be returning to this dispositional sense a little later, but I will give most attention to the first two senses of need—as motive and lack. These uses have been more widely recognized and discussed than the dispositional one.[4] Indeed one sometimes suspects that there is more talk about need as motive and need as deficit state than actual *use* of the expression in either way. At any rate, it will not be necessary to dwell on the much discussed aspects of these uses. In the discussion to follow I will concentrate on some of the special problems and puzzles which arise in connection with these uses. We will find that each use is plagued by conceptual difficulties that in one case at least render the very use itself questionable. Yet these difficulties are often ignored by edu-

[4] For a few of the discussions see Reginald D. Archambault, "The Concept of Need . . . ," *Harvard Educational Review* (Winter, 1957), pp. 40f.; Donald C. Doane, *The Needs of Youth* (New York: Bureau of Publications, Teachers College, Columbia University, 1942), pp. 3f.; Ralph W. Tyler, *Basic Principles of Curriculum and Instruction* (Urbana, Ill.: University of Chicago Press. 1950), pp. 5f.; and Herbert F. Wright, "How the Psychology of Motivation is Related to Curriculum Development," *Journal of Educational Psychology* (March 1948), pp. 149f.

cators who introduce the expression into all aspects of education.

### NEEDS AS MOTIVES

Sporadically among educators generally and more commonly among educational psychologists in particular there has developed a practice of using the expression "need" to refer to a certain type of happening. This event has been characterized in a variety of ways—as a state of tension, a psychological condition of sensitivity to respond, a condition of disequilibrium, or less grandly, as an "inner urge" or desire or want, etc. Whatever we call it, "need" is being used to report the motive itself and not, as in the dispositional use, the tendency for the motive to recur.

Furthermore, in pedagogical language, "need" is usually a general motive expression; it is used to refer to any kind of motive or any goal-seeking behavior. The definition given by Gates and others illustrates this general applicability of "need":

A need exists as a state of tension in a person which serves to direct his behavior toward certain goals. . . . "Need" . . . is used as an inclusive term to embrace drives, impulses, goal sets, urges, motives, cravings, desires, wants, and wishes.[5]

The first point to note is that this usage is not encountered outside education (and the social sciences generally). In ordinary discourse, "need" is not a general motive expression but a specific one, referring only to a motive that is particularly persistent and compelling. Thus, one feels truly "driven" by a need, and if motives were scaled by reference to their intensity or strength, feelings of need would top the scale.

The restricted use is represented in education also. Cronbach, for example, speaks cryptically of needs as "persistent and recurrent wants," not simply as wants.[6] And the attempt made by some educators to separate needs from whims and "mere" desires indicates that the ordinary usage still retains followers in education.

The use of "need" as a motive expression has yet another feature which warrants particular attention. There is considerable variation in the type of word that can be employed to refer to the object of the motive. In the same or similar circumstances a relatively abstract term might be employed ("he has a need for recreation") or a more specific one ("he has a need to go fishing").

What makes this divergence particularly intriguing is that it concerns only the choice of word (or phrase) used to refer to the goal. It is not a disagreement over the criteria for the motivational use of "need" itself.

Let me explain this point a little more fully. The actual specific or concrete criteria for the use of motive expressions are numerous and differ (though not completely) from situation to situation. For example, the pleas of a boy to be taken fishing and the boy's preparations are all criteria for the assertion "he wants to go fishing." However, we can abstract from the *specific* criteria to form the *general* rule that a motive expression is used in a situation where some subject is actively pursuing a goal.

We recognize that a great variety of activities may constitute an acitve pursuit. In one case it may be asking a

[5] Arthur I. Gates, Arthur T. Jersild, T. R. McConnell, and Robert Challman, *Educational Psychology*, 3rd ed. (New York: The Macmillan Company, 1948), p. 617.

[6] Lee J. Cronbach, "The Learning Process and Text Specification," *Text Materials in Modern Education* (Urbana: University of Illinois Press, 1955), p. 66.

question and skimming through an encyclopedia ("he wants to know the area of Spain"). In another it may be spurts of running, or fretting over the lateness of the hour ("he wants to see the batting practice"). There is no reason to concern ourselves with this issue, for the disagreement we are discussing does not concern the presence or absence of the criteria. All would agree that a student must actively be pursuing (in some way) a goal before we say he has a need for that goal. In spite of this agreement, however, there might still be variations in the generality of the word employed to characterize the goal.

The more general terms like "status," "achievement," and "adventure" are also employed when "need" is used *dispositionally*. This is understandable, for in the dispositional use we are trying to summate, generalize from, many individual motivational episodes. A need in this sense is not a report of the actual goal being pursued. So the use of general terms in dispositional reports does not mean that the *goals* are necessarily general, only that the goals—whether they be specific or general—fall into a certain class.[7]

However, when exclusively general terms are used to refer to goals then we *are* committed to the proposition that motives themselves are general. And general motives are characterized by transitory goal-objects and wavering goal-directed behavior, among other things. The original choice of abstract terms implies the above as character-

---

[7] "Needs describe the relatively permanent tendencies in persons to be motivated in specific ways, and *we infer them from the commonalities among the goals that the person appears to be seeking* [italics not in the original]." Frederick J. McDonald, *Educational Psychology* (Belmont, Calif.: Wadsworth Publishing Company, 1959), p. 81.

istics of human goal-seeking behavior. Similarly one who employs only specific labels for goals is prejudging the empirical traits motivated behavior will be found to possess.

Furthermore, the fact that goals are given abstract labels has at least one other important consequence. We find that the same terms are applicable to many students and to the same student at various times in his career. Thus the step to the universality of motives (needs) is a smooth one. For example, a student who studies furiously for a test and requests guidance in eradicating errors is said to have a need to gain status. The same is said of the pupil whose antics gain the attention of his classmates. What is more natural than to conclude that both students are having the "same" need? The transition is more difficult when the more idiosyncratic expressions like "get an A in the spelling test" rather than "recognition" are used to label the goals. Thus many educators who claim to *discover* common motives in students may be deluding themselves. Their discovery may simply be a consequence of a previous *decision* to employ abstract language. The choice of words to report needs in the motive sense is a serious matter. For the choice itself may commit one to empirical claims concerning motivational phenomena.

## NEEDS AS LACKS

Considering the popularity of the notion of need as a state of deficiency, it is surprising that there is so little agreement on descriptions of the use. However, many educators who agree on the notion diverge considerably in their more detailed accounts of it.

First, there seems to be no consensus on whether the need is the *object* that is lacking or the *condition* of absence.[8,9] But having noted this particular divergence, let me put it aside and adopt the language of "condition."

A more serious difficulty is revealed when we attempt to clarify the way in which motives are related to lacks in this conception. One view of the relationship has been described by James Olds as follows:

The physiological phenomenon of need is this: without certain needed conditions the organism will perish. The animistic theory proceeds to make the following assumptions: (1) the organism wants to survive, (2) therefore, the organism wants the conditions that will permit survival. The conclusion is that when we say something is needed we mean not only (*i*) that without the condition the organism will perish, but also (*ii*) the organism will want and therefore pursue the condition. . . . My contention is that the term *need* refers only to the fact that the organism would perish without the needed conditions; and I believe the assumption that "need" is intrinsically related to "want" or "pursuit" is something akin to the presumption that an automobile low on fuel will always automatically head for the nearest gasoline station.[10]

Putting aside for the moment Olds' proposal to restrict the expression, let us consider the view he criticizes. The claim (or assumption) that needs arouse motives has at least two interpretations. First, we might view it as

an empirical assertion, as a prediction that a motivated state reliably follows a deficient one. Secondly, the claim could be taken as a defining characteristic of need. Thus "need" would be *defined* as a deficit state that reliably initiates a motive.

Educators seem to vacillate between these two interpretations. Thus, Stephens begins with the empirical position by making the factual assumption that needs and motives are related. But a little later he seems to be *defining* a need state as one which brings on action:

Just as it is convenient to assume that some force or drive is giving direction and continuity to a series of individual acts, so it is convenient to assume that the drive is operating in the service of some *need*. A need is the thing which sets a drive in motion. . . . Need is a condition which calls for action toward a certain goal.[11]

On the other hand, Thayer and his associates, in their well-known study of secondary education, begin with the definitional conception:

Hence a working concept of an educational need must always be both personal and social in reference; it must always incorporate both the present desires of the individual and what they should desirably become.[12]

However, in the second half of the study they slip back into the empirical view. The authors simply identify the important student deficiencies and seem to assume, as a matter of fact, that students will be motivated to overcome the lacks so identified.

But even if educators agreed on one

[8] "Anything that is requisite to the maintenance of a state of affairs is a need." Asahel D. Woodruff, *The Psychology of Teaching*, 3rd ed. (New York: David McKay Co., Inc., 1951), p. 80.

[9] "A need is the lack of something that, if present, would further the welfare of the individual." Robert T. Beck, Walter W. Cook, and Nolan C. Kearney, *Curriculum in the Modern Elementary School*, 2nd ed. (Englewood Cliffs, N.J.: Prentice-Hall, Inc., 1960).

[10] James Olds, "A Physiological Study of Reward," in *Studies of Motivation*, edited by David C. McClelland (New York: Appleton-Century-Crofts, 1955), p. 135.

[11] J. M. Stephens, *Educational Psychology*, rev. ed. (New York: Holt, Rinehart & Winston, Inc., 1956), pp. 478f.

[12] V. T. Thayer, Caroline B. Zachry, and Ruth Kotinsky, *Reorganizing Secondary Education* (New York: Appleton-Century-Crofts, 1939), p. 38.

view of the lack-motive relation, difficulties would not disappear. For "needs (lacks) arouse motives" as an empirical claim is manifestly false. The world is full of things we do not have and do not want. To retain at least the hope of truth, "need" will have to refer to a subclass of lacks. However, there has been little success in specifying this subclass. If "need" refers to a state of deprivation, a loss of things once possessed, the motivational claim fares no better. Chronic failure, disease, poverty, and submission are not typically in demand when absent from lives they once afflicted. There are other possibilities. We can take some norm or end-state and use "need" to refer to deviations from the norm or the absence of conditions necessary for achieving the end-state. Survival is the most common nominee for this role, but "the welfare of the individual"[13] and "comfortable adjustment in some stage in life"[14] have also been proposed. Survival, however, is too miserly a conception, since there are deficiencies which arouse us without the threat of death (e.g., affection). On the other hand, the other proposed norms are too vague to be used as criteria (what constitutes "comfortable" adjustment?).

The definitional interpretation avoids most of these difficulties for on this view "need" is defined as a deficit state that initiates a motive. The price of this avoidance, however, is vagueness. For example, it is not clear whether this use of the expression requires present motivation or only past instances of motivation in similar circumstances. That is, when I say "$A$ needs $X$" am I saying that $X$ is now being sought or only that $X$ is now lacking and has been sought in

the past when absent? Discussion and use of "need" in education does not supply an answer. Yet if present motivation is required, then this use would differ very little from the motive use of "need."

Clarity is lacking on at least one other point. Here, as with motives, it is pertinent to ask about the degree of generality in the labels used to report the lacks. If I say someone needs $X$, precisely what is lacking? Do I say he lacks some particular friend, or just a friend, or affection? This question also goes unanswered in the literature. Yet if specific terms are allowable, it is possible that in some cases the teacher will encounter legitimate needs for things—like breaking windows—which go unrecognized in educational texts.

Finally, we can adopt Olds' suggestion and simply employ "need" to refer to deficiencies associated with certain norms or end-states. Any claim, definitional or empirical, that these deficiencies are related to motives could be dropped. What is immediately apparent is that such a practice would differ little from "need" in the prescriptive sense. We would then have two uses of "need," one to report deficiencies and another to prescribe for their alleviation. Surely this is linguistic luxury. We have discussed enough of the use of "need" as lack to suggest its confused state.

## 3. THE NEEDS-CURRICULUM

The needs concept has been made to carry a heavy theoretical load in many areas of education. This is especially true in the area of curriculum theory, as witnessed by the popularity of the claim that the public school curriculum should meet the needs of the students. For ease of reference, let me refer to this view as the "needs-policy"

---

[13] Beck, op. cit., p. 53.
[14] Woodruff, op. cit., p. 81.

and the resulting educational program as the "needs-curriculum." The needs-policy is considered to be a significant and certainly a controversial approach to public education. Thus it is not uncommon for someone to object to new proposals and practices by claiming that they will fail to meet some or all of the needs of some or all of the students. Also, some educational textbooks explicitly distinguish the needs-curriculum from other types of curricular organization.[15] And at least one major educational association has made need-meeting its clarion call.[16] By applying some of the results of the earlier analysis, I hope to show that this widespread belief in the significance of the needs-policy is unjustified. Depending upon the way "need" is interpreted, the needs-policy turns out to be sometimes trivial, sometimes indeterminate, and sometimes unsupported, but always unimportant.

PRESCRIPTIVE MEANINGS

When applying prescriptive meanings to the needs-policy, it is possible to treat the rule and directive uses together. We fulfill general requirements (rules) by applying them to specific cases (in directives), and the directives in turn presuppose rules. Therefore a curriculum derived from students' needs in either of these senses will inevitably invoke the other as well. When these uses are adopted, the needs-policy has two possible interpretations. The interpretation depends on whether *school* requirements or *social* requirements are employed for determining students' needs.

If the school requirements are viewed as the source of the curriculum, then the needs-policy is trivial. For, then, to say that the school should meet needs would be the same as asserting that the school should do what is necessary to fulfill its assigned tasks. No one could sensibly dispute this claim since it is a tautology. For the acceptance of something as one's objective already *implies* that one should do what is necessary to achieve it. And as expected, the denial of the needs-policy, so interpreted, involves a self-contradiction. With this interpretation, then, the needs-policy receives unanimous support, but only because it makes the trivial claim that schools should do what they should do.

If, on the other hand, needs are general social requirements, then the claim is significant (it says something), but what it says is either preposterous or incomplete. For affirming the needs-policy would now commit us to the view that the school should take responsibility for *all* the requirements imposed on children in our society. Such a school is barely conceivable.

Someone who supports this form of the needs-policy probably does not want us to take it literally. Rather he merely wants to emphasize that the school should assume a broader social responsibility. But if this is so, then the needs-policy is of secondary importance. For the real dispute arises not in answer to (1) "should the curriculum be based on needs of youth?" but in answer to (2) "which needs should the school be concerned with?" The needs-policy is an answer to (1) only; it is indeterminate with respect to (2), and a policy that does not offer an answer to (2) is incomplete.

There is one other prescriptive use

[15] Kenneth H. Hansen, *Public Education in American Society*, 2nd ed. (Englewood Cliffs, N. J.: Prentice-Hall, Inc., 1963). Galen J. Saylor and William M. Alexander, *Curriculum Planning* (New York: Holt, Rinehart & Winston, Inc., 1955), Chap. 9.

[16] National Association of Secondary-School Principals, *Planning for American Youth*, rev. ed. (Washington: The Association, 1951).

of "need"—the hypothetical use. The adoption of this meaning, however, would also culminate in a policy that was either preposterous or indęterminate.

## MOTIVATIONAL MEANINGS

The proposal fares no better when a motivational meaning is adopted. If we take needs to be very general motives or dispositions (need for recognition, affection, achievement, etc.), even then, as Bode has demonstrated, it is not enough to say that schools should meet needs. There are different ways of gaining affection, status, achievement, and the like;[17] that is, there is a great variety of "objects" that these general terms can cover. The needs-policy is again incomplete; it does not tell us which of these to teach. Yet debates arise over the *mode* of satisfaction, not over satisfaction per se.

There is another point to note here. Looked at as a proposal about our most general goals or propensities (i.e., "basic needs"), the needs-policy once more resembles a mere truism. Any curriculum can be said to assist students in meeting their needs. Every curriculum is a needs-curriculum. Of course, the needs-policy is not a tautology; it would be possible to deny it without self-contradiction. But it would be decidedly odd to find a curriculum that is said to be unrelated to the students' basic needs. The reason is that the very conception of basic needs makes them so ubiquitous and all-embracing that no such sustained activity as schooling could be completely alien to them.

However, one can *choose* whether or

[17] Boyd H. Bode, *Progressive Education at the Crossroads* (New York: Newson & Company, 1938), Chap. 4.

not to talk the language of basic needs when discussing curricula. It is still possible to ignore the relation of schooling to students' needs without denying that there is some connection.

In contradistinction to the general approach, one can take a microscopic view and use "need" to refer to specific motives ("have a bicycle," "build a boat"). If "meet needs" is taken to mean "assist the student to reach his goal," then the needs-policy is more determinate and certainly not redundant. The difficulty with this interpretation is that it has no supporters.

To summarize the discussion thus far, I have tried to show that the general proposal that schools meet students' needs is trivial or indeterminate or unsupported, depending on what a need is taken to be. This might account for the popularity of the needs-policy. For by a nimble equivocation on the meaning of "need" a supporter of the needs-policy can feel as if he were making a daring proposal which could not possibly be wrong (no mean feat!).

These conclusions should not be overgeneralized. There are many specific contexts in education in which the claim "we should meet this need for $X$" is significant. This might be said, for example, to report the discovery of a condition necessary to the achievement of some accepted goal. Or on some particular occasion it might be uttered to warn a teacher against unnecessary activities. My strictures apply only to the attempt to use "need" in a general policy statement, but even here there may exist another way of saying it.

Thus far I have been treating the proposal "schools should meet needs" as a prescriptive generalization from which one can deduce that if $X$ is a need then the schools should deal with it. This is certainly a reasonable approach to proposals of this sort. Thus, if someone proposed that schools develop intellectual discipline, our very first step would be to discover the meaning of "intellectual discipline." For this information is necessary if we are to deduce the kind of curriculum being proposed.

One sign of the usualness of this treatment is the widespread use of the *reductio ad absurdum* argument in educational debate. But to claim that some proposal is unjustified because one can deduce foolish consequences, is to assume that one can deduce consequences at all. To do so is to treat the proposal as a prescriptive generalization.

But suppose the needs-policy is not a prescriptive generalization. Then it would not necessarily have the weaknesses enumerated earlier. But what else could it be? It could be the *title* given to a set of curriculum practices. When the needs-policy is viewed as a title, it is not necessary that there be any logical relation between the policy itself and the parts of the proposed curriculum. The "relation" is similar to that which obtains between the title and content of novel. Titles of novels are chosen because they are suggestive of the content (in *some* way) and appealing in their own right. So it is with the needs-policy (on this interpretation). Actually the needs-curriculum could conceivably ignore students' needs. The term "need" might be employed in the title because it suggests necessity, and necessity connotes importance, and the proposed studies are considered important. This example borders on the absurd, but it typifies the connection that exists between policy statement and curriculum in this view.

Other assertions in education seem to function similarly. "Education for life adjustment" and "teach the child, not the content" are ludicrous when cast in the role of generalizations. The first, because of the appalling vagueness and ambiguity of "adjustment." The second, because the notion of teaching someone without teaching him something is nonsense. We call such assertions slogans; they have the "logic" of titles and are chosen because of their appeal. I am suggesting that the needs-policy might belong to this group.

This interpretation becomes even more plausible when carried a step further. For it would explain why the ambiguous term "need" survives and even thrives in educational writing and discussion. Its vagueness and multiplicity of meaning, far from impairing its usefulness, enhances it. For its utterance in a slogan in a suitable setting may further or maintain some educational enterprises.

Consider the role of the administrator with its attendant conflicts and dilemmas. The person occupying such a position is frequently called upon to announce policy statements to a public replete with competing and incompatible educational expectations. The energy given in defense of a seemingly partisan policy would detract from other vital administrative functions. Such assertions as "our schools meet needs . . ." may help, in part at least, to avoid these impairments. For a task is performed and a "policy" announced which is least apt to require lengthy debilitating defense. Similarly, the administrator must maintain authority when dealing with teachers more competent in some subject than himself. What better directive can he give than "be sure to meet the needs of the student."

The appraisal of the needs-policy as a slogan calls for a new approach. For here the triviality, the vagueness, and the indeterminacy are boons, not failings. The t∍rms employed in slogans must appeal, yet be flexible; they must arouse without suggesting anything definite. If "need" has become too closely identified with a definite and controversial program, as I believe it has, then whatever utility it once possessed as a slogan has vanished.

# 41

# Pressures to Learn Can Be Blocks to Learning

## JOHN I. GOODLAD

Certain pressures block children's learning. Sometimes these pressures stem from beyond the schools; they are part of the larger society. Sometimes these pressures arise inside the classroom; they are part of the teaching-learning environment. We shall concern ourselves here with the latter type.

### PREPACKAGED CONTENT
### AND INAPPROPRIATE REWARDS

Schools often proceed as though the thinking already had been done. Somebody, somewhere, thought up everything in advance. There's just no more thinking to be done. Or, worse still, nobody had anything to do with it in the first place. Ideas are the product of immaculate conception!

The task of curriculum construction, following this concept of learning, be-

John I. Goodlad, "Pressures to Learn Can Be Blocks to Learning," *Childhood Education*, XXXVI, No. 4 (December 1959), 162-65. Reprinted by permission of the Association for Childhood Education International, 3615 Wisconsin Avenue, N. W., Washington, D.C., and the author.

comes the prepackaging of content into neat, consumable bundles. These bundles are then stored away in a curricular deep-freeze and, ultimately, displayed before the eager eyes of hopeful pupils. But, alas, once removed from cold storage, the fast-thawing goods quickly spoil and swiftly smell. The pupils are less than enchanted.

Such a concept of learning leads naturally to fixed patterns of teaching. If the purpose of learning is to consume, then the purpose of teaching is to dispense. Successful consumption is easily recognized and approved.

In the process of dispensing and consuming, both teacher and learner often become confused over ends. For example . . . Miss Manton tells a story to her second-grade class. (Of course, there's no such thing as a "second-grade" class but we'll abide by the conventions.) Before completing it, she asks, "How do you think this story ends?" So far, so good. The children eagerly pose conclusions. To Tommy's response, Miss Manton answers, "No, I don't quite see how that could be." To Susan's, "No, I don't think so." To Mildred's, "No, that's not *what I'm thinking of.*"

A shift has occurred, a subtle but significant shift. A process of inquiry, a process of putting ideas together to infer a logical conclusion, has shifted to a mere guessing game. Guess the right answer and the teacher's warm beam of approval floods down upon you. Learning becomes not a search for meaning, not an exciting pursuit whetted by surprise and the satisfaction of true accomplishment, but a search for responses that bring rewards. Press the right button and gain approval.

Some students learn the process well. They go through high school, college, and life burdened with this misguided conception of education. So many nods of approval add up to a B, so many B's add up to an A.B. and an A.B. opens certain doors. In graduate school they ask, "Mr. Professor, what do I need to do [to gain your approval] in your course?" In business they become good organization men.

This is education? I think not. This is pressure to conform, social pressure of the most insidious sort, worming its way like a bacterial infection into the heart of the learning-teaching process, distorting and contaminating it until true education withers and dies.

Some educators writhe in horror over the imminent danger of machines taking over part of the learning-teaching act. Perhaps, for some aspects of learning, machines are more promise than threat. At least they focus on learning for learning's sake. You press the button and you're right or you're wrong. No syrupy words of commendation, no halos, for guessing the teacher's mind. The machines, too, will become monsters to be feared when they dispense peanuts, candy and chewing gum for pressing the right button. Once more, the ends of education will be contaminated and distorted.

## PERCEPTIONS OF COVERAGE

A crippling perception of coverage often is part of the teaching-learning environment. We must be up to here by Hallowe'en, this much farther by Thanksgiving. Heaven help us if we aren't halfway there by Christmas. Halfway where? Don't ask silly questions. *There*, of course! On to Easter. By May, we're loping out in front, all by ourselves. And the children? Don't be ridiculous. We're almost *there*! A little prodding, a little pushing, a little skipping—and it's June. We're *there* for another year.

Such a concept of coverage creates immeasurable pressures to learn. It, too, is based on a "sacred cow" view of the curriculum. Here are the important things to be learned, laid out in neat order, to be "covered" at a set pace one after the other in the process of getting an education.

There is, indeed, a fairly respectable theory of knowing to support this view of the curriculum. But imagine, for a moment, the problem of selection in to-day's world! How do teachers determine what is of most worth among all from which to select? The little that can be put into the curriculum in relation to all that is available is as a handful of straw in relation to thousands of silos filled with straw.

And yet, we often act as though *the* most important content already had been selected for all time and appropriately arranged for consumption. We have, indeed, our sacred cow standing stubbornly in the path of reason. Do we dare to kill it?

## EXTERNAL STANDARDS

When one troubles to push beyond the criticisms, the panaceas, and the slogans mouthed in the name of educational betterment, one sees that many seeking to be heard conceive standards to be something external to the learning process. "Higher standards, more rigor, better quality," come the pleas. "If they can't learn," says one, "kick 'em out. That's what we did at West Point."

It is difficult (and unwise) for teachers to ignore the clamor, ever mindful as most are of the need to do better. But, sometimes, we ignore our own beliefs about learning. Short-route methods take on a special attractiveness. Drill replaces the search for meaning. Children repeat their incorrect responses along with correct ones. Teacher presentation replaces pupil exploration. Routes that *appear* to be most direct take precedence.

Learning is seldom the shortest distance between two points. Learning often is oblique and circuitious. The means that appear to be most roundabout often lead most directly to the ends sought.

The net result of the pressure of inappropriate standards is likely to be less, not more, learning.

True standards are found within, not outside of, the learning process. True standards relate means most appropriately to ends. True standards free rather than restrict the human mind in its search for order and truth. Standards perceived to be outside of learning itself are blocks to learning.

## SOME GROUND TO STAND ON

Each of us readily identifies with some part of the foregoing. In recognizing ourselves we can in part right ourselves—but only in part. We're all caught up in a massive piece of machinery that answers not to our commands. Some basic changes are needed.

*First, we need a concept of curriculum that better defines our freedoms.* Freedom is a disciplined thing. It comes to the individual with increased understanding of his areas of choice as well as his areas of no choice. The sailor who sails strange waters is free to cruise and to explore if he possesses good charts. The sailor who lacks such charts must either pine away on the shore or then grope his way cautiously, ever fearful of lurking reefs.

A curriculum plan that better defines our freedoms separates the relatively variable from the relatively constant. A few facts—particularly in the linguistic and mathematical realms—are here for a while, unless the structure of knowing of which they are a part collapses. The learning of them does not call for undue imagination, as though there were wide degrees of choice. In fact, imagination may well be a block to the learning of such facts.

Some facts are transitory or, at best, quite incidental (even accidental) to the learning of larger concepts. Such facts should be subordinated to the larger ends of formulating and employing concepts. The teacher is free to use whatever data seem appropriate to the clarification of larger concepts.

Most curriculum plans now in existence fail to recognize distinctions such as those suggested above. As a result, everything in a plan (even when labeled "for consideration only") becomes relatively constant—to be learned by all. Thus we get our sacred cow.

*Second, we need a better understanding of the learner realities before us.* We act as though there were only shades of difference among learners—as though, perhaps, the brightest child were twice as bright as the dullest. Actually, the differences in reasoning among slow and bright children almost defy mathematical comparison. One is thousands of times more proficient than the other in certain kinds of abstract reasoning.

In seeking appropriate teaching

techniques, we do well to approach these differences as differences in kind (as between a cat and a human) rather than in degree. Thus, the pedagogical road to learning for the slow may not be more of what was good for the bright. Similarly, the best procedure for the bright may not be just a little less of methods that worked for the average. We need experimental studies designed to find the optimal learning conditions for many kinds and degrees of differences among learners. The studies needed will not be conducted until potential experimenters catch a vision of pupil variability radically different from the view presently in vogue.

*Third, we need a concept of learning embracing unlimited expectancy for human creativity.* We know little about the potential creativity inherent in the human organism. We know only that our school practices tend to recognize and reward certain abilities out of proportion to other abilities. In a very real sense, then, creativity comes to be defined sociologically rather than biologically and psychologically. What we value most shifts with the ebb and flow of societal tides. What we value in peacetime we value not in time of war.

There is little likelihood of social pressure ceasing to reward only certain kinds of creativity. Social pressure is part of a real world. But the schools can do much to keep open-ended the drive that is human creativity. Schools must avoid like the plague external rewards for certain kinds of learning that freeze the creative process in its infancy. They do well to encourage creativity as an end in itself—creativity is many things—rather than to promote and reward accomplishment in those limited aspects of human activity that happen to be currently popular.

There are appropriate as well as inappropriate pressures to learn. Somewhere along the educative and miseducative road that is life the learner must respond to compelling forces within him, forces seeking to repeat the satisfactory experience of coming to know for one's self. The best way to make sure that these forces never will hold sway is to substitute for them pressures from without—pressures to please, pressures to cover and pressures to conform.

# 42

# Intellectual Mastery and Mental Health

## MILLIE ALMY

A pencilled slogan, "Kill mental health," has appeared on so many billboards of late that it no longer excites comment. Is the demise of "mental health" perhaps to date from the moment it became a cliché? So far as the schools are concerned, the answer seems all too clear.

Since the 1930's most American schools have had an avowed concern for children's social relations, their personal problems, and their personal adjustment. In many instances extensive psychological services have been developed for the early detection of emotional disturbance and mental illness. But the main responsibility for the promotion of mental health has lain with the teachers. Imbued with the notion that they must teach the "whole child" (as though there were some other kind), they have struggled to understand the complexities of a child growing up in his family and the intricacies of his life with his peers.

Millie Almy, "Intellectual Mastery and Mental Health," *Teachers College Record*, LXIII, No. 6 (March 1962), 468-78. Reprinted by permission.

Beyond this, many have attempted in various ways to help children to cope more or less directly with these problems.

### LIMITS ON TEACHERS

But the teacher's influence, however good it may be, is spread over some 25 individuals (or in the case of many high school teachers, 125). How effective can he be? This question becomes particularly acute, in view of the fact that the mental health function of the teacher has so often been seen as something apart from his teaching functions. One of the first mental hygiene specialists to call attention to this was Ruth Kotinsky.

In an article with Jules Coleman (9), she put the issue very directly: What is the school's business? Have the schools the personnel, the facilities, the time to take on mental health responsibilities beyond those inherent in carrying through the functions traditionally accepted as their business? Are there not potentialities for influencing mental health in teaching the skills and understandings necessary to cope with the environment, the skills of communication, the ways of identifying and solving problems rationally, and the rudiments needed for a vocation?

The decade in which Ruth Kotinsky raised these questions was, by and large, a decade of retreat for the schools. Beset by criticism from within and without, many schools abandoned so-called frills and fads and placed renewed emphasis on the fundamentals, on skills and content and subject matter.

So far as mental health is concerned, the decade may perhaps be labeled one of beginning clarification. The appearance in 1958 of *Current Concepts in Mental Health* by Marie Jahoda (7) indicated initial progress toward the eventual establishment of some empirical indicators for mental health. One of the six components of the multiple criteria proposed by Jahoda seems especially relevant for the school. This is the component of environmental mastery.

Environmental mastery encompasses adequacy in love, work, play, and in interpersonal relationships, in adaptation and adjustment, and in problem solving. The child undoubtedly formulates his basic attitudes toward love, work, play, and other people in considerable part before he enters school, but the school confronts the child with new possibilities. It introduces him to persons whose ways of responding are different from those he has known at home. It provides him with knowledge of many sorts of work and play. It develops skills that enable him to investigate and to cope more effectively with the world of people and things. Although the knowledge and the skills the school offers can be acquired elsewhere, no other agency can be held so directly responsible for this aspect of mental health.

To say this does not deny that developments in other components of the personality may affect environmental mastery. Mastery obviously also involves attitudes toward self, the development of autonomy, and the perception of reality. Conversely, progress toward mastery has repercussions on each of the other facets of the mental health criterion.

## CHILDREN'S REACTIONS

We can only conjecture about how effectively the schools further environmental mastery at the present time. Everyone knows youngsters who have not only found satisfaction from their schooling, but have emerged from it with real convictions about their own abilities and their future. They anticipate mastery. One 15-year-old, shortly following the announcement of Sputnik, wrote this about his reactions:

What a time to live! In five years we'll be on the moon!

Every time I hear someone moaning about how he should have lived in the days of the Old West when men were men and about how the world today is a hopeless mess, I nearly throw up.

And I want to be a part of it. So the Russians did it first. More power to them. They're going to need it to keep ahead of us now. 18,000 miles an hour. Ten years ago Bell had just finished going eight hundred and astonishing the world. Now, we're on our way. Vanguard will succeed, and Sputnik will have a couple U.S.-type companions.

And then in a few years, I come along. I and my generation are going to be the ones to see this thing off. We may not get to Mars, but the first men to leave the earth's atmosphere are going to be my contemporaries. Maybe me, if I can be so lucky. What a chance! How can a pioneer of three thousand miles of earth be compared to a pioneer of forty thousand miles of space? I'm on my way. Just watch my smoke!

But in contrast to the youngsters who regard the future with equanimity and see themselves taking active part in it, there are others who are resigned to passivity. They spend their days in waiting —waiting to be old enough for first grade, waiting to graduate from elementary school, waiting to graduate from high school, and then waiting for college, or waiting for marriage, or waiting for a job that involves waiting for quitting time. Then they wait for the coming of their children, who, unless war comes, will carry on the endless waiting, the endless rounds of meaningless activity. Or, as one commentator on the American scene has put it, "America will not perish from a bomb. It will perish from boredom."

The picture is exaggerated of course. But its prototype does exist. And to the extent that youngsters emerge from our schools without commitments, with little sense of personal challenge, beset by apathy, the schools appear to have failed in furthering environmental mastery. Furthermore, children who lack any real feelings of involvement, who evade using their intellectual powers, are probably to be found both in schools that are clearly traditional and in schools that still bear some of the trappings of progressivism.

The crucial test of any school's contribution to mental health lies not so much in the skills and knowledge it purports to teach as in its effectiveness in helping youngsters to incorporate these into their day-to-day living. It is a matter of using such skills and knowledge to strengthen and enhance each child's personal resources. But the question of whether the average school makes an appreciable difference in these respects is an open one. It is a question unlikely to be answered satisfactorily until certain basic issues have been resolved.

One such issue has to do with the matter of individuality in learning and thinking. To what extent can the school, predicated on the notion that children are to be taught in groups, provide adequately for each individual? Related to this is the problem of differences in the ways of learning and of thinking at different ages. When there is so much to be learned, how much leeway can the school have to adapt its instruction to these differences?

Still another issue relates to the fact that the glib use of words does not always reflect genuine understanding. Traditionally, the school has emphasized the verbal transmission of knowledge to the exclusion of other ways of knowing. How long can this continue if students are to develop the critical, creative thinking demanded for mastery in a complex modern world?

## TEACHING VS. LEARNING

An issue of somewhat different but nonetheless critical order has to do with the relationship between teaching and learning. Schools are prone to describe their curriculum in terms of what is taught. The more important question, of course, is "What has been learned?" But the nature of the learning very likely turns as much on *how* something is taught as it does on *what* is taught.

Around each of these issues are many questions that schools must face before they can hope to fulfill their mental health roles adequately.

First, the matter of *individuality in learning*. Although schools have long paid lip service to "individual differences," most school practice assumes common, average, or typical ways of learning. Yet, it is a specific emotional concern, a specific tendency to see a problem differently from the way others see it, a specific sensitivity to what one sees or hears or feels, that either inhibits or enhances learning. Clinical studies have shown that children's propensities for learning are related to their ways of coping with the emotional conflicts inherent in growing up. The accomplishment of a particular learning task may lead toward a constructive resolution of conflict for one child. The same task may be unproductive or even defeating for another child. Without training in recognizing the influence of these deeper motivations, can a teacher adequately diagnose the child's needs as a learner? To what extent can the curriculum provide leeway for the child to make the appropriate use of his unique ways of learning at the same time that he adapts to the ways of others? To further environmental mastery, where shall the balance between the nurturance of individuality and conformity to group trends be struck?

At a time when the furore of "keeping up with the Russians" puts a premium on the acceleration of learning, many persons press the schools to begin the "fundamentals" earlier, to start mathematics, science, and foreign languages sooner, and to push the "gifted" ahead. Although many children have already demonstrated their abilities to learn more than has typically been expected, many questions about pacing learning to development arise. For example, evidence from the administration of thousands of IQ tests, from other studies of conceptual development, from Piaget's research on children's thinking, as well as from psychoanalytic studies of young children, indicates that the young child's learning and his thinking is of an imaginative, manipulative, exploratory kind. Not until

the middle school years does he begin to organize and systematize his knowledge in a truly logical fashion. Even then, he is still very much bound to the concrete in his thinking, and not until near adolescence do abilities to deal meaningfully with abstractions emerge.

## PRICE OF HURRY

What are the effects of the early introduction of generalizations and abstractions for which the child may have few experimental referents? Is it possible to further a kind of verbal environmental mastery at an early age, but at a price? The price, perhaps, of a lack of empathy toward one's fellows or what Jerome Bruner (4) has termed a lack of "passion" for ideas? Conversely, what happens to the child who is held in school to a concrete level when his mind is already taken up with the abstract? Is the concrete *always* enriching?

Many schools, from the kindergarten through the college, have reacted to current criticisms by putting more stress on "knowledge," which may be anything from the alphabet and the multiplication tables to the dates of the Punic Wars or the basic principles of atomic theory. Such knowledge often is acquired largely by memorization and repetitive drill and all too often is tested in similar fashion. No one doubts the importance of many of the facts youngsters are supposed to learn, but in relation to a mental health criterion of environmental mastery, the crucial question is their relevance to an individual coping with and understanding a changing world. A youngster needs to know facts; he also needs to know how and when to apply them. He needs, further, to know how to appraise and evaluate a given situation. Above all, he needs to know that there are many ways of knowing. The scientist does not always arrive at new ideas through processes of logical deduction. New insights often arise from undirected fantasy or from periods of conscious preoccupation with some other activity. A particular event can be "known" through direct sensory participation; it can be weighed, measured, analyzed into its components, put into a larger context, but often it may also be played with, painted, or danced.

Does the school contribute to environmental mastery when it leaves the student with the impression that there are so few ways of knowing? Or are *all* the ways of knowing not the business of the school?

With appalling frequency, many young teachers say today, "What I learned in my education courses does not help me in the classroom." Those of us who teach teachers often retort that they are merely looking for "recipes." But are they? Are they not saying that we have taught them about children, about learning, and about thinking without teaching them *how* to direct learning or *how* to change thinking?

In dealing with the nature of teaching as related to the nature of the learning and the thinking that ensues, we have come to what is likely the basic issue for mental health in the schools. Not until we know more specifically how teaching affects thinking can we know how extensively teachers can influence the development of environmental mastery.

When John Dewey formulated his ideas about learning and thinking, he surely intended to help youngsters toward a meaningful, intellectual mastery of the environment. But neither Dewey nor his followers spelled out in sufficient detail how a teacher may appraise the many kinds of thinking

he encounters among his pupils, nor how he may help them to shift from ineffective to effective kinds. Too often the teacher, receiving his notions of Dewey's philosophy fourth or fifth hand, has been left with no better criterion for the value of a particular activity than "they learn by doing." Once a teacher loses sight of the intellectual goals to be realized in the pursuit of any activity, it often deteriorates into a free-for-all in which the immediate emotional concerns and needs of the youngsters dominate the situation. Many teachers are ill-equipped to deal directly with these and retreat from them to a more stereotyped and sterile but "safe" kind of teaching.

When the teacher's *primary* function is clearly seen to be that of teaching skills and understandings and ways of solving problems, it is clear that knowledge of children's ways of thinking and learning is an essential part of his professional repertoire. But, in addition, he needs skill in influencing that thinking and learning. Without such skills, it is doubtful that any teacher can effectively fulfill the mental health functions which are inherent in his role.

A few educators and psychologists are now beginning to examine the nature of the relationship between what the teacher does and what the children think. Such examination promises much for eventual understanding of the specific ways teachers can further environmental mastery. Current research programs at Bank Street College (3), for example, include an analysis of the teacher's involvement in the processes of the child's learning and thinking. Along with this goes study of the various ways the teacher offers emotional support to the child and helps him to build inner controls.

Many other centers are carrying on research related to thinking, and interest in the nature of teaching increases steadily. Examination of some of the research dealing with the nature of teaching on the one hand, and the nature of thinking on the other, suggests that both of these areas constitute important new resources for mental health in education.

## ANALYSES OF TEACHING

Most of the research related to teaching is directed toward the questions of what it means to be teacher and what it is that a teacher *does* in relation to his pupils that results in their learning and their thinking.

There is nothing new in the notion that effective teachers present material, ask questions, clarify understandings, and so on, in different ways from less effective teachers. What is new is the attempt to arrive at a framework for analyzing the teacher's behavior so that it becomes possible to pinpoint the places where his questions or his comments either enhance or forestall good thinking.

Interest in such analysis has arisen spontaneously in several different centers. Bellack and Huebner (2), discussing the need for a theory of teaching, point out that in the 25 years prior to 1956 little if any research was directed specifically toward teaching. Apparently, in what would seem to be equally important activities in the school—the *giving* and the *taking* of instruction—much more systematic attention has been given to taking than to giving. B. O. Smith (14), an educational philosopher at the University of Illinois, is engaged in an attempt to describe and classify the actions, both verbal and expressive, that compose the teacher's repertoire. A colleague of

Smith's, M. J. Aschner (1), describes the teacher as a strategist and tactician in the campaign for learning, noting that the teacher's repertoire includes not only what he does to instruct pupils, such as defining, explaining, showing, and admonishing, but also observing what his pupils do and say in response to these actions. "He does so in order to predict—to diagnose and adapt his teaching to the pupils' present state of comprehension and progress in learning, to appraise the quality of their reasoning and to assess their emotional reactions to the situation of the moment." This notion of prediction, Dr. Aschner cautions, is not the same as that implied in much current research in the psychological laboratory. Teachers do not see themselves as manipulators of student behavior by push-button techniques: "It is the teacher's task and purpose not to condition the responses or the learnings of his pupils, but to develop in them their own capacities to think and to act responsibly."

Marie Hughes (5) and her colleagues at the University of Utah have also attempted to analyze teachers' behavior in the classroom. They have studied teaching functions relating to the obviously intellectual content of the classroom experience, such as stimulating interest, clarifying content, and evaluating results, and also functions relating to the affective aspects of the learning situation. Many of the immediate outcomes of their study offer real cause for discouragement about the effectiveness of teachers in furthering active environmental mastery. Teachers judged "good" by their administrators exercised the controlling functions most frequently and most pervasively. They told the children both what they should do and how they should do it, what they should answer and how they should answer. The teachers gave the children very little opportunity to explore or expand ideas, or to make comparisons and inferences. The thinking processes they demanded were almost exclusively limited to identification and memory.

Dreary as these findings are, they also seem to hold some promise. These teachers were not "bad" teachers; they were not mean; they were simply ineffective. The reason for this probably lies in the fact that no one had ever helped them to see the variety of specific ways they could respond to children and, having so responded, the specific ways they could build on the ideas of the children. Given an opportunity to study an analysis of their own behavior and to discuss it with a nonthreatening consultant or counselor, could they not learn to modify their approach and to direct it toward opening new and richer avenues of inquiry?

## SAUCE FOR THE GOOSE

Lawrence Kubie (10), in a devastating critique of education, has suggested that overemphasis on repetitive drill (and much that these teachers were doing *would* fall under the heading of repetitive drill) is symptomatic of anxiety, anger, and repression. But we may ask whether some (though by no means all) of the anxiety and the anger which teachers bring to the teaching situation may not arise in part out of the frustration involved in knowing that they are expected to do *something* about the learning of these children, while they remain basically uncertain as to *what* to do.

If we expect the acquisition of knowledge, skills, and understandings to enhance the ego development of youngsters, it is no less reasonable to anticipate that knowledge, skills, and understandings—provided always that their rele-

vance to the teaching situation is clear—should also strengthen the teacher.

Some oblique evidence on this point comes from a current study by Jersild (8), relating to the effects of personal psychotherapy and psychoanalysis on teachers. Some of these teachers reported that as their therapy progressed, they were able to see more clearly and specifically how their own behavior in the classroom influenced the learning and the thinking of their pupils. At the same time, some of them noted an increasing ability to understand and hence to clarify the youngsters' confusions. Although, in these instances, the teachers' insights into their own functioning as teachers came only after therapy, their comments often suggested that they would not only have welcomed but could have benefited at an early point in their careers from a more penetrating analysis of what was involved in teaching.

Studies of teacher behavior by Levin (11) and others provide good evidence that teachers who have a high interest in children are most likely to remain in teaching. Such individuals, it would seem, would not be frightened but, rather, rewarded by an opportunity to examine their own techniques. They might welcome study of their own ways of relating to children with a view to seeing how these affect children's learning and thinking.

The notion that teachers and teachers-in-training would benefit from analysis of their teaching implies that such analysis would not be directed toward a single "right" way. Rather, consideration of the *variety* of ways one might respond in a given situation should lead to flexibility and help in the quick "on the spot" decisions which are part of the challenge and the fun of teaching.

Ultimately, of course, any analysis

of the task of teaching leads back to the question of its effectiveness in relation to the achievement of the pupil. Some of the teacher's actions may further the pupil's learning and thinking. Others may serve only to block and confuse him. It is no accident that much of the current interest in the analysis of teaching comes from centers where there has also been continuing research related to thinking as revealed in the classroom.

## RESEARCH ON THINKING

The theoretical views on thinking held by two psychologists, Jean Piaget and Jerome Bruner, appear to have particular significance for the eventual resolution of some of the issues raised earlier.

Piaget's position, although well formulated, has been difficult for American investigators to interpret. But, many former skeptics are now impressed by his later work and by independent research validating a number of his ideas. These relate particularly to the question of developmental differences in thinking. Piaget uses the principles of formal logic as a basis for his analysis of thinking. He has arrived at a schematization of the emerging developmental stages of the abilities to deal either with increasingly complex problems or with simple problems in more efficient ways. Within the period covered by the years of schooling, there are three such stages. A preoperational or representational stage extends into the early childhood period. During this phase, much of the child's thinking is characterized by an inability to separate his own goals from the means for achieving them. In the later stage of concrete operations, extending from approximately 7 to 11 years, the child becomes increasingly able to organize

the means for achievement of the goal independently of the goal itself. His operations are internalized and reversible, but he is still bound very closely to the immediately present object world. In the stage of formal operations, beginning around the age of 12, a stage which is preparatory to adult thinking, the ability to use hypothetical reasoning and controlled experimentation develops. The child is no longer bound to the concrete, but can deal directly with abstractions.

By and large, Piaget has seemed to his American colleagues to neglect the important role of motivation in thinking. Indeed, he has specified that the "structures" of intellect and affect must be regarded separately. Nevertheless, as various psychoanalytic writers have shown, and as he and his colleague, Inhelder (6), have brilliantly demonstrated in an analysis of adolescent thinking, the shift from one level of thinking to another is in many ways very closely bound up with the individual's life situation and with the changing nature of his needs, wishes, and desires.

Piaget is a genetic psychologist and biologist. He has never fully developed the implications of his position for the schooling of children. The main implication is, however, almost immediately apparent. If there are, as his theory indicates, built-in limitations in thinking at a particular level, then to confront the pupil with problems whose solutions are based on logical operations beyond his comprehension at that level must be to confront him with a meaningless task. If the solution his teacher expects is beyond him, it appears that for the moment at least, he and his teacher are really speaking in different languages. The student can, perhaps, if the teacher demands it, learn a solution by rote memory; but the words he mouths are little more than gibberish so far as real insight is concerned.

Jerome Bruner, unlike Piaget, does not deal with developmental differences in thinking, and his emphasis on motivation is somewhat different. Nevertheless, his viewpoint is in many ways compatible with Piaget's. His mode of attack on the nature of thinking seems likely to provide new insights into both the problem of individuality and that of the variety of ways of knowing.

Bruner views thinking as a complex process involving categorization, organization, transformation, and evaluation. Motivation is implied in and gives direction to each of these. This scheme for analyzing intellectual performance is currently being tested with children. Although children younger than ten years have not been involved in this study, the results are assumed to have general application, certainly to older children and probably to younger ones.

These youngsters under Bruner's observation have encountered a wide range of intellectual tasks, many of them clearly parallel to those usually involved in school learning. Examination of their performances in detail has indicated some of the dimensions on which this theory can be measured. One such dimension is *power*, which has to do with the youngster's perseverance and the range and order of approaches he uses in attempting to solve a problem. Another dimension involves individual *style* in thinking, a matter of the way the concepts the child brings to the problem are organized. A third, referred to as *conceptual distance*, reflects the child's ability to avoid becoming bound in the immediate and obvious and to keep his eventual goal in view. A dimension of *involvement* measures the degree of separation of the task from personal needs and demands. In this connection, it may be noted that some children appear to be almost exclusively task-oriented, whereas others are always much more directed toward pleasing the experimenter. Finally, there is a *rigidity-flexibility* dimension, related to the ability to recognize errors and change one's plans accordingly.

Bruner (4), has recently reported a study comparing learning effectiveness in normal children and in children with learning blocks—those with adequate or superior intelligence who were unable to learn in school.

## LEARNING BLOCKS

The findings bear directly on the question of the school's responsibility for mental health. The children with learning blocks revealed cognitive organizations differing radically from those of the normal youngsters. Their thinking was dominated by what Bruner calls "preemptive metaphors," principles of organization biased toward overinclusion and overgeneralization. For example, a child whose early experiences have reinforced the idea that "things can hurt me" views his environment as a source of potentially disruptive events. A youngster of this sort is so busy reading possible destruction into the learning problems set for him and defending himself against it that he never copes with the reality problems.

Bruner believes that the thinking of persons who are "defenders" rather than "copers" has never moved beyond the action-and-affect-laden conceptualization characteristic of the young child. Such conceptualization, of course, also survives in the creativity of the artist and sometimes serves the disciplined thinking of the inventor and initiator. But it is not preemptive and distorting as it is in the child who thinks only defensively.

Bruner theorizes that the prevention of learning difficulties is dependent on three factors in the early history of the child. These include opportunities for play, opportunities for identification, and freedom from excessive drive and anxiety. Undoubtedly the family contributes most importantly to these, but the influence of the school is not negligible. A closer examination of these factors indicates some of the ways the school may function to further children's abilities to think adequately and to cope with their environment realistically rather than merely defensively.

Play, according to Bruner and others, reduces the pressures of impulse and incentive and makes intrinsic learning possible. Piaget also indicates that play is important, especially during the period when the child is developing basic notions about the nature of the world. Thus, a first step toward the conviction that intellectual activity has an inherent worth comes in doing things for fun, and an early childhood education program based on play takes on added significance.

So far as identification is concerned, the child first emulates the models he finds in his own family. But teachers, provided they are individuals for whom children can have warm and positive feelings, may also serve as models and, if they are competent, importantly influence children's ways of thinking.

The third factor mentioned by Bruner also relates to the behavior of the teacher. Excessive drive and anxiety inhibit effective thinking. Too much pressure on learning, too many external rewards and punishments, lead to blocking and functional stupidity on the part of the would-be learner.

Illustrative of the inevitable enmeshing of teaching and thinking is a recent six-year study by Sarason (12) and others. This inquiry revealed many children with good intellectual potential who were unable to function adequately in school. It appeared that very often the techniques used by their teachers mobilized rather than allayed these children's anxieties. Unfortunately, relatively few of the teachers were able to identify the anxiety-prone children in their classrooms. Nor were they able to avoid anxiety-arousing techniques in dealing with them.

Undoubtedly, many teachers are benignly unaware of the inhibiting effects certain comments and expressions have on many children. Others deliberately push and prod in the mistaken notion that they are thus providing needed motivation. They assume that learning is necessarily painful and overlook the fact that success in learning often provides a powerful incentive to further learning.

## LEARNING BY MACHINE

Evidence on this point comes from current research on teaching machines. This research also throws considerable light on many of the relationships between teaching and thinking. Teaching machines, as developed under the direction of B. F. Skinner (13), operate on the principle that a very complex concept can be broken down into a series of related ideas—learning these ideas step by step according to a "program" leads to eventual comprehension of the large idea. Unlike a textbook, which may skip an essential step for the student, each step in the program for the machine must be made explicit. The person who sets up a program must not only know the subject matter to be taught, but also the thinking processes through which it can be mastered. The record of the student's errors indicates the places where the programmer failed to anticipate confusion. The machines may thus contribute to improved knowledge of both teaching and thinking.

Many educators have taken a dim view of the development of the machines for a variety of reasons. The machines do involve the manipulation of student behavior by push-button techniques. Some of their appeal to the learner may depend on their novelty, and that appeal may diminish. They promote some kinds of thinking and learning, but are inappropriate for others. The effectiveness of any machine is entirely dependent on the nature of the program given it. This, in turn, depends on the person who develops the program, how well he understands the subject the machine is to teach, and the thinking processes involved in mastering it.

But the machines appear to have some very positive attributes. The student makes an active response. He does not parrot an answer, but must compose or select the appropriate idea. The machine is set up so that he makes progress through making the correct responses in a sequence intended to lead him to increasing competence and understanding. The machine eliminates the kinds of verbal and expressive behavior on the part of the teacher that may either enhance or confuse learning in the usual classroom situation. The child is "in contact" only with the person who made the program on which the machine operates. For some children, a machine may be considerably less threatening than a teacher! In general, however, the purposes of mental health and environmental mastery would seem best served only when the machine is used as an adjunct to the teacher. It could provide opportunities for individuals to proceed at their own rates, obviate much of the needless repetition which is now so prevalent, and free the teacher to

function in a more truly creative and individualized way with youngsters.

In the long run, of course, the question of whether or not the school can promote mental health lies directly with the teacher. The teacher, more than most other persons can, I believe, further the youngster's efforts toward active, healthy mastery. He can help him with the specific skills and knowledge traditionally held to be the business of the school. He can also help him toward the critical, evaluative, creative kinds of thinking needed to cope with an environment that is ever changing.

But if the teacher is to accomplish these things, he too must have help. His mental health function needs to be clarified and reduced to comprehensible size. He needs more than a firm grasp of the skills and knowledge he is expected to teach his pupils. He needs to understand thinking processes. He needs to know very specifically what it means to teach and how what he does as a teacher influences the thinking and the learning of those he teaches.

## REFERENCES

1. Aschner, M. J., "The Language of Teaching," *Teachers College Record*, LXI (1960), 242-52.
2. Bellack, A. and D. Huebner, "Teaching," *Review of Educational Research*, XXX (1960), 246-50.
3. Biber, Barbara, "Integration of mental health principles in the school setting," in G. Caplan, ed., *Prevention of Mental Disorders in Children*. New York: Basic Books, Inc., 1961.
4. Bruner, J., "On coping and defending." Address to the American Psychological Association, September 1959.
5. Hughes, Marie *et al.*, *Assessment of the Quality of Teaching in Elementary Schools*. Salt Lake City: University of Utah, 1959.
6. Inhelder, Barbel and J. Piaget, *The*

*Growth of Logical Thinking from Childhood to adolescence.* New York: Basic Books, Inc., 1958.

7. Jahoda, M., *Current Concepts of Positive Mental Health.* New York: Basic Books, Inc., 1958.

8. Jersild, A. T. and E. A. Lazar, *The Meaning of Psychotherapy in the Teachers Life and Work.* New York: Bureau of Publications, Teachers College, Columbia University, 1962.

9. Kotinsky, Ruth and J. V. Coleman, "Mental Health as an Educational Goal," *Teachers College Record*, LVI (1955), 267-76.

10. Kubie, L., *Education and the Process of Maturation.* New York: Bank Street Publications, 1958.

11. Levin, H. *et al.*, "Studies of Teacher Behavior," *Journal of Experimental Education*, XXVI (1957), 81-92.

12. Sarason, S. B., *Anxiety in Elementary School Children.* New York: John Wiley & Sons, Inc., 1960.

13. Skinner, B. F. "Teaching Machines," *Science*, CXXVIII (1958), 969-77.

14. Smith, B. O., "A Concept of Teaching," *Teachers College Record*, LXI (1960), 229-41.

# 43

# Are We Educating for Maturity?

## LAWRENCE S. KUBIE

I am impatient with educators and psychiatrists, with scientists and artists—with all of us in fact—for our failure to implement criticism of education by an experimental search for new ways.

My central thesis here is that we do not need to be taught to *think;* indeed that thinking is something that cannot be taught. Memorizing (i.e., the recording and recalling of factual data) and also creative thinking (i.e., the assembling of such data in new combinations) are automatic, swift, and spontaneous processes, if these are allowed to proceed undisturbed by other influences.

Under ideal circumstances, memory and thinking are carried on neither consciously nor unconsciously but in the preconscious stream of automatic mentation, which proceeds at phenomenal speed. Of this swift stream, conscious processes provide us with tentative summaries and fragmentary samples; but conscious and, even more, unconscious processes combine

Lawrence S. Kubie, "Are We Educating for Maturity?" *N.E.A. Journal* (January 1959), pp. 58-63. Reprinted by permission.

to distort and delay and impede and sometimes wholly to block the processes of conscious summary and sampling by which the data from the preconscious stream can be put to work in human affairs.

For this, there is abundant clinical and experimental evidence, the crucial implications of which have been largely neglected by educators. What we need is to learn how to avoid interfering with this inherent preconscious capacity of the human mind.

This concept of a preconscious core of all human mentation is essential to my thesis. It implies that there is an incessant current of thought and feeling which is incredibly swift, which is neither conscious nor unconscious, which can learn, record, recall, and respond appropriately and also creatively, and all this without conscious awareness of any one of these steps.

We need also to be helped to improve the tools of conscious sampling and communication: i.e., how to read and listen to words, how to speak and write them. Yet even this is only one component in the complex art of communication, since here again the imperative need is to learn how not to let unconscious conflicts, affects, and defenses distort the work of even the fully educated eye and ear and tongue and hand.

Eventually, education must accept the full implications of the fact that the free creative velocity of our thinking apparatus is continually being braked and driven off course by the play of unconscious forces. As long as educational procedures refuse to recognize this, they will continue to increase this interference from masked and unrecognized neurotogenic processes. This happens in school today from the first grade through the highest echelons of postgraduate study.

It has long been known that in early years children have extraordinarily inventive imaginations, and use delightful and original figures of speech and allegory. What happens to this poetic gift when it is exposed to formal education? Or to rephrase the question: What happens to the free play of preconscious (spontaneous, "intuitive") functions in the course of conventional education?

It has been the assumption of education that learning would make man wise, mature, and creative. It is my unhappy conviction that learning alone achieves none of these goals, but more frequently is a mask for immaturity, neurosis, and a lack of wisdom. Furthermore, much of the learning which has traditionally been looked upon as an essential attribute of the educated man has no necessary relevance either to creativity or to maturity. Instead many ingredients in the very process by which men become learned tend actively to prevent psychological growth. It is not learning or the learning process which matures men; it is maturity, however won, which makes it possible for men to learn and to be creative with their learning.

I must warn that I am not going to prescribe remedies for this state of affairs, or to describe preventive measures. We must diagnose before we can cure or prevent; and educators must first acknowledge that something is amiss, before they will even tolerate a search for remedies.

I will be content if I am able to convince even a few that there is something quite basically wrong with our approach to education, and then to define what is wrong in terms of the crippling influence on the creative process of much of what now occurs in school. Only at the end will I suggest a few directions in which it is reasonable to seek for corrective or preventive techniques.

This is as far as I will presume to go; but I hope that experienced educators, with their more intimate knowledge of the details of educational procedures, may be able to offer more definitive remedies. Indeed, some educators and certain special schools have begun to attack the problems that I will describe. But I must leave this to them. My function is to challenge, not to offer panaceas.

The premises from which I start are not happy ones. Nor are they pessimistic, since they carry the implication that if we face these problems, we can solve them and that if we solve them, we will open a new era in human. culture. Let me then state my premises.

The great cultural institutions of human society, including art and literature, science, education in general, the humanities and religion, have three essential missions: namely, to enable human nature itself to change; to enable each generation to transmit to the next whatever wisdom it has gained about living; to free the enormous untapped creative potential which is latent in varying degrees in all men.

It is my belief that in all of these respects our great cultural efforts and institutions have failed, and will continue to fail until new techniques of education are developed.

Evidence for this is found in the fact that our knowledge of the external world and our ability to represent the world as it is or as we would like it to be has grown enormously, while our ability to meet wisely the challenge of how to be human beings has not developed. Everyone acknowledges this intellectually; yet few have accepted the full implications which this failure entails for education itself as an instrument of human growth.

The failure of education to make it possible for man to change is due to a specific component in human nature; to wit, that psychological rigidity which is the basic and universal expression of the neurotic process. Indeed, this neurotogenic rigidity is so universal that it is frequently accepted as normal (even among some psychiatrists), as though the mere fact that everybody is rigid in one or more aspects of his personality means that rigidity is normal.

Since all that I will say is predicated upon what I regard as this basic failure of human culture, I will list the indices of this failure:

1. There is the universality of the neurotic process itself, which is manifested with minor variations in every culture about which we know anything.

2. There is the resulting failure of the race as a whole, and of men as individuals, to evolve and change psychologically.

3. There is the failure of all traditional methods to impart to successive generations that wisdom about living which a few individuals in each generation slowly acquire. Specifically, the kinds of behavioral conventions which protect the association of men into livable societies are well known. We call these ethical principles. Yet we do not know how to perpetuate and inculcate such ethical principles, nor how to seat them firmly in the saddle of human affairs.

These are basic gaps in our knowledge of how to transmit the fruits of experience from one generation to the next. The consequence is that in forms which change only in detail, country after country and generation after generation repeat the errors of their predecessors.

These manifestations of the failure of culture signify that the universal masked neurotic component in "normal" human nature is the major obstacle to progress. No system of education which fails to accept this challenge can educate in any meaningful sense. Therefore, we must ask ourselves whether the educational process as we know it increases or decreases in the student the sway of hidden neurotic forces in his life. It is my contention that education as it is increases the power of the neurotic processes in our culture, and that this need not be true.

Every adult bears the imprint of the child. The unconscious projection of the years of childhood onto the screen of adult years anchors us to the past. Consequently, the educator who is interested in making education assist the individual to move toward maturity must study how such projections from the past influence education, and whether the educational process tends to perpetuate their influence.

First of all, we face the obvious fact that the schoolroom and school as a whole confront the child with substitute parents and siblings. This provides an opportunity to resolve the fateful and destructive conflicts of the nursery. Yet the opportunity is not utilized. Instead, the child in school merely relives and buries even deeper the hates and loves and fears and rivalries which had their origins in his home.

The schoolroom may partially balance or neutralize these conflict-laden feelings; but it fails utterly to render them less fixed and less rigid *by bringing them within the reach of conscious selection, direction, and control.* Self-control, as it is taught, is almost invariably concentrated on control of the secondary consequences of such conflicts, rather than focusing on the elimination of their inner sources.

One could choose at random a number of illustrations of the consequences of this. There is the child who in his struggle with authority becomes an obsessional dawdler. This will have begun in the nursery in dawdling about eating, washing, or dressing. Unless this neurotic deviation has been effectively resolved in the home before the youngster reaches school, it will warp his every activity in this new setting.

At the opposite pole from the obsessional dawdler is the compulsive rusher, the youngster who has to plunge headlong from one half-finished task to another, afraid to tarry long enough to complete anything lest he be overtaken by some nameless fate, some dreaded exposure. These two oppositely paced obligatory patterns may alternate in the same individual, and may arise out of almost identical unconscious conflicts.

The relevant and disconcerting point is that both of these opposing neurotic patterns (as well as others) tend to be reinforced and not lessened by the pressure of our formal educa-tional processes. Yet instead of giving the child insight into and freedom from this reaction to authority, the school usually increases its paralyzing influence. Consequently, it persists to plague the lifework of potentially brilliant and creative adults.

Many such adults are seduced by the illusory freedom of a blind automatic rejection of all external authority. Yet because the road to external freedom is never found by submitting to irresponsible internal compulsion, these obligatory rebels pay for this in the stereotyped and repetitive quality of their pseudorebellious productions, whether these are in literature, art, music, politics, or science.

In considering how to deal with these difficult and ubiquitous problems, we do not need to conjure up a Utopian school in which no nursery battles would be reenacted. Whether the immediate and remote effects of such conflicts upon each child and adult are creative or destructive will depend not upon the mere fact that such struggles occur, but upon the *level on which they are waged,* i.e., whether this level is preponderantly conscious, preconscious, or unconscious.

Therefore the schools face the challenge to see what they can do to make sure that these battles will be fought out on conscious and preconscious levels. It would seem that an essential aspect of any truly educational experience would be to enable each child to face in himself those painful conflicts from which he shrinks, but which shape his character.

Neither traditional disciplinary education nor progressive education solves the technical problems which this goal involves. Disciplinary techniques alone, even when seemingly successful, give the child a sense that he must control *something*, but fail to make clear what there is inside that needs controlling or redirecting.

In its early years, progressive education encouraged the child to act out his problems, but failed to realize that acting out will not alone bring any increase in self-understanding or in self-mastery. Indeed, like blind discipline, blind acting out can distort and block insight—as it does in the case of the psychopath.

In addition to its failure to accept the challenge of buried neurotogenic processes, even at its current best, the educative process tends to reinforce the neurotic process through the misuse of the techniques of repetitive drill.

In the tangled interweaving of the processes of learning and the neurotic process, repetition plays a major role. By imperceptible gradations, the repetitive drills of the learning process shade over into the automatic involuntary repetitions of the neurosis. This intensification of the neurotic process through repetitive drill mars our educational system from primary grades through professional and graduate levels.

Limitless repetition without the guidance of insight is not merely self-defeating; it does deeper damage by hampering spontaneous, "intuitive," i.e., preconscious, functions.

Nevertheless, in the acquisition of skills, many teachers continue to place major emphasis on repetitive drill; and this in spite of the well-known and repeatedly demonstrated fact that the most efficient learning is essentially effortless and almost instantaneous.

For example, under hypnosis enormous amounts of material can be recorded effortlessly, almost as on a photographic plate. Here drill and repetition play no role, and their introduction would merely interfere with automatic recording and recall. In general, the degree to which learning depends upon repetitive drill is a measure of the degree to which guilt, anxiety, anger—whether conscious or unconscious—are blocking the assimilative component of education.

For a number of reasons, therefore, we are forced to conclude that there is a continuous conflict rather than a happy alliance between erudition and maturity. This conflict begins in the primary grades and continues unabated to and through postgraduate education.

Every educator knows scholars who lack the least quality of human maturity and wisdom, yet who are technical masters of their own fields, whether this field is the humanities, art, music, philosophy, religion, law, science, the history of ideas, or the languages by which men communicate ideas. The measure of our wisdom about living is determined neither by the breadth of the area of our knowledge nor by the sharpness of the focus of our specialization.

It might shed some light on the elusive relationship between formal education and maturation to consider what happens to medical students when they are brought into contact with the sufferings of patients. This is a moment which forces them to accept some measure of responsibility for human suffering other than their own. For each student, this is an experience which precipitates a powerful, if masked, internal struggle among conflicting impulses.

Shall he cling to the unrecognized prerogative of childhood to shut out the suffering of others or even secretly to exult in it? Or shall he yield to those simultaneous, powerful internal and external pressures of medical tradition to accept the challenge of human needs other than his own? Will it extricate him from the cocoon of his childhood to identify with other individuals through ministering to them?

This may give us a clue to other basic defects in our educational process. Perhaps above anything else, the adolescent needs not only to be exposed to human suffering, but also to be given the responsibility of ministering to it. Yet instead of this, the educational years cultivate in each student a maximal concentration on himself. Moreover, we know that the essence of maturity can come only through the insight which arises out of the interaction between living and blundering, and then of studying and dissecting our blunders. Neither living without self-study nor study without living is enough.

One obvious implication runs through everything I have said; namely, that if education is to become a matter not only of the mind but of the spirit, and if it is ever to facilitate the maturing process instead of limiting and distorting it, then it must deal with the universal, masked, neurotic ingredient in human nature. Clearly then, self-knowledge in depth is essential for any solution.

It is my conviction that education without this understanding can never mean wisdom or maturity; and that self-knowledge in depth is a process which, like education itself, is never complete. It is a process which goes on throughout life. Like the fight for external freedom, the fight for this inner freedom from the internal tyranny of unconscious processes demands eternal vigilance and continuous struggle.

This is because in every one of us, from the beginning of life until its end, active forces are at work which tend repeatedly to confuse and obscure our images of ourselves. Consequently, those who do not struggle continuously throughout life to attain and then to retain self-knowledge in depth cannot be creative. Without such

knowledge, society has no adults, but only aging children, armed with words and paint and clay and atomic weapons, none of which they understand.

And since self-knowledge has been a neglected aspect of our educational system, and indeed of human culture in general, most scholars have been only erudite rather than wise. Wisdom when it has graced any one of us has come not by design but as a happy accident. This challenges us to have the courage to face this failure of education as we have always known it, with a determination to do something effective about it.

Even if we do not already possess the technique by which to implement fully our determination, we can at least formulate our goals.

The increasing duration of the process of formal education tends to imprison the student for many decades in an adolescence of limited responsibility in which he lives on a dole from an adult world toward which—whether or not he manifests it openly—he harbors much unconscious hostility. Thus we obstruct the very processes of maturation for which we are striving.

I take it for granted that our educational processes must continue to last longer and longer. This means, however, that unless the student is exposed concurrently to maturing experiences, he will continue to end up as an erudite adolescent. The need to achieve the fullest degree of intellectual preparation without emotional stunting challenges us to find ways in which without limiting education we can facilitate those aspects of emotional maturity which emanate only from the direct experience of living and from carrying a sobering responsibility for others.

Yet the amount of data which

every educated man must master is enormous already and is constantly increasing. Moreover, we know that if we hold him at the student level too long, the process of emotional maturation which is so essential an ingredient of education is in danger of being stunted. Obviously, then, some means must be found to remake the life of the student, so that in itself it will become a maturing experience. Alternatively, periods of study must be interspersed with periods devoted to other types of experiences, or techniques of psychotherapy must be adapted to the educational scene to supplement formal education in the service of greater emotional maturity.

When we meet the currently popular and all too easy assumption that the humanities will solve our problems, we should remind the optimist that the humanities have never served us that well in the past.

We cannot be wise, yet remain immature. Maturity requires the capacity to change, to become different, to react in varied and unanticipated ways. The emotional and intellectual maturity which the returning veteran brought to his studies after World War II, the subtle birth of maturity in the medical student as he first experiences the suffering of others and participates in its alleviation, what we have learned about the imprisoning of the human spirit by the neurotic process—all these indicate the directions toward which we must move as we seek solutions to these fundamental problems of how education for the first time in human history can enable the human spirit to grow and change. Progress will not come just from sitting back and hoping. It will come only as a reward for an uncompromising defense of the creative value of doubt, and from an unsparingly critical reexamination of every educational premise.

# 44

# Teacher Training and Emotional Needs

## LOUIS E. RATHS

Within the past twenty-five years there has been a very great emphasis within professional education on the desirability of "meeting the emotional needs of children." It is probably true that throughout all recorded history there are writings which touch upon this point. It is also undoubtedly true that the pioneering work of Freud in the study of neurotic personalities contributed very greatly to an increased understanding of the role of emotional needs in the behavior of people, and it was also due to the work of Freud that educators came to see the great significance of experiences in early childhood on the later development of personality. Simultaneously, with the great depression of the early thirties, various leaders in education saw the necessity for some systematic, organized attack on the problem of how to identify these needs and how best to try to meet these needs.

The Progressive Education Associa-

Louis E. Raths, "Teacher Training and Emotional Needs," *Journal of Educational Sociology*, XXIV, No. 7 (March 1951), 369-80. Reprinted by permission.

tion became the organizing center for this more and more, so far as this accelerated emphasis was concerned. Through the planning of people in the Association, with the aid of consultants from a number of fields, with the cooperation of many public and private school administrators, they submitted a plan which resulted in the organization of The Eight Year Study which included thirty secondary schools of the United States. A number of commissions and committees were organized to study and to report on significant developments that had bearing on the education of children. One of these commissions, under the untiring and intelligent leadership of Caroline Zachry, concentrated much of its attention on the needs of youth. At the same time, Dr. Alice Keliher headed up the Commission on Human Relations and she and her associates produced books, pamphlets, and motion picture excerpts which paid particular attention to some of the emotional problems of youth and growing up in our society. The work of these two outstanding leaders influenced considerably the educational thinking of that time. Other committees working within the framework of the Progressive Education Association produced a number of books and reports dealing with the role of various academic subjects in the education of youth, and nearly all of these writings stressed the great importance of certain needs of secondary-school students. At the same time, a number of educational leaders associated with The Eight Year Study were often invited to speak at meetings of educational associations, at faculty meetings, at particular schools, to parents' meetings, and over and over again there was a great stress on the role of emotional needs in the adjustment of adolescents. These leaders had been associated with psychologists, with psychoanalysts, with anthropologists, with sociologists, with physicians, with frontier thinkers in the field of teacher education, and with teachers, parents, and children. Out of these associations had come a firm conviction that emotions had been neglected in the educative processes; that attention had been given almost exclusively to intellectual factors in the learning process, and that a concern for the all-around growth and development of children required a reconstruction of our beliefs and practices as these related to the emotional needs that were pressing for recognition.

In many of these writings a great variety of such emotional needs were postulated and leaders were exhorted to pay more attention to meeting the needs of children. Among the needs most frequently mentioned were: (1) the need for belonging, (2) the need for achievement, and (3) the need for love and affection. Studies of delinquency seemed to show a correlation between the neglect of these needs and delinquent behavior. Studies of difficulty in the learning process seemed to indicate that emotional maladjustment was often associated with the blocking of normal progress in educational achievement. Studies of social acceptance and rejection seemed to indicate that students with frustrated emotional needs had greater difficulty in making friends and getting along with people. The theory was suggested that aggression directed toward minority groups might well have its origin in the frustrated needs of those who were aggressive. Because the depression was affecting family life so significantly, it was suggested that economic insecurity brought with it anxiety and tension, and that under these conditions adjustment was more difficult and learning more difficult too.

Over and over again it was suggested to teachers that one of their most important jobs was "to meet the needs of children." Just how this could be done was often left as an exercise for the individual teacher who had heard the speech or who had read the materials in which this directive was laid down. It was pretty clear that before one could meet the needs of children it was certainly necessary to be able to identify some of those needs. It was also pretty clear that some kind of systematic procedure had to be developed for teaching procedures and curriculum development, once the needs had been identified.

A significant contribution was made by H. A. Murray in his book, *Personality, a Psychological Approach.* He listed 44 needs and described them in some detail. He also suggested ways of getting evidence bearing upon these needs, and his writings were widely discussed and many of his techniques were used in experimental researches. One of his methods included a projective procedure called the Thematic Aperception Test. He also called attention to a number of other projective types of procedures.

One important development of Keliher's work was represented by a series of motion picture film excerpts. These represented problems in human relationships, and the excerpting was done in such a manner that solutions were not presented. The audience, composed usually of secondary-school students, were then invited to discuss the excerpt that they had seen. In general, these discussions by adolescent youth tended to show that they projected their own problems and their own needs into the pictures thus shown. Skillful observers were able to note some of the more pressing needs of the discussants. Both the work of Murray and the work of Keliher seemed to depend upon very highly informed and very expertly trained leaders. The writer may be doing an injustice to these contributors, but it does seem clear that their work did not penetrate into the classrooms of the country to the extent that was expected.

It seemed evident that the rank and file of teachers were in need of some more direct attack on the problem of meeting needs. The rank and file of the teaching profession were hardly prepared to understand and to apply what had thus far been discovered. Moreover, no systematic proof was then available that these needs did exist or that they did have serious influence on learning and on the total growth and development of children. There was a wealth of illustrations, a wealth of anecdotes, but there was no conclusive evidence that attempts to meet needs would result in significantly changed behavior. There was a faith that this would happen, there was a faith that this could happen and that the effort should be made.

With respect to learning, the theory received support from a great many teachers who had met with failure as they repeatedly addressed themselves to the so-called "intellectual analyses" of difficulties in learning. The recommended techniques for the improvement of reading, for example, often resulted in little or no progress, and teachers who used these techniques came to see that emotional problems were involved in these learning difficulties. Here again there was no proof with respect to this point but there was a widespread sharing of experiences, and out of these experiences there came the feeling on the part of many leaders in education that more attention needed to be given to the emotional needs of children.

Twenty-five years have now passed since this trend began to assume importance in professional educational circles. It can truly be said that teachers all over the nation have become much more sensitive to the role of emotions in the learning process and in the social adjustment of children. It can also truly be said that even now we do not have any conclusive proof, experimental proof, of the existence of emotional needs and their direct relationships to learning, or to behavior. This relationship seems to be one "that everybody knows and that no one has demonstrated."

Moreover, there is no listing of needs which has received the blessings of leaders in psychology, anthropology, or education. Human personality is conceived to be infinitely varied. Needs are thought to be infinite in their number and widely varying in their expression. A concept so vague and so all-embracing with respect to personality leaves much to be desired with respect to the organization of teacher education, both preservice and in-service. The facts, however, seem to support such a generalization about the infinite variability of human needs and the expression of these needs in behavior.

Nonetheless, teachers were anxious and often expressed intense desire to have some organized systematic training in identifying needs and also some training in ways of helping to meet these needs. The practical problem which these teachers faced day by day was one which demanded attention. There was an urgent demand for some kind of training which would help teachers to gain some insight into the role of emotional needs, some systematic training in trying to identify some of the emotional needs of children who are having difficulty in school, and some systematic training in ways of trying to meet the needs of these youngsters. When one thinks of ways of helping teachers in these several directions, one thinks immediately about the necessity for a curriculum that has continuity and sequence to it; a curriculum that would focus directly upon some emotional needs, a curriculum which would illustrate the behavior of people who seem to have these needs, and a curriculum which would allow teachers to engage in activities that would test out different procedures in attempting to meet these needs.

Dollard and others had brought out a book entitled *Frustration and Aggression*. In their writings they postulated that aggressive behavior was an outcome of the frustration of emotional needs. They indicated also that submissive behavior was a possible outcome of the frustration of these needs. Flanders Dunbar conducted an investigation relating to psychosomatic illness and it was her conclusion that many of these illnesses had their origin in emotional disturbances. Amongst teachers it was widely held that the child who was an isolate, a fringer, a nonparticipant, was also a student whose emotional needs were not being met. With this basis it became possible to meet with groups of teachers and to ask them to identify children in their classrooms who were unusually and characteristically aggressive, who were unusually and characteristically submissive, who were unusually and characteristically withdrawn from the group, and who were unusually and characteristically "ill" when emotional pressures became intense. It was not a very difficult matter to identify children who represented extremes in these behaviors. They were the source of "trouble" in the classrooms, and they were more or less "problems" with the teachers. The most common, of course, were the so-called "aggressive" ones.

If the theory was sound, children exhibiting these behaviors to a marked extent were the children who were supposed to have intense emotional needs. The next step in the process was to try to study the behavior of these children and to identify, if possible, any emotional needs that seemed to be present. At this time, efforts were made, in working with groups of teachers, to have no finite list of needs which would direct observations. The long list suggested by Murray was singled out for attention. The writings of Prescott, of Zachry, of Kotinsky, and of Alberty and others became a basis for studying the behavior of children. In general, the attempts failed and the opinion was held that until some more simplified method of attack was developed, success was highly improbable so far as in-service teacher education was concerned. It seemed fairly clear that some listing of needs was necessary as a framework. It seemed clear also that materials had to be found which teachers could study and which would focus upon this simplified listing.

An attempt was then made to solicit

from teachers their own opinions about needs which seemed to have direct relationships to problems in the classroom. In these discussions suggestions were made to the teachers which derived from Freud, Zachry, Keliher, Frank, Plant, Prescott, Rogers, and many others. Out of these discussions the writer generalized a list of eight emotional needs that seemed to find acceptance with teachers with whom he had worked, and that had some support in the literature that was then current. It was decided to concentrate upon the following needs:

1. The need for belonging
2. The need for achievement and recognition
3. The need for economic security
4. The need to be relatively free from fear
5. The need for love and affection
6. The need to be relatively free from intense feelings of guilt
7. The need for self-respect and sharing in the values that direct one's life
8. The need for guiding purposes in understanding of the world in which one lives

The decision to concentrate on these *eight* needs was a matter of convenience. The teachers with whom the writer was working seemed to agree that these offered a starting point and that if these could be defined fairly clearly, illustrated profusely, then attempts could be made to develop procedures which would be helpful in trying to meet those needs. The next problem became one of organizing some kind of curriculum for teachers out of which these understandings might come.

Professor Alberta Young of the University of Tennessee agreed to accept the major responsibility for undertaking this task. Over a period of two years she worked on the problem of developing a curriculum that could be used in the training of teachers with primary emphasis on an understanding of these eight selected needs. Her work resulted in a doctoral dissertation at Ohio State University. It was a pioneering work and of great importance in the subsequent chain of events.

After she had developed a resource unit in this area, Professor Anna Carol Fults, now with the University of Florida, used this curriculum as a basis for training teachers in an experiment which she conducted in Arkansas.[1] In her work with these junior high school teachers, the group identified the so-called "problems" in their classrooms. They then tried to identify some of the needs of these youngsters and they limited themselves to a study of the eight needs listed above. Working together, they started to devise a list of "do's and don'ts" in working with children who had specific emotional needs. They tried to carry through a systematic educational treatment of these needs over a period of a semester. They took measures before and after, of academic achievement, of IQ of social acceptance, and they kept anecdotal records of manifest behavior. The conclusions of the study pointed conclusively to the fact that the teachers' attempts to meet needs seemed to be accompanied by significant changes in the measurements that were made. This was not, of course, any proof of the existence of needs as such. It was a demonstration that if teachers worked with children in these ways, certain changes took place.

A number of similar studies were carried on at different age levels. One was done by Professor Katheryn Feyereisen now on the faculty at Wayne University in Detroit. Still a third was carried on by Professor Anna Porter Burrell now on the faculty of Buffalo

[1] Anna Carol Fults, "Improving Learning Through an Emphasis on Human Relations in an In-service Teacher Education Program." Ph.D. Dissertation, Ohio State University, 1946.

State Teachers College. In these studies the same general procedures were followed and the curriculum materials developed by Professor Alberta Young were utilized in the in-service training of teachers. In general, again, the results showed positive changes in an overwhelming majority of the children selected for remedial work with respect to emotional needs.

In 1949 Professor Robert Fleming of the University of Tennessee attempted a study in which with the aid of nurses, physicians, teachers, and parents certain school children were identified as having chronic symptoms of psychosomatic illness. These children became the focus of further study in an attempt to identify whether or not any of the eight needs previously listed were being thwarted. The same curriculum materials were used for an in-service training program with teachers and in some instances with parents. . . . His conclusions support the general idea that if attempts are made to meet some of these emotional needs, the frequency of the symptoms and the intensity of the symptoms of illness tend to decline. Other gains were also reported.

Dr. Frank A. Mann, now of Temple University, set for himself the task of surveying a relatively large number of classrooms in order to determine the frequency with which needs made themselves manifest in the behavior of children and to determine how frequently teachers characterized children as overly aggressive, overly submissive, overly withdrawn or chronically ill in a psychosomatic sense. His results are also reported in this issue and they tend to reinforce what has previously been expressed as opinion so far as the frequency of unmet needs are concerned and the frequency with which deviant behavior of a serious kind tends to assert itself.

In all of these studies, not one of the investigators has taken the position that these particular eight needs constitute the range of needs which are important in the lives of children. They have taken the position that among the many emotional needs of children these eight appear frequently, seem to be closely related to certain kinds of behavior, and tend to affect the learning process rather significantly. It follows from this that perhaps other needs should be given equal attention, should be clearly defined, should be illustrated in terms of children's behavior, and should be identifiable through close observation of behavior. In the same fashion, those "to be added" needs should be studied in terms of what teachers can do to help children more satisfactorily to meet these needs. The work of many of these graduate students and cooperating teachers, children and parents in the several studies have culminated in the publication of two booklets which have had extensive distribution in more than twenty-five states of the nation. The first of these, *An Application to Education of the Needs Theory*, contains rather specific directions and procedures for trying to identify these eight emotional needs. The second booklet, *Do's and Don'ts of the Needs Theory*, consists almost exclusively of hundreds of ideas for teachers who are anxious to make some attempt to meet the needs of children in their classrooms. The publications have proved to be of great help to classroom teachers who are seeking to bring about desirable change in the growth and development of their children. The booklets themselves, however, do not provide a design for "proving" the existence of a particular need or a pattern of needs. The various researches that have been carried on have not been designed to verify the existence of particular needs or groups of needs as such. Instead, all of these researches have had as their purpose an attempt to do something with children *who seem to have one or more of these needs.* The significance of each of these studies has consisted in demonstrating worthwhile changes which have occurred in the behavior of children. The studies have not proved that attempts to meet these needs caused the changes to occur; neither have these studies proved the existence of the needs. Over and over again, however, they have demonstrated that as teachers try to work with disturbed children in the ways that are suggested, in a very, very large proportion of the cases desirable changes have taken place. Perhaps we should not hope for more, and yet designs need to be worked out which extend this list of needs, and designs need to be worked out which will give us a better basis for estimating the causal character of needs in the learning process.

Before bringing this report to a close, a few additional points should be noted. The curriculum materials developed by Professor Alberta Young depended very heavily upon the pioneering work done by Professor Alice Keliher. Some of these materials are now badly dated and seem anachronistic. Very recently, Professor Henry Singer of the New York State Teachers College at Fredonia, New York, in collaboration with New York University professors and graduate students, made significant contributions by developing further film excerpts. Details concerning this project will appear in the next general number of this journal.

Finally, something should be said about the role of frustration of needs and intercultural education. There are some who tend to believe that frustrated needs are a primary cause of the aggression that is directed toward and against minority groups. Those who have worked long in the field are less likely to place the cause of hostility or aggression in any one category. Certainly there seem to be causes that inhere in our social organization. There are causes that seem to inhere in the way in which we produce and distribute goods in our society. There are causes that seem to inhere in learned behavior that is a product of child training patterns, that differ from cultural group to cultural group. There may be factors associated with heredity which play a part here. There may be factors that are associated with accident and trauma in the life experience of individuals. It is also probably true that frustrated emotional needs play some part in aggravating tensions that exist between intercultural groups.

Professor Lawrence Park of Pennsylvania State College conducted an investigation which tended to show that a relationship existed between the changing status of needs and the changing status of prejudice.

We seem to be at the beginning of more intelligent planning of curriculum so far as the meeting of needs is concerned. We seem to be at the beginning of more intelligently devised plans in research in this area. It may be that further exploration will reveal that these initial studies are the directions that we should take. At the present time, however, the data that are available indicate that a curriculum directed specifically toward the training of teachers in identifying needs, and in attempts to meet needs, has a positive and beneficial effect on the children who are under the supervision of these teachers.

# ACTIVITIES

1. What are some techniques you may use to meet "emotional needs" in your teaching?

2. Describe the methods you can employ to monitor your efforts as regards meeting the emotional needs of your students?

3. Compare the articles by Kubie and Goodlad. On what issues do these authors agree? Where do they seem to disagree? What evidence from learning theory would support their premises? Which of their premises may be discredited by evidence from research in this area?

4. Read a section on "the needs of children" in an educational-methods text. How does the author define "need"? If his definition is not explicit—or perhaps not given at all—state your own, drawing on contextual clues. Compare the various meanings of the word as outlined in Komisar's discussion.

5. Consider, for example, that a new child has entered your class in the middle of the year and is having difficulty making friends. You assume that he has a need for belonging, as yet unmet. What are some things you might do as a teacher? What are some things you should try to avoid? Prepare lists of other needs similar to those mentioned by L.E. Raths in his paper.

6. Louis E. Raths has identified eight needs that are predominantly unmet in our students. Which of these needs do you consider the most unrealistic? Which do you think is the most important? Defend your choices.

7. The Supreme Court decision concerning the desegregation of public schools held that separate school facilities are inherently unequal. Do you imagine that the Court was referring to emotional needs in its decision?

## Chapter Eight

# DISCIPLINE

For many beginning teachers, as well as for some who have been teaching for many years, one of the greatest concerns is whether or not the students will cooperate with them. They are fully aware—in fact, some have learned by experience—that the most imaginative ideas, the finest plans, the best of intentions are of no value if a class is "out of control."

Just what is meant by classroom control? Obviously this term means something quite different to the art teacher, the science teacher, the math teacher, the physical education teacher, and the reading teacher. The definition which may generally apply is: students and teacher work toward a commonly held goal, and behave in a manner which is mutually acceptable. Now, while this means the students have to cooperate with each other and with the teacher, the important consideration for us here is the job of the teacher. And it should be apparent that there is no one prescription for success. Teachers' personalities vary a great deal, so that even identical approaches to the problem of class control do not always have the same results.

There are some principles on which one can base his plan of operation. The following articles will offer several alternatives for your consideration. Do you have any criteria for evaluating these alternatives? Will your ideas on planning and interaction in the classroom force you to take a particular stand on discipline?

# 45

# Power in Small Groups

## LOUIS E. RATHS

All serious writers about power speak of its interpersonal nature and its reciprocal relationships: to have power one must be empowered. The power comes from others.

Much of the writing about power concerns itself with definitions and illustration of what is meant by one or more conceptions of power. What is communicated in these writings are the personal conviction and opinions of the writers. Many of these are intelligent guideposts for the researcher in the field, particularly the inference that *power* is not a simple unitary concept, and that its meanings and effects may differ from one situation to another.

It is probably true that all knowledge starts with opinion, but on many occasions it delays overlong at the starting position. Opinion may or may not be verifiable but the conscious increase of knowledge requires the reformulation of opinion into testable form.

Louis E. Raths, "Power in Small Groups," *Journal of Educational Sociology*, XXVIII, No. 3 (November 1954), 97-103. Reprinted by permission.

With respect to the concept of power there have been two prevailing trends: the expressions of opinion and the tendency to simplify a very complex phenomenon: power is force; power is influence; power is the ability to get work done; power is what is behind the decision-making activity of the topmost level of a social hierarchy; power is authority.

Oversimplification is not necessarily to be condemned. There may be great advantage in focusing upon a single factor in a situation involving many variables. The restatement of opinion into the form of a hypothesis may or may not lead to further clarification, depending upon the designs of the researcher and also upon the relevance of the hypothesis to the *theory* under consideration.

We need an explicitly formulated theory from which hypotheses can be derived for experimental testing.

In the absence of experimental data or a systematized organization of fact we may take as a basis the informed opinion of authorities in the field, such as Bertrand Russell,[1] Lasswell and Kaplan,[2] de Jouvenel,[3] Homans,[4] and L. L. Whyte. The latter says, "The unity of society depends on the existence of a hierarchical order which gives each section its special status and function within the whole, and this order may be effective even when it is not recognized."[5]

Given the interpersonal nature of power, the *power-empowering* relationship, and the suggestion of the need for hierarchical order, we may formulate a theory as follows:

1. In a small group if everyone were equal in all respects to every other person, the potentials for the development of power would be at a minimum.
2. Effective social power arises out of the operation of inequalities present in small group situations.
3. These inequalities may be few or many in number and may relate to different status categories. They come into being through the consent of those in the group. In other words, differences in status in one or more categories are recognized by the group members.
4. To preserve itself, leadership utilizes these inequalities; in part it tends to preserve them.
5. The utilization and preservation of inequalities is more likely if the leader is *aware* of them.
6. Group effectiveness is likely to be superior in those situations where the operations of the group leader support

the several status systems created by the members of the group.

This theory assumes that power is created when a status system is brought into being. The source of the power is the status system itself. The functioning of power is dependent upon the continuance of a stable status system.

Power, then, arises in situations where there is imbalance or inequality of status and where the inequality in status is recognized by the members of the group. A particular status leader is chosen on the assumption that he will preserve the inequalities in the status system. The leader will not "rock the boat" for if he does he threatens his own leadership position. A leader may seize the power which has been created by the status system but does not create it. It is recognized that in addition to the differences between the statuses within a system there may be significant status differences between the several different status systems.

It is argued that to be effectively utilized power must be channeled through the different status systems which exist in the groups. The group system is, of course, dynamic and with change in the focus of attention, developing status systems may assume more or less importance from time to time. As the situation changes certain individuals in the group may appear to have more status at one time than another.

Another assumption is involved. Given a primary group whose associations are concerned with common problems, who meet under regularly prescribed conditions, and who get to know each other quite well on a "person to person" or "person to group" basis, *statuses become known*. Individuals "earn" a regard from their fellows in the group. Thus each person "comes to have status" and this status is a product of his interaction with others

[1] Bertrand Russell, *Power, A New Social Analysis* (London: George Allen & Unwin, 1938), p. 103.

[2] Harold D. Lasswell and Abraham Kaplan, *Power and Society* (New Haven, Conn.: Yale University Press, 1950), p. 67.

[3] Bertrand de Jouvenel, *On Power: Its Nature and the History of Its Growth* (New York: The Viking Press, Inc., 1949), p. 63.

[4] George C. Homans, *The Human Group* (New York: Harcourt, Brace & World, Inc., 1950), p. 59.

[5] L. L. Whyte, *The Next Development in Man* (New York: New American Library of World Literature, Inc., 1950), p. 102.

in that group. For any individual the status which he has achieved for himself may not be the one that he desires; moreover the status which he has earned may not be a sound reflection of his abilities. Status is used in the sense that it is that place or position in the hierarchy which members of the group bestow upon a participant.

In ordinary life we often see applications of this theory of power. A new man coming into an important post asks to be briefed on "Who's who around here?" The principal of a school has "to go through channels." Our bureaucracy, in one sense, represents an attempt to systematize, to mechanize, and perhaps to publicize the status levels within the several organizations in which bureaucracy is characteristic.

In many groups, however, this all takes place at almost an unconscious level. Individuals in a group, in some manner now unknown to us, come to identify the status level of individuals in the group with respect to many different categories. Also there is a sense in which one makes a kind of composite of all the status systems and tends to place people in dominant or deferential classifications. The theory suggests that this gradation of status is the vehicle through which power is most effectively expressed in our culture. By implication there is the suggestion that an effective leader, one who gets work done and gets it done under circumstances where the group morale is high, is a person who distributes rewards directly in proportion to status and distributes penalties or neglect inversely in proportion to status. On the other hand there is the implication that the appointed or elected status leader who goes against the channels, who goes against the status systems, will get less work done and will do it less effectively, and will have problems of morale of a serious nature.

There is the further implication that as committees are chosen in such a way that all of the members seem to be of about equal status, or if they are ignorant of each other's status and if their continued efforts do not allow an opportunity for them to become aware of each other's status, the work of that group will be largely ineffective. The situation will be somewhat confusing to the members. They will be aware that things are not going along well and that they are not accomplishing much and often they will wonder why.

Are there some systems of status in group situations which are crucial for the development of the group's power potential? Lasswell has suggested eight status categories which he seems to believe are intimately associated with power. All eight seem to be interrelated but the correlations are not extremely high. Their actual impact upon classroom morale will be discussed in the other articles which follow.

1. *Well-being*: Refers to qualities of physical strength and endurance, capacity for work and play, and to the general idea of well-being.
2. *Skills*: These refer to what we ordinarily think of as special abilities and special proficiencies.
3. *Enlightenment*: This refers to knowledge, insight, and information.
4. *Power*: The ability to influence the behavior of others and to participate in the making of decisions.
5. *Wealth*: Meaning the personal economic resources of the individual himself rather than family wealth.
6. *Rectitude*: Which includes uprightness, virtue, and conscience.
7. *Respect*: The term is related to social position and to favorable reputation.
8. *Affection*: Which includes not only social acceptance but friendship and regard.

If we may assume that in primary groups these different status categories are influential in relation to power, we are in a position to formulate research.

We need to get information from every one of the group members about his estimate of every other member in terms of these eight status categories. Having that information, we can combine these results and get the total status of each member in each category, or we can combine one or more categories into a larger composite.

We tend to associate effective group work with a desirable group climate. We may call this *morale* or social climate, or good group atmosphere. If the theory is sound it seems to follow that where there is good social climate, power is being effectively channeled through the status system. Another implication would be that where there is good social climate that status leader would be more *aware* of the differences in status among the group members with respect to these categories.

If the power is being effectively channeled it would imply that the status leader supports more frequently the individuals of higher status and supports less frequently those of lower status. In the two articles which follow, the investigators report research bearing directly on these ideas.

Mr. Bogen's data support the theory in part and in part throw doubt upon it. His evidence suggests that there are combinations of status categories which, when related to teachers' awareness of status, show a statistically significant difference between teachers with high morale and teachers with low morale. In each group of teachers an exception occurs. On the basis of his own personal experience during the inquiry Mr. Bogen has some reason for believing that the exceptions were not as inconsistent with the theory as might at first be observed.

All kinds of errors might be creeping into such a study: the differences might be associated with errors in the selection of teachers; the means of measurement may be inadequate and inaccurate. Even our statistics may be inappropriate in the circumstances. The sample is very small indeed. There is a grave danger in generalizing from a classroom group in a school to other kinds of populations and to other kinds of groups, and correlation does not imply causation.

Notwithstanding all of these hazards, the evidence which Mr. Bogen presents suggests that the theory deserves much more exploration. Mr. Bogen's investigation dealt with the status leader's *knowledge* of the status positions of children in the classroom group. His hypothesis was that *knowledge* of children's status systems would be greater with teachers who had better group morale. When Lucy Polansky initiated her inquiry she was concerned not at all with the teacher's conscious *knowledge* of status systems. She was concerned with whether or not teacher, as status leader, tended *to give more verbal support* to children of higher status, and less verbal support to children of lower status.

Her results are not in absolute agreement with the theory. She also found an inconsistency in her evidence. By and large, however, the teachers with good group morale tended to support the status systems of children and those with poor group morale tended to be less supportive. Exceptions, however, were noted. In the presence of favorable data and with other data not favorable to the theory it is necessary to say "not proved." It should be added that a single experiment seldom constitutes socially accepted truth. In both studies there is some consistency in the evidence which supports the theory. In both cases there is some negative evidence—but the supporting evidence is much greater in extent. To this writer it seems that the theory is worthwhile exploring in many areas.

It should be possible to secure evidence of status in many different kinds of groups; it should be possible to secure data which indicate whether or not status leaders tend to support individuals with high status in the group and to give less support to individuals of lower status. It should be possible to identify groups which are *accomplishing* a great deal and other groups with the same tasks confronting them who are not *accomplishing* very much. An hypothesis related to the theory would suggest that where group accomplishment was high the theory is at work and where accomplishment is relatively low the theory is not being applied.

Space is too limited for an extensive discussion of related ideas but perhaps one or two words should be said about the relationships. The status systems as such are the results of the interaction of individuals in the group and hence were determined more or less by assent and consent. It seems to follow that these status systems cannot be imposed upon a group; they come from the group itself and are in that sense an expression of that group's experience.

In another sense the theory implies that as new status systems have opportunity to come being, new sources of power are being created so far as group work is concerned. That teacher or leader who tries to limit the status systems to one or two which relate only to academicism, is limiting opportunities for the development of group power. It is in this sense that a group or nation becomes powerful as it increases opportunities for a group to differentiate themselves, but to differentiate themselves in group situations where status may be earned—a *status* that is cherished and is also approved by other members of that group.

The theory opens up many opportunities for further research. It is possible that the committee system which is such a fundamental in our social operations might be considerably improved if we knew how to select a group whose self-accepted differentials might allow for a maximum of power with a maximum of social climate.

The theory might be very helpful in the organization of individual groups. The relationships of such groups to departments and departments to divisions and divisions to the central authority may all be examined if this theory is used as a tentative base for experimentation. It is indeed possible that problems of discipline in all of our social institutions including the school can be approached from this point of view and aid in the discovery of solutions.

Although it has been implied throughout, a final word might be said to the effect that hierarchy was not considered as something permanent, unyielding, or fixed. The concept here dealt with a multitude of hierarchies in a situation so flexible that change was an ever-present possibility. It may indeed be true that this is a great strength of our society as it is presently organized.

# 46

# Social Perception and Teacher-Pupil Relationships

N. L. GAGE & GEORGE SUCI

How two or more persons interact in a given situation depends on many variables, only a few of which have been isolated even conceptually. Properties of the persons and of their situations, all considered as interdependent aspects of a field of forces, obviously provide handles by which to grasp the interaction phenomena. This paper seeks to throw light on interactions between teachers and pupils as a function of one property of the teachers: the accuracy of their perception of pupils' attitudes.

We are concerned with the more affective dimensions of the interaction, rather than with cognitive ones. Our reasoning goes as follows: Behavior in any situation is a function of one's perception of the situation. The "appropriateness" of the behavior will hence depend, at least in part, on the correctness or accuracy of the perceptions. But mere perceptions do not govern behavior completely; the motivational system of the person will determine the ends to which his perceptions are used. Similarly, his "integration," or freedom from neuroticism, will determine how well he can control his behavior to accord with his motivations and perceptions. Thus, even if John perceives a stoplight accurately, he will not stop for it unless he wants to and is sufficiently unexcited to be able to react in time. If John perceives his date's boredom with a movie, he will not suggest that they leave unless he wants to please her and this motive is integrated in a given way with his own feelings about the movie.

So far, however, this formulation ignores the relationships between these determiners; motivation and perception, at least, are themselves linked together. As Bruner (1) recently summarized it:

a. Personally relevant objects in the perceptual field, whether the relevance is a function of positive or negative value to the individual, undergo accentuation. . . .

b. Perceptual selectivity . . . is shown to

N. L. Gage and George Suci, "Social Perception and Teacher-Pupil Relationships," *Journal of Educational Psychology*, XLII (1951), 144-52. Reprinted by permission.

favor the recognition of valued objects and objects associated with the prevailing interests of the subject.

Applied to teachers' perceptions of pupils' attitudes and their interaction with pupils, this implies that the accuracy of teachers' perceptions will be a function of the way in which teachers value pupils and relationships with them. Miss Smith will tend to become aware of how her pupils feel about various issues to the degree that she is interested in those pupils and in getting along smoothly with them. Similarly, she will probably act upon her awareness of their attitudes in positive ways for the same reasons that motivated her to perceive them accurately. Thus certain patterns of motivation, perception, and behavior tend to go together. At the one extreme of a continuum, we may have teachers who do not value pupils positively, do not perceive their attitudes accurately, and behave in ways conducive to negative reactions. At the other extreme are teachers who "need" their pupils more, perceive them with greater sensitivity and understanding, and conduct themselves in ways that elicit positive affect from pupils.

But, it may be objected, need does not necessarily lead to accuracy of perception. The more an object is valued, the more indeed may perception of it be distorted. In our framework, this leads us to examine what it is we are asking teachers to perceive. This, as will be described below, was the attitudes of pupils as reported by themselves in answer to direct Yes-No questions. Whether the attitudes so reported are "true" or "real" ones, we cannot know. It is reasonable to suppose, however, that what pupils report about themselves in a nonclinical, classroom situation are probably opinions of an ego-supporting kind. The

opinions of the pupils tended, in other words, to be those which would enhance their own view of themselves. When teachers are then asked to estimate these opinions, they are being asked to judge what are the ego-supporting responses of pupils. Teachers who value pupils positively then should come closer to the pupils' own picture of themselves. Such a "coming closer" is what we have here termed "accuracy of social perception."

In short, this should mean that teachers who perceive their pupils' attitudes more accurately should be regarded more favorably by their pupils. To test this inference, we need estimates of (a) the accuracy of teachers' perceptions of pupils' attitudes, (b) the favorableness of pupils' attitudes toward their teachers, and (c) the relationship between (a) and (b).

## THE ESTIMATE OF ACCURACY OF SOCIAL PERCEPTION

Ideally, we should deal with the teacher's perception of attitudes of individual pupils on matters that are deeply relevant to each pupil. This would mean, first, the identification of attitude-objects that are highly salient for each pupil and, second, asking the teacher to estimate that pupil's attitude toward those objects. The attitudes to be perceived would then differ from one pupil to the next. Such a procedure was manifestly too difficult for the present study. We compromised by selecting areas of attitude that we surmised to be significant to the pupils en masse, and we asked the teachers to estimate the group attitude on each topic. This procedure is admittedly gross; but whatever support for our hypothesis might emerge from such an approximation might then be considered an underestimate of its true validity.

Accordingly, we proceeded as follows: The 20 teachers of a high school were asked to estimate what per cent of the two hundred pupils in the school would respond affirmatively to a set of 67 opinion items. The items dealt with scholastic, recreational, and student government issues in their school.[1] An illustrative item of each kind follows:

Scholastic: Should students with high scholastic ratings be allowed to skip classes?

Recreation: Could the time spent in school activities be used better for studying or working?

Student government: Should Student Council members be appointed by teachers rather than elected by students?

The students responded anonymously, underlining "Yes" or "No" for each item. The pupils' "Yes" responses were tabulated and the percentage of Yes's found for each item. These percentages comprised the scoring key. Each teacher was scored by taking the difference between his estimate and the actual percentage for each item, summing, and, because a few teachers omitted some items, averaging overall items. The signs of the differences were disregarded. Such "mean error" scores were also obtained separately for each of the three subgroups of items.

These "mean error" scores are directly dependent on the absolute accuracy with which each percentage is predicted. But a teacher, although not able to predict accurately in terms of absolute percentages, may be able to rank the items in order of relative acquiescence of the pupils. Accordingly, we also computed for each teacher a

Pearsonian $r$ between actual and predicted percentages. This we called an "$r$" score. It correlated .77 with the "mean error" score, showing a possibly important difference between the two scoring methods.

## PUPILS' INTERACTION WITH THEIR TEACHERS

At a separate meeting, with the teacher absent, the pupils rated their 6 current teachers on 52 Yes-No items[2] typified by the following:

Is this teacher often "bossy"?

Does this teacher think he or she is always right and the student wrong?

Again the papers were unsigned and pupils were assured their responses would remain anonymous. A score for each teacher was obtained by scoring favorable and unfavorable pupil responses as 1 and 0, respectively, summing overall items and averaging overall pupils rating the given teacher. This measure we considered an approximation, adequate for this study, to the positive affect elicited in pupils by their interaction with a given teacher.

Furthermore, for an appraisal of each teacher's system of values in teacher-pupil relationships, we used the *Teacher Attitude Inventory* developed by Leeds and Cook.[3] The 239 items in this device had been empirically selected and weighted by Leeds and Cook for their ability to discriminate between teachers known to maintain very satisfactory and very unsatisfactory relations with pupils, in the judgment of the teachers' local school administrators.

---

[1] These items were adapted from those used by Wood (4).

[2] These were a slight modification of those used by Leeds and Cook (3).

[3] We are grateful to Professor W. W. Cook for permission to use this device.

## RESULTS

Our first task in analyzing the data was to estimate the generality over items, or the internal consistency, of our approach to accuracy of social perception. Table 1 shows the corrected odd-even coefficients for the "mean error" scores on all items and on each of the three subgroups. The coefficient for all items, .73, indicates that the accuracy of teachers in estimating percentages of acquiescence was fairly general over the items. Thus we have evidence that the task of judging opinion revealed individual differences among teachers that were substantially loaded with nonerror variance. For the subgroups of items, these estimates yielded much lower coefficients.

Secondly, what is the reliability of the pupils' ratings of their teachers? Table 2 shows the results obtained from an application of Horst's formula (2). This coefficient, .93, indicates that the mean ratings we obtained would correlate very highly with subsequent sets of similar ratings, when our estimate of the variability of such further mean ratings is based on an average of the standard errors of those obtained. In short, the variance among the mean ratings is even more a nonerror one; the ratings discriminated well among the teachers.

Having established these estimates of reliability, we turned to the relationships with which we were primarily concerned. Is social perception, defined operationally as mean error in estimating students' percentages of acquiescence to opinion items, related to acceptance of the teachers by pupils, defined as the mean rating of teachers by pupils? Table 3 shows the pertinent coefficients of correlation. The $r$'s between mean rating and mean error for all items and for the three subgroups of items are $-.37$, $-.16$, $-.30$, and $-.18$, respectively. It is evident that all $r$'s are in the direction inferred from our hypothesis: the greater the teacher's mean error in estimating student opinion, the lower his mean rating by students. None of these $r$'s are statistically significant. Our interpretation of this fact may, however, be tempered somewhat by the consistency in direction and size of the three subtest coefficients. These subtests provide in a sense three semi-independent trials of our investigation. The consistency of their results may therefore be construed as favorable evidence in addition to that provided by the overall test's $r$.

When the teachers' estimates of student opinion were scored in terms of their correlation with, rather than their difference from, the actual percentages, we obtain the results also shown in Table 3. Here the relationships, using $r$ and $z_r$ as measures of accuracy of social perception, increase to .50 and .45, respectively. Both these coefficients meet the requirement for statistical significance at the 5 per cent level.

Why do the $r$ scores correlate more highly than the mean error scores with the pupils' ratings? We can only conjecture as follows: The $r$ scores are not influenced, as are the mean error scores, by individual differences among teachers in "adaptation level," or "anchor point." The teachers differed very significantly beyond the 1 per cent level, in the means of their predicted percentages. The $r$ scores eliminate the effect of these differences. They render the measure of accuracy in social perception dependent solely on relative rather than absolute judgments of degree of acquiescence.

Two further findings should be mentioned. First, as shown in Table 3,

TABLE 1

**Corrected Odd-Even Reliability Estimates for the "Mean Error" Scores on Opinion Estimates.** $N = 20$

| Type of Items | No. of Items | Odd Items | | Even Items | | Corrected Odd-Even r |
|---|---|---|---|---|---|---|
| | | Mean | SD | Mean | SD | |
| All Items 1–67 | 67 | 20.19 | 2.81 | 18.64 | 2.97 | .73 |
| Scholastic 1–23 | 23 | 22.50 | 5.03 | 19.74 | 4.05 | .17 |
| Recreation 24–45 | 22 | 15.47 | 3.13 | 18.16 | 4.28 | .28 |
| Student Government 46–67 | 22 | 20.50 | 5.07 | 17.26 | 4.95 | .47 |

TABLE 2

**Estimate by Horst's Method of the Reliability of Pupils' Ratings of Their Teachers**

$$r = 1 - \frac{\sum \dfrac{\sigma_i^2}{n_i - 1}}{N \sigma_{M_i}^2} = 1 - \frac{47.45}{648.46}$$
$$= .93$$

where

$N$ = number of teachers
$n_i$ = number of pupils rating teacher $i$
$M_i$ = mean of the ratings for teacher $i$
$\sigma_i$ = standard deviation of ratings for teacher $i$
$\sigma_{M_i}$ = standard deviation of means for the $N$ teachers

TABLE 3

**Means, Standard Deviations, and Intercorrelations\* of Various Measures**

| | No. of Teachers | Mean | SD | (2) | (3) | (4) | (5) | (6) | (7) | (8) |
|---|---|---|---|---|---|---|---|---|---|---|
| 1. Mean Rating by Pupils | 20 | 33.20 | 5.49 | −.37 | −.16 | −.30 | −.18 | .50 | .45 | −.20 |
| 2. Mean Error (All Items) | 20 | 19.35 | 2.45 | | | | | −.77 | | −.57 |
| 3. Mean Error (Scholastic Items) | 20 | 21.65 | 3.54 | | | .13 | .18 | | | |
| 4. Mean Error (Recreational Items) | 20 | 16.70 | 3.28 | | | | .48 | | | |
| 5. Mean Error (Student Government Items) | 20 | 19.15 | 4.60 | | | | | | | |
| 6. r-score (All Items) | 20 | .67 | .08 | | | | | | | .46 |
| 7. $z_r$-score (All Items) | 20 | .82 | .16 | | | | | | | |
| 8. Teacher Attitude Inventory | 19 | 154.08 | 18.35 | | | | | | | |

\* When $N = 20$, an $r$ of .44 is significant at the 5 per cent level.

the scores on the Cook-Leeds inventory correlated .57 and .46 with our mean error and $r$ scores, respectively. This indicates that the attitudes and understandings concerning pupils which are tapped by that test are significantly related to ability to estimate student's opinions. But what of the relation of the Cook-Leeds instrument to mean ratings by pupils? Contrary to the Cook-Leeds findings, our coefficient was negative, −.20, although not significantly different from zero. In this school, at any rate, this test did not yield results in corroboration of the significant positive relationships with pupils' ratings (about .45) previously reported by Cook and Leeds.

### DISCUSSION

All our conclusions must be tempered by an awareness of the smallness of our sample and its lack of replication in other schools. For example, our impression that a curvilinear relationship exists between pupil ratings and accuracy of perception cannot adequately be pursued. It should be reported, however, that six teachers with high mean ratings nevertheless made only mediocre "mean error" or "$r$" scores. None of the teachers with very low ratings made high accuracy in social perception scores. This could have occurred if some of the well-liked teachers did not attack the task of estimating pupils' opinions with sufficient motivation. Thus low ratings seem sufficient to indicate poor perception scores, but the converse is not true.

The instability of our results is further indicated when we omit one extreme case from calculations of the $r$'s between the two scoring methods and the mean ratings. With the one case

retained, $r$'s of −.37 and .50 were obtained with the "mean error" score and the "$r$" score, respectively. With the extreme case omitted, the $r$'s became −.24 and .18, respectively—a considerable reduction. Nevertheless some degree of correlation, in the expected direction, persisted.

### SUMMARY

To test the hypothesis that accuracy of social perception is positively related to effectiveness of interpersonal relations, we asked the 20 teachers of a high school to predict the percentage of the 200 students who would answer "Yes" to each of 67 items eliciting opinions on various aspects of the school. Teachers' predictions were scored in terms of ($a$) "mean error" from actual percentages and ($b$) correlation with actual percentages. The teachers were rated by their pupils on a 52-item inventory. Finally, the teachers filled out the Cook-Leeds *Teacher Attitude Inventory*.

Results support the hypothesis. The teachers' "mean error" scores had fair internal consistency (corrected odd-even $r$, .73) and correlated −.37 with mean rating by pupils. Their "$r$" scores correlated .50 with mean rating. The teachers' scores on the *Teacher Attitude Inventory* correlated .57 with the "mean error" scores but, unexpectedly, −.20 with mean ratings. (For $N = 20$, an $r$ of .44 is significant at the 5 per cent level.)

Our results must, of course, be pursued through replications in other schools and other situations. Tentatively, however, we conclude that teachers' accuracy of social perception is positively related to their effectiveness in eliciting positive affect in pupils.

## REFERENCES

1. Bruner, J. S., "Social Psychology and Group Processes," in C. P. Stone and D. W. Taylor, eds., *Annual of Psychology*, I (1950), 119-50.

2. Horst, Paul, "A Generalized Expression for the Reliability of Measures," *Psychometrika*, XIV (1949), 21-31.

3. Leeds, C. H. and W. W. Cook, "The Construction and Differential Value of a Scale for Determining Teacher-Pupil Attitudes," *Journal of Experimental Education*, XVI (1947), 149-59.

4. Wood, Homer, "An Analysis of Social Sensitivity." Unpublished Ph. D. Thesis, Yale University, 1948.

# 47

# Permissiveness, Permission, and Aggression: The Effect of Adult Presence or Absence on Aggression in Children's Play

ALBERTA ENGVALL SIEGEL & LYNETTE GAYLE KOHN[1]

It has become conventional to think of an adult's permissiveness toward a child as representing neutralization of adult control. By behaving permissively (acceptantly, nonjudgmentally, etc.), the adult is thought to be "freeing" the child from his presence and authority, and in some loose sense to be permitting the child to behave as he would in the absence of any adult. Such thinking has emphasized the punitive or threatening aspects of adult-child relations. Adult permissiveness is seen as a way of reducing the child's fear of adult punishment and thus as a way of encouraging him to express in behavior those impulses whose expression he knows to be normally unacceptable to adults.

Such thinking about permissiveness has been the basis for explanations which have been advanced for a frequent finding about aggression in doll play. It has repeatedly been observed that aggression in doll play increases over time or from session to session (1, 2, 5, 6, 8, 9). This finding has typically been explained by reference to the adult experimenter's acceptant and nonjudgmental interaction with the child and the fear-reducing effect this interaction has. For example, in discussing recent evidence confirming the finding, Levin and Sears state that

> For both sexes, there was a significant session-to-session increase in the proportion of aggression units. This finding . . . has been interpreted to mean that the deliberate permissiveness of the experimental procedure progressively acts to reduce the inhibitions about aggression that the child has heretofore acquired (2, pp. 149-50).

Support for the notion that the increase of aggression over time "might

Alberta E. Siegel and Lynette G. Kohn, "Permissiveness, Permission, and Aggression: The Effect of Adult Presence or Absence on Aggression in Children's Play," *Child Development*, XXX (1959), 131-41. Reprinted by permission.

[1] We acknowledge with gratitude the skilled services of Miss Lyn Kuckenberg as the observer in this study, and the generous cooperation of Dr. Edith M. Dowley, Director, and Miss Patricia Rowe, Head Teacher, of the Stanford Village Nursery School, where the study was conducted.

indicate a lessening of inhibition on the part of the child, due to the fact that his earlier aggressive actions have met with no criticism from the experimenter" (6, p. 164) is given by two findings from Pintler's study. The first is that the latency of aggressive acts is significantly shorter under a condition of high experimenter-child interaction (which was deliberately permissive and nonjudgmental) than under a condition of low experimental-child interaction. The second is that the amount of thematic aggression is significantly greater under conditions of high experimenter-child interaction.

If the increase over time is explainable in terms of diminution of fear alone, we would expect an increase of aggression from session to session in the *absence* of an adult as well as in an adult's presence. This expectation, however, was disconfirmed in a study of children's social play in two sessions in the absence of any adult (12). Contrary to the prediction that would be drawn from the assertion that inhibition of aggression is caused by fear of adult punishment, it was observed that aggression *decreased* from session to session in the absence of any adult. In the light of the findings already mentioned, this finding was interpreted to mean that whether aggression increases or decreases with time depends on whether a permissive adult is present, for:

The evidence of this study . . . suggests that the presence of a permissive adult in a play session may have a cumulatively facilitating or releasing effect on children's aggression. . . . This interpretation . . . forces a somewhat more positive conception of the result of experimenter permissiveness than might otherwise be held. Lack of fear of punishment is not a sufficient explanation. . . . A more adequate explanation seems to be that in the presence of an adult experimenter the young child abdicates superego and ego control functions

to him, whereas in the absence of any adult the child's own internalized standards are invoked (12, p. 376).

The explanation of the finding by reference to adult presence or absence, however, was admittedly based on only rough evidence, for it was drawn from a comparison of session difference findings in studies which differed in other ways than in the presence or absence of an adult. The increase in aggression from session to session was observed in doll-play studies of a single child in the presence of an adult; the decrease in aggression from session to session was observed in a study of the social play of two children in the absence of an adult. This means that the interpretation of these findings together as demonstrating the positive or facilitating effect of adult permissiveness "may properly be viewed as a hypothesis which should be tested in a direct comparison of two play situations which differ only in the presence or absence of a permissive adult" (12, p. 377). The present paper reports a study designed to permit just such a direct comparison.

Rather than thinking of permissiveness as adult self-neutralization, we may conceive of permissiveness positively as a way of expressing judgments or employing imputed authority. According to this conception, adult behavior which is intended by the adult to be "acceptant" is seen by the child as permission-giving, and an adult attempt at being "nonjudgmental" is interpreted by the child as being in fact affirmatively judgmental.

A conception of permissiveness approaching this one is used by Sears, Maccoby, and Levin (10) in their ratings of mothers' statements about their practices concerning aggression. A mother is categorized as "entirely permissive" if she "never interferes, never tells child she does not want him to fight," and if she considers aggression to be "natural, part of growing up" (10, p. 243). These researchers found that, according to maternal reports, high permissiveness in the sense just defined is associated ($r = .23$) with high aggression in children. They account for this association by referring to the mutual expectations of mother and child as well as to punishment and fear of punishment:

When a mother adopts a permissive point of view about aggression, she is saying to her child, in effect, "Go ahead and express your angry emotions; don't worry about me." She gives few signals in advance that would lead the child to fear to be aggressive. On the contrary, her behavior is one of expectancy that he *will* be, and that such behavior is acceptable. It is scarcely surprising that a child tends to fulfill her expectations (10, p. 259).

An adequate account of aggressive behavior must acknowledge the force of a number of influences in determining the amount and kind of aggression a child exhibits. One of these, of course, is the strength of his aggressive drive, and this is presumably a resultant of a range of experiences in his personal history and of the operation of certain characteristics of the immediate setting. A second influence of importance is the child's own attitude toward aggression—his own evaluation of its goodness or badness. This may be presumed to be a distillation and internalization of the attitudes of significant people in his life. These two influences—the strength of the child's aggressive drive and the nature of his attitudes toward aggressiveness—together undoubtedly account for much of the variability in aggression from child to child and also for at least some of the systematic variability between the sexes. A third influence is the expressed attitudes and values of the other people

in the setting in which aggression may be displayed. In our culture, with its extremely complex code about when, where, how, and to whom aggression may appropriately be displayed, people learn to derive cues about what behavior is acceptable at any given time and place by observing the behavior and communications of others in the setting. Children learn especially to rely on adult behaviors and communications to provide hints as to what is suitable or appropriate. This third sort of influence probably accounts for many differences in children's behavior from one setting to another, and also is probably important in shaping sex differences in both incidence and modes of aggression.

A fourth influence is the expectation that aggression will elicit counter-aggression (punishment). Presumably, such an expectation typically acts to inhibit overt expression of aggression.

It is by reference to the fourth factor that the finding of an increase in aggression from session to session has been explained. We believe that an adequate account of the session-to-session increase in an adult's absence must include reference to all of the influences which have been enumerated, and especially the second, third, and fourth.

In either the presence or the absence of an adult, we may expect wide individual differences in incidence of aggression, because of the wide range of strength of aggressive drives in children and because of individual differences in attitudes toward aggression. In addition to these individual differences irrespective of condition, however, we may expect systematic group differences dependent on the condition of adult presence or absence.

In the presence of a permissive adult, a child's aggression may be expected to increase because (a) he will infer from the behavior of the adult that this is a setting in which aggression is suitable or appropriate, and (b) with experience he will undergo a progressive decrease in inhibition based on fear of punishment. That is, changes in the nature of the third and fourth influences mentioned above account for an increase over time.

In the absence of any adult, however, a child's aggression may be expected to decrease from session to session. Lacking any adults to define the social situation and to express expectations of his behavior in it, the child will, after an initial "release" or testing of the limits, rely increasingly on his own learned standards of conduct (the second influence mentioned above) which, in the middle class child, will typically be that aggression is unacceptable in social play.

## HYPOTHESIS

The study reported here was conducted to test the hypothesis derived from the above account, one concerning session-to-session differences in aggression in children's play in the absence of an adult relative to such differences in the presence of an adult. The hypothesis is that *children under the two conditions will exhibit different session-to session changes in aggression, in that the aggression of the children under the adult-absent condition will tend to decrease in comparison to the aggression of the children under the adult-present condition, which will tend to increase.*

## METHOD

### Subject

The Ss were boys enrolled in a university nursery school. Boys were used exclusively because the amount of ag-

gression they display in the play setting used in the study is much greater than the amount displayed by girls (11, p. 374) and therefore boys' aggression scores may be presumed to be more sensitive to change. The boys served in the experiment in pairs, both members of any pair being from the same play group in the school. One member of each pair was chosen from the older boys in the group (among the upper 50 per cent in age) and one from among the younger. The boys were paired by the director of the nursery school on the basis of their usual friendliness to each other and the supportiveness they could be expected to have for each other in an unfamiliar play setting. The older boy of each pair was a S in the experiment. Eighteen pairs were selected, and the older boys (Ss) in these pairs ranged in age from 4-1 (4 years, 1 month) to 5-0. The younger boys (who were not Ss— their aggression in play was not scored) ranged in age from 2-11 to 4-9, the great majority being 3-year-olds or early 4-year-olds. There were three independent play groups in the school; therefore, some minor overlap occurred between the age ranges of "older" and "younger" boys.

After the pairs had been selected, they were assigned at random (by the toss of a coin) to the two conditions: Adult-Absence and Adult-Presence. Nine pairs were assigned to each condition. The average age of Ss in both groups was 4-7.

### Procedures with Subjects

Each pair participated in two play sessions. These occurred two days apart. Any pair's two sessions were held at the same time of day, insofar as this could be accomplished without destroying the informal and permissive nature of

*E*'s interactions with the *Ss*. (In the Adult-Absent group, the difference between time of day for initiation of one session and time of day for initiation of the other was 22 minutes on the average, and these differences ranged from 0 to 50 minutes. In the Adult-Present group, the average difference in time of day of initiation was 16 minutes, with a range from 0 to 40 minutes.)

All play sessions were conducted in a small playroom in the same building as the nursery school classrooms. This room is reserved for testing and research sessions, and is familiar to the children in the school.

The sessions were initiated in an identical manner for all pairs. *E* invited the pair to come to the playroom so that she could read a story to them and then let them play with some special toys there. As soon as the children entered the room, they were asked to be seated in two chairs, and *E* read a story to them.

The two stories used for the two sessions were rather similar in content, each being a simple animal story which was neutral with respect to aggression and which was printed in a brightly illustrated book. These stories were selected during a pilot study for their interest and appeal for young boys. A counterbalanced design determined which story was read first and which second for any pair.

After the story had been read, *E* invited the children to play as they wished with any of the toys in the room. The toys, selected to be similar to those used in the earlier study (12), were these: two rubber daggers, two small plastic toy guns, one singing spinning top, two lumps of clay, a small wooden train composed of detachable cars, three small metal automobiles, five or six inflated balloons, a small clown toy which was weighted to remain erect, and a large inflated plastic punching

toy (a clown) which stood child height. The arrangement of the room, which was furnished with three chairs and a table, was the same at the beginning of each session.

For the pairs in the Adult-Present condition, *E* sat quietly in a chair at one side of the playroom during both sessions. Her attitude was friendly, acceptant, interested, but nonintrusive. She did not initiate any conversations, and she replied only briefly and noncommittally to any initiations from a child.

For the pairs in the Adult-Absent condition, *E* followed her invitation to the children to play with another statement indicating that she had to leave the room for a while to work at her desk. (*E* had shown this desk to the Adult-Absent pairs while walking with them to the playroom; the desk was in a hall some distance from the room.) She explained that they were to stay in the room until she returned for them. She said that she would knock at the door before entering the room upon her return, and that during her absence they would be alone and their privacy would not be disturbed. The purpose of these remarks, which were restated or amplified when necessary to assure their being understood, was to assure the children of freedom from adult intrusion, supervision, or observation during their play.

Some children under the Adult-Absent condition left the room during the play session, usually to carry some item of information to *E* at her desk. In such instances, *E* walked back to the playroom door with them, repeated her instructions, and returned them to the playroom.

Each pair remained in the room for a 14-minute play period. During this period their play was observed by an observer behind the one-way-vision mirror on one wall of the room. At the conclusion of the period, *E* terminated the play session and walked with the children back to the nursery school. For the Adult-Absent pairs, her conduct was exactly as she had told them it would be: she returned to the door of the playroom, knocked, and waited for their invitation before entering. Moreover, she ignored the state of the room, and she responded in an uninquisitive and noncommittal way to their remarks about what went on during her absence.

## SCORING OF AGGRESSION

All play sessions were observed and scored by the same person, a graduate student in psychology who was kept ignorant of the purposes of the study and of the hypothesis under test. The scoring procedure was identical to that reported earlier (11, 12). Scoring began as soon as the instructions to the children were concluded in the Adult-Present sessions, and soon as $E$ left the room in the Adult-Absent sessions. Paced by an electric timer and using prepared scoring sheets, $O$ entered a rating of aggression for every 20-second interval. The rating was either a 0 (no aggression), 1 (mild or playful aggression), 2 (stronger or more forceful aggression), or 3 (intense aggression in which the child seemed highly involved). $O$'s rating of intensity represented, by convention, the *most extreme* aggressive behavior of the child during the 20-second interval. In judging intensity, $O$ considered both the quality of the instrumental act and the nature of the goal response; an act might be judged intensely aggressive because its aim was highly destructive or hostile or because its mode of execution was highly forceful and showed much self-involvement. Only the behavior of the older member of each pair, the $S$, was scored. A $S$'s aggression score for a play session was the sum of the ratings he received for the 42 20-second inter-

vals during that session. Thus, theoretically, scores could range from 0 to 126. In fact, the observed range of scores for these $S$s was from 10 to 114. In previous work (11, 12), this scoring method has been shown to have high interobserver reliability: the agreement between total scores from 48 protocols of two independent observers was indicated by the Pearson correlation, $r = .97$. For the present study, pilot sessions were conducted to train $O$ in the scoring technique and to conduct a preliminary check on interobserver reliability, which was found to be satisfactory. In the course of the experiment itself, 12 play sessions (including some of each type— first Adult-Absent session, second Adult-Absent session, first Adult-Present session, and second Adult-Present session) were observed and scored independently by a second $O$, and the interobserver agreement for these sessions is given by the Pearson correlation, $r = .98$.

## SUMMARY OF EXPERIMENTAL CONTROLS

Summarized below are the controls which were instituted in the experiment in order to enable isolation of the effects of Adult-Presence or Adult-Absence on session differences inaggression:

1. Any $S$'s partner in play was the same child for both sessions. Thus, any differences between sessions cannot be attributed to systematic differences in interpersonal stimulation.

2. Only one member of each pair served as a $S$. The statistical test's requirement that the scores be independent was thus met.

3. A counterbalanced design determined which story was read first and which second for any pair, so that any possible systematic differential effect of any story would not appear as an experimental effect.

4. The pairs were assigned to the two

conditions by a random procedure. Any significant differences between the *S*'s behavior under the two conditions, therefore, cannot reasonably be attributed to any probable prior systematic differences between the *Ss* in the two groups.

5. Possible time-of-day effects on incidence of aggression were held constant; any pair participated in both sessions I and II at the same time of day.

6. Timing effects were controlled by separating sessions I and II by a constant interval of time (48 hours) for every pair.

7. Possible observer bias was controlled by keeping *O* ignorant of the hypothesis under test. *O* knew whether or not *E* was present at any play session, of course, but she did not know that *E*'s presence or absence was the experimental effect under study, and she was not familiar with the research literature concerning the influence of an adult on children's play.

8. The *E* was the same person for all sessions, and she attempted to interact with all children similarly except with respect to those acts of hers which necessarily depended on whether she was present or absent during the play sessions.

## RESULTS

The hypothesis was tested by a Mann-Whitney test (13, pp. 116-27) on the difference scores (each *S*'s session II score for aggression subtracted from his session I score). The data are shown in Table 1. The scores for the *Ss* in the Adult-Absent sessions show changes significantly different ($p = .01$) from those shown by the scores for the *Ss* in the adult-present sessions. As inspection of Table 1 will reveal, all *Ss* in the Adult-Absent settings showed *less* aggression in session II than in session I, whereas two-thirds of the *Ss* in the Adult-Present settings showed *more* aggression in

TABLE 1

**Session Differences in Aggression**

| Subject and Condition | AGGRESSION SCORE Session I | Section II | Difference |
|---|---|---|---|
| Ab-1 ................... | 65 | 10 | 55 |
| Ab-2 ................... | 73 | 46 | 27 |
| Ab-3 ................... | 58 | 52 | 6 |
| Ab-4 ................... | 90 | 30 | 60 |
| Ab-5 ................... | 56 | 50 | 6 |
| Ab-6 ................... | 80 | 74 | 6 |
| Ab-7 ................... | 103 | 97 | 6 |
| Ab-8 ................... | 41 | 26 | 15 |
| Ab-9 ................... | 97 | 72 | 25 |
| Pr-1 ................... | 46 | 48 | − 2 |
| Pr-2 ................... | 17 | 22 | − 5 |
| Pr-3 ................... | 97 | 114 | −17 |
| Pr-4 ................... | 75 | 59 | 16 |
| Pr-5 ................... | 30 | 53 | −23 |
| Pr-6 ................... | 55 | 42 | 13 |
| Pr-7 ................... | 86 | 107 | −21 |
| Pr-8 ................... | 58 | 39 | 19 |
| Pr-9 ................... | 72 | 93 | −21 |

session II than in session I. Thus, the hypothesis is confirmed.

This finding does not imply an over-all difference in incidence of aggression under the two conditions: when each $S$'s scores for the two sessions are considered together, the mean of these totals for the Adult-Absent $S$s (124.4) is less than a point different from the comparable mean for the Adult-Present $S$s (123.7). Thus, it is not the total incidence of aggression which was shown to vary under the two conditions, but rather the timing of its occurrence.

## DISCUSSION

The results of this study confirm the hypothesis drawn from the contention that adult permissiveness must be conceived in more positive terms than simply as a way of reducing a $S$'s fear of punishment.

In their discussion of ego functions, Redl and Wineman have described a phenomenon similar to that under study. They describe the "spontaneous establishment of substitute controls":

Even in normal children, the control system of the ego does not always have to stay switched on to its full volume just to keep things from getting disorganized. Much of the time, ego vigilance and ego control can be switched back to low, just because there are adequate outside control forces at work. In those cases, the ego gets its flow of support from the presence of authority figures, the soothing awareness of a relaxed and friendly atmosphere, the perception of existing routines or well-oiled rules and regulations. . . . Sometimes, especially when impulsivity runs high, even well-adjusted children have trouble keeping to the level on which they were performing when such "outside controls" suddenly drop out. Thus . . . the teacher leaving the room may find noise rising in the classroom in spite of the warnings or pleas she left behind, the change over from a more highly pressured classroom to one with

a wider range of permissiveness may cost ten minutes of temporary disorganization.

The normal child is supposed to have some reserves to institute inside controls quickly after the outside ones have petered out. . . . In fact, we could think of no better test for the emergency vigilance of ego functions than just such moments of withdrawal or breakdown of outside structures or controls (7, pp. 110-11).

In terms of these authors' discussion, $S$s under the Adult-Absent condition in the present study were observed spontaneously to establish "substitute controls," to "switch to high," to demonstrate the "emergency vigilance of ego functions." On the other hand, $S$s under the Adult-Present condition could "switch to low," and could get a flow of support from the existence of an accepting authority figure and the perception of rules and regulations consonant with their behavior. It may be suggested that a technique for assessing a child's ego strength or maturity of controls would be to compare his behavior in the two settings of this study (Adult-Absence and Adult-Presence) and especially to observe the swiftness and ease with which he "switches to high."

Also relevant here is the psychoanalytic account of the relations between leader and follower. As presented by Munroe, this theory sees a leader as a substitute for internalized controls. "The leader and the admonitions of the leader are substituted for the ego ideal or superego. The great man . . . takes over the individual conscience" (4, p. 146). In the terms of the psychoanalytic account, the present study concerns children who abdicate superego functions to an adult leader when in her presence—"Interestingly enough, people usually do not feel acute remorse for actions committed under conditions of leadership conscience" (4, p.146)—but who increasingly rely on their own ego ideal or superego for standards of behavior in the absence of any adult.

The importance of the presence of an adult, and the differential effects of adults in different role relations to the $S$s, has also been highlighted by the findings of Levin and Turgeon (3) who studied changes in children's aggression in two sessions of doll play. The first session was attended by only the child and the experimenter. During the second session, the child's mother was in attendance for one group of $S$s and an adult woman who was a stranger to the children was in attendance for the other group. Each of the children watched by their mothers was more aggressive in the second than in the first session, whereas four-fifths of the children watched by a stranger were less aggressive. These session differences are in the opposite direction from what had been predicted in a hypothesis drawn from displacement theory, and it is of interest to note that Levin and Turgeon refer to the nature of superego development in the child in their attempt to account for the unexpected finding. They suggest the plausibility of a "'transfer of superego'" explanation, one which posits that the child returns impulse control to the mother in her presence. "Self control is a worrisome burden for the child, so that he is ready to transfer his newly acquired control to his mother when she is available. Anecdotally, we know that mothers often complain that their children are so well behaved only when they are not around" (3, p. 307).

The findings of the present study, as well as those of other related studies (1, 3, 6, 12), also have direct methodological implications. They emphasize the significance of the behavior of any adult $E$ in a laboratory situation with children, pointing to the *social* nature of the play situations typically used in research with young children, and demonstrating that children's play responses are extremely sensitive to variations in the social setting of the play.

## SUMMARY

The social play of pairs of young boys was observed in two sessions separated by two days, and the aggression of the older member of each pair was scored. Half the pairs' play sessions were in the presence of a permissive adult, and half were in the absence of any adult. Two-thirds of the $S$s in the Adult-Present sessions were more aggressive in the second than in the first session, and all the $S$s in the Adult-Absent sessions were less aggressive in the second than in the first session. This finding is in confirmation of the hypothesis, which was drawn from a consideration of the nature and effects of adult permissiveness with children and of the nature of young children's controls for aggression.

## REFERENCES

1. Hollenberg, Eleanor and Margaret Sperry, "Some Antecedents of Aggression and Effects of Frustration in Doll Play," *Personality*, I (1951), 32-43.
2. Levin, H. and R. R. Sears, "Identification with Parents as a Determinant of Doll-Play Aggression," *Child Development*, XXVII (1956), 135-53.
3. —— and Valerie F. Turgeon, "The Influence of the Mother's Presence on Children's Doll-Play Aggression, *Journal of Abnormal & Social Psychology*, LV (1957), 304-8.
4. Munroe, Ruth L., *Schools of Psychoanalytic Thought.* New York: The Dryden Press, Inc., 1955.
5. Phillips, Ruth, "Doll Play as a Function of the Realism of the Materials and the Length of the Experimental Session,"

*Child Development*, XVI (1945), 123-43.

6. Pintler, Margaret H., "Doll Play as a Function of Experimenter-Child Interaction and Initial Organization of Materials," *Child Development*, XVI (1945), 145-66.

7. Redl, F. and D. Wineman, *The Aggressive Child*. I. *Children Who Hate*. New York: Free Press of Glencoe, Inc., 1957.

8. Sears, Pauline S., "Doll-Play Aggression in Normal Young Children,"*Psychological Monographs*, LXV, No. 6 (1951).

9. Sears, R. R., "Influence of Methodological Factors on Doll-Play Performance," *Child Development*, XVIII (1947), 190-97.

10. ——, Eleanor E. Maccoby, and H. Levin, "Patterns of Child Rearing." Evanston, Ill.: Row, Peterson & Company, 1957.

11. Siegel, Alberta E., "Film-Mediated Fantasy Aggression and Strength of Aggressive Drive," *Child Development*, XXVII (1956), 365-78.

12. ——, "Aggressive Behavior of Young Children in the Absence of an Adult," *Child Development*, XXVIII (1957), 371-78.

13. Siegel, S., *Nonparametric Statistics for the Behavioral Sciences*. New York: McGraw-Hill Book Company, 1956.

# 48

# A New Look at Classroom Discipline

### DAVID P. AUSUBEL

A few years ago, in one of our better New England high schools, two members of the school's counseling staff happened to be walking in the building when their attention was drawn to sounds of a disturbance in an adjoining corridor. Investigating further, they found that two boys, surrounded by a knot of curious onlookers, were engaged in an all-out switchblade fight. One counselor quickly whispered to the other, "We'd better break this up in a hurry before there's bloodshed." The latter replied heatedly, "For heaven's sake leave them alone or you'll ruin everything! Do you want the kids to think we are *disciplinarians?*" Fortunately, however, the native common sense of the first counselor prevailed over the doctrinaire permissiveness of his colleague, and a near-tragedy was averted.

This true story is admittedly a bit extreme and unrepresentative of disciplinary attitudes in American public

schools. Nevertheless, somewhat less extreme versions occur frequently enough to suggest that American teachers are more confused and disturbed about matters of discipline today than at any previous time in the history of our public school system.

It is true that superficial observation does not support this conclusion. On the surface, practically everything *appears* the same as it was ten years ago when, except in the so-called "Blackboard Jungles," these same teachers seemed supremely confident that the ideal of democratic discipline had been achieved in the American classroom. Substantially the same disciplinary philosophy is still preached in our teachers colleges; and teachers, by and large, still practice the same kind of discipline they practiced a decade ago.

To be sure, there is still an appreciable gap between the theory of discipline as taught in colleges of education and discipline as it is actually conceived and practiced in the schools. For example, in a recent survey conducted by the National Education Association,

David P. Ausubel, "A New Look at Classroom Discipline," *Phi Delta Kappan*, XLIII, No. 1 (October 1961), 25-30. Reprinted by permission.

72 per cent of the responding classroom teachers favored the judicious use of corporal punishment in the elementary school. But the gap is no greater now than it has ever been. In everyday disciplinary practice, American teachers have never gone along completely with the more extreme ideas of educational theorists. Elementary and high-school teachers, after all, have to be realistic in handling problems of discipline because they encounter them daily in doing their jobs. Unlike professors of education, who rarely if ever have to cope with disciplinary problems in the classroom, they can ill afford to be starry-eyed about these matters.

Why then should teachers be suddenly confused and disturbed about issues of discipline? Closer scrutiny reveals that everything is not *really* the same as it used to be. One important factor in the situation has undergone significant change: Although educational theory in the field of classroom discipline has remained virtually unchanged over the past two decades, the pendulum of public opinion in recent years has been swinging further and further away from the formerly fashionable cult of permissiveness. As a result, a growing estrangement has arisen between the general public, on the one hand, and educational and psychological theorists on the other—with the classroom teacher and the rank-and-file school administrator caught squarely in the middle. Teachers, of course, were also in the middle throughout the entire period of approximately 1935–1955, when American classroom discipline underwent a process of extensive democratization. But this middle position was decidedly more comfortable then than it is now, because all three groups—educational theorists, teachers, and the public at large—were moving toward the same

culturally desirable goal of a less authoritarian classroom climate.

It is true that these three groups were moving toward this goal at quite different rates. Permissiveness, nondirective guidance, and the cults of extroversion, conformity, and social adjustment were much more extreme among child-centered educators, client-centered counselors, and psychoanalytically trained child-study experts than among American parents and teachers generally. By 1955, however, the entirely laudable objective of more democratic pupil-teacher relationships had been reached, and perhaps overreached. Public opinion began moving away from permissiveness, but educational and psychological theorists and professors of education, with few exceptions, stood their ground tenaciously. The same relatively extreme permissive doctrines of discipline are still dominant in teachers colleges, even though educational philosophy in the post-Sputnik era has generally become less permissive in most other areas, such as curriculum.

Now, it was one thing for teachers to swim in the middle of two streams moving in the same historically necessary direction, and to enjoy the approbation of both the general public and of their own professional leaders. It is quite another for them to be caught between two opposing streams, and to be faced with the problem of having to choose between the spirit of the times, on the one hand, and the historically obsolete ideological extremism of their former professors on the other.

## HISTORICAL AND CULTURAL PERSPECTIVE

Before examining how particular concepts and practices of discipline have gone astray, it might be profitable first to view the problem in historical perspective within a broader cultural context. The revolution in classroom discipline that swept American schools between 1935 and 1955 was as necessary as it was inevitable. Teacher-pupil relationships had to be brought into closer alignment with the general spirit of adult egalitarianism in American society; and a more desirable balance had to be achieved between the actual dependence of children on adult direction and their realistic capacities for exercising self-direction and self-discipline. It was inevitable, of course, that we would go too far in redressing the balance—in overdoing the permissiveness and in cutting back adult control and guidance too drastically. Much more serious, however, were the deplorable consequences of de-emphasizing certain other traditional American values in the enthusiasm of democratizing adult-child relationships.

Thus, in stressing the inherent right of children to receive the consideration to which they are entitled, we have neglected the equally valid claims of age and maturity. In debunking superficial and unilateral forms of etiquette, we have lost sight of the importance of genuine courtesy in human relationships. And in attacking despotic and abusive adult rule, we have failed to cultivate appropriate respect for just and rightful authority.

By respect for age I do not mean uncritical veneration or ancestor worship, but simply the consideration that is due all human beings at any stage in the life cycle. Yet our cultural attitude toward middle-aged and elderly persons tends to be patronizing and slightly contemptuous. Because they quite understandably lack the exuberance and venturesomeness of youth, they are often cavalierly dismissed as "has-beens" or as bumbling, ineffectual fuddy-duddies.

Courtesy is another of our most valuable cultural assets that was overlooked in the frenzy of extending democracy to home and school. It is fashionable in many quarters—not only among the younger set—to regard good manners and the more subtle amenities of interpersonal relationships as hollow formalities. But even the highly stylized bowing ceremony of the Japanese is far from being an empty gesture. It symbolizes deep and culturally ingrained respect for the dignity of the individual and genuine concern for his pride and feelings. Although bowing is obviously incongruous with our modern way of life, concern for the pride, feelings, and dignity of every human being is one of our most cherished American values. Hence, since courtesy is basically an institutionalized set of rules designed to safeguard and implement this legitimate cultural concern, those who sneer at courtesy, whether they realize it or not, sneer at nothing less than human dignity.

Finally, our culture has tended to put authority figures in an anomalous and untenable position, particularly in the school environment. We have assigned them the necessary and often distasteful task of authority figures the world over, that is, to enforce certain basic standards of conduct; but in too many instances we have failed to give them the respect, the authority, and the protection commensurate with this responsibility. When they conscientiously attempt to apply without fear or favor the community approved sanctions for violating these standards, we accuse them of being punitive, vindictive, and authoritarian. School administrators, of course, are not above criticism and reproach when they use poor judgment or exceed their authority; but society has an obligation to protect them from disrespect and abuse for simply doing their duty and exercising their just and necessary disciplinary prerogatives. In our present cultural climate, therefore, it is small wonder that many principals and super-intendents of schools are more concern-ed with courting general popularity than with enforcing desirable norms of pupil behavior.

## THE BRIGHTER SIDE OF THE COIN

In pointing out some of the failings of our recent approach to discipline, I do not mean to detract in any way from our genuine accomplishments. The latter are extremely impressive when compared with disciplinary prac-tices in many other countries. I recently had an opportunity to study secondary schools in New Zealand, an English-speaking welfare state of British origin with a pioneering tradition not unlike our own. School discipline in New Zea-land high schools connotes explicit sub-jection to authority and implicit habits of obedience that are enforced by a very heavy-handed set of controls and punishments. It implies a very identifi-able atmosphere of classroom control which the teacher maintains with much deliberate effort—in much the same sense that he strives to have his pupils understand and assimilate the subject matter he teaches. For example, it is not uncommon for a New Zealand high-school teacher to begin the school year by exhibiting a cane to his class and announcing that he fully intends to use it on the first pupil who steps out of line.

By contrast, the American approach to discipline seems laudably incidental. Our teachers tend to feel that the cause of discipline is adequately served if pupils exercise sufficient self-control and observe a minimum set of rules with sufficient decorum to enable classroom work to proceed in an orderly, efficient manner. They do not, in other words, strive deliberately for discipline as an explicit goal in its own right. They assume instead that good discipline is *ordinarily* a natural by-product of interesting lessons and of a wholesome teacher-pupil relationship; that the vast majority of pupils respond posi-tively to fair and kindly treatment; that respect for the teacher is a usual accompaniment of the latter's superior knowledge, experience, and status as a leader, and does not have to be rein-forced by such artificial props and status symbols as differences in clothing, mode of address, and fear of the strap. Hence they treat adolescents as matur-ing young adults rather than as unruly children, and implicitly expect them to respond in kind—which they usually do. And it was a very gratifying ex-perience to discover that despite the absence of strict authoritarian controls, American high-school students, on the whole, behave more decorously than their New Zealand counterparts—particularly when not under direct supervision.

## SCIENCE OR OPINION ?

Discipline today is much less a science than a matter of opinion. It not only shifts in response to various social, economic, and ideological factors, but also manifests all of the cyclical proper-ties of fads and fashions. Objective scientific evidence about the relative merits of different types of discipline is extremely sparse. Indeed it is highly questionable to what extent valid objective data are obtainable and even relevant in matters of discipline. Wheth-er or not particular disciplinary prac-tices are appropriate depends, in the first place, on the particular values, institutions, and kinds of personal relationships prevailing in a given culture; and, second, any definitive empirical test of appropriateness would have to be conducted over such an extended period of time that its conclusions would tend to be rendered obsolete by intervening changes in significant social conditions. For all practical purposes, therefore, the choice of disciplinary policy involves taking a rationally defensible and self-consistent position based on value preferences, on relevant considerations of child development, and on individual experience and judgment.

The fact that discipline cannot be placed on a largely scientific basis, however, does not mean that one position is as good as another or that no public policy whatsoever is warranted. Society is continually obliged to resolve issues of much greater moment with even less objective evidence on which to base a decision. Under the circumstances, all we can reasonably expect is greater humility and less dogmatism on the part of those engaged in formulating disciplinary policy. Thus, the most disturbing aspect of the entire problem is not the fact that there is precious little scientific evidence to support the disciplinary doctrines expounded in our colleges of education and educational journals and textbooks, but rather the ubiquitous tendency to represent purely personal opinions and biases as if they were the incontrovertibly established findings of scientific research.

## THE DEFINITION AND FUNCTIONS OF DISCIPLINE

By discipline I mean the imposition of *external* standards and controls on individual conduct. Permissiveness, on the other hand, refers to the absence of such standards and controls. To be permissive is to "let alone," to adopt a laissez-faire policy. Authoritarianism is an excessive, arbitrary, and autocratic type of control which is diametrically opposite to permissiveness. Between the extremes of laissez-faire permissiveness and authoritarianism are many varieties and degrees of control. One of these, to be described in greater detail below, is democratic discipline.

Discipline is a universal cultural phenomenon which generally serves four important functions in the training of the young. First, it is necessary for socialization—for learning the standards of conduct that are approved and tolerated in any culture. Second, it is necessary for normal personality maturation—for acquiring such adult personality traits as dependability, self-reliance, self-control, persistence, and ability to tolerate frustration. These aspects of maturation do not occur spontaneously, but only in response to sustained social demands and expectations. Third, it is necessary for the internalization of moral standards and obligations or, in other words, for the development of conscience. Standards obviously cannot be internalized unless they also exist in external form; and even after they are effectively internalized, universal cultural experience suggests that external sanctions are still required to insure the stability of the social order. Lastly, discipline is necessary for children's emotional security. Without the guidance provided by unambiguous external controls, the young tend to feel bewildered and apprehensive. Too great a burden is placed on their own limited capacity for self-control.

## DEMOCRATIC DISCIPLINE

The proponents of democratic classroom discipline believe in imposing the minimal degree of external control necessary for socialization, personality maturation, conscience development, and the emotional security of the child. Discipline and obedience are not regarded as ends in themselves but only as means to these latter ends. They are not striven for deliberately, but are expected to follow naturally in the wake of friendly and realistic teacher-pupil relationships. Explicit limits are not set routinely or as ways of showing "who is boss," but only as the need arises, i.e., when they are not implicitly understood or accepted by pupils.

Democratic discipline is as rational, nonarbitrary, and bilateral as possible. It provides explanations, permits discussion, and invites the participation of children in the setting of standards whenever they are qualified to do so. Above all, it implies respect for the dignity of the individual and avoids exaggerated emphasis on status differences and barriers between free communication. Hence it repudiates harsh, abusive, and vindictive forms of punishment, and the use of sarcasm, ridicule, and intimidation.

The aforementioned attributes of democratic classroom discipline are obviously appropriate in cultures such as ours where social relationships tend to be egalitarian. This type of discipline also becomes increasingly more feasible as children become older, more responsible, and more capable of understanding and formulating rules of conduct based on concepts of equity and reciprocal obligation. But contrary to what the extreme permissivists would have us believe, democratic school discipline does not imply freedom from all external constraints, standards, and direction, or freedom from discipline as an end in itself. And under no circumstances does it presuppose the eradication of all distinctions between pupil and teacher roles, or require that teach-

ers abdicate responsibility for making the final decisions in the classroom.

## DISTORTIONS OF DEMOCRATIC DISCIPLINE

Many educational theorists have misinterpreted and distorted the ideal of democratic discipline by equating it with an extreme form of permissiveness. These distortions have been dogmatically expressed in various psychologically unsound and unrealistic propositions that are considered sacrosanct in many teachers colleges. Fortunately, however, most classroom teachers have only accepted them for examination purposes—while still in training—and have discarded them in actual practice as thoroughly unworkable.

According to one widely held doctrine. only "positive" forms of discipline are constructive and democratic. It is asserted that children must only be guided by reward and approval; that reproof and punishment are authoritarian, repressive, and reactionary expressions of adult hostility which leave permanent emotional scars on children's personalities. What these theorists conveniently choose to ignore, however, is the fact tht it is impossible for children to learn what is *not* approved and tolerated simply by generalizing in inverse from the approval they receive for behavior that *is* acceptable. Merely by rewarding honesty and good manners one cannot, for example, teach children that dishonesty and rudeness are socially unacceptable traits. Even adults are manifestly incapable of learning and respecting the limits of acceptable conduct unless the distinction between what is proscribed and what is approved is reinforced by punishment as well as by reward. Furthermore, there is good reason to believe that acknowledgement of wrongdoing and acceptance of punishment are part and parcel of learning moral accountability and developing a sound conscience. Few if any children are quite so fragile that they cannot take deserved reproof and punishment in stride.

A second widespread distortion of democratic discipline is reflected in the popular notion that there are no culpably misbehaving children in the classroom, but only culpably aggressive, unsympathetic, and punitive teachers. If children misbehave, according to this point of view, one can implicitly assume that they must have been provoked beyond endurance by repressive and authoritarian classroom discipline. Similarly, if they are disrespectful, then the teacher, by definition, must not have been deserving of respect. It is true, of course, that some pupil misconduct *is* instigated by harsh and abusive school discipline; but there are also innumerable reasons for out-of-bounds behavior that are completely independent of the teacher's attitudes and disciplinary practices. Pupils are also influenced by factors originating in the home, the neighborhood, the peer group, and the mass media. Some children are emotionally disturbed, others are brain-damaged, and still others are aggressive by temperament; and there are times when even the best-behaved children from the nicest homes develop an irresistible impulse—without any provocation whatsoever—to test the limits of a teacher's forebearance.

Both of the aforementioned distortions of classroom democracy are used to justify the commonly held belief among educators that pupils should not be reproved or punished for disorderly or discourteous conduct. I have, for example, observed classrooms where everybody talks at once; where pupils turn their backs on the teacher and engage in private conversation while the latter is endeavoring to instruct

them; and where pupils verbally abuse teachers for exercising their rightful disciplinary prerogatives. Some educators contend that all of this is compatible with wholesome, democratic teacher-pupil relationships. Other educators deplore this type of pupil behavior but insist, nevertheless, that punishment is unwarranted under these circumstances. In the first place, they assert, reproof or punishment constitutes a "negative" and hence axiomatically undesirable approach to classroom management; and, secondly, the misbehavior would assuredly have never occurred to begin with, if the teacher's attitudes had been less autocratic or antagonistic. I have already answered the second group of educators, and to the first group I can only say that I am still sufficiently old-fashioned to believe that rudeness and unruliness are not normally desirable classroom behavior in any culture.

When such misconduct occurs, I believe pupils have to be unambiguously informed that it will not be tolerated and that any repetition of the same behavior will be punished. This action does not preclude in any way either an earnest attempt to discover why the misbehavior occurred or suitable preventive measures aimed at correcting the underlying causes. But, by the same token, the mere fact that a pupil has a valid psychological reason for misbehaving does not mean that he is thereby absolved from moral accountability or rendered no longer subject to punishment.

Still another related distortion of democratic discipline is reflected in the proposition that it is repressive and authoritarian to request pupils to apologize for discourteous behavior or offensive language. However, if we take seriously the idea that the dignity of the human being is important, we must be willing to protect it from affront;

and apology is the most civilized and effective means mankind has yet evolved for accomplishing this goal. In a democratic society nobody is so important that he is above apologizing to those persons whom he wrongfully offends. Everybody's dignity is important—the teacher's as well as the pupil's. It is no less wrong for a pupil to abuse a teacher than for a teacher to abuse a pupil.

If apologies are to have any real significance in moral training, however, it is obvious that, even though they are explicitly requested, they must be made voluntarily, and they must be reflective of genuine appreciation of wrongdoing and of sincere regret and remorse. Purely formal and mechanical statements of apology made under coercion are less than worthless. Apologies are also without real ethical import unless their basis is reciprocal, i.e., unless it is fully understood that under comparable circumstances the teacher would be willing to apologize to his pupils.

A final distortion of democratic classroom discipline associated with the extreme child-centered approach to education is the notion that children are equipped in some mysterious fashion for knowing precisely what is best for them. "Scientific proof" of this proposition is adduced from the fact that nutrition is adequately maintained and existing deficiency conditions are spontaneously corrected when infants are permitted to select their own diet. If the child can successfully choose his diet, runs the argument, he must certainly know what is best for him in *all* areas, including curriculum and classroom management.

This doctrine, however, has even less face validity than the three other distorted concepts of school discipline. Because the human being is sensitive in early childhood to internal cues of physiological needs, we cannot con-

clude that he is similarly sensitive to complex intellectual and moral needs, or that he has sufficient experience, perspective, and judgment to make intelligent decisions in these latter areas. Even in the field of nutrition, self-selection is a reliable criterion of need only during early infancy. The current interests and opinions of immature pupils can hardly be considered reliable guideposts and adequate substitutes for seasoned judgment in designing a curriculum or in formulating rules of classroom behavior. Hence, while it is reasonable to consider the views of pupils in these matters, teachers and school administrators cannot abdicate their responsibility for making the final decisions.

## WHAT NEEDS TO BE DONE

In seeking to correct these undesirable permissive distortions of classroom democracy, it would be foolhardy to return to the equally undesirable opposite extreme of authoritarianism that flourished in this country up to a quarter of a century ago, and still prevails in many Western nations. Democratic school discipline is still an appropriate and realistic goal for American education; hence there is no need to throw away the baby with the bath water. It is only necessary to discard the aforementioned permissivist doctrines masquerading under the banners of democracy and behavioral science, and to restore certain other traditional American values that have been neglected in the enthusiasm of extending democracy to home and school.

More specifically, we first have to clear up the semantic confusion. We should stop equating permissiveness with democratic discipline, and realistic adult control and guidance with authoritarianism. Permissiveness, by definition, is the absence of discipline, democratic or otherwise. We should cease instructing teachers that it is repressive and reactionary to reprove or punish pupils for misconduct, or to request them to apologize for offensive and discourteous behavior.

Second, we should stop misinterpreting what little reputable evidence we have about discipline, and refrain from misrepresenting our personal biases on the subject as the indisputably established findings of scientific research. The available evidence merely suggests that, in our type of cultural setting, authoritarian discipline has certain undesirable effects—*not* that the consequences of laissez-faire permissiveness are desirable. As a matter of fact, research studies show that the effects of extreme permissiveness are just as unwholesome as are those of authoritarianism. In the school situation a laissez-faire policy leads to confusion, insecurity, and competition for power among pupils. Assertive pupils tend to become aggressive and ruthless, whereas retiring pupils tend to withdraw further from classroom participation. The child who is handled too permissively at home tends to regard himself as a specially privileged person. He fails to learn the normative standards and expectations of society, to set realistic goals for himself, or to make reasonable demands on others. In his dealings with adults and other children he is domineering, aggressive, petulant, and capricious.

Third, we should stop making teachers feel guilty and personally responsible for all instances of misconduct and disrespect in the classroom. We do this whenever we take for granted, without any actual supporting evidence, that these behavior problems would never have arisen in the first place if the teachers involved were truly deserving of respect and had been administering genuinely wholesome and democratic discipline.

Finally, teachers colleges should terminate the prevailing conspiracy of silence they maintain about the existence of disciplinary problems in the public schools. Although discipline is the one aspect of teaching that the beginning teacher is most worried about, he receives little or no practical instruction in handling this problem. Colleges of education, as pointed out above, rationalize their inadequacies in this regard by pretending that disciplinary problems are relatively rare occurrences involving the disturbed child, or more typically the disturbed teacher. Due respect for the facts of life, however, suggests that prospective teachers today not only need to be taught more realistic propositions about the nature and purposes of democratic discipline, but also require adequately supervised, down-to-earth experience in coping with classroom discipline.

# 49

# Corrective Measures, Punishment, and Discipline

## HENRY H. BATCHELDER

Following is material for a series of bulletins on classroom disciplines that has been used for faculty discussions in a number of secondary schools. Some have used them for posting or faculty circulation only. Some teachers have used sections for classroom discussions, debates, compositions, student paper editorials and articles, etc. The reader may find still other methods of using them.

Basically, these ideas came from a book whose title and author's name have long escaped me. They have been refined, changed, added to, and modernized by teachers, students, articles, lectures, institutes, discussions, and practice. The author regrets his inability to give credits (or ask permission) to the originators of these ideas or to those who have contributed corrections and/or refinements.

If, perchance, a reader recognizes

Henry H. Batchelder, "Corrective Measures, Punishment, and Discipline," *Journal of Secondary Education*, XXXIX, No. 2 (February 1964), 86-93. Reprinted by permission.

some of this, be thankful that it is here published and will be profitably used again by some of the readers of our journal—that it will help teachers and children of our schools.

## Bulletin # 1

### SIMPLE CONTROL

By simple control is meant: a look at an offender, a shake of the head, a frown signifying disapproval, waiting for attention before continuing the instruction, a mild reproof, posing a question to a pupil whose attention has wandered, switching seats of offenders, movement of the teacher about the room to trouble centers, and laughing off minor infractions, etc.

#### ADVANTAGES

1. Simplicity
2. Allows instruction to proceed
3. Avoids unpleasant scenes

4. Has few harmful effects on the personality

DISADVANTAGES

1. Attacks surface behavior only
2. May be ineffective
3. Depends largely on the personality of the teacher

Much of the success in the use of simple control measures rests upon the tacitly implied dissatisfaction on the part of the teacher. Most adolescents comply quickly with methods of simple control, since they are unaware of the exact nature of what the teacher is thinking. This system rests upon the authority of the teacher and/or on approval and disapproval, but may be found expedient in maintaining order in the classroom for instructional purposes for the general welfare of the group.

If this appeal to simple authority is coupled with genuine understanding on the part of the teacher, and if it is employed to teach the pupil that his behavior is unacceptable to the social welfare of the group, then these measures may be justified and very valuable. In difficult, unruly classes, however, simple measures of control may be ineffective (at times).

## Bulletin ♯ 2

### INDIVIDUAL CONFERENCES WITH PUPILS

The individual conference between the pupil and the teacher is, by far, the most desirable single major corrective measure to be employed by the teacher. A serious and frank talk would appear to be the logical first step in the understanding of behavior problems.

ADVANTAGES

1. The individual conference provides an opportunity for a private talk between the teacher (as a guidance person) and the pupil who has exhibited a behavior problem.
2. It affords the teacher an opportunity to obtain further information.
3. It provides the pupil with an opportunity to express himself and to air his problems.

DISADVANTAGES

1. Some teachers find difficulty in carrying on an interview or a conference with an offender because of (a) lack of knowledge, (b) lack of time, (c) lack of interest, (d) lack of understanding of adolescent problems, (e) feeling of moral indignation at the offender's actions, and (f) some difficulty in achieving rapport between teacher and pupil.

All of us have had some study in the use of interview techniques. Conferences are helpful techniques, if they are designed to understand the causes of misbehavior, to learn the problems the pupil faces, and to interpret school or class regulations to the pupil as desirable for individual and group welfare.

*Note*: There is little or no relationship to effective value because some of these methods seem to have more itemized numbers of disadvantages or advantages. For instance, *one advantage* may outweigh ten disadvantages or vice versa.

## Bulletin ♯ 3

### HOME-SCHOOL COOPERATION AND COACTION

This measure of correction recognizes the fact that the behavior problems are rooted in the home environment as well as in the school environment. Genuine cooperation between home and school through conferences, home visits, and social contacts can achieve remarkable results, provided both parties are willing to understand the pupil's behavior in terms of causes and are sincere about wanting to help the pupil in his adjustment problems.

### ADVANTAGES

1. Opportunity for establishing rapport between the home and the school.
2. Parent and teacher may supply each other with valuable information.
3. Provides opportunity for concerted attack upon the causes of misbehavior.
4. Visits to the home provide an opportunity to see the pupil in his home environment.

### DISADVANTAGES

1. Some teachers are not trained to conduct interviews with adults nor to make home visits. A few teachers do not desire to make the effort.
2. Some teachers do not understand some causes of behavior themselves. It is then difficult to carefully interpret pupil behavior to parents.
3. It is difficult to get the parents into the school or the teacher into the home. Some teachers cannot seem to realize how valuable this type of visit can be.

Home-school cooperation can produce fruitful information and lead to correction of misbehavior. The method of handling the conferences or visits is important. Teachers must usually avoid "summoning" a parent to school. Parents readily resent this authoritarian display. The teacher-parent conference is certainly not an occasion for the teacher to "lay down the law" to the parent. This antagonizes, creates ill will, destroys good public relations, and defeats the purposes of the conference

as an attempt to solve the youth's problems.

# Bulletin ♯ 4

## RESTITUTION AND REPARATION

Restitution of things taken and reparation for things damaged or destroyed willfully are generally conceded effective and fair forms of punishment.

### ADVANTAGES

1. Associates the punishment in a natural way with the offense.
2. Teaches the child that damages done through willful action on his part must be rectified.
3. Can be administered justly, fairly, impartially, and unemotionally.

### DISADVANTAGES

1. Pupils and parents may not have the money to pay for damages.
2. Children may obtain the money too readily from parents (or steal it), thus destroying the educative values of the punishment.

To be effective, this form of punishment must educate the immature pupil to realize that what he destroys affects the welfare of the entire group. It teaches him that he must make amends. The teacher's responsibility lies in explaining to him the reasons for the punishment and in following through to see that restoration is made. If the pupil is financially unable to pay expenses of reparation, the school should find a way by which he may work out the damages and pay off his debt. Where parents are too free with money, the school should solicit their cooperation to make the punishment educative by permitting the pupil to work out his own debt to society.

## Bulletin ♯ 5

### A. LOSS OF PRIVILEGE

The loss of privileges, particularly those of a social nature, is generally a well-accepted method of punishment in the interest and training of the pupil.

ADVANTAGES

1. This form of punishment enables the child to feel that, if his behavior destroys the group's effectiveness, society will disapprove of that action by not associating with him.
2. This measure corresponds to the type used to a large extent in the home.

DISADVANTAGES

1. This measure of control may, if wrongly used, deny the child the very thing that he may need most, social participation.

When "loss of privilege" is applied, it should follow as a natural, logical form of correction with no sort of retributory attitude on the part of the teacher. Care must be exercised not to apply this sanction too long. Ways must be made available so that, after the child has had time to examine his conduct with the help of the teacher, he can restore himself to full privileges. This is one method of teaching the child the relationship of duties to privileges.

### B. REWARDS AND PRIZES

ADVANTAGES

1. It is a positive method.

DISADVANTAGES

1. Rewards may become ends in themselves instead of means to good conduct.

2. Rewards may not be made available to all students on an equal basis.
3. Marks (for citizenship as well as for scholarship) are sometimes used as rewards.
4. Tangible rewards such as money and material prizes appeal to greed.

*Note:* The use of rewards is justified if the rewards are available (and obtainable) to all and if they appeal to higher motives such as group welfare, citizenship and service. Praise from the group, recognition of useful service by the school paper and the local press, privileges, the use of students in assisting others, certification cards and plaques for achievement, the use of honor rolls, and the use of honor study halls under student leadership may be suitable types of the use of this method.

## Bulletin ♯ 6

### DETENTION AFTER SCHOOL

ADVANTAGES

1. Substitutes for more harsh forms of punishment.
2. Deterrent for those pupils who have something to do after school.
3. Easily administered.
4. Students can do constructive work while detained.
5. Teacher and student can repair damaged rapport.
6. Teacher can investigate causative factors and have helpful conferences.

DISADVANTAGES

1. The pupil can readily sense that he is detaining the teacher at the same time.
2. It prevents the pupil from getting recreation and exercise outside after school.
3. It prevents the teacher from getting recreation and exercise outside after school.

4. It makes unnecessary demands on the teacher's time.
5. Parents may need the child at home. This system can alienate the parents.
6. The pupil may work after school. The home may need the income from his work. This situation may increase parental antagonism.
7. After-school appointments with the dentist, doctor, music teacher, or tutor cause conflicts.
8. Conflicts arise with other school activities, particularly with sports, clubs, and extracurricular activities. Frequently, this system causes friction among faculty members who want the pupil for some purpose after school.
9. It becomes a problem of what to have the pupil do during detention.
   a. If he does nothing but sit, there is no worthwhile learning taking place. He may sit nursing his resentment.
   b. If he does homework, he is learning further to detest school, since his homework becomes punishment.
   c. If he does homework, he may take the attitude that this is an opportunity to get his homework done so he will not have to do it later. This destroys the punishment effect of detention.
   d. If he does tasks other than homework, the punishment is no longer associated with the behavior in the class where he caused the trouble.
10. This type of control is often used for all types of offenders, and makes little or no distinction in fitting the measure of correction to the offense and to the offender.

## Bulletin ♯ 7

### DISMISSAL FROM CLASS AND ISOLATION

#### ADVANTAGES

1. This gets rid of the troublemaker or silences him.

2. It has some effectiveness since it bars a pupil from association with his group.
3. It "saves the day"—for the other students.
4. It tells the administrator or other staff member that this child needs attention and/or correction.

#### DISADVANTAGES

1. Dismissal from class.
   a. Bars a pupil from necessary instruction.
   b. Creates a scene; can be humiliating to the offender.
   c. The pupil gets considerable attention and may become a hero to the class.
   d. It may be exactly what the pupil wants, relief from the "boredom" of classroom work.
2. Sending a pupil elsewhere in the building.
   a. The teacher, in sending a pupil elsewhere in the building, may be shifting his burden to another faculty member.
3. Sending pupils to the "office."
   a. Bars the pupil from instruction.
   b. Transfers the teacher's problem to other authority (this may or may not be good).
   c. Consumes some one else's time.
4. Isolation.
   a. May not be harmful when the pupil is isolated in the same classroom; bars a pupil from instruction when he is sent out to an "isolation" room.
   b. Other supervision is required if the pupil is isolated in a room other than the classroom.

*Note:* The practice of sending pupils to an "office" may be justified in severe cases. But we all frown upon a *large number* of cases being sent anywhere. The teacher may be shirking his responsibilities and creating a "bogeyman" in the principal and/or counselor and/or vice-principal.

## Bulletin ♯ 8

### A. PUNISHING THE GROUP FOR THE OFFENSES OF ONE PERSON

ADVANTAGES

1. It may be expedient in arousing group disapproval toward the offender.

DISADVANTAGES

1. It may align the group against the teacher.
2. It may create a hostile group teaching climate.

*Note:* This procedure is condemned by all educational authorities. This applies whether *or not* the teacher can identify the offender.

### B. EXTRA TASKS

ADVANTAGES

1. There are few worthwhile advantages.

DISADVANTAGES

1. Punishment bears little connection with the behavior.
2. It creates added distaste for school work and destroys incentive to learn.

### C. ENFORCED APOLOGIES

ADVANTAGES

1. It is often for teacher satisfaction only.
2. If the pupil can be shown how his actions are undesirable and if he can be induced to apologize with sincerity, this method may be useful.

DISADVANTAGES

1. It stirs up resentment on the part of the pupil and of the group.
2. It embarrasses the pupil.
3. It teaches the pupil to be hypocritical, if he gives an apology without meaning it.

## Bulletin ♯ 9

### LOWERING THE MARKS

(Citizenship and/or scholarship.) This is quite different from giving low marks that have been earned. It means lowering marks already given!

ADVANTAGES

1. It satisfies the teacher's need for surface order or revenge.

DISADVANTAGES

1. It does not treat causes of behavior.
2. This is a misuse of marks, which are for indications of citizenship and scholarship achievement only.

The teacher who uses marks as a major disciplinary device is often considered a weak teacher.

Further undesirable practices most educators do not sanction for regular use are personal indignities and tortures, threats, humiliation before others, ridicule, satiation or saturation by repetition of the offense *ad nauseam*, fines, and nagging, scolding, tongue lashings, and diatribes.

Questionable is the practice of demerits. Though they may be effective in maintaining order, they do not attack causes of behavior. They entail unnecessary bookkeeping for already burdened teachers. Such time could be better employed in counseling and in-service study and work.

Fixed penalties for offenses should not be set. Some pupils may be willing to "pay the price" if they know the penalty attached to the offense. Fixed penalties cannot anticipate the many types of behavior that will arise.

## Bulletin # 10

### CORPORAL PUNISHMENT

(Including: grabbing, shaking, punching, holding, slapping, hitting, standing in the corner, *forcing of the will*, etc.)

#### ADVANTAGES

1. Dramatic!
2. Associates punishment with pain.
3. Relieves the teacher's need.

#### DISADVANTAGES

1. Humiliates pupil.
2. Ineffective with some pupils, who may not dread it at all.
3. May create personal battle between the pupil and the teacher. Pupil may act in self-defense.
4. Deepens resentment and hostility of the pupil, creates a further hatred for school, arouses hostility toward all authority.
5. May alienate parents.
6. This measure of control is controlled by law.

Corporal punishment is based on the psychology of fear. It is often administered by the punisher in a state of anger. Corporal punishment may arouse the entire group against the teacher, thus augmenting the troubles.

Corporal punishment should be used by school administrators only after every other avenue is exhausted. In applying it the following precautions must be taken:

1. The pupil must be guilty of some major offense (proven, not suspected).
2. The teacher must know the laws regarding corporal punishment.
3. Obtain the parents' consent first.
4. Administer in private with one adult witness.
5. Do not be brutal. Do not leave scars or bruises.
6. Do not strike the face, ears, or head.
7. Do not administer in a rage or anger.
8. Record the offense and the punishment. Report is filed in the office of the superintendent of schools.

Teachers may find it just as useful to inform the parents of the child's misbehavior. Parents, in some cases, will administer the corporal punishment themselves. This too, must be done with caution, since parents, at times, can be brutal. Generally speaking, corporal punishment should not be used with adolescents or older students.

## Bulletin # 11

### A. SUSPENSION FROM SCHOOL

Those who recommend suspension do so with the reservation that it is an extreme form of punishment.

#### ADVANTAGES

1. Removes the offender from the situation.
2. Allows the pupil time for reflection and time for parental and/or other corrective measures and study of the case. (Pupils should have home assignments and should remain at home during the school day.)

#### DISADVANTAGES

1. Bars the pupil from instruction and causes him to fall behind in his work.
2. Does not treat the causes of behavior.
3. May be exactly what the pupil wants, reprieve from the scholastic setting.

4. Involves parents, who may resent this extreme action.

Suspension may be justified only in very unusual circumstances. Though action may start with the teacher, the principal and the board of education are the only authorities to suspend a pupil from school. Pupils who are suspended must be permitted the opportunity to make up the work they have missed. Suspension should be concluded as soon as the pupil is aware of the seriousness of his action.

## B. EXPULSION FROM SCHOOL

Expulsion is considered desirable only as the very last measure which a board of education can take. It is reserved for those cases of erratic behavior for which there is no hope for improvement under school conditions. The welfare of the group, or others, has to be seriously endangered to justify expulsion.

### ADVANTAGES

1. Empowers the school to get rid of extreme cases such as mentally deranged youths, severe delinquents, homosexuals, etc.

### DISADVANTAGES

1. Removes the pupil from a normal setting.

Expulsion is generally regulated by state law. The principal, superintendent, and the board of education must be the final authorities for expulsion. In expelling a student who is within the compulsory age limits of education, provision should be made for other instruction, such as committal to an institution. Expulsion arouses public interest, but if it is justifiable, public sympathy will support the administration.

## Bulletin ♯ 12

### GENERAL CONSIDERATION AND SUMMARY

1. Corrective measures should be based upon understanding of the student and sound guidance procedures.
2. The purpose of any correctional device is the improvement of the adjustment of the individual or of the group.
3. Measures must be taken for the welfare of the individual and for the welfare of the group. A measure applied to an individual must be destructive neither of the individual's personality nor of the group climate. In case a choice has to be made between the welfare of the individual and the welfare of the group, the welfare of the group must take precedence.
4. In using punishment, the simple measures should be used before resorting to the more severe ones.
5. Punishment should usually be administered impersonally, objectively, unemotionally, and privately.
6. The corrective measure should fit the offender and the offense. Intent of the offender should affect the choice of the corrective measure.
7. All sources of idleness and lack of interest and preventive measures should be exhausted prior to using corrective measures.
8. Punishment has to be certain. Certainty acts as a deterrent to future would-be offenders.
9. Fixed penalties *should not be established*. They cannot anticipate all forms of misconduct. They may encourage pupils to "pay the price." They erroneously assume that all offenses of the same type are actually the same and

that the same corrective measures should be applied.

10. Punishment should be exercised swiftly, though at times a short delay may be effective to enable the pupil to consider his actions.

11. Teachers must remember that most offenses are *not* personally directed against them, though *it may seem so* on the surface.

12. Desirable corrective measures are simple classroom control, individual conferences, cooperation with parents, restitution and reparation, loss of privileges, and the use of rewards.

13. Undesirable or questionable measures are detention after school, dismissal from class, sending to the office, punishing the group, extra tasks, enforced apologies, lowering the marks, personal indignities, threats and warnings, humiliation, sarcasm and ridicule, satiation, nagging, scolding, and *demerits.*

14. Corporal punishment, suspension, and expulsion are to be used in extreme situations only, and then with appropriate precautions and care by the school administrators.

# 50

# The Ripple Effect in Discipline

JACOB S. KOUNIN & PAUL V. GUMP

Discipline is a serious concern to many teachers, especially beginners. The teacher who seeks help in discipline is likely to get advice that draws heavily on lore. The counsel may carry the name of a respected authority or the prestige of a widely accepted educational philosophy.

But how much advice on classroom discipline, even advice offered under such auspices, meets the test of experimentation? How many widely accepted beliefs and practices have been upheld by careful research?

In Detroit, we are studying classroom management (1). In one phase of our study, we are paying special attention to the "ripple effect," or the influence that control techniques have—not on the children who are being disciplined—but on the other children who are watching and listening.

Briefly, the problem may be put in this way: While the teacher is correcting

Sally, what effect is the disciplinary measure having on Ruth, who is sitting nearby, taking in what is happening?

Answers were sought in the kindergartens of twenty-six representative Detroit schools. In the study reported here, fifty-one undergraduates served as observers. The students began their observations on the first days of the new school year.

The observers were carefully instructed on their assignment. They were to note any incident in which a kindergartner watched the teacher correct another child for misbehavior. They were to report in detail on three phases of each incident: the behavior of the watching child immediately before the incident, the behavior of the teacher and the child who was being corrected during the incident, and the behavior of the watching child for two minutes after the incident.

Four hundred and six such incidents were analyzed. In our analysis, we classified the control technique itself, the behavior of the watching child before the incident, and the behavior of the watching child after the incident.

Jacob S. Kounin and Paul V. Gump, "The Ripple Effect in Discipline," *Elementary School Journal*, LIX, No. 3 (1962), 158-62. Copyright ©1962 by the University of Chicago Press. Reprinted by permission.

## THE CONTROL TECHNIQUE

Three dimensions of the control techniques used by the teachers were measured: clarity, firmness, and roughness.

*Clarity* involved the teacher's directions to the children. How clearly did the directions define the misbehavior the teacher wanted to bring to an end?

A teacher might say: "Tommy, stop it!" Or "Tommy, you can't do that!" Or "Tommy, that will do!" However emphatically uttered, these directions did not make it clear what Tommy was to stop doing.

A teacher who wanted to make sure that a pupil understood what was expected of him might use one of several approaches. The teacher might give directions that defined the pupil's misbehavior: "Tommy, don't take the blocks away from Johnny while he's using them." Or the teacher might give the child an acceptable standard of behavior: "Tommy, in kindergarten we ask for things. We don't grab." Or the teacher might tell Tommy how to stop the misbehavior: "Tommy, put those blocks down and look at the picture books."

*Firmness* involved how much "I-mean-it" the teacher packed into the disciplinary technique. How did the teachers say "I mean it"?

By touching or guiding the child. By speaking emphatically. By walking close to the child. Or by following through, that is, by focusing steadily on the misbehaving child until he conformed. If the teacher brushed over the trouble lightly, the correction conveyed little firmness.

*Roughness* described techniques in which the teacher expressed hostility or exasperation. If the teacher touched the child, the touch had more pressure than was necessary. If the teacher gave the child a warning look, the look was angry rather than serious. The samples in the study showed no extremely harsh techniques. No child, for example, was shaken or spanked.

## THE CHILDREN'S REACTIONS

The children who watched while a classmate was being corrected responded in various ways, which we classified in five categories. Sometimes boys and girls showed no reaction. They simply went about their business, making no observable response to the episode. If the children happened to be drawing when a classmate was admonished, they simply continued with their drawing.

At other times, children reacted sharply to the correction of a classmate. They lost interest in what they had been doing and became worried, confused, and restless. This type of reaction was classified under "behavior disruption."

At still other times, children responded with a special effort to be good. They stopped a misbehavior of their own, sat up taller, paid closer attention to the lesson, or tried in some other way to show that they were not misbehaving. These reactions were grouped under "conformance."

Sometimes the correction had no deterrent effect whatsoever. Even though a child had just seen a classmate corrected for misbehaving, he launched some mischief of his own. This response was classified as "nonconformance."

At times, children in the audience vacillated between conformance and nonconformance. During the two minutes after the teacher had corrected a classmate, they both conformed and misbehaved.

We related the children's reactions to the teacher's control techniques (2). When the teachers made it very clear what they expected of a child, the children in the audience responded with increased conformance and decreased nonconformance. When the teachers did not make it clear what they expected of the child they were correcting, the effect on the young observers was reversed, that is, they responded with less conformance and more nonconformance. The probability level (3) for this difference, by the chi-square test, was .01.

The clarity of the teachers' directions was plainly related to the responses of the children in the audience, but the firmness of the teachers' technique, the researchers found, only tended to be related to the reactions of these children. In other words, the knowledge that a control technique was firm or lacking in firmness did not enable us to predict how a watching child would react.

Finally, we found a relation between the roughness of the control technique and the response of the watching child. Roughness did not lead to increased conformance and decreased nonconformance. Instead, rough techniques were followed by an increase in behavior disruption. Severe techniques did not make for "better" behavior in the watching child. Severe techniques simply upset him.

Our study recognized that control techniques alone do not determine how a watching child reacts. Other influences are also at work.

## THE IMPACT OF THE SETTING

We investigated three possibilities. First of all, we asked: "What was the watching child doing just before the incident?" Our next concern: Was the watching child psychologically close to the child who was being corrected? Was the child in the audience watching his misbehaving classmate with considerable interest? Finally, how long had the watching child been in kindergarten?

Children who were themselves misbehaving—or even innocently related to misbehavior—were much more responsive as they watched the teachers' efforts to control than were the children who were free of any connection with misbehavior. Children who at the moment were free of misbehavior were quite likely to show no reaction. Children who were misbehaving showed more conformance, more nonconformance, and markedly more vacillation between conformance and nonconformance (probability level .001).

It was instructive to compare the effects of clarity and firmness on the various groups. The effects already noted for clarity were obtained regardless of whether or not the watching child was associated with misbehavior. However, firmness affected only groups that had some connection with misbehavior. In these groups, high firmness increased conformance and decreased nonconformance (probability level .05).

The length of time the children had been in kindergarten, we found, affected their reactions. On the first day the children were highly sensitive to control techniques. They showed some outward reaction to 55 per cent of all control incidents. On the next three days they reacted outwardly to only 34 per cent of the incidents (probability level .001).

## AMONG OUR FINDINGS

To the extent that we can generalize on cause and effect, the study indicates that the reaction of watching children to a teacher's control of a misbehaving child is related to at least three factors.

First, the newness of the situation. On the first day in kindergarten, watching children showed the strongest responses.

Second, the behavior of the watching children. Pupils who were themselves misbehaving or interested in children who were misbehaving were more likely to show the strongest reactions; the particular response was most likely to be vacillation.

Third, the disciplinary technique itself, that is, the clarity, the firmness, and the roughness of the technique.

When the teacher made it clear what behavior she objected to or what behavior she expected, the watching children responded with increased conformance and decreased nonconformance.

If the teacher's behavior conveyed firmness, the watching children sometimes responded with increased conformance and decreased nonconformance. This reaction occurred if the watching children had been misbehaving or interested in a child who was misbehaving.

If the teacher used rough techniques, the children showed behavior disruption but not conformance or nonconformance.

It should be kept in mind that clarity in the teacher's directions led to greater conformance and less nonconformance in a new and unstructured situation. When children are new to kindergarten or to the teacher, they may be especially sensitive to his directions and desires. As the child feels more at home in kindergarten and more at ease with the teacher, we would expect clarity to be less important. Several studies are now in progress to check this expectation.

## FACT AND LORE

What meaning does the study have for teachers of children who are just beginning kindergarten? It is clear

that a ripple effect does exist. What a teacher does to control children's behavior affects the children who watch as well as the children who are corrected.

The teacher who is interested in controlling ripple effects can generally do so best by giving clear instructions to the child rather than by exerting pressure on him. However, some intensity or firmness is effective if the children who are watching are themselves inclined to "deviancy."

The study does not support the notion that the teacher must "bear down" on the first day or "make an example" of a child. Such steps are not necessary to induce conformity in children who are entering kindergarten. Nor does the study support the contention that roughness and anger are simply firmness intensified. Firmness and roughness are different qualities. Witness the different effects they have on watching children.

## NOTES

1. The research is sponsored by the Department of Educational Psychology, College of Education, Wayne State University. Financial support has been provided by the National Institute of Mental Health, National Institutes of Health, Public Health Service, Grant 1066.

2. The inter-coder reliability on a 24-item control technique code was 78 per cent agreement; on a 34-item audience reaction code, 83 per cent. Since the former was collapsed to three dimensions and the latter to five categories, the functional reliability would be even higher. To avoid possible bias, different teams coded the control techniques used by teachers and the reactions of the watching children.

3. Probability levels refer to the probability that the differences obtained could be due to chance. For example, a probability level of .01 means that the difference obtained would occur by chance less than one time in a hundred.

# 51

# The Dynamics of Learning

## NATHANIEL CANTOR

Mr. Robin was called to a conference with me. He had failed to hand in several previous assignments. He came 45 minutes late for the appointment. Another time was arranged and he was 10 minutes late.

*Robin:* What did you want to see me about?

*I:* I thought we might discuss your work in relation to the class. (Robin remained silent.) How do you feel about the quality of work you are doing?

*Robin:* I'm very much interested in the course as you can tell by my discussions in class.

*I:* Apparently your interest doesn't extend to handing in the written assignments.

*Robin:* Oh, those. The reason for that is simple. I don't like to hand in papers written in my sloppy handwriting, I prefer typing them.

*I:* Yes, I find it much easier to read. But I've received no typewritten papers.

*Robin:* I want to do good papers and haven't got 'round to complete them.

*I:* I believe they were all due weeks ago.

Nathaniel Cantor, *The Dynamics of Learning* (Buffalo, N.Y.: Henry Stewart, Inc., 1946), pp. 169-73. Reprinted by permission.

*Robin:* Well, you wouldn't want me just to hand in a paper for the sake of being on time if I haven't anything to say?

*I:* It may be that if you have nothing to say, the course isn't giving you enough, and you should resign from it. That sometimes happens.

*Robin:* I don't want to do that, I'm getting lots out of the course.

*I:* What are you giving to it?

*Robin:* You mean the papers, again?

*I:* That is your responsibility.

*Robin:* I am interested in the course, but I carry three lab courses and am taking the course in flying. The trips to and from the flying field take an awful lot of time, and I can't get around to writing the papers.

*I:* You mean typewriting the papers.

*Robin:* Well, that was the original reason I gave.

*I:* If you are too busy with others matters, I suppose the wise thing to do is to select what interests you most. If you haven't time to carry out the responsibility of this class, perhaps it's best that you drop it.

*Robin:* I don't want to drop out.

(There was a half minute of silence.) Suppose I accept whatever penalty goes with not handing in papers?

*I:* It isn't a matter of penalty which should interest us, but whether you are doing the best kind of work of which you are capable.

*Robin:* Well, what do you want me to do?

*I:* That's up to you. What do you want to do?

*Robin:* What's the point of going through the motions and just handing in black scribbling on white paper—just to hand something in?

*I:* There isn't much point to that.

*Robin:* Well, I could do that like others are doing.

*I:* Perhaps some of the others who just hand in anything also aren't meeting their responsibility, doing their best work? I suppose, too, that what they do is irrelevant to our problem. (There was silence for about a minute.)

*Robin:* Will you do something for me, Dr. Cantor?

*I:* If I can.

*Robin:* I've been in a jam in my other work, too. I don't know what's the matter. I'm having trouble with my girl and my parents. Can you understand what I mean? (Tears started to appear.)

*I:* I appreciate something of the difficulties which must be involved. And in addition you have the problem of doing something about your work in criminology.

*Robin:* You're the only professor I feel like talking to.

*I:* What would you like me to do about helping you in your work in criminology?

*Robin:* Will you give me a week's time to think the whole matter over?

*I:* What is there to think about?

*Robin:* I want to decide what to do about the course.

*I:* Very well, suppose we meet a week from today at the same hour.

*Robin:* Thanks, I know it's my problem and I'll settle it.

Mr. Robin was not doing satisfactory work, he failed to hand in written assignments, and when he did participate in discussion I felt his remarks were perfunctory. He was late for both appointments. His first direct remark, "What did you want to see me about?" carried a defensive tone. His first defense for not handing in the assigned papers was his failure to typewrite them. The second justification was lack of time. (He gives himself away when I remark he meant "typewriting" instead of "writing" by stating, "Well, that was the original reason I gave.") The third reason was that writing papers is formal and worthless, "black scribbling on white paper." He was unwilling, as yet, to face the fact that he has tried to escape his responsibility. My criticism gave him something to think about and feel about. He could not continue in the same way. Some new direction had to be defined one way or another, and he had to discover it for himself.

He was, apparently, dissatisfied with his work not only in CS but in his other courses. My holding him to account led him into another attitude. He suddenly dropped his slightly belligerent attitude, and asked me to help him out of a jam.

He wanted to talk about the backgrounds of his difficulty. It was a temptation to which I almost yielded since I felt that he would be immensely relieved if he could express what was troubling him. But by talking *about* what led up to his poor work would have been another way of avoiding doing something about it. I could offer my help to him only insofar as his difficulty was reflected in the kind of work he did in the CS course. I am not a therapist. My function is to deal with a student's difficulty only insofar as his work in CS is involved. My firm stand gave Mr. Robin a chance to come to grips with one definite obstacle if he would.

Sooner or later, the movement initiated by my cricitism must have led to a reorganization on Mr. Robin's part with reference to the course, or he would have to leave it. If he accepted and assimilated my difference, it meant he recognized the legitimacy of it, i.e., his positive self was criticizing his negative self (represented by my negative criticism).

Two days after this conference, Mr. Robin handed in, at the regular time, his reactions to a long chapter in the text:

"The chapter makes clear the extensive disorganization and lack of effective policy in the treatment of prisoners. The problems involved in treatment are complicated and far from being solved.—Impressions not completed."

The last three words were hastily added in pencil. I had observed his writing this brief paper in class. Mr. Robin was again asked to see me. An appointment was made. He did not appear. I subsequently learned that he resigned from the college, having also been in difficulties with his other courses. (Some of the administrative officers of the college had tried to help Mr. Robin and had not succeeded. I do not know whether I would have helped him if I had permitted him to discuss his personal affairs with me. I feel, however, that that is not my function. I could, perhaps, have suggested, but failed to, that Mr. Robin make an appointment with the school psychiatrist.)

# 52

# Control in an Educational Organization

DONALD J. WILLOWER & RONALD G. JONES

The study[1] reported briefly here examined certain social processes in a single educational organization, a junior high school in a middle-sized city in Pennsylvania. The school had an enrollment of approximately 1600 students and a faculty of 72. Its administrative staff consisted of a principal, three guidance counselors, one of whom was half-time, and eight department heads. The principal was new to the school, having succeeded a long-term principal who retired shortly after the study began.

Our purposes were simple ones: to describe social behavior in an educational organization, and to apply and develop concepts which might be theoretically useful and lead to further research. The techniques used were basically observation and interview. Numerous observations were made at the school over a 14-month period beginning in April, 1962, and more than 60 interviews were conducted. Since the study was limited to a single organization, it should be clear that only very tentative generalizations can be made from it.

During the study, we were quite naturally confronted by a multitude of data provided by our observations of behavior in the faculty lounge, in faculty and administrative meetings, in classes, in the corridors, in the cafeteria and the assembly, and by the feelings, perceptions and opinions expressed by those we interviewed. A central task was to give clearer meaning, order, and some unity to these diverse data.

In their study of organizations and of societies, sociologists and anthropologists have often employed concepts which are integrative and which portray social systems as unified wholes

The original paper is reprinted here by permission of the authors. An edited version appears as: "When Pupil Control Becomes an Institutional Theme," *Phi Delta Kappan*, XLV, No. 2 (November 1963), 107-9.

[1] The study was supported by a grant from the Research Fund of the College of Education, The Pennsylvania State University. We also owe a considerable debt to the administration and faculty of the school studied for their cooperation and assistance.

rather than as fragmented and unrelated parts. We sought and found such an integrative theme in the school under study; it was clearly that of pupil control.[2] While there were certainly many matters which could not be particularly related to this concept, pupil control appeared to be a dominant motif within the school.

## SELECTED DATA

Faculty informal structure was characterized by a number of groupings. One such grouping was based on differences in age, number of years at the school, and certain attitudes. On the one hand, those teachers who had been teaching at the school for a number of years and who were older held generally conservative views. On the other hand, those teachers who had been teaching at the school for shorter periods of time, usually five years or less, and who were younger held more liberal and permissive views. Members of the older group placed great stress on pupil control and discipline, and did not hesitate to communicate their views to the younger teachers whom they often viewed as being lax and failing to maintain sufficient social distance between themselves and students. Younger teachers sometimes tried to win the approval of their more conservative colleagues by talking or acting "tough" with regard to students. These attempts met with mixed success, one teacher reporting that "no matter how strict you are, they still think you're soft on discipline."

A good deal of the "tough talk"

[2] Pupil control is a form of social control. Social control is the process by which social order is established and maintained. See Paul H. Landis, *Social Control* (Philadelphia: J. B. Lippincott Co., 1956), p. 4.

regarding students occurred in the faculty lounges. There were separate lounges for men and women teachers in the school, and while data concerning the men's lounge were based on direct observation, information regarding the women teachers' lounge was based entirely upon interviews. Talk in the men's lounge was primarily concerned with students and sports. The sports talk focused on the national level and on the school's extensive athletic program. With regard to students, the following kinds of discussion predominated: boasting about the tough and uncompromising manner in which a particularly difficult discipline problem was handled, ridiculing students, especially their answers to teacher questions and tests, and more pointedly aggressive references to students who were considered to be hopelessly uncooperative. Interviews indicated that talk in the women's lounge followed a similar pattern except that sports were not much discussed. The term "gossiping" was used in several interviews to describe teacher behavior there. This included more talk about a student's family, particularly about brothers and sisters who had preceded him at the school, than occurred in the men's lounge.

Another type of teacher behavior of some interest occurred in the "circle meetings," which were held prior to each marking period. A circle consisted of those teachers of the four "solid subjects" teaching the same students; it also included guidance personnel, and the principal who was an ex officio member of every circle but did not attend every meeting. The formally stated purpose of the meetings was to better meet student needs by coordinating the work of teachers, counselors, and administrators with regard to the problems of students. However, the circle meetings actually were used to come to a united front in the grading of students, particularly in the assignment of failing grades. While a variety of data led to this conclusion, the following occurrence illustrated it rather well: A circle chairman had some difficulty setting a suitable meeting time for the circle and became quite anxious because "I don't want to be out on a limb with my F grades."

With regard to teacher-administrator relations, two points relative to the pupil control theme should be made. The first concerns the retired principal and occurred prior to the study but was mentioned frequently in interviews. During the last few years of his tenure, the principal was in poor health. The faculty, to use a term employed by one of the teachers, "carried" the principal; that is, they handled things themselves wherever possible so as not to add to his work load. Instead of sending the more serious discipline cases to the principal's office, the teachers handled them or, more often, these cases were sent to the guidance counselor. The counselor, then the only full-time guidance person at the school, clearly recognized the undesirability of mixing guidance and discipline, but all involved gave higher priority to the maintenance of the discipline function.

When the new principal took over, the greatest single concern of the faculty was that he might be weak on discipline. This was mentioned by teachers again and again during interviews. He had to win his spurs with the faculty by showing that he was a stern disciplinarian. In so doing, he separated guidance and discipline, took full responsibility for discipline on himself, and worked hard to show the faculty that he was not "soft." While he has generally succeeded, many teachers appear ready to change their opinions at the slightest provocation. Thus, in tallying

up at the close of the school year, a number of teachers noted that the new principal had suspended fewer pupils over the year than had typically been the case with his predecessor. Also, a number of the women teachers were annoyed when the new principal moved into a somewhat less accessible office than had been occupied by the former principal. We were told the reason for their annoyance was that they could not get to him as easily when they had a discipline case to bring to his attention.

The theme of pupil control fits the general climate of the school as the writers developed a "feel" for it, and it fits the behavior, particularly of teachers, which we observed in the corridors, in the assembly, and in the cafeteria. A symbolic referent was the single roll of toilet tissue found in the boys' lavatories; it hung by padlocked chain from a post near the door.

A final observation does not seem to fit the theme of pupil control: The concept of social obligations[3] appeared to be particularly useful in explaining certain relationships, especially those between the faculty and the old principal. The following incident illustrates this: At a faculty meeting a teacher objected strongly to a proposal made by the principal. The teacher expected the support of most of the faculty since the proposal involved extra duty for teachers. However, he spoke alone in opposition; our interviewees stated that this happened because most of the teachers were obligated to the principal for favors done. The concept of social obligations applied less well to relationships between the faculty and the new principal probably because it takes time for a new system of social obligations to develop after an administrator enters upon a new position.

[3] Peter M. Blau, *Bureaucracy in Modern Society* (New York: Random House, Inc., 1956), pp. 72-73.

## DISCUSSION

On the basis of our observations and interviews, we are convinced that the theme of pupil control is an apt one in the school studied. We are less sure that the school is a representative one. One factor which makes us particularly cautious in this respect is that the school exists in an area of high unemployment and low income.[4] On the other hand, all who are familiar with schools know the stress placed on pupil control in most of them, and the Tom Sawyer attitude which many students have toward school is too well known to chronicle here.

On a more theoretical level, public schools can be viewed as an organizational type. Carlson[5] notes that in some service-type organizations, the organization controls the selection of its clients while in others, it does not; in some cases, clients can refuse to participate in the organization while in others, they cannot. These considerations lead to a four-category classification scheme. Public schools fall in the category of organizations which have no control over client selection and where clients have no choice concerning their participation. That control should be identified as central in such organizations does not seem surprising. Indeed,

studies of other organizations of the same type, e.g., mental hospitals and prisons, focus on control as a major variable. While mental hospitals and prisons are, in Goffman's[6] terms, total institutions and public schools are not, studies of the former organizations can provide helpful leads in analyzing schools. The concept of displacement of goals has been used extensively in such studies where it has been observed that control goals frequently replace treatment or rehabilitative goals. The circle meetings in the present study provided an example of goal displacement, and the general emphasis on control goals in the school could hardly fail to lead to displacement of instructional goals at certain points.

Whether stress on pupil control is viewed as functional or dysfunctional depends upon one's perspective. In terms of the limitations faced by many schools—overcrowding, low teacher pay, student apathy—an emphasis on control could be seen as functional, enabling the school to make the best of a difficult situation. In terms of a broader view of what education might become and ought to be, such an emphasis is largely dysfunctional. A strong emphasis on control usually returns definite but short-range gains and may be self-defeating in the long run. Clearly, the teachers in the school under study insisted upon the shorter range objective.

New teachers are quickly exposed to informal norms as well as to more formal expectations in the process of socialization into the organization. New teachers and sometimes student teachers were frequently silent but interested listeners in the faculty lounge discussions described earlier. They

[4] Another feature which seemed unusual to us was that nearly one-fourth of the teachers had themselves attended the school as students and more than one-half had attended the local high school. We do not know how this compares with other schools but it does seem meaningful to the relationships between older and younger teachers. The question of what kind of person returns is also interesting.

[5] Richard O. Carlson, "Environmental Constraints and Organizational Consequences: The Public School and Its Clients." Draft of a paper prepared for the 1964 Yearbook of the National Society for the Study of Education, 1962.

[6] Erving Goffman, *Asylums* (Ganden City, N. Y.: Doubleday & Company, Inc., 1961), especially pp. 3-124.

learned that they had to be "tough on discipline" to get along; and they knew that they were restricted in the kinds of innovations they could employ in their classrooms, since the use of more permissive methods left them open to the charge of softness. This created a serious problem for the more idealistic new teachers. As one teacher put it: "These new teachers come out of college filled with ideas, then they meet opposition from the old-timers who have been going over the same problems in the same ways for years." Ideals need reinforcement. If that is lacking, it seems logical that the idealistic teacher will, in consequence, employ certain adaptive behaviors. Thus, he may go along, submerge his ideals and not act on them, he may engage in conflict with his colleagues, or he may leave the organization. In the event that the first of these adaptations is employed, energies might be directed toward some other facet of the organization's activity. In this connection, it should be recalled that we observed unusual commitment and activity on the part of the male teachers with regard to the school's athletic program.

The "scapegoating" of students observed in the faculty lounge also deserves comment. Blau and Scott[7] dis-

cuss the same kind of behavior on the part of staff members in a public employment agency. They point out that such behavior has several functions. It furnishes an escape valve for releasing aggressive feelings against clients in a relatively harmless form and it provides social approval from peers, which helps to relieve feelings of guilt for not having done a more effective job with clients. While such behavior led to the reduction of staff tensions and increased social support, it also legitimated inconsiderate treatment of clients. These points appear to apply to the teacher behavior observed in this study.

It seems obvious yet important to note that the study reported here points to the kinds of issues which lie at the core of educational administration—the individual and the organization, idealism and disillusion, stability and the difficulty of instituting innovation and change, short-run and long-range goals, and the very purposes for which administrative leadership in education ought to be employed. While its limitations have been noted, this research, among other things, points to pupil control as an integrative concept of some value in studying educational organizations. We have only scratched the surface. Further studies which focus on pupil control in schools are needed. Such studies may reveal still other useful integrative concepts.

[7] Peter M. Blau and W. Richard Scott, *Formal Organizations* (San Francisco: Chandler Publishing Co., 1962), pp. 84-85.

*excuse for failure to try to teach*

*Displacement of instructional goals with control goals. More conducive to short-range goals.*

# ACTIVITIES

1. What realistic alternatives are open to you in the area of discipline?

2. In what way can you monitor your behavior to help you determine what approach to discipline is best for you?

3. Is there a persistent theme that pervades the articles you have now read on classroom control? If so, what implications does it have for you as a classroom teacher? If not, are there some important contradictions which you will have to resolve before entering your classroom?

4. How could you, as a teacher, determine if you were accurately appraising the attitudes of your students? Assuming you could successfully conduct such an evaluation, of what practical value would it be to you as a classroom teacher?

5. What implications do you see in L. Raths' paper for preventing discipline problems?

6. How would you define "democratic discipline"? What consequences would your interpretation have for you as a classroom teacher?

7. Are Batchelder's recommendations consistent with Ausubel's point of view?

8. Do the recommendations of Batchelder in any way conflict with the research findings of Siegel and Kohn? of Kounin and Gump?

9. Recall several situations from your own school experience in which the teacher "disciplined" a student or group of students. Do you think your teacher would have agreed with Ausubel? With Batchelder? With Willower and Jones?

10. In what ways might the approach taken by Cantor in his interview with the student be related to the findings of Siegel and Kohn?

11. If it were safe to generalize the findings of Willower and Jones to the school in which you will teach, what statements might you make to other teachers, and to the principal, about how you maintain or expect to maintain classroom control?

# Chapter Nine

# MOTIVATING STUDENTS

Did you ever do something just because you felt that you wanted to do it? Wasn't it different—more exciting—didn't it seem easier and more worthwhile simply because no one told you to do it? Since the answer is obviously in the affirmative, teachers sometimes ask in despair: "How can I get my students to *want* to work in this course? There is no pat answer to this age-old question, and there is no indication that such an answer will soon be forthcoming. Nevertheless, there is some research which identifies various approaches available to a teacher. Most motivation research directs attention to those student characteristics that a teacher can watch for when trying to develop the student's interest in some aspect of a given subject. The utility of this research is not always evident; in addition there are times when one report will contradict another, leaving the teacher in a quandary. A review of the articles in Chapter 5, "The Act of Discovery" and "Learning by Discovery" by Bruner and Ausubel, respectively, readily verifies this.

Many of the ideas about how a teacher may be able to motivate students have not been put to experimental test. All one can do about these ideas is to guess which are likely to work and to try them out. Do you think a classroom teacher could test the effectiveness of such techniques reliably?

The teacher must realize that a single approach probably will not stimulate all students equally. For this reason, as was pointed out by Virgil Herrick in his article, "Curriculum Decisions and Provision for Individual Differences," one would do well to utilize several techniques when making a conscious effort to motivate a class of students.

So the question still remains: "How can I get my students to *want* to work in this course?" You probably have formed some definite ideas on the subject of motivation; it is hoped that some of the articles in earlier chapters have given you additional insight. The articles that follow are intended to acquaint you with some of the research findings in the field of motivation and to help resolve some of the major problems.

## 53

# Motivation: The Educator's Dilemma

WALTER B. WAETJEN

The typical curriculum developer, supervisor, and teacher is highly interested in what pupils do in the classroom and how well they do it. Their interest is along the lines of how well a student conjugates irregular verbs or the extent to which he understands the mitosis of cells. On the other hand, there are curriculum specialists and teachers who are not only interested in *what* pupils do, but *why* they do it. It becomes clear that there are two orders of consideration involved. The first order is that of behavior; the second order of consideration, however, is that of motivation. One is always tempted to make judgments as to which type of teacher or curriculum developer is the better one. Obviously, these two factors cannot be discreetly separated in practice, although we can for the

Walter B. Waetjen, "Motivation: The Educator's Dilemma." The original paper is reprinted by permission of the author. The manuscript is a part of the *Proceedings* (1965) of the Ohio Association for Supervision and Curriculum Development Research Institute.

moment separate them for the purposes of discussion.

When a teacher asks himself the question "What motivated this pupil's behavior?" he is asking to have identified one or more of three different things. The first of these is an environmental determinant which caused the behavior to occur. This could be the pressure of a parent to have his child learn, a provocative bulletin board display in the classroom, or a well presented demonstration by the teacher. Second, it may be an internal instinct: want, desire, aspiration, plan, motive, purpose, urge, feeling, wish, or drive, which precipitated the behavior. Third, it may be the goal which either attracted the learner or repelled him. Thus, we can see that when we raise questions about the motivation of pupils, we are not asking easy questions. The complexity of the questions has given rise to a number of theories of motivation. It is unfortunate that teachers and curriculum developers seem to subscribe to none.

In order that this discourse not fall into the same trap, a theory of motivation will be presented; but prior to that we shall make explicit our use of the term "motivation."

For the purposes of this paper we shall define motivation as ". . . the process of arousing action, sustaining the activity in progress, and regulating the pattern of activity" (24). This definition makes it clear that there must be some mobilization of energy and there must be continuous flow of activity in order to assure attainment of the goal.

## A POINT OF VIEW
## ABOUT MOTIVATION

In the process of growing up and experiencing, a child has many contacts with varied aspects of his environment. These "contacts" become incorporated into the cognitive structure, which is much like a private map the individual has of his world. It is the cognitive structure that the teacher tries to develop by teaching the curriculum content. When a teacher gives a demonstration, has youngsters work on projects, shows a film or gives a lecture, he is attempting to introduce information into the cognitive structure of the youngsters. It seems clear, then, that teachers must be knowledgeable about the functioning of the cognitive structure since this strikes at the heart of the dynamics of learning and motivation.

A person uses his cognitive map to make predictions from the past to the present situation. For example, a pupil uses his previous experience with teachers and classrooms to make predictions about the classroom which he has just entered. In so doing he assumes the present environment to be identical to or highly similar to what it

was in the past. Ordinarily this is a good assumption and benefits the pupil since his expectancies permit him to make optimal use of both time and intellectual resources. What must be emphasized is that the pupil is actually making hypotheses about the stimuli he will be receiving. Sometimes the environment has changed in relatively important ways and hypotheses are not fulfilled.

It is entirely probable that the learner does not expect or anticipate that the present situation will be *identical* to those of the past. A young child may make such predictions from his cognitive structure, but with increased experience he would anticipate some difference. Thus, the anticipation of change is partially an *experiential matter*. The pupil faces the present situation, then, with two anticipations: (1) the environment will be, in the main, comparable to what it was in the past, and (2) there will be change in the environment. As experience accumulates, it is probable that the child savors the novelty of change in the environment and this becomes the basis for epistemic behavior.

It is not too uncommon to find teachers who assume that they are able to transmit curriculum content to the cognitive structure of a pupil. This assumption means that we can teach directly, that nothing intervenes between what the teacher teaches and what the learner learns. It is believed that if the teacher makes the curriculum content "interesting" by a few audiovisual devices or by introducing a note of excitement into his voice, the students will be motivated to learn. To make such assumptions means that we minimize strategic individual differences as factors in learning rather than maximize them.

If the material to be taught to youngsters is already similar to or contained in their existing cognitive structure, learning is not facilitated. This is portrayed in Fig. 1. It will be noted in Fig. 1 that the curriculum content and the instructional methods (indicated by the arrows) are designed to communicate to the youngster. In the event the curriculum content is already known to the youngster or is inconsequential to him, there is little behavior elicited from the learner himself. For the learner, such a situation is extremely lacking in and probably devoid of meaningful content. Instead of engaging in learning activity, it is more likely that nonproductive verbal behavior will increase, that motor activity of a random nature will increase, and that the person will become increasingly unable to give attention to specific ideas or tasks.

In this instance, there is practically 100 per cent match between what the teacher is attempting to teach and the preexisting content of the cognitive map. In such situations learning is not enhanced. As a matter of fact, that situation which we shall call the *100 per cent match situation* is indeed an enemy to learning. The type of behavior elicited from the learner is not learning behavior, but is random and nonproductive in nature.

Figure 2 portrays a different state of affairs in which there is for the most part a match between the curriculum content (including the instructional procedures) and the cognitive structure of the learners. Since there is a generous portion of match between these two elements, it means that the youngster is familiar with the material

or the situation because they fit into his predictions. On the other hand, there is also some degree of "mismatch," meaning there are some elements of either the content or the instructional procedures which the learner does not know and did not predict. This is a dissonant situation which results in arousal of conflict with a consequent need for the learner to assimilate or articulate the unknown, incongruous, or unfamiliar material into his cognitive structure (5). To do this, he engages in exploratory behavior. Exploratory behavior, as it is being used here, means that the learner scans the classroom looking for new experiences and materials. Likewise, it means that the learner avoids the more familiar aspects of the classroom. There is an increase in the type of verbal activity which evokes information from other people. In this condition the learner is a *seeker* of knowledge. It would be improper to believe that all youngsters who are in the motivated condition engage in similar exploratory behaviors. We must recognize that the modes or strategies by which youngsters seek information and by which they process it into the cognitive structure are unique. We emphasize that this is an individual difference in learning.

In passing, we noted that verbal activity of the learner increased so as to cause him to evoke information from people. This is but another way of saying that a youngster engaging in exploratory behavior asks questions. It is altogether proper to speculate as to who asks questions in the typical

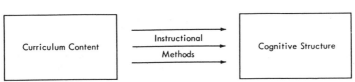

Fig. 1.

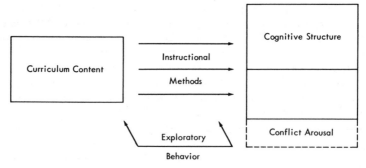

**Fig. 2.**

classroom situation. The usual classroom situation is one in which teachers ask most of the questions. This is indeed a paradox for it should not be the teacher who is seeking knowledge by question asking. Herein lies one implication of this discussion: teachers can begin to reexamine the matter of *who* asks questions in the classroom and the *type* of questions asked.

Occasionally a teacher will attempt to get pupils to learn something by presenting them with a vast array of entirely new and different kinds of material. Literally, the learners are bombarded with new stimuli. The teacher is rather chagrined to find that the learners do not respond as anticipated and may even resist this seemingly rich learning environment. In this instance there is great mismatch between the learners' predictions and the material with which they came in contact. Figure 3 portrays the two things which eventuate when a great amount of mismatch occurs. In either case the information is unassimilated and usually is held in a context of anxiety. The learner is aware that he should be able to articulate the curriculum content with his present knowledge; but he is equally sensitive to the

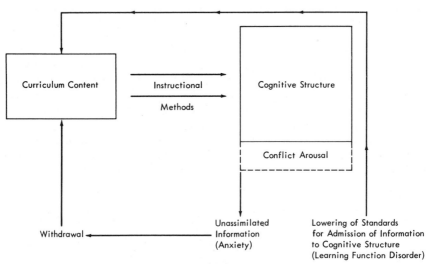

**Fig. 3.**

fact that he cannot do so and therefore he becomes anxious about the matter. To cope with this situation the learner may engage in a variety of withdrawing behaviors. He may withdraw from the conceptual material by being a gross dilettante in work production or by daydreaming to excess. On the other hand, he may physically withdraw by virtue of cutting classes or being a truant.

The second way of handling unassimilated information is more insidious and should cause teachers to be introspective. In this instance the learner abandons his usual strategies for admitting information to his cognitive domain. In abandoning these strategies he lowers his standards for admission of information into the cognitive structure. Instead of integrating simple facts into higher levels of organization the individual holds them at a lower level. This person can be thought of as having a learning disability, for good learning involves orchestrating simple acts or relatively simple ideas into higher and more complex acts or ideas. What is unfortunate about this type of learner is that he is often judged to be at least an adequate and maybe a good learner because he is able to retain facts even though he is not able to integrate them within the cognitive structure. When tests measure only the student's ability to retrieve data at the factual level, these students are erroneously perceived as progressing well even though they cannot be said to be effective learners. By lowering the standards for admission of information to their cognitive structure, they have at once put themselves in a position where they are functioning at a much lower level in their learning.

In summary, we have presented three conditions of learning based on the predictions that a pupil makes stemming from his cognitive structure.

Condition One is when the classroom events entirely match the predictions the student has made (a consonant condition). Learning is not facilitated when there is this high degree of consonance. Condition Two is when the predictions of the learner are for the most part met but there is slight dissonance. Such a condition is highly favorable to learning, for the slight dissonance causes the learner to seek information (motivation) so as to reduce the conflict or dissonance. Condition Three is when there is great dissonance between the learner's predictions and the classroom events. Under such conditions the learner either withdraws from the situation, or he lowers the standards for admitting new material into the cognitive domain. Great dissonance, then, is the enemy of motivation and learning.

Although teachers tend to acknowledge motivating students to be one of their most important functions and they frequently complain about the lack of motivation in certain students or classes, the motive concept itself is generally invoked to explain or account for a pupil's behavior. Currently, little is known about the cues (from a child's behavior) which determine the basis for a teacher's judgments of motivation that underlie students' behavior. Also, there is precious little evidence as to how a teacher's subsequent behavior toward a learner is influenced by his perceptions of what causes or guides the learner's behavior. The main focus of an investigation by Johnson and others (9) was to discover how the characteristics and/or the behaviors of the student (the actor and his act) affect the teacher's perceptions of the locus of motivation, the attribution of characteristics by the teacher to the child, and the expressions of teacher's sentiment about the learner. In this experiment subjects attempted to teach an arithmetic unit (multiplying by 10's) to two fourth-grade boys, A and B (actually fictitious), who were situated in another room. After a subject had presented the concept, the student supposedly worked on problems that were based on the arithmetical concept. After a short period of time the experimentor returned with a previously prepared work sheet which was allegedly pupil A's work up to that time. At this time the subject was allowed to converse with B briefly by using a one-way intercom system. Later the experimentor returned with all of A's work and the rest of B's work on the task and the subject was permitted to talk briefly to A. The subjects were divided into 4 groups of 20 each.

The subjects were then given two "fictitious" cumulative record folders containing the personal history of A and B. They were asked to familiarize themselves with this material and then to attempt to teach a second arithmetic unit (multiplying by 20's) after which the students again worked related problems. After a period of time the subjects were asked whose work they would like to see and they were allowed to talk with that student. Since the subjects were free to select either student A or B, these choices can be interpreted as expressions of sentiment. This choice was made again at the end of the task and the subjects communicated briefly with their choice. The experiment was designed to permit variation of B's performance on an initial task as well as it permitted variation of information concerning B's task, relevant characteristics from the accumulative record and also permitted variation of B's performance on the second task, that of multiplying by 20's. Throughout the experiment, A

was constant on performance and on his characteristics as evidenced in the cumulative record.

The results on the perception of the locus of motivation are of particular interest since they suggest the manner in which these perceptions may be related to the problem of student motivation. A teacher's judgment that a student is internally motivated will tend to occur only when a student's performance is high or has improved and the perceived locus of motivation is internal. If the perceived locus is external, if the teacher sees himself as responsible for the student's good performance, the student will not be judged to be internally motivated. At the same time, judgments about lack of motivation also occur when performance is low and the perceived locus of motivation is internal. A large number of subjects perceived a positive external locus for B's good performance and few subjects perceived a negative external locus for B's poor performance. It is not surprising therefore that teachers should acknowledge that motivating students is an important problem. These findings suggest that students' motivation may be as much a perceptual problem involving the teacher as it is a psychological problem involving the learner.

It was noted that after the first teaching task, the subjects in all four groups expressed positive sentiments that reflected trust of A, and negative sentiments reflecting distrust of B. It should be kept in mind that these expressions of sentiment came before the subjects supposedly had information from the cumulative record about the students. It should also be borne in mind that they had never seen the student but had only communicated with him through a one-way intercom system. It is equally interesting to note the kinds of characteristics that the subjects attributed to A and B following their first experience at teaching them on the first teaching task. For example, a significantly greater number of subjects attributed higher intelligence, higher achieving rate, more motivation, and more ambition to A and considered B to be least dependable, of lower social class, and most troublesome. What this seemingly adds up to is that these teachers vastly oversimplified what seemed to be involved in the motivation of A and B in the two learning tasks. It can be seen that even though the "teachers" had never seen A nor B, had only communicated with them through a one-way intercom system, and had seen their work sheets on only one learning task, they were prone to make many judgments about these students. Also, these teachers perceived themselves to be involved in B's good performance but did not see themselves as being involved in B's poor performance. In both cases, the locus for motivation was external but the teachers judged that it did not involve them.

Recently, research and theoretical formulations have tended to specify certain kinds of motives when human behavior is discussed. The following motives have been identified: achievement, power, affiliation, aggression, fear, dependency, and anxiety. It is usually conceded that almost all motives are learned. As such, one would assume that research on learned motives would be of a developmental or historical nature. Paradoxically, the research has tended to be of a cross-sectional nature. This state of affairs has led to great confusion and lack of any systematic clarification of learned motives.

It is generally conceded that motives are arranged in a hierarchy. Each individual has certain motives arranged in priority order and the priority order differs from one individual to another. It would follow that those motives high in the hierarchy would take precedence over those motives lower in the hierarchy. Recently, there has come to be another point of view (4) about the importance of a given motive. Specifically, this view holds that the master motive which underlies all other apparent motives is anxiety. This paper does not embrace such a point of view, but it does concede that anxiety may be present with other motives even if not generic to all of them.

## ACHIEVEMENT MOTIVATION

As early as 1950, McClelland (16) began a series of investigations designed to establish a procedure for measuring the achievement motive and also to determine some of the behavioral correlates of this motive. Two major assumptions underlie this research. One is that motivation may have some effects on fantasy or imagery. The other assumption is that motives can be brought into play by suitable conditions and that the degree of arousal can be varied by altering the conditions that cause the arousal. The first assumption gave rise to the basic methodology by which the achievement motive has been measured; namely, that of using a modified TAT technique.

The research having to do with achievement motivation indicates there are at least two components to the achievement motivation, doing things well and doing them alone. Rosen and D'Andrade (20) demonstrated that these two components are related to the degree of achievement training provided by parents to their youngsters and also the degree of independence training provided the youngsters. They concluded that the former component was somewhat the more important of the two. In essence they found that when parents provide a high degree of achievement training as well as training in independence, the achievement motive tends to be rather high in youngsters. It should be pointed out that this experiment was conducted with ten-year-old elementary school boys. More recently, Mitchell (18) factor-analyzed the dimensions of the achievement motive. This investigation came about as the result of a larger study of the cultural and situational determinants of achievement motivation for a large group of college students. The purpose of the study was to determine whether achievement motivation was a unitary construct with invariable meaning, or a complex of relatively independent dimensions. Twenty-nine different indices of achievement motivation were subjected to factor analysis. Ultimately, six factors were identified: academic motivation and efficiency (the only factor highly predictive of academic performance), wish-fulfillment motivation, nonacademic achievement motivation, self-satisfaction, external pressure to achieve, and imputed generalized motivation without attendant effort. What this seems to indicate is that the achievement motive is a rather complex psychological phenomenon which cannot be reduced to a simple construct for immediate application in the classroom.

Other studies have attempted to ascertain behavioral correlates of the achievement motive. For example, Atkinson (1) investigated the affect of individual differences in strength of achievement motive on risk-taking behavior. It was hypothesized that persons having high achievement motivation scores would prefer intermediate risk (or difficulty) to a greater extent than a person having low achievement motivation scores. The subjects for this study were sophomore-level psychology students at the University of Michigan. Achievement motivation was measured by the Test of Insight developed by French, which is a projective test consisting of single sentence descriptions of behavior which the subject is required to "explain." An example: "Tom always lets the other fellow win." An individual who is predominantly achievement oriented would be expected to see Tom's behavior as stemming from that motive and might say, "He's afraid that if he tried to win he would fail so he makes a big show of not trying." Each group of subjects was shown a shuffleboard arrangement consisting of a chalk circle one foot in diameter. Fifteen lines, 1 foot apart, were marked on the floor. The closest line was 1 foot away from the target; the farthest line was 15 feet away. The subjects were given ten practice shots and then told the "big game" would begin. They were told to try to get the highest possible score, the score being the sum of the distances of the hits, in five attempts, from any of the lines. The probability of success was written for each line beside them on the floor.

The results indicated that the high achievement motivation group took more shots from lines closer to the target than the low motivation group. On the first trial of test shots, 64 per cent of the high achievement motivation group shot from 2 feet to 6 feet, while only 39 per cent of the low achievement motivation group shot from this region. Five of the low achievement motivation group but none of the high achievement motivation group shot from the 15-foot line. Men who were high in achievement motivation showed a fairly strong preference for intermediate risk in a game requiring activity in which the outcome was contingent upon successful exercise of skill and a relative preference for intermediate risk in a game of chance where their own skill and confidence could not control the outcome. Men who were low in achievement motivation generally preferred extreme probability alternatives in the same games. It is good armchair sport to speculate as to whether or not these findings are related to pupil behaviors which teachers encounter frequently. For example, is it possible that the student who delays his studying until the night before an examination is engaging in a high risk activity, possibly indicating low achievement motivation? Is it equally possible that the student who postpones working on a long-term assignment, such as a term paper, until the evening before it is due, is also engaging in a high risk activity, again indicative of low achievement motivation?

Another behavior that appears related to achievement motivation is that of delay of gratification. Studies having to do with the relationship between delay of gratification, achievement motivation, and actual achievement are multitudinous. We shall select one of these studies because it seems to be typical of the relationship with which we are primarily concerned. The interesting part of this study is that it was done in a culture somewhat different from that of the United States. Mischel (17) tested the relationship between the need for achievement (achievement motivation) and patterns of preference for reinforcement with respect to delay of gratification. A total of 112 Trinidadian

Negro children (68 boys and 44 girls) all in the age group 11–14 were tested in a government school. There were three measures of preference for reinforcement, of which one was a behavioral choice and the other two were questionnaire items. The behavioral measure consisted of a choice between immediate reinforcement or delayed reinforcement in the form of a small candy bar available immediately, or a much larger candy bar for which the subject must wait a week. The two questionnaire items were: (1) I would rather get $10.00 right now than have to wait a whole month and get $30.00 then; (2) I would rather wait to get a much larger gift much later rather than get a smaller one now. Need achievement was measured using the procedure developed by McClelland. The finding that is of particular importance to this discourse is that subjects showing greater preference for the delayed reinforcement had significantly higher need achievement scores than did subjects with lesser preference for delayed reinforcement. This seems to highlight the findings of other researches, namely that persons with high achievement motivation appear to be able to postpone immediate gratification for the sake of long-range goals.

## THE AFFILIATION MOTIVE

The research on this motive has attempted to describe the degree to which people are motivated to affiliate or form relationships with other people and the degree to which they move away from affiliation. While not a great deal of research has been done on this motive, that which has been done deals in the main with adult subjects. This, of course, raises the question as to whether the dynamic is developmentally the same in youngsters, and whether the same instruments might be used to measure affiliation motivation with children as are used with adults.

French (7), using a projective test called the Test of Insight, measured achievement and affiliation motivation and the relationship of these motives to behavior in various situations. It will be recalled from an earlier discussion that the Test of Insight contains single sentence descriptions of behavior which the subject is required to "explain." The example was presented of a sentence which reads, "Tom always lets the other fellow win." An individual who is predominantly achievement oriented might be expected to reply, "He's afraid that if he tried to win he would fail so he makes a big show of not trying." A person who is primarily affiliation motivated might say, "He wants to make the other guy feel good." The first aspect of this study tested the hypothesis that groups of subjects with achievement motivation would give better task performances when they were given task-relevant feedback than when they were given feeling feedback; that is, feedback concerned with the interpersonal relations of the group members. All four subjects in any given group had either high achievement and low affiliation motivation scores or the reverse. They were given a task (a story reconstruction problem) to work on and at intervals their progress was discussed with them in either task-relevant terms or in terms of the friendliness of the group members. At the conclusion of the experimental period, each group was given a score based on the amount of work correctly done. The evidence made it clear that subjects with high achievement motivation scores working in a situation where achievement was stressed, and subjects with high affilia-

tion motivation scores working in a situation where good performance was given an affiliation value, made significantly better scores than subjects for whom the inappropriate goal was stressed.

The final aspect of this study tested the hypothesis that the behavior of an individual who must make a work partner choice between a competent nonfriend and a less competent friend will be related to his relative levels of achievement motivation and affiliation motivation. The subjects with high achievement motivation should select the competent nonfriend; those with high affiliation motivation should choose the less competent friend, while those high in both aspects of motivation should show evidence of conflict. The subjects for this experiment were basic airmen. Members of the individual groups ranked each other according to friendship, had a sorting task explained to them as an important concept formation task, and then took the Test of Insight. On the basis of the friendship ratings, groups of four men were formed so that they contained three usual friends and a fourth man toward whom the others expressed indifference. The four worked individually on the sorting test, success on which was under the control of the experimenter. The nonfriend was made to succeed and the others to fail. The subjects were then told that they were to work on a similar task in pairs and were asked to write down their choice of a work partner. There were large differences in the distribution of choices from group to group and all in the predicted direction. That is, subjects with only high achievement motivation made more single choices of the successful subject but those with high scores in both achievement motivation and affiliation motivation made more double choices involving both a friend and a successful subject, while those with only high affiliation scores made more double friend choices.

## EPISTEMIC MOTIVATION

In rather simple terms, epistemic motivation can be described as the drive individuals have to seek knowledge. For generations, teachers have described such knowledge-seeking pupils as "inquisitive" or "curious." We prefer to use the term curiosity not only because it has been used by those who research this motive but because its simplicity communicates well.

It is worth noting that the study of curiosity is in its relative infancy, but we are reassured by the fact that some of the investigations of curiosity have been done with school-age children in school situations. Typical of these studies is that done by Mittman and Terrell (19) who sought to determine the effects of three levels of curiosity on the selection by first- and second-grade children of size and form discrimination problems. Each of the 42 subjects was required to learn the size and form of a given object. With each trial he could then connect two successive dots on dot drawing (either an elephant standing on its hind legs, or a dog begging). The subjects were randomly divided into three groups representing levels of curiosity: high curiosity, moderate curiosity, and low curiosity. For the low curiosity group the experimenter presented the completed dot drawing immediately following the instructions and just prior to the first trial in size and form discrimination. The completed drawing was shown to subjects of the moderate and high curiosity groups after the eighth and twenty-ninth correct responses, respectively, to the size and form discrimination. There was a

significant difference in the number of errors committed by Ss of the high, moderate and low curiosity groups. The rank order of the three groups in terms of number of errors committed was low, moderate and high.

What is particularly noteworthy about the study cited above is that the Ss were not selected on the basis of some measures of curiosity. Instead, the environment was structured in such a way as to create uncertainty or curiosity in the children. This would suggest that we may create curiosity by the instructional procedures used. The study suggests also that high curiosity enables a person to gain greater precision in his learning (fewer errors in size and form discrimination).

As we shall see, many investigations of curiosity, novelty, or uncertainty focus on the degree to which ambiguity is tolerable to the individual. This is reflected in the research done to determine the relation between qualitatively different types of environmental novelty and curiosity in children (23). The subjects were 44 first-grade children, half of whom were boys. Each of the subjects was seated before a mock TV set in which two film strips were placed. The strips contained sets of stimuli presented in different order for a variety of tasks. The mock TV set contained a response panel on which there were a button and a lever. Each time the subject pressed the button, a picture was repeated on the TV screen for 250 milliseconds. Pulling the lever permitted the subject to change to a new picture. The subjects were tested on three tasks: stimulus ambiguity (SA) in which one set of stimuli was patterned and the other random; perceptual conflict (PC) in which two sets of pictures of animals and birds were presented that were congruous or incongruous with their previous perceptions; and conceptual conflict

(CC) in which six pictures were utilized which began with a circle and by progressive addition of details ended with a complete picture.

When the data were analyzed it was found that novel (incongruous, random) stimuli elicited significantly more responses than non-novel pictures (P .001). One could say on the basis of this finding that novelty generally evoked positive approach behavior. There was also a significant difference between the boys' and girls' performance. The girls were curious when confronted with an environment lacking in information necessary to complete a spatial or temporal pattern of events, but were relatively lacking in response when incongruous objects were presented them. In short, the girls were found to be more rigid and less curious than the boys. Apparently, rigidity and curiosity are negatively associated.

In the studies cited above, it was assumed that to a certain degree all of the subjects possessed curiosity, and an attempt was made to ascertain the impact of a modified environment upon curiosity. The studies to be discussed take a somewhat different theoretical position in the respect that groups of children are identified as having different degrees of curiosity motivation and their performance on certain types of tasks is assessed.

A recent experiment (15) hypothesized that children with high curiosity amass a larger store of general information than do children of the same intelligence who have low curiosity. The hypothesis was tested by selecting groups of fifth-grade children of high and low curiosity and comparing their scores on a test of general information. The curiosity groups were established on the basis of teacher and peer judgments of curiosity. Intelligence was statistically controlled. The groups were similar in age, popularity, and tested intelligence. A test of general information, consisting of items based on material in encyclopedias available to children, discriminated in favor of the high curiosity children.

A skeptic might raise the question as to whether children with high curiosity retain their knowledge after it has once been learned. Maw and Maw (13) addressed themselves to such a question in a study using approximately 800 fifth-grade children as subjects. In this study, it was hypothesized that retention is due, at least in part, by the level of curiosity children have about their environment. Children high and low in curiosity were identified, using teacher and peer judgments. The children were given copies of a story which was a collection of strange but true facts, mostly about animal subjects. As far as the children were concerned the experience ended with the experimenter asking if they had liked the story and the one thing they liked best about it. Seven days later, a 40-item true-false test was given the pupils. Tests of significance showed that in every case the difference between the means of the groups was highly significant and always favored the high curiosity group.

The evidence from this study seems to indicate that children with a high level of curiosity either learn more in a given period of time or they retain more of what they experienced. Perhaps the high curiosity children savor the story in their thinking and the details of it are more available to consciousness at the time of testing. It matters little whether there was more learning or greater retention. What is important is that children of comparable intelligence, but differing in curiosity, performed differently in the learning situation.

The usual school is one in which

learners take part in a variety of activities over a relatively short period of time. If one were to look for a common element in many of these school experiences he would discover reading to be that element. This would surprise no one since our schools employ the written word as a major means of communication and learning. It is, therefore, entirely proper to inquire as to whether curiosity has some influence on reading comprehension.

Using much the same procedure as in other studies, two groups were established to test the relationship between reading comprehension and high and low curiosity. The groups were matched on sex, race, popularity, and intelligence. A Foolish Sayings Test was developed containing 22 items designed to measure the child's ability to sense important aspects of sentences. Some of the items in the test were common absurdities while others were straightforward statements. When the test results were analyzed it was found that the difference between means of the groups was significant beyond the .05 level (12). This leads to the interpretation that children with high curiosity tend to comprehend the meaning of sentences more accurately than do low curiosity children of equal intelligence.

From these studies it might be deduced that children with a high degree of curiosity motivation move out from a familiar position and attempt to make contact with aspects of the environment that are novel. One might also deduce that children with low curiosity are prone to seek a balanced or homeostatic environment. Such was the basic position of a study (14) conducted to discover how varying degrees of curiosity in children affect their response to balanced and unbalanced stimuli. A group of high curiosity and a group of low curiosity fifth-grade students were established by using teacher judgments, peer judgments, and self-judgments of curiosity. Each child in each group was then administered a test which measured his acceptance of the unbalanced and unfamiliar. The test was a paper-and-pencil instrument consisting of 20 pairs of geometric figures. One figure in each pair was more symmetrical and/or presumably more familiar than the other to the children. Comparison of the test means of the two groups indicated there was a difference significant at the .02 level. The evidence lends support to the idea that children of high curiosity select unbalanced and unfamiliar aspects of their environment more frequently than do fifth-grade children having low curiosity.

Historically, educational research findings have had little impact on the educative process. One reason for this is that we are prone to discount the research because of its alleged sampling deficiencies, the inadequacy of the instruments used, or because it used subjects of one age group. With regard to the last criticism, the research on curiosity has dwelt mainly on the elementary-age child but there are a few studies done with high school or college students. For example, Berlyne (3) used two groups of college freshmen and two groups of high school juniors to investigate the relation between uncertainty and curiosity. A series of 28 quotations, each 1 to 2 sentences in length, was put into a test booklet and students were told that prominent men in English or American literature had made the statements. Three alleged authors were given for each of the quotations but in no case was the true author's name one of those. The subjects were told that 100 high school teachers had read the quotes and indicated which of the 3 names given was the name of the true author.

Each quote, therefore, had three authors' names after it, each followed by a number indicating how many teachers had chosen it. Uncertainty was introduced by virtue of the evenness or unevenness of distribution of the numbers that followed each author's name. Some quotes were designated *hi-uncertainty quotations* because the distribution of teachers' choices was 34-33-33 (100 teachers); *medium uncertainty quotations* had a distribution of teacher choices that was 77-13-10; and, the *low uncertainty quotations* had a distribution of teacher choices that was 90-10. The quotations were read aloud, then the students were instructed to go back over the 28 quotations and mark the 12 whose true author they would most like to know. Then they were instructed to rank-order the twelve selections they had made. For all 135 students who participated in the experiment the mean curiosity score for even-distribution (uncertainty) items was 2.98, while the mean curiosity score for uneven distribution quotations was 2.56. The difference in these means was significant at the .01 level. This suggests that curiosity increases with evenness of distribution of alleged teachers' guesses. In turn, it suggests that when alternatives approach the level of equal-probability there is greater uncertainty as to the response that an individual will make.

The research on curiosity does not have immediate recommendations as to how the teacher may improve his instruction, but certain techniques used in the conduct of research sometimes suggest ways in which teaching might be altered so as to improve learning of students. One such suggestion emerges from a study (2) which sought to determine the effects of prequestioning on learning and curiosity. An experimental group of 24 high school biology students received a questionnaire about invertebrate animals prior to any other information about the animals. A control group did not receive the same fore-questionnaire. The 12 animals consisted of 8 familiar and 4 unfamiliar of which 2 of the latter were fictitious. Following this, both the experimental and control groups were given 120 word paragraphs describing the animals (information input). After the word paragraphs had been read a 48-item test was given each subject. The test was constructed in such a way that the subjects answered either that they were certain of the answer from previous knowledge or that they were surprised.

It was hypothesized that the experimental group would learn more effectively and would recall more answers than the control group, because their curiosity would be aroused by the fore-questionnaire. The findings support this hypothesis inasmuch as the experimental group made 32.41 correct responses on the post test and the control group made 27.15 correct responses. The difference in these was significant at the .01 level of probability. Apparently, the prequestions did arouse curiosity and the surprising statements were more likely to be recalled as answers in the posttest than other statements. The prequestioning apparently "tuned" the organism by arousing curiosity which, in turn, predisposed it toward acquisition of information.

One might take the position that curiosity is an inherent human factor and, therefore, it should be manifest in varying degrees at all levels of intellectual ability. Conversely, one might argue that curiosity and intellectual ability are negatively correlated, and that low intelligence makes a person less sensitive to dissonant elements in his environment. The dissonant elements are the genesis of curiosity.

Spitz and Hoats (23) contribute evidence that supports the latter point of view. Using a group of institutionalized high-grade retardates, a group of equal CA normals and a group of equal MA normals, they made comparisons as to "perceptual curiosity" of the subjects. The Ss were shown two patterns of a pair side by side for 3 seconds. One pattern of the pair was balanced and/or symmetrical or less irregular (LI), while the other pattern was more unbalanced and/or more irregular (MI). The subject was allowed after the 3-second viewing to press a button and to see for as long as he chose, either pattern of the pair. Thus, two scores were obtained, the pattern chosen and the length of time the chosen pattern was retained for viewing. There was a marked tendency for Ss to choose the less irregular over the more irregular patterns in all categories, even though there was variation among the groups. One of these variations was that normals, to a greater extent than the retardates, tended to look at complex stimuli relatively longer than at simpler stimuli.

Perhaps the findings of this study deviate with those of others because the methodology was different. Yet, it was not too different and, therefore, the study leads one to speculate as to why the retardates avoided the asymmetrical or uneven figures and apparently were more attracted to the redundant and balanced figures. It should be noted that balance rather than amount of information was the key factor in selection since each pattern of the pair contained the *same amount* of information but its arrangement was different. A brief excursion into the realm of "hunches" might suggest that the world of the retardate is one of relative chaos and complexity; his need therefore is to bring stability and balance into the picture. The work of Griffith, Spitz, and

Lipman (8) on the difficulty of the retardate in neatly categorizing incoming information is related to the idea expressed above.

## ATTEMPTS TO INFLUENCE MOTIVATION

Because of the very nature of the classroom setting, there is little question that teachers have impact on the motivation of learners. What impact they have is much less well known, but a variety of researches have attempted to ascertain this. One such study is that conducted by Kennedy and Willcut (10), who investigated the effects of praise and blame on a discrimination task under the variables of grade, intelligence, sex, race, social class, school, and examiner. The 720 subjects in the study were divided into 3 reward conditions: praise, blame, and no incentive; 4 grade levels: 2, 4, 7, and 10; three levels of intelligence: high, medium, and low; 2 sexes and 2 races. Thirty-two oddity-problems stimulus cards presented four patterns, one of which was different from the other three. The task was to identify the odd pattern as quickly as possible by depressing the correct key on a discrimination box. Subjects were administered the 32 stimulus cards followed by the experimental reward condition and then a second trial was given on the same stimulus cards. The same procedure was followed with the other two groups except that one group was given blame after the first trial and the third group received no incentive. The reaction time between the stimulus card appearing on the viewing screen and the depression of the key on the discrimination box was the criterion measure. The findings indicate that all subjects regardless of sex, race, grade level, or level of intelligence reacted to praise with decreased mean reaction time from trial one to trial two. Likewise, all subjects reacted to no incentive with decreased mean reaction time from trial one to trial two. Also, all subjects, regardless of sex, race, grade level, or level of intelligence responded to blame with increased mean reaction time on the second trial with some few exceptions. The results of this study indicate that the effects of praise and blame are quite obvious and quite consistent.

The impact of the teacher upon the motivation of youngsters became apparent in an investigation by Sechrest (21). Interviews were conducted with 128 kindergarten, first-, second-, and third-grade children about the experiences they were having in school. An attempt was made to gain knowledge about the motivational factors operating in the classroom and their effects on the children. The interviews were relatively structured and consisted of ten questions requiring an extensive reply by the child and ten additional questions on specific motivational procedures which could be answered "yes" or "no." Examples of the questions are "When you begin a new lesson at school, what kinds of things does your teacher do to get you started?" and "What does your teacher do that makes it fun to learn new things?" The results indicated that young children are able to report reasonably well the things that go on at school. It would appear that one of the most powerful motivating factors available to the teacher is her attention to the child, which she may give or withhold at will. Children are sensitive to the motivational devices such as stars and marks on their papers and also seem very likely to be affected very much by praise or reproof administered to other children. Verbal feedback, particularly of a positive nature, is apparently the most salient technique

by which the teacher keeps the children motivated; but a substantial number of children mentioned that their teacher used nonvocal ways of giving them information about their performance. Interestingly enough, the use of nonverbal techniques apparently declined by the third grade. If this decline is general it would seem that teachers deny themselves a great means by which they can influence the motivation of students through nonverbal techniques.

To this point we have discussed the way in which a variety of motives have been measured by a variety of techniques. No matter the motive and no matter the technique of assessment, none of the studies dealt with the learner's perception of his motivation, which presumably could be an important factor in motivation and in learning. One study that considered this dimension was conducted by Fisher (6) in which eighth-grade students were separated into all-boy or all-girl classes for 1 hour per day for English instruction. A hypothesis of this study was that since boys would be removed from the unfair competition of the girls and since girls would be removed from the retarding effect of the boys, English achievement for both sexes would increase. It was also hypothesized that with increase in achievement, the pupils' perception of their motivation would become more positive. This was assessed by an instrument devised by one of the investigators which measured one's self-concept as a learner. One of the four components of this scale is the youngster's perception of his motivation. He responded on a Likert type-scaling to such items as "I am usually eager to go to class," "I do only the work I have to do and don't do extra work," and "I do things without being told several times." On a comparison of premeasures and postmeasures for both boys and girls no significant differences were found on the motivation index of this scale. This was not surprising for in only one out of five dimensions of English achievement was there any gain and that was by girls. It should be noted that teachers were not instructed to change their teaching style in this experiment. This study would seem to suggest that grouping alone without some type of different teacher intervention has little impact upon pupil's perception of their motivation and also upon pupil achievement.

Much earlier in this discourse it was mentioned that most motives are learned. But the question of when a motive is learned in relation to a certain task is considerably less clear. Many teachers believe that a youngster must be motivated *before* he learns. They are much less aware of the fact that motivation may be acquired *while* learning. That is, the youngster not only learns the curriculum content at a given moment but at the same instant he is acquiring or learning something about his own motivational pattern. This would seem to be exemplified in the study conducted by Kolodner (11) which compared the self-concepts of nonachieving readers and achieving readers in order to test the relationship between self-concept and reading disabilities in children. The sample consisted of 15 boys in grades 4, 5, and 6 with average or higher than average IQ, and a matched comparison group of 15 boys who demonstrated ability to read at what the school called a "normal level." The Self-Concept As a Learner scale (SCAL) was used to measure the boys' image of self as a learner. The four components of this test are: motivation, task orientation, problem solving or intellectual ability, and class membership. On all four components of this test there was found to be a significant difference at the

1 per cent level between the self-concepts of nonachieving and achieving readers. This study did not determine if an initial low concept interferes with learning ability or if the self-concept falls after a child has had difficulty with reading. Nevertheless, it gives some evidence that youngsters are achieving at levels commensurate with their estimate of their motivation and apparently are behaving consistently with that estimation.

In summary, this paper has presented various aspects of motivation. Also presented was a cognitive dissonance theory of motivation. Implicitly the position was taken that the research cited was related to the cognitive dissonance theory.

## REFERENCES

1. Atkinson, J. W., "The Achievement Motive, Goal Seeking and Probability Preferences," *Journal of Abnormal & Social Psychology*, LX, No. 1 (1960).
2. Berlyne, D. E., "An Experimental Study of Human Curiosity," *British Journal of Psychology*, XLII, No. 3 (1951).
3. ——, "Uncertainty and Epistemic Curiosity," *ibid.*, LIII, No. 1 (1962).
4. Cofer, C. N. and M. H. Appley, *Motivation: Theory and Research.* New York: John Wiley & Sons, Inc., 1964.
5. Festinger, L., *A Theory of Cognitive Dissonance.* Stanford, Calif.: Stanford University Press, 1957.
6. Fisher, J. K., "An Investigation of the Relationship Between Separation by Sex of Eighth-Grade Students and English Achievement and Self-Concept." Unpublished doctoral dissertation, University of Maryland, 1964.
7. French, Eliz., "Some Laboratory Studies of the Role of Motivation in Behavior." Air Force Human Engineering, Personnel, and Training Research. *National Academy of Sciences*, Publication 516, 1958.
8. Griffith, B. C., H. H. Spitz, and R. S.

Lipman, "Verbal Mediation and Concept Formations in Retarded and Normal Subjects," *Journal of Experimental Psychology*, LVIII (1959), 247-51.

9. Johnson, Thos., Rhoda Feigenbaum, and Marcia Weiby, "Some Determinants and Consequences of the Teacher's Perception of Causation." Unpublished manuscript, University of Wisconsin, 1963.

10. Kennedy, W. A. and H. C. Willcutt, "Motivation of School Children." Unpublished research report, Florida State University, 1964.

11. Kolodner, F. K., "The Self-Concept of Nonachieving Readers." Unpublished Master of Arts thesis, University of Maryland, 1964.

12. Maw, Wallace H. and Ethel W. Maw, "Children's Curiosity as an Aspect of Reading Comprehension," *The Reading Teacher*, XV, No. 4 (1962), 236-40.

13. ——, "Information Recognition by Children with High and Low Curiosity," *Educational Research Bulletin*, XL, No. 8 (November 1961).

14. ——, "Nonhomeostatic Experiences As Stimuli of Children with High Curiosity," *California Journal of Educational Research*, XII, No. 2 (March 1961).

15. ——, "Relationship Between Curiosity and Scores on a Test of General Information," *Association for Research in Growth Relationships*, I (1960), 27-32.

16. McClelland, D. C. *et al.*, *The Achievement Motive*. New York: Appleton-Century-Crofts, 1953.

17. Mischel, W., "Delay of Gratification, Need for Achievement, and Acquiescence in Another Culture," *Journal of Abnormal & Social Psychology*, LXII (1961).

18. Mitchell, J. V., "An Analysis of the Factorial Dimensions of the Achievement Motivation Construct," *Journal of Educational Psychology*, LII, No. 4 (1961).

19. Mittman, L. R. and Glenn Terrell, "An Experimental Study of Curiosity in Children." Unpublished paper read at Society for Research and Child Development, April 1963.

20. Rosen, B. C. and R. D'Andrade, "The Psychosocial Origins of Achievement Motivation," *Sociometry*, XXII (1959).

21. Sechrest, L. B., "The Motivation in School of Young Children: Some Interview Data," *Journal of Experimental Education*, XXX, No. 4 (1962), 327-35.

22. Smock, Charles D. and B. G. Holt, "Chidren's Reactions To Novelty: An Experimental Study of Curiosity Motivation," *Child Development*, XXXIII (1962), 631-42.

23. Spitz, H. H. and D. L. Hoats, "Experiments on Perceptual Curiosity Behavior in Mental Retardates." Final report on NIMH M-4533. Bordentown, N. J.: E. R. Johnstone Training and Research Center, 1961.

24. Young, P. T., *Motivation and Emotion; a Survey of the Determinants of Human and Animal Activity*. New York: John Wiley & Sons, Inc., 1961, p. 24.

# 54

# A Descriptive Approach to Classroom Motivation

EVAN R. KEISLAR

In developing a useful conceptual structure for education, the topic of motivation appears to require a central position. And yet motivational terms are exceedingly difficult to clarify; in fact, in psychology itself the status of the word "motivation" is very unclear. Richard Littman[1] has given a definition for motivation which appears to comprise no more than what investigators have at one time or another included under this term; the definition, as Littman himself points out, unfortunately encompasses just about everything which psychologists study.

In this report it is proposed that, for certain kinds of problems in the classroom, motivation be discussed without recourse to the usual constructs such as "motive" or "interest." Some motivational phenomena might be treated profitably in purely descriptive terms, that is, with words which refer only to observable events and their mathematical relations. As an illustration of the application of this purely descriptive approach to motivation a series of experiments is briefly reviewed. This attack upon problems of motivation is to be evaluated in terms of its usefulness in providing hypotheses for the control of student behavior, a process important for teacher and experimenter alike. When the utility of other motivational words becomes more clearly established, this descriptive approach could at such times become easily enriched.

## MOTIVATION AS STIMULUS CONTROL

Motivation is usually assessed in education by noting the kind and amount of behavior of the learner. When we say that a student is motivated, we generally mean that he is or probably will be active. Pupils who read a good deal are said to be "interested" in reading, those who are aggressive have a "need" for aggression, students

Evan R. Keislar, "A Descriptive Approach to Classroom Motivation," *Journal of Teacher Education*, XI, No. 2 (June 1960), 310-15. Reprinted by permission.

[1] Richard A. Littman, "Motives, History, and Causes," in M. R. Jones (ed.), *Nebraska Symposium on Motivation* (Lincoln, Nebraska: University of Nebraska Press, 1958), pp. 114-68.

who study many hours a week have a strong achievement "motive," and persons who answer a set of items in certain ways have a particular vocational "interest." If motivational terms such as interest, motive, desire, goal, level of aspiration are inferred entirely from behavior, they have little use in attempts to produce such behavior. Such circularity of reasoning is found, for example, when it is said, "You can tell that Bill is interested in reading, since he spends so much time at it! His interest in reading is what makes him read so much."

As descriptions of observable behavior, these motivational terms possess considerable value. In the first place they are useful in predicting other behavior. On the basis of correlational data we may be able to predict, better than chance at least, that a student with a particular interest score on some test will engage in certain other kinds of activities, or that a child who says he is interested in tractors will read books about tractors. Secondly, such information about the "motives" of students can be used to supply parameters in the statement of relationships dealing with control; this description of prior behavior is therefore useful in the same way that data are about the student's age, intelligence, and socioeconomic status.

But when we infer, on the basis of observations alone, some internal motivational state, the usefulness of such language in education may well be questioned. Even from a practical point of view, a word like "interest" often adds little to the teacher's effectiveness. For example, it isn't very helpful for a teacher to make the hypothesis, "If I arouse my pupils' interest in arithmetic they will do their problems regularly," if such interest can be identified only by the way the pupils act. Since it is still necessary to clarify what must be done to "arouse" the interest, she might just as well formulate a hypothesis which suggests what she must do to get pupils to do their problems; she does not need to use the word "interest" at all.

Motivational terms will have far greater utility for education when they refer to antecedent as well as consequent conditions. In other words, we must identify the conditions which have to occur before the child is active or "motivated." The establishment of these conditions will then permit control of student behavior for teacher and experimenter alike; the conditions are then said to have "stimulus control."[2]

In the series of investigations being reported there was an attempt to distinguish "motivating" stimuli from other kinds of stimuli. Incentives, or "motivating" stimuli, control broad classes of behavior. General instructions may be regarded as stimuli which control behavior classes of intermediate breadth while cues are stimuli which control very narrow classes. While this concept of "breadth of class of behavior" is admittedly imprecise, it suggests that on occasion teachers might be helped by viewing their presentation in terms of incentives, instructions, and cues. This classification system may have "engineering" value in some school situations; in many others it may be quite adequate simply to describe the situations students face without regard to these categories.

Loosely speaking, an incentive may be regarded as a "promise" of a reinforcement. A grade of "A," social approval, or money are not incentives for a student; these are the reinforcements. The situations which "promise" these things are the incentives. Although a stimulus may become both an

---

[2] B. F. Skinner, *Science and Human Behavior* (New York: The Macmillan Company, 1953).

incentive and a reinforcement, when we refer to it as an incentive we are emphasizing its property of arousing a broad class of behavior subsequently. (Which particular responses in this class will be emitted depend upon the other stimuli, the instructions, and the cues which are present.) When we refer to a stimulus as a reinforcement we are talking about its usefulness in strengthening behavior which has just previously occurred. Parenthetically, it should be noted that the term "incentive" is here used with about the same functions as the term "drive-arousing stimulus" proposed by Dollard and Miller.[3]

## DEVELOPMENT OF STIMULUS CONTROL OF PROBLEM-SOLVING BEHAVIOR

While it is valuable to continue normative studies of our pupils to find out what stimuli are effective incentives for them, it is even more important to find out how new incentives are developed. An attempt was made to conceptualize one such process in Experiment I. The hypothesis for this experiment was that if a neutral stimulus (a bell and light combination) is present when the child is reinforced for solving a variety of problems but is not present when he is not reinforced, then this stimulus will gain control of the problem-solving behavior; it will become an incentive.

Twenty-two second-grade children were tested individually. When presented with a picture card, each child moved a knob along any of three grooves. Moving the knob in the correct groove was reinforced with marbles to be exchanged later for trinkets. For each of three different cards, the chil-

dren learned to give the correct response a variable number of times only when a bell and light were presented with the card; responses to the card alone were never reinforced.

On the test, in which no responses were reinforced, each child was shown a new card for just one trial. Half the children were presented with the bell and light (the incentive) in addition; the other half were given no such stimulus pattern. The number of responses each child gave before stopping was then recorded. Ten of the group with the incentive present and one of the group without the incentive were above the median $(p < .01)$. Since the children were clearly more active in this new problem when the incentive was present than in its absence, we may conclude that, under these conditions, by associating a neutral stimulus with reinforcement in a variety of problems, its presence in a new task will bring about problem-solving activity.

This descriptive approach to motivation may have some utility in suggesting hypotheses for researcher and teacher. For the researcher it means that particular attention must be given to the prior reinforcements his subjects have had with the stimuli present during the experiment. In Hurlock's classic study,[4] for example, pupils who had been praised for several days were found to do better on an arithmetic test than pupils who had been reproved. That this may reflect nothing about a general change of skill in arithmetic may easily be tested by changing the incentives (but not the instructions or cues); if, after the experiment, the same type of test had been given by the local Kiwanis club with a promise of bicycles for superior performance,

[3] J. Dollard and N. E. Miller, *Personality and Psychotherapy* (New York: McGraw-Hill Book Company, 1950).

[4] Elizabeth Hurlock, "An Evaluation of Certain Incentives Used in School Work," *Journal of Educational Psychology*, XVI (1925), 145-59.

both groups might have done equally well.

Many school children appear inactive in school situations although they act differently on the playground or in the shop. Instead of saying that these children are "disinterested" or "nonmotivated," it may be more helpful to the teacher to say that the school setting is no incentive for such children. She might act upon a hypothesis which states that if such children are provided with a wealth of appropriately administered reinforcements in the classroom setting, they will participate actively in school.

## STIMULUS CONTROL AND THE ENERGIZING FUNCTION OF DRIVE

It will be objected that the illustration of "motivating stimulus" given in the previous experiment was inadequate, that the bell and light merely informed the child when it would be worth his effort, or that the "real motivators" were somewhere inside the child. But we do not yet have any way of determining the "real motivators." If these motive states are inferred entirely from behavior, they have little value for control. In the field of primary motivation such as hunger, the energizing function of drive is a respectable intervening variable, anchored between data on antecedent conditions such as hours of deprivation and data on consequent conditions like eating behavior. But even here Estes[5] has proposed a stimulus-response theory of drive which places the energizing function in a position subordinate to that of stimulus. When we come to secondary or learned motivation, the energizing function of drives is even

[5] W. K. Estes, "Stimulus-Response Theory of Drive," in M. R. Jones, *op. cit.* pp. 35-68.

more confused. In very few instances have we a way of using secondary drive as a true intervening variable. Most of the time it is simply a construct which offers no value for the purposes of control of behavior. By regarding the stimuli as the "motivators" we can move ahead with our research in certain areas of education without waiting for psychologists of motivation to clarify the nature of secondary drives.

## LEARNING SETS

A central "motivational" problem in education is that of getting students to change their behavior as a result of being presented with information or a pattern of stimuli. For example, when students are given a lecture, shown a film, presented with printed material, or provided with a demonstration, it is hoped that they will learn (i.e., change their behavior) as a result. This "motivational" problem has been frequently stated as one of teaching students to "pay attention," to "study hard," to "concentrate," or to "remember." With a descriptive approach to motivation, the above problem is regarded as one of developing stimulus control of a learning set. "Motivating students to study or to pay attention" is thus looked upon as a matter of presenting stimuli which control the appropriate learning sets.

A learning set was defined in this study as the relationship between a pattern of stimuli, which is not contingent upon the subject's responses, and a change in operant behavior. The distinctive feature of a learning set, as used in this study, is that learning results from sheer exposure to stimuli; there is apparently no three-term contingency (stimulus, response, and reinforcement) recognized generally as essential for operant learning. It is true that one can observe an orientation of sense receptors to the information; the student, for example, stops doing other things and looks directly at the material. But every teacher is familiar with the danger of assuming that students learn just because they appear attentive. The teacher (or experimenter) usually observes neither the response students ultimately learn to make nor the reinforcements contingent upon such responses. While one may explain such learning by assuming that students reinforce themselves for their covert responses or by discussing the phenomena in terms of some form of cognitive activity, the pressing problem, at the operational or practical level, is to find out under what conditions a set to learn is acquired and displayed. The position taken in this study is that a stimulus can acquire control of a learning set in exactly the same fashion as stimuli which control problem-solving behavior.

## DEVELOPMENT OF STIMULUS CONTROL OF A LEARNING SET

The general hypothesis of Experiments II and III was that a learning set (this relationship) is brought under the control of a stimulus through a reinforcement program. For example, if students exhibit this set in a variety of situations where a common distinctive stimulus is present and if they are reinforced for the appropriate learning in each case, this stimulus will acquire control of the learning set. In other words, students will learn if this stimulus is present, or, this stimulus will act as an incentive and will "motivate" them to learn. On the other hand, if subjects learn in a variety of situations where a distinctive stimulus

*and attitude*

is present but are not reinforced for this learning, this stimulus will lose control of the learning set; subjects will not learn when this stimulus is present, or, in this situation they will remain "apathetic" or "nonmotivated."

In Experiment II, 22 second-grade children (not those used in Experiment I, of course) were tested individually. Each subject was shown, through a window in a panel board, a series of 48 "information" cards, each of which presented pictures and colors to be associated. After each information card was exposed, there followed randomly either a blank card or a set of question cards, one question card for each pair presented in the information card. If the pupil indicated the correct color he received a marble from the automatic dispenser.

For half the subjects a green light was turned on when the information card was exposed, if the pupil was to be questioned on this card; a white light with black stripes was on when no questions, just the blank card, were to follow. The functions of these two lights were reversed for the other half of the subjects.

Information Card 49 was presented with a "test" light and Information Card 50 with a "no-test" light but three questions followed each information card, one question for each pair on the card. To counterbalance item difficulty these two cards and their three questions were interchanged for half the group. Fourteen children learned more when the "test" light was on; two children learned more when the "no-test" light was on. This difference, when tested by the Wilcoxon matched-pairs signed-ranks method, is significant at the .01 level. It may be concluded that these children learned more from information accompanied by a light previously associated with a test than they did from information presented with a light with no such association. Assuming that the test provided opportunities for reinforcement, the principles of operant conditioning appear to apply to the development of stimulus control of a learning set.

### EFFECT OF KNOWLEDGE OF RESULTS UPON A LEARNING SET

In Experiment III an attempt was made to assess the effect of giving knowledge of results upon the learning set. Knowledge of results usually includes both positive and negative reinforcements. The material, apparatus, and general procedure were identical with the previous experiment, but the experimental and control conditions both involved test questions; pupils were given questions following each information card. When one light (the "KR" light) was turned on with the information card, pupils were given marbles for each right answer to the test question on this information. When the other light (the "No-KR" light) was on with the information card, pupils were never informed in any way as to whether their answers were right or wrong.

The criterion consisted of the nine questions on the last three information cards for each light condition. The pupils obtained a score of 6.3 when the "KR" light was on, and 4.8 when the "No-KR" light was on. This difference is significant at the .05 level. (Using the last half of the cards, seven under each light condition, the difference was proportionately about the same but was significant at the .01 level.) It has been well known that knowledge of results is an important factor in the acquisition of specific behavior. But the findings of Experiment III point up the fact that knowl-edge of results can also strengthen a learning set.

### SHAPING OF A LEARNING SET

In the previous two experiments, the emphasis was placed upon the development of stimulus control of a learning set. Although this set to learn may have been altered, the relationship between the stimuli presented on the information card and the kind of change of behavior was not deliberately modified. This relationship was brought under the control of one stimulus and not another. In other words, pupils were taught *when* to learn.

In Experiment IV an attempt was made to alter the relationship, to modify what students learned. Students were reinforced for learning certain kinds of things from the information and not other kinds. This process of shaping a learning set may be regarded as analogous to response differentiation. In this experiment, therefore, students were taught *what* to learn.

What most high school and college students learn from their study in a course is less likely to be influenced by the stated objectives of the course, objectives which are often expressed in "high-sounding and broad" terms. Students are far more likely to learn those things for which they get reinforced on course examinations. The learning sets of students are shaped largely by the kind of reinforcements teachers actually provide. The specific hypothesis of Experiment IV was that pupils would learn better (1) the kind of information from a paragraph for which they had been previously tested than they would (2) the kind for which they had not been previously tested. Forty sixth- and seventh-grade children were tested individually. Each was presented with 22 paragraphs of pseudohistorical information containing a date, a name, and a place as well as three reasons for this event. Immediately after each paragraph was exposed, one half of the group was tested on the date, name, and place; the other half was tested on the reasons. Correct answers were immediately reinforced.

On Paragraph No. 23 both groups were asked questions on both kinds of material (order of presentation of the two sets of test items being counterbalanced). The mean score (1.5) made by the group on the questions about the information of the type on which they had previously been tested was higher, at the .05 level, than the mean score (1.0) on the questions of the other kind. It was concluded that, at this level of confidence, the learning set of these pupils in reading these paragraphs was altered by a program of differential reinforcement; the two groups of pupils had acquired different learning sets for this situation.

When students are shown the same film, given the same lecture, or taken on the same field trip, different students learn different things. This is often "explained" by saying that students differ in their "interests" and therefore "pay attention" to different things. But such language is of little value in making education more effective; it merely describes the phenomena we observe. It is far more fruitful, for purposes of controlling what students learn, to suggest that such learning sets have been shaped differently by virtue of different reinforcement histories. With appropriate reinforcement programs such learning sets might be altered and improved to make the students' educational experiences more effective.

## CONCLUSION

This discussion of motivation has emphasized the stimuli in the presence of which the child is active or learns. But it has also stressed the fact that such stimuli function as they do because of prior reinforcements. The crucial aspects of motivation are therefore to be found in the systems of reinforcements which a school provides for pupils. Such a discussion of reinforcements already has been extensively presented by other writers, notably B. F. Skinner,[6] with implications for education. The descriptive approach presented in this paper may, however, bring many research problems in education more clearly within the framework of reinforcement theory.

[6] *Op. cit.*

# 55

# Experience and the Development of Motivation: Some Reinterpretations [1]

## J. McV. HUNT

A recent issue of the *Saturday Evening Post* carried a cartoon that some of you may have noted. It depicts a boy entering his house, perhaps from school, where his father is sitting with his paper. The boy appears to be fixing his father with an accusing glare. The punch line reads, "Somebody goofed. I'm improperly motivated."

This cartoon depicts the vantage

J. McV. Hunt, "Experience and the Development of Motivation: Some Reinterpretations," *Child Development*, XXXI (1960), 489-504. Reprinted by permission of the Society for Research in Child Development, Inc. Copyright © 1960 by the Society for Research in Child Development, Inc.

[1] Earlier versions of this paper were read at the Eleventh Annual Institute in Psychiatry and Neurology of the Veterans Administration Hospital at North Little Rock, Arkansas, February 27, 1959, and at colloquia of the Department of Psychology at Vanderbilt University and of the Department of Psychiatry at the Medical School of Colorado. The paper was prepared in connection with a survey of the implications of the work in behavioral science for child rearing which has been supported by the Russell Sage Foundation.

point from which I have been examining what we think we know about the relation between experience and motivation. When a child's behavior fails to fit the standards somebody in our society holds for him, it is pretty well agreed among us who are supposed to be experts on human nature that "somebody goofed." And that somebody is usually considered to be a parent.

The question is: What is the proper formula? If one examines the accruing evidence relevant to what has been the dominant conception of the experiential sources of motivation, one can hardly escape the conclusion that this conceptual scheme needs some revisions. If we based our child rearing entirely on our dominant theory of motivational development, we would probably goof as often and as badly as run-of-the-mill parents.

Today I wish, first, to remind you of three of the most basic and general of the propositions in that theory of motivation which has been dominant for the past 30 to 40 years.

These are propositions which, although stated in somewhat varied forms, have been shared by both psychoanalysts and academic behavior theorists. Secondly, I wish to cite evidence which calls these propositions into question, and thirdly, to suggest tentatively three new interpretative principles which appear to me to be congruent with a large number of facts and which have interesting implications.

Our conceptions of motivation have traditionally been concerned with three large questions: (a) Why does an organism or person become active? (b) Why does the organism or person act one way rather than another? and (c) How do you get the organism or person to change his behavior to something conceived to be more desirable or appropriate?

## THE DOMINANT THEORY

### DRIVE

According to our dominant theory, it is claimed, first of all, that "all behavior is motivated," and that the aim or function of every instinct, defense, action, or habit is to reduce or eliminate stimulation or excitation within the nervous system. It is not easy to state when this view was first presented. Signs of it appear in the seventh chapter of Freud's *Interpretation of Dreams* (15) in 1900, and the idea is full-blown in his paper entitled *Instincts and Their Vicissitudes* (17) in 1915. The idea also appears in Woodworth's *Dynamic Psychology* (68), published in 1918, where the term *drive* was first introduced into the glossary of American psychology. The idea was full-blown in Dashiell's *Fundamentals of Objective Psychology* (11) in 1928.

Although Freud (17) believed that the source of motivation lay outside the domain of psychology in physiology, American psychologists, untroubled by such limits to their domain, have gone on to answer the first question concerning what motivates organisms to become active by saying that they are *driven.* Organisms have been conceived to be driven, first, by those so-called primary, inner stimuli which arise from homeostatic imbalances or needs. With no shame whatsoever, psychologists have long cited the evidence from the work of such physiologists as Claude Bernard (5) and his successors, and especially of Walter B. Cannon (10), and also of the psychologist Curt Richter (59) to document this answer. Organisms are driven, second, by various forms of intense and painful external stimulation. It has been assumed that these two forms of stimulation arouse an inner state of excitement which has usually been called *drive.*

It is also assumed, as the proposition that "all behavior is motivated" implies, that the organism would be inactive unless driven by either inner or outer stimuli. Freud (17) has been highly explicit about this assumption, and the assumption lies implicitly behind the notion of conditioned or learned drive in behavior theory and behind the traumatic notion of anxiety in psychoanalysis. It is sometimes obvious, of course, that animals and people are sometimes active when it is hard to see how either homeostatic drive or painful external stimulation could be operative. It is then assumed that some of the weak, innocuous stimuli present must have been associated in the past with either painful stimuli or homeostatic needs. In such a way the weak stimuli which are present must have acquired the capacity to arouse the drive, often now called anxiety by psychologists as well as psychoanalysts, and it is such acquired or conditioned drive that is conceived to activate the organism.

Such conditioned drive or anxiety has been well demonstrated in the laboratory. Before World War II, Miller (45, 46) at Yale showed that rats which had been repeatedly shocked in a white box would, when later returned to the white box, make an effort to escape. Moreover, in the course of these efforts, they could be got to learn new skills such as that of turning a wheel to open a door. Rats which had not been shocked in the white box made no such efforts to escape. In another demonstration Solomon and Wynne (64) have shown that dogs which have experienced a tone or a buzzer paired a few times with a sub-tetanizing shock will run away from that tone or buzzer for hundreds of trials, with the average reaction time of starting continuing to decrease through 600 such trials. In my own work (31) rats fed irregularly in infancy ate more and sometimes (32) hoarded more than their litter-mate controls in adulthood after a period without food. Here, as I conceived it, the cues of hunger were conditioned to intense hunger excitement during the infantile experience. In adulthood the conditioned hunger drive facilitated the rate of eating and, sometimes, hoarding.

Such work has demonstrated that this notion of conditioned drive or anxiety, which goes back to the work of Bechterev (2) and Watson and Raynor (67), has a solid basis in reality. But in what has been the dominant theory of motivation, as epitomized by Freud's (18) later traumatic theory of anxiety and by the Hull (30) and Dollard-Miller (13, 47) theory of acquired drives, conditioning is conceived to be the only way in which an organism can become fearful of innocuous stimuli.

## HABIT

Habit has been the answer to the second question concerned with why an animal or person acts one way rather than another. The organism is controlled by the habits which have served to reduce drive in the past when that organism was in the presence of the inner and outer drive stimuli and the cue stimuli impinging upon him at any given now. Under the term *habit*, I am including psychoanalytic modes, which have supposedly been fixated during infancy in the course of either too much gratification or too much frustration, and I am including also ego defenses, or anxiety equivalents, and cathexes, as well as the instrumental responses and traits commonly investigated in psychological laboratories.

Changing behavior has been conceived to be a matter of motivating the organism with either punishment or homeostatic need to make the desired behavior which can then be reinforced by arranging for it to reduce the drive aroused by the punishment or the need. Although the conditions and conceptions of psychotherapy in the clinic differ considerably from the conditions and conceptions of the behavior theorist investigating learning in laboratory animals, in either case it is conceived that motivation is a necessity, and motivation means changing the emotional or drive conditions which are quite extrinsic to either the instrumental behavior or the cognitive, informational processes concerned.

This dominant theory has been a conceptual edifice of large dimensions and of considerable detail. It has provided a plausible account of both personality development and social motives. The experimental facts of homeostasis and of conditioned drive and fear are sound. Nevertheless, it has become more and more evident in the past 10 years that some of the basic assumptions of this dominant theoretical scheme and some of the explanatory extrapolations contradict facts and call for reinterpretation.

## REINTERPRETATIONS

### IS ALL BEHAVIOR MOTIVATED?

The first of the assumptions to be called into question is the one that *all behavior is motivated* and that *organisms become inactive unless stimulated* by homeostatic need or painful stimulation or conditional stimuli for these. A large variety of observations contradict this assumption and imply spontaneous molar activity. Beach (1) has reviewed the observations of play in the young to show that playful activities are most likely to occur when either young animals or children are homeostatically satisfied and also comfortably warm. The very occurrence of either homeostatic need or strong external stimulation stops play and turns the young animal or child to activities calculated to relieve such stimulation. Berlyne (3, 4) has shown that well-fed and watered rats will explore areas new to them if given only the opportunity. Montgomery (49), moreover, has shown that hunger and thirst tend to limit the exploratory behavior of rats rather than facilitate it, and Montgomery and Monkman (50), as well as others, have shown that conditioned fear inhibits exploration. Harlow, Harlow, and Meyer (23) have demonstrated that well-fed monkeys will learn to unassemble a three-device puzzle with no other drive and "no other reward than the privilege of unassembling it." In another study Harlow (20) found two well-fed and

well-watered monkeys worked repeatedly at unassembling a six-device puzzle for 10 continuous hours, and they were still showing what he characterized as enthusiasm for their work on the tenth hour of testing. From his observations of the human child, moreover, Piaget (55) remarks repeatedly on the enthusiastic and repeated performance of such emerging skills as the release of a toy, sitting up, standing, etc.

Such evidences of spontaneous behavior, which is unmotivated in the traditional sense, have led to the naming of such new motives as a curiosity drive by Berlyne (4), an exploratory drive by Montgomery (48), and exteroceptive and curiosity drives by Harlow (21). I would like to object that merely naming such drives explains nothing. If we continue, we shall be revisiting McDougall's (44) practice of postulating a separate drive for almost every variety of activity. Let us stop with noting that such observations do contradict our assumption that organisms will become inactive unless driven by homeostatic needs and painful stimuli and give up this ancient Greek notion that living matter is inert substance to which motion must be imparted by extrinsic forces. We can then embrace the thermodynamic conception of living things as open systems of energy exchange which exhibit activity intrinsically and upon which stimuli have a modulating effect, but not an initiating effect.

This notion of activity being intrinsic in living tissue is receiving support from studies of organ systems as well as studies of molar organisms. The EEG, for example, shows that brain cells are continuously active (33, 58). In sleep the slow waves of large amplitude are taken to imply that large numbers of cells are firing synchronously, and the effect of waking and stimulation and exciting the brain-stem reticular formation is to asynchronize this firing which shows in rapid waves of low magnitude (42).

Granit (19) points out that the spontaneous firing of retinal cells increases with dark adaptation and thereby functions to prevent the deafferentization of visual contex with darkness. Twenty years ago, this spontaneous firing was considered, at worst, to be due to some failure of experimental control, or at best, noise in the channel of information. Recently, the Laceys (36) have found spontaneous fluctuations of sudomotor activity and cardiac activity which they also see as functioning in the control of the organism's relations with its environment. Especially intriguing is their notion that the carotid sinus mechanism functions as a feedback loop which participates in the directing of attention inward or outward by inhibiting or facilitating receptor inputs. But the point of mentioning these evidences of spontaneous activities of organ systems here is merely to help inter for good the notion that activity of living systems requires homeostatic need or painful external stimulation and to foster the idea that to live means to be active in some degree.

## REINFORCEMENT

This idea of activity being intrinsic in living organisms has implications for our conception of reinforcement. It makes it unnecessary to see all activity as a matter of either reducing or avoiding stimulation which is implied in the assumption that organisms become inactive unless stimulated. This is a second fundamental assumption of the dominant theory which has been shared by psychoanalysts and behavior theorists alike.

On the one hand, there is still a place for drive reduction. It is clear that under conditions of homeostatic need and painful stimulation, and perhaps under circumstances when the conditions of stimulation are changing with too great rapidity, both animals and persons learn techniques and strategies leading to gratification or reduction in external stimulation. The evidence that led Thorndike to formulate the "law of effect" is as convincing as ever. Moreover, in association with reductions of homeostatic need, animals and men may also learn cathexes or emotional attachments. The facts referred to are those highly familiar in secondary reinforcement (30, 54).

On the other hand, the facts implying that organisms show spontaneous molar activity also imply that, when animals and human beings have been living under conditions of low and unchanging stimulation for a time, increases of stimulation become reinforcing. Butler has shown that rhesus monkeys will learn quite complex discriminations with the only reward being a peek through a glass window (7) at the things in the next room or a few seconds of auditory experience (8). Berlyne (3) has shown that, the greater the variety of stimulation in an area which rats are permitted to explore, the longer they continue their explorations.

Especially important in this connection are the studies of human behavior under conditions of minimal variation in stimulation. I refer to the studies of perceptual isolation by Bexton, Heron, and Scott (6) at McGill and also the work of Lilly (41). At McGill, college students were paid 20 dollars a day to do nothing. They lay for 24 hours a day on a comfortable bed.

The temperature was optimal and constant. Eyes, ears, and hands were shielded to minimize stimulus variation. Few subjects could endure more than two or three days of such conditions. They developed a desire for variation which was almost overwhelming.

While interpreting such facts in terms of a multiple set of drives for curiosity, exploration, or stimulation will get us only to a redescription of them, Hebb's (26) notion of an optimal level of activation—and, I would like to add, stimulus variation below which *increases* are reinforcing and above which *decreases* are reinforcing—is an integrative conception of fair magnitude. Moreover, the drive-reduction principle of reinforcement may be seen to be but half of this more general curvilinear principle.

But this is probably not the whole story. It looks as if there were natively both positive and negative forms of exciting stimulation. Sheffield, Roby, and Campbell (61) have argued that the reinforcing effect of eating is not a matter of reduction of the hunger drive but rather a matter of the positive value of the consummatory act of eating. Moreover, Sheffield, Wulff, and Backer (62) have shown that male rats will learn mazes to get to females in heat even when they are allowed only intromission but not allowed to continue coitus to the point of drive-reducing ejaculation. From the fact that Davis (12) and his collaborators at Indiana have shown that showing pictures of nude women to college males increases excitement as shown by increased palmar conductance and the arrest of EEC-alpha, it is clear that such stimulation is exciting rather than excitement-reducing. Young (69) has long emphasized the importance of the hedonic quality of experience for reinforcement, and he has shown that speed of running in rat subjects increases with the concentration of sucrose in the incentive drink.

The suggestion that the two forms of excitation, one positive and one negative, are built into organisms comes also from the work of Olds and Milner (53). Electrical stimulation of the septal area is positively reinforcing, but electrical stimulation of the brainstem reticular formation is negatively reinforcing. Perhaps, it is not without significance that the septal area is part of the old olfactory brain which has been considered to have an especially important part in the mediation of sexual and consummatory behavior in mammals. At any rate, it looks as though certain types of stimulation may be positively reinforcing even though they be intense and exciting. This may mean that the curvilinear principle may be limited in its domain to strong stimulation via the exteroceptors when homeostatic needs are minimized.

The suggestion of innate, positive, and negative exteroceptive stimulation comes secondly from recent work by Harlow (22). It has been customary to see an infant's cathexis or love for its mother developing as secondary reinforcement largely out of its feeding experiences. Freud (16), of course, contended that the pleasure from stimulation of the oral erogenous zone furnished the experiential basis for both pleasure-sucking and maternal attachment, a contention which contradicted his most definitive formulations of drive theory (17). The fact that an infant must suck for its nourishment, according to libido theory (16, p. 587), merely guaranteed discovery of the pleasures of oral stimulation. Behavior theorists have seen both sucking and love of mother as forms of secondary reinforcement deriving from the fact that the child satisfies its hunger by means of sucking the mother's breasts (51, pp. 137ff.). Harlow (22), however, has recently compared the degree of attachment of young monkeys to a wire mother-surrogate on which they nursed at a bottle with attachment to a padded and cloth-covered mother-surrogate on which they received nothing but the feel of the softness. In terms of the amount of time spent on each of the two mother-surrogates, the monkeys showed more than 10 times the attachment to the soft-padded surrogate as to the wire surrogate. When various fear-evoking stimuli were presented to the baby monkeys in their cages, it was to the padded and cloth-covered surrogate that the frightened, infant monkey turned, not to the wire surrogate on which it had been nursed. Harlow argues from these findings that it is the sensory quality of softness which gives the reinforcement. His study suggests, moreover, that it is important to investigate the capacity for various kinds of stimuli for positive and negative reinforcement in the very young. Pratt (57) cites a monograph by Canestrini (9) on the sensory life of the newborn for an observation that certain stimuli are associated with decreases in the rate of the heart rate, and are therefore pleasant, while others are associated with increases in heart rate and are unpleasant.[2] In view of

---

[2] An examination of Canestrini's (9) monograph shows that Pratt was mistaken in stating that Canestrini remarked upon decreases in heart rate being associated with pleasure, but some of his published kymograph records do indicate decreases in heart rate. It may well be that heart rate could serve as an indicator of the emotional value of various sensory inputs, and these might be tested for their reinforcement values. I am indebted to Dr. William Gerler for reading this monograph carefully to check my own impressions of Canestrini's text.

the finding by Davis (12) and his collaborators that seeing a picture of a nude female results in reduction in the heart rate of male college students, it is possible that this physiological indicator may provide a technique for determining the direction of the reinforcing effect of stimuli in the newborn. At any rate, what is suggested is that McDougall's (44) old notion of natively positive and negative values for receptor inputs be reexamined.

CONDITIONED FEAR AND ANXIETY

The third assumption that I wish to examine in the light of empirical evidence is the notion that fear and anxiety are *always* inculcated as a consequence of traumatic experiences of helplessness in the face of homeostatic-need or painful external stimulation. Note that I am not denying that such conditioned fears do exist. I am only questioning the word *always* ... are always inculcated as a consequence of traumatic experiences.

The first relevant studies go way back to the 1920's. Harold and Mary Cover Jones (34) attempted to test the claims of Watson (66) and Watson and Raynor (67) concerning conditioned fears. They exposed their subjects of various ages, ranging from early infancy to adult, to a large but sluggish and harmless bull snake. Fear of the snake was exceedingly common among adults, teenagers, and latency-age children, but it was absent in children below three years of age. It began to appear among children older than three and was typical of children six and older. From the fact that the fear appeared at a younger age in those of higher intelligence than those of lower intelligence, the Joneses argued that fear of snakes is a response which comes automatically into the developing child's repertoire through maturation. This remains as an alternative hypothesis to that of conditioned fear.

A study by Frances Holmes (29), which is seldom cited, calls both of these interpretations into question. Holmes compared the fearfulness of the children of lower-class background, who were attending a day nursery, with the fearfulness of children of upper-class background, who were attending a private nursery school. She got her fear scores by indicating that the child could get some attractive toys with which to play by going into the dark room adjacent to the examining room, or by taking them off a chair situated beside that of a strange woman dressed in a large floppy black hat and a long gray coat, or by climbing along a plank some three feet off the floor. If the child started immediately for the toys, he got a score of one for that item. If he hesitated but ultimately went ahead on his own, he got a score of two. If he would go only if accompanied by the examiner, the score was three. If he refused to go at all, the score was four. There were seven such situations. The results show that the fear scores of the lower-class children averaged only about half the size of those for the upper-class children, and the fear scores for boys were lower than those for girls. Yet it would be the lower-class children who had experienced the more homeostatic need and painfully rough treatment than the upper-class children, and the boys had probably experienced more painful experiences than the little girls. That intelligence is not the factor is shown by the fact that the fear scores showed a correlation of only about $+.2$ with mental age, and the differences were still significant when intelligence was partialed out.

Something besides either conditioned fear or the correlation between fear and intelligence is required to make these results comprehensible.

Recently evidence even more contradictory to the notion of conditioned fears has been coming from the work of Seymour Levine. Levine, Chevalier, and Korchin (40) have compared the adult behavior of rats shocked and rats petted daily from birth to their 20th day with the adult behavior of rats left continuously in their nests with their mothers. When he started this work, Levine expected to find that the shocked animals would show traumatic effects of their shock experiences in heightened emotionality and damaged capacity to learn adaptive responses. On the contrary, the shocked animals, along with the handled animals, gained weight faster than those left in the nest (37, 38, 39, 40). Byron Lindholm, working with the writer, has repeated and confirmed this finding. Moreover, Levine's shocked and handled animals both showed less emotionality than those left continuously in the nest with their mothers, i.e., less emotionality in the sense that they defecated and urinated less frequently when placed in a strange situation. Finally, the shocked and handled animals, which have appeared alike in all of these experiments, learned an avoidance response more rapidly and drank more readily after 18 hours without water than did the rats left in the nest with their mother.

Clearly these results on both human children and rats imply that fear and anxiety must sometimes have some other basis than that of being associated with painful stimulation. As many of you know, Hebb (24, 25) has formulated a radically different explanation of fear which may be termed either an incongruity or a dissonance theory.

The facts which suggested Hebb's conception came largely from observing chimpanzees being raised under controlled conditions at the Yerkes Laboratory. Fear, defined as withdrawal behavior in response to the appearance of some object, does not appear in young chimpanzees until they are approximately four months old. Then, the objects feared are familiar objects in unfamiliar guise. Fear of strangers is an example. This appears spontaneously to the first stranger seen, so it cannot be based on associating strangers with painful stimulation. Fear of strangers does not appear in chimpanzees—or in children, I might add—who have always been exposed to a large number of persons. While the avoidance response is unlearned, the familiar, expected aspects of objects must be learned. The young animal must have established as residues of his experience cortical firing patterns (or cognitive structures—whichever term you like) from which new receptor inputs can be incongruous. Consider the kinds of objects regularly feared. They are, for instance, the familiar keeper or experimenter in strange clothes, the experimenter in a Hallowe'en mask, a plaster cast of a chimpanzee head (which lacks, of course, the familiarly attached body), an anesthetized chimpanzee infant (from which the familiar patterns of motion are absent). On the other hand, objects which have never entered into the young chimpanzee's life may be strange without evoking withdrawal. In other words, the feared object is one which excites receptors in a fashion which is incongruous with the central, sequential pattern of neural firing which has accrued as a residue of the chimpanzee or human infant's past experience. Until

the central pattern has been learned, incongruous stimulation is impossible.

Such a conception can well account for Holmes' findings that lower-class children are less fearful than higher-class children and that boys are less fearful than girls even though both lower-class children and boys of nursery school age are likely to have had the wider experience with the sorts of situations used by Holmes to evoke fear. It may well be that being shocked and handled provides a variety of experience which leaves the rat pups which have been subjected to it less disturbed by such things as open fields and 18 hours without water, but these effects may ultimately be found to be a matter of still another mechanism. It is too early to say.

Taking seriously this incongruity-dissonance conception of the genesis of fear leads to interesting reinterpretations of a great many of the motivational phenomena of child development. Consider these few. In considering separation anxiety, the incongruity principle makes it unnecessary to puzzle about how the absence of mother could be the conditional stimulus for the traumatizing and helpless distress that has been supposed to have occurred in her absence. In considering fear of the dark, it also becomes unnecessary to puzzle about how the absence of light stimulation could so widely have been associated with painful stimulation. Multiple mothering need not be seen as a traumatizing experience in the light of this conception, but rather as an innoculation against social shyness and fear. The timidity of the overprotected child and the social shyness of the rural mountain people get an explanation which has been difficult in terms of the theory of conditioned fear.

## MOTIVATION IN TERMS
## OF THE INCONGRUITY-DISSONANCE
## PRINCIPLE

This introduction of the incongruity-dissonance principle concludes the three reinterpretations I wish to present today, but I do wish to call your attention to the pervasive character of this incongurity-dissonance principle. It appears to have great explanation power which figures, in one guise or another, in several systematic theories, besides that of Hebb, all of which have been characterized as nondynamic.

Hebb's (25) theorizing is physiological, at least in a verbal sense, in that he conceives the residues of past inputs to be stored in semiautonomous, reverberating cerebral circuits which he terms *cell assemblies*. These cell assemblies are the neural analogue of concepts, and they get sequentially integrated into what he calls *phase sequences*. The sequential organization in time provides for the subjective phenomenon of expectation. When markedly incongruous receptor inputs disrupt this sequential organization, behavior is changed and the process is felt as unpleasant emotion. Slight degrees of incongruity, which can readily be accommodated, lend interest and may provide attractive problems, but the larger ones are repelling and perhaps even devastating.

Piaget (55, 56) utilizes very much the same incongruity notion to account for the development of intelligence and concepts in human children. In his system, the child comes at birth with certain sensory-motor coordinations which he terms *schemata*. Variation in stimulus situations call for adaptive *accommodations* or changes in these schemata, which changes are *assimilated* or stored as residues. Piaget also finds limited incongruities between central schemata and receptor inputs to be interesting and facilitative of growth, but incongruities which extend beyond the child's capacity for accommodation instigate withdrawal or fear and even terror. In Piaget's theory the child's gestalt-like conceptions of reality (space, time, and number) are schemata which develop through a continuous process of accommodations and assimilations and become fixed or static only when the child's schemata come to correspond so well with reality that no further accommodations are required. Here agreement among people is dictated by reality.

Helson (27, 28) has called the residues of immediate past experience in the typical psychophysical experiment an *adaptation level*. Both he and McClelland (43) have seen affective arousal to be a matter of the size of the discrepancy between receptor inputs and the adaptation level. Small discrepancies may be attractively pleasant, large ones repellingly unpleasant. As an example, some of you will readily recall having experienced the affective startle that comes when you have been set to pick up what you thought was a full pail, only to find it empty.

Festinger (14) has recently written a book entitled *A Theory of Cognitive Dissonance* in which he shows that a discrepancy between belief about a situation and perception of that situation acts like a drive. The subject acts to reduce the *dissonance* by either withdrawing from the incredible situation or by changing his beliefs, and, not incidentally, he finds the dissonance highly unpleasant.

Rogers (60) has described the basis for anxiety as discrepancy between the "phenomenological field" and the perceived reality as represented by his two circles. Rogers' phenomenological field, however, is not the perceptually-given phenomenal field of such German phenomenologists as Delthei and Husserl. It is rather the inferred storehouse of past experience and represented in the present by expectations, aspirations, self-concept, and the like. Thus, his conceptual scheme appears to fall within the domain of the incongruity-dissonance principle.

Kelly's (35) *Psychology of Personal Constructs* also makes central use of this principle. The term *personal constructs* refers to the ways in which individuals construe and anticipate events. These each person derives from the way in which he has experienced such events in the past. When a person's constructions fail to predict events, this is disturbing, even anxiety-producing, and it motivates some kind of change, but the change may take place in defenses against such change of constructs or in avoiding such events, or in the constructs themselves.

Perhaps, it is worth noting in closing that this incongruity-dissonance principle makes both motivation and reinforcement intrinsic to the organism's relations with its environment, intrinsic, if you will, to the organism's information-processing. It is as if the organism operated like an error-actuated, feedback system where the error is derived from discrepancy between receptor-inputs of the present and the residues of past experience which serve as the basis for anticipating the future. The dominant view of the past half century has seen both motivation and reinforcement as extrinsic to the information-processing. This has put a tremendous burden of responsibility for the management of affective

motivation on parents, teachers, and all those in positions of authority and control. Visions of man completely controlled, as examplified by George Orwell's *1984*, are conceivable only by assuming that the extrinsic motivating forces of homeostatic need and painful stimulation are completely dominant. In this light the terror of the baby chimp at seeing his keeper in a Hallowe'en mask and the irritation of the believer when his beliefs are disconfirmed are perhaps symbols of hope. They may justify Abraham Lincoln's well-known dictum that "you can fool some of the people all the time, and all the people some of the time, but you cannot fool all the people all the time."

To return to the cartoon of the lad who was improperly motivated: Perhaps, the task of developing proper motivation is best seen, at least in nutshell form, as limiting the manipulation of extrinsic factors to that minimum of keeping homeostatic need and exteroceptive drive low, in favor of facilitating basic information-processing to maximize accurate anticipation of reality.

## REFERENCES

1. Beach, F. A., "Current Concepts of Play in Animals," *American Naturalist*, LXXIX (1945), 523-41.

2. Bechterev, V. M., *La Psychologie objective* (trans. by N. Kostyleff). Paris: Alcan, 1913.

3. Berlyne, D. E., "Novelty and Curiosity As Determinants of Exploratory Behavior," *British Journal of Psychology*, XLI (1950), 68-80.

4. ——, "The Arousal and Satiation of Perceptual Curiosity in the Rat," *Journal of Comparative & Physiological Psychology*, XLVIII (1955), 238-46.

5. Bernard, C., *Leçons sur les propriétés physiologiques et les alterations pathologiques des liquides de l'organisme*, 2 vols. Paris: Ballière, 1859.

6. Bexton, W. H., W. Heron, and T. H. Scott, "Effects of Decreased Variation in the Sensory Environment," *Canadian Journal of Psychology*, VIII (1954), 70-76.

7. Butler, R. A., "Discrimination Learning by Rhesus Monkeys to Visual Exploration Motivation," *Journal of Comparative & Physiological Psychology*, XLVI (1953), 95-98.

8. ——, "Discrimination Learning by Rhesus Monkeys to Auditory Incentives," *ibid.*, L (1957), 239-41.

9. Canestrini, S., "Über das Sinnesleben des Neugeborenen," eds. A. Alzheimer and M. Lewandowsky, *Monographien der gesamten neurologischen Psychiatrie* (Heft 5). Berlin: Springer Verlag, 1913.

10. Cannon, W. B., *Bodily Changes in Pain, Hunger, Fear, and Rage.* New York: Appleton-Century-Crofts, 1915.

11. Dashiell, J., *Fundamentals of Objective Psychology.* Boston: Houghton Mifflin Company, 1928.

12. Davis, R. C. and A. M. Buchwald, "An Exploration of Somatic Response Patterns: Stimulus and Sex Differences," *Journal of Comparative & Physiological Psychology*, L (1957), 44-52.

13. Dollard, J. and N. E. Miller, *Personality and Psychotherapy.* New York: McGraw-Hill Book Company, 1950.

14. Festinger, L., *A Theory of Cognitive Dissonance.* Evanston, Ill.: Row, Peterson & Company, 1957.

15. Freud, S., "The Interpretation of Dreams" (1900), in *The Basic Writings of Sigmund Freud* (trans. by A. A. Brill). New York: Modern Library, Inc., 1938. Pp. 179-548.

16. ——, "Three Contributions to the Theory of Sex" (1905), in *The Basic Writings of Sigmund Freud* (trans. by A. A. Brill). New York: Modern Library, Inc., 1938. Pp. 553-629.

17. ——, "Instincts and Their Vicissitudes" (1915), in *Collected Papers*, Vol. IV. London: Hogarth Press, Ltd., 1950. Pp. 60-83.

18. ——, *Inhibition, Symptom and Anxiety* (1926). Trans. by H. A. Bunker as *The Problem of Anxiety*. New York: W. W. Norton & Company, Inc., 1936.

19. Granit, R., *Receptors and Sensory Perception*. New Haven, Conn.: Yale University Press, 1955.

20. Harlow, H. F., "Learning and Satiation of Response in Intrinsically Motivated Complex Puzzle Performance by Monkeys," *Journal of Comparative & Physiological Psychology*, XLIII (1950), 289-94.

21. ——, "Motivation As a Factor in the Acquisition of New Responses," in *Current Theory and Research in Motivation: A Symposium.* Lincoln, Nebr.: University of Nebraska Press, 1953. Pp. 24-49.

22. ——, "The Nature of Love," *American Psychologist*, XIII (1958), 673-85.

23. ——, M. K. Harlow, and D. R. Meyer, "Learning Motivated by a Manipulation Drive," *Journal of Experimental Psychology*, XL (1950), 228-34.

24. Hebb, D. O., "On the Nature of Fear," *Psychological Review*, LIII (1946), 259-76.

25. ——, *The Organization of Behavior.* New York: John Wiley & Sons, Inc., 1949.

26. ——, "Drives and the CNS (Conceptual Nervous System)," *Psychological Review*, LXII (1955), 243-54.

27. Helson, H., "Adaptation-Level As Frame of Reference for Prediction of Psychophysical Data," *American Journal of Psychology*, LX (1947), 1-29.

28. ——, "Adaptation-Level As a Basis for a Quantitative Theory of Frames of Reference," *Psychological Review*, LV (1948), 297-313.

29. Holmes, Frances B., "An Experimental Study of the Fears of Young Children," in A. T. Jersild and Frances B. Holmes, "Children's Fears," *Child Development Monographs*, XX (1935), 167-296.

30. Hull, C. L., *Principles of Behavior.* New York: Appleton-Century-Crofts, 1943.

31. Hunt, J. McV., "The Effects of Infant Feeding-Frustration Upon Adult Hoarding in the Albino Rat," *Journal of Abnormal & Social Psychology*, XXXVI (1941), 338-60.

32. ——, H. Schlosberg, R. L. Solomon, and E. Stellar, "Studies on the Effects of

Infantile Experience on Adult Behavior in Rats. I. Effects of Infantile Feeding Frustration on Adult Hoarding," *Journal of Comparative & Physiological Psychology*, XL (1947), 291-304.

33. Jasper, H. H., "Electrical Signs of Cortical Activity," *Psychological Bulletin*, XXXIV (1937), 411-81.

34. Jones, H. E. and Mary C. Jones, "A Study of Fear," *Child Education*, V (1928), 136-43.

35. Kelly, G. A., *The Psychology of Personal Constructs*. New York: W. W. Norton & Co., Inc., 1955.

36. Lacey, J. I. and Beatrice C. Lacey "The Relationship of Resting Autonomic Activity to Motor Impulsivity," in *The Brain and Human Behavior*. Baltimore: The Williams & Wilkins Co., 1958. Pp. 144-209.

37. Levine, S., "Infantile Experience and Consummatory Behavior in Adulthood," *Journal of Comparative & Physiological Psychology*, L (1957), 609-12.

38. ——, "Infantile Experience and Resistance to Physical Stress," *Science*, CXXVI (1957), 405.

39. ——, "Noxious Stimulation in Infant and Adult Rats and Consummatory Behavior," *Journal of Comparative & Physiological Psychology*, LI (1958), 230-33.

40. ——, J. A. Chevalier, and S. J. Korchin, "The Effects of Shock and Handling in Infancy on Later Avoidance Learning," *Journal of Personality*, XXIV (1956), 475-93.

41. Lilly, J. C., "Mental Effects of Reduction of Ordinary Levels of Physical Stimuli on Intact, Healthy Persons," *Psychiatric Research Reports*, V (1956), 1-9.

42. Lindsley, D. B., "Psychophysiology and Motivation," in M. R. Jones (ed.), *Nebraska Symposium on Motivation*. Lincoln, Nebr.: University of Nebraska Press, 1957. Pp. 44-105.

43. McClelland, D. C., J. W. Atkinson, R. A. Clark, and E. L. Lowell, *The Achievement Motive*. New York: Appleton-Century-Crofts, 1953.

44. McDougall, W., *An Introduction to Social Psychology*. Boston: John W. Luce & Company, 1915.

45. Miller, N. E., "An Experimental Investigation of Acquired Drives," *Psychological Bulletin*, XXXVIII (1941), 534-35.

46. ——, "Studies of Fear As an Acquirable Drive: I. Fear As Motivation and Fear-Reduction As Reinforcement in the Learning of New Responses," *Journal of Experimental Psychology*, XXXVIII (1948), 89-101.

47. ——, and J. Dollard, *Social Learning and Imitation*. New Haven, Conn.: Yale University Press, 1941.

48. Montgomery, K. C., "The Relation Between Exploratory Behavior and Spontaneous Alternation in the White Rat," *Journal of Comparative & Physiological Psychology*, XLIV (1951), 582-89.

49. ——, "The Effect of the Hunger and Thirst Drives Upon Exploratory Behavior," *ibid.*, XLVI (1953), 315-19.

50. ——, and J. A. Monkman, "The Relation Between Fear and Exploratory Behavior," *Journal of Comparative & Physiological Psychology*, XLVIII (1955), 132-36.

51. Mussen, P. H. and J. J. Conger, *Child Development and Personality*. New York: Harper & Row, Publishers, 1956.

52. Olds, J., "Physiological Mechanisms of Reward," in M. R. Jones (ed.), *Nebraska Symposium on Motivation*. Lincoln, Nebr.: University of Nebraska Press, 1955. Pp. 73-139.

53. ——, and P. Milner, "Positive Reinforcement Produced by Electrical Stimulation of Septal Area and Other Regions of the Rat Brain," *Journal of Comparative & Physiological Psychology*, XLVII (1954), 419-27.

54. Pavlov, I. P., *Conditioned Reflexes* (trans. by G. V. Anrep). London: Oxford University Press, 1927.

55. Piaget, J., *The Origins of Intelligence in Children*. New York: International Universities Press, Inc., 1952.

56. ——, *The Construction of Reality in the Child* (trans. by Margaret Cook). New York: Basic Books, Inc., Publishers, 1954.

57. Pratt, K. C., "The Neonate," in L. Carmichael (ed.), *Manual of Child Psychology* (2nd ed.). New York: John Wiley & Sons, Inc., 1954. Pp. 215-91.

58. Prosser, C. L., "Action Potentials in the Nervous System of the Crayfish: I. Spontaneous Impulses," *Journal of Cellular & Comparative Physiology*, IV (1934), 185-209.

59. Richter, C. P., "Animal Behavior and Internal Drives," *Quarterly Review of Biology*, II (1927), 307-43.

60. Rogers, C. R., *Client-Centered Therapy*. Boston: Houghton Mifflin Company, 1951.

61. Sheffield, F. D., T. B. Roby, and B. A. Campbell, "Drive Reduction Versus Consummatory Behavior As Determinants of Reinforcement," *Journal of Comparative & Physiological Psychology*, XLVII (1954), 349-55.

62. ———, J. J. Wulff, and R. Backer, "Reward Value of Copulation Without Sex Drive Reduction," *ibid.*, XLIV (1951), 3-8.

63. Solomon, R. L. and Elinor S. Brush, "Experimentally Derived Conceptions of Anxiety and Aversion," in M. R. Jones (ed.), *Nebraska Symposium on Motivation*. Lincoln, Nebr.: University of Nebraska Press, 1956. Pp. 212-305.

64. ———, and L. C. Wynne, "Traumatic Avoidance Learning: Acquisition in Normal Dogs," *Psychological Monographs*, LXVII, No. 4 (1953); whole No. 354.

65. Thorndike, E. L., *Educational Psychology*. (Vol. I, *The Original Nature of Man;* Vol. II, *The Psychology of Learning.*) New York: Teachers College, 1913.

66. Watson, J. B., *Psychological Care of the Infant and Child*. New York: W. W. Norton & Company, Inc., 1928.

67. ———, and Rosalie Raynor, "Conditional Reactions," *Journal of Experimental Psychology*, III (1920), 1-4.

68. Woodworth, R. S., *Dynamic Psychology*. New York: Columbia University Press, 1918.

69. Young, P. T., "The Role of Hedonic Processes in Motivation," in M. R. Jones (ed.), *Nebraska Symposium on Motivation*. Lincoln, Nebr.: University of Nebraska Press, 1955. Pp. 193-237.

# ACTIVITIES

1. What alternative do you see open to you for motivating your students to learn your subject?

2. How can you determine the success of the motivation techniques you employ?

3. Is there a relationship between who asks questions in a classroom and who is motivated to learn the curriculum content? What implications does your answer have for you as a teacher?

4. What is the relationship between Waetjen's description of what is transpiring in Fig. 3 and J. Raths' description of the rationale behind advanced organizers? Herrick's organizing center? Bruner's discussion of discovery?

5. Apply the research reported by Waetjen on achievement motivation to your teaching area.

6. Waetjen describes a pretest in biology which, he says, apparently stimulated the curiosity of the students who took it. What arguments might Ausubel use as an alternative hypothesis to describe the students' success on the posttest? What kind of a pretest might you use as a curiosity stimulant?

7. Waetjen reports that nonverbal feedback of a positive nature is an effective, but seldom used, motivational technique. Can you think of some nonverbal techniques you might try as a teacher? How might you determine their effectiveness?

8. Are tests stimulants to learning? In what way may a test inhibit learning? Do you propose to test in a manner which will stimulate or inhibit learning? How can you tell if you are achieving this goal?

9. Do the "reinterpretation" research findings reported by Hunt reinforce or refute the theories and findings of Waetjen? Of Keislar? Of Suchman (see Chapter 5)?

10. How would you answer in a positive fashion the question: "How can I get my students to want to do work in a given subject?"

11. What implication for motivating students in the classroom can you see in the findings of Waimon ("Feedback in the Classroom," found in Chapter 2)?

# Chapter Ten

# RESEARCH AND TEACHING

If education is to be regarded as a true profession, its practitioners at all levels must pay close attention to empirical evidence in making decisions. To make decisions based only on good faith, only on tradition or on authority is not desirable.

Teachers may argue that they do not have time to collect research data *and* teach. Yet many admit to problems in their teaching and will try to solve them, of course. However, to be able to evaluate their efforts—to tell whether their solutions are successful or unsuccessful—they will of necessity have to turn to research. And it is this need to "know" that makes the collection of data so very important to the teacher. Answers based primarily on feelings, impressions, or haphazard samplings of student opinions cannot be tolerated by the profession.

Among the research findings, the endeavor of the behavioral scientists is also to be considered. Although many times they are outraged with what some educators call research, and although they assert that research is an activity only suited to a laboratory or a college campus, it is our view that there are many different levels of research—from the pure, highly controlled research that is reported in journals to the field testing of ideas in the less-than-ideal "laboratory" setting—the classroom. We need all sorts of data gathering because, again, we cannot build a profession unless its decisions are empirically based.

# 56

# Let Us Research—An Invitation

JAMES RATHS

At a recent meeting for teachers and administrators, a teacher voiced a common complaint. "I'm sick and tired of hearing professors raise questions about teaching. I'm looking for answers." Whose job is it to find the answers? For years, the education profession has been divided into the producers of research and the consumers of research (1). Ideally, the producers (mostly college professors or research directors of the larger school systems) are charged with the task of finding the answers. The producers, again in the ideal situation, are to communicate their findings to the consumers, primarily groups of teachers and principals. These practitioners then will apply the findings and eliminate the day-to-day problems found in the classroom. Needless to say, this ideal arrangement has not worked out. The findings of researchers in the areas of teaching and learning are not easily applicable to the problems teachers face in the classrooms. What has caused

the breakdown in this ideal arrangement?

Essentially, there are several reasons. First, teachers know many times where their difficulties lie; the producers of research, for the most part, do not. Secondly, producers do not have convenient access to students in order to test out solutions to problems. Finally, if an occasional "producer" does identify a crucial problem and does find positive support for his proposed solution, he has difficulty communicating his results to the practitioners in the field. These reasons effectively militate against prolonging the dichotomy between producers and consumers. All of us must join the search for answers, but most important, college professors and school administrators must encourage teachers to take on a major role in the process. In brief, "research befits the teacher"—both in the sense that he has raw materials (students and problems) with which to work and in the light of the apparent ineffectiveness of the current division of labor.

Asking teachers to take on a research

James Raths, "Let Us Research—An Invitation," *The Instructor*, LXXIV, No. 7 (March 1965), 3, 158. Reprinted by permission.

role has drawbacks too. First, few teachers receive training in research techniques. Of course, as for any process, researching requires a good number of skills and understandings. Two rather recent trends may help to alleviate this barrier to teacher-research. More and more schools are employing research directors to assist teachers in testing their own ideas. Secondly, as salary increments and prerequisites for professional positions require more and more advanced degrees, more and more teachers are being trained in research skills.

A second objection to expecting teachers to do research is that of time. A teacher is a very busy person just taking care of the day-to-day responsibilities of her assignment. Can such a busy involved person be expected to do everything a teacher is required to do *and* do research too? My position is that there is really no alternative. Suppose a teacher finds a problem in her teaching for which there are no "answers" in the research literature, in her own personal experiences, or in the personal experiences of her colleagues or supervisors. What can she do? Certainly she must try to solve the problem in some manner. She must spend time planning how to deal with the problem. I suggest that her planning be disciplined by the research process, and my hunch is that in the long run, a teacher will be saving time by working at her problems in such a systematic way.

What are some ways to become familiar with the research process? I can think of none better than to become immersed in a research study and to that end I propose that interested readers undertake a partial replication of the very fine study conducted by E. B. Page (2). Many of us, Page suggests, write comments on students papers. Does this time-consuming process lead to significant improvement in student performances? His experiment was an attempt to answer this question.

To test the efficacy of teacher comments, Page applied three treatments to students. To some he only wrote the number correct and the letter grade on their papers. To others, in addition to the grade, he wrote comments that seemed suitable to him—as he usually did. To a third group, fixed comments determined by the grade received on the test (see below) were also included with the grade on the students' papers. He hoped to see a difference in the performances of these students on the very next test given in class. To carry out Page's plan, we must divide our students into three groups, treat their test papers in different and prearranged ways, and then observe the results. Teachers interested in "getting their feet wet" in the research process may follow the detailed paragraphs below to carry out the experiment using their own students as subjects.

1. Consider any test that you are about to give in one of your classes. The subject of the test is not important, but a longer test is more suitable than a shorter one. After giving the test, mark each paper with the number correct and, if customary, the appropriate letter grade. Next rank the test papers from highest to lowest using raw scores. Form temporary teams of three students each by putting the three highest papers together; the next three highest papers together, and so on. A teacher with 30 students will have 10 teams of 3 students each. (If the original number of students in a teacher's class is not divisible by three, one or two students must be dropped from consideration in this experiment before teams are formed. For example, a teacher with 32 students will first drop two names. The names dropped must be selected by drawing them out

of a hat containing all the names of the students, or some other unbiased way.)

2. Choose by lot a student from each team of three and consider these students as members of the no-comment group—Group A. Group A will contain one person from the team with the highest three papers; another person from the team with the second highest three papers, etc. To form Group B, the free-comment group, go back to the two students left in each team and assign one by lot to group B. The students left over in each team will make up Group C—the fixed-comment group. Teachers should now have three groups equal in number. For example, a teacher with 30 students will now have 3 groups of 10 students each. At this point it is important to stress that the selection of each group from the teams must be done by a procedure that is based on chance. Names may be drawn out of a hat or the test papers of each team of three may be shuffled and dealt like cards into the three groups, A, B, or C. These procedures ensure that chance alone determines which group a student becomes assigned to for the purposes of the experiment. This process, called randomization, is a *sine qua non* of any legitimate and accepted study.

3. Return all test papers with letter grades to the students. Group A students should receive no other comment on their papers. Page's instructions for Group B's treatment were that teachers should write anything that occurs to them in the circumstances. A comment is "right" for the study if it conforms with a teacher's own feelings and practices. Group C should receive specific comments suggested by Page and the letter grade assigned to the test determines the specific comment as follows:

Grade A:  Excellent! Keep it up.
Grade B:  Good work. Keep at it!
Grade C:  Perhaps try to do still better?
Grade D:  Let's bring this up.
Grade F:  Let's raise this grade.

Further, teachers were instructed to administer the comments rapidly and automatically trying not to notice which students were in which group.

4. The effect of the comments can be judged by the scores received by students on the very next objective test given in the class regardless of the subject. Teachers can judge the merits of commenting on papers by inspecting the median test scores of the three groups, A, B, and C. If the medians are very similar, a teacher may conclude that comments apparently had little effect. If the medians of Groups B and C are higher than that of Group A, then it would seem that writing comments is well worthwhile.

Page analyzed the data using the Friedman test to see if observed differences were greater than chance (3). Space does not allow a discussion of this technique here but teachers who wish to go beyond merely inspecting differences may (*a*) consult a person trained in statistics in her school system, or (*b*) write to the author at the Bureau of Educational Research and Field Services, University of Maryland for additional information.

In order to whet research appetites, I will not summarize Page's own findings (of course, the reference will allow you to look it up). I will say they were surprising and not at all what "common sense" would predict. Also, his results may not be valid in other schools or in other classrooms. This paper is an invitation to get started in researching by repeating a significant and important study that may have many implications for your teaching and your students. A next step may be for you to test an idea of your own. Let us begin!

**REFERENCES**

1. Barnes, Fred P., "Research Methods In Education." (Mimeo) University of Illinois.

2. Page, E. B., "Teacher Comments and Student Performance," *Journal of Educational Psychology*, XLIX, No. 4 (August 1958), 173.

3. Siegel, S., *Non-Parametric Statistics*. New York: McGraw-Hill Book Company, 1956, pp. 166-72.

# 57

# Research in Education

## THOMAS H. BRIGGS

Research has a halo. The lay public correctly respects it for contributions to the advancement of civilization. Many professional educators reverence it like a mystic religion. All people, whether or not formally educated, often use simple research in solving their everyday problems, and those who have sought and found its higher secrets by persistent study use it as an inviolate habit. Roger Bacon wrote a half millennium ago, "Mind perceives certainty and rests in the possession of truth, which could not be given by argument, but only by regulated experience," meaning sensible research.

But as not everyone who cries "Lord, Lord" shall enter into the Kingdom, so not everyone who proclaims himself a research scientist carries on his work with devoted understanding of what is *required* of its priests. As with the Black Knight in Arthurian legend, the accouterments of research sometimes conceal weakness rather than strength. Penetrated by the lance of cold crit-

icism, the conclusions of such "research" lose their assumed potency and he who publishes them fails to gain even the respect of good knights of the order.

Research is badly needed in the field of education, but it has its limitations. They must be recognized before educational research becomes a fetish. The basic problem in education is, of course, to ascertain what should be taught. Ideally, the curriculum should determine everything—the financing of our schools, the buildings and equipment needed, and the kind of teachers employed. Generous financial support, adequate or even architecturally attractive buildings, and skilled teachers are not sufficient. The curriculum is paramount. The best of teachers with a poor curriculum will simply turn out more of a poor product.

An accepted philosophy of life, of civilization, and of education should determine what is to be taught and to whom. Research cannot make this determination. It can, however, and it should furnish reliable information

Thomas H. Briggs, "Research in Education," *Phi Delta Kappan*, XLVI, No. 3 (November 1964), 99-103. Reprinted by permission.

**481**

with regard to results as evaluated in terms of the accepted philosophy. And of course it can supply much other valuable information that is more reliable than mere opinions, however confidently expressed by those who set themselves up as experts. Only as research is regarded as ancillary to the promotion of a sound philosophy can it be of real importance to education.

Incidentally, it should be recognized that philosophy need not be abstruse and difficult to understand. If it is to be an effective guide, it should be simply stated, understandable by every practitioner, and applicable to all situations, everywhere and at any time. For more than a century the Germans used effectively such a simply stated guiding philosophy of education, holding that the school's purpose was to develop "God-fearing, country-loving, self-supporting subjects of Imperial Germany." In 1749 Benjamin Franklin stated another simple philosophy in his "Proposals Relating to the Education of Youth," which every educator should know and ponder in formulating his own philosophy. The Golden Rule in the New Testament was not written in professional philosophic jargon, and yet for ages it has proved a potent guide to the making of any and all moral decisions.

## THE MEANING OF RESEARCH

What is research? As understood by the scientist, research is a careful and systematic inquiry, usually requiring considerable time and using the best-developed techniques. It has one or more of the following purposes:

1. To ascertain facts presumably useful in the solution of some recognized problem. (Under this rubric should be subsumed historical research for whatever reason undertaken.)

2. To prove—that is, to test the soundness of—a theory or hypothesis.
3. To discover a principle or law useful as a criterion of conclusions tentatively reached, or to direct future thinking or actions.
4. To test the conclusions reached by previous research or a conclusion stated arbitrarily without supporting evidence.
5. To develop techniques that will be useful in further research.
6. To make comparisons of the relative effectiveness of two or more procedures.

True research starts with a purpose, an intent to solve a clearly conceived problem, which frequently breaks down into a number of minor problems, the solutions of which are contributory to success. Edison was confronted with a challenge to find a material that would be effective as a filament in his vacuum light bulb. To achieve success he used empiricism, a wasteful kind of research, whereas a better scientist would have used theory to lead to a hypothetic material, which he would then test to prove its ability to incandesce without being consumed.

True research is also objective. It seeks to find truth regardless of desire or prejudice. It is scrupulous in procedure, and both patient and persistent. It seeks truth rather than personal promotion. And, as Einstein declared, "Concern for man himself and his fate must always form the chief interest of all technical endeavors." This is particularly true regarding research in education—it should always seek, directly or indirectly, the betterment of our schools for the betterment of mankind.

The importance of research has been recognized especially by industry, which now spends on it annually more than the total cost of all of our elementary and secondary schools. As a result, industry has grown wondrously in the past generation and is now producing goods that make possible comforts that our forefathers never dreamed of. By using research wisely education can in like manner increase its contribution to the advancement of civilization.

Research in education is relatively new in history. It was only in the early 1890's that Joseph M. Rice made the first ventures, focusing his attention on the teaching of spelling. His crude studies were followed by the work of G. Stanley Hall and his students, and a current began that has never ceased to flow.

Hall and his followers were primarily interested in assembling facts about the psychology of human beings, regardless of their application to the improvement of educational practices. The collecting of facts, regardless of their practical significance, rapidly became a fetish. It was easy to collect data, count cases, and report means and medians with sigmas carried to meaningless refinements, and even by the Spearman-Brown formula to make guesses as to their probable soundness when applied to larger populations.

But facts in isolation have no real meaning. As Voltaire once said, "Facts are to history what baggage is to an army, impedimenta." Of course he did not mean that facts and baggage are unimportant for use; but they are of neither significance nor value until used. In too many cases researchers in education have been content to present accumulated facts without pressing on to see that they were used for any practical achievement. And unfortunately this practice too often continues.

## QUESTIONABLE FASHIONS IN RESEARCH

The questionnaire, with all of its booby traps, soon became the most popular means of acquiring data, especially by aspirants for a doctoral degree. But besides selecting a problem important enough to warrant the collection of facts contributory to its solution, which too often was not done, the student was faced by a challenge to state his questions with absolute clarity and without being "leading," to select knowledgeable people to whom he would submit them—people who could be expected to answer honestly and fully—to consider why those who did not respond failed to cooperate, to interpret the answers that he did receive, and to apply imaginatively and practically his interpretations to solution of the original problem. The questionnaire seems to be the easiest instrument of research, whereas actually it is extremely difficult to prepare well when scientific criteria are used to judge it.

There have been fashions in research methodology. Besides the early popularity of the questionnaire, another fashion was emphasis on the mechanics of statistics. Anyone with a knowledge of even elementary mathematics can learn to find medians, means, modes, probable errors, and mean square deviations, and to compute correlations of relationship by several methods. But to apply formulae without a thorough understanding of their significance does not qualify one to conduct research by statistical methods or even to use statistics intelligently. A little learning is a dangerous thing in research, as it is in medicine or the handling of explosives. As a result of little learning we have had seriously reported correlations like .327, an index of little significance, made ridiculous by probable errors like .254, obviously an absurdity. Statistics have too often been used "as a drunken man uses a lamppost, for support rather than for illumination."

There seems to be a tendency in recent years to use statistics more elaborate and refined than the data being studied warrant. Terms like stanine scores and T-scores are impressive to the uninitiated, but neither such terms nor extrapolation are likely to make crude measures more useful. Human beings are too complex and too variable to be measured by the refined tools effective in the physical sciences. In research on human learning, simple techniques used with common sense in all probability are sufficient to produce findings that can confidently be used for improving educational practices. As we are all today to an extent pragmatists, so we should be more concerned with results than with virtuosity.

## IS USOE DEALING
## WITH MAJOR PROBLEMS ?

The problems to be attacked by research in education should be major problems, the solutions of which will make practical contributions of the greatest value. Examination of the projects that have been supported by the United States Office of Education through its Cooperative Research Program during the past seven years with grants in aid of some $25,000,000 evidence that warnings against waste are in order. Few of the hundreds of supported projects promise findings that are likely to be of practical value, and fewer still are concerned with major problems of practical education.

Increasingly since the publications by G. Stanley Hall and his followers, interest in educational research has increased. Many studies have been published by researchers of high competence, and many more have been made by students who were qualifying for the doctorate degree. The requirement by most universities of completion of an "original research" project has of course had some good results, such as

giving to school administrators an understanding of what research is and of the techniques that it uses. But unfortunately it has led neither to continued research by most men who have achieved the doctorate nor to daring application in practice of what research has proved.

What is needed now is, first of all, appreciation of what research can contribute to the improvement of education. When carried on by experts it attacks and solves problems of major importance. There are too many such major problems for research to be spent on trivial or abstruse questions or on those that do not promise practical application of proved findings. It may be interesting and in some remote way valuable for research to report, for example, on "Motor Characteristics of the Mentally Retarded." But certainly it is more worthwhile to report what can confidently be done to better day-to-day procedures in educating the young.

## " WILDCATTING " IS
## SELDOM PROFITABLE

The major problems for educational research are too big and too complex to be solved by a single piece of research carried on by one person. They need to be broken down into minor problems which, more quickly solved, will yield findings important to the solution of the grand major problem. Independent "wildcatting" is seldom profitable.

Directors of educational research can well learn from the procedures of petrogeologists. Instead of sinking expensive wells here and there at random, they select an area which they judge promising and stake out sections for intensive study. At assigned locations they drill exploratory holes, and then by assembling the reported results they gain information of directive value. By coordinating minor studies they learn what they need to know, the location of an oil pool that can be profitably exploited.

Scientists say that they can in time solve any problem that is clearly defined, and that such definition is more challenging and difficult than working out a solution. Graduate students working toward a doctorate usually worry and spend much time trying to find a problem for research. They often end up by accepting one suggested by their major professor. Any good problem assigned by an ingenious instructor, especially if it promises a contribution in a related group, is far better than a poor one proposed after wasteful worry by a student of limited understanding of relative values. His competence can be tested by the work that he does on the accepted assignment.

Professors in universities, where most educational research is carried on, would do well to follow the example of oil prospectors and stake out for exploration an important area in which they will become specialists. Then they should map out sections that need to be explored and allocate them eventually to students for individual research. The results of those minor studies, when approved as sound, they would then assemble and coordinate for contributions to the solution of the major problem. Centers of research on a simple grand project promise far more valuable results than scores of unrelated—and later unused—small problems, however good in themselves they may be.

### THE NEED FOR POPULARIZATION

Another obvious need is popularization of proved findings that research has already made and the promotion of general practical use in our schools. Unfortunately, the results of sound research are not now made widely known to administrators and teachers, for education has no professional magazine, such as medicine has, that reports approved findings by research. At present the influence of research findings on practice comes mainly from the translation by textbook writers into practical application. But authors, with an eye on sales, do not often dare include much that is revolutionary.

The United States Office of Education Cooperative Research Program has announced that it will undertake preparation of a catalog of research findings and "synthesize the results." Such a project can not be too highly commended, for it should make dependable information easily available to school people. The project will require much time and large financial support and also workers of high competence. The results will be small, however, unless the studies selected for report are important and carefully evaluated for soundness of the conclusions reached. In all probability it will be necessary for the project to concern itself with one area at a time, such as the teaching of English; and that means a series of publications in the years to come. Of course the project should continue indefinitely, as new research studies are completed.

Even after the proved results of research on major problems are made widely available, something more is still needed. For several reasons, the majority of school administrators and teachers are not adventurous. Already they know more about what has been proved superior to traditional practices than they attempt to put into practice. It is their cardinal sin to give verbal approval and then do nothing. It is easier, and sometimes safer, to continue doing what one knows how to do than to introduce innovations that the supporting public may neither understand nor approve. And, moreover, teachers need guidance and help in translating new theory into practice.

Industry has found it necessary and profitable to supplement its research staff with what is called a development engineer. He takes the theory and the blueprints from ingenious inventors and attempts to make what works in a test tube work in a vat. He knows the workers—both their limited skills and their prejudices. He knows the machines available or needed. He knows the raw material that must be used. And with such knowledge he is challenged to turn out products that will result in profits.

Ideally, every school or school system should have a development engineer who is skilled in translating research findings into an effective practical program. He would know the teachers and their potentialities; he would know the availability of necessary equipment; he would know the pupils, who are the raw material to be turned into educated citizens; and he would know how far he dared go without alarming the local public.

Without the probability of such an ideal being achieved, the desired translation of research findings into practice can to an extent be achieved by some central body, be it federal, state, or local, undertaking the stated duties. It could evaluate reported research studies, select those that are most promising of contributions to the betterment of practice, and indicate to administrators and teachers how desired innovations can best be introduced into the going program. Lacking such information, many schools are ignorant of what they ought to do, are not daring enough to adopt new practices, or adopt the form without guidance as to the most promising procedures. The disappointing results in some schools from introducing televised programs, the new mathematics, or lay readers of English compositions have doubtless been caused by inadequate guidance to teachers in preparing and promoting promising proposals of procedure.

## IN SUMMARY

Unquestionably, research is needed on educational problems. But it should focus on problems of recognized importance that promise application to the improvement of programs and of practices. Instead of permitting graduate students to spend their time on unrelated and sometimes piddling studies, our universities, recognizing what are the truly major problems in education, should formulate a master plan of research and direct minor studies that promise to contribute to its completion. And when solutions of even minor problems are found, machinery should be developed to see that proved and promising findings are used practically in our schools. The goal is a greater contribution to society, which depends on education for its continuation and progress.

# 58

# Comment on the Briggs Proposals

## DAVID R. KRATHWOHL

No doubt you found yourself nodding your head in agreement as you read the preceding article. There is good reason. Dr. Briggs, at 87, writes with a stylistic flair that presents his ideas forcefully and vividly. More important, there is common concern among both researchers and nonresearchers about many of the points he raises—the gross use of quesionnaires to query everyone; the indiscriminate use of statistics to count everything; the fracturing of important educational problems into myriads of noncomparable, isolated research exercises; and the difficulties of translating any of this research into practice with school-shaking impact.

Although his proposal that we assign dissertation topics to our students sharply contradicts current practice, the principle behind thesis topic assignment—that of focusing research effort on a problem—seems good common sense. He suggests that the educational researcher like the oil geologist

David R. Krathwohl, "Comment on the Briggs Proposals," *Phi Delta Kappan*, XLVI, No. 3 (November 1964), 103-4. Reprinted by permission.

should concentrate the wells drilled so as to learn the nature of the oil-bearing substrata. You should recognize, however, that from the first use of this analogy to the end of the article, the writer is describing a reasonable sounding strategy of research which may or may not increase payoff.

By definition research seeks to plot the unknown. One can hardly accept with assurance any prescription for such a venture. So many of the things that we depend on, from penicillin to scotch tape or birth control pills, resulted not from any direct attack on the problem for which they proved to be a solution, but an attack on a different problem entirely—sometimes, as in the case of the birth control pills, from an attack on the opposite problem —in this case, increased fertility. Can we then be sure that massing our efforts will result in the expected payoff?

The public has come to believe that the concentration of funds and resources will solve any problem. Would that they were right! But cancer cures have leveled off over the past several years despite massive research expenditures, the most capable talent, and increasingly sophisticated equipment and techniques.

We venture into the unknown territory to be researched, seeking solutions to problems in terms of what knowledge we have and our best guesses regarding the areas of likely payoff. But we often find little agreement as to where the payoff is. The apparent obvious does not always prove true. Gage[1] points out that it seems reasonable to assume that a group of pupils given considerable practice and instruction in developing a skill will become more alike in that skill, since they are all subjected to a uniform experience. But research shows us that individual differences increase with training. Gage cites five other "obvious" truisms disproved by research. Is the *obvious* area of payoff the best place to concentrate our efforts? Must we so concentrate our efforts, as Dr. Briggs seems to suggest?

Perhaps it is clear by now that this is an impossible question to answer. Dr. Briggs is entitled to his opinion. For our own part, while some concentration of effort seems reasonable and desirable, we feel it must be accompanied by strong support for the researcher whose pet area may not be in the focal arena. There is no certainty that the payoff may not indeed be as high or higher in the unfettered program.

We should recognize too that we do not have enough funds available in educational research to mount concentrated efforts commensurate to the size of our problems. Despite a rapid growth in funds available through USOE, it is estimated that considerably less than 1 per cent of the annual education budget goes for research. Clearly, if we are not careful, too great a concentration of expenditures could absorb all the funds from the nonprogramed research areas without still covering the vast voids in our programing efforts.

Perhaps too we expect too much from our research efforts. That these projects have borne fruit has been pointed out in earlier *Phi Delta Kappans*.[2] But if these fruits seem inconsiderable compared to the money spent, remember that industry expects only 1 to 5 per cent of its projects to yield a return. We are so used to pinching research pennies that we expect each one to cry out with some new truth.

The USOE Cooperative Research Program is to be commended for its efforts to find the minmax solution to the problem of administering research funding. It has attempted to achieve concentration of resources with a minimum of coercion into expected payoff areas, combined with a funding of those projects perceived likely to achieve maximal payoff. Strong support has continued to be given the basic and applied part of the program which supports *any* researcher in *any* education area. A concentration of expenditures in areas needing research but devoid of funds has resulted in such efforts as Project English, Project Social Studies, and Project Talent. Even these did not indicate which approaches would alone be supported. All approaches were invited to compete. Still tighter concentration of research efforts appeared in last year's invitation for proposals involving any method

---

[1] Nathaniel Gage, "Psychological Theory and Empirical Research for Teacher Education," in *Freedom With Responsibility*, Seventeenth Yearbook, 1964 Annual Meeting, American Association of Colleges for Teacher Education. Washington, D. C.: The Association (1964), pp. 7-8.

[2] Lindley J. Stiles, "The Cooperative Research Program," *Phi Delta Kappan* (March 1962), pp. 231-36, and Gerald R. Smith, "Progress Through the Cooperative Research Program," *Phi Delta Kappan* (March 1964), pp. 303-10.

of teaching reading to be tested against any other in a common design with common evaluation instruments.

Thus the USOE has been hedging its bets. It fosters some concentration of resources in areas of particular problems, yet makes funds available in quantity to a researcher free of any such restrictions. This covering both sides of the board makes good intuitive sense as a strategy to approaching the unknown.

Briggs proposes concentration of effort both at the national level as just discussed and at the local level as well. The latter would be achieved by assigning dissertation topics to the student, as is so often done in chemistry, mathematics, and physics. There seems to be no evidence that researchers in these sciences are less competent because they did not have the opportunity to discover and limit their own dissertation problem. Yet most educators would, no doubt, feel that the research experiences of our students are too few to omit this important step. Perhaps this points to other deficiencies in our research training.

One of Briggs' constructive suggestions is that we give greater emphasis to developmental engineering research. Programing research resources at the application end of the research pipeline seems much more possible and acceptable than at the discovery end. Perhaps this step is a hurdle (in the developmental task sense) that, once achieved, will promote greater maturity in the Cooperative Research Program. A proposal now receiving careful consideration by program personnel suggests the following: a concentration of resources on engineering solutions in needy areas where the basic research has been largely completed; a careful evaluation of the engineered products with competing possibilities; and, finally, a concentrated dissemination of those solutions that successfully pass the evaluation stage. Such a proposal seems quite consistent with a developmental engineering viewpoint.

Finally, it is of interest to compare Briggs' description of the "true scientist" with his proposals. Briggs indicates that such a scientist is objective; he seeks ". . . to find truth regardless of desire or prejudice." He seeks "truth rather than personal promotion." Is it consistent to ask such a scientist, free to pursue his topic as the subject dictates, to turn his efforts in certain directions and to concentrate on certain problems? If his pursuit of truth leads him to examine the "Motor Characteristics of the Mentally Retarded," are we not compromising our ideal if we ask him to concentrate instead on "Day-to-Day Procedures in Educating the Young?" From a realistic standpoint we must realize that, being human beings, researchers are not entirely selfless. They will seek out areas where research is well supported and where through the successful development of their projects their needs may be fulfilled. We can seduce many of them into well-funded areas by concentrating and programing fund availability. But we should, true to the ideal, maintain free access to ample and unrestricted funds for those who, in pursuit of new knowledge, find themselves outside the area currently designated for attention.

Articles such as Dr. Briggs' challenge the researcher to seek greater self-awareness of his role as a scientist. Through such self-perception he can better be aware of the foibles of his daily activities, and researchers and research fund administrators alike may find greater insight and perspective on our research approaches. Hopefully, we can thus maintain the flexibility needed to use whichever routes appear currently to maximize progress.

# ACTIVITIES

1. What teaching practices are supported by research findings?

2. If you have identified some practices that are not supported by research findings, plan methods for collecting data to support these practices.

3. Compare the points of view of Professor Briggs and Professor Krathwohl. Are their points of view essentially in disagreement?

4. What are some findings stemming from research sponsored by the Cooperative Research Program of the United States Office of Education that are especially relevant to your teaching?